Are you an Elvis expert? See how you rate by taking
the Elvis trivia quiz.
(Answers are below.)

1. When was Elvis born? When did he die?
2. What was Elvis's first movie?
3. What is the correct spelling of his middle name?
4. Was Elvis really a twin?
5. Who was America's "female Elvis"?
6. What was the Memphis Mafia?
7. Who was Elvis's girlfriend at the time of his death?
8. Where and how did Elvis meet his wife Priscilla?
9. What was Elvis doing before he became famous?

So you don't know it all?
Don't feel bad! You're about to find out
All About Elvis . . .

1. Born January 8, 1935. Died: August 16, 1977.
2. *Jailhouse Rock* in 1957
3. Aron. A misspelling of the Biblical Aaron. Elvis later had it changed to the correct spelling.
4. Yes, his twin brother, Jesse Garon Presley, died at birth.
5. Ann-Margret
6. Close friends, associates and employees of Elvis who protected him from his fans and the press.
7. Ginger Alden
8. When he was in Germany with the Army, Elvis met Priscilla at a party given by her father, Air Force Captain Joseph Beaulieu. She was 14 years old at the time.
9. He was a truck driver.

ALL ABOUT ELVIS

Fred L. Worth
and
Steve D. Tamerius

BANTAM BOOKS
TORONTO • NEW YORK • LONDON • SYDNEY

ALL ABOUT ELVIS
A Bantam Book / August 1981

ISBN 0-553-14129-5

Published simultaneously in the United States and Canada

PRINTED IN THE UNITED STATES OF AMERICA

0 9 8 7 6 5 4 3 2 1

Dedicated to

Gertrude Worth
Dean and Bonnie Tamerius

ACKNOWLEDGMENTS

Special thanks to our super typists, Susan Worth and Sharon Bowen, and another special thanks to our photographers, Don Fink and his assistant Bonnie Redelings.

We wish to thank the following people for helping us to bring you this book: Howard DeWitt, Bob and Cathy Nicholas (Elvis Video Club), Marie Fletcher, Tony and Donna Russo, Mary Garret, Tom Kirby, Mary Cannedy, Judy and Greg Bickford, Bonnie Burnette, Kathy Burnette, George Owens, Stan Kesler, Lori Bowen, Tom Bowen, Ron Hicks, Gary Stone, Jeff Roberts, Jeff Wheatcraft, Eddie Hudson, William T. Booth, LeRoy Green, Jr., Charlette Bond, Kelli Bond, Bob Reed, Ernest Bowen, the Lee County Library in Tupelo, and the Memphis City Library.

AUTHORS' NOTE

In order to keep *All About Elvis* as accurate and as up-to-date as possible, it will be necessary to constantly update this work. This is where you, the reader, can help. Compilers of encyclopedias are constantly updating and correcting their vast works. We intend on doing the same. We want this to be *the* Elvis bible, the book that Elvis fans can use for information on Elvis A. Presley. If you have any items to add, or if you wish to correct any existing items, please write to us and to the best of your ability substantiate your information, including sources whenever possible. Even if you can't substantiate the information send it along anyway—it may give us a lead. This is *your* book.

All About Elvis is not just about Elvis, it is about the people he loved and the people who loved him. It is a book about Elvis and the Elvis mystique.

Our goal in future years is to constantly expand this work so that in five, ten, or twenty years one can look back and relive those wonderful days of the 1950s, '60s, and '70s, when Elvis was King.

For the next edition we need unique photographs of Elvis, his friends, his cars, or any associated facts. We also need signed releases to publish the photos.

We also need photos of promotional products that were manufactured in the 1950s and '60s.

Remember, the more we get on Elvis Presley, the more reliable and important *All About Elvis* will become.

As far as we are concerned, the Elvis fan clubs are a part of the Elvis story also. Any information on fan clubs—names, dates, originals or copies of their newsletters—would be greatly appreciated. Hopefully in the next edition we can include entries on the more popular clubs.

Write to:

> Steve Tamerius
> Box 30088
> Lincoln, Nebraska 68503

Since this book is basically about Elvis Presley, his name is mentioned in at least ninety percent of the entries. With that in mind, we the authors have decided to refer to Elvis Presley simply as Elvis.

Many of the songs that appear on Elvis's albums were recorded live at concerts. When referring to any song that Elvis sang and was pressed on record, we have used the word *recorded*. Although certainly he did not go into a studio to record many of his concert songs, it is much easier to use the word for both his studio and his concert releases.

To the best of our ability, we have listed every song, single release, Extended Play album, and Long Playing album associated with Elvis. Under the individual song titles, we have listed every EP and LP on which that song can be found. No RCA Record Club releases, RCA special promotional releases, or bootleg records have been used for cross-reference. We have used only those EPs and LPs readily available to the public.

We have entries on as many bootleg records as we could locate. Unfortunately, there will be some that we missed.

Finally, we used a cut-off date of January 1, 1980, on all musical entries.

THE PROS

"Without Elvis none of us could have made it."—Buddy Holly

"Nothing really affected me until Elvis."—John Lennon

"If I could find a white man who had the Negro sound and the Negro feel, I could make a million dollars."—Sam Phillips

"To command such a large following, he must be a great performer."—Paul Anka

"He taught white America to get down."—James Brown

"Elvis is the greatest blues singer in the world today."—Joe Cocker

"Elvis Presley was a symbol of the country's vitality, rebelliousness and good humor."—President Jimmy Carter

"When I met him, he only had a million dollars' worth of talent. Now he's got a million dollars!"—Col. Tom Parker

AND THE CONS

"He can't last, I tell you flatly, he can't last."—Jackie Gleason

"He can't sing a lick."—Jack O'Brien (*Journal-American*)

"I wouldn't have Presley on my show at any time."—Ed Sullivan

"I wouldn't let my daughter walk across the street to see Elvis Presley perform."—Billy Graham

"I want to count Elvis' hound dogs 20 years from now. Only time will tell if Elvis is collecting Cadillacs in 1976."—Spike Jones (1956)

"Mr. Presley has no discernible singing ability."—Jack Gould (*New York Times*)

ELVIS AARON PRESLEY
(1935-1977)

A Mini-biography

Shortly after 12:00 noon, on January 8, 1935, in East Tupelo, Mississippi, Elvis Aron Presley was born. The son of Vernon and Gladys Presley, Elvis was an identical twin. His twin brother, Jesse Garon, was stillborn and buried in the Priceville Cemetery the next day.

In his early childhood, Elvis loved to sing the gospel songs that were sung in the First Assembly of God Church, the church that he and his parents attended.

While in the fifth grade at Lawhon Elementary School, Elvis's teacher, Mrs. J. C. (Oleta) Grimes, discovered that Elvis had an unusual singing talent when he extemporaneously sang "Old Shep" in class one day. Mrs. Grimes informed the school's principal, J. D. Cole, of Elvis's talent and, on October 3, 1945, he entered Elvis in the annual talent show at the Mississippi-Alabama Fair and Dairy Show. The talent show was sponsored and broadcast live by Tupelo radio station WELO. Singing "Old Shep," Elvis garnered second place, receiving five dollars and free admission to all of the amusement rides.

On Elvis's next birthday, January 8, 1946, he received his first guitar—a $12.75 model purchased by his mother at the Tupelo Hardware Store. According to the proprietor, Forrest L. Bobo, Elvis wanted a shotgun and raised quite a ruckus in the store when it became evident that Gladys Presley was not about to buy him the gun. Mrs. Presley finally persuaded Elvis to accept the guitar.

Late in the summer of 1948, the Presleys moved to Memphis, Tennessee. Though the circumstances remain clouded, it appears that Vernon Presley was in trouble with the law. Apparently he had been selling moonshine whiskey. (Earlier, in 1938 and 1939, Vernon Presley served an eight-month sentence in Parchman Penitentiary for forgery.) Reportedly, the local Tupelo authorities gave Presley two weeks to leave town. In any case, the Presleys moved from Tupelo to Memphis in September of 1948 and Elvis was immediately enrolled in L. C. Humes High School.

Elvis's career at Humes High was uneventful except for his senior year. During that year (1952–1953), Elvis was persuaded by his history and home room teacher, Mrs. Mildred Scrivener, to perform in the annual Humes High variety show which she produced. He received more applause than any of the other contestants and was asked to do an encore.

After graduating from Humes High School on June 3, 1953, Elvis went to work for the Precision Tool Company. He was employed there only a short time. (Reportedly, Elvis was fired because of a fight with his foreman over the length of his hair.) Soon after leaving the Precision Tool Company, Elvis was employed by the Crown Electric Company as a truck driver. His job consisted primarily of delivering supplies to the men on location.

During a lunch break on a Saturday afternoon in the summer of 1953 (the exact date is unknown, but it was probably in August or September), Elvis stopped the Crown Electric pickup he was driving in front of the Memphis Recording Service at 706 Union Avenue. The Memphis Recording Service was a lucrative sideline of Sam Phillips, the owner of Sun Records. For four dollars, a person could record two songs on a ten-inch acetate record. While there were several similar companies in Memphis, Elvis chose the Memphis Recording Service because it was owned by Sam Phillips. Elvis knew he had a good voice. His sole purpose for stopping at 706 Union Avenue was to be "discovered" by Phillips. Legend has it that Elvis wanted to make a record for his mother's birthday; however, Gladys Presley's birthday was on April 25, so that story can be discounted.

Marion Keisker, who was a former Miss Radio of Memphis and Sam Phillips's secretary, was in the studio when Elvis arrived. Phillips was not in that day. Although disappointed that Phillips was not there, Elvis proceeded to record two songs—"My Happiness" and "That's When Your Heartaches Begin." Midway through "My Happiness," Marion Keisker recognized in Elvis the quality that Sam Phillips was looking for—"a white singer with a Negro voice." She immediately threaded a piece of discarded recording tape onto the Ampex tape recorder used in the studio and succeeded in recording the last third of "My Happiness" and all of "That's When Your Heartaches Begin." Prior to Elvis leaving the studio with his record, Miss Keisker asked for his address and telephone number.

When Sam Phillips returned to the studio, Marion played Elvis's tape for him. He was impressed, but not unduly so.

A few months later, on Monday, January 4, 1954, Elvis again returned to the Memphis Recording Service to make another four-dollar record. Since Sam Phillips was not in the previous time, a Saturday, Elvis figured that he had a better chance of meeting Phillips if he stopped by during the week. He was correct. Phillips *was* in and Elvis recorded two songs—"Casual Love Affair" and "I'll Never Stand in Your Way." Though Phillips was impressed with Elvis's talent, he concluded that Elvis needed a lot of work.

In the spring of 1954, Sam Phillips couldn't locate the Negro singer of a demo record of "Without You" which he had brought back from Nashville. He decided to record it with someone else and Marion Keisker suggested that he try Elvis. A recording session was booked, but Elvis didn't project the sound for which Phillips was looking. Elvis was then asked to sing several songs that he knew. He sang "Rag Mop" and several Dean Martin hits. None of them were satisfactory to Sam Phillips.

In July Sam Phillips asked Scotty Moore to invite Elvis over to his apartment to rehearse some numbers—which he did. On Sunday, July 4, Elvis and Scotty got together to rehearse. Later that afternoon Bill Black stopped by. Neither Scotty Moore nor Bill Black was greatly impressed with Elvis's talent.

The next evening, on Monday, July 5, 1954, Elvis Presley had his first commercial recording session at Sun Records. The first song actually put on tape was "I Love You Because." During a refreshment break, Elvis began cutting up and singing an upbeat version of Arthur "Big Boy" Crudup's blues standard, "That's all Right (Mama)." Scotty and Bill joined in. Phillips was so impressed with the sound that he immediately had them put it on tape. After a short while, they decided on an up-tempo version of Bill Monroe's "Blue Moon of Kentucky" for the flip side of the record.

Sam Phillips took several acetates of Elvis's first record to many of the local disc jockeys. On the evening of July 7, on his WHBQ radio program, "Red, Hot, and Blue," disc jockey Dewey Phillips (no relation to Sam) played "That's

All Right (Mama)." The response was so terrific that Phillips called Elvis's home to arrange to interview him. Elvis wasn't home. He was at the Suzore No. 2 theater watching a movie. Vernon Presley went to the theater to tell Elvis about Phillips's call. Later that night, Elvis gave his first media interview. The interview and record made him an overnight celebrity in Memphis.

Elvis signed a managerial contract with Scotty Moore on July 12 and, later that week, he signed a recording contract with Sun Records. The following week, on July 19, "That's All Right (Mama)"/"Blue Moon of Kentucky" (Sun 209) was released. Eventual sales totaled less than twenty thousand, but it was the beginning of a career that would be unmatched by anyone in the entertainment industry.

Elvis's first professional appearance after signing with Sun Records was at the Overton Park Shell on July 30. Slim Whitman was the featured performer that day. Elvis soon began making many professional appearances, among them the grand opening of the Katz Drug Store in September. That same month, he made his first and only appearance on the Grand Ole Opry, singing "Blue Moon of Kentucky." The audience response was lukewarm and Jim Denny, the talent coordinator for the Opry, suggested that Elvis go back to truck driving. In October, however, he performed on the "Louisiana Hayride" and the response was so good that he was asked to become a regular.

On January 1, 1955, Scotty Moore, no longer able to fully devote his time to the management of Elvis's career, relinquished his managerial duties to WMPS disc jockey Bob Neal.

Elvis, Scotty, and Bill auditioned for "Arthur Godfrey's Talent Scouts" in New York City in April of 1955, failing to make the show.

In the fall of 1955, Sam Phillips was faced with a problem: should he continue to devote his energies to promoting Elvis, or should he sell Elvis's contract to the highest bidder and use the money to develop several of the potential stars he had at Sun Records? He chose the latter avenue. At the Warwick Hotel in New York City, on November 22, Sam Phillips sold Elvis's Sun contract to RCA Victor for the total sum of $40,000 ($25,000 to RCA and $15,000 to the Hill and Range Music Company) plus a $5,000 bonus to Elvis to cover the amount he would have received in royalties from Sun Records. With the $5,000 bonus, Elvis bought his family a pink Cadillac.

Though he was with Sun for only sixteen months, Elvis recorded five records: Sun 209 ("That's All Right (Mama)"/ "Blue Moon of Kentucky"); Sun 210 ("Good Rockin' Tonight"/ "I Don't Care If the Sun Don't Shine"); Sun 215 ("Milkcow Blues Boogie"/"You're a Heartbreaker"); Sun 217 ("Baby, Let's Play House"/"I'm Left, You're Right, She's Gone"); and Sun 223 ("Mystery Train"/"I Forgot to Remember to Forget").

Early in 1955, Colonel Thomas Andrew Parker, a former carnival worker, began taking an interest in Elvis's career and it was he who helped to secure the RCA Victor contract. Parker had been born in the carnival and, when his parents died, he went to work for the Great Parker Pony Circus, an outfit run by his uncle. At the age of seventeen, he started his own animal act and toured the South.

After World War II, Colonel Parker began booking and managing several Country music stars, among them Eddy Arnold and Hank Snow. In February of 1955, Parker assisted Bob Neal in booking a performance for Elvis in Carlsbad, New Mexico. It was the start of his involvement with Elvis. Although it was Bob Neal who was Elvis's legal manager, it was Colonel Thomas Parker who was guiding his career in late 1955 and early 1956. On March 15, 1956, Parker officially took over the managerial duties.

After signing with RCA Victor, all of Elvis's Sun singles were re-released on RCA's label and, on January 10, 1956, Elvis had his first recording session for RCA in Nashville. The first song actually put on tape was "I Got a Woman," but the big hit from the session was "Heartbreak Hotel," a tune written by Tommy Durden and Mae Boren Axton (Country singer Hoyt Axton's mother). "Heartbreak Hotel" backed with "I Was the One" was released on January 27, and the following evening, Elvis, Scotty, and Bill made their national television debuts on the Dorsey Brothers' "Stage Show." Five more appearances followed. By the time of the last appearance on March 24, "Heartbreak Hotel" was the #1 song on *Billboard* magazine's popularity chart and Elvis was on the way to becoming a millionaire.

Elvis made a screen test for Hal Wallis of Paramount Studios on April 1. He did a scene from *The Rainmaker* with veteran actor Frank Faylen and sang "Blue Suede

Shoes." Two days later, Elvis made his first of two appearances on "The Milton Berle Show." A disastrous one-week stand at the New Frontier Hotel in Las Vegas followed later in April. Originally, scheduled for two weeks, Elvis's Las Vegas debut was cut short after the first week because of the poor audience response. On June 5, Elvis made his second appearance on "The Milton Berle Show," and "The Steve Allen Show" followed on July 1. Elvis's real big break came when he performed on "The Ed Sullivan Show" on September 9. After that, he was truly a national phenomenon. His performance was viewed by an estimated 54,000,000 people.

Elvis's first movie, *Love Me Tender*, premiered in November and he was on his way to becoming a successful movie star. Three other films were made in the 1950s: *Loving You*, *Jailhouse Rock*, and *King Creole*.

Prior to filming *King Creole*, Elvis received his draft notice. Originally scheduled to report for duty on January 20, 1958, Elvis requested and received a deferment to March 24 so that he could finish filming *King Creole*.

On Monday morning, March 24, Elvis Presley was inducted into the U.S. Army. He received his indoctrination at Fort Chaffee, Arkansas, and was then sent to Fort Hood, Texas, for boot camp. Though Elvis's Army career was primarily uneventful, two events *did* happen that were to change his life.

While Elvis was stationed at Fort Hood, his mother became ill. She died on August 14, 1958, at the Baptist Memorial Hospital in Memphis. Gladys Presley was forty-six, though popular opinion has it that she was forty-two.

In September, Elvis was assigned to the Third Armored Division in West Germany. During his stay in Germany, Airman Curry Grant introduced Elvis to his future wife, Priscilla Beaulieu.

Vernon Presley also met his future wife in West Germany. Davada "Dee" Stanley was in the process of divorcing her husband, an Army sergeant, when Vernon met her. On July 3, 1960, Vernon Presley and Dee Stanley were married in a private ceremony in Huntsville, Alabama. Elvis was unable to attend because he was filming *G.I. Blues.*

Soon after Elvis's discharge on March 5, 1960, he traveled to Miami, Florida, to film "The Frank Sinatra-Timex Special" for ABC-TV. It was billed as his "welcome home party." Just before Christmas, Elvis placed a call to Col. Joseph Beaulieu (Priscilla's father) to ask for permission for Priscilla to spend the holiday at Graceland. After talking with Vernon Presley, Col. Beaulieu said yes. In 1961, Elvis arranged for Priscilla to live at Graceland and enrolled her in Immaculate Conception High School.

Elvis gave a benefit concert for the U.S.S. *Arizona* Memorial Fund in Honolulu on March 25, 1961. It was to be his last live performance until eight years later. "Good Luck Charm," Elvis's last #1 single until 1969, was released the following year.

Throughout the 1960s, Elvis busied himself with making movies and he filmed twenty-seven of them during the decade. His most successful movie was *Blue Hawaii* in 1961. None of the movies received rave reviews from the critics, but Elvis's legion of fans made certain that they all showed a profit at the box office.

Musically, the mid-1960s was a period of decline for Elvis. None of his single releases reached #1 and almost all of them were from his movies. His records weren't the giant hits they were in his golden years of the 1950s and early 1960s. Elvis's decline can be attributed to several factors. Foremost among them was the advent of the British invasion and, specifically, the Beatles. The number of instrumental and vocal groups and single performers represented on the music charts simply diluted the market. There was more competition for the public's record-buying dollar and it took a much stronger record to reach #1 and become a million-seller.

On May 1, 1967, Elvis Presley and Priscilla Beaulieu were married at the Aladdin Hotel in Las Vegas. Nine months later, February 1, 1968, the Presleys' only child, Lisa Marie, was born. Elvis's marriage and the birth of Lisa Marie seemed to give him a new drive for success and the urge to perform before a live audience again.

After seven years of concert inactivity, Elvis decided the time was ripe to start performing before the public once again. The first step on his comeback trail was an NBC television special titled "Elvis." He filmed the special in June of 1968 at NBC's Burbank, California, studios. The special, which aired on December 3, received critical acclaim and good ratings. Elvis was truly back!

If there were any doubters as to Elvis's comeback, they were quickly dispelled the next year. In January, 1969, Elvis had his first Memphis recording sessions since his days with Sun Records. His recordings at the American Sound Studios were among the most dynamic of his career. On July 26,

Elvis began a spectacular one-month engagement at the International Hotel in Las Vegas—his first appearance in Las Vegas since the disastrous week at the New Frontier Hotel thirteen years earlier. In November of 1969, Elvis once again reached the top of the music charts with "Suspicious Minds," his first #1 song since 1962. At the same time, *Change of Habit,* his last movie (excepting two documentaries), was released.

Elvis was presented an award by the U.S. Jaycees for being one of the "Ten Outstanding Young Men of America" in 1971. Two years later one of the crowning achievements of Elvis's career occurred. On January 14, 1973, he performed to a worldwide television audience in a special called "Elvis: Aloha from Hawaii." A taped and expanded version of the special was televised by NBC-TV in the United States on April 4.

Everything seemed to be coming up roses for Elvis in the early 1970s—at least professionally, but the constant touring, filming, and long periods of separation from Priscilla put a strain on Elvis's marriage. In addition, Priscilla had to compete with Elvis's entourage, the Memphis Mafia, for his attention. So, in February 1972, Priscilla left Elvis for Mike Stone, her karate instructor. Elvis and Priscilla were divorced in October 1973.

Even before his divorce, and shortly after his separation, Elvis began dating other women. Although he dated Sheila Ryan, Malessa Blackwood, and several others, Linda Thompson was foremost in Elvis's life and was his steady companion from 1972 to 1976. Linda was Miss Tennessee of 1972.

Toward the end of 1976, Elvis had a new steady girlfriend—Ginger Alden, a first runner-up in the 1976 Miss Tennessee beauty pageant. According to Ginger, Elvis proposed to her on January 26, 1977, and they were to be married on Christmas Day of that year. That day was to never come.

Elvis made several concert appearances in 1977, the last being in Indianapolis, Indiana, on June 26. After that tour, Elvis retired to Graceland for rest and recuperation before embarking on his next tour. In August, Lisa Marie came to visit a few days.

On the night of August 15–16, just one day prior to leaving on yet another tour, Elvis visited the office of dentist Lester Hoffman to get a cavity filled. A few hours later, he played racquetball with Rick Stanley (a step-brother) and Billy

Smith (a cousin). After playing racquetball, Elvis went to bed. He awoke late in the morning to go to the bathroom, taking a book, *The Scientific Search For the Face of Jesus*, with him to read. Ginger said, "Don't fall asleep," and Elvis replied, "Okay, I won't." Those were the last words ever spoken by Elvis Presley.

Shortly after 2:00 P.M., Ginger awoke and noticed that Elvis was not in the bedroom. She became worried and, upon entering the bathroom, found Elvis slumped over on the floor. Ginger called for Joe Esposito who tried to revive Elvis. At approximately 2:30, paramedics Charlie Crosby and Ulysses S. Jones, Jr., arrived at Graceland to render assistance and take Elvis to Baptist Memorial Hospital. All attempts by the doctors at resuscitation failed, and Elvis Presley was pronounced dead at 3:30.

Throughout the world, Elvis's fans went into mourning and many booked flights into Memphis. Reverend C. W. Bradley officiated at the private funeral service at Graceland on Thursday, August 18, and Elvis's body was later entombed at Forest Hill Cemetery next to that of his mother. Because of an attempted body snatching on August 29 and the tremendous crowds at Forest Hill Cemetery, the bodies of Elvis and Gladys Presley were moved to the grounds of Graceland on the night of October 2.

Much speculation tends to surround the death of Elvis Presley. He did have a history of health problems and drugs did contribute to his death; however, to what degree the drugs contributed to his death is still unknown. No matter what the cause of death, the world lost a great entertainer and the King of Rock 'n' Roll—Elvis Aaron Presley.

CHRONOLOGY OF THE LIFE OF ELVIS PRESLEY

April 10, 1865—Date of the opening scene of *Love Me Tender*.

June 17, 1893—Elvis's paternal grandmother, Minnie Mae Hood Presley, born.

June 26, 1909—Colonel Thomas Andrew Parker born.

April 25, 1912—Elvis's mother, Gladys Love Smith Presley, born.

April 19, 1916—Elvis's father, Vernon Presley, born.

June 7, 1933—Vernon Presley and Gladys Love Smith married in Verona, Mississippi.

January 8, 1935—Elvis Presley born at approximately 12:20 P.M. in East Tupelo, Mississippi. A twin brother, Jesse Garon Presley, was stillborn.

January 9, 1935—Jesse Garon Presley buried in the Priceville Cemetery northeast of Tupelo, Mississippi.

June 1, 1938–February 6, 1939—Vernon Presley served a term of imprisonment for forgery in the Parchman (Miss.) Penitentiary.

October 3, 1945—Elvis won second place in the talent show of the Missississippi-Alabama Fair and Dairy Show.

January 8, 1946—Elvis received a $12.75 guitar—his first —for his eleventh birthday.

September 12, 1948—The Presleys moved from Tupelo, Mississippi, to Memphis, Tennessee, and obtained a one-bedroom apartment at 572 Poplar Avenue.

September 13, 1948—Elvis enrolled at L. C. Humes High School.

February 1949—Vernon Presley began work for the United Paint Company.

June 17, 1949—Mrs. Jane Richardson, an advisor from the Memphis Housing Authority, interviewed the Presleys to see if they qualified for financial assistance. They did.

September 20, 1949—The Presleys moved from 572 Poplar

Avenue to a two-bedroom apartment in the Lauderdale Courts at 185 Winchester Street.

1950—Memphis Recording Service founded by Sam Phillips.

Fall 1950—Elvis obtained a part-time job at Loew's State Theater. He soon had to quit because his school work suffered.

Summer 1951—Elvis returned to work for Loew's State Theater, but was fired when he punched a fellow usher for telling the manager that Elvis was getting free candy from the girl at the concession stand.

September 1951—Elvis attended a few football practices at Humes High.

Fall 1951—Elvis began working for MARL Metal Products, but soon had to quit when his mother discovered that he was falling asleep in school.

March 1, 1952—Sun 174 ("Blues In My Condition"/"Sellin' My Whiskey" by Jackie Boy and Little Walter) became the first release for Sun Records.

January 7, 1953—The Presleys evicted from 185 Winchester and moved into an apartment house at 398 Cypress Street.

April 1953—The Presleys moved from 398 Cypress Street to a two-story apartment house at 462 Alabama Street.

June 3, 1953—Elvis graduated from L. C. Humes High School.

Elvis took the General Aptitude Test Battery at the Tennessee Employment Security in Memphis.

June 1953—Elvis began work for the Precision Tool Company.

July 1953—Elvis was fired from the Precision Tool Company and began working for Crown Electric Company.

Summer 1953—On a Saturday afternoon, Elvis recorded "My Happiness" and "That's When Your Heartaches Begin" on a ten-inch acetate record at the Memphis Recording Service. He left with the only copy.

January 4, 1954—Elvis recorded "Casual Love Affair" and "I'll Never Stand In Your Way" on a ten-inch acetate at the Memphis Recording Service. He first met Sam Phillips.

Spring 1954—Sam Phillips had Elvis try to record "Without You." It wasn't the sound Phillips was looking for, so he had Elvis sing several other songs that he knew. None of them suited Phillips.

July 4, 1954—Elvis first met Scotty Moore and Bill Black at

Moore's house. They rehearsed several songs prior to recording the following night at Sun Records.

July 5, 1954—Elvis's first commercial recording session at Sun Records. The first song put on tape was "I Love You Because." "That's All Right (Mama)" was recorded that evening as was "Blue Moon of Kentucky."

July 7, 1954—Disc jockey Dewey Phillips of Memphis radio station WHBQ became the first person to play an Elvis Presley record on the air when he played "That's All Right (Mama)." It was played on his program, "Red, Hot, And Blue," shortly after 9:30 P.M. Later that night, Elvis gave his first media interview on Phillips's program.

July 12, 1954—Scotty Moore became Elvis's first manager when Elvis and his parents signed a one-year contract with Moore.

July 19, 1954—Sun 209 ("That's All Right (Mama)"/"Blue Moon of Kentucky") became Elvis's first commercial record release.

July 28, 1954—Elvis's first newspaper interview (by Edwin Howard) appeared in the Memphis *Press-Scimitar*.

July 30, 1954—Elvis made his first concert appearance at the Overton Park Shell in Memphis. The appearance was advertised in both Memphis newspapers. Slim Whitman was the featured performer.

August 10, 1954—Elvis made an unbilled appearance at the Overton Park Shell.

September 9, 1954—Elvis, Scotty, and Bill played for the grand opening of the Katz Drug Store in Memphis.

September 25, 1954—Elvis made his first and only appearance on the "Grand Ole Opry" singing "Blue Moon of Kentucky."

Sun 210 ("Good Rockin' Tonight"/"I Don't Care If The Sun Don't Shine") released.

October 16, 1954—Elvis made his first appearance on the "Louisiana Hayride" singing "That's All Right (Mama)" and "Blue Moon of Kentucky."

Late 1954—The Presleys moved from 462 Alabama Street to a house at 2414 Lamar Avenue.

January 1, 1955—Scotty Moore let Elvis out of his managerial contract. Bob Neal became Elvis's new manager.

January 8, 1955—Sun 215 ("Milkcow Blues Boogie"/"You're a Heartbreaker") released.

February 1955—Colonel Thomas Parker first became involved with Elvis's career. He helped Bob Neal book Elvis into Carlsbad, New Mexico.

March 5, 1955—Elvis made television debut by appearing on the regionally telecast "Louisiana Hayride."

April 1, 1955—Sun 217 ("Baby, Let's Play House"/"I'm Left, You're Right, She's Gone") released.

April 1955—Elvis auditioned for "Arthur Godfrey's Talent Scouts" TV program in New York City and was rejected. It was Elvis's first trip to New York City and his first airplane flight.

May 13, 1955—Elvis made a concert appearance in Jacksonville, Florida. It was the first Presley concert to cause a riot. Future singer Johnny Tillotson was in the audience.

May 26, 1955—Elvis made a concert appearance at the Jimmie Rodgers Memorial Day Celebration in Meridian, Mississippi.

June 24, 1955—Bob Neal first met Colonel Parker at the Big D Jamboree in Dallas, Texas.

Mid-1955—The Presleys moved from 2414 Lamar Avenue to 1414 Getwell Street.

August 1955—Sun 223 ("Mystery Train"/"I Forgot to Remember to Forget") released.

September 1955—*Country Song Roundup* magazine became the first magazine to feature an article on Elvis Presley.

September 7, 1955—Both sides of Sun 223 ("Mystery Train"/"I Forgot to Remember to Forget" reached #1 on Billboard's Country chart becoming Elvis's first #1 record.

October 15, 1955—Elvis played the Cotton Club in Lubbock, Texas. The warm-up act was Buddy and Bob—Buddy Holly and Bob Montgomery. Thirteen-year-old future songwriter Mac Davis was in the audience.

Fall 1955—Bill Randle of WERE in Cleveland, Ohio became the first disc jockey in the North to play an Elvis Presley record.

November 22, 1955—RCA purchased Elvis's contract from Sun Records for $25,000 and Hill and Range Music purchased Sam Phillips's Hi-Lo Music publishing company for $15,000, making a total purchase of $40,000. In addition, Elvis received a $5,000 bonus from RCA to cover the future royalties he would have gotten from Sun Records.

December 17, 1955—Elvis made his last regular appearance

on the "Louisiana Hayride" doing a benefit for the YMCA in Shreveport.

January 10, 1956—Elvis's first RCA recording session took place in Nashville. The first song taped was "I Got A Woman."

January 27, 1956—RCA 20/47-6420 released—Elvis's first RCA release of new material ("Heartbreak Hotel"/"I Was The One").

January 28, 1956—Elvis made his national television debut on the Dorsey Brothers' "Stage Show" on CBS.

February 4, 1956—Elvis's second appearance on "Stage Show."

February 11, 1956—Elvis's third appearance on "Stage Show."

February 18, 1956—Elvis's fourth appearance on "Stage Show."

March 15, 1956—Colonel Thomas A. Parker officially became Elvis's manager.

March 17, 1956—Elvis's fifth appearance on "Stage Show."

March 24, 1956—Elvis's sixth and last appearance on "Stage Show."

Elvis purchased a red and black Messerschmitt automobile which he later gave to Bernard Lansky.

April 1956—The Presleys moved from 1414 Getwell Street to a house on 1034 Audubon Drive.

April 1, 1956—Elvis made his screen test performing a scene from *The Rainmaker*.

April 3, 1956—Elvis's first appearance on "The Milton Berle Show."

April 11, 1956—While flying to Nashville for a recording session, Elvis's plane experienced trouble and almost crashed. Later that day, Elvis recorded "I Want You, I Need You, I Love You."

April 23–29, 1956—Elvis's first appearance in Las Vegas at the New Frontier Hotel. His scheduled two-week engagement was cancelled after the first week because of the poor reception.

June 5, 1956—Elvis's second appearance on "The Milton Berle Show."

July 1, 1956—Elvis made an appearance on "The Steve Allen Show" and introduced "Hound Dog."

July 2, 1956—First Presley recording session to include The Jordanaires (RCA studios in New York City). "Hound

Dog," "Don't Be Cruel," and "Any Way You Want Me" were recorded at the session.

August 22, 1956—Elvis began filming *Love Me Tender*.

September 3, 1956—Elvis bought his mother a pink Cadillac.

September 8–14, 1956—*TV Guide* featured Elvis on the cover and contained an article by Paul Wilder.

September 9, 1956—Elvis's first appearance on "The Ed Sullivan Show."

September 26, 1956—Elvis Presley Day in Tupelo, Mississippi.

October 18, 1956—"Ed Hopper" incident in Memphis.

October 28, 1956—Elvis's second appearance on "The Ed Sullivan Show."

November 16, 1956—*Love Me Tender* released.

November 23, 1956—"Louis Balint" incident in Toledo.

December 4, 1956—Million-dollar session at the Sun studios. Participants included Elvis, Johnny Cash, Jerry Lee Lewis, and Carl Perkins.

1957—During the year, Elvis was interviewed twice by Wink Martindale on WHBQ-TV's "Dance Party."

January 4, 1957—Elvis took his pre-induction Army physical at the Kennedy Veterans' Hospital in Memphis.

January 6, 1957—Elvis's third and last appearance on "The Ed Sullivan Show." This was the only television performance by Elvis on which he was shown only from the waist up.

January 30, 1957—The NBC-TV program, "Kraft Theater," presented "The Singing Idol," starring Tommy Sands. The main character, Ewell Walker, was modeled after Elvis.

March 1957—Elvis purchased Graceland from Mrs. Ruth Brown Moore.

April 2, 1957—Elvis made a concert appearance in Toronto, Ontario, Canada.

April 3, 1957—Elvis made a concert appearance in Ottawa, Canada.

April 20–June 15, 1957—"All Shook Up" was number one on Billboard's Hot 100 Chart for eight weeks—the longest of any Presley song.

July 9, 1957—*Loving You* released.

August 31, 1957—Elvis made a concert appearance in Vancouver, British Columbia, Canada.

October 21, 1957—*Jailhouse Rock* released.

December 20, 1957—Memphis draft board chairman Milton Bowers hand-delivered Elvis's draft notice to Graceland.

December 21, 1957—Frank Freeman, Paramount Studio Production Chief, sent Elvis's draft board a letter asking for a sixty-day deferment so Elvis could complete filming of *King Creole*. Freeman was told that Elvis would have to ask for the deferment himself.

December 26, 1957—Elvis donated a truckload of teddy bears to the National Foundation for Infantile Paralysis.

January 20, 1958—Original date Elvis was to have entered the U.S. Army. He received a deferment to March 24.

March 24, 1958—Elvis inducted into the U.S. Army.

March 25, 1958—Elvis received his Army haircut from James Peterson at Fort Chaffee, Arkansas.

March 26, 1958—Elvis given medical inoculations at Fort Chaffee, Arkansas (typhoid, tetanus, and Asian flu).

March 28, 1958—"The Phil Silvers Show" aired an episode titled "Rock And Roll Rookie," which was a parody of Elvis.
Elvis, along with the other recruits, bused to Fort Hood, Texas, for basic training.

June 4, 1958—*King Creole* released.

August 11, 1958—Elvis received his first Gold Disc Award from the Recording Industry Association of America for "Hard Headed Woman."

August 14, 1958—Gladys Presley died in Memphis of a heart attack complicated by hepatitis.

August 16, 1958—Gladys Presley buried in Forest Hill Cemetery in Memphis.

September 19, 1958—Elvis and his Army unit began train trip from Fort Hood, Texas, to Brooklyn, New York.

September 22, 1958—Elvis and his Army unit left the Military Ocean Terminal in Brooklyn aboard the U.S.S. *General Randall* for Bremerhaven, West Germany.
Elvis interviewed by Pat Herron in the library of the U.S.S. *General Randall*.

October 1, 1958—Elvis, aboard the U.S.S. *General Randall*, arrived in Bremerhaven, West Germany.

December 27, 1958—Elvis promoted to private first class.

January 8, 1959—Elvis's twenty-fourth birthday. Dick Clark's "American Bandstand" dedicated its program to Elvis. Clark spoke with Elvis by telephone.

February 18, 1959—Elvis sang impromptu at the Lido night club in Paris while on leave.

June 1, 1959—Elvis was promoted to specialist fourth class.

January 14, 1960—Elvis promoted to sergeant.

March 3, 1960—Elvis left West Germany by plane for the United States, stopping briefly at Prestwick Airport in Scotland. Late that day, he arrived at McGuire Air Force Base in New Jersey.

March 5, 1960—Elvis discharged from the U.S. Army.

March 26, 1960—Elvis taped "The Frank Sinatra-Timex Special" at the Fontainebleau Hotel in Miami, Florida.

May 12, 1960—"The Frank Sinatra-Timex Special" aired on ABC-TV at 9:30 E.S.T.

July 3, 1960—Vernon Presley and Davada "Dee" Stanley married in Huntsville, Alabama.

October 20, 1960—*G.I. Blues* released.

October 30–December 25, 1960—"It's Now Or Never" was #1 in the United Kingdom for eight weeks—the longest of any Presley single in the U.K.

December 20, 1960—*Flaming Star* released.

December 25, 1960—Priscilla Beaulieu visited Elvis at Graceland.

February 25, 1961—Elvis gave live concert in the Ellis Auditorium in Memphis—his last live performance (except for the U.S.S. *Arizona* benefit) until 1968.

March 25, 1961—Elvis gave a benefit concert for the U.S.S. *Arizona* Memorial Fund. The concert was to have been the 26th, Palm Sunday, but Elvis thought that that would be in bad taste.

June 8, 1961—*Wild In The Country* released.

November 1, 1961—*Blue Hawaii* released.

January 8, 1962—Elvis's twenty-seventh birthday. Dick Clark's "American Bandstand" dedicated its program to Elvis.

April 11, 1962—*Follow That Dream* released.

August 1, 1962—*Kid Galahad* released.

October 31, 1962—*Girls! Girls! Girls!* released.

April 3, 1963—*It Happened at the World's Fair* released.

June 14, 1963—Priscilla Beaulieu graduated from Immaculate Conception High School in Memphis.

November 28, 1963—*Fun in Acapulco* released.

December 11, 1963—*Love Me Tender* became the first Elvis Presley film to be shown on television.

January 30, 1964—Elvis purchased Franklin D. Roosevelt's former presidential yacht, *Potomac.* He then gave it to the St. Jude's Children's Hospital.

March 11, 1964—*Kissin' Cousins* released.

April 20, 1964—*Viva Las Vegas* released.

November 12, 1964—*Roustabout* released.

April 14, 1965—*Girl Happy* released.

May 28, 1965—*Tickle Me* released.

August 27, 1965—Elvis met The Beatles at his Perugia Way mansion in Bel Air.

October 22, 1965—Bill Black, Elvis's former bass player, died during surgery.

November 24, 1965—*Harum Scarum* released.

Late 1965—Elvis moved from his house at 565 Perugia Way in Bel Air to one located at 10550 Rocca Place.

March 31, 1966—*Frankie And Johnny* released.

May 25–28, 1966—In Nashville, Felton Jarvis produced his first Elvis Presley recording session.

June 15, 1966—*Paradise, Hawaiian Style* released.

November 23, 1966—*Spinout* released.

February 9, 1967—Elvis purchased the Circle G ranch near Walls, Mississippi.

March 22, 1967—*Easy Come, Easy Go* released.

May 24, 1967—*Double Trouble* released.

May 1, 1967—Elvis and Priscilla Beaulieu are married at the Aladdin Hotel in Las Vegas.

May 7, 1967—Elvis moved from 10550 Rocca Place in Bel Air to a house located at 1174 Hillcrest.

May 29, 1967—Elvis held a second wedding reception at Graceland for his friends and employees.

September 29, 1967—Elvis Presley Day in Tennessee.

December 13, 1967—*Clambake* released.

Late 1967—Elvis moved from his home at 1174 Hillcrest to 144 Monovale.

February 1, 1968—Lisa Marie Presley born.

March 8, 1968—*Stay Away, Joe* released.

June 12, 1968—*Speedway* released.

June 27–29, 1968—Elvis taped his NBC-TV special at the Burbank, California, studios. These sessions became known later as the "Burbank Sessions." The TV special aired on December 3, 1968.

October 23, 1968—*Live a Little, Love a Little* released.

December 3, 1968—Elvis appeared on his own TV special on NBC-TV. It was sponsored by Singer and was Elvis's first appearance before an audience since 1961.

January 13–23, 1969—Elvis's first recording session at the American Sound Studios in Memphis.

February 17–22, 1969—Elvis's second and last recording session at the American Sound Studios.

March 13, 1969—*Charro!* released.

May 28, 1969—Elvis sold the Circle G ranch to Lou McClellan.

July 26–August 28, 1969—Elvis's first Las Vegas appearance since 1956. He began his comeback at the International Hotel.
Opening date in the 1979 ABC-TV movie *Elvis*.

May 8, 1969—*The Trouble with Girls (And How to Get into It)* released.

November 10, 1969—*Change of Habit* released.

November 11, 1970—*Elvis—That's The Way It Is* released. Elvis Presley Day in Portland, Oregon.

January 9, 1971—U.S. Jaycees presented an award to Elvis for being one of the "Ten Outstanding Young Men of America."

May 4, 1971—Elvis appeared on the cover of *Look* magazine.

June 1, 1971—Elvis's birthplace in Tupelo, Mississippi, was opened to the public.

September 8, 1971—Elvis received the Bing Crosby Award.

January 18, 1972—Southern portion of Bellvue Street (Highway 51 South) in Memphis renamed Elvis Presley Boulevard.

February 23, 1972—Elvis and Priscilla separated.

November 1, 1972—*Elvis on Tour* released.

January 8, 1973—Elvis sued Priscilla for divorce.
Elvis's thirty-eighth birthday.

January 14, 1973—TV special, "Elvis: Aloha From Hawaii," was broadcast worldwide.

April 4, 1973—NBC-TV broadcast an expanded version of the "Elvis: Aloha From Hawaii" TV special to the United States.

October 11, 1973—Elvis and Priscilla's divorce final.

January 8, 1974—Elvis Presley Day in Georgia by proclamation of Governor Jimmy Carter.

June 18, 1975—Elvis underwent a face lift at Mid-South Hospital in Memphis.

July 19, 1975—Elvis played the piano in public for the first time at a concert in Uniondale, New York.

December 31, 1975—Elvis broke the record for a single performance at a concert in Detroit, Michigan, when the gate receipts totaled $816,000.

January 14, 1976—While vacationing in Vale, Colorado, Elvis gave away five automobiles.

April 20, 1976—Presley Center Courts, Inc., established to build and manage racquetball courts.

August 26, 1976—After Elvis became ill, Peggy Lee replaced him as headliner at the Las Vegas Hilton.

December 1–12, 1976—Elvis's last Las Vegas appearance (at the Las Vegas Hilton).

January 26, 1977—According to Ginger Alden, she accepted Elvis's proposal.

March 3, 1977—Elvis's last will and testament filed.

April 1, 1977—Elvis entered Baptist Memorial Hospital in Memphis. He left on the 6th.

May 29, 1977—Elvis walked off the stage at a concert in Baltimore, Maryland—the first time he had ever quit in the middle of a concert except for health reasons.

May 30, 1977—Psychic Gloria James predicted on a talk show on radio station WMEX in Boston, Massachusetts, that Elvis would soon die.

June 18, 1977—Elvis received two Photoplay Gold Medal Awards for Favorite Variety Star and Favorite Rock Music Star. These were the last awards presented to Elvis before he died.

June 26, 1977—Elvis gave his last public performance at the Market Square Arena in Indianapolis, Indiana.

July 19, 1977—Psychic Jacqueline Eastland predicted, on the "Nine in the Morning Show" in Los Angeles (KHJ-TV), that Elvis would soon die.

August 12, 1977—The book, *Elvis—What Happened?*, released.
Philadelphia psychic, Marc Salem, predicted Elvis's death, including the headlines in the Philadelphia newspapers.

August 15, 1977—Elvis got a cavity filled during the evening at the office of dentist Lester Hoffman.

August 16, 1977—Elvis found dead by Ginger Alden at approximately 2:30 P.M. in a bathroom on the second floor of the Graceland mansion.

August 17, 1977—Elvis was to have begun another tour starting with a concert in Portland, Maine.

August 18, 1977—Elvis's funeral at Graceland. He was buried next to his mother in Forest Hill Cemetery.

In the early morning hours, Tammy Baiter was injured and Alice Hovatar and Juanita Johnson were killed in front of Graceland by a car driven by Treatise Wheeler III.

August 27, 1977—According to Ginger Alden, Elvis was going to announce his engagement to her.

August 29, 1977—Ronnie Lee Adkins, Raymond M. Green, and Bruce Eugene Nelson arrested for trespassing at Forest Hill Cemetery. Speculation was that they were going to steal Elvis's body and hold it for ransom.

September 6, 1977—*National Enquirer* ran cover photo of Elvis lying in his open coffin.

October 2, 1977—The bodies of Elvis and Gladys Presley were moved from Forest Hill Cemetery to Graceland.

October 3, 1977—The CBS-TV special, "Elvis in Concert", was telecast at 8:00 P.M. E.S.T.

October 5, 1977—Charges against Ronnie Lee Adkins, Raymond M. Green, and Bruce Eugene Nelson were dismissed.

October 17, 1977—Dr. Jerry Francisco stated at a press conference that Elvis died of a heart attack—not drugs.

November 15, 1977—Dee Stanley obtained a Dominican Republic divorce from Vernon Presley.

December 25, 1977—According to Ginger Alden, Elvis and she were to have been married on Christmas Day.

February 1, 1978—Elvis inducted into the *Playboy* magazine's Musical Hall of Fame.

September 8, 1978—Bronze, 400-pound statue of Elvis dedicated in the lobby of the Las Vegas Hilton Hotel.

October 18, 1978—"The Gong Show," on NBC-TV, aired an entire show of Elvis impersonators.

February 11, 1979—ABC-TV movie, *Elvis,* telecast, beating *Gone With the Wind* and *One Flew Over the Cuckoo's Nest* in the ratings.

June 26, 1979—Vernon Presley died at the age of sixty-three.

June 28, 1979—Vernon Presley buried next to Elvis and Gladys.

August 19, 1979—The Elvis Presley Chapel in Tupelo, Mississippi, was dedicated.

September 13, 1979—The ABC-TV series, "20/20," telecast an episode titled "The Elvis Cover-up" concerning Elvis's drug problems and the probable cause of his death.

October 31, 1979—Priscilla Presley made her national TV commercial debut appearing for the Wella Corporation.

A

Aaron. Correct spelling of Elvis's middle name, although it was misspelled A-r-o-n on his birth certificate. Elvis legally changed his name to Aaron and that is how it appears on his gravestone. (See: Aron)

Abbott and Costello Meet Frankenstein. Universal movie in 1948 starring Bud Abbott and Lou Costello with Bela Lugosi, Lon Chaney, Jr., and Glenn Strange. It played at a theatre in Tupelo when Elvis was fourteen years old and was believed to be the first motion picture he ever saw.

Abel, Robert. Producer and director (with Pierre Adidge) of the 1972 documentary, *Elvis on Tour*.

Acapulco Hilton. One of the two Acapulco hotels at which Mike Windgren (Elvis) performed in the 1963 movie *Fun in Acapulco*. The other hotel was the Ambassador.

Ace, Johnny. Rhythm and blues artist (real name: John Marshall Alexander, Jr.) whose biggest hit was "Pledging My Love" (Duke 136). Johnny Ace was once B.B. King's piano player. On Christmas Eve, 1954, Ace shot himself while playing Russian roulette prior to going on stage at the Houston Civic Auditorium. "Pledging My Love" had just entered the charts.

Elvis's recording of "Pledging My Love" also was on the charts at the time of his death.

A Company. Elvis's assignment at Fort Hood, Texas, while taking Army basic training. A Company was a part of the Second Medium Tank Battalion, Second Armored Division.

Action of the Tiger. A 1957 adventure film, directed by Terrance Young, which starred Van Johnson, Martina Carol, and Herbert Lom. *Action of the Tiger* appeared on the bill with *Loving You* in most cities.

Adam and Evil. Song that Elvis sang in the 1966 movie *Spinout*. "Adam and Evil" was written by Fred Wise and Randy Starr and appeared in the Long Playing album "Spinout" (RCA LPM/LSP-3702).

Adams, Faye. Rhythm and blues singer who reached the top of the R & B charts in 1953 with "Shake a Hand" (Herald 416). Elvis recorded "Shake a Hand" in March 1975. Faye Adams was known as "Atomic Adams."

1

Adams, Jack. Rancher from whom Elvis purchased the 163-acre Circle G Ranch in February 1967 for the sum of $300,000.

Adams, Nick. Hollywood actor who debuted in a Pepsi-Cola TV commercial with James Dean in 1951. Nick Adams was a good friend of James Dean and appeared with him in the 1955 movie *Rebel Without a Cause.* (Ironically, James Dean was selected to play a character named Nick Adams in the television presentation of Ernest Hemingway's "The Battler" on October 18, 1955. Due to Dean's death, the part went to Paul Newman.) Adams had a starring role as Johnny Yuma (a part that he created) in the television series "The Rebel."*

Elvis and Nick Adams were very good friends, until Adams's death. Elvis tried to get him the role of one of the Reno brothers in the 1956 movie *Love Me Tender,* but he was rejected for the role because he was considered too young (he was twenty-six). On February 7, 1968, the day after Lisa Marie Presley was taken home from Baptist Memorial Hospital, Nick Adams committed suicide by taking an overdose of pills. (See: Sing, Boy, Sing)

Adidge, Pierre. Producer and director (with Robert Abel) of the 1972 documentary *Elvis on Tour.*

Adkins, Ronnie Lee. One of the three men—the other two were Raymond Green and Bruce Nelson—who were arrested for trespassing at Forest Hill Cemetery on August 29, 1977. The charges were later dismissed. According to speculation, the men were going to steal Elvis's body and hold it for a $1 million ransom. It has never been proved.

Persons who know Adkins, Green, and Nelson say that the men believed Elvis wasn't dead and that they wanted to prove to the world that his crypt was empty. If the crypt was empty, they felt, that would show that Elvis was still alive.

After Loving You. Song recorded by Elvis on February 18, 1969, at Chip Moman's American Sound Studios in Memphis. Sandy Posey is among the backup vocalists on this recording. Written by Eddie Miller and Johnny Lantz, "After Loving You" appeared in the Long Playing album "From Elvis in Memphis" (RCA LSP-4155).

"After Loving You" was originally recorded by Eddy Arnold in 1962 (RCA 8048).

After Midnight. Title originally considered for the 1966 movie *Spinout. Always at Midnight* was another title considered.

Aida. Opera written by Giuseppe Verdi in 1871 to commemorate the opening of the Suez Canal. The opera was first performed in Cairo, Egypt, on December 24, 1871. The opera was mentioned by Betty (Nicole Jaffe) in the 1969 movie *The Trouble with Girls (And How to Get Into It).*

---

*The series' theme song, "The Ballad of Johnny Yuma," was sung by Johnny Cash.

Ain't That Loving You, Baby. RCA 47-8440. Released in September 1964 as a 45 rpm single. It reached #16 on *Billboard*'s Hot 100 chart and sold over a million copies. "Ask Me" was on the flip side. Elvis's recording of "Ain't That Loving You, Baby" was spliced from two or more takes. Although Elvis recorded the song on June 10, 1958, it wasn't released until six years later.

"Ain't That Loving You, Baby" was written by Clyde Otis and Ivory Joe Hunter and was originally recorded by Jimmy Reed (Vee Jay 169) in 1955. It appeared in the Long Playing albums "Elvis' Gold Records, Volume 4" (RCA LPM/LSP-3921) and "Elvis: Worldwide 50 Gold Award Hits, Volume 1" (RCA LPM-6401).

Ain't That Loving You, Baby. RCA 447-0649. Gold Standard Series re-issue of RCA 47-8440.

Airport Inn. Memphis nightclub where, in 1955, Thomas Parker's advance man, Oscar Davis, first saw Elvis perform.

Airway's Used Cars. Car lot in Memphis that sponsored a Saturday radio show on KWEM on which brothers Johnny and Dorsey Burnette and Paul Burlitson performed as a trio in late 1953. Elvis supposedly asked to sing a few songs with the group on one or two occasions.

Ajax Market. Grocery store that Sister Barbara Bennett (Jane Elliot) picketed in the 1969 movie *Change of Habit*.

Ajax Market—Unfair to Consumers. Words on the picket sign carried by Sister Barbara Bennett (Jane Elliot) in the 1969 movie *Change of Habit*.

Alabama Fieldstone. Material from which the walls surrounding the grounds at Graceland are constructed. The walls were built in 1957.

Aladdin Hotel. Las Vegas hotel where Elvis Presley and Priscilla Beaulieu were married in a double-ring ceremony on May 1, 1967, at approximately 9:41 A.M., in the private suite of Milton Prell, the hotel's owner.

Albert. Bernice's (Michelle Carey) pet Great Dane in the 1968 movie *Live a Little, Love a Little*. Albert slept in a baby crib. Brutus (Elvis's real-life dog) played the part of Albert.

Albright, Lola. Female lead (as Dolly Fletcher) in the 1962 movie *Kid Galahad*. Lola Albright portrayed Edie Hart, Peter Gunn's girlfriend, on the "Peter Gunn" TV series (1958/61). Briefly, in the fall of 1965, she assumed the role of Constance Mackenzie for the ailing Dorothy Malone in the TV series "Peyton Place." Lola Albright was married to actor Jack Carson from 1952 to 1958.

Alden, Ginger. Elvis first saw Ginger's sister Terry Alden on local television. Elvis wished to meet Terry, so a meeting was set up by a Memphis disc jockey. Ginger accompanied her sister Terry. Upon meeting the two Alden sisters, Elvis became fascinated with Ginger.

3

Memphis's "Miss Traffic Safety of 1976," Ginger Alden was Elvis Presley's fiancee at the time of his death. Elvis bought her an eleven-and-a-half-carat diamond engagement ring valued at $60,000. It was Ginger who discovered Elvis's body on the day of his death. Elvis and Ginger were to be married on Christmas Day, 1977. Ginger Alden appeared in the fictionalized biographical movie *The Living Legend*.

Alden, Jo. Mother of Ginger Alden. After Elvis's death, she filed a $40,000 claim against the Elvis Presley estate, stating that Elvis had promised to pay the remainder of her home mortgage. In addition, Mrs. Alden said that Elvis had agreed to pay for some home improvements and legal fees in a divorce.

Alden, Walter. U. S. Army officer who inducted Elvis into the Army on March 24, 1958. Walter Alden is the father of Ginger Alden, Elvis's fiancee at the time of his death.

Alexander, Arthur. Rhythm and blues singer who was discovered working as a bellhop. Alexander's original versions of "Burning Love," "Anna," and "You Better Move On" were covered by Elvis (1972), the Beatles (1964), and the Rolling Stones (1964), respectively. "Burning Love," by Arthur Alexander, never made the pop charts. (See: Hound Dog Man's Gone Home)

Ali, Muhammad. Three-time Heavyweight Boxing Champion (only man to accomplish this feat).

In 1964, Ali (real name: Cassius Marcellus Clay, Jr.) recorded "Stand By Me" backed with "I Am the Greatest" on Columbia Records (Columbia 43007).

Elvis once gave Muhammad Ali a robe with Ali's name and the phrase THE PEOPLE'S CHAMPION embossed on the back. He wore the robe when he lost to Ken Norton on March 31, 1973. Ali then considered it to be bad luck and never wore it again.

All About Elvis, Part 1/Part 2. Novelty song recorded in 1956 on Pelvis Records by Milt Oshins (Pelvis 169).

All About Elvis, Volume 1. Novelty album featuring songs about Elvis by several artists. Songs included—Side 1: United Press News—Comments About Elvis, "Dear Elvis, Part 1," "Dear Elvis, Part 2," "Hey, Mr. Presley," "My Boy Elvis," "I'm Lonesome for Elvis," "Bye Bye, Elvis," "Marching Elvis." Side 2: "Elwood Pretzel Fan Club, Part 1," "Elwood Pretzel Fan Club, Part 2," "All About Elvis, Part 1," "All About Elvis, Part 2," "Oh, Elvis," "Elvis Presley for President," "I'm in Love with Elvis Presley," "I Wanna Spend Xmas with Elvis."

All About Elvis, Volume 2. Novelty album featuring songs about Elvis by several artists. Songs included—Side 1: "All American Boy," "Dear Elvis, Part 1," "Dear Elvis, Part 2." Side 2: "My Boy Elvis," "Hey, Mr. Presley," "Bye Bye Elvis," Dear 53310761," "Gonna Get Even with Elvis' Sergeant," "Elvis and Me."

All American Boy. An Elvis novelty song released in December

1958 by Fraternity Records (Fraternity 835). Written by Orville Lunsford, "All American Boy" was sung by Bobby Bare* although it was credited to Bill Parsons. It was the most successful of the novelty songs about Elvis, reaching #2 on *Billboard*'s Hot 100 chart in February 1959.

Allen, Rex. The last of the singing cowboys in the movies while under contract with Republic Pictures. Rex Allen, who was nicknamed "the Arizona Cowboy," was voted into the top ten Money Making Western Stars of 1951, '52, '53, and '54 by *Motion Picture Herald-Fame* polls. He is perhaps best known as the narrator of most of the Walt Disney nature films.

In 1953 Rex Allen had a million-seller with "Crying in the Chapel" (Decca 9-28758), which Elvis recorded on October 31, 1960. Elvis's version was released in 1965 and it also became a million-seller.

All I Needed Was the Rain. Song that Elvis sang in the 1968 movie *Stay Away, Joe*. Written by Ben Weisman and Sid Wayne, "All I Needed Was the Rain" appeared in the following Long Playing albums: "Singer Presents Elvis Singing Flaming Star and Others" (RCA PRS-297), "Elvis Sings Flaming Star" (RCA Camden CAS-2304), and "Elvis Sings Flaming Star" (Pickwick CAS-2304).

The film version of "All I Needed Was the Rain" has Elvis talking at the end of the song with dogs howling in the background.

All My Trials. Traditional song (author unknown) that was one of three songs included in "An American Trilogy." In 1959 the Kingston Trio recorded a version of the song, titled "All My Sorrows" (Capitol 4221). (See: An American Trilogy)

All Right Private. An Elvis novelty song by Mo Klein and the Sargents on Crystalette Records (Crystalette 727) in 1959.

All Shook Up. RCA 20/47-6870. Released in March 1957 both as a 78 rpm single and a 45 rpm single. It reached #1 on *Billboard*'s Hot 100 chart (for eight weeks, April 20–June 15—the longest of any Presley single), #1 on the Country chart (for four weeks), and #1 on the Rhythm and Blues chart (for four weeks). "All Shook Up" was one of four Presley songs to reach #1 on all three *Billboard* charts. (The other three songs were: "Don't Be Cruel," "Teddy Bear," and "Jailhouse Rock.") It was the first Presley record to reach #1 in the United Kingdom (for seven weeks, July 12–August 30). "All Shook Up" remained on *Billboard*'s Hot 100 chart for thirty weeks— the longest of any Presley song—and sold well over two million copies. "That's When Your Heartaches Begin" was on the flip

---

*During a Bill Parsons recording session, Bobby Bare recorded a couple of songs, one of which was "All American Boy." All the tapes, with Bill Parsons's name on them, were sold to Fraternity Records of Cincinnati. Fraternity Records assumed that "All American Boy" was sung by Parsons. Bobby Bare sold the rights to his recording for fifty dollars.

side. Dudley Brooks can be heard playing piano on this record. Elvis sang "All Shook Up" in his 1968 NBC-TV special and in the 1970 documentary *Elvis—That's the Way It Is*. In 1974, Suzi Quatro recorded "All Shook Up." Written by Otis Blackwell (Elvis's name also appeared, for copyright reasons), "All Shook Up" appeared in the Extended Play album "A Touch of Gold, Volume 3" (RCA EPA-5141) and the following Long Playing albums: "Elvis' Golden Records" (RCA LPM-1707); "Elvis' Golden Records" (RCA LSP-1707 [e]); "Elvis—TV Special" (RCA LPM-4088); "From Memphis to Vegas/from Vegas to Memphis" (RCA LSP-6020); "Elvis: Worldwide 50 Gold Award Hits, Volume 1" (RCA LPM-6401); "Elvis in Person" (RCA LSP-4428); "Elvis As Recorded at Madison Square Garden" (RCA LSP-4776); "Elvis" (RCA DPL2-0056 [e]); "Pure Gold" (RCA ANL1-0971).

All Shook Up. RCA 447-0618. Gold Standard Series re-issue of RCA 47-6870.

All That I Am. RCA 47-8941. Released in October 1966 as a 45 rpm single. It reached #41 on *Billboard*'s Hot 100 chart and was a million-seller. "Spinout" was on the flip side. Elvis sang "All That I Am" in the 1966 movie *Spinout*.

"All That I Am" was written by Sid Tepper and Roy C. Bennett and appeared in the Long Playing album "Spinout" (RCA LPM/LSP-3702).

All That I Am. RCA 447-0658. Gold Standard Series re-issue of RCA 47-8941.

Almost. Song that Elvis sang in the 1969 movie *The Trouble with Girls (And How to Get Into It)*. The film version of "Almost" is a different take from the one on the record. "Almost" was written by Florence Kaye and Ben Weisman and appeared in the Long Playing albums "Let's Be Friends" (RCA Camden CAS-2408) and "Let's Be Friends" (Pickwick CAS-2408).

Almost Always True. Song that Elvis sang in the 1961 movie *Blue Hawaii*. The film version of "Almost Always True" has an added commentary by Joan Blackman. "Almost Always True" was written by Fred Wise and Ben Weisman and appeared in the Long Playing album "Blue Hawaii" (RCA LPM/LSP-2426.)

Almost in Love. RCA 47-9610. Released in September 1968 as a 45 rpm single. It reached #95 on *Billboard*'s Hot 100 chart. "A Little Less Conversation" was on the flip side. "Almost in Love" was written by Rick Bonfa and Randy Starr and was sung by Elvis in the 1968 movie *Live a Little, Love a Little*. It appeared in the Long Playing albums "Almost in Love" (RCA Camden CAS 2440) and "Almost in Love" (Pickwick CAS-2440). The album verison of "Almost in Love" has a shorter instrumental introduction than does the film version.

Almost in Love. RCA 447-0667. Gold Standard Series re-issue of RCA 47-9610.

Almost in Love. RCA Camden CAS-2440. A 33⅓ rpm Long Playing album that was released in November 1970. It reached #65 on *Billboard*'s Hot LP chart. When initially released, this album contained a take of "Stay Away, Joe" that was not included in the film, in which Elvis messed up the lyrics. Actually, "Stay Away" was to have been included in the album, instead of "Stay Away, Joe." In March 1973, RCA corrected the problem by re-issuing "Almost in Love" with "Stay Away" on it. (The original album is a rare collector's item). The March 1973 version is the one that was released by Pickwick in January 1976. Songs on "Almost in Love" included—Side 1: "Almost in Love," "Long-Legged Girl (With a Short Dress On)," "Edge of Reality," "My Little Friend," "A Little Less Conversation." Side 2: "Rubberneckin'," "Clean Up Your Own Backyard," "U.S. Male," "Charro," "Stay Away, Joe" (take #2), (replaced in March 1973 with "Stay Away").

Almost in Love. Pickwick CAS-2440. A 33⅓ Long Playing album that was a re-issue of the March 1973 version of RCA Camden CAS-2440. It was released in December 1975.

Aloha Oe. Traditional Hawaiian ballad that Elvis sang in the 1961 movie *Blue Hawaii*. "Aloha Oe" had previously been recorded by Bing Crosby (Decca 880). Although arranged and adapted by Elvis, "Aloha Oe" was written in 1878 by Queen Liliuokalani and appeared in the Long Playing album "Blue Hawaii" (RCA LPM/LSP-2426).

Along Came Jones. One of a number of songs that Elvis sang parts of in a concert in the 1970s.

"Along Came Jones" was written by Jerry Leiber and Mike Stoller and was originally recorded by the Coasters (Atco 6141) in 1959.

Also Sprach Zarathustra. Classical number composed in 1894 by Richard Strauss (1864–1949). It was the theme song of Staney Kubrick's 1968 movie *2001: A Space Odyssey*.*

A rock version of "Also Sprach Zarathustra" was a #2 hit for Deodato (Eumir Deodato) in 1973 (CTI 42).

In later years Elvis opened his live concerts with "Also Sprach Zarathustra." It appeared in the following Long Playing albums: "Elvis as Recorded at Madison Square Garden" (RCA LSP-4776); "Elvis: Aloha from Hawaii Via Satellite" (RCA VPSX-6089); "Elvis in Concert" (RCA APL2-2587).

Alvis Presley. Spelling of Elvis's name on the 1956 Los Angeles concert tickets.

Always Elvis. Ten-day convention for Elvis fans held at the Las Vegas Hilton, 1-10 September 1978. Carl Romanelli was the show's master of ceremonies. The four special guests were: Vernon Presley, Priscilla Presley, Henri Lewin (president of

---

*Segments of the song also appear in the movies *Catch-22* (1970) and *The Big Bus* (1976).

the Hilton Hotel chain), and Barron Hilton (the owner of the hotel).

Always Elvis. Hour-long documentary film prepared in 1978 by Vernon Presley and Col. Tom Parker.

Always Elvis/Blanc D'Oro. Wine first marketed in 1979 by Italy's Frontenac Vineyards with the authorization of Factors, etc. The white wine with Elvis's face on the label retails for four dollars. On the back label is a poem written by Colonel Tom Parker.

Always Late (With Your Kisses). Unreleased Presley Sun recording of October 1954. Actually, "Always Late (With Your Kisses)" is on a radio transcript from a "Louisiana Hayride" performance. Lefty Frizzell composed and originally recorded the song in 1951 (Columbia 20837).

Always on My Mind. RCA 74-0815. Released in November 1972 as a 45 rpm single. It reached #10 on *Billboard*'s Hot 100 chart. "Separate Ways" was on the flip side. "Always on My Mind" was written by Mark James, Wayne Carson, and Johnny Christopher and appeared in the Long Playing albums "Separate Ways" (RCA Camden CAS-2611) and "Separate Ways" (Pickwick CAS-2611).

Always on My Mind. RCA GB-10486. Gold Standard Series reissue of RCA 74-0815.

Amazing Grace. Traditional hymn written by the Reverend John Newton of the Church of England in 1779. "Amazing Grace" uses only six different notes in the sixteen-bar melody.

Judy Collins had a million-seller with "Amazing Grace" in 1971, as did the Royal Scots Dragoon Guards Band* in 1972. Elvis Presley recorded "Amazing Grace" on March 15, 1971, and it appeared in the Long Playing album "He Touched Me" (RCA LSP-4690).

Ambassador Hotel. One of the two Acapulco hotels at which Mike Windgren (Elvis) performed in the 1963 movie *Fun in Acapulco*. The other hotel was the Acapulco Hilton.

Amen. Song that Elvis sang at several of his live concerts. At his last public concert (at the Market Square Arena in Indianapolis, Indiana, on June 26, 1977), Elvis sang "Amen." On the 1976 Long Playing album "Elvis Recorded Live on Stage in Memphis," Elvis sang a short version of the song but it was not credited on the album jacket or the record label.

In the 1963 movie *Lilies of the Field,* Homer Smith (Sidney Poitier) taught five German nuns to sing "Amen."

America. Song title that erroneously appeared on the label of RCA PB-11165. The actual song on the record was "America, the Beautiful." (See: America, the Beautiful)

---

*The Royal Scots Dragoon Guards Band had the only million-seller using bagpipes. A segment of their version can be heard in the 1978 movie *Invasion of the Body Snatchers.*

American Bandstand. Dick Clark's* ABC-TV series, originating from Philadelphia over WFIL-TV (first broadcast nationally on August 5, 1957). The theme song, "Bandstand Boogie," was composed by Charles Albertine and performed by Les Elgart. The current closing theme is sung by Barry Manilow. On January 8, 1959, Clark dedicated the program to Elvis's birthday. He talked with Elvis by telephone from West Germany. On January 8, 1962, Clark again devoted the show to Elvis. Rick Nelson and Elvis were the only major rock stars of the 1950s and '60s never to appear on "American Bandstand." From 1957 to 1964, Elvis was voted the most popular artist by the "American Bandstand" Popularity Poll.

American Hot Wax. A 1978 movie starring Tim McIntire as disc jockey Alan Freed. Elvis was mentioned in the movie.

American Music. One of the number of music-publishing companies owned by Elvis. American Music owned the publishing rights to numerous country classics, including "Sixteen Tons," "A Dear-John Letter," and "Smoke, Smoke, Smoke (That Cigarette)."

American Pie. A 1971 song by Don McLean, on United Artists, that referred to the tragic death of rock 'n' roll star Buddy Holly. "American Pie" was a #1 song and a million-seller. In the song, McLean made reference to the King and the Queen, meaning Elvis Presley and Connie Francis.

American Sound Studios. Memphis recording studio, located at 827 Thomas Street, founded by Chips Moman and Bob Crew† in 1964. Singer Sandy Posey was once a secretary at American Sound Studios. The Box Tops and Dusty Springfield recorded there in the late 1960s.

In 1969 Elvis held two recording sessions at American Sound Studios: January 13–23 and February 17–22. It was the first time since his Sun Records days that Elvis recorded in Memphis. Country artist Ronnie Milsap was one of the session men in January. Many consider the thirty-five songs he recorded there to be among his best.

Some of the songs Elvis recorded at American Sound Studios are: "Kentucky Rain"; "In the Ghetto"; "Suspicious Minds"; "Don't Cry, Daddy."

The studio musicians who performed on the Elvis sessions were: Bobby Wood, Tommy Cogbill, Mike Leech, Reggie Young, John Hughey, Gene Chrisman, Ed Kollis, and Bobby Emmons. Those same musicians backed up various artists at the studio to place 125 recordings on the record charts for a five-year period.

---

*The show's original host, Bob Horn, was the first DJ to be tried and convicted on charges of payola.
†Bob Crewe was the cowriter of the Rays' 1957 hit "Silhouettes" and cowriter of many of the Four Seasons' hits. In 1966 he had the hit "Music to Watch Girls By" (Dyno Voice 229), which became a theme song for Pepsi-Cola.

America, the Beautiful. RCA PB-11165. Released in November 1977 as a 45 rpm single. "My Way" was on the flip side. Elvis sang "America, the Beautiful" at many of his concert appearances and this release is a "live" version.

"America, the Beautiful" was a poem written by Katherine Lee Bates, an English teacher at Wellesley College in Massachusetts. She was inspired to write the poem in the summer of 1893 after taking in the view from the summit of Pike's peak. "America the Beautiful" was first published on July 4, 1895, in *The Congregationalist*, a Boston periodical.

The poem was later set to music (exact date unknown), using the melody of "Materna." Samuel Augustus Ward composed "Materna," which was first published on July 12, 1888, in *The Parish Choir* in Boston. It was used as a setting for the hymn "O Mother Dear Jerusalem."

Elvis's version of "America, the Beautiful" was erroneously called "America"* on the record label.

"America, the Beautiful" has never appeared in a Long Playing album.

"America, the Beautiful" was played by three children on kazoos in the 1969 movie *The Trouble with Girls* (*And How to Get Into It*).

Amigos. Vocal group that backed Elvis on songs in the 1963 movie *Fun in Acapulco*. They appeared as the Four Amigos in that film.

Am I Ready. Song that Elvis sang in the 1966 movie *Spinout*. Written by Sid Tepper and Roy C. Bennett, "Am I Ready" appeared in the following Long Playing albums: "Spinout" (RCA LPM/LSP-3702); "Burning Love and Hits from His Movies, Volume 2" (RCA Camden CAS-2595); "Burning Love and Hits from His Movies, Volume 2" (Pickwick CAS-2595).

Am I to Be the One. Song recorded by Jerry Lee Lewis in the late 1950s. The duet version of the song first appeared on Lewis's "Duets" album (Sun 1011) and was released as a single (Sun 1139) in 1978. The song was composed by Otis Blackwell and R. Stevenson. Charlie Rich is the unlisted singer with whom Lewis is singing the duet. The flip side of the single is "Save the Last Dance for Me." (See: Save the Last Dance for Me) When the duet version of "Am I to Be the One" was first released, there was much speculation by many uninformed writers who reported that the unlisted singer was Elvis, thus playing into the hands of Shelby Singleton, who packaged the album.

---

*"America" was written in February 1832 by Samuel Francis Smith. Educator Lowell Mason asked Smith to write a song for a children's choir. While looking through a book of hymns, Smith spotted a melody he liked—a German song called "Heil, Dir im Siegerkranz." Not until later did he discover that he had used the melody of "God Save the King (Queen)," the British national anthem. "America" was first sung in public by a children's choir on July 4, 1832, at the Park Street Church in Boston. (Ten-year-old Edward Everett Hale, who in 1863 wrote *Man Without a Country*, was a member of that choir).

Amory, Mississippi. Site of a historic concert in the summer of 1955. Elvis Presley, Johnny Cash, and Carl Perkins performed there that day. It was while Elvis was on stage that Carl Perkins wrote his biggest hit song, "Blue Suede Shoes," on a piece of brown paper sack. (See: Blue Suede Shoes)

An American Trilogy. RCA 74-0672. Released in April 1972 as a 45 rpm single. It reached #66 on *Billboard*'s Hot 100 chart. "The First Time Ever I Saw Your Face" was on the flip side. This single release of "An American Trilogy" is a live recording from a performance at the Las Vegas Hilton on February 17, 1962. Elvis sang "An American Trilogy" in the 1972 documentary *Elvis on Tour* and the 1973 TV special "Elvis: Aloha from Hawaii."

"An American Trilogy" is a medley of three songs arranged by Mickey Newbury: "Dixie," "The Battle Hymn of the Republic," and "All My Trials."

"Dixie" was written on Sunday, April 3, 1859, by Dan Emmett for a minstrel show. The following night, April 4, "Dixie"* was introduced by the Bryant Minstrels at Mechanics Hall in New York City. The first southern performance of the song occurred at Charleston, South Carolina, in December 1860. Rumsey and Newcomb performed it in a minstrel show. "Dixie" was played prior to General Pickett's charge at Gettysburg in order to pick up the troops' morale. Abraham Lincoln asked it to be played by the Union band upon hearing the news of Lee's surrender on April 9, 1865.†

The words to "The Battle Hymn of the Republic" were written by Julia Ward Howe in December 1861 at the Willard Hotel in Washington, D.C. A friend of Mrs. Howe, the Reverend James Freeman Clarke, suggested that she write new war lyrics to the melody of "John Brown's Body."‡ In February 1862, the *Atlantic Monthly* published Julia Ward Howe's poem under the title "The Battle Hymn of the Republic." The title was suggested by the editor. For her poem Mrs. Howe received five dollars.

"All My Trials" (a.k.a. "All My Sorrows") is a traditional song whose composer is unknown.

"An American Trilogy" was to have been included in the Long Playing album "Standing Room Only" (RCA LSP-4762), but the album was never released. The song did appear in the following Long Playing albums: "Elvis as Recorded at Madison Square Garden" (RCA LSP-4776); "Elvis: Aloha from Hawaii

---

*The term *dixie*, a synonym for the South, came from a ten-dollar bill that was circulated throughout the South. It was issued by the Citizen's Bank of Louisiana. The New Orleans French population referred to ten as "dix."
†The story is recounted in the song "Johnny Reb" by Johnny Horton (Columbia 41437).
‡"John Brown's Body" was based on the song "Glory, Halleluja," written by William Steffe in 1862.

Via Satellite" (RCA VSPX-6089); "Elvis Recorded Live on Stage in Memphis" (RCA CPL1-0606).

An American Trilogy. RCA 447-0685. Gold Standard Series original that was released in July 1973. Although "An American Trilogy" had previously been released as a single (RCA 74-0672), this Gold Standard Series issue had a different flip side ("Until It's Time for You to Go"), making it a different record.

Andersen, Ellen. Member of the Norwegian Consulate in Los Angeles who presented Elvis with three Norwegian Silver Records in 1962 for a "Good Luck Charm." Elvis was the first artist to receive three Norwegian Silver Records.

And How to Get Into It. Subtitle of the 1969 movie *The Trouble With Girls.* This was the only Elvis movie that had a subtitle.

And I Love You So. Song written and originally recorded by Don McLean* in 1970. Bobby Goldsboro (in 1971) and Perry Como (in 1973) had hit versions of "And I Love You So." Elvis recorded the song in 1975 and it appeared in the October 1977 TV special "Elvis in Concert." Subsequently it appeared in the Long Playing albums "Today" (RCA APL1-1039) and "Elvis in Concert" (RCA APL2-2587).

Andress, Ursula. Female lead (as Margarita Dauphine) in the 1963 movie *Fun in Acapulco.* Ursula Andress has appeared in two James Bond movies: *Dr. No* (1963) and *Casino Royale* (1967). She was once married to actor John Derek. For a short time Ursula Andress was romantically involved with Elvis, as she once was with James Dean.

And the Grass Won't Pay No Mind. Song written and originally recorded by Neil Diamond in 1970 (Uni 55224). Later, another version was released by Mark Lindsay with Paul Revere and the Raiders (Columbia 45229).

Elvis recorded "And the Grass Won't Pay No Mind" at the American Sound Studios in Memphis on February 18, 1969. It appeared in the Long Playing albums "From Memphis to Vegas/From Vegas to Memphis" (RCA LSP-6020) and "Elvis —Back in Memphis" (RCA LSP-4429).

An Evening Prayer. Religious song recorded by Elvis on May 18, 1971, in Nashville. Written by C. M. Battersby and Charles H. Gabriel, and backed by the Imperial Quartet, "An Evening Prayer" appeared in the Long Playing albums "He Touched Me" (RCA LSP 4690) and "He Walks Beside Me" (RCA AFL1-2772).

Angel. Song that Elvis sang in the 1962 movie *Follow That Dream.* Written by Sid Tepper and Roy C. Bennett, "Angel" appeared in the Extended Play album "Follow That Dream" (RCA

---

*The song is from McLean's debut album, "Tapestry" (United Artists 5522). Carole King also had an album titled "Tapestry" (Ode 34946), which today is the second-best-selling non-soundtrack album.

12

EPA-4368) and the following Long Playing albums: "C'mon Everybody" (RCA Camden CAL-2518); "Elvis Sings for Children (And Grownups Too)" (RCA CPL1-2901); "C'mon Everybody" (Pickwick CAL-2518).

Animal Instinct. Song recorded by Elvis and originally scheduled to appear in the 1965 movie *Harum Scarum*. It was cut from the final print, although it is believed that some prints do exist with "Animal Instinct" included. Written by Bill Giant, Bernie Baum, and Florence Kaye, "Animal Instinct" appeared in the Long Playing album "Harum Scarum" (RCA LPM/LSP-3468).

Anita Kerr Singers, The. Vocal group that backed Elvis on the song "Tomorrow Night." Elvis recorded the song in 1955 while he was at Sun Records. On march 18, 1965, the Anita Kerr Singers, who have backed numerous artists on RCA Records, recorded the vocal backing to "Tomorrow Night."

Under the name the Little Dippers, the Anita Kerr Singers had the 1960 hit "Forever" on the University label (University 210).

Anka, Paul. Singer-songwriter who made his first public appearance at the age of twelve as an impersonator. Paul Anka's first chart hit was "Diana"* in 1957. "Diana," which has sold over 9 million copies, was written about Diana Ayoub, the twenty-year-old babysitter of Anka's younger brother. Paul had a crush on Ms. Ayoub.

Paul Anka was the first Canadian solo artist to have a million-selling record, and through the years he has done just about everything in the entertainment world. He has written over 225 songs, including four movie themes and the theme for the "Tonight Show Starring Johnny Carson." One of the movie themes Paul Anka wrote was for *The Longest Day*—a movie in which he also had an acting role.

At an Elvis Presley concert at Lake Tahoe on August 1, 1971, Elvis and Paul Anka exchanged friendly quips. After singing "One Night," Elvis remarked to Anka: "Look, Anka! When I'm singing and you're in the audience, you listen to me! I go to hear you sing—I listen! You don't talk when I sing!" Elvis reached over the stage and gave Anka a gentle nudge. Later in the show he introduced Paul Anka as "Paul Anchor."

Paul Anka wrote the English words to "My Way" in 1969 for Frank Sinatra. Elvis recorded "My Way" in 1973.

Ansara, Michael. Actor who protrayed Prince Dragna in the 1965 movie *Harum Scarum*. Michael Ansara played an Apache Indian in two TV series: Cochise on "Broken Arrow" and Deputy U. S. Marshal Sam Buckhart on "Law of the Plainsman." His wife, Barbara Eden, costarred with Elvis in *Flaming Star* (1960). Michael Ansara and Barbara Eden are the only

---

*Paul Anka's first record was "I Confess" in 1956 (RPM 499). The vocal back-up was provided by the Jacks.

married couple to have costarred with Elvis. (See: Eden, Barbara)

Any Day Now. RCA 47-9741. Released in April 1969 as a 45 rpm single. "In the Ghetto" was on the flip side. Written by Bob Hilliard and Burt Bacharach, "Any Day Now" was originally recorded by Chuck Jackson (Wand 122) in 1962. Elvis recorded the song at American Sound Studios in Memphis on February 21, 1969. "Any Day Now" appeared in the Long Playing albums "From Elvis in Memphis" (RCA LSP-4155) and "Elvis —The Other Sides: Worldwide Gold Award Hits, Volume 2" (RCA LPM-6402).

Any Day Now. RCA 447-0671. Gold Standard Series re-issue of RCA 47-9741.

Anyone (Could Fall in Love with You). Song recorded by Elvis for the soundtrack of the 1964 movie *Kissin' Cousins*. It was cut from the final print of the movie. "Anyone (Could Fall in Love with You)" was written by Bennie Benjamin, Sol Marcus, and Louis A. DeJesus and appeared in the Long Playing album "Kissin' Cousins" (RCA LMP/LSP-2894).

Anyplace Is Paradise. Song that Elvis recorded at Radio Recorders Studio in Hollywood on September 3, 1956. That recording session of September 1–3 was the first of many sessions at Radio Records through the years. "Anyplace Is Paradise" was written by Joe Thomas and appeared in the Extended Play album "Elvis, Volume 2" (RCA EPA-993) and the Long Playing albums "Elvis" (RCA LPM-1382) and "Elvis" (RCA LSP-1382 [e]).

Anything That's Part of You. RCA 47-7992. Released in February 1962 as a 45 rpm single. It reached #31 on *Billboard*'s Hot 100 chart. "Anything That's Part of You" sold over a million copies. "Good Luck Charm" was on the flip side. Written by Don Robertson, "Anything That's Part of You" appeared in the Long Playing albums "Elvis' Golden Records, Volume 3" (RCA LPM/LSP-2765) and "Elvis: Worldwide 50 Gold Award Hits, Volume 1" (RCA LPM-6401).

Anything That's Part of You. RCA 447-0636. Gold Standard Series re-issue of RCA 47-7992.

Any Way You Want Me (That's How I Will Be). RCA 47-6643. Released in September 1956 as a 45 rpm single. It reached #27 on *Billboard*'s Hot 100 chart and sold over a million copies. "Love Me Tender" was on the flip side. "Any Way You Want Me (That's How I Will Be)" was written by Aaron Schroeder and Cliff Owens and was recorded by Elvis on July 2, 1956, at RCA's New York City studios—the first session to include the Jordanaires. The song appeared in the Extended Play album "Any Way You Want Me" (RCA EPA-965) and the following Long Playing albums: "Elvis' Golden Records" (RCA LPM-1707); "Elvis' Golden Records" (RCA LPM-1707 [e]); "Elvis: Worldwide 50 Gold Award Hits, Volume 1" (RCA LPM-6401).

Any Way You Want Me (That's How I Will Be). RCA 447-0616. Gold Standard Series re-issue of RCA 47-6643.

Any Way You Want Me. RCA EPA-965. This was a 45 rpm Extended Play album released in October 1956. It reached #74 on *Billboard*'s Hot 100 chart. Songs included—Side 1: "Any Way You Want Me," "I'm Left, You're Right, She's Gone." Side 2: "I Don't Care if the Sun Don't Shine," "Mystery Train."

Anzaldua, Nathan. Youngest professional Elvis impersonator (as of 1978) at the age of six.

Apex 350 C. Tape-recorder used to record the sessions at Sun Records. It was on this machine (Serial No.: 54L-220) that Elvis was first taped. Marion Keisker used this Ampex 350 C (made in Redwood City, California) to tape the last third of "My Happiness" and all of "That's When Your Heartaches Begin." The control panel connected to the tape-recorder was of RCA manufacture. (See: Memphis Recording Service; RCA Consolette)

Apollo 15. NASA moon mission (July 26–August 7, 1971) that took the photograph of the earth used on the cover of the Long Playing album "Elvis: Aloha from Hawaii Via Satellite." Astronauts on that mission were David R. Scott, Alfred M. Worden, and James B. Irwin.

Apollo Theater. Biggest theater in Harlem, it seats 1800 patrons. Amateur Night was broadcast 11:00 p.m. on Wednesday nights over WMCA. The theater is owned by Frank Schiffman. Prior to Schiffman's purchase, it was called Hurtig and Seamon's Theater. The first white performers to appear at the Apollo Theater were Buddy Holly and the Crickets* in 1957.

While playing the Apollo Theater in 1940, Sarah Vaughn was discovered by Billy Eckstine while singing "Body and Soul." She had been singing at an amateur-night show.

Doris Troy, who in 1963 had a hit with "Just One Look," once worked at the Apollo as an usherette. It was while working there that she was discovered by James Brown.

While in New York City in 1956 to appear on the Dorsey Brothers' "Stage Show," Elvis spent time at the Apollo Theater. One of the entertainers Elvis enjoyed watching was Bo Diddley (real name: Elias McDaniels), whom he met there. (See: Diddley, Bo)

The Apollo is located at 125th St. and Eighth Ave., N.Y., N.Y. Telephone: 864-4490

Appreciation. Song that Ann-Margaret sang in the 1964 movie *Viva Las Vegas.* "Appreciation" has never been released on record.

April 10, 1865. Day after General Robert Edward Lee surrendered to General Ulysses Simpson Grant at the Appomattox Court

---

*The person who booked Buddy Holly and the Crickets thought they were a black group.

House in Virginia, ending the Civil War. April 10, 1865, is the opening date in the 1956 movie *Love Me Tender*.

Arcade Records. Legitimate record label on which the album "Elvis Presley's 40 Greatest Hits" was released in Great Britain in 1974. It was released by arrangement with RCA and sold over 1½ million copies in Great Britain.

Are You Laughing Tonight. Parody of "Are You Lonesome Tonight" that Elvis sang at the International Hotel in Las Vegas on July 26, 1969.

Are You Lonesome Tonight. RCA 47-7810. Released in November 1960 as a 45 rpm single. It reached #1 on *Billboard*'s Hot 100 chart (for six weeks, from November 28, 1960, to January 9, 1961), #22 on the Country chart, and #3 on the Rhythm and Blues chart. "Are You Lonesome Tonight" also reached #1 in the United Kingdom (for four weeks, from January 15, 1961, to February 12). "I Gotta Know" was on the flip side. "Are You Lonesome Tonight" sold over 4 million copies. Elvis borrowed the song's phrasing and recitation from the rendition used by the Blue Barron Orchestra (with Franklin McCormick). It is a spliced version of "Are You Lonesome Tonight" that exists on the 45 rpm single—no master exists. The song was sung by Elvis on his 1968 NBC-TV special. Written by Roy Turk* and Lou Handman in 1926, "Are You Lonesome Tonight" was first recorded by Al Jolson. It appeared in the Extended Play album "Elvis By Request" (RCA LPC-128) and the following Long Playing albums: "Elvis' Golden Records, Volume 3" (RCA LPM/LSP-2765); "From Memphis to Vegas/From Vegas to Memphis" (RCA LSP-6020); "Elvis: Worldwide 50 Gold Award Hits, Volume 1" (RCA LPM 6401); "Elvis in Person" (RCA LSP-4428); "Elvis—A Legendary Performer, Volume 1" (RCA) CPL1-0341); "Elvis in Concert" (RCA APL2-2587). On the last album Elvis forgot the words to part of the song.

Are You Lonesome Tonight. RCA 447-0629. Gold Standard Series re-issue of RCA 47-7810.

Are You Lonesome Tonight. RCA 61-7810. A 45 rpm "Living Stereo" release. "I Gotta Know" was on the flip side.

Are You Sincere. RCA PB-11533. Released in April 1979 as a 45 rpm single. It reached #10 on *Billboard*'s Country Chart. "Solitaire" was on the flip side. "Are You Sincere" was written by Wayne P. Walker in 1957 and first popularized by Andy Williams (Cadence 1351) in 1958. The vocal group Voice backed Elvis on this recording. "Are You Sincere" appeared in the Long Playing albums "Raised on Rock/For Ol' Times Sake" (RCA APL1-0388) and "Our Memories of Elvis" (RCA AQL1-3279).

---

*Roy Turk, with Fred Ahlert and Bing Crosby, also wrote Crosby's theme song "Where the Blue of the Night Meets the Gold of the Day," in 1931. The song was originally titled "Where the Gold of the Day Meets the Blue of the Night."

Arizona, U.S.S. United States battleship sunk by Japanese bombers on December 7, 1941. The ship's skipper, Captain Frank van Valkenburg, was posthumously awarded the Congressional Medal of Honor. The U.S.S. *Arizona* is still the only commissioned battleship in the Navy. On March 25, 1961, Elvis performed at a benefit concert for the U.S. *Arizona* Memorial Fund and helped to raise $62,000 (See: Bloch Arena)

Arnold, Eddy. Country Music Hall of Fame (1966) singer whom Col. Tom Parker managed from 1945 to 1953. Eddy Arnold's first big professional break came when he appeared with Pee Wee King's Golden West Cowboys on the "Grand Ole Opry." He was nicknamed The "Tennessee Plowboy" by George D. Hay, host of the "Grand Ole Opry."

Through the years, Eddy Arnold has had seventy-one records in the top ten of *Billboard*'s charts—the most by any performer. In 1948 he had nine records in the top ten and four #1 records.

Hank Houghton (Mickey Shaughnessy), in the 1957 movie *Jailhouse Rock,* claimed to have performed on the same bill with Eddy Arnold and Roy Acuff.

Elvis recorded the following Eddy Arnold hits: "I Really Don't Want to Know," "Make the World Go Away," "It's a Sin," "I'll Hold You in My Heart," "You Don't Know Me."

Arnold, James "Kokomo." Chicago blues singer who composed "Milk Cow Blues," which Elvis recorded in 1955 as "Milkcow Blues Boogie." The name "Kokomo" was taken from the 1934 blues song "Old Original Kokomo Blues," which James Arnold recorded.

Aron. Spelling of Elvis's middle name on his birth certificate. It was the result of Vernon Presley's misspelling of the biblical name Aaron. In later years Elvis legally changed his middle name to Aaron.

Arthur Godfrey's Talent Scouts. CBS-TV series (1948–58) hosted by Arthur Godfrey. The Blue Moon Boys (Elvis, Scotty Moore, and Bill Black) went to New York City in April 1955 to audition for "Arthur Godfrey's Talent Scouts."* They were turned down.† At nearly the same time, Pat Boone auditioned for the show and won first place when he appeared, later becoming a regular on Godfrey's other TV series, "Arthur Godfrey and Friends."

Buddy Holly and the Crickets also failed an audition for "Arthur Godfrey's Talent Scouts" in 1957. In the same week that George Hamilton IV failed to win first place on the show,

---

*Godfrey's orchestra leader (1948–54) Archie Bleyer formed Cadence Records in 1952 and signed Julius La Rosa as his first artist. Bleyer and La Rosa had both been fired by Godfrey. Julius La Rosa was fired on the air on October 19, 1953, just after he finished singing "I'll Take Manhattan." Godfrey later said he fired him because "he lacked humility."
†Had the trio decided to sing "I Believe," they might have appeared on the show since no one who sang "I Believe" on the show ever lost.

in 1956, his recording of "A Rose and a Baby Ruth" (Colonial 420 and ABC Paramount 9725) had just been released. The song reached #6 on the charts. Other artists who made their TV debuts on "Arthur Godfrey's Talent Scouts" include: Steve Lawrence, Connie Francis, Jimmie Rodgers, Tony Bennett, Guy Mitchell, Rosemary Clooney, the Chordettes,* Carmel Quinn, and Patsy Cline, who made her debut in 1957, singing "Walkin' After Midnight."

Ashley, Edward. Man who brought a $5 million lawsuit against Elvis, claiming that Elvis's bodyguards beat him at the Sahara Tahoe Hotel. The suit was dismissed.

As Long as I Have You. Song that Elvis sang in the 1958 movie *King Creole.* "As Long as I Have You" was written by Fred Wise and Ben Weisman and appeared in the Extended Play albums "King Creole, Volume 1" (RCA EPA-4319) and "King Creole, Volume 1" (RCA EPA-5122) and the following Long Playing albums: "King Creole" (RCA LPM-1884); "King Creole" (RCA LSP-1884 [e]); "Elvis: The Other Sides—Worldwide Gold Award Hits, Volume 2" (RCA LPM-6402).

In the movie *King Creole,* Ronnie (Carolyn Jones) sang a few bars of "As Long as I Have You" without instrumental accompaniment.

Ask Me. RCA 47-8440. Released in September 1964 as a 45 rpm single. It reached #12 on *Billboard*'s Hot 100 chart. "Ain't That Loving You, Baby" was on the flip side. A different version of "Ask Me" appeared on a French 45 rpm single. One of the stereo channels was omitted and all that was heard was Elvis and Floyd Cramer (on piano). The Jordainaires and some instrumentation were not heard.

Originally, "Ask Me" was the Italian folk song "Io," written by Domenico Modugno.† The English words and music were written by Bill Giant, Bernie Baum, and Florence Kaye. "Ask Me" appeared in the Long Playing albums "Elvis' Gold Records, Volume 4" (RCA LPM/LSP-3921) and "Elvis—The Other Sides: Worldwide Gold Award Hits, Volume 2" (RCA LPM-6402).

Ask Me. RCA 447-0649. Gold Standard Series re-issue of RCA 47-8440.

Atkins, Chet. Guitarist who recorded a number of instrumental albums and played on and later produced many recording sessions for RCA artists. Chester Burton Atkins‡ is a member

---

*The Chordettes were Dick Clark's first live guests on "American Bandstand."

†In 1958, Domenico Modugno had the best-selling song of the year with "Nel Blu, Dipinto Di Blu" ("Volare") on Decca Records (Decca 30677). Modugno's cowriter, Franco Migliacci, received the inspiration for the song from the back of a cigarette pack.

‡In 1974, Atkins and Floyd Cramer, with a group called the Country Hams, recorded a record titled "Walking in the Park with Eloise" (Apple 3977). The Country Hams was an assumed name used by Paul McCartney and Wings. Paul McCartney's father, James McCartney, wrote the song.

of the Country Music Hall of Fame. For fourteen consecutive years he won the Best Instrumentalist award in the *Cashbox* magazine poll.

Atkins played on Elvis's Nashville recording sessions of January 10–11, 1956; April 11, 1956; and June 10–11, 1956. He and Boudleaux Bryant composed "How's the World Treating You," which Elvis recorded in September 1956.

In 1960 Chet Atkins became the A & R manager for RCA and in 1968 became RCA's vice-president.

Atlantic Records. The most successful independent record label of the 1950s. Atlantic was founded in October 1947 by Ahmet Ertegun (the son of a Turkish ambassador to the United States) and Herb Abramson.

Ertegun* is the present owner of the New York Cosmos soccer team. Atlantic recorded mostly rhythm and blues artists, such as Chuck Willis, the Clovers, Joe Turner, LaVerne Baker, Ruth Brown, and the Drifters. In 1952 the New York City-based company paid L.A.'s Swingtime Records $2,500 for Ray Charles's contract.

Atco Records (founded in 1955), the label on which the Coasters and Bobby Darin recorded, was a subsidiary of Atlantic.

Atlantic Records unsuccessfully bid $25,000 for Elvis in 1955.† (Had they been successful, Atlantic would have had both Elvis Presley and Ray Charles on the same label.)

Atomic Powered Singer, The. Billing for Elvis Presley at the New Frontier Hotel in April 1956. In California he was billed as the "Nation's Only Atomic Powered Singer."

Audio Recorders of Arizona. Phoenix, Arizona, studio where Elvis is alleged to have recorded the song "Tell Me Pretty Baby" with the Red Dots. (See: Tell Me Pretty Baby)

Aura Lee. Traditional song written in 1861 by W. W. Fosdick and George R. Poulton. "Aura Lee" was a favorite with the Union Army in the Civil War. With new words and retitled "Army Blue," it was adopted as the class song of the West Point graduates in 1865.

Actress Frances Farmer sang "Aura Lee" in the 1936 movie *Come and Get It.*

Elvis's 1956 hit "Love Me Tender" was based on "Aura Lee." (See: Love me Tender)

Elvis sang "Violet (The Flower of N.Y.U.)" which has the same melody as "Aura Lee," in the 1969 movie *The Trouble with Girls (And How to Get Into It).* However, it was re-

*Frank Zappa named his son, Ahmet Rodan Zappa, after Mr. Ertegun.
†It is interesting to speculate how Elvis would have been handled on Atlantic. Would he have been given country songs, as Atlantic had no country artists; would he have been given R & B songs, their main releases; or would he have recorded on the Atco label singing many of the same Leiber and Stoller compositions that he did on RCA? He certainly would not have had the Jordanaires or Chet Atkins or Floyd Cramer.

19

corded on the film set—not in a recording studio. "Violet" ("Aura Lee") has never been released by RCA, but it does appear on several bootleg albums such as "Behind Closed Doors."

Austin, Gene. Crooner/composer (1900–72) who in 1927 recorded "My Blue Heaven," which became a multimillion-seller. It was the best-selling record of all time until it was surpassed by Bing Crosby's "White Christmas" in 1942. Col. Tom Parker was once the agent for Gene Austin. Country artist Tommy Overstreet is a nephew of the late Gene Austin.

Autry, Orvon Gene. Cowboy actor, singer, composer (over 275 songs), and successful investor. Early in his career Gene Autry was known as "Oklahoma's Singing Cowboy." He made his film debut in 1934 with *In Old Sante Fe.* Autry was the first cowboy to make recordings, the first to make singing Western movies, and the first cowboy to head a rodeo in New York. As a successful investor, he has owned Challenge Records,* Republic Records (with which Pat Boone began his recording career), the California Angels baseball team, and the Golden West radio network.

Gene Autry's biggest record was "Rudolph the Red-Nosed Reindeer" (Columbia 38610) in 1949, which is Columbia Records' all-time best-seller (over 8 million sold). Autry recorded a number of songs that Elvis later recorded. They included: "Frankie and Johnny" (1929), "The Yellow Rose of Texas" (1933), "Blue Hawaii" (1937), "Blueberry Hill" (1941), "I'll Never Let You Go (Little Darlin')" (1941), "Here Comes Santa Claus" (1947).

Avon Theater. One of the Memphis theaters that Elvis rented for his private showings. The Avon Theater is located at 124 W. Broadway in West Memphis.

Axton, Hoyt. Oklahoma-born composer and singer Hoyt Axton is the son of Mae Axton, co-composer of "Heartbreak Hotel." He composed "Greenback Dollar," which the Kingston Trio recorded in 1963 (Capitol 4898). Three Dog Night recorded two Hoyt Axton compositions, "Joy to the World" (Dunhill 4272) and "Never Been to Spain" (Dunhill 4299), both in 1971. Elvis recorded "Never Been to Spain" in February 1972.

Axton, Mae Boren. Cowriter (with Tommy Durden) of "Heartbreak Hotel." She worked as a publicist for country singer Hank Snow and is the mother of singer-songwriter Hoyt Axton. Previously, she and her husband, John Thomas Axton, taught English at Paxton High School in Jacksonville, Florida. Mae Axton is the sister of U.S. Senator David Boren of Oklahoma. In 1956 she composed the novelty song "Flying Saucer," recorded

---

*The Champs recorded "Tequila" on Challenge Records (Challenge 1016) in 1958 (Glen Campbell, Jimmy Seals, and Dash Crofts joined the group a short time later). Autry named the Champs after Champion, his Wonder Horse.

by Bill Buchanan and Dickie Goodman on the Luniverse label. Mae Axton also worked for the Grand Ole Opry for a time. (See: Axton, Hoyt; Velvet, Jimmy)

Ayers, Rick. One of Elvis's hairdressers in the 1970s.

B

B6. Guy Lambert's (Elvis) London apartment number in the 1967 movie *Double Trouble*.

Baba. Midget who befriended Johnny Tyronne (Elvis) in the 1965 movie *Harum Scarum*. Baba was played by Billy Barty.

Baba. Collie owned by Elvis at Graceland—one of the favorites of his many pets.

Baby, Baby, Baby. Song that Stella Stevens sang in the 1962 Elvis movie *Girls! Girls! Girls!*

(You're So Square) Baby, I Don't Care. Song that Elvis sang in the 1957 movie *Jailhouse Rock*. "(You're So Square) Baby, I Don't Care" was written by Jerry Leiber and Mike Stoller and appeared in the Extended Play album "Jailhouse Rock" (RCA EPA-4114) and the following Long Playing albums: "A Date with Elvis" (RCA LPM-2011); "A Date with Elvis" (RCA LSP-2011 [e]); "Elvis: The Other Sides—Worldwide Gold Award Hits, Volume 2" (RCA LPM-6402).

Baby, If You'll Give Me All of Your Love. Song that Elvis sang in the 1967 movie *Double Trouble*. "Baby, If You'll Give Me All of Your Love" was written by Joy Byers. It appeared in the Long Playing albums "Double Trouble" (RCA LPM/LSP-3787) and "Mahalo from Elvis" (Pickwick CL-7064).

Baby, Let's Play House. Sun 217. Released on April 1, 1955, as a 78 rpm single and a 45 rpm single. "Baby, Let's Play House" was the first song by Elvis to make the *Billboard* national charts (it reached #10 on the Country chart on July 6, 1955). "I'm Left, You're Right, She's Gone" was on the flip side. Written and originally recorded by Arthur Gunter (Excello* 2047) in 1954, "Baby, Let's Play House" inspired John Lennon to write "Run for Your Life." In 1956 Conway Twitty, using his real name, Harold Jenkins, recorded a version for Sun Records that was never released. (See: Oh Baby Babe)

Baby, Let's Play House. RCA 20/47-6383. A 78 rpm and a 45 rpm re-issue of the Sun original (Sun 217). "Baby, Let's Play House" appeared in the following albums: "A Date with Elvis"

*Excello was founded by Ernie Young in 1953. Arthur Gunter's "Baby, Let's Play House" was the first hit on the Excello label.

(RCA LPM-2011); "A Date with Elvis" (RCA LSP-2011 [e]); "The Elvis Presley Sun Collection" (RCA Starcall Hy-1001); "The Sun Sessions" (RCA APM1-1675); "The Sun Years" (Sun 1001).

Baby, Let's Play House. RCA 447-0604. Gold Standard Series reissue of RCA 20/47-6383.

Baby, What You Want Me to Do. Song written and originally recorded by Jimmy Reed in 1960 (Vee Jay 333). Elvis sang "Baby, What You Want Me to Do" on the 1968 NBC-TV special "Elvis." It appeared in the Long Playing albums "Elvis—TV Special" (RCA LPM-4088) and "Elvis—A Legendary Performer, Volume 2" (RCA CPL1-1349).

Bacarolle. Classic song by Jacques Offenbach that was the basis of "Tonight Is So Right for Love." Elvis sang "Tonight Is So Right for Love" in the 1960 movie *G.I. Blues.*

Bacharach, Burt. Composer of numerous movie themes and musical director for Dionne Warwick (later spelled Warwicke). He composed numerous hit songs with lyricists Hal David and is the husband of actress Angie Dickinson. Burt Bacharach, with Bob Hilliard, composed "Any Day Now," which Elvis recorded in 1969.

Badges. One of Elvis's hobbies was collecting badges. Former President Nixon personally saw to it that he received a Narcotics Bureau Badge that had previously been denied by Deputy Director John Finlater.

Bad Moon Rising. The 1969 hit song by Creedence Clearwater Revival (Fantasy 622). Written by John Fogerty, it appeared on the flip side of "Lodi." It reached #1 in both the U.S. and U.K. Elvis sang the song at several of his live concerts.

Baer, Herbert. Manitowoc, Wisconsin, foundry worker who, on December 18, 1978, legally changed his name to Elvis Presley. Previously, Elvis impersonators had been refused the name change because by doing so they would have made financial gains with their new name. Herbert Baer's wife and children retained the Baer name.

Baer, Max, Jr. Actor, director, and son of Heavyweight Boxing Champion Max Baer (June 14, 1934, to June 13, 1935). As an actor, Max Baer, Jr., played Jethro Bodine in the TV series "The Beverly Hillbillies" (1962–71). He directed the 1967 movie *Ode to Billie Joe.* Max Baer, Jr., was a close personal friend of Elvis and played on Elvis's football team.

Baiter, Tammy. St. Clair, Missouri, girl who was seriously injured by a car driven by Treatise Wheeler III on August 18, 1977, in front of Graceland. Two other girls (Alice Hovatar and Juanita Johnson) were killed in the accident. Miss Baiter's pelvis was shattered in four places.

Tammy Baiter was born on Elvis's birthday in 1960. (See: Hovatar, Alice; Johnson, Juanita Joan; Wheeler, Treatise, III)

Baize, Bill. Singer with J.D. Sumner and the Stamps. Elvis considered Bill Baize to have one of the finest voices in the world.

Baker, LaVern. Rhythm and blues artist of the 1950s and early '60s, nicknamed "Little Miss Sharecropper."* LaVern Baker had three million-sellers: "Tweedle Dee"† (Atlantic 1047) in 1955; "Jim Dandy" (Atlantic 1116) in 1957; "I Cried a Tear" (Atlantic 2007) in 1959. In the early 1950s she and singer Johnnie Ray appeared at Detroit's Flare Club together.

Elvis recorded two songs that LaVern Baker also recorded: "Saved" and "See See Rider." He also sang "Tweedle Dee" at the "Louisiana Hayride" in 1955. LaVern Baker recorded "Hey Memphis" (Atlantic 2119) as an answer to Elvis's "Little Sister."

Baker's Grand Prix Garage. Las Vegas garage where Lucky Jackson (Elvis Presley) kept his race cars in the 1964 movie *Viva Las Vegas*.

Bakir Oil Company. Petroleum corporation that wanted to drill for oil in the Valley of the Moon in the Arab kingdom of Lunarkand (1965 movie *Harum Scarum*).

Balint, Louis John. Unemployed Toledo, Ohio, sheetmetal worker who took a swing at Elvis on November 23, 1956. He claimed that his wife's love for Elvis broke up their marriage. Balint was fined $19.60 for assault and was jailed. Later, he claimed that a Presley aide had paid him $200 plus payment of any fine to pull the stunt. Balint's story was considered phony.

Ballad of Elvis Presley, The. A 1977 Elvis tribute record by Rita Bevis and California Gold on Larupin Records (Larupin 100).

Ballads of the King. An Elvis tribute album by the Johnny Mann Singers.‡ "Ballads of the King" contained twelve Elvis songs and was released on Liberty Records (Liberty 3198).

Ballard, Caroline. Elvis's first girlfriend (he was nine). Her father was the Reverend James Ballard—at that time, the Presley's pastor in East Tupelo.

Ballard, Reverend James. Pastor, in the mid-1940s, of the First Assembly of God Church in East Tupelo—the church attended by the Presleys. (See: First Assembly of God)

Ball, George. Security guard at Graceland and coauthor of Harold Loyd's book *The Gates of Graceland*.

Baltimore, Maryland. Site of a May 29, 1977, Elvis Presley concert. During this concert Elvis walked off the stage—the first time he had ever quit in the middle of a concert (except for health reasons).

---

*LaVern Baker chose the nickname "Little Miss Sharecropper" because another popular singer had the nickname "Little Miss Cornshucks."

†"Tomorrow Night," another song later recorded by Elvis, was on the flip side.

‡Thurl Ravenscroft, a member of the Johnny Mann Singers, is the voice of Tony the Tiger on the Kellogg's Sugar Frosted Flakes commercials.

Banana. Song that "Forty" Nina (Liliane Montevecchi) sang in the 1958 movie *King Creole*. "Banana" was written by Sid Tepper and Roy C. Bennett.

Baptist Memorial Hospital. Memphis, Tennessee, medical facility, at 899 Madison Avenue, which Elvis entered on April 1, 1977, suffering from both fatigue and intestinal flu. He left on April 6. His previous visits were: January–February 1975 (two weeks), August–September 1975 (two weeks), and October 1973 (two weeks). It is also the hospital where Lisa Marie Presley was born on February 1, 1968. Musician Bill Black died there on October 22, 1965; he was a victim of a heart attack. Elvis's body was brought to the hospital on the day of his death, August 16, 1977.

Baraso, Tony. Memphis accordianist who played at Elvis and Priscilla's second wedding reception, on May 29, 1967, at Graceland. Their first reception was on May 1 in Las Vegas.

Barbee, Sam. Disc jockey with whom Elvis talked in a telephone interview while in West Germany.

Bardot, Brigitte. French actress and ballerina whom Elvis wanted to meet while in the Army. In 1958, as Private Presley, Elvis stated, "The first place I want to go is to Paris and look up Brigitte Bardot." Miss Bardot didn't wish to meet Elvis at the time.

Ironically, on December 3, 1968, Brigitte Bardot's TV special immediately followed the NBC-TV special "Elvis."

Barefoot Ballad. Song that Elvis sang in the 1964 movie *Kissin' Cousins*. "Barefoot Ballad" was written by Dolores Fuller and Lee Morris and appeared in the Long Playing album "Kissin' Cousins" (RCA LPM/LSP-2894).

Barrett, Rona. Popular gossip columnist (real name: Rona Burstein) who announced in 1967 that Elvis and Priscilla were to be married in Palm Springs, California. In reality, they were married in Las Vegas. In the 1950s, as a teenager, Rona Barrett was the president of Eddie Fisher's National Fan Club.

Barris, George. One of the country's leading automobile customizers. George Barris customized Elvis's touring bus, which was later given to country singer T. G. Sheppard.

Barron Hilton. Las Vegas hotel where Vernon Presley and Priscilla unveiled a life-size statue of Elvis on September 14, 1978.

Bartholomew, Dave. New Orleans band leader who backed up Fats Domino* on his 1950s hits. Bartholomew also cowrote with Fats a number of hit records. Bartholomew previously was a trumpet player with Duke Ellington's band. He ranks third (tied with Fats Domino) behind Paul McCartney and John Lennon for composing the most million-selling songs. Dave Bartholomew with Pearl King composed "One Night," which Elvis recorded in 1957.

---

*Actually, Fats Domino began as a member of Dave Bartholomew's band.

Dave Bartholomew has been credited with having composed 22 million-selling records.

Barton Memorial Hospital. Recipient of the proceeds of Elvis's special Mother's Day concert at Lake Tahoe, Nevada, on May 13, 1973. The concert was in memory of Elvis's mother, Gladys.

Battle Hymn of the Republic, The. Civil War song, written by Julia Ward Howe, which was one of three songs included in "An American Trilogy." (See: An American Trilogy)

Battling Bellhop, The. The name to which the original 1937 movie *Kid Galahad* was changed whenever shown on television after 1962. *The Battling Bellhop* starred Edward G. Robinson, Bette Davis, Humphrey Bogart, and Wayne Morris.* The movie's title was changed so as not to be confused with the Elvis Presley version of 1962.

Beach Boy. Book by Allan Weiss on which the 1961 movie *Blue Hawaii* is based.

Beach Boy Blues. Song that Elvis sang in the 1961 movie *Blue Hawaii*. "Beach Boy Blues" was written by Sid Tepper and Roy C. Bennett and appeared in the Long Playing album "Blue Hawaii" (RCA LPM/LSP-2426).

Beach Shack. Song that Elvis sang in the 1966 movie *Spinout*. "Beach Shack" was written by Bill Giant, Bernie Baum, and Florence Kaye, and appeared in the Long Playing album "Spinout" (RCA LPM/LSP-3702).

Bean, Orville S. Tupelo, Mississippi, dairy farmer for whom Vernon Presley worked, prior to Elvis's birth. Bean bought lumber for Mr. Presley so that he (Presley) could build himself a house. Bean then rented the house to the Presleys. It was the same home in which Elvis was born.

Bear Cat. First Sun Records release for Rufus Thomas (Sun 181), recorded on March 8, 1953. "Bear Cat" was recorded as an answer to Big Mama Thornton's "Hound Dog." Don Robey, of Peacock Records in Houston, sued Sam Phillips of Sun, claiming that "Bear Cat" was a plagiarism of "Hound Dog." After a U. S. district court ruled in favor of Don Robey, an agreement was reached whereby Hi-Lo Music would pay to Lion Publishing a royalty of two cents on every sold copy of "Bear Cat." Phillips also agreed to change the record label from "Bear Cat (The Answer to Hound Dog)" by Rufus "Hound Dog" Thomas, Jr., to "Bear Cat" by Rufus Thomas, Jr. Rufus Thomas's band was thereafter known as the Bear Cats.

Beard, Eldene. Fifteen-year-old Memphis girl who may have been the first person to purchase an Elvis Presley record. She

---

*During World War II, Wayne Morris (who played the same role Elvis would later play) was one of the most decorated of the U. S. pilots. He shot down seven Japanese aircraft and sank two destroyers. Wayne Morris was awarded four Distinguished Flying Crosses. Enlisting as an ensign, he was discharged as a lieutenant commander.

purchased "That's All Right (Mama)"/"Blue Moon of Kentucky" (Sun 209) at 9:00 A.M. on July 19, 1954, at Charles Records on Main Street, across from the Suzore Theater.

Beatles. Most successful musical group in the history of show business. Members of the group were John (Winston) Lennon, (James) Paul McCartney, George Harrison, and Ringo Starr (Richard Starkey).

The Fab Four visited Elvis at his house in Bel-Air (565 Perugia Way) on August 27, 1965, during their second U. S. tour. They arrived at Elvis's home at 10:00 P.M. and stayed until 2:00 A.M.

Elvis sent the Beatles a telegram congratulating them on their first "Ed Sullivan Show" appearance, February 9, 1964. The Beatles sent Elvis a toy water pistol during their first American tour.

Elvis mentioned the Beatles by name in the altered lyrics of the song "I've Never Been to Spain" sung by Elvis in the 1972 documentary *Elvis on Tour.*

Elvis and the Beatles appeared on the same album in 1964. It was a U. S. Marines release for military stations. The lp was titled "Sounds of Solid Gold"; "Kissin' Cousins" by Elvis and "I Want to Hold Your Hand" by the Beatles were among the songs.

In a sad note, Elvis would later denounce the Beatles as a subversive group.

Beau. Priscilla Presley's nickname for herself.

Beaulieu, Joseph P. Priscilla Presley's father, who adopted her when she was a child (her real father died when she was four). His wife's name was Ann. Major Beaulieu was attached to the 1405 Support Squadron at the Weisbaden (West Germany) Air Base when Priscilla first met Elvis. He was later transferred to Travis Air Force Base near San Francisco, California, and was a colonel when he retired.

Beaulieu, Michelle. Younger sister of Priscilla Beaulieu. She served as the maid of honor at Priscilla's wedding to Elvis on May 1, 1967. Priscilla's brothers are Jeffrey, Donald, and twins Timothy and Thomas. They are all younger than Priscilla.,

Beaulieu, Priscilla. Adopted daughter of Joseph and Ann Beaulieu. Priscilla's real father died when she was four. Joseph Beaulieu, her stepfather, was a captain in the U. S. Air Force, stationed with his family in Germany at the same time that Elvis was there in the Army. At the age of fourteen, Priscilla met Elvis at a party in 1959; they were introduced by U. S. Airman James Curry. Elvis began seeing Priscilla shortly afterward and soon the two fell in love. With the help of Elvis's grandmother and stepmother, Priscilla was invited to spend Christmas with Elvis at Graceland in 1960. After the stay Priscilla returned to Germany. It was then that Elvis realized how much he missed her. In January 1961 Elvis called Priscilla's father, Captain Beaulieu, and asked if Priscilla could finish her schooling in Memphis under the watchful guardianship of Elvis's family. Priscilla's father finally agreed, and Priscilla completed her schooling at Immaculate Conception High while living at Graceland. In June 1963 Priscilla graduated from the school and enrolled in the Patricia Stevens Finishing School. On May 1, 1967, Elvis and Priscilla were married in a private ceremony held in Milton Prell's private suite at the Aladdin Hotel in Las Vegas. The couple then honeymooned at Palm Springs, California. After the honeymoon the couple moved into a mansion at 1174 Hillcrest Road in Beverly Hills, California. On February 1, 1968, nine months after the marriage, Lisa Marie Presley was born to the Presleys. Lisa would be the couple's only child. Priscilla left Elvis on February 23, 1972, becoming romantically involved with karate instructor Mike Stone, who himself was obtaining a divorce from his wife. It was Elvis who suggested that Stone teach Priscilla karate. Elvis sued Priscilla for divorce on January 8, 1973, in Santa Monica, California, and, on October 11, 1973, the divorce was granted. The divorce settlement put Priscilla economically well off. After her divorce from Elvis, Priscilla entered into several ventures including the Bis and Beau's boutique in Los Angeles, which was sold in 1976. Priscilla made her TV debut as a guest on Tony Orlando's NBC special in 1978. In the 1979 TV movie *Elvis*, Priscilla was portrayed by Season Hubley (Season married her costar Kurt Russell, who portrayed Elvis, after the completion of the TV movie).

Beautiful Dreamer. Stephen Foster song written in 1864, just a few days before his death. A Union soldier played "Beautiful Dreamer"* on his harmonica in the opening scenes of the 1956 Elvis movie *Love Me Tender*.

Because Of Love. Song that Elvis sang in the 1962 movie *Girls! Girls! Girls!* "Because of Love" was originally recorded by British singer Billy Fury.† It was written by Ruth Batchelor and Bob Roberts and appeared in the Long Playing album "Girls! Girls! Girls!" (RCA LPM–LSP-2626).

Becker, Joyce. Girl whom Elvis dated in 1961 during the filming of *Blue Hawaii*.

Bee Gees. Australian vocal group composed of the Gibb brothers: Robin, Barry, and Maurice. Barry and Maurice Gibb are twins. The Bee Gees were once managed by the Beatles' manager, Brian Epstein. Scottish singer Lulu (real name: Marie McDonald McLaughlin Lawrie), of Lulu and the Luvvers, was once

---

*"Beautiful Dreamer" was the favorite song of Mighty Joe Young, the ape in the 1949 movie *Mighty Joe Young*, and of Walter Mitty (Danny Kaye) in the 1947 movie *The Secret Life of Walter Mitty*.
†Billy Fury (real name: Ronald Wyncherley) once met Elvis on the set of *Girls! Girls! Girls!* Early in their career the Beatles once *failed* an audition to become the back-up band for Fury.

married to Maurice Gibb. The Bee Gees' album "Saturday Night Fever" has become the all-time best-selling album.

In 1969 Elvis recorded the Bee Gees' 1967 composition "Words."

Beene, Wally. Staff writer for the Armed Forces newspaper *Stars and Stripes.** Wally Beane was the only reporter to obtain an exclusive interview with Elvis Presley (late February 1960) while Elvis was in the Army.

Beginner's Luck. Song that Elvis sang in the 1966 movie *Frankie and Johnny*. "Beginner's Luck" was written by Sid Tepper and Roy C. Bennett and appeared in the Long Playing albums "Frankie and Johnny" (RCA LPM/LSP-3553) and "Frankie and Johnny" (Pickwick ACL-7007).

Bel Air Club. Memphis nightclub, located at 1850 S. Bellevue, in which Elvis appeared as a guest artist with Doug Poindexter and the Starlight Wranglers in 1954. The Bel-Air Club was a lounge at the Bel Air Motel. Jack Clement and his band once backed Elvis at the club.

Belew, Bill. Tailor who designed Elvis's jumpsuits and capes.

Bellevue Boulevard. The main north-south street in Memphis, Tennessee. The southern portion† of Bellevue Boulevard (Highway 51 South) was renamed Elvis Presley Boulevard on January 18, 1972.

Bell, Freddie, and the Bellboys. Obscure mid-1950s vocal group. Elvis, Scotty Moore, and Bill Black heard them sing "Hound Dog" while they were in Las Vegas in April 1956. Elvis liked the song and recorded it exactly as Freddie Bell and the Bellboys sang it (July 2, 1956). Interestingly, Freddie Bell first made a recording of "Hound Dog" twenty-two years later, in 1976, on the Penn label.

Members of the group were: Freddie Bell—lead singer, Jack Kane—saxophone, Frank Brent—bass guitar, Jerry Mayo—trumpet, Russ Conti—piano, Chick Geeney—drummer.

The band appeared in the 1956 movie *Rock Around the Clock* and the 1964 movie *Get Yourself a College Girl* (British title: *The Swingin' Set*). Roberta Linn sang with the band in the later movie.

Benevolent Con Man, The. Title of the autobiography (subtitled: *How Much Does It Cost If It's Free*) that Col. Tom Parker was writing in 1956. He turned down a $100,000 offer for it from a publisher with this reply: "Well, I guess I could let you have the back cover for that!"

Benjamin, Francis "Whitey" Ford. "Grand Ole Opry" comedian,

---

*The father of singer Jackson Browne was also a reporter for *Stars and Stripes* in West Germany.

†The reason that the entire Bellevue Boulevard wasn't renamed was due to the protests of the Bellevue Baptist Church (70 Bellevue), stating that they did not wish their church's name to be affiliated with that of a rock 'n roll singer (Elvis Presley Baptist Church).

28

known as the Duke of Paducah, who served as a scout for Col. Tom Parker. Whitey Benjamin helped persuade Parker to sign Elvis.

Bennett, Tony. Nightclub singer and recording artist (real name: Anthony Dominick Benedetto) who in 1953 recorded "Rags to Riches" (Columbia 40048), which Elvis recorded in September 1973.

Benny, Jack. Comedian whose house was pointed out during a Hollywood bus tour on which Vince Everett (Elvis) was an interested passenger in the 1957 movie *Jailhouse Rock*.

Bergen, Edgar. Late ventriloquist who featured dummies Charlie McCarthy, Mortimer Snerd, Effie Klinker, and Podine Puffington. His daughter is actress Candice Bergen.

Ventriloquists Edgar Bergen and Jimmy Nelson, along with Abe Saperstein, the founder of the Harlem Globetrotters basketball team, attended Lake View High School in Chicago.

Elvis took New York model Sandy Preston to see Edgar Bergen at the Sahara Hotel in 1956. Also featured was the Mary Kaye Trio.

Berle, Milton. Talented television comedian of the 1950s, nicknamed Uncle Miltie "The Thief of Bad Gags." He hosted the "Milton Berle Show." Milton Berle made his screen debut as a baby being thrown from a train in an episode of the 1914 silent serial *Perils of Pauline*. (See: Milton Berle Show, The)

Bernard, Judd, and Winkler, Irwin. Producers of the 1967 movie *Double Trouble*.

Berry, Chuck. Highly imaginative and talented composer/singer who recorded for Chicago's Chess Record label. His first hit record, "Maybelline," was actually written by Berry as a country song titled "Ida Red." His songs have been recorded by the Beatles, the Rolling Stones, and Elvis Presley, among others. Elvis recorded Chuck Berry's "Memphis, Tennessee," "Johnny B. Goode," "Too Much Monkey Business," and "The Promised Land." The Beatles recorded two of Berry's songs, "Rock and Roll Music" and "Roll Over Beethoven." The Rolling Stones recorded eight of his songs: "Carol"; "Don't Lie to Me"; "Around and Around"; "You Can't Catch Me"; "Talking About You"; "Little Queenie"; "Bye Bye Johnnie"; "Come On." Although Elvis, the Beatles, and the Rolling Stones all recorded a total of fourteen Chuck Berry compositions, none recorded the same song. Chuck Berry's first million-seller was "My Ding-a-Ling" in 1972.

Best Legs in the State of Maine. Former title won by Ronnie (Carolyn Jones) in the 1958 movie *King Creole*.

Best Years of Our Lives, The. Academy Award winning 1946 movie starring Fredric March, Myrna Loy, Dana Andrews, Harold Russell, and Cathy O'Donnell. *The Best Years of Our Lives* won several Academy Awards, including Best Picture,

Best Actor (Fredric March as Al Stephenson), and Best Supporting Actor (Harold Russell* as Homer Parrish).

On the night of July 7, 1954, Elvis went to the Suzore Theater No. 2 to see *The Best Years of Our Lives.* That same night, at approximately 9:30, Dewey Phillips became the first disc jockey to play an Elvis record ("That's All Right [Mama]"). The response from Phillips's listeners was so overwhelming that he decided to phone the Presleys to see if Elvis would do an interview. Since Elvis was at the Suzore Theater No. 2, Vernon Presley had to go to the theater to tell Elvis that Dewey Phillips wanted him at the radio station. Later that night, Elvis did his very first interview.

Beverly Hillbillies, The. Popular CBS-TV comedy series (1962–71). "The Beverly Hillbillies" was TV's top-rated program its first two seasons on the air. Four members of the cast had a connection with Elvis Presley. Max Baer, Jr., was a good friend of Elvis and played on Elvis's football team; Donna Douglas costarred with Elvis in the 1966 movie *Frankie and Johnny;* Raymond Baily appeared in *King Creole* (1958); Percy Helton was in *Jailhouse Rock* (1957).

The theme song of "The Beverly Hillbillies," "The Ballad of Jed Clampett," was composed by Lester Flatt and Earl Scruggs and sung by Jerry Scoggins. It reached #44 on *Billboard*'s Hot 100 chart. (See: Baer, Max, Jr.; Douglas, Donna; Flatt, Lester)

Beverly Wilshire Hotel. Beverly Hills, California, hotel where Elvis and his parents stayed while he was making the 1958 movie *King Creole.*

Beyond the Bend. Song that Elvis sang in the 1963 movie *It Happened at the World's Fair.* The Mello Men back Elvis on this song. "Beyond the Bend" was written by Fred Wise, Ben Weisman, and Delores Fuller, and appeared in the Long Playing album "It Happened at the World's Fair" (RCA LPM/LSP-2697).

Beyond the Reef. Song composed in 1950 by Jack Pitman and recorded by Jimmy Wakely and Margaret Whiting (Capitol 1234). Elvis recorded "Beyond the Reef" on May 27, 1966. It was voided because of a faulty backing track. A new backing track was cut on August 9, 1968, with personnel consisting of Ray Edenton (guitar), Norbert Putham (bass), Jerry Byrd (steel guitar), and Buddy Harman (drums). "Beyond the Reef" has never been released in any form.

B.F. Wood Music Company. Music-publishing firm that owns the British rights to Elvis's songs.

Bible, The (In the Beginning). A 1966 movie directed by John

---

*Harold Russell, who played the handless veteran in the movie, had lost his hands in a dynamite explosion during training maneuvers in North Carolina. Because of the two awards, he became the only person in Academy Award history to be awarded two Oscars for the same role.

Huston.* Elvis, Priscilla, and some of the Memphis Mafia attended a Hollywood premier showing of *The Bible* in 1966. (The world premier of *The Bible* (*La Biblia*) was in Rome, Italy.)

Elvis didn't care for the movie and wanted to leave at the intermission. Priscilla tried to persuade him to stay, but he and the boys left the theater.

Bienstock, Freddie. Manager of Elvis's music-publishing company who collected all the material from which Elvis would select the songs for his recording sessions.

Big Boss Man. RCA 47-9341. Released in September 1967 as a 45 rpm single. It reached #38 on *Billboard*'s Hot 100 chart. "You Don't Know Me" was on the flip side. "Big Boss Man" was written by Al Smith and Luther Dixon. In 1961 Jimmy Reed had a very successful recording of "Big Boss Man" (Vee Jay 380).

Elvis sang "Big Boss Man" in the Million-Dollar Session in 1956 and in the 1968 NBC-TV special "Elvis." It appeared in the following Long Playing albums: "Clambake" (RCA LPM/LSP-3893); "Elvis—TV Special" (RCA LPM-4088); "Elvis Sings Hits from His Movies, Volume 1" (RCA Camden CAS-2567); "Elvis Sings Hits from His Movies, Volume 1" (Pickwick CAS-2567); "Double Dynamite" (Pickwick DL2-5001). (See: Million-Dollar Session.)

Big Boss Man. RCA 447-0662. Gold Standard Series re-issue of RCA 47-9341.

Big Blue. Code name for the Pentagon during Operation Big Smokey in the 1964 movie *Kissin' Cousins*.

Big Boots. Song that Elvis sang in the 1960 movie *G.I. Blues*. The film and record versions are a combination of two takes. "Big Boots" was written by Sid Wayne and Sherman Edwards and appeared in the Long Playing albums "G.I. Blues" (RCA LPM/LSP-2256) and "Elvis Sings for Children (And Grown-ups Too)" (RCA CPL1-2901).

Big Bunny. Hugh Hefner's all-black DC-9 jet (N950PB). The aircraft was used by Elvis on his 1974 concert tour.

Big "D" Jamboree. Concert held in Dallas, Texas, April 16, 1955. Elvis appeared on the same bill with Sonny James, Hank Locklin, and the Maddox Brothers and Rose. Roy Orbison was a staff member at the time Elvis played the Big D. It was later, on June 24, that Bob Neal and Col. Parker met there for the first time.

Big E. One of the many nicknames Elvis acquired.

Big El. Affectionate nickname conferred upon Elvis.

---

*John Huston was the son of actor Walter Houston (who was the first person to record the classic song "September Song" from the 1938 musical play *Knickerbocker Holiday*). John Huston's first directorial attempt was with *The Maltese Falcon* (1941), starring Humphrey Bogart.

Biggs, Delta Mae. Aunt of Elvis and sister of Elvis's father, Vernon. She moved to Graceland in 1963, after her husband died, and served as housekeeper.

Big Hunk o' Love, A. RCA 47-7600. Released in June 1959 as a 45 rpm single. It reached #1 on *Billboard*'s Hot 100 chart (for two weeks, August 10–24) and #10 on the Rhythm and Blues chart. "A Big Hunk o' Love" sold over a million copies. "My Wish Came True" was on the flip side. Elvis sang "A Big Hunk o' Love" in the 1972 documentary *Elvis on Tour* and in the 1973 TV special "Elvis: Aloha from Hawaii." It was written by Aaron Schroeder and Sid Wyche and appeared in the following Long Playing albums: "50,000,000 Elvis Fans Can't Be Wrong—Elvis' Gold Records, Volume 2" (RCA LPM-2075); "50,000,000 Elvis Fans Can't Be Wrong—Elvis' Gold Records, Volume 2" (RCA LSP-2075 [e]); "Elvis: Worldwide 50 Gold Award Hits, Volume 1" (RCA LPM-6401); "Elvis: Aloha from Hawaii Via Satellite" (RCA VPSX-6089); "Elvis" (RCA DPL2-0056 [e]).

Big Hunk o' Love, A. RCA 447-0626. Gold Standard Series re-issue of RCA 47-7600.

Big Love, Big Heartache. Song that Elvis sang in the 1964 movie *Roustabout*. "Big Love, Big Heartache" was written by Dolores Fuller, Lee Morris, and Sonny Hendrix, and appeared in the Long Playing album "Roustabout" (RCA LPM/LSP-2999).

Big Smokey Mountain. Site in North Carolina that the U. S. Air Force tried to purchase from the Tatum family in the 1964 movie *Kissin' Cousins.*

Bill Bailey, Won't You Please Come Home. An early ragtime classic written in 1902 by Hugh Cannon, which Donna Butterworth sang in the 1966 movie *Paradise, Hawaiian Style.* Bill Bailey was a real person who died in 1966 in Singapore. Bailey had been a member of the vaudeville team Bailey and Cowan.

Hugh Cannon stated that the song was based on fact. He said that Bill Bailey was locked out of his apartment by his wife and that he (Cannon) gave Bailey money to rent a hotel room. Cannon further stated that he consoled Bailey and told him that his wife would forgive him. From that episode, Cannon wrote "Bill Bailey, Won't You Please Come Home." To his dying day, Bill Bailey said that Cannon's story was a complete fabrication.

Bobby Darin had a hit with "Bill Bailey, Won't You Please Come Home" in 1960 on Atco Records (Atco 6167) but titled "Won't You Come Home Bill Bailey."

A variation of the song was sung by Glenda Farrell as "Pappy, Won't You Please Come Home" in the 1964 movie *Kissin' Cousins.*

Billboard Magazine. Publication of current music trends, founded in 1894. In 1954 *Billboard* magazine voted Elvis Presley the eighth Most Promising Artist of the Year.

Bill's Motorcycles. Motorcycle shop that repaired Charlie Rogers's (Elvis) Honda after it was run off the road by Joe Lean (Leif Erickson) in the 1964 movie *Roustabout*.

Billy Easter. Title of the screenplay that was in the works at the time of Elvis's death in 1977. Financed by Elvis, it was to have been Elvis's best dramatic, nonsinging role.

Billy Goat Song, The/Swinging in the Orchard. Record cut by Jessie Presley, grandfather of Elvis, on Legacy Records in the 1950s.

Bing Crosby Award. Award presented to Elvis on September 8, 1971, by Bing's son Chris Crosby. The award was previously named the Golden Achievement Award. Previous recipients have been Irving Berlin, Frank Sinatra, and Edward Kennedy "Duke" Ellington.

Biondi, Dick. Disc jockey for Buffalo, New York, radio station WKBW who was fired on the air in 1956 for playing an Elvis Presley record.

Bio Science Laboratories. Los Angeles medical research facility, headed by Dr. Raymond Kelly, that analyzed the tissue from Elvis's body. Bio Science Laboratories concluded that the following depressant drugs were present in Elvis's body at the time of his death: Butabarbitol, Codeine, Morphine, Nembutal, Pentobarbital, Phenobarbital, Placidyl, Quaalude, Valium, Valmid.

Bis and Beau's. Beverly Hills boutique opened by Priscilla Presley and Olivia Bis in 1974. The shop was located at 9650 Santa Monica Boulevard. Bis and Beau's was sold on April 1, 1976.

Bitter They Are, Harder They Fall. Song written and originally recorded by country singer Larry Gatlin (Monument 8602). Elvis recorded "Bitter They Are, Harder They Fall" at Graceland on the night of February 2–3, 1976. It appeared in the Long Playing album "From Elvis Presley Boulevard, Memphis, Tennessee" (RCA APL1-1506).

Black. Color that Elvis dyed his naturally brown hair. Clairol hair dye was used.

Black and White. Only three Elvis Presley movies were filmed in black and white: *Love Me Tender* (1956), *Jailhouse Rock* (1957), and *King Creole* (1958).

Black Belt. Ranking designation used in karate. Elvis earned an eighth-degree black belt. He used karate in the following movies: *G.I. Blues* (1960); *Wild in the Country* (1961); *Blue Hawaii* (1961); *Kid Galahad* (1962); *Follow That Dream* (1962); *Harum Scarum* (1965).

Black, Bill. Bass player who backed Elvis on many of his early recordings. Prior to joining Elvis, he played with the Starlight Wranglers (a Sam Phillips group that Scotty Moore also played for). Bill Black, Scotty Moore, and Elvis were briefly known as the Blue Moon Boys. Bill Black played Eddy the bass player in the 1957 movie *Loving You*. After Black and Moore left Elvis in September 1957, because of a salary squabble, Black formed the Bill Black Combo. The last time that Bill Black backed up Elvis was on February 1, 1958. The group recorded a number of hit records, including the 1960 hit "Smokie Part 2" (Hi 2018) and the 1960 hit "White Silver Sands" (Hi 2021). Black also recorded an instrumental version of "Don't Be Cruel" (Hi 2026), (1960). All songs were released on the Memphis' Hi record label. The Bill Black Combo appeared in the 1961 movie *Teenage Millionaire*. His brother Johnny Black can be seen playing bass for the Johnny Burnette Trio in the 1957 movie *Rock, Rock, Rock*. (The Burnette Trio disbanded soon after the movie.) At one time Bill Black owned a recording studio located across the street from American Sound Studios in Memphis. In 1965 Bill Black was hospitalized at the Baptist Memorial Hospital three times from June to October 8 (when he went into a coma). On October 22, 1965, Bill Black died during surgery. Vernon Presley attended the funeral but Elvis did not. Ace Cannon took over the Bill Black Combo after his death.

Black Elvis, The. Name conferred upon singer Jackie Wilson. The late singer-guitarist James Marshal "Jimi" Hendrix (1942–70) was also called "The Black Elvis."

Blackman, Joan. Female lead (as Maile Duval) in the 1961 movie *Blue Hawaii*. Reportedly, Elvis disliked working with Joan Blackman.

Black Star. Title originally considered for the 1960 movie *Flaming Star*. Another title considered was *Flaming Heart*.

Blackwell, Otis. Prolific songwriter, born in Brooklyn on February 16, 1932. Under the pseudonym John Davenport, he cowrote "Fever" in 1958. In 1977 Stevie Wonder presented Otis Blackwell with a rock-music award in recognition of his accomplishments. Some of Blackwell's compositions are: "Great Balls of Fire"; "Priscilla"; "Just Keep It Up"; "Hey Little Girl"; "Breathless." Elvis recorded a number of Otis Blackwell songs, including "Fever"; "Don't Be Cruel"; "All Shook Up"; "Paralyzed"; "Return to Sender"; "(Such an) Easy Question"; "One Broken Heart for Sale"; "Don't Drag That String Around"; and others which have never been released. Otis Blackwell and Elvis never met.

Blackwood, Malessa. Nineteen-year-old beauty whom Elvis dated in 1976.

Blackwood Brothers. Gospel quartet from Ackerman, Mississippi, that formed their group in 1939. The original members were R. W. Blackwood, James Blackwood, Bill Lyles, and Bill Shaw. On June 30, 1954, a day after returning from the "Arthur Godfrey's Talent Scouts" show, where they won first place, R. W. Blackwood was killed in his twin Beech aircraft. Cecil Blackwood then became the group's lead singer. Elvis was once asked to join the Blackwood Brothers' younger group, the

Songfellows, which Cecil Blackwood had just vacated to become the lead of the Blackwood Brothers. Elvis wanted to join the Songfellows but couldn't because he was just then beginning to record for Sun Records. On July 24, 1957, Elvis attended a concert featuring the Blackwood Brothers. Because the group was the favorite of Gladys Presley, at her funeral they sang the spirituals "Rock of Ages" and "Precious Memories."

Blanton, Raymond. Former governor of Tennessee. On the day of Elvis's funeral Governor Blanton ordered all flags in the state flown at half-mast. He attended the funeral services. In 1978 Governor Raymond Blanton was involved in a major scandal that involved the selling of clemency for prisoners (he gave over fifty pardons). Brian Christie, the singing weatherman for WNGE-TV, recorded the song "Pardon Me, Ray" on Nashville's Sound Factory label in January 1979.

Bloch Arena. Four-thousand-seat facility at Pearl Harbor, Hawaii, where Elvis did a benefit concert for the U.S.S. *Arizona* Memorial Fund on March 25, 1961. The concert, sponsored by the Pacific War Memorial Commission, was originally scheduled for Palm Sunday, March 26, but Elvis didn't think that date was appropriate. Elvis and Col. Parker purchased the first two tickets (at $100 each). (See: Arizona, U.S.S.).

Blong, Larry. Elvis impersonator originating from the Philadelphia area.

Blossoms, The. Female vocal trio that backed Elvis on the 1968 NBC-TV special "Elvis." The members of the Blossoms were Darlene Love, Jean King, and Fanita James. They began singing together in 1957 when they recorded "He Promised Me"/"Move On" (Capitol 3822). Under the name of the Rebelettes, the Blossoms provided the vocal backing on several Duane Eddy hits, including "Guitar Man" (RCA 8087) and "Boss Guitar" (RCA 8131). They have also recorded under the name of the Wildcats. With Bobby Sheen, the Blossoms recorded as Bob B. Soxx and the Blue Jeans, scoring a hit in 1962 with "Zip-a-Dee-Doo-Dah" (Phillies 107). The Blossoms were regulars on the ABC-TV series "Shindig." (See: Love, Darlene)

Blue. Color of Elvis Presley's eyes.

Blue. Word that appeared in the title of nineteen songs that Elvis recorded. They are: "Beach Boy Blues," "Blueberry Hill," "Blue Christmas," "Blue Eyes Crying in the Rain," "Blue Guitar," "Blue Hawaii," "Blue Moon," "Blue Moon of Kentucky," "Blue River," "Blue Suede Shoes," "G.I. Blues," "Indescribably Blue," "Mean Woman Blues," "A Mess of Blues," "Milkcow Blues Boogie," "Moody Blue," "Something Blue," "Steamroller Blues," "When My Blue Moon Turns to Gold."

Blue Album. Nickname for Elvis's 1977 album "Moody Blue" because the first pressing was made of translucent blue plastic. This record was RCA Victor's two-billionth disc. (See: Moody Blue)

Blueberry Hill. Song written by Al Lewis, Larry Stock, and Vincent Rose in 1940. Gene Autry sang "Blueberry Hill" in the 1941 movie *The Singing Hill*. Glenn Miller's orchestra (with a vocal by Ray Eberle) first popularized the song with a recording on the Bluebird label (Bluebird 10768). In 1956 "Blueberry Hill" (Imperial 5407) became Fats Domino's biggest recording, selling over a million copies and reaching #4 on *Billboard's* Hot 100 chart. It was the only million-seller by Fats Domino that was not written by himself or by Dave Bartholomew.

Elvis sang "Blueberry Hill" in the famous Million-Dollar Session in December 1956. Elvis's recorded version of 1957 appeared on the Extended Play album "Just for You" (RCA EPA-4041) and the following Long Playing albums: "Loving You" (RCA LPM-1515); "Loving You" (RCA LSP-1515 [e]); "Elvis Recorded Live on Stage in Memphis" (RCA CPL1-0606). (See: Million-Dollar Session)

Blue Christmas. RCA 47-0808. A 45 rpm promotional release. "Blue Christmas" was featured on both sides of the record. The version used was that found on the Long Playing album "Elvis' Christmas Album" (RCA LOC-1035).

Blue Christmas. RCA 447-0647. Gold Standard Series original released in November 1965 as a 45 rpm single. Although "Blue Christmas" was released in 1964, this Gold Standard Series issue had a different flip side ("Santa Claus Is Back in Town"), making it a different record. "Blue Christmas"/"Santa Claus Is Back in Town" has been released during the Christmas season in subsequent years.

Blue Christmas. RCA 447-0720. Gold Standard Series original released in November 1964 as a 45 rpm single. "Wooden Heart" was on the flip side. "Blue Christmas" was recorded on September 5, 1957—seven years before it was released as a single. Elvis sang the song on the 1968 NBC-TV special "Elvis." Written by Bill Hayes and Jay Johnson, "Blue Christmas" appeared in the Extended Play album "Elvis Sings Christmas Songs" (RCA EPA-4108) and the following Long Playing albums: "Elvis' Christmas Album" (RCA LOC-1035); "Elvis' Christmas Album" (RCA LPM-1951); "Elvis' Christmas Album" (RCA LSP-1951 [e]); "Elvis—TV Special" RCA LPM-4088); "Elvis' Christmas Album" (RCA Camden CAL-2428); "Elvis' Christmas Album" (Pickwick CAS-2428); "Elvis—A Legendary Performer, Volume 2" (RCA CPL1-1349).

Blue Cross. Insurance company that insured Elvis's employees. The employees paid the premiums themselves and there were no retirement benefits, although they got time off for Elvis's movie openings. In earlier years, Elvis had paid for his employees' insurance.

Blue Eyes Crying in the Rain. Song written by Fred Rose and originally recorded by Roy Acuff (Columbia 37822). Willie Nelson later had a hit record with "Blue Eyes Crying in the Rain" (Columbia 33326). Elvis recorded the song at Graceland on February 8, 1976, and it appeared in the Long Playing album "From Elvis Presley Boulevard, Memphis, Tennessee" (RCA APL1-1506).

Blue Guitar. Song written and originally recorded by Sheb Wooley (MGM 13241) in 1954 and also recorded by Red Foley (Decca 29626). Elvis recorded "Blue Guitar" in 1955 at Sun Records. It has never been released.

BLUE HAWAII. Paramount, 1961. Premiered Los Angeles November 22, 1961 (101 min). Elvis's eighth movie. Producer, Hal B. Wallis. Associate Producer, Paul Nathan. Director, Norman Taurog. Cast: Chad Gates/Elvis Presley, Maile Duval/Joan Blackman, Abigail Prentace/Nancy Walters, Fred Gates/Roland Winters, Sarah Lee Gates/Angela Lansbury, Jack Kelman/John Archer, Mr. Chapman/Howard McNear, Mrs. Manaka/Flora Hayes, Mr. Duval/Gregory Gay, Tucker Garvey/Steve Brodie, Enid Garvey/Iris Adrian, Patsy/Darlene Tompkins, Sandy/Pamela Akert, Beverly/Christian Kay, Ellie Corbett/ Jenny Maxwell, Ito O'Hara/Frank Atienza, Carl/Lani Kai, Ernie/José De Vega, Wes/Ralph "Tiki" Hanalie, Waihila/ Hilo Hattie, Convict/Richard Reeves, Lt. Grey/Michael Ross, The Jordanaires/The Jordanaires. Screenplay, Hal Kanter. Photography, Charles Lang, Jr. Music, Joseph J. Lilley. Choreography, Charles O'Curran. Art Direction, Hal Pereira and Walter Tyler. Set Decoration, Sam Comer and Frank McKelvy. Special Effects, John P. Fulton. Costumes, Edith Head. Technical Adviser, Col. Tom Parker. Assistant Director D. Michael Moore. Editors, Warren Low and Terry Morse. Songs sung by Elvis: "Blue Hawaii," "Almost Always True," "Aloha Oe," "No More," "Can't Help Falling in Love," "Ku-u-i-Po," "Rock-a-Hula Baby," "Moonlight Swim," "Ito Eats," "Slicin' Sand," "Hawaiian Sunset," "Beach Boy Blues," "Island of Love," "Hawaiian Wedding Song." "Stepping Out of Line" was cut from the film. This was Elvis's most financially successful movie.

Blue Hawaii. Title song of the 1961 movie *Blue Hawaii,* which Elvis sang. Additional horn and string instruments were added to the film version. Elvis recorded "Blue Hawaii" for the worldwide TV concert "Elvis: Aloha from Hawaii," but it was not included.

"Blue Hawaii" was written by Leo Robin and Ralph Rainger in 1937 and was introduced in the movie *Waikiki Wedding* by Bing Crosby (Decca 1175). It appeared in the following Long Playing albums; "Blue Hawaii" (RCA LPM/LSP-2426); "Elvis in Hollywood" (RCA DPL2-0168); "Elvis—A Legendary Performer, Volume 2" (RCA CP1-1349); "Mahalo from Elvis" (Pickwick ACL-7064).

Blue Hawaii. RCA LPM/LSP-2426. A 33⅓ rpm Long Playing album that was released in October 1961. It reached #1 (for twenty weeks) on *Billboard*'s Hot LP chart. "Blue Hawaii" remained #1 longer than any other album by a rock performer or rock group until Fleetwood Mac's "Rumours" album in 1977. It sold over 5 million copies and received a Gold Disc award from the R.I.A.A. "Blue Hawaii" was Elvis's most successful album. Songs included—Side 1: "Blue Hawaii," "Almost Always True," "Aloha Oe," "No More," "Can't Help Falling in Love," "Rock-a-Hula Baby," "Moonlight Swim." Side 2: "Ku-u-i-po," "Ito Eats," "Slicin' Sand," "Hawaiian Sunset," "Beach Boy Blues," "Island of Love (Kauai)," "Hawaiian Wedding Song."

Blue Moon. RCA 20/47-6640. Released in September 1956 as a 78 rpm single and a 45 rpm single. It reached #55 on *Billboard*'s Hot 100 chart. "Just Because" was on the flip side. "Blue Moon" was composed by Richard Rodgers (music) and Lorenz Hart (words) in 1934. "Blue Moon" was originally titled "Prayer" and was to have been sung by Jean Harlow in the movie *Hollywood Revue of 1933*. However, that film project was scratched. Lorenz Hart changed the lyrics and retitled the song "The Bad in Every Man." Shirley Ross sang it in the 1934 movie *Manhattan Melodrama*,* starring Clark Gable.

In 1948 Billy Eckstine had a million-seller with "Blue Moon" —the third time the title and lyrics had been changed. In 1952 Ivory Joe Hunter recorded "Blue Moon" (MGM 11132). The Marcels also had a million-seller with "Blue Moon" (Colpix 186) in 1961. Their version reached #1 on the charts.

Elvis recorded "Blue Moon" in 1954 and it appeared in the Extended Play album "Elvis Presley" (RCA EPA-830) and the following Long Playing albums: "Elvis Presley" (RCA LPM-1254); "Elvis Presley" (RCA LSP-1254 [e]); "The Elvis Presley Sun Collection" (RCA Starcall Hy-1001); "The Sun Sessions" (RCA APM1-1675).

Blue Moon. RCA 447-0613. Gold Standard Series re-issue of RCA 20/47-6640.

Blue Moon Boys. Trio consisting of Elvis Presley, Bill Black, and Scotty Moore. The group used the name briefly in 1954.

Blue Moon of Kentucky. Sun 209. Released on July 19, 1954, as a 78 rpm single and a 45 rpm single. "That's All Right (Mama)" was on the flip side. "That's All Right (Mama)"/"Blue Moon of Kentucky" sold less than twenty thousand copies. "Blue Moon of Kentucky" was recorded by Elvis on July 5, 1954— his first commercial recording session. Later that week the song was first played on the radio by Sleepy-Eyed John Leply, a disc jockey with country station WHHM. Elvis sang "Blue Moon of

---

Manhattan Melodrama was the movie that Public Enemy No. 1, John Dillinger, had just watched at Chicago's Biograph Theater when he was shot and killed by F.B.I. agents led by Melvin Purvis (July 22, 1934).

Kentucky" at the Grand Ole Opry on September 25, 1954, where he bombed.

Bill Monroe wrote and originally recorded "Blue Moon of Kentucky" (Columbia 20370) in 1947, which was quickly rereleased after Elvis recorded it. (See: Grand Ole Opry; Phillips, Dewey; That's All Right [Mama]).

Blue Moon of Kentucky. RCA 20/47-6380. A 78 rpm and a 45 rpm re-issue of the Sun original (Sun 209). "Blue Moon of Kentucky" appeared in the Extended Play album "A Touch of Gold, Volume 3" (RCA EPA-5141) and the following Long Playing albums: "A Date with Elvis" (RCA LPM-2011); "A Date with Elvis" (RCA LSP 2011 [e]); "The Elvis Presley Sun Collection" (RCA Starcall Hy-1001); "The Sun Sessions" (RCA APM1-1675); "The Sun Years" (Sun 1001).

Blue Moon of Kentucky. RCA 447-0601. Gold Standard Series re-issue of RCA 20/47-6380.

Blue Moon of Kentucky. Sun 1129. A 45 rpm single originally released without any artist listed on the label. After a lawsuit by RCA, Sun reissued the record, listing Jimmy Ellis as the artist. Conjecture is that "Blue Moon of Kentucky" is an outtake from an early Sun session and that it's really Elvis on the record.

Blue River. RCA 47-8740. Released in January 1966 as a 45 rpm single. It reached #95 on *Billboard*'s Hot 100 chart. "Tell Me Why" was on the flip side. A different version of "Blue River" appeared in the French Extended Play album "Elvis Presley" (86508). Though released in 1966, "Blue River" was actually recorded on May 27, 1963. "Blue River" was written by Paul Evans and Fred Tobias and appeared in the Long Playing album "Double Trouble" (RCA LPM/LSP-3787).

Blue River. RCA 447-0655. Gold Standard Series re-issue of RCA 47-8740.

Blue Quail. Code name for Lt. Josh Morgan's (Elvis) search party. Captain Salbo's (Jack Albertson) squad used the code name Magpie (1964 movie *Kissin' Cousins*).

Blue Shade. New Orleans nightclub, located in the French Quarter on Bourbon Street, where Danny Fisher (Elvis) worked as a busboy in the 1958 movie *King Creole*. The Blue Shade was owned by Maxie Fields (Walter Matthau). Danny Fisher later began singing at the King Creole club.

Blue Suede Shoes. RCA 20/47-6636. Released in September 1956 as a 78 rpm single and a 45 rpm single. It reached #24 on *Billboard*'s Hot 100 chart. "Tutti Frutti" was on the flip side. "Blue Suede Shoes" was written and originally released by Carl Perkins* in 1956 (Sun 234). Perkins's version was a million-

---

*Carl Perkins wrote "Blue Suede Shoes" in Amory, Mississippi, in the summer of 1955. Perkins, Johnny Cash, and Elvis all performed at that concert. It was while Elvis was performing on stage that Carl Perkins wrote "Blue Suede Shoes" on a brown paper sack. "The Blue Suede Shoes" was

seller. Three versions of "Blue Suede Shoes" reached the charts in 1956: Perkins (#4), Elvis (#24), and Roy Bennett (King 4903) (#63). Several other recorded versions of "Blue Suede Shoes" in 1956 include Sid King, Pee Wee King, Jim Lowe, and Roy Hall.

Elvis sang "Blue Suede Shoes" in his screen test for Hal Wallis in April 1956, and in the following TV programs: "Stage Show" (January 28 and March 17, 1956); "Milton Berle Show" (April 3, 1956); "Elvis: Aloha from Hawaii" (January 14, 1973, and the NBC-TV telecast of April 4, 1973). "Blue Suede Shoes," by Elvis, was sung on a jukebox in the 1960 movie *G.I. Blues*. He also sang it in the 1970 documentary *Elvis—That's the Way It Is.*

"Blue Suede Shoes" appeared in the following Extended Play albums; "Elvis Presley" (RCA EPA-747); "Elvis Presley" (RCA EPB-1254); "Elvis Presley" (RCA SPD-22); "Elvis Presley" (RCA SPD-23); and the following Long Playing albums: "Elvis Presley" (RCA LPM-1254); "Elvis Presley" (RCA LSP-1254 [e]); "G.I. Blues" (RCA LPM/LSP-2256); "From Memphis to Vegas/From Vegas to Memphis" (RCA LSP-6020); "Elvis in Person" (RCA LSP-4428); "Elvis: Aloha from Hawaii Via Satellite" (RCA VPSX-6089); "Elvis—A Legendary Performer, Volume 2" (RCA CPL1-1349).

Blue Suede Shoes. RCA 447-0609. Gold Standard Series re-issue of RCA 20/47-6636.

Blue Suede Shoes. RCA 47-6492. A 45 rpm disc jockey "record preview." "I'm Counting on You" was on the flip side. On the regular release, RCA 20/47-6636, "Tutti Frutti" was on the flip side.

BMW (Bavarian Motor Works). One of several cars Elvis owned while in Germany. The German press referred to the automobile as the "Presley Wagen."

Bobo, Forrest L. Proprietor of the Tupelo Hardware Company, who, in January 1946, sold Gladys Presley a $12.75 guitar that she bought for Elvis. Elvis had wanted a .22 rifle. When Mrs. Presley told him he couldn't have a rifle, Elvis had a temper tantrum. After several minutes of discussions, Mrs. Presley and Mr. Bobo persuaded Elvis to get a guitar that was in a glass showcase on the other side of the store. The Tupelo Hardware Company had three different prices of guitars: $3.50, $6.25, and $12.75. Elvis received the most expensive model.

Bon Air Club. Memphis nightclub, located at 4862 Summer Ave. (at Mendenhall Road), where, in July 1954, Elvis made his

---

suggested by a statement made to Perkins by Johnny Cash. Cash mentioned a black sergeant he knew in the Air Force, named C. V. White, who coined the phrase, "Just don't step on my blue suede shoes." Interestingly, both sides of Perkins's record were covered by the two biggest institutions in rock music—Elvis rcorded "Blue Suede Shoes" and the Beatles recorded the flip side, "Honey Don't."

first public appearance after recording his first record ("That's All Right (Mama)"/"Blue Moon of Kentucky").

Bond, Eddi. EKKO recording artist who toured with the Elvis Presley unit September 5–9, 1955.

Bond, Johnny. Cowriter (with Ernest Tubb) of "Tomorrow Never Comes," which Elvis recorded in 1970. Johnny Bond, who was discovered by Gene Autry, appeared in movies with Roy Rogers, Gene Autry, Tex Ritter, and William Boyd (Hopalong Cassidy). In 1960 Johnny Bond reached the Pop charts with "Hot Rod Lincoln" (Republic 2005).

Bonus Tracks. Nonmovie songs placed in Elvis's soundtrack albums to reach a total of twelve songs.

Boola Boola. Yale University school song that was sung along with other school songs by a group of college men in the 1969 movie *The Trouble with Girls* (*And How to Get Into It*).

Boone, Pat (Eugene Charles Patrick Boone). Popular "clean cut" singer of the 1950s and early '60s. While performing he always wore white buck shoes, which became his trademark. Pat Boone had been president of David Lipscomb High School, while Shirley Foley, his future wife and daughter of Country Music Hall of Fame member Red Foley, was voted homecoming queen. He is the great-great-great-grandson of frontiersman Daniel Boone.

Pat Boone is surpassed only by Elvis for having the most #1 records by a single artist. Elvis had fourteen and Boone had five.

In the 1960s Pat Boone recorded an Elvis tribute album titled "Pat Boone Sings . . . Guess Who?"

Elvis Presley and Pat Boone first crossed paths when Pat won first place on the "Arthur Godfrey's Talent Scouts" TV series. Elvis was turned down at the show's rehearsal.

Boone and Presley, who appeared together in a show in Cleveland in 1955, were always good friends, despite the competition they supposedly created for each other in the 1950s. In Red Robinson's August 31, 1957, interview with Elvis in Vancouver, B.C., Elvis stated that Pat Boone was "undoubtedly the finest voice out now, especially on slow songs" and that he had been a collector of Pat Boone's records.

In 1977 Pat's daughter Debby Boone recorded the best-selling song in twenty-three years (and best ever by a female) —"You Light Up My Life" (Warner Bros. 0354). (See: Foley, Red)

Pat Boone has for years been accused of recording white covers of black records such as: "Two Hearts" by the Charms (Deluxe 6065), "Ain't It a Shame" by Fats Domino (Imperial 5348), "At My Front Door" by the El Dorados (Vee Jay 147), "Gee Whittakers" by the Five Keys (Capitol 3267), "Tutti Frutti" by Little Richard (Specialty 561), "I'll Be Home" by the Flamingos (Checker 830), "Long Tall Sally" by Little

Richard (Specialty 572), "Chains of Love" by Joe Turner (Atlantic 939), "I Almost Lost My Mind" by Ivory Joe Hunter (MGM 10578), "Tra La La" by LaVern Baker (Atlantic 1116).

Elvis Presley covered a vast amount more than Pat Boone ever did. The reason why Elvis was never accused of covering other people's songs was that he recorded obscure songs that the public either never knew existed or had never heard the original. For example, checking the top-ten rhythm and blues single for January–July 1955, these songs appeared: "Reconsider Baby" by Lowell Fulson, "Tweedle Dee" by LaVern Baker, "Pledging My Love" by Johnny Ace, "I've Got a Woman" by Ray Charles, "My Babe" by Little Walter, "Flip Flop & Fly" by Joe Turner, "Unchained Melody" by Roy Hamilton.

There are at least fifty more R & B songs from 1935 to '64 that Elvis either "covered" or recorded, whichever way one wishes to look at it.

Boppin' Hillbilly. One of the early nicknames for Elvis.

Borgnine, Ernest. Actor who won the Academy Award for Best Actor in 1955 for his portrayal of Marty Pilletti in the movie *Marty*. On TV, Ernest Borgnine portrayed Lt. Commander Quinton McHale in the series "McHale's Navy." He became good friends with Elvis (and Col. Parker) in 1956 while both were filming at Twentieth Century-Fox. Elvis was filming *Love Me Tender* and Borgnine, *Three Brave Men*.

Bosom of Abraham. RCA 74-0651. Released in March 1972 as a 45 rpm single. "He Touched Me" was on the flip side. Elvis sang "Bosom of Abraham" in the 1972 documentary *Elvis on Tour.* Ten thousand copies of "Bosom of Abraham"/"He Touched Me" were released with a 45 rpm hole but which played at 33⅓ rpm. RCA found out about the error and recalled the copies. "Bosom of Abraham" was recorded by the Trumpeteers on Score Records in the late 1940s (Score 5031). "Bosom of Abraham" was written by William Johnson, George McFadden, and Ted Brooks and appeared in the Long Playing album "He Touched Me" (RCA LSP-4690).

Bossa Nova Baby. RCA 47-8243. Released in October 1963 as a 45 rpm single. It reached #8 on *Billboard*'s Hot 100 chart and #20 on the Rhythm and Blues chart. "Bossa Nova Baby" was the only Bossa Nova* song that Elvis recorded and was the last Elvis single to appear on the Rhythm and Blues chart. It sold over a million copies. "Witchcraft" was on the flip side. "Bossa Nova Baby" was written by Jerry Leiber and Mike Stoller and was originally recorded by Tippie and the Clovers (Tiger 201) in 1963. Their version did not make the charts.

Elvis sang "Bossa Nova Baby" in the 1963 movie *Fun in Acapulco,* and it appeared in the Long Playing albums "Fun in

---

*The only other Bossa Nova song to reach the charts was "Blame It on the Bossa Nova" (Columbia 42661) by Edie Gorme in 1963.

Acapulco" (RCA LPM/LSP-2756), "Elvis: Worldwide 50 Gold Award Hits, Volume 1" (RCA LPM-6401), and "Elvis in Hollywood" (RCA DPL2-0168).

Bossa Nova Baby. RCA 447-0642. Gold Standard Series re-issue of RCA 47-8243.

Boucher, Ralph. Ranch hand at Elvis's Circle G Ranch who took care of the cattle.

Bourtiere, Carol. Stewardess on board Elvis's Convair 880 jet, *Lisa Marie.*

Bowers, Milton. Chairman of Local Draft Board #86 in Memphis, who personally delivered Elvis's draft notice at Graceland on December 20, 1957. The draft board gave Elvis a deferment to March 24, 1958 (from the original January 20), so that he could finish filming *King Creole* (1958).

Boxcar Records. Record label, based in Madison, Tennessee, begun by Elvis Presley and Col. Tom Parker. It was on this label that the 1974 album "Having Fun with Elvis on Stage" was first released. RCA later distributed it on its label (RCA CPM-0818).

Boy. Elvis's pet dog in the 1950s.

Boyce, Coach Rube, Jr. Elvis's football coach at Humes High School. Elvis went out for a few football practices in the fall of 1951.

Boyle Investment Company. Memphis firm that bought the Circle G Ranch from Elvis in 1969 after Elvis had bought it back from Lou McClellan. (See: Lou McClellan, Lou)

Boy Like Me, a Girl Like You, A. Song that Elvis sang in the 1962 movie *Girls! Girls! Girls!* It was written by Sid Tepper and Roy C. Bennett and appeared in the Long Playing album "Girls! Girls! Girls!" (RCA LPM/LSP-2621).

Boyd, Billie (Virginia). Custodian of Elvis's birthplace in Tupelo, Mississippi. In 1971 Mrs. Boyd created the idea for the Elvis museum. Jeanette McCombs then became head of the organization and with $80,000 built a chapel on the grounds next to Elvis's birthplace.

Bradley, Reverend C. W. Pastor of the Memphis Woodvale Church of Christ who conducted Elvis's funeral ceremony at Graceland on August 18, 1977, at 2:00 P.M.

Brand, Neville. Actor who played Mike Gavin (the man who killed "Elvis") in the 1956 movie *Love Me Tender.* Neville Brand was the fourth most decorated American soldier in World War II. (Audie Murphy was the most decorated.)

Brando, Marlon. Popular method actor of the 1950s, '60s, and '70s. Marlon Brando's second wife, Movita Castanada, played opposite Clark Gable in the 1935 movie *Mutiny on the Bounty.* Ironically, Brando played the same role in the 1962 remake and became romantically involved with the actress Tarita, who played the same role as Movita had played. He fathered a son by Movita and one by Tarita.

Marlon Brando has been nominated for Best Actor seven times, winning twice: 1954 (*On the Waterfront*) and 1972 (*The Godfather*).

The role of Pacer Burton in the 1960 movie *Flaming Star* was originally written for Marlon Brando. Elvis eventually received the part.

Elvis once stated that his favorite actors were Marlon Brando and Spencer Tracy, and he referred to James Dean as a genius.

Breath of a Nation. National television show, broadcast from prison, in which Vince Everett (Elvis) sang "I Want to be Free" in the 1957 movie *Jailhouse Rock*.

Bremerhaven, West Germany. Port city where Elvis arrived on the troop ship *General Randall* on October 1, 1958. Elvis then traveled by train to Friedberg, his permanent post in West Germany.

Brewer, Teresa. 1950s singer who made her singing debut at the age of two on the "Uncle August Kiddie Show" on radio station WSPD in Toledo. Teresa Brewer became a regular on the "Major Bowes Amateur Hour" at the age of five. In early 1950, at the age of eighteen, she had her first and biggest seller—"Music, Music, Music" (Coral 65520).

Elvis met Teresa Brewer for the first time when he and some friends attended one of her Las Vegas shows in 1972. Elvis spent an hour backstage talking with Ms. Brewer.

Bridge Over Troubled Water. Song written by Paul Simon and recorded by Simon and Garfunkel in 1970 (Columbia 33187).* "Bridge Over Troubled Water" sold over 5 million copies and was the top song of 1970. It was #1 for six weeks and received Grammy Awards for Record of the Year (1970), Song of the Year (1970), and Best Contemporary Song (1970).

Elvis sang "Bridge Over Troubled Water" in the documentaries *Elvis—That's the Way It Is* (1970) and *Elvis on Tour* (1972). It appeared in the Long Playing album "Elvis—That's the Way It Is" (RCA LSP-4445).

Briggs, David. Boyfriend of Linda Thompson after she and Elvis split. He played piano on a number of Elvis's record sessions and at his live concerts.

Brightest Stars of Christmas, The. RCA SP-0086. A 33⅓ rpm Long Playing album that was a collection of Christmas songs by various RCA artists. Elvis sang "Here Comes Santa Claus" on the album. "The Brightest Stars of Christmas" was a special release for J. C. Penney stores.

Brindley, Thomas C. Principal of Humes High School while Elvis was a student there (1948–53).

Bringing It Back. RCA PB-10401. Released in October 1975 as a

---

*A second 45 rpm record by Simon and Garfunkel was later released, this time titled "Bridge Over Troubled Waters" (note the s), backed with "Keep the Customer Satisfied" (Columbia 45079).

44

45 rpm single. It reached #65 on *Billboard*'s Hot 100 chart. "Pieces of My Life" was on the flip side. "Bringing It Back" was written by G. Gordon and appeared in the Long Playing album "Today (RCA APL1-1039).

Britches. Song recorded by Elvis on August 8, 1960, for the movie *Flaming Star*. Written by Sid Wayne and Sherman Edwards, "Britches" was cut from the final release of the film and remained unreleased until 1978, when it appeared on the Long Playing album "Elvis—A Legendary Performer, Volume 3" (RCA CPL1-3082).

Brock, Robert. Attorney picked by Gregory Hookstratten (Elvis's attorney) to represent Priscilla during the divorce proceedings in 1973.

Brockaw, Norman. Priscilla Presley's agent.

Bronson, Charles. Actor (real name: Charles Buchinsky) who graduated from playing Igor in the 3-D movie *House of Wax* (1953) to become one of the highest-paid actors in the world. Charles Bronson, Clark Gable, and Sabu all served as tail gunners in bombers during World War II. Bronson is married to actress Jill Ireland,* who usually appears in her husband's films.

Charles Bronson played Lew Nyack in the 1962 movie *Kid Galahad*.

Brooklyn Army Depot. (See: Military Ocean Terminal)

Brooks, Dudley A. Piano player on many of Elvis's recording sessions from 1956 to '64. Some of the cuts Dudley Brooks appeared on include: "(Let Me Be Your) Teddy Bear," "Treat Me Nice," "Don't," and "Jailhouse Rock."†

Brown, Aubrey. One of the Memphis gas station attendants whom Elvis punched on October 18, 1956, in the "Ed Hopper" incident. (See: Hopper, Ed)

Brown, James. Black singer and entertainer who is called "Soul Brother Number One." In his youth, James Brown spent three years in a Georgia reform school. He shined shoes outside of an Augusta, Georgia, radio station. Today, James Brown is the owner of that station. As a professional, James Brown won sixteen of seventeen bantamweight boxing matches.

Both Elvis and James Brown were referred to as "Mr. Dynamite." Brown, Richard Penniman (Little Richard), and Otis Redding all hail from Macon, Georgia.

James Brown was one of several celebrities who attended Elvis's private funeral.

Brown, Roy. Rhythm and blues singer and composer who wrote

---

*Prior to her marriage to Bronson, Jill Ireland was married to actor David McCallum.

†Because the song's cocomposer Mike Stoller made a cameo scene in the 1957 movie *Jailhouse Rock*, playing the piano while Elvis sang "Jailhouse Rock," this led to the erroneous belief that Stoller played the piano on the recording.

"Good Rockin' Tonight" in 1947. Elvis recorded the song in 1954. Roy Brown was an unusual rhythm and blues singer in that, while Elvis was a white singer with a black sound, Brown was a black with a white sound. His favorite singer was Bing Crosby.

Roy Brown claimed that in 1953–54, Elvis tried on a number of occasions to join his band on stage in several Memphis clubs. Elvis, who befriended them, would buy the band wine. At the time, Brown wouldn't let Elvis perform with him.

Interestingly, both Roy Brown's mother and Elvis's mother had the same middle name—Love.

Brown, Tony. Piano player with Elvis's touring band (1974–77). Tony Brown replaced Glenn D. Hardin. Previously, he was a member of Voice.

Brown Suede Combat Boots. Short parody on "Blue Suede Shoes" that Sgt. Bilko (Phil Silvers) sang in an episode of the "Phil Silvers Show" about rock 'n' roll singer Elvin Pelvin. (See: Elvin Pelvin; Phil Silvers Show, The)

Bryant, Boudleaux. Songwriter and violinist. In 1938 Boudleaux Bryant played violin for the Atlanta Philharmonic Orchestra. Bryant, along with his wife, Felicia, are best known as writers of country songs. They have written "Bye Bye Love," "Wake Up Little Susie," "All I Have to Do Is Dream," and "Bird Dog" for the Everly Brothers. In 1961 Boudleaux wrote the instrumental "Mexico," which Bob Moore successfully recorded (Monument 446).

Boudleaux Bryant co-wrote with Chet Atkins "How's the World Treating You," which Elvis recorded in 1956.

Buchanan and Goodman on Trial. A 1956 novelty record by Bill Buchanan and Dickie Goodman on the Luniverse label (Luniverse 102). A few seconds of Elvis's version of "Hound Dog" appeared in the record.

Buddah Records. Record label on which the 1972 album "Current Audio Magazine" was released. In August 1972, RCA sued Buddah. The court ruled in favor of Buddah Records, stating that a press conference is public domain. This, then, accounts for the various legitimate record labels that carry Elvis interviews. (See: Current Audio Magazine)

Buddy Holly Story, The. A 1978 movie starring Gary Busey in the role of Buddy Holly. Elvis was mentioned in the movie.

Buergin, Margarite. Seventeen-year-old German stenographer whom Elvis dated while he was stationed in West Germany.

Bullfighter Was a Lady, The. Song that Elvis sang in the 1963 movie *Fun in Acapulco*. "The Bullfighter Was a Lady" was written by Sid Tepper and Roy C. Bennett and appeared in the Long Playing album "Fun in Acapulco."

Bumble Bee, Oh Bumble Bee. Tentative title of Elvis's 1968 movie *Stay Away, Joe*. The title was then changed to *Born Rich* before finally becoming *Stay Away, Joe*.

Bunny. Code name that Ann-Margret used when telephoning Elvis. It later evolved into "Thumper" (after the rabbit in the 1942 Walt Disney animated movie *Bambi*).

Bunting. One of Linda Thompson's nicknames for Elvis.

Burbank Sessions, Volume 1, The. A two-record bootleg album released in November 1978. The album contained the entire live shows that Elvis gave at the NBC studios in Burbank, California, on June 27, 1968. Excerpts from the two shows were used for the NBC-TV special "Elvis" (December 3, 1968). Songs included—Side 1: Dialogue, "That's All Right," "Heartbreak Hotel," "Love Me," "Baby, What You Want Me to Do," Dialogue, "Blue Suede Shoes," "Baby What You Want Me to Do," Dialogue, "Lawdy, Miss Clawdy." Side 2: "Are You Lonesome Tonight," "When My Blue Moon Turns to Gold Again," "Blue Christmas," "Tryin' to Get to You," "One Night" (2 Versions), "Baby, What You Want Me to Do," Dialogue, "One Night," "Memories." Side 3: Dialogue, "Heartbreak Hotel," "Baby What You Want Me to Do," Dialogue, "Thats All Right," "Are You Lonesome Tonight," "Baby What You Want Me to Do," "Blue Suede Shoes," "One Night." Side 4: "Love Me," Dialogue, "Tryin' to Get to You," "Lawdy, Miss Clawdy," Dialogue, "Santa Claus Is Back in Town," "Blue Christmas," "Tiger Man," "When My Blue Moon Turns to Gold Again," "Memories."

Burbank Sessions, Volume II, The. A two-record bootleg album released in November 1978 on the German Audifön record label. The album contains the entire live show that Elvis gave at the NBC Studios in Burbank on June 29, 1968. Songs included—Side 1: Intro and Dialogue, "Heartbreak Hotel"/ "One Night," Medley: "Heartbreak Hotel"/"Hound Dog"/"All Shook Up," "Can't Help Falling in Love," "Jailhouse Rock," "Don't Be Cruel," "Blue Suede Shoes." Side 2: "Love Me Tender," Dialogue, "Trouble," Dialogue, "Baby, What You Want Me to Do," "If I Can Dream." Side 3: Intro and Dialogue, Medley: "Heartbreak Hotel"/"Hound Dog"/"All Shook Up," "Can't Help Falling in Love," "Jailhouse Rock," "Don't Be Cruel," "Blue Suede Shoes," "Love Me Tender." Side 4: Dialogue, "Trouble No. 1," Dialogue, "Trouble"/ "Guitar Man," Dialogue, "Trouble"/"Guitar Man," Dialogue, "If I Can Dream."

Burke's Florist. Memphis florist, located at 1609 Elvis Presley Blvd., where Elvis and Priscilla purchased their flowers.

Burnette, Johnny. Popular country rock-a-billy recording artist of the 1950s and '60s and brother of country star Dorsey Burnette. In his youth Johnny Burnette was a Golden Gloves boxing champion.* While playing football for Catholic High

---

*As were Jackie Wilson, Screamin' Jay Hawkins, Billy Ward, and Willie Dixon.

School in Memphis he played in a game opposite Red West, who knocked him out of the game. Both brothers had also attended Humes High in Memphis. Johnny Burnette sang and played in a trio consisting of Bill Black and Scotty Moore, prior to the two backing Elvis. Johnny and Dorsey Burnette both worked as electricians at Crown Electric in Memphis in 1952, a year prior to the time that Elvis was employed there as a truck driver. In 1953 Johnny Burnette formed the Johnny Burnette Trio (Johnny, Dorsey, and Paul Burlison).* All three members of the band were Memphis Golden Glove fighters. The trio disbanded in 1957. Elvis once sang and played with the Johnny Burnette Trio, backing Johnny on one occasion in 1954 at a used-car-lot show. The Johnny Burnette Trio made some recordings for Sun Records but none of them was ever released. In 1955 the trio won three weeks in a row on the "Ted Mack Amateur Hour," making it to the finals, which were broadcast at 9:00 P.M., September 9, 1956, on ABC (this was the same night that Elvis made his national television debut on the "Ed Sullivan Show" one hour earlier on CBS). (Johnny Burnette made his national TV debut on the "Steve Allen Show.") The trio made their movie debut in the 1957 movie *Rock, Rock, Rock,* singing "Lonesome Train." Carl Perkins's cousin Tony Austin later became a drummer for the trio. When Dorsey left the trio to become a solo artist ("Tall Oak Tree" and "Hey Little One") he was replaced by Johnny Black, the brother of Bill Black. Johnny and Dorsey Burnette composed "It's Late," "Just a Little Too Much," and "Believe What You Say." At his peak as a successful solo artist (Dreamin'" and "You're Sixteen") Johnny Burnette drowned, on August 1, 1964, in a fishing accident at Clear Lake,† California.

Burning Love. RCA 74-0769. Released in August 1972 as a 45 rpm single. "Burning Love" reached #2 on *Billboard*'s Hot 100 chart and sold over a million copies. "It's a Matter of Time" was on the flip side. "Burning Love" was written by Dennis Linde and was originally recorded by Arthur Alexander. Alexander's version never reached the charts. Elvis sang "Burning Love" in the 1972 documentary *Elvis on Tour* and in the 1973 TV special "Elvis: Aloha from Hawaii." It appeared in the following Long Playing albums: "Elvis: Aloha from Hawaii Via Satellite" (RCA VPS-6089); "Burning Love and Hits From His Movies, Volume 2" (RCA Camden CAS-2595); "Burning Love and Hits from His Movies, Volume 2" (Pickwick CAS-2595).

Burning Love. RCA GB-10156. Gold Standard Series original re-

---

*Paul Burlison, who hailed from Walls, Mississippi, was the spitting image of Carl Perkins.
†Ironically, it was at Clear Lake, Iowa, that on February 3, 1959, Buddy Holly, Ritchie Valens, and Jiles Perry Richardson (the Big Bopper) died in a plane crash.

leased in January 1975. Although "Burning Love" had been released previously (RCA 74-0769), this Gold Standard Series issue had a different flip side ("Steamroller Blues"), making it a different record.

Burning Love and Hits from His Movies, Volume 2. RCA Camden CAS-2595. A 33⅓ rpm Long Playing album released in November 1972. It reached #22 on *Billboard*'s Hot LP chart. "Burning Love and Hits From His Movies, Volume 2" achieved sales of over 1 million, qualifying it for a Gold Record. The album contained "Burning Love," "It's a Matter of Time," and eight movie songs. Songs included—Side 1: "Burning Love," "Tender Feeling," "Am I Ready," "Tonight Is So Right for Love," "Guadalajara." Side 2: "It's a Matter of Time," "No More," "Santa Lucia," "We'll Be Together," "I Love Only One Girl."

Burning Love and Hits from His Movies, Volume 1. A 33⅓ rpm Long Playing album that was a re-issue of RCA Camden CAS-2595. It was released in December 1975.

Burning Sands. Actor Johnny Tyronne's (Elvis) latest movie (1965 movie *Harum Scarum*).

Burton Boat Company. Firm from which Scott Hayward (Elvis) obtained the boat that he entered in the Orange Bowl Regatta boat race in the 1967 movie *Clambake*.

Burton, James. Lead guitarist in many of Elvis's later recording sessions. James Burton's first recording session was with Dale Hawkins, appearing on Hawkins's 1957 hit "Susie Q" (Checker 863). Burton then played lead guitar for Ricky Nelson in the 1960s, before joining Elvis's band.

Butch. Word Elvis used for "milk" from childhood until his death.

Butch Cassidy and the Sundance Kid. A 1969 movie starring Paul Newman (as Butch Cassidy), Robert Redford (as the Sundance Kid), and Katharine Ross (as Etta Place). The movie's theme song, "Raindrops Keep Fallin' on My Head,"* was sung by B. J. Thomas (Billy Joe Thomas) and reached #1 selling over a million copies. Elvis attended a showing of *Butch Cassidy and the Sundance Kid* at the Memphian Theater in Memphis on September 27, 1969.

By and By. Gospel song arranged and recorded by Elvis in 1966. "By and By" appeared in the Long Playing album "How Great Thou Art" (RCA LPM/LSP-3758).

Bye Bye Birdie. Broadway musical that ran from 1960 to '62. It told the story of the induction into the Army of a rock 'n' roll singer named Conrad Birdie. Dick Gautier starred as Conrad Birdie. The musical was written by Michael Stewart, with music by Lee Adams and Charles Strouse. *Bye Bye Birdie* parodied Elvis's career. Today Paul McCartney owns the musical rights.

---

*Bob Dylan received an offer to sing "Raindrops Keep Fallin' on My Head," but he turned it down.

In 1963 *Bye Bye Birdie* was made into a movie starring Dick Van Dyke, Janet Leigh, Ann-Margret, and Jesse Pearson as Conrad Birdie.

The movie's producers almost got Elvis to appear in the movie to sing two songs, but they couldn't meet the price of $100,000 asked by Col. Tom Parker. Ed Sullivan had a cameo role in the movie.

Bye Bye Elvis. An Elvis novelty record by Gene Harris that mentioned Elvis, "Hound Dog," and "Don't Be Cruel" in the lyrics. It was released on ABC Paramount Records (ABC Paramount 9900) in 1958.

C

C42597. Nevada license-plate number of the black Cadillac that brought Elvis (Kurt Russell) to the International Hotel July 26, 1969 (1979 TV movie *Elvis*).

Cabot, Sebastian. Actor who was best known for his role as Giles French, the butler on the TV series "Family Affair."* Other TV series of Sebastian Cabot include "Checkmate," "Ghost Story" (host), and "Suspense." Cabot was one of several celebrities who died (August 23, 1977) within a short time of Elvis's death. (See: Marx, Groucho; Mostel, Zero)

Cactus Coca. Character played by Imogene Coca to Elvis's Tumbleweed character on the "Steve Allen Show" (July 1, 1956).

Cadets, The. Rhythm and blues group who in 1956 recorded a cover version of "Heartbreak Hotel" (Modern 985). The flip side was "Church Bells May Ring," a hit for the Diamonds (Mercury 70835) and the Willows† (Melba Records), for both in 1956. The Cadets, whose biggest hit was "Stranded in the Jungle" (Modern 994), in 1956, also recorded ballads, such as "Why Don't You Write Me" (RPM 428), in 1955, under the name of the Jacks. (See: Anka, Paul)

Cadillac Club. New Orleans nightclub, on St. Claude Avenue, where Elvis was turned down as a performer by owner Lois Brown in 1954 because he was an unknown. The club did book two brothers—the Everly Brothers. (It was not until 1957 that the Everly Brothers had their first hit, "Bye Bye Love.")

Cadillac Elvis. A 33⅓ rpm bootleg album containing various interviews and spoken tributes, plus the following songs—

---

*Anissa Jones, who played Buffy on "Family Affair," appeared as Carol in the 1969 Elvis movie *The Trouble with Girls (and How to Get Into It).*
†On the Willows' original version of "Church Bells May Ring," the chimes were dubbed in by Neil Sedaka.

Side 1: "Polk Salad Annie" (Recorded live—January 26, 1970), "Heartbreak Hotel" (Recorded live—February 16, 1972), "Rags to Riches" (Previously released), "The Lady Loves Me" (Duet with Ann Margret), "That's All Right (Mama)" (Recorded live—June 27, 1968), "Blue Suede Shoes" (Recorded live—August 4, 1972), "All Shook Up" (Recorded live—August 4, 1972). Side 2: "Shake a Hand" (Recorded live—July 22, 1975), Medley: "Young and Beautiful," "Happy Birthday," "The Mickey Mouse March" (Recorded live—May 30, 1976), "I Want You, I Need You, I Love You," "Hound Dog" (Recorded live—July 1, 1956), "Blueberry Hill" (Recorded live—July 19, 1975), "Lawdy, Miss Clawdy" (Recorded live—March 5, 1974.

Café Europa. Title originally considered for the 1960 movie *G.I. Blues.*

Calhoun, Charles E. Composer of many rhythm and blues songs of the early 1950s, including "Shake, Rattle, and Roll." Charles Calhoun is a pen name used by composer Jesse Stone. Elvis recorded "Shake, Rattle, and Roll" in February 1956.

California Holiday. British title of the 1966 Elvis movie *Spinout.*

Call from Mitch Miller, A. Short story by Mary Agnes Thompson that appeared in *Good Housekeeping* magazine. The screenplay for *Loving You* is based on this story.

Camden. Record label on which Elvis's discount albums were released. Camden is a subsidiary of RCA, named after Camden, New Jersey, the site of the RCA pressing plant. Usually, Camden had ten songs on each album. (See: Pickwick) The 1972 album "Burning Love and Hits from His Movies, Volume 2" is the only Gold album that Camden has ever produced.

Camp, Mrs. Quay Web. Elvis's sixth-grade teacher at Milam Junior High School in Tupelo, Mississippi.

Campbell, Glen. Talented singer, composer, and musician, Glen Campbell began as a studio musician. He played for both the Champs and the Beach Boys. In 1967 Glen Campbell recorded his first hit, "Gentle on My Mind," which Elvis recorded in 1969. Glen Campbell played guitar on the soundtrack of many of Elvis's movies. Glen Campbell's former wife, Sarah, had previously been married to Mac Davis. (See: Davis, Mac)

Glen Campbell does an excellent imitation of Elvis in his nightclub act.

Canada. Country where Elvis made only three appearances: April 2, 1957, (Toronto); April 3, 1957 (Ottawa); August 31, 1957 (Vancouver).

Candy Bars for Elvis. A tribute song to Elvis recorded in 1977 by Barry Tiffin. (Tiffin International 300.)

Candy Kisses. Song written by George Morgan in 1948 and recorded by him on Columbia Records (Columbia 20547). Georgia Gibbs also had a recording of "Candy Kisses," on Mercury Records. Bill Haley and the Four Aces of Western Swing

51

recorded "Candy Kisses" on Cowboy Records (Cowboy 1701) in 1948. Elvis is believed to have recorded "Candy Kisses" for the 1957 movie *Loving You,* although it was cut from the final print of the film. Throughout the movie, however, "Candy Kisses"* can be heard being played by Tex Warner's (Wendall Corey) Rough Ridin' Ramblers.

Cane and a High Starched Collar, A. Song that Elvis sang in the 1960 movie *Flaming Star.* Written by Sid Tepper and Roy C. Bennett, "A Cane and a High Starched Collar" remained unreleased until 1976, when it appeared on the Long Playing album "Elvis—A Legendary Performer, Volume 2" (RCA CPL1-1349). The false start (take 2) and the film version (take 3) were included.

Can't Help Falling in Love. RCA 47-7968. Released in November 1961 as a 45 rpm single. It reached #2 on *Billboard*'s Hot 100 chart and #1 in the United Kingdom (for four weeks, February 24–March 24). "Can't Help Falling in Love" sold over a million copies. "Rock-a-Hula Baby" was on the flip side. Based on the classical "Plaisir d' Amour" by Giovanni Martini (1741–1816), "Can't Help Falling in Love" was written by George Weiss, Hugo Peretti, and Luigi Creatore. It was sung by Elvis in the 1961 movie *Blue Hawaii,* the 1970 documentary *Elvis—That's the Way It Is,* and the 1972 documentary *Elvis on Tour.*

In the movie *Blue Hawaii,* "Can't Help Falling in Love" was played on a music box.

In addition, "Can't Help Falling in Love" appeared in the following TV specials: "Elvis" (NBC-TV, 1968); "Elvis: Aloha from Hawaii" (NBC-TV, 1973); "Elvis in Concert" (CBS-TV, 1977).

Elvis ended every concert of the 1960s and '70s with "Can't Help Falling in Love." (In the 1950s, he ended with "Hound Dog.") It appeared in the following Long Playing albums: "Blue Hawaii" (RCA LPM/LSP-2426); "Elvis—TV Special" (RCA LPM-4088); "From Memphis to Vegas/From Vegas to Memphis" (RCA LSP-6020); "Elvis: Worldwide 50 Gold Award Hits, Volume 1" (RCA LPM-6401); "Elvis in Person" (RCA LSP-4428); "Elvis as Recorded at Madison Square Garden" (RCA LSP-4776); "Elvis: Aloha from Hawaii Via Satellite (RCA VPSX-6089); "Elvis" (RCA DPL2-0056 [e]); "Elvis—A Legendary Performer, Volume 1" (RCA CPL1-0341); "Elvis Recorded Live on Stage in Memphis" (RCA CPL1-0606); "Elvis in Concert" (RCA APL2-2587).

Can't Help Falling in Love. RCA 447-0635. Gold Standard Series re-issue of RCA 47-7968.

Capital Casino. Albany, New York, site of Kid Galahad's (Elvis)

---

*It also appeared in the 1949 movie *Down Dakota Way,* starring Roy Rogers.

first fight in the 1962 movie *Kid Galahad*. He fought Ezzard "Baba" Bailey.

Caplan, Harry. Producer of the 1969 National General Pictures movie *Charro!*

Capricorn. Astrological sign of Elvis.

Captain of the Louisiana State Highway Patrol. Honorary award, with badge, conferred upon Elvis in 1956.

Cardiac Arrhythmia. Irregular and ineffective heartbeat due to hypertensive heart disease relating to high blood pressure. Cardiac arrhythmia was the official cause of Elvis's death.

Carlsbad, New Mexico. City where Elvis performed in February 1955. The concert appearance was Col. Tom Parker's first involvement with Elvis. He assisted Bob Neal in getting Elvis booked in Carlsbad.

Carlson, Richard. Actor who played Bishop Finley in the 1969 movie *Change of Habit*. Richard Carlson and Vincent Price have appeared in more 3-D movies than have any other actors (three each). In 1953 Carlson starred in the syndicated TV series "I Led Three Lives," based on the book by Herbert Philbrick.

Carny Town. Song that Elvis sang in the 1964 movie *Roustabout*. "Carny Town" was written by Fred Wise and Randy Starr and appeared in the Long Playing album "Roustabout" (RCA LPM/LSP-2999).

Carpenter, John. Director of the 1979 TV movie *Elvis*. John Carpenter is married to actress Adrienne Barbeau.

Carter, Billy. Brother of former President Jimmy Carter and proponent of Billy Beer. Billy Carter handles the Carter family's peanut business in Plains, Georgia. He once visited Elvis in Memphis, commenting, "My gosh, you're guarded better than the president!"

Carter, Jack. Comedian who hosted the talent contest in which Lucky Jackson (Elvis) and Rusty Martin tied for first place. Lucky became the winner after a toss of a coin (1964 movie *Viva Las Vegas*).

Carter, Jimmy. President Jimmy Carter's tribute to Elvis: "Elvis Presley's death deprives our country of a part of itself. His music and his personality, fusing the styles of white country and black rhythm and blues, permanently changed the face of American popular culture. His following was immense and he was a symbol to the people of the world over of the vitality, rebelliousness, and good humor of this country."

Carter, June. One of the three daughters of mother Maybelle Addison Carter. June Carter's great-great-great-grandfather was Henry Addington Sidmouth, prime minister of England (1801–1804). She is also related to former President Jimmy Carter (as claimed by the chief executive himself). She has been married to two country artists: Carl Smith and Johnny Cash. Elvis first met June at the Grand Ole Opry. The two were touring together, with Col. Tom Parker as their manager. June first became a Johnny Cash fan when, while touring with Elvis, he played Johnny Cash songs on juke boxes. Elvis then introduced June to Johnny at a North Carolina concert in 1955.

Caruso, Enrico. Operatic singer who was the first person to sell a million records (collectively). Caruso recorded a version of "O Sole Mio," on which "It's Now or Never" was based. He was in San Francisco on April 18, 1906, when the Great Earthquake struck. Caruso never again returned to the city. In the 1951 movie *The Great Caruso*, Mario Lanza portrayed Caruso.

Elvis collected Enrico Caruso's recordings.

Caruso, Paul. Attorney for Patricia A. Parker in her paternity suit against Elvis. (See: Parker, Patricia)

Carver's Combined Shows. Rival carnival in the 1964 movie *Roustabout*.

Carwile, Bill. Memphis dry cleaner who in 1979 bought the two tons of gray marble that was Elvis's first tomb. He carved the marble into 44,000 chunks, each measuring 2″ x 1″, and asked eighty dollars per chunk.

Cash, Johnny. Singer, guitarist, and songwriter, born in Kinsland, Arkansas, on February 26, 1932. He was born J. R. Cash; it was only at the time of his induction into the U. S. Air Force that he was given the name Johnny. While stationed in Germany, Cash's first poem, which later became his first record, "Hey Porter," was published in *The Stars and Stripes*. Johnny Cash began recording for the Sun label in 1955 with the Tennessee Two (Luther Perkins and Marshall Grant). His first public appearance was on the same bill with Elvis Presley and Carl Perkins in Amory, Mississippi, in 1955. Cash left Sun Records in 1958 to record for Columbia Records. Cash's wife, June Carter, is the daughter of Maybelle Carter and was the previous wife of country singer Carl Smith.

Johnny Cash was one of the participants in the famed Million-Dollar Session.

At a live concert at the International Hotel in Las Vegas in August 1969, Elvis jokingly introduced himself by saying, "Hello, I'm Johnny Cash," prior to singing "Folsom Prison Blues" and "I Walk the Line." (See: Million-Dollar Session; Perkins, Luther)

CASINO APPEARANCES OF ELVIS. 1956: Frontier Hotel, Las Vegas, April 23–29. 1969: International Hotel, Las Vegas, July 26–August 28, 1970: International Hotel, Las Vegas, January 26–February 23; International Hotel, Las Vegas, August 30–September 7. 1971: International Hotel, Las Vegas, January 26–February 23; Sahara Tahoe, Lake Tahoe, July 20–August 2; International Hotel, Las Vegas August 9–September 6. 1972: International Hotel, Las Vegas, January 26–February 23; International Hotel, Las Vegas, August 4–September 4. 1973: Sahara Tahoe, Lake Tahoe, May 4–20; Las

Vegas Hilton, Las Vegas, January 26–February 23; Las Vegas Hilton, Las Vegas, August 6–September 3. 1974: Las Vegas Hilton, Las Vegas, January 26–February 9; Sahara Tahoe, Lake Tahoe, May 16–26; Las Vegas Hilton, Las Vegas, August 20–September 2; Sahara Tahoe, Lake Tahoe, October 11–14. 1975: Las Vegas Hilton, Las Vegas, March 18–31; Las Vegas Hilton, Las Vegas, August 18–September 2; Las Vegas Hilton, Las Vegas, December 2–15. 1976: Sahara Tahoe, Lake Tahoe, April 30–May 9; Las Vegas Hilton, Las Vegas,* August 20–September 1; Las Vegas Hilton, Las Vegas, December 1–12.

Casual Love Affair. One of two songs recorded by Elvis at the Memphis Recording Service on January 4, 1954. The other song was "I'll Never Stand in Your Way (Little Darlin')." "Casual Love Affair" was recorded on a ten-inch acetate at a cost of four dollars. Elvis retained the only copy. It was at this time that Elvis first met Sam Phillips. Marion Keisker was not present. (See: Memphis Recording Service)

Catchin' on Fast. Song that Elvis sang in the 1964 movie *Kissin' Cousins*. "Catchin' on Fast" was written by Bill Giant, Bernie Baum, and Florence Kaye and appeared in the Long Playing album "Kissin' Cousins" (RCA LPM/LSP-2894).

Catholic. Religion of Mike Windgren (Elvis) in the 1963 movie *Fun in Acapulco*. Priscilla Presley was also Catholic.

Caught in the Act. An Elvis novelty album by Betty Reilly on RKO Records (RKO 118). One track on the album was called "The Saga of Elvis Presley."

Cedars of Lebanon Hospital. Los Angeles hospital where Elvis was rushed on May 15, 1957, after experiencing chest pains. The previous day, Elvis had inhaled a porcelain cap from one of his front teeth during a dance number from *Jailhouse Rock*. It had become lodged in a lung and was removed on May 15.

Century Plaza Hotel. Hotel used as the Las Vegas Hilton in the 1979 TV movie *Elvis*.

Chad Gates. Elvis's role in the 1961 movie *Blue Hawaii*.

Chain Gang. Song composed by Sam Cooke and Charles Cook. Recorded by Sam Cooke in 1960, it sold a million copies. Sam Cooke, son of a minister, sang for a gospel group called the Pilgrim Travelers, in which Lou Rawls was a member. When Cooke left the group to record "You Send Me," he was replaced by Johnnie Taylor. The song was sung by Elvis at several live concerts.

CHANGE OF HABIT. Universal, 1969. Premiered November 10, 1969 (93 minutes). Elvis's thirty-first movie. Producer, Joe Connelly. Associate Producer, Irving Paley. Director, William Graham. Cast: Dr. John Carpenter/Elvis Presley, Sister Michelle/Mary Tyler Moore, Sister Irene/Barbara McNair, Sister Barbara/Jane Elliot, Mother Joseph/Leora Dana, Lt. Moretti/Ed-

---

*After three nights the show was canceled due to Elvis being ill.

ward Asner, The Banker/Robert Emhardt, Father Gibbons/
Regis Toomey, Rose/Doro Merande, Lily/Ruth McDevitt, Bish-
op Finley/Richard Carlson, Julio Hernandez/Nefti Millet, An-
gela/Lorena Kirk, Desiree/Laura Figueroa, Miss Parker/Virginia
Vincent, Colom/David Renard, Robbie/Bill Elliott, Mr. Her-
nandez/Rodolfo Hoyos, Hawk/Ji-Tu Cumbuka. Screenplay,
James Lee, S.S. Schweitzer, and Eric Bercovici. Story, John
Joseph and Richard Morris. Photography, Russell Metty. Music,
Billy Goldenberg. Songs, Ben Weisman and Buddy Kaye. Art
Direction, Alexander Golitzen and Frank Arrigo. Set Decoration,
John McCarthy and Ruby Levitt. Costumes, Helen Colvig. Assistant Director, Phil Bowles. Editor, Douglas Stewart. Songs
sung by Elvis: "Change of Habit," "Let Us Pray," "Rubberneckin'," "Have a Happy." Elvis played "Lawdy, Miss Clawdy"
on piano.

Change of Habit. Song that Elvis sang in the 1970 movie *Change
of Habit.* "Change of Habit" was written by Ben Weisman and
Buddy Kaye and appeared in the Long Playing albums "Let's Be
Friends" (RCA Camden CAS-2408) and "Let's Be Friends"
(Pickwick CAS-2408).

Chapel, Jean. Sun recording artist who, like Elvis, switched to
RCA Records in 1956. Jean Chapel recorded an answer to
Elvis's "Good Rockin' Tonight" titled "I Won't Be Rockin'
Tonight" (Sun 244).

Charge at Feather River, The. A 1953 movie filmed in 3-D, starring
Guy Madison and Vera Miles. *The Charge at Feather River*
was shown on the "Three O'Clock Movie," which Elvis (Kurt
Russell) watched in his Presidential Suite at the International
Hotel on August 26, 1969 (1979 TV movie *Elvis*).

Charities. Some of the charities to which Elvis donated money in-
cluded: Boys Town; Father Tom's Indian School; Salvation
Army; Girls' Club; Boys' Club; Y.M.C.A.; Y.W.C.A.; Jewish
Community Center; St. Jude Hospital Foundation; Muscular
Dystrophy; Cerebral Palsy; March of Dimes; Motion Picture
Relief Fund. Between 1957 and 1967, Elvis gave over $1
million to charities.

Charles, Ray. Blind rhythm and blues/jazz/country/pop musician,
born Ray Charles Robinson, on September 23, 1930, in Albany, Georgia. Ray Charles began recording for the Swing Time
label in Los Angeles in the early 1950s in the style of his idol
Nat "King" Cole. In 1952 he began recording for Atlantic
Records, producing such hits as "I've Got a Woman" and "The
Right Time." In 1961 Ray Charles joined the ABC Paramount
label, where he recorded a number of million-sellers including
two albums of country hits. Elvis recorded two Ray Charles
hits: "I've Got a Woman," (Atlantic 1050) and "What'd I Say,"
(Atlantic 2031). Both men have recorded "I Can't Stop Loving
You"; "You Don't Know Me"; "Your Cheating Heart"; "I'm
Moving On"; "Blue Moon of Kentucky"; "Yesterday."

Charles Street. New Orleans location of the five-and-dime store where Nellie (Dolores Hart) was employed in the 1958 movie *King Creole*. To divert attention while Shark and his pals shoplifted in the store, Danny Fisher (Elvis) serenaded the customers by singing "Lover Doll."

Charlie. Jess Wade's horse in the novel version of *Charro!*, written by Harry Whittington.

Charlie Rogers. Elvis's role (as a carnival roustabout) in the 1964 movie *Roustabout*.

Charlotte 600. Race that Steve Grayson (Elvis) won in the 1968 movie *Speedway*.

CHARRO! National General Pictures, 1969. Premiered San Antonio, Texas, March 13, 1969 (98 min). Elvis's twenty-ninth movie. Executive Producer, Harry Caplan. Producer/Director/Writer, Charles Marquis Warren. Cast: Jess Wade/Elvis Presley, Tracy/Ina Balin, Vince/Victor French, Sara Ramsey/Barbara Werle, Billy Roy/Solomon Sturges, Marcie/Lynn Kellogg, Opie Keetch/Paul Brinegar, Gunner/James Sikking, Heff/Harry Landers, Lt. Rivera/Tony Young, Sheriff Ramsay/James Almanzar, Mody/Charles H. Gray, Lige/Rodd Redwing, Martin Tilford/Gary Walberg, Gabe/Duane Grey, Jerome Selby/John Pickard, Henry Carter/J. Edward McKinley, Will Joslyn/Robert Luster, Christa/Christa Lang, Bartender/Robert Karnes. Photography, Ellsworth Fredericks. Music, Hugo Montenegro. Art Direction, James Sullivan. Set Decoration, Charles Thompson. Special Effects, George (Bud) Thompson, Woodrow Ward, and Robert Beck. Associate Producer and Assistant Director, Dink Templeton. Editor, Al Clark. Song sung by Elvis: "Charro!" This is the only film in which Elvis wore a beard.

Charro. RCA 47-9731. Released in March 1969 as a 45 rpm single. "Memories" was on the flip side. "Charro" is the title song of the 1969 movie of the same name. "Charro" was written by Billy Strange and Mac Davis and arranged by Hugo Montenegro. The Jordanaires and Hugo Montenegro's orchestra backed Elvis on this recording. "Charro" appeared in the Long Playing albums "Almost in Love" (RCA Camden CAS-2440), "Almost in Love" (Pickwick CAS-2440), and "Elvis in Hollywood" (RCA DPL2-0168).

Charro. RCA 447-0669. Gold Standard Series re-issue of RCA 47-9731.

Chautauqua. Novel by Day Keene and Dwight Babcock on which the 1969 movie *The Trouble with Girls (And How to Get Into It)* is based. In the movie Chautauqua* was a traveling college headed by Walter Hale (Elvis).

Checker, Chubby. Popular rock singer and dance-craze innovator

---

*Chautauqua was originally a summer vacation school held at Chautauqua, New York, near Lake Chautauqua. Founded by Lewis Miller and Reverend John Heyl Vincent. (Lewis Miller was the father-in-law of Thomas Alva Edison, the inventor of the phonograph.)

(the Twist, the Pony, the Fly, the Hucklebuck, the Limbo Rock, etc.). Born Ernest Evans, Chubby Checker received his stage name from Dick Clark's wife (it was a parody of Fats Domino's name). As a teenager, he attended South Philadelphia High with Frankie Avalon and Fabian.

Chubby Checker's first release was "The Class" (Parkway 804), in 1959, in which he did impersonations of Fats Domino, the Coasters, Elvis Presley, Cozy Cole, and the Chipmunks (Ricky, Frankie, and Fabian)—all singing "Mary Had a Little Lamb."

Chubby Checker's version of "The Twist" (Parkway 811), which was an exact copy of Hank Ballard and the Midnighters' version (King 5171), reached #1 in 1960 (September 19–26) and again in 1962 (January 13–27). Actually, it was "The Twist" that replaced Elvis's "It's Now or Never" as #1 in 1960.

Chubby Checker married Miss World of 1962, Catherine Lodders.

Chenault's. Memphis restaurant, located at 1402 Bellevue Blvd. South, where Elvis threw parties—especially on New Year's Eve. Tommy Sands was once given a birthday party at Chenault's by Col. Tom Parker, his manager.

Cher. Popular singer of the 1960s and '70s. Cher (real name: Cherilyn Sakisian LaPierre) began singing as a duet with her husband Sonny Bono (originally using the names Caesar and Cleo). They divorced in 1975. Cher then married guitarist Greg Allman and has been romantically linked with Gene Simmons of Kiss.

The first concert that Cher ever attended featured Elvis Presley; she was eleven years old at the time.

Chesay. Song that Elvis sang in the 1966 movie *Frankie and Johnny.* In the film version of "Chesay," the opening lines are sung by another voice and Harry Morgan adds two lines to the song. It was written by Fred Karger, Sid Wayne, and Ben Weisman and appeared in the Long Playing album "Frankie and Johnny" (RCA LPM/LSP-3553).

Chess Records. 2120 S. Michigan Avenue.* Chicago rhythm and blues record company founded in 1947 by Polish immigrants Leonard and Phil Chess. The label was originally called Aristocat Records and recorded such artists as Chuck Berry, Muddy Waters, Bo Diddley, and Lowell Fulson. In 1969 Chess Records was sold to GRT.

Sam Phillips recorded many black artists at Sun Records, selling the tapes to Chess.

At one time Sam Phillips attempted to sell to Chess his entire

---

*"2120 So. Michigan Avenue" became the title of a song recorded by the Rolling Stones who, in October 1964, cut four songs at the Chess Studios, including their song "It's All Over Now."

group of Sun artists, including Elvis. The Chess brothers turned him down.

Chess Records was located directly across the street from another successful R & B label, Vee Jay Records (the second label* that released the Beatles in the U.S.).

Chevrolet. The 1954 Bel Air model automobile that Elvis, Scotty Moore, and Bill Black purchased so that they could tour in 1954.

Chicken of the Sea. American television sponsor for the "Elvis: Aloha from Hawaii" special, broadcast on April 4, 1973.

Chicken 101. Bootleg record label from Catahoula, Louisiana. "That's All Right (Mama)" and "Blue Moon of Kentucky" appeared on this 45 rpm record released in the 1970s. They were recorded live on the "Louisiana Hayride" in December 1954. On the label of the record appeared the phrase THE STILL SMALL VOICE OF TRUTH.

Chief, The. One of the many nicknames Elvis acquired.

Childress, Hubert. U. S. Army Captain from Coleman, Texas, who was Elvis's company commander in West Germany.

Chrissie and Midnight. Pet cats of Thomas and Marie Parker.

Christmas Tribute, A. A 1977 Elvis tribute record by Bob Luman on Polydor Records (Polydor 14444).

Christmas with Elvis. RCA EPA-4340. This was a 45 rpm Extended Play album released in November 1958. Songs included— Side 1: "White Christmas," "Here Comes Santa Claus (Right Down Santa Claus Lane)." Side 2: "O Little Town of Bethlehem," "Silent Night."

Christmas without Elvis. A 1977 Elvis tribute record by Patsy Sexton on the Delta Record label (Delta 1151).

Chuck Norris Studios. Los Angeles martial-arts studio where Mike Stone taught Priscilla Presley karate in 1972.

Church, Charles R. Memphis businessman who installed the closed-circuit TV system (with the master controls in Elvis's bedroom) in Graceland. RCA televisions were used. Church owned an indoor shooting range (Memphis Indoor Shooting Center) and police-accessories store in Whitehaven, a suburb of Memphis.

Cilla. Elvis's nickname for Priscilla.

Cindy, Cindy. Song recorded by Elvis in 1970. "Cindy, Cindy" was written for Elvis by Buddy Kaye, Ben Weisman, and Dolores Fuller and appeared in the Long Playing album "Love Letters from Elvis" (RCA LSP-4530).

Circle G. Name of Elvis Presley's 163-acre cattle ranch (later to be renamed the Flying Circle G because there was already a Circle G in Texas), located at the corner of Horn Lake and

---

*Swan Records released the third Beatles record in the U. S. with "She Loves You" (Swan 4152). The first was early in 1962 when Decca Records released "My Bonnie" by Tony Sheridan and the Beat Brothers (Decca 31382).

Goodman roads near Walls, Mississippi. Elvis bought it on February 9, 1967, for $300,000. It was sold on May 28, 1969, to Lou McClellan for $440,100.

Circle Theater. Cleveland theater where Elvis and Pat Boone performed in a concert in 1955. That was the first time that the two singers met.

Circle Z Ranch. Guest ranch where Lonnie Beal (Elvis) worked in the 1965 movie *Tickle Me.*

City by Night. Song that Elvis sang in the 1967 movie *Double Trouble.* The film version had added instrumentation. "City by Night" was written by Bill Giant, Bernie Baum, and Florence Kaye and appeared in the Long Playing album "Double Trouble" (RCA LPM/LSP-3787).

CLAMBAKE. United Artists, 1967. Premiered December 13, 1967 (100 min). Elvis's twenty-fifth movie. Producers, Arnold Laven, Arthur Gardner, and Jules Levy. Associate Producer, Tom Rolf. Director, Arthur H. Nadel. Cast: Scott Heyward/Elvis Presley, Dianne Carter/Shelley Fabares, James Jamison III/Bill Bixby, Tom Wilson/Will Hutchins, Sam Burton/Gary Merrill, Duster Heyward/James Gregory, Ellie/Amanda Harley, Sally/Suzie Kaye, Gloria/Angelique Pettyjohn, Gigi/Olga Kaye, Olive/Arlene Charles, Mr. Hathaway/Jack Good, Doorman/Hal Peary, Race Announcer/Sam Riddle, Cigarette Girl/Sue England, Lisa/Liza Slagle, Bartender/Lee Krieger, Waiter/Herb Barnett, Crewman/Melvin Allen, Bellhop/Steve Cory, Barasch/Robert Lieb, Ice Cream Vendor/Red West. Screenplay, Arthur Browne, Jr. Photography, William Margulies. Music, Jeff Alexander. Choreography, Alex Romero. Art Director, Lloyd Papez. Set Decoration, James Red. Special Effects, Bob Warner. Assistant Director, Claude Binyon, Jr. Editor, Tom Rolf. Songs sung by Elvis: "Clambake," "Who Needs Money?" (duet with Will Hutchins)* "The Girl I Never Loved," "Confidence," "A House That Has Everything," "Hey, Hey, Hey," "You Don't Know Me."

Clambake. Title song of the 1967 movie *Clambake,* sung by Elvis. The film version had added instrumentation. Written by Sid Wayne and Ben Weisman, "Clambake" appeared in the Long Playing album "Clambake" (RCA LPM/LSP-3893).

Clambake. RCA MTR-244. Special 45 rpm Extended Play promotional release (1967). Songs included—Side 1: "Clambake," "Hey, Hey, Hey." Side 2: "You Don't Know Me," "A House That Has Everything."

Clambake. RCA LPM/LSP-3892. A 33⅓ rpm Long Playing album released in November 1967. It reached #33 on *Billboard*'s Hot LP chart. A full color wedding photo of Elvis and Priscilla was included inside the album. "Clambake" featured songs from

---

*The singer who dubbed the singing voice for Will Hutchins is unknown.

the 1967 movie of the same name, plus five bonus songs. Songs included—Side 1: "Guitar Man" (bonus), "Clambake," "Who Needs Money," "A House That Has Everything," "Confidence," "Hey, Hey, Hey." Side 2: "You Don't Know Me," "The Girl I Never Loved," "How Can You Lose What You Never Had" (bonus), "Big Boss Man" (bonus), "Singing Tree" (bonus), "Just Call Me Lonesome" (bonus).

Clark, Albert, Jr. One of Elvis's groundkeepers and handymen at Graceland. Albert Clark, Jr., worked for Elvis for twelve years.

Clark, Dick. Philadelphia disc jockey who in the mid-1950s hosted the TV series "American Bandstand." During Elvis's Army career Dick Clark interviewed him several times via telephone. In 1979 Dick Clark produced the TV movie *Elvis*.

Clark, Petula. One of the leading female performers of the 1960s. Petula Clark made her singing debut auditioning for a BBC-radio show in England in 1941 (at the age of eight). During the audition, a German air raid began. In order to prevent panic, she was asked to continue singing. Petula Clark was soon given her own BBC-radio show called "Pet's Parlor."

From her first big American hit, "Downtown" (Warner Bros. 5494), in 1964, to the end of the 1960s Petula Clark was rarely absent from the *Billboard* charts. She was the second British female to reach #1 on the charts in America (Vera Lynn, in 1952, was the first).

Petula Clark turned down the female lead of Susan Jacks for the 1968 Elvis movie *Speedway*.

Class Prophecies. Item in the L. C. Humes High School yearbook, *The Herald*: "Donald Williams, Raymond McCraig, and Elvis Presley leave, hoping there will be someone to take their places as teacher's pet."

Claude Thompson Dancers, The. Dance troupe that appeared in Elvis's 1968 NBC-TV special.

Clayton, Merry. Solo artist who was a previous member of Ray Charles's Raelets. She sang duet with Bobby Darin on "You're the Reason I'm Living" (Capitol 4897). Merry Clayton sang back-up on the Rolling Stones' "Let It Bleed" album. She has also sung back-up for such artists as the Supremes, Pearl Bailey, Joe Cocker, and Elvis Presley.

Clean Up Your Own Backyard. RCA 47-9747. Released in June 1969 as a 45 rpm single. It reached #35 on *Billboard*'s Hot 100 chart and #74 on the Country chart. "The Fair Is Moving On" was on the flip side. "Clean Up Your Own Backyard" was written by Billy Strange and Mac Davis and sung by Elvis in the 1969 movie *The Trouble with Girls* (*And How to Get Into It*). It appeared in the Long Playing albums "Almost in Love" (RCA Camden CAS-2440) and "Almost in Love" (Pickwick CAS-2440).

Clean Up Your Own Backyard. RCA 447-0672. Gold Standard Series re-issue of RCA 47-9747.

Clement, Jack Henderson. Memphis band leader and vocalist with whom Elvis appeared in 1954 at the Eagle's Nest, a Memphis ballroom on Lamar Ave. Elvis sang between sets, earning ten dollars a night.

Jack Clement was later the producer of many recordings by Johnny Cash, Carl Perkins, Roy Orbison, Jerry Lee Lewis, and Charlie Rich. He also composed the Johnny Cash hits "Ballad of a Teenage Queen" and "Guess Things Happen That Way."* He produced Floyd Cramer's 1960 hit "Last Date" (RCA 7775).

It was Jack Clement who recorded the famed Million-Dollar Session. (See: Million-Dollar Session) In 1959 Jack Clement left Sun Records. He was later responsible for the discovery of black country singer Charley Pride.

Clement, Frank G. Governor of Tennessee who, in 1953, conferred upon Thomas Andrew Parker the honorary title of Colonel.

Climax Studios. Hollywod movie company that first put Vince Everett (Elvis) into films in the 1957 movie *Jailhouse Rock.*

Climb, The. Song written by Jerry Leiber and Mike Stoller and originally recorded by the Coasters (Atco 6234) in 1962. "The Climb" was an attempt to capitalize on the various dance crazes in the early 1960s. In the 1964 movie *Viva Las Vegas*, a group called the Forte Four sang "The Climb" (Decca 32029) while Elvis and Ann-Margret danced.

Clint Reno. Elvis's role in the 1956 movie *Love Me Tender.*

Club El Florita. Club run by Sam Brewster (Percy Helton) where Vince Everett (Elvis) met Peggy Van Alden (Judy Tyler) (1957 movie *Jailhouse Rock*).

C'mon Everybody. Song that Elvis sang in the 1964 movie *Viva Las Vegas.* The movie version had a heavier beat and extra voices. "C'mon Everybody" was written by Joy Byers.

Eddie Cochran had a hit in 1958 with a completely different song called "C'mon Everybody" (Liberty 55166).† It was originally called "Let's Get Together."

"C'mon Everybody" by Elvis appeared in the Extended Play album "Viva Las Vegas" (RCA EPA-4382) and the Long Playing albums "C'mon Everybody" (RCA Camden CAL-2518) and "C'mon Everybody" (Pickwick CAS-2518).

C'mon Everybody. RCA Camden CAL-2518. A 33⅓ rpm Long Playing album released in July 1971. It reached #70 on *Billboard*'s Hot LP chart. "C'mon Everybody" featured songs from four of Elvis's movies (*Follow That Dream, Kid Gala-*

---

*The song was first offered to Marty Robbins.
†The first rock 'n' roll record ever purchased by singer Rod Stewart was "C'mon Everybody" (Liberty 55166) by Eddie Cochran.

had, Viva Las Vegas, and *Easy Come, Easy Go*). Songs included—Side 1: "C'mon Everybody," "Angel," "Easy Come, Easy Go," "A Whistling Tune," "Follow That Dream." Side 2: "King of the Whole Wide World," "I'll Take Love," "Today, Tomorrow and Forever," "I'm Not the Marrying Kind," "This Is Living."

C'mon Everybody. Pickwick CAS-2518. A 33⅓ rpm Long Playing album that was a re-issue of RCA Camden CAL-2518. "C'mon Everybody" was released in December 1975.

Coasters, The. Popular novelty group of the 1950s–'60s. Beginning as the Robins in 1955, they recorded for Jerry Leiber and Mike Stoller's Spark Records. They spawned a chain of hit records for Atco Records, beginning in 1956, most of which were Leiber-Stoller compositions. In 1961 they recorded "Little Egypt" and "Girls! Girls! Girls!" both of which were also recorded by Elvis. (See: Climb, The)

Cochran, Hank. Composer of numerous hit songs, including "Make the World Go Away" recorded by Elvis in June 1970. In his youth Hank Cochran teamed musically with another youth named Eddie Cochran. Although they billed themselves as the Cochran Brothers they were unrelated. (Eddie Cochran was killed in a London taxicab accident on April 17, 1960, in which Gene Vincent and Sharon Sheeley were injured.)

Coffee Cup, The. West Memphis, Arkansas, restaurant where Elvis and other recruits stopped to eat on March 24, 1958. Elvis ate spaghetti. The meal was cut short when fans converged on the restaurant and the recruits had to get back on the bus. The chartered Greyhound bus was en route to Fort Chaffee, where Elvis was to receive his Army indoctrination.

Coffman, Richard L. U. S. Army first lieutenant from Nevada, Missouri, who served as Elvis's platoon leader in West Germany.

Cold, Cold Icy Fingers. Song that Elvis sang at the Humes High annual variety show as a senior (1952–53). Another song Elvis sang was "Old Shep." He got the most applause and was asked to do an encore. (See: Scrivener, Mildred)

Cole, J. D. Principal of the Lawhon Grammar School, which Elvis attended as a child. He entered Elvis in the annual talent show at the 1945 Mississippi-Alabama Fair and Dairy Show. Singing "Old Shep," Elvis won second prize—five dollars and free admission to all amusement rides. (See: Harris, Becky; Mississippi-Alabama Fair and Dairy Show)

Coleman, George. Electrician who worked at Graceland.

Coley, Henry. Elvis's master sergeant at Fort Hood, Texas.

Colgate. Brand of toothpaste preferred and used by Elvis.

Colonel. Honorary title conferred on Elvis by Tennessee Governor Buford Ellington in 1961.

Colonel John Burrows. Code name that Vernon Presley sometimes used for receiving personal telephone calls.

Colonel Midnight. Vernon Presley's horse at Graceland.

Colonel Snow. Code name Col. Tom Parker used to identify himself when calling Vernon Presley at Graceland.

Color My Rainbow. A 1973 studio recording that has never been released in any form. The band recorded the instrumental track of "Color My Rainbow" but Elvis never recorded a vocal track.

Colossus of New York, The. A 1958 Paramount horror film, starring Otto Kruger and Mala Powers, that appeared on the same bill with *King Creole*.

Columbia Records. Record label that bid $15,000 for Elvis in 1955. One can only speculate what A & R man Mitch Miller would have done with Elvis, since Miller was strongly against rock 'n' role music.

Columbia Records bought the contracts of both Johnny Cash and Carl Perkins from Sun Records in 1958.

Combat. World War II drama series on ABC-TV, starring Rick Jason and Vic Morrow. It aired from October 2, 1962, to August 29, 1967. Reportedly, it was one of Elvis's favorite television shows. Vic Morrow earlier appeared in the 1958 movie *King Creole*.

Come Along. Song that Elvis sang in the 1966 movie *Frankie and Johnny*. "Come Along" was written by David Hess and appeared in the Long Playing albums "Frankie and Johnny" (RCA LPM/LSP-3553) and "Frankie and Johnny" (Pickwick ACL-7007).

Come Back to Sorrento. Melody on which Doc Pomus and Mort Shuman based their song "Surrender."

Come Hell, Come Sundown. Original title of the 1969 movie *Charro!*

Come Out, Come Out. A 1969 studio recording that has never been released in any form. The band recorded the instrumental track of "Come Out, Come Out" but Elvis never recorded a vocal track.

Come What May. RCA 47-8870. Released in June 1966 as a 45 rpm single. "Love Letters" was on the flip side. "Come What May" was written by Table Porter and originally recorded by Clyde McPhatter in 1958 (Atlantic 1185). Elvis's version never appeared in an RCA album.

Come What May. RCA 447-0657. Gold Standard Series re-issue of RCA 47-8870.

Comin' Home Baby. Instrumental that the band played whenever Elvis introduced the members to the audience. Mel Torme had a hit with "Comin' Home Baby" (Atlantic 2165) in 1962, as did Kai Winding (Verve 10295) in 1963.

Commodore Perry Hotel. Toledo, Ohio, hotel where, in the Shalimar Room, Louis Balint attempted to hit Elvis Presley on November 23, 1956. (See: Balint, Louis)

Compact 33 Double. A RCA Victor 33⅓ rpm record the size of a

45 rpm single, with four songs on it. The first one released was "Elvis by Request" in 1961. (See: Elvis by Request)

Concert Jumpsuits. Custom-made jumpsuits worn by Elvis included: Peacock, American Eagle, Indian, Sundial, Burning Love, Red Lion, Nail Studded Suit, White Prehistoric Bird, Flame, Blue Prehistoric Bird, White Eagle, Tiffany, Black Eagle, Blue Aztec, Red Eagle, Blue Rainbow, Sleak, Inca Gold Leaf, Gypsy, Mexican Sundial, Blue Braid, Blue Swirl, Flower, Blue Rainbow, Mad Tiger, King of Spades.

CONCERT TOURS OF ELVIS. 1970: Houston, February 27–March 1. Phoenix, September 9. St. Louis, September 10. Detroit, September 11. Miami, September 12. Tampa, September 13. Mobile, September 14. Oakland, November 10. Portland, Ore. November 11. Seattle, November 12. San Francisco, November 13. Los Angeles, November 14. San Diego, November 15. Oklahoma City, November 16. Denver, November 17. 1971: Minneapolis, November 5. Cleveland, November 6. Louisville, November 7. Philadelphia, November 8. Baltimore, November 9. Boston, November 10. Cincinnati, November 11. Houston, November 12. Dallas, November 13. Tuscaloosa, November 14. Kansas City, Mo., November 15. Salt Lake City, November 16. 1972: Buffalo, April 5. Detroit, April 6. Dayton, April 7. Knoxville, April 8. Hampton Roads, April 9. Richmond, April 10. Roanoke, April 11. Indianapolis, April 12. Charlotte, April 13. Greensboro, April 14. Macon, April 15. Jacksonville, April 16. Little Rock, April 17. San Antonio, April 18. Albuquerque, April 19. New York City, Madison Square Garden, June 9–11. Fort Wayne, June 12. Evansville, June 13. Milwaukee, June 14–15. Chicago, June 16–17. Fort Worth, June 18. Wichita, June 19. Tulsa, June 20. Lubbock, November 8. Tucson, November 9. El Paso, November 10. Okaland, November 11. San Bernardino, November 12–13. Long Beach, November 14–15. Honolulu, November 17–18. 1973: Honolulu—"Aloha from Hawaii," January 14. Phoenix, April 22. Anaheim, April 23–24. Fresno, April 25. San Diego, April 26. Portland, Ore., April 27. Spokane, April 28. Seattle, April 29. Denver, April 30. Mobile, June 20. Atlanta, June 21. Uniondale, N.Y.—Nassau Coliseum, June 22–24. Pittsburgh, June 25–26. Cincinnati, June 27. St. Louis, June 28. Atlanta, June 29–30. Nashville, July 1. Oklahoma City, July 2. Atlanta, July 3. 1974: Tulsa, March 1–2. Houston—Astrodome, March 3. Monroe, La., March 4. Auburn, Ala. March 5. Montgomery, March 6. Monroe, La., March 7–8. Charlotte, March 9. Roanoke, March 10. Hampton Roads, March 11. Richmond, March 12. Greensboro, March 13. Murfreesboro, Tenn., March 14. Knoxville, March 15. Memphis, March 16–17. Richmond, March 18. Murfreesboro, Tenn. March 19. Memphis, March 20. San Bernardino, May 10. Los Angeles—Forum, May 11. Fresno, May 12. San Bernardino, May 13. Fort Worth, June

15–16. Baton Rouge, June 17–18. Amarillo, June 19. Des Moines, June 20. Cleveland, June 21. Providence, June 22. Philadelphia, June 23. Niagara Falls, June 24. Columbus, June 25. Louisville, June 26. Bloomington, June 27. Milwaukee, June 28. Kansas City, Mo., June 29 Omaha, June 30–July 1. Salt Lake City, July 2. College Park, Md., September 27–28. Detroit, September 29. South Bend, September 30–October 1. St. Paul, October 2–3. Detroit, October 4. Indianapolis, October 5. Dayton, October 6. Wichita, October 7. San Antonio October 8. Abilene, Tex. October 9. 1975: Charlotte, March 19. Johnson City, March 20. Cincinnati, March 21. Macon, April 24. Jacksonville, April 25. Tampa, April 26. Lakeland, Fla. April 27–28. Murfreesboro, Tenn., April 29. Atlanta, April 30–May 2. Monroe, La., May 3. Lake Charles, May 4. Jackson, May 5. Murfreesboro, Tenn., May 6–7. Huntsville, May 30–June 1. Mobile, June 2. Tuscaloosa, June 3. Houston, June 4–5. Dallas, June 6. Shreveport, June 7. Jackson, Miss. June 8–9. Memphis, June 10. Oklahoma City, July 8. Terre Haute, July 9. Cleveland, July 10. Charleston, W. Va., July 11. Niagara Falls, N.Y. July 12. Springfield, Mass., July 14–15. New Haven, July 16. Cleveland. July 18. Uniondale, N.Y.—Nassau Coliseum, July 19. Norfolk, July 20. Greensboro, July 21. Asheville, N. C. July 22–24. Pontiac, Mich.—New Year's Eve Show, December 31.1976: Johnson City, Tenn., March 17–19. Charlotte, March 20. Cincinnati, March 22. Kansas City, Mo., April 21. Omaha, April 22. Denver, April 23. San Diego, April 24. Long Beach, April 26. Spokane, April 27. Seattle, April 28. Bloomington, Ind., May 27. Ames, Iowa, May 28. Oklahoma City, May 29. Odessa, Tex., May 30. Lubbock May 31. Tucson, June 1. El Paso, June 2. Fort Worth, June 3. Atlanta, June 4–6. Buffalo, June 25. Providence, June 26. Largo, Md., June 27. Philadelphia, June 28. Richmond, June 29. Greensboro, June 30. Shreveport, July 1. Baton Rouge, July 2. Fort Worth, July 3. Tulsa, July 4. Memphis, July 5. Louisville, July 23. Charleston, July 24. Syracuse, July 25. Rochester, N.Y., July 26. Syracuse, July 27. Hartford, July 28. Springfield, Mass. July 29. New Haven, July 30. Hampton Roads, July 31–August 1. Roanoke August 2. Fayetteville, N.C., August 3–5. San Antonio, August 27. Houston, August 28. Mobile, August 29. Tuscaloosa, August 30. Jacksonville, September 1. Tampa, September 2. St. Petersburg, September 3. Lakeland, Fla., September 4. Jackson, Miss., September 5. Huntsville, September 6. Pine Bluff, September 7–8. Chicago, October 14–15. Duluth, October 16. Minneapolis, October 17. Sioux Falls, October 18. Madison, October 19. South Bend, October 20. Kalamazoo, October 21. Champaign, October 22. Cleveland, October 23. Evansville, October 24. Fort Wayne, October 25. Dayton, October 26. Carbondale, Ill., October 27. Reno, November 24. Eugene, November 25. Portland, Ore., November 26. Eugene, November 27. San Francisco, November 28–29. Anaheim, November 30. Wichita, December 27. Dallas, December 28. Birmingham, December 29. Atlanta, December 30. Pittsburgh—New Year's Eve Show, December 31. 1977: Hollywood, Fla., February 12. West Palm Beach, February 13. St. Petersburg, February 14. Orlando, February 15. Montgomery, February 16. Savannah February 17. Columbia, S.C., February 18. Johnson City, Tenn., February 19. Charlotte, February 20–21. Phoenix, March 23. Amarillo, March 24. Norman, Okla., March 25–26. Abilene, Tex., March 27. Austin March 28. Alexandria, La., March 29–30. Greensboro, April 21. Detroit, April 22. Toledo, April 23. Ann Arbor, April 24. Saginaw, April 25. Kalamazoo, April 26. Milwaukee, April 27. Green Bay, April 28. Duluth, April 29. St. Paul, April 30. Chicago, May 1–2. Sagina, May 3. Knoxville, May 20. Louisville, May 21. Largo, Md., May 22. Providence, May 23. Augusta, Me., May 24. Rochester, N.Y., May 25. Birmingham, N.Y. May 26–27. Philadelphia, May 28. Baltimore*, May 29. Jacksonville, May 30. Baton Rouge, May 31. Macon, June 1. Mobile, June 2. Springfield, Mo., June 17. Kansas City, Mo., June 18. Omaha—Filmed for the CBS special, June 19. Lincoln, Nebr. June 20. Rapid City, S.D. Filmed for the CBS special, June 21. Sioux Falls, June 22. Des Moines, June 23. Madison, Wis., June 24. Cincinnati, June 25. Indianapolis—Elvis's farewell performance, June 26.

Concert Tour That Was Canceled Because of Elvis's Death. Portland, Me., August 17–18. Utica, N.Y., August 19. Syracuse, August 20. Hartford, August 21. Uniondale, N.Y.—Nassau Coliseum, August 22. Lexington, August 23. Roanoke, August 24. Fayetteville, N.C., August 25. Asheville, N.Y., August 26. Memphis, August 27–28.

Concerts West. The firm that did the concert bookings for Elvis, headed by Tom Hulett. They also took care of the bookings for Neil Diamond and John Denver.†

Confidence. Song that Elvis sang in the 1967 movie *Clambake*. The film version was longer than that on record and included a children's chorus. "Confidence" was written by Sid Tepper and Roy C. Bennett and appeared in the following Long Playing albums: "Clambake" (RCA LPM/LSP-3893); "Elvis Sings Hits from His Movies, Volume 1" (RCA Camden CAS-2567); "Elvis Sings Hits from His Movies, Volume 1" (Pickwick CAS-2567).

Connelly, Joe. Producer of the 1969 movie *Change of Habit*.

Cook's Hoedown Club. Houston, Texas, nightclub where Elvis performed in early 1955. The appearance was unprofessionally recorded and can be heard via bootleg albums. He sang: "Good

---

*This was the first time in Elvis's career that he walked out on his audience.
†In 1961, John Denver's father, Henry Deutschendorf, Sr., set a world's speed record in a B58 Hustler bomber, traveling 1,200 mph.

Rockin' Tonight"; "Baby, Let's Play House"; "Blue Moon of Kentucky"; "I Got a Woman"; "That's All Right (Mama)."

Copas, Lloyd "Cowboy". Popular country artist with whom Elvis toured in mid-September 1955. Elvis headlined the tour, which covered North Carolina and Virginia. Cowboy Copas died in a private-plane crash on March 5, 1963, with Patsy Cline and Harold "Hawkshaw" Hawkins. The trio was returning from Kansas City, Kansas, where they had given a benefit performance for D. J. Cactus Jack Call, who had been killed in an automobile accident. En route to the funerals of Copas, Cline, and Hawkins, Jack Anglin, singing partner of Johnny Wright* (Johnny and Jack), was killed in an automobile accident, on March 7, 1963.

Corvair. First automobile (among many) that Elvis bought for Priscilla.

Cotton Candy Land. Song that Elvis sang in the 1963 movie *It Happened at the World's Fair*. The Mello Men backed Elvis on this song. The film version of "Cotton Candy Land" has added strings and a shorter ending. It was written by Ruth Batchelor and Bob Roberts and appeared in the Long Playing albums "It Happened at the World's Fair" (RCA LPM/LSP-2697) and "Elvis Sings for Children (And Grownups Too)" (RCA CPL1-2901).

Could I Fall in Love. Song that Elvis sang in the 1967 movie *Double Trouble*. Charlie Hodge sang duet with Elvis. In the film, "Could I Fall in Love" was a hit record on the KCA label by Guy Lambert (Elvis). Randy Starr wrote "Could I Fall in Love." It appeared in the Long Playing album "Double Trouble" (RCA LPM/LSP-3787).

Country and Western Disc Jockeys' Association. In November 1955 the association held their annual convention at the Andrew Jackson Hotel in Nashville, Tennessee. Elvis was named the thirteenth Most-Played Singer on radio, was sixteenth on the disc jockeys' favorite-singer list ("Baby, Let's Play House" was also #16 for the year on the Country charts), and Elvis was the Most Promising Country Artist of 1955. It was also announced that Elvis had just been signed by RCA Victor Records.

Country Song Roundup. First magazine to feature an article on Elvis. The article, which was titled "Folk Music Fireball," appeared in the September 1955 issue of *Country Song Roundup*.

Cowboy Copas Show. Concert held in Kingsport, Tennessee, on September 22, 1955, in which Elvis sang "Rock Around the Clock," "Mystery Train," "I Love You Because," and "Milkcow Blues Boogie." The Louvin Brothers were also on the bill.

---

*The son of Johnny Wright and singer Kitty Wells, John Wright, played Seaman Willy Moss on the TV series "McHale's Navy."

Craig, Yvonne. Actress who played the roles of Dorothy Johnson in the 1963 movie *It Happened at the World's Fair* and Azalea Tatum in the 1964 movie *Kissin' Cousins*. She dated Elvis, briefly, during the making of the films. During the 1967–68 television season, Yvonne Craig portrayed Barbara Gordon (Batgirl) on the ABC-TV series "Batman."

Cramer, Floyd. Nashville piano player who became well known for his slipnote style of playing (taught to him by Don Robertson). Floyd Cramer has played as a session musician for numerous RCA artists, including Elvis Presley. Cramer's first recording session with Elvis, on January 10, 1956, produced "Heartbreak Hotel."

In 1960 Floyd Cramer had a #2 hit and million-seller with "Last Date" (RCA 7775). Cramer provided the clanging metal sound on Jimmy Dean's 1961 hit "Big Bad John" (Columbia 42175). When Elvis sang "Tweedle Dee" on the "Louisiana Hayride" on December 17, 1955, Floyd Cramer backed him on piano.

Cranberry County. Arkansas setting of the 1962 movie *Follow That Dream.*

Crawfish. Song that Elvis sang in the 1958 movie *King Creole.* In the film version of "Crawfish," Kitty White sang with Elvis. "Crawfish" was written by Fred Wise and Ben Weisman and appeared in the Extended Play album "King Creole, Volume 2" (RCA EPA-4321) and the following Long Playing albums: "King Creole" (RCA LPM-1884); "King Creole" (RCA LSP-1884 [e]); "Elvis: The Other Sides—Worldwide Gold Award Hits, Volume 2" (RCA LPM-6402).

Crawford, Christina. Actress who played Monica George in the 1961 movie *Wild in the Country.*

Christina is the adopted daughter of late actress Joan Crawford. In 1978 Christina wrote a best-selling autobiography about their relationship, titled *Mommie Dearest.*

Crayle, Donna Lee. Elvis Presley fan who headed the movement to have Congress declare January 8 (Elvis's birthday) a national holiday called National Elvis Presley Day.

Crazy. Memphis Mafia's nickname for Elvis.

Cream Valley. Setting for Kid Galahad's (Elvis) training camp in the 1962 movie *Kid Galahad.*

Creedence Clearwater Revival. Very popular rock group of the late 1960s and early '70s. Creedence Clearwater Revival* recorded one of Elvis's hits ("My Baby Left Me") and Elvis recorded one of their hits ("Proud Mary"). The group also recorded Roy Orbison's "Ooby Dooby." If it can be said that any band of the 1960s captured the early Sun sound, it was Creedence.

---

*Creedence Clearwater Revival, originally named the Blue Velvets, then the Golliwogs, chose part of their name from a line from a popular beer commercial.

Crosby, Bing (Harry Lillis Crosby). Popular crooner (1904–77) and movie actor (Best Actor Oscar for *Going My Way* [1944]). He recorded the best-selling record of all time, "White Christmas" (Decca 18429A). Bing Crosby was second only to Elvis Presley in the record of most records sold (by a solo artist). Bing Crosby's son Gary Crosby appeared as a guitarist in the 1965 movie *Girl Happy*. Crosby first sang with a trio called the Rhythm Boys. Harry Barris, a member of the trio, was the father of TV game-show host Chuck Barris. Both Crosby and Elvis recorded versions of "White Christmas" and "Hey Jude." (See: White Christmas) Bing Crosby died on October 14, 1977, fifty-nine days after the death of Elvis Presley.

Crosby, Charlie and Jones, Ulysses S., Jr. Paramedics for the Memphis Fire Department (unit 6) who arrived at Graceland on August 16, 1977, in response to an emergency call. They attempted to revive Elvis but he was already dead.

Crosby, Gary. Actor and son of crooner Bing Crosby. He played Andy, a musician, in the 1965 movie *Girl Happy*.

Crossing, The. White settlers' village in the 1960 movie *Flaming Star*.

Cross My Heart and Hope to Die. Song that Elvis sang in the 1965 movie *Girl Happy*. Written by Sid Wayne and Ben Weisman, "Cross My Heart and Hope to Die" appeared in the Long Playing album "Girl Happy" (RCA LPM/LSP-3338).

Crosstown Theater. Memphis movie theater, located at 400 N. Cleveland, that Elvis rented for his private showings. Other theaters were also used. (See: Avon Theater; Memphian Theater)

Crown Electric Company. Memphis electrical contracting firm, located at 353 Poplar Ave., for which Elvis worked after leaving the Precision Tool Company in the summer of 1953. Crown Electric (telephone number: JA5-4625) was owned by Jim and Gladys Tipler. In early 1954, Crown Electric moved from 475 No. Dunlap to its 353 Poplar Ave. location. Elvis made a little over $41.00 each week ($1.25/hour). His job consisted of driving either the company's Ford pickup truck or their blue panel truck and delivering supplies to the men on the job. In addition, Elvis worked in the warehouse.

Ironically, a few years before, singer Dorsey Burnette also drove a truck for Crown Electric.* (It is also ironic that two other rock superstars worked for electrical firms prior to becoming musicians: George Harrison was employed by Blackers in Liverpool, England, while Paul McCartney was employed by

---

*The odds of two future rock stars working for the same firm at the same time are not as remote as one would think. Michael Zager and Barry Manilow were fellow employees in the CBS-TV mailroom in Los Angeles, while Kris Kristofferson and Billy Swan were both janitors at the Columbia Studio in Nashville.

the Liverpool firm of Massey and Coggins.) (See: Burnette, Johnny; Tipler, Gladys)

It was while he was with Crown Electric that Elvis began recording for Sun Records. In the fall of 1954, Elvis left Crown Electric to pursue his singing career full-time.

Today, B & H Hardware stands at 353 Poplar Ave.

Crudup, Arthur "Big Boy." Black rhythm and blues singer who wrote and recorded three songs that Elvis later recorded: "That's All Right (Mama)", "So Glad You're Mine," and "My Baby Left Me." Leonard Chess of Chess Records discovered Arthur Crudup (August 24, 1905–March 28, 1974) singing in Forest, Mississippi. In addition to his real name, Crudup recorded under the names of Perry Lee Crudup and Elmer James. Elvis credited Arthur Crudup (who was born illegitimate) with influencing his style. In later years Elvis financed Crudup's recording sessions with Fire Records, though the two never did meet each other. A 1973 TV movie was made, titled *"Arthur Crudup: Born in the Blues."* Arthur Crudup died of a stroke on March 28, 1974. (See: My Baby Left Me; That's All Right [Mama]; Fire Records)

Cry, Cry a Few Tears for Elvis. A 1977 Elvis tribute song by Leda Ray on Allied Artists Records (Allied Artists 008).

Crying. Song written by Roy Orbison and Joe Melson and recorded by Roy Orbison in 1961, going to #2 on the charts (Monument 447). Elvis recorded this song and "Runnin' Scared" in December 1976. Elvis was dissatisfied with the songs, and they were never released.

Crying 'Bout Elvis. A 1977 Elvis tribute song by the Songwriters on Adam's Rib Records (Adam's Rib 1112).

Crying Heart Blues. Unreleased Sun recording by Elvis. Elvis sang "Crying Heart Blues" on the "Louisiana Hayride" in October 1954.

Crying in the Chapel. RCA 447-0643. Released in April 1965 as a 45 rpm Gold Standard Series original. "Crying in the Chapel" reached #3 on *Billboard*'s Hot 100 chart and #1 in the United Kingdom (for two weeks, June 19–July 3). It sold well over a million copies. "I Believe in the Man in the Sky" was on the flip side.

"Crying in the Chapel" was written by Artie Glenn in 1953 and introduced by the composer's son, Darrell Glenn (Valley 105). It was popularized by Sonny Til and the Orioles (Jubilee 5122) and Rex Allen (Decca 28758) in the same year.

Little Richard later had a successful revival of the song (Atlantic 2181).

Though released in 1965, "Crying in the Chapel" was recorded on October 31, 1960. It was Elvis's first recording to reach #1 in the United Kingdom after the advent of the Beatles. "Crying in the Chapel" appeared in the following Long Playing albums: "How Great Thou Art" (RCA LPM/LSP-

3758); "Elvis: Worldwide 50 Gold Award Hits, Volume 1" (RCA LPM-6401); "Elvis—A Legendary Performer, Volume 3" (RCA CPL1-3082).

Crying Time. Song originally written and recorded by Buck Owens in 1964. Ray Charles had a very successful recording of "Crying Time" in 1966 (ABC Paramount 10739). Elvis can be seen singing "Crying Time" in a rehearsal in the 1970 documentary *Elvis—That's the Way It Is*. The song has never been released by RCA.

Cugat, Xavier. Famed orchestra leader who was seen as a member of the audience in the 1970 documentary *Elvis—That's the Way It Is*.

Xavier Cugat's* ex-wife, Charo, has the same name (but different spelling) as the 1969 Elvis Presley movie *Charro!*

Culver City. California town in which Col. Tom Parker's West Coast headquarters are located. (See: Madison, Tennessee)

Cultural Phenomenon of Elvis Presley: The Making of a Folk Hero. Four-credit course offered by the University of Tennessee in 1980.

Cummings, Jack, and Sidney, George. Producers of the 1964 movie *Viva Las Vegas*.

Cunningham, Buddy. Musician who could be heard on "I Don't Care If the Sun Don't Shine," playing what sounded like bongos but what in actuality is a cardboard record box. He has never been credited on the record session. (See: Holiday Inn Records)

Current Audio Magazine. Buddah CM—Volume 1. A 33⅓ rpm Long Playing album released in September 1972 (the August–September edition). "Current Audio Magazine" was an attempt to have up-to-date news events available on record. Elvis appeared on only one cut—his June 1972 Madison Square Garden press conference. After only sixty days on the market, the album was deleted. (See: Buddah Records) Selections included—Side 1: Mick Jagger Speaks, Manson Will Escape, Robert Klein, Teddy Kennedy, Angela Davis, Monty Python's Flying Circus—Spam, Sensuous You. Side 2: Elvis Presley: His First and Only Press Conference, The Killer Was a Narc, Bella Abzug Loses, Scoop's Column, Nader Group Hits Vega, Crime Watch.

Curtis, Tony. Pseudonym of actor Bernie Schwartz. Curtis made his movie debut in 1948 in *Criss Cross*. Tony Curtis was Elvis's favorite actor in the early 1950s, even to the point of copying Curtis's ducktail hairstyle. Tony Curtis's first wife, Janet Leigh, played in the 1963 movie *Bye Bye Birdie*. (See: Bye Bye Birdie)

Curtiz, Michael. Director of the 1958 movie *King Creole*. Previous film credits include *Casablanca* (1942) and *Yankee Doodle Dandy* (1942).

---

*It was in an Xavier Cugat movie, *Holiday in Mexico* (1946), that future Cuban premier Fidel Castro made his movie debut.

D

Dainty Little Moonbeams. Song that Elvis sang part of in the 1962 movie *Girls! Girls! Girls!* Written by Jerry Leiber and Mike Stoller, "Dainty Little Moonbeams" was fifty seconds in length and was incorporated into the track of "Girls! Girls! Girls!" (end title version), which was spliced with "Girls! Girls! Girls!" (main title version). It has never been legitimately released.

Dance Party. A 1950s Memphis TV program on WHBQ (Channel 13), hosted by Wink Martindale. Elvis appeared on "Dance Party" twice in 1957.

Dancing Guitars Rock Hits of the King. A tribute album to Elvis, by Jerry Kennedy, which included eleven Elvis songs. It was released on Smash Records (Smash 27004).

Dancing Jewels. Trio of beautiful dancing girls, named Sapphire, Emerald, and Amethyst (Gail Gilmore, Brenda Benet, and Wilda Taylor), in the 1965 movie *Harum Scarum*.

Dancing on a Dare. Song that Elvis is believed to have recorded for the 1957 movie *Loving You*. It was cut from the final print of the film. There is no record of "Dancing on a Dare" in RCA's recording sessions.

Danny. Title originally considered for the 1958 movie *King Creole*. *Danny Boy* was also considered.

Danny. Song that Elvis recorded in January 1958. Written by Fred Wise and Ben Weisman, "Danny" was originally to have been the title song for the 1958 movie *King Creole*—but it was not included in the film or any of the soundtrack albums. In 1959 it was recorded by Gene Bua on Warner Brothers Records and by Cliff Richard on his Columbia LP, "Cliff." Conway Twitty recorded "Danny"—then retitled "Lonely Blue Boy" (MGM 12857)—in 1960 and had a million-seller with it. Elvis's version of "Danny" remained unreleased until 1978, when it appeared in the Long Playing album "Elvis—A Legendary Performer, Volume 3" (RCA CPL1-3082).

Danny Boy. Popular song written by Frederick Edward Weatherly in 1913, with music adapted from the Irish song "Londonderry Air." "Danny Boy" has been recorded by several artists through the years, including Conway Twitty (MGM 12826) (1959) and Ray Price (Columbia 44042) (1967). The song serves as entertainer Danny Thomas's theme song and was the theme song of the radio series "The O'Neills." Elvis recorded "Danny Boy" in 1976 and it appeared in the Long Playing album

73

"From Elvis Presley Boulevard, Memphis, Tennessee" (RCA APL1-1506).

Danny Fisher. Role portrayed by Elvis in the 1958 movie *King Creole*.

Danzig, Fred. Reporter who interviewed Elvis on January 31, 1956, at RCA Victor's New York studio.

Darby, Ken. Singer, composer, and musical conductor. During the 1940s Ken Darby was a member of the popular singing group the King's Guards (later known as the King's Men). The King's Men sang on the long-running radio series "Fibber McGee and Molly." In 1942 the Ken Darby Singers, along with John Scott Trotter's orchestra, backed up Bing Crosby on the now-famous Decca Records release "White Christmas." Ken Darby later served as Marilyn Monroe's voice coach. In the 1950s the Ken Darby Singers sang the theme song of the TV Western series "The Life and Legend of Wyatt Earp."*

Ken Darby was the musical director of Elvis's first movie, *Love Me Tender*. He was asked to write four songs for the film. He wrote "Love Me Tender," "We're Gonna Move," "Let Me," and "Poor Boy." The Ken Darby Trio did the back-up vocals for Elvis in those recordings.

Ken Darby's wife, Vera Matson, and Elvis are officially credited with writing the four songs for *Love Me Tender* because of copyright problems. Darby was a writer affiliated with ASCAP (American Society of Composers, Authors, and Publishers) and Elvis's publishing company was affiliated with BMI (Broadcast Music, Inc.).

Darin, Bobby. Popular rock 'n' roll singer of the 1950s and '60s. Bobby Darin's (real name: Walden Robert Cassotto) recording career began in 1956 with his first two releases, "Rock Island Line"/"Timber" (Decca 29883) and "Silly Willy"/"Blue-Eyed Mermaid" (Decca 29922). In March of the same year he made his national TV debut on "Stage Show" (just as Elvis had, two months before).

Bobby Darin's first big hit was "Splish Splash" on the Atco label (Atco 6117) in 1958.† The idea for the song came from New York disc jockey Murray the K's mother. "Splish Splash" reached #3 on the charts and was a million-seller. Bobby's biggest hit was "Mack the Knife" in 1959. It was #1 for six weeks and sold over 2 million copies. "Mack the Knife" was the Record of the Year and became Bobby Darin's trademark.

---

*Douglas Fowley, the father of musician Kim Fowley, portrayed Doc Holliday on the series.

†Earlier in 1958, when he thought that Atco was going to drop him because he hadn't produced a hit record, Bobby Darin recorded a song, under the name of the Ding Dongs, called "Early in the Morning." He sold the recording to Brunswick Records (Brunswick 55073). When "Early in the Morning" started moving up the charts (and "Splish Splash" became a hit), Atco bought the recording from Brunswick and released it on their label (Atco 6121), changing the group's name to the Rinky Dinks.

74

In 1963 Bobby Darin was nominated for Best Supporting Actor for his role in the movie *Captain Newman M.D.* He died on December 20, 1973, at 12:15 A.M., during heart surgery.

Bobby Darin was introduced as a guest at one of Elvis's Las Vegas concerts at the International Hotel. The introduction appeared in the bootleg album "To Know Him Is to Love Him" (Black Belt Records).

Dark Cloud Over Memphis. A 1977 Elvis tribute record by Johnny Tollison on Klub Records (Klub 5515).

Darktown Strutter's Ball. Song written by Shelton Brooks and first recorded by Al Jolson in 1917. "Darktown Strutter's Ball" was sung by Carol (Anissa Jones) and Willy (Pepe Brown) in the 1969 movie *The Trouble with Girls* (*And How To Get Into It*). The song also appeared in the following movies: *The Story of Vernon and Irene Castle* (1939); *Broadway* (1942); *The Dolly Sisters* (1945); *Incendiary Blonde* (1945).

Date with Elvis, A. RCA LPM-2011. A 33⅓ rpm Long Playing album that was released in September 1959. It reached #32 on *Billboard*'s Hot LP chart. The album had a double cover. It opened up, revealing a telegram from Elvis and photos of Elvis's departure from the U. S. for West Germany. The back cover originally featured a 1960 calendar with Elvis's discharge date circled. Songs included—Side 1: "Blue Moon of Kentucky," "Young and Beautiful," "(You're So Square) Baby I Don't Care," "Milkcow Blues Boogie," "Baby, Let's Play House." Side 2: "Good Rockin' Tonight," "Is It So Strange," "We're Gonna Move," "I Want to Be Free," "I Forgot to Remember to Forget."

Date with Elvis, A. RCA LSP-2011 (e). This record was the electronically reprocessed stereo re-issue of LPM-2011.

Datin'. Song that Elvis sang in the 1966 movie *Paradise Hawaiian Style*. In the film, Donna Butterworth sang in duet with Elvis. "Datin'" was written by Fred Wise and Randy Starr and appeared in the Long Playing album "Paradise, Hawaiian Style" (RCA LPM/LSP-3643).

Davenport, John. Cowriter (with Eddie Cooley) of "Fever" in 1956. John Davenport was a pseudonym of Otis Blackwell.
Elwood David reportedly earned $43,000 a year.

David, Elwood. Pilot of Elvis's Convair 880 jet, the *Lisa Marie*.

David, Hal and Mack. Composer brothers who have both written songs that Elvis recorded. Hal David was the lyricist with Burt Bacharach on dozens of hit songs, Mack David, Hal's elder brother, wrote the theme songs for the TV series "77 Sunset Strip," "Hawaiian Eye," "Lawman," and "Surfside 6," and others.

Davis, Mac. Country-oriented singer and composer Scott Davis. On October 15, 1955, in Lubbock, Texas, thirteen-year-old Mac Davis attended a show at the Cotton Club, which featured Elvis Presley. Buddy Holly was on the same bill.

In the late 1960s and early '70s, many Mac Davis compositions began to be recorded by major artists, including Lou Rawls ("You're Good for Me"), Bobby Goldsboro ("Watching Scotty Grow"*), and Glen Campbell ("Within My Memory").

Glen Campbell gave Mac Davis the nickname the "Song Painter." (Davis's wife, Sarah, divorced him to marry Glen Campbell.)

At one time Mac Davis changed his pen name to Scott Davis so as not to be confused with songwriter Mack David.

Mac Davis has hosted his own TV variety series on three occasions: July–August 1974 (as a replacement for the "Flip Wilson Show"); December 1974 to May 1975; and March–June 1976.

Elvis recorded several Mac Davis compositions, including "Clean Up Your Own Back Yard"; "Charro"; "A Little Less Conversation"; "Nothingville"; "Memories"; "In the Ghetto"; "Don't Cry Daddy."

Davis, Oscar. Agent, nicknamed "The Baron," who worked for Col. Tom Parker. Oscar Davis performed in vaudeville between 1910 and 1917. He has worked with country artists Hank Williams, Eddy Arnold, Hank Snow, Ernest Tubb, Roy Acuff, and others. It was Oscar Davis who first told Col. Parker about Elvis. He then helped Parker promote Elvis. Davis was also Jerry Lee Lewis's manager. (See: Airport Inn)

Davis, Richard. Elvis's personal valet for seven years (1963–'69). Richard Davis had a bit part in the 1967 movie *Clambake*.

Davis, Sammy, Jr. Black entertainer, singer, musician, dancer, mimic, and actor who attended Elvis's private funeral on August 18, 1977. Sammy Davis, Jr., who made his professional debut at the age of two, was a member of Frank Sinatra's Rat Pack.† In 1954 he had his first chart record, "Hey, There" (Decca 29199). Sammy added Broadway to his career when he starred in *Mr. Wonderful* in 1956. Although he has been recording for over a quarter of a century, Sammy Davis, Jr., has had only one #1 record—"Candy Man" (from the 1971 movie *Willy Wonka and the Chocolate Factory*). On TV, he has hosted his own musical variety series, "The Sammy Davis, Jr. Show" (1966), and sang the theme song of the TV detective series "Baretta" ("Keep Your Eye on the Sparrow").

Sammy Davis, Jr., appeared with Elvis on the 1960 "Frank Sinatra-Timex Special" on ABC-TV. He can be seen as a member of the audience in the 1970 documentary *Elvis— That's the Way It Is.*

---

*"Watching Scotty Grow" was about Mac Davis's real-life son.
†Members of the Rat Pack included, from time to time: Frank Sinatra, Sammy Davis, Jr., Peter Lawford, Dean Martin, Joey Bishop, Shirley Mac-Laine, Tony Curtis, Jimmy Van Heusen, Sammy Cahn, Irving Paul Lazar, and Harry Kurnitz.

Prior to Elvis recording "In the Ghetto," the song was offered to Sammy Davis, Jr., who failed to project the song with the proper feeling.

Day, James Clayton. Steel guitarist with Ray Price's Cherokee Cowboys. Jimmy Day backed up Elvis at the Louisiana Hayride in 1954 and can be heard on "Tweedle Dee." Day played guitar on the Everly Brothers' 1957 hit, "Bye Bye Love" (Cadence 1315).

Day in the Life of a Number One D.J., A. Film in which Pat Boone appeared in 1957. *A Day in the Life of a Number One D.J.* was about Cleveland disc jockey Bill Randle. While in Cleveland making the film, Boone met Elvis, who was performing at a nearby high school. (See: Circle Theater; Randle, Bill) The film, which is also known by the title *The Pied Piper of Cleveland,* has never been released. This was Elvis's first movie appearance.

Day the Beat Stopped, The. A 1978 Elvis tribute record by Ral Donner on Thunder Records (Thunder 7801).

Dean, Dizzy. Baseball pitcher for the St. Louis Cardinals (1930–'37) and later TV baseball announcer. In the 1952 movie *The Pride of St. Louis,* Dizzy Dean (real name: Jerome Herman Dean) was portrayed by Dan Dailey. (It was Dizzy Dean who gave Roy Acuff the nickname the "King of Country Music.")

Dizzy Dean was one of the featured performers, along with Elvis Presley, at the Jimmie Rodgers Memorial Day Celebration, May 26, 1955. (See: Jimmie Rodgers Memorial Day Celebration)

Dear Elvis with Love From Audrey, Part 1/Part 2. An Elvis novelty record by Audrey on Plus Records (Plus 104). It was recorded in the form of a fan letter and included cuts from Elvis versions of "Baby, Let's Play House" and "I Don't Care If the Sun Don't Shine."

Dear 53310761. An Elvis novelty record by the Three Teens. The record was released by Rev Records (Rev 3516) in 1958 and made reference to Elvis's stay in the U. S. Army. The music publisher, Trinity Music, gave away 50,000 Elvis Presley dog tags to disc jockeys to promote the record.

DeCordova, Frederick. Director of the 1966 movie *Frankie and Johnny.* In addition to movies, Fred DeCordova has directed several television shows, including "Leave it to Beaver"* and the "Tonight Show Starring Johnny Carson."

Dedicated to the King. A tribute album to Elvis, by Chuck Jackson† which included ten Elvis songs. It was released on Wand Records (Wand 680).

---

*Even Jerry Mathers made a record, in 1962, for Atlantic Records, titled "Don't Cha Cry"/"Wind Up Toy (Atlantic 2156).
†Lead singer of the Del Vikings from 1957 to 1959.

Deke Rivers. Elvis's role in the 1957 movie *Loving You.* "Deke" stood for Deacon. Deke's real name was Jimmy Tompkins and he was an orphan. He borrowed the name Deke Rivers from a tombstone in Woodbine Cemetery (Deke Rivers 1878–1934).

Del Rio, Dolores. Actress who portrayed Neddy Burton in the 1960 movie *Flaming Star.* Dolores Del Rio was called the "First Lady of the Mexican Cinema" and the "First Lady of the Mexican Stage." *Flaming Star* was Dolores Del Rio's first Hollywood movie since *Journey into Fear* (1942).

Delta Airlines. Airline company that previously flew Elvis's Convair 880 jet, the *Lisa Marie.*

DeMille, Cecil Blount. Veteran Hollywood director who became famous for his religious spectaculars (his father was a minister). DeMille, who was born in Demille Corners, Massachusetts, in 1881, was the only man to successfully film the same movie three times—*The Squaw Man* (1913, '18, '31). He filmed his favorite, *The Ten Commandments,** twice (1923 and '56). In 1937 the Republican party of California nominated DeMille for senator, but he turned it down. It was Cecil B. DeMille who designed the Service Alpha uniform for the cadets at the Air Force Academy.

When Elvis met the director in 1956, DeMille asked him if he had seen his film *The Ten Commandments.*† Elvis is supposed to have replied, "Crazy, man, real crazy."

Dene, Terry. First British Elvis impersonator. He began copying Elvis in the mid 1950s. Dene's back-up band was the Dene-Agers.

Dennis Roberts Optical Boutique. Los Angeles firm where Elvis purchased his prescription sunglasses. They cost about $200 each. Elvis also bought his bodyguards sunglasses with "TCB" printed on them.

Denny, James R. The talent cordinator for the Grand Ole Opry from 1951 to 1954. Denny (1911–63) booked the stars through the Artists Service Bureau. After Elvis performed on the "Grand Ole Opry," in September 1954, Jim Denny told Elvis that he should return to truck driving.‡

In 1955 Jim Denny was selected *Billboard*'s Man of the Year and in 1966 he was voted into the Country Music Hall of Fame.

Deputy Sheriff. Honorary law-enforcement designation given to Elvis by the Shelby County, Tennessee, Sheriff's Department.

---

*The movie *The Ten Commandments* is mentioned in the 1957 movie *Loving You.*
†In this 1956 version (the 1923 version was silent), a young Herb Alpert can be seen with his back to the audience playing a drum as Moses descends from Mt. Sinai. (In 1966, Herb Alpert and Jerry Moss would establish A & M Records on the site of the old Charlie Chaplin studio in Hollywood where Elvis recorded some movie songs.)
‡Ironically, it was Jim Denny who, in 1956, took great interest in another rock 'n' roller—Buddy Holly. He helped Holly to be signed by Decca Records.

Because he was appointed Deputy Sheriff, Elvis was allowed to carry a loaded pistol.

DeShannon, Jackie. Singer-composer who has written over six hundred songs, including "Put a Little Love in Your Heart" and "Dum Dum" (cowritten with Sharon Sheeley, a good friend). Jackie DeShannon (real name: Sharon Myers) dated Elvis for a six-month period in the mid-1960s. (see: O'Neill, Jimmy)

Detour. Song that Sweet Susie Jessup (Dolores Hart) sang on stage in the 1957 movie *Loving You.* "Detour" had been a hit in 1951 for Patti Page (Mercury 5682).

Detroit, Michigan. Site of December 31, 1975, Elvis Presley concert where he broke the record for a solo artist when he earned $816,000 for a single performance.

Deusenberg (1929 Model J.) Antique automobile driven by Mike McCoy (Elvis) in the 1966 movie *Spinout.*

(You're The) Devil in Disguise. RCA 47-8188. Released in July 1963 as a 45 rpm single. It reached #3 on *Billboard*'s Hot 100 chart, #9 on the Rhythm and Blues chart, and #1 in the United Kingdom (for one week, August 3–10). "(You're The) Devil in Disguise" sold over a million copies. "Please Don't Drag That String Around" was on the flip side. Written by Bill Giant, Bernie Baum, and Florence Kaye, "(You're The) Devil in Disguise" appeared in the Long Playing albums "Elvis' Gold Records, Volume 4" (RCA LPM/LSP-3921) and "Elvis: Worldwide 50 Gold Award Hits, Volume 1" (RCA LPM-6401).

(You're The) Devil in Disguise. RCA 447-0641. Gold Standard Series re-issue of RCA 47-8188.

Devore, Sy. Fashion designer who created a new wardrobe for Elvis in 1962, costing $9,000.

Diamond, Neil. Popular singer-songwriter who originally recorded for Columbia Records, then Bang Records,* Uni Records, and, finally, back to Columbia. Neil Diamond's first record release was "Clown Town"/"At Night" (Columbia 42809) in 1963. It didn't reach the charts. His next release, "Solitary Man," for the Bang label (Bang 519) in 1966, did make the charts and was a big hit.

While at Erasmus Hall High School in Brooklyn, Neil Diamond and Barbra Streisand sang in the same choral group.

In 1973 Neil Diamond added to his many achievements by scoring the soundtrack of the motion picture *Jonathan Livingston Seagull.*

Among the compositions Neil Diamond has written for other artists are "I'm a Believer" for the Monkees and "Sunday and Me" for Jay and the Americans.

Elvis recorded Neil Diamond's 1969 hit "Sweet Caroline," in

---

*Bang Records was founded by Bert Berns, Ahmet Ertegun, Nesuhi Ertegun, and Gerald "Jerry" Wexler.

1970, at the International Hotel in Las Vegas. Elvis also recorded the Diamond composition "And the Grass Won't Pay No Mind."

Diddley, Bo. Rhythm and blues guitarist and singer of the 1950s and '60s. Bo Diddley (real name: Elias McDaniels) received his nickname while in grade school in Chicago. He used the nickname when he boxed in the Golden Gloves. In 1955 Bo Diddley walked into Chess Records and auditioned for the owners, Phil and Leonard Chess. He performed a song that he wrote, called "Uncle John" (the catchy tune was based on the old English folk song "Hush Little Baby"). The Chess brothers signed Bo to a contract and recorded "Uncle John", changing the title to "Bo Diddley" (Checker 814).

While Elvis was in New York City in 1956, appearing on the "Stage Show" TV program, he went to the Apollo Theater to see Bo Diddley perform. Many people believe that Elvis copied Diddley's style of performing, since Bo Diddley was one of the first artists to wriggle his hips while singing. Bo Diddley once stated: "If he copied me, I don't care. More power to him, I'm not starving."

Didja Ever. Song that Elvis sang in the 1960 movie *G.I. Blues*. The regular release of "Didja Ever" has the backing of the Jordanaires, while the film version has several voices answering Elvis. "Didja Ever" was written by Sid Wayne and Sherman Edwards and appeared in the Long Playing album "G.I. Blues" (RCA LPM/LSP-2256).

Dirty, Dirty Feeling. Song that Elvis sang in the 1965 movie *Tickle Me*. "Dirty, Dirty Feeling" was recorded five years earlier, on April 4, 1960. It was written by Jerry Leiber and Mike Stoller and appeared in the Extended Play album "Tickle Me" (RCA EPA-4383) and the Long Playing album "Elvis Is Back" (RCA LPM/LSP-2231).

Diskin, Tom. One of Col. Tom Parker's assistants. Tom Diskin is Parker's brother-in-law.

Dixie. Traditional southern song—thought to be written by Dan Emmett* and first performed in the north. "Dixie" is one of three songs included in "An American Trilogy" and was one of several tunes the U. S. Army band played as Elvis boarded the U.S.S. *Randall* to sail to West Germany (September 22, 1958). (See: An American Trilogy)

Dixieland Rock. Song that Elvis sang in the 1958 movie *King Creole*. "Dixieland Rock" was written by Aaron Schroeder and R. Frank and appeared in the Extended Play album "King Creole, Volume 2" (RCA EPA-4321) and the following Long Playing albums: "King Creole" (RCA LPM-1884); "King Cre-

---

*Daniel Decatur Emmett was portrayed by Bing Crosby in the 1934 movie *Dixie*.

ole" (RCA LSP-1884 [e]); "Elvis: The Other Sides—Worldwide Gold Award Hits, Volume 2" (RCA LPM-6402).

The version of "Dixieland Rock" on the "King Creole" LP is different—it has seven downbeats instead of two.

Dixon, Willie. Blues artist and Golden Gloves boxing champion in Chicago in 1936. Willie Dixon composed three songs that Elvis recorded: "Big Boss Man," "Doncha Think It's Time," and "My Babe."

D.O.A. A 1977 Elvis tribute record ("*Dead On Arrival*") by Misty. It was released on Sun Records (Sun 1136).

Doc Hayes—Vernon Presley Motor Sales. Memphis used-car dealership with which Vernon Presley was affiliated for a brief time in the 1960s.

Dodgems. Bumper cars at the Fairgrounds Amusement Park in Memphis. Dodgems were Elvis's favorite ride.

Dodger. Elvis's pet name for his grandmother, Minnie Mae Presley.

Dog's Life, A. Song that Elvis sang in the 1966 movie *Paradise, Hawaiian Style*. The film version had barking dogs. "A Dog's Life" was written by Sid Wayne and Ben Weisman and appeared in the Long Playing album "Paradise, Hawaiian Style" (RCA LPM/LSP-3643).

Doin' the Best I Can. Song that Elvis sang in the 1960 movie *G.I. Blues*. "Doin' the Best I Can" was written by Doc Pomus and Mort Shuman and appeared in the Long Playing album "G.I. Blues" (RCA LPM/LSP-2256).

Dolan, Kitty. Brunette Las Vegas showgirl whom Elvis dated in 1956. Elvis met Kitty Dolan while she was performing at the Tropicana.

Dominick. Song that Elvis sang in the 1968 movie *Stay Away, Joe*. Dominick was a bull and Elvis sang the song to him. RCA never released "Dominick," although it did appear on the English bootleg LP "Please Release Me."

Dominick XII. Champion bucking bull owned by Joe Lightcloud (Elvis) in the 1968 movie *Stay Away, Joe*.

Domino. Priscilla Presley's favorite horse, given to her by Elvis.

Domino, Fats. New Orleans rhythm and blues piano player and singer. Fats Domino (real name: Antoine Domino) ranks #3 on the all-time list of performers with the most million-selling singles records. He has twenty-three. (Elvis is #1 and the Beatles are #2.) Fats's first million-seller (and the derivation of his nickname) was "The Fat Man" (Imperial 5058),* which was released in 1948. Most of his tunes have been written by him, in collaboration with Dave Bartholomew. As a matter of fact, Fats Domino and Dave Bartholomew rank #3 on the list of songwriters with the most million-selling songs. Each has twenty-two. (Paul McCartney is #1, with thirty-nine, and John

---

*Many rock historians consider this the first rock 'n' roll record.

Lennon is #2, with thirty-seven.) Although he has had twenty-three million-sellers, Fats Domino has never had a #1 record.

Fats Domino's biggest hit (and only million-seller *not* written by him and Dave Bartholomew) was "Blueberry Hill" (Imperial 5407) in 1956. Elvis recorded "Blueberry Hill" in 1957.

Doncha' Think It's Time. RCA 20/47-7240. Released in April 1958 as a 78 rpm single and a 45 rpm single. It reached #21 on *Billboard*'s Hot 100 chart. "Wear My Ring Around Your Neck" was on the flip side. "Doncha' Think It's Time" was written by Clyde Otis and Willie Dixon and appeared in the following Long Playing albums: "50,000,000 Elvis Fans Can't Be Wrong—Elvis' Gold Records, Volume 2" (RCA LPM-2075); "50,000,000 Elvis Fans Can't Be Wrong—Elvis' Gold Records, Volume 2" (RCA LSP-2075 [e]); and "Elvis: The Other Sides—Worldwide Gold Award Hits, Volume 2" (RCA LPM-6402).

Doncha' Think It's Time. RCA 447-0662. Gold Standard Series reissue of RCA 47-7240.

Donna Reed Show, The. ABC-TV series (1958–66) featuring Donna Reed, Carl Betz, Shelley Fabares, Paul Peterson,* and Jimmy Hawkins. Three of the stars were in Elvis movies. Betz, Fabares, and Hawkins appeared in the 1966 movie *Spinout,* while Fabares and Hawkins were in *Girl Happy* (1965). Shelley Fabares also appeared in the 1967 movie *Clambake.* Paul Peterson had a 1962 hit, "She Can't Find Her Keys" (Colpix 620), which made reference to Elvis. Together, in 1962, Paul Peterson and Shelley Fabares recorded "What Did They Do Before Rock & Roll" (Colpix 631), which also mentioned Elvis's name.

Donner, Ral. One of the more successful Elvis sound-alikes. Ral Donner's (real name: Ralph Stuart Emanuel Donner) 1961 version of "The Girl of My Best Friend" (Gone 5102) is almost identical to Elvis's version. His back-up group was called the Starfires.†

Ral Donner first saw Elvis perform at Chicago's International Amphitheater in 1957.

In 1978 Ral Donner recorded the Elvis tribute record "The Day the Beat Stopped" (Thunder 7801). A portion of the record's royalties was donated to the Elvis Presley Memorial in Memphis.

Do Not Disturb. Song that Elvis sang in the 1965 movie *Girl Happy.* "Do Not Disturb" was written by Bill Giant, Bernie Baum, and Florence Kaye and appeared in the Long Playing album "Girl Happy" (RCA LPM/LSP-3338).

Don't. RCA 20/47-7150. Released in December 1957 as a 78 rpm single and a 45 rpm single. It reached #1 on *Billboard*'s Hot

---

*Paul Peterson's real-life sister, Patty, portrayed Trisha Stone, his stage sister, on the "Donna Reed Show."
†Originally called the Gents.

100 chart (for one week, March 10–17), #2 on the country chart, and #4 on the Rhythm and Blues chart. "Don't" sold over a million copies (*advance* orders were over a million!). "I Beg of You" was on the flip side. "Don't" was recorded on September 6, 1957, during the first Elvis recording sessions that used a female voice (Millie Kirkham). Jerry Leiber and Mike Stoller wrote "Don't" and it appeared in the Extended Play album, "A Touch of Gold, Volume 1" (RCA EPA-5088) and the following Long Playing albums: "50,000,000 Elvis Fans Can't Be Wrong—Elvis' Gold Records, Volume 2" (RCA LPM-2075); "50,000,000 Elvis Fans Can't Be Wrong—Elvis' Gold Records, Volume 2" (RCA LSP-2075 [e]); "Elvis: Worldwide 50 Gold Award Hits, Volume 1" (RCA LPM-6401); "Elvis" (RCA DPL2-0056 [e]).

Don't. RCA 447-0621. Gold Standard Series re-issue of RCA 20/47-7150.

Don't. RCA SP-45-76. Special 45 rpm promotional release. "Wear My Ring Around Your Neck" was on the flip side.

Don't Ask Me Why. RCA 20/47-7280. Released in June 1958 as a 78 rpm single and a 45 rpm single. It reached #28 on *Billboard*'s Hot 100 chart and #2 on the Rhythm and Blues chart. "Hard Headed Woman" was on the flip side. Elvis sang "Don't Ask Me Why" in the 1958 movie *King Creole*. "Don't Ask Me Why" was written by Fred Wise and Ben Weisman and appeared in the Extended Play Album "A Touch of Gold Volume 3" (RCA EPA-5141) and the following Long Playing albums: "King Creole" (RCA LPM-1884); "King Creole" (RCA LSP-1884 [e]); "Elvis: The Other Sides—Worldwide Gold Award Hits, Volume 2" (RCA LPM-6402).

Don't Be Cruel. RCA 20/47-6604. Released in July 1956 as a 78 rpm single and a 45 rpm single. It reached #1 on *Billboard*'s Hot 100 chart (for seven weeks, September 15–November 3), #1 on the Country chart, and #1 on the Rhythm and Blues chart. "Don't Be Cruel" was the first of four Presley songs to be #1 on all three *Billboard* charts. (The other three songs were "All Shook Up," "(Let Me Be Your) Teddy Bear," and "Jailhouse Rock.") "Hound Dog" was on the flip side. Together, "Don't Be Cruel" and "Hound Dog" sold over 9 million copies.

Elvis recorded "Don't Be Cruel" on July 2, 1956—the first Elvis Presley recording session to include the Jordanaires. Musicians in that session were Scotty Moore (guitar), Bill Black (bass), Shorty Long (piano), and D. J. Fontana (drums). In 1960 Bill Black recorded "Don't Be Cruel" with his combo on Hi Records (Hi 2026). Scotty Moore played guitar in that session. Elvis sang "Don't Be Cruel" on all three "Ed Sullivan Show" appearances, in the 1972 documentary *Elvis on Tour,* and in the 1977 CBS-TV special "Elvis in Concert." "Don't Be Cruel" was written by Otis Blackwell and appeared in the following Extended Play albums: "The Real Elvis" (RCA EPA-940); "The Real Elvis" (RCA EPA-5120); "Elvis Presley" (RCA SPD-23); and the following Long Playing albums: "Elvis' Golden Records" (RCA LPM1707); "Elvis' Golden Records" (RCA LSP-1707 [e]); "Elvis: Worldwide 50 Gold Award Hits, Volume 1" (RCA LPM-6401); "Elvis as Recorded at Madison Square Garden" (RCA LSP-4776); "Elvis" (RCA DPL2-0056 [e]); "Elvis—A Legendary Performer, Volume 1" (RCA CPL1-0341); "Pure Gold" (RCA ANL1-0971); "Elvis in Concert" (RCA APL2-2587).

Don't Be Cruel. RCA 447-0608. Gold Standard Series re-issue of RCA 20/47-6604.

Don't Blame It on Elvis. An Elvis novelty record by the Famous McClevertys. It was released on Verve Records (Verve 10029).

Don't Cry, Daddy. RCA 47-9768. Released in November 1969 as a 45 rpm single. It reached #6 on *Billboard*'s Hot 100 chart and #13 on the Country chart and sold over a million copies. "Rubberneckin'" was on the flip side. "Don't Cry, Daddy" was written by Mac Davis. Ronnie Milsap sang harmony with Elvis in the recording. The title "Don't Cry, Daddy" came from Mac's son Scotty, who told his dad, "Don't cry, Daddy' upon seeing Mac's tearful reaction to the TV showing of a Vietnamese hamlet massacre. "Don't Cry, Daddy" appeared in the Long Playing album "Elvis: Worldwide 50 Gold Award Hits, Volume 1" (RTCA LPM-6401).

Don't Cry, Daddy. RCA 447-0674. Gold Standard Series re-issue of RCA 47-9768.

Don't Cry for Christmas/Dr. X-Mas. A 45 rpm record, released by Sun Records, which has a question mark instead of the artist's name on the label. The singer is an Elvis sound-alike (possibly Jimmy Ellis)—it is not Elvis, as Shelby Singleton would like listeners to believe.*

Don't Cry Lisa. A 1977 Elvis tribute song by Pamela Nichols, released on the Heartsong label (Heartsong 458).

Don't Knock Elvis. An Elvis novelty record by Felton Jarvis, released by Viva Records (Viva 1001) in 1959.

Don't Leave Me Now. Song that Elvis sang in the 1957 movie *Jailhouse Rock*. It was sung three times in the film. The version of "Don't Leave Me Now" that appeared on the "Loving You" album was recorded on February 23, 1957, and is different from the version of the "Jailhouse Rock" EP (which was recorded in May). The South African LP, "Jailhouse Rock," contained the EP version. "Don't Leave Me Now" was written by Aaron Schroeder and Ben Weisman and appeared in the Extended Play album "Jailhouse Rock" (RCA EPA-4114) and

---

*Many Elvis fans accept the theory that Singleton releases these "Elvis" songs this way because he can't legally credit Elvis on his Sun label since RCA Victor owns the rights to Elvis's releases. This belief only encourages Singleton to release more "mysterious" records.

the Long Playing albums "Jailhouse Rock" (RCA LPM-1515) and "Loving You" (RCA LSP-1515 [e]).

Don't Think Twice, It's All Right. Song written and originally recorded by Bob Dylan in 1963 (Columbia 42856). It was based on the traditional folk tune "Who'll Buy Your Chickens When I'm Gone." Peter, Paul, and Mary had a bigger hit with "Don't Think Twice, It's All Right" (Warner Brothers 5385) in late 1963. Elvis's version of the song was the result of an eight-minute jam session on May 16, 1971. The unedited version appeared in the bootleg albums "The Entertainer" and "Behind Closed Doors." The edited version of "Don't Think Twice, It's All Right" (2 minutes, 45 seconds) appeared in the Long Playing albums "Elvis" (RCA APL1-0283) and "Our Memories of Elvis, Volume 2" (RCA AQL1-3448).

Don't Want Your Letters. Answer record by Gerri Granger to "Return to Sender." Released on Big Top Records (Big Top 3128) in 1962.

Doors Incorporated. Memphis firm, located at 911 Rayner Street, that built the Music Gates at Graceland (1957).

Dorsey Brothers. (See: Stage Show)

Dorsey Shows, The. A 33⅓ rpm bootleg album released on the Golden Archives label (Golden Archives GA-100). The album featured songs from Elvis's appearances on the Dorsey brothers' "Stage Show."

Dorsey, Thomas A. Chicago bluesman, born on July 1, 1899, songwriter, and one-time bandleader for Gertrude "Ma" Rainey. Prior to 1932 Thomas Dorsey composed mostly blues and jazz tunes. After 1932 he became America's foremost writer of gospel songs. Dorsey composed "Peace in the Valley" and "Take My Hand, Precious Lord," both of which Elvis recorded. Thomas Dorsey coined the term *gospel song*.

Do the Clam. RCA 47-8500. Released in March 1965 as a 45 rpm single. It reached #21 on *Billboard*'s Hot 100 chart. "Do the Clam," written by Sid Wayne, Ben Weisman, and Dolores Fuller, was tremendously successful in Japan. "You'll Be Gone" was on the flip side. Elvis sang "Do the Clam" in the 1965 movie, *Girl Happy*. It appeared in the Long Playing album, "Girl Happy" (RCA LPM/LSP-3338).

Do the Vega. Song that Elvis recorded for the 1964 movie, *Viva Las Vegas*. It was cut from the final print of the film. Written by Bill Giant, Bernie Baum, and Florence Kaye, "Do the Vega" appeared in the following Long Playing albums: "Singer Presents Elvis Singing Flaming Star and Others" (RCA PRS-279); "Elvis Sings Flaming Star" (RCA Camden CAS-2304); and "Elvis Sings Flaming Star" (Pickwick CAS-2304).

Double Dynamite. Pickwick DL2-5001. A 33⅓ rpm Long Playing album released in December 1975. "Double Dynamite" was a Pickwick original—not a re-issue. Songs included—Side 1: "Burning Love," "I'll Be There (If Ever You Want Me),"

"Fools Fall in Love," "Follow That Dream," "You'll Never Walk Alone." Side 2: "Flaming Star," "Yellow Rose of Texas"/ "The Eyes of Texas," "Old Shep," "Mama." Side 3: "Rubber-neckin'," "U.S. Male," "Frankie and Johnny," "If You Think I Don't Need You," "Easy Come, Easy Go." Side 4: "Separate Ways," "(There'll Be) Peace in the Valley (For Me)," "Big Boss Man," "It's a Matter of Time."

DOUBLE TROUBLE. MGM, 1967. Premiered New York City, May 24, 1967 (90 min.). Elvis's twenty-fourth movie. Produc-ers, Judd Bernard and Irwin Winkler. Director, Norman Taurog. Cast: Guy Lambert/Elvis Presley, Jill Conway/Ann-ette Day, Gerald Waverly/John Williams, Claire Dunham/ Yvonne Romain, The Wiere Brothers/The Wiere Brothers, Archie Brown/Chips Rafferty, Arthur Babcock/Norman Rossington, Georgie/Monty Landis, Morley/Michael Murphy, Inspector De Grotte/Leon Askin, Iceman/John Alderson, Capt. Roach/Stanley Adams, Frenchman/Maurice Marsac, Mate/ Walter Burke, Gerda/Helene Winston, Desk Clerk/Monique Lemaire, The G Men/The G Men. Screenplay, Jo Heims. Photography, Daniel L. Fapp. Music, Jeff Alexander. Choreog-raphy, Alex Romero. Art Direction, George W. Davis and Merrill Pye. Set Decoration, Henry Grace and Hugh Hunt. Special Visual Effects, J. McMillan Johnson and Carroll Shep-phird. Costumes, Don Feld. Technical Adviser, Col Tom Par-ker. Assistant Director, Claude Binyon, Jr. Editor, John McSweeney. Songs sung by Elvis: "Double Trouble," "Baby if You'll Give Me All Your Love," "City by Night," "There's So Much World to See," "Could I Fall in Love," "Long Legged Girl (With the Short Dress On)," "Old MacDonald," "I Love Only One Girl." "It Won't Be Long" was deleted from the film.

Both Elvis and Ray Charles appeared in movies titled *Double Trouble*. *Double Trouble* was the title (released as *Swinging Along* in Britain) of the 1962 movie in which Ray Charles and Bobby Vee appeared. It starred Tommy Noonan and Peter Marshall.

Double Trouble. Title song of the 1967 movie, *Double Trouble*, which Elvis sang. "Double Trouble" was written by Doc Pomus and Mort Shuman and appeared in the Long Playing albums, "Double Trouble" (RCA LPM/LSP-3787) and "Elvis in Holly-wood" (RCA DPL2-0168).

Double Trouble. RCA LPM/LSP-3787. A 33⅓ rpm Long Playing album released in June 1967. It reached #47 on *Billboard*'s Hot 100 chart. "Double Trouble" featured eight songs from the 1967 movie of the same name, plus four bonus songs. Songs included—Side 1: "Double Trouble," "Baby if You'll Give Me All Your Love," "Could I Fall in Love," "Long Legged Girl (With the Short Dress On)," "City by Night," "Old MacDon-ald." Side 2: "I Love Only One Girl," "There Is So Much

World to See," "It Won't Be Long" (bonus), "Never Ending" (bonus), "Blue River" (bonus), "What Now, What Next, Where To" (bonus).

Douglas, Donna. Actress who played Frankie in the 1966 movie, *Frankie and Johnny*. Donna Douglas is probably best known for her role of Elly Mae Clampett on the TV series, "The Beverly Hillbillies." She was formerly a Miss New Orleans. In *Frankie and Johnny*, Donna Douglas sang "Petunia, the Gardener's Daughter" with Elvis. She introduced Elvis to yoga. (See: Beverly Hillbillies, The)

Douglas, Gordon. Director of the 1962 movie, *Follow That Dream*. Gordon Douglas also directed several Frank Sinatra movies, including *Robin and the 7 Hoods* (1964) and *Tony Rome* (1967). He is the only person to have directed both Elvis Presley and Frank Sinatra.

Down by the Riverside/When the Saints Go Marching In. Medley sung by Elvis in the 1966 movie, *Frankie and Johnny*. "Down by the Riverside" was an old standard that Bill Giant, Bernie Baum, and Florence Kaye adapted for the movie.

"When the Saints Go Marching In" was a New Orleans funeral hymn and jazz classic, author unknown. It gained national popularity from a 1930 Decca recording by Louis Armstrong. In 1956 Bill Haley and the Comets recorded a version titled "The Saints Rock 'n Roll" (Decca 29870). Giant, Baum, and Kaye adapted it for the movie.

"Down by the Riverside"/"When the Saints Go Marching In" appeared in the following Long Playing albums: "Frankie and Johnny" (RCA LPM/LSP-3553); "Frankie and Johnny" (Pickwick ACL-7007); "Elvis Sings Hits from His Movies, Volume 1" (RCA Camden CAS-2567); "Elvis Sings Hits from His Movies, Volume 1" (Pickwick CAS-2567).

Down in the Alley. Song written by Jesse Stone and originally recorded by the Clovers in 1957 on Atlantic Records (Atlantic 1152). Elvis recorded "Down in the Alley" in 1966 and it appeared as a bonus song on the Long Playing album, "Spinout" (RCA LPM/LSP-3702). "Down in the Alley," an excellent R & B version by Elvis, was a cut above the movie songs that he was recording at the same time.

Down the Line. Unreleased Sun recording of 1955. In addition to Elvis, Jerry Lee Lewis also recorded "Down the Line," appearing on the flip side of "Breathless," released by Sun Records (Sun 288) in 1958. The song, also known by the title of "Move on Down the Line," was composed by Sam Phillips.*

Do You Know Who I Am. Song written by Bobby Russell† in

---

*The actual composer of the song is difficult to trace. In 1955 Roy Orbison recorded the song as "Go! Go! Go!" (flip side of "Ooby Dooby" on Sun 242), listing himself as composer. When Ricky Nelson recorded the same song as "Down The Line," the composer was listed as Allen Matthews.

†Ex-husband of comedienne and singer Vicki Lawrence.

1969 and recorded by Elvis at the American Sound Studios on February 19 of that year. "Do You Know Who I Am" appeared in the Long Playing albums, "From Memphis to Vegas/ From Vegas to Memphis" (RCA LSP-6020) and "Elvis—Back in Memphis" (RCA LSP-4429).

Do You Remember. Song by the Beach Boys, on Capitol Records, in which the following phrase was heard: "Elvis Presley is the King, he's the giant of the day, paved the way for the rock 'n' roll sound."

Drake, Peter. Steel guitarist, known as the "Talking Steel Guitar Man," who achieved national notoriety in 1964 with the million-selling record, "Forever." Peter Drake played steel guitar in many Elvis Presley recordings, including "Guitar Man," "Big Boss Man," and "You'll Never Walk Alone." In 1968 Drake founded Stop Records.

Draper, David. Former Mr. America and Mr. Universe who was a member of one of the film crews for the 1973 documentary, *Elvis on Tour*. Draper's crew filmed Elvis at Graceland in 1972.

Dr. Ben Casey/Roaring 20's Rag. An Elvis novelty record by Mickey Shorr and the Cut-ups on Tuba Records (Tuba 8001) in 1962. The record included a cut from Elvis's version of "Good Luck Charm."

Drifters, The. Popular rhythm and blues vocal group of the 1950s and '60s. Among the Drifters' lead singers were Clyde McPhatter, David Baughan, Johnny Moore, Bobby Hendricks, Ben E. King, Rudy Lewis, and Charlie Thomas.

There were actually two different groups called the Drifters. The original Drifters disbanded* in 1958. The group's manager, George Treadwell, wanted the name to continue. So, in late 1958, he signed the Five Crowns, who began performing under the name the Drifters. The new Drifters' first hit was "There Goes My Baby" (Atlantic 2025)—the first rhythm and blues recording to incorporate strings. Ben E. King sang the lead.

Dionne Warwick was "discovered" while singing back-up for the Drifters in some of their recording sessions.

Elvis recorded four songs that the Drifters had previously recorded: "Money Honey"; "Fools Fall in Love"; "Such a Night"; "White Christmas." Elvis also recorded "Without Love (I Have Nothing)" in 1969, a hit for Clyde McPhatter in 1957.

Dr. Strangelove. The 1964 Stanley Kubrick movie (subtitled *Or, How I Learned to Stop Worrying and Love the Bomb*) starring Peter Sellers and George C. Scott. It was one of Elvis's favorite movies. (See: Shot in the Dark, A)

Drums of the Islands. Song that Elvis sang in the 1966 movie *Paradise, Hawaiian Style*. Elvis sang "Drums of the Islands"

---

*They were all fired by George Treadwell, husband of Sarah Vaughan.

twice during the film. The film versions were longer and slightly different from that on the record. "Drums of the Islands" was written by Sid Tepper and Roy C. Bennett and appeared in the Long Playing album "Paradise, Hawaiian Style" (RCA LPM/LSP-3643).

Dubrovner, Mrs. The Presleys' landlady while living at 462 Alabama Street in Memphis.

Duckling. Word Elvis used, as a small boy, for water.

Duet. Bootleg label that offered (for three dollars) the "Love Me Tender" duet by Elvis and Linda Ronstadt (Duet 101).

Duets. Sun 1011. This is a 33⅓ rpm album by Jerry Lee Lewis and Friends that Shelby Singleton released in 1978. Some of the cuts on this album sound like Elvis singing duet with Jerry Lee Lewis—which is precisely what listeners are supposed to believe. However, music experts are aware of the fact that Jimmy Ellis appeared in "Save the Last Dance for Me" and Charlie Rich is heard on "Am I to Be the One." Elvis doesn't sing on any of the songs in the album. Songs included—Side 1: "Save the Last Dance for Me," "Sweet Little Sixteen," "I Love You Because," "C. C. Rider," "Am I to Be the One," "Sail Away." Side 2: "Cold, Cold Heart," "Hello, Josephine," "It Won't Happen with Me," "What'd I Say," "Good Golly, Miss Molly."

Duets. Elvis sang duets with the following people in movies: "Crawfish," Kitty White, *King Creole* (1958). "Husky Dusky Day," Hope Lang, *Wild in the Country* (1961). "Earth Boy," Ginny and Elizabeth Tiu, *Girls! Girls! Girls!* (1962). "Happy Ending," Joan O'Brien, *It Happened at the World's Fair* (1963). "How Would You Like to Be," Vicki Tiu, *It Happened at the World's Fair* (1963). "Mexico," Larry Domasin, *Fun in Acapulco* (1963). "The Lady Loves Me," Ann-Margret, *Viva Las Vegas* (1964). "Petunia, the Gardener's Daughter," Donna Douglas, *Frankie and Johnny* (1966). "Datin" and "Queenie Wahine's Papaya," Donna Butterworth, *Paradise-Hawaiian Style* (1966). "Yoga Is as Yoga Does," Elsa Lanchester, *Easy Come, Easy Go* (1967). "Who Needs Money?", Will Hutchins,* *Clambake* (1967). "There Ain't Nothing Like a Song," Nancy Sinatra, *Speedway* (1968). "Signs of the Zodiac," Marlyn Mason, *The Trouble with Girls* (*And How To Get Into It*) (1969).

Duke. Name of Gladys Presley's French poodle. Duke was named for actor John Wayne.†

Dunavant, Bobby. Probate court clerk who handled Elvis Presley's will.

---

*An unknown singer dubbed Hutchins's voice.
†John Wayne, whose real name was Marion Michael Morrison, in turn received his nickname "Duke" after his pet Airdale. Firemen called him "Big Duke" and the dog "Little Duke." Wayne's horse in six films beginning in 1932 was also named "Duke," named after John Wayne himself. Prior to John Wayne, Tom Mix rode the horse.

Dunne, Philip. Director of the 1961 movie *Wild in the Country*.

Dutch Elvis Presley Fan Club. An Elvis fan club located in Voorschoten, The Netherlands.

Dvorin, Al. Producer of Elvis's 1961 Hawaiian benefit concert for the U.S.S. *Arizona*. He was the show's master of ceremonies. Al Dvorin was the leader of a twenty-piece orchestra that provided the music for some of Elvis's concerts. He was the announcer on the 1974 album "Elvis as Recorded Live on Stage in Memphis."

Dwyer, Ronald. Elvis's attorney who successfully defended him in the lawsuit brought by Kenneth MacKenzie, Marlo Martinez, Roberta MacKenzie, and Marcelo Elias. They claimed that Elvis and his friends attacked them at the Las Vegas Hilton on February 19, 1973. Superior Court Judge Robert Weil, in Los Angeles, dismissed the $4 million lawsuit.

Dylan, Bob. Popular poet and folk artist known for his songs of social consciousness and protest. Bob Dylan (born Robert Allen Zimmerman)* was once a member of Bobby Vee's touring band, the Strangers. Bobby Vee fired Dylan because he believed music was not the field in which Dylan should be. Bob Dylan's very first record was "Mixed Up Confusion" (Columbia 4-42656), released in December 1962. Immediately after its release, Columbia took the record off the market because it didn't fit the image of their new "folk" artist!

Elvis recorded two Bob Dylan tunes: "Don't Think Twice, It's All Right" (in 1971) and "Tomorrow Is a Long Time" (in 1966).

E

8. *Blue Hawaii,* filmed in 1961, was Elvis's eighth movie (1961 = 1 + 9 + 6 + 1 = 17 = 1 + 7 = 8 [eighth movie]).

8-Track Tapes. Beginning in 1965, Elvis's entire stereo catalog was put on 8-track tape cartridges.

8 Weeks. Longest time that any Elvis single remained #1 on the Pop charts: "All Shook Up" in the U.S. (April 20–June 15, 1957) and "It's Now or Never" in the United Kingdom (October 30–December 25, 1960). (See: Mystery Train)

8-3667. Memphis business telephone number in the 1950s of Bob Neal (at 160 Union Ave.). His home phone number was 4-4029.

*Bob Dylan is today his legal name.

11. Uniform number worn by Walter Hale (Elvis) in a football game in the 1969 movie *The Trouble with Girls* (*And How to Get Into It*).

11 Miles. Distance to Nashville on a road sign in the 1979 TV movie *Elvis*.

11. Number of Tulsa McLean's (Elvis) tank in the 1960 movie, *G.I. Blues*.

11A 3142491. Serial number of the U. S. Army jeep driven by Lt. Josh Morgan (Elvis) in the 1964 movie *Kissin' Cousins*. The jeep figured in a blooper in the movie: it was the same jeep that was used to bring General Donford (Donald Woods) to Big Smokey Mountain.

11½ Carat. Size of ring that Elvis bought for Ginger Alden just prior to his death. Elvis paid $35,000 for the ring.

$80.00 to $145.00. Range of Elvis's pay from the time he was inducted into the U. S. Army until his discharge (March 24, 1958–March 5, 1960).

$85. Beginning weekly pay scale for Danny Fisher (Elvis) at the King Creole club in the 1958 movie *King Creole*.

86. Local board number of Elvis Presley's Memphis draft board, where, on Monday morning, March 24, 1958, Elvis was sworn into the U. S. Army.

1870. Time setting of the 1969 movie *Charro!*

E. Affectionate nickname for Elvis.

Eagle's Hall. Site of the Grand Prize Jamboree in 1955, featuring Elvis Presley ("Louisiana Hayride" star) and Hoot Gibson* (famous Western-movie star), among other artists.

Eagle's Nest. Memphis ballroom, located on Highway 78 at Lamar Avenue and Clearpool, where Elvis supposedly made one of his first professional appearances, early in 1954. He earned ten dollars a night singing there. (See: That's Amore—That's Love)

E. A. Presley. Elvis signed all his checks using his first two initials and last name.

Early Mornin' Rain (Early Morning Rain). Song written and originally recorded by Gordon Lightfoot in 1965 and first popularized both by the Kingston Trio (Capitol) and by Peter, Paul, and Mary (Warner Brothers 5659). In 1966 Chad and Jeremy had another version of "Early Morning Rain" (Columbia 43490). Elvis recorded "Early Morning Rain" in 1971. He sang it in the 1977 CBS-TV special "Elvis in Concert." "Early Morning Rain" appeared in the following Long Playing albums: "Elvis—Now" (RCA LSP-4671); "Elvis in Concert" (RCA APL2-2587); "Mahalo from Elvis" (Pickwick ACL-7064), "Elvis—A Canadian Tribute" (RCA KKL1-7065).

Earth Boy. Song that Elvis sang in the 1962 movie *Girls! Girls!*

---

*Born Edward Richard Gibson, he was called the "Champion Cowboy of the World." He won the title All-Around Champion Cowboy at the Pendleton Roundup in 1912.

Girls!. The film version of "Earth Boy" is different from that on record. In the film, Chinese girls sing the first portion in Chinese and Elvis follows with a narration of the lyrics while they continue to sing. Elvis then begins singing in Chinese and ends the song in English. "Earth Boy" was written by Sid Tepper and Roy C. Bennett and appeared in the Long Playing album "Girls! Girls! Girls!" (RCA LPM/LSP-2621).

East Go-Go. Discotheque in the 1966 movie *Easy Come, Easy Go*.

East Heights Garden Club. Organization that restored Elvis's birthplace in Tupelo, Mississippi. The house is now a monument and was opened to the public on June 1, 1971.

Easter Sunday. Day on which Elvis flew to Nashville for a recording session (April 11, 1956). The plane experienced some trouble and came to within a few feet of the ground before the trouble was corrected. That same day, Elvis recorded "I Want You, I Need You, I Love You."

Eastlund, Jacqueline, and James, Gloria. Two psychics who predicted Elvis's death. Mrs. Eastlund made her prediction on the "Nine in the Morning" show on KHJ-TV in Los Angeles (July 19, 1977). Mrs. Gloria James made her prediction on a radio talk show on WMEX in Boston (May 30, 1977).

East Tupelo, Mississippi. Town of Elvis's birth. East Tupelo had a population of a little less than 6,000 in 1935. It merged with Tupelo in 1948.

EASY COME, EASY GO. Paramount, 1967. Premiered San Francisco March 22, 1967 (95 min.). Elvis's twenty-third movie. Producer, Hal B. Wallis. Associate Producer, Paul Nathan. Director, John Rich. Cast: Ted Jackson/Elvis Presley, Jo Symington/Dodie Marshall, Dina Bishop/Pat Priest, Judd Whitman/Pat Harrington, Gil Carey/Skip Ward, Mme. Neherina/Elsa Lanchester, Captain Jack/Frank McHugh, Lt. Schwartz/Sandy Kenyon, Cooper/Ed Griffith, Lt. Tompkins/Read Morgan, Lt. Whitehead/Mickey Elley, Vicki/Elaine Beckett, Mary/Shari Nims, Zoltan/Diki Lerner, Tanya/Kay York, Artist/Robert Isenberg, The Jordanaires/The Jordanaires. Screenplay, Allan Weiss and Anthony Lawrence. Photography, William Margulies. Music, Joseph J. Lilley. Choreography, David Winters. Art Direction, Hal Pereira and Walter Tyler. Set Decoration, Robert Benton and Arthur Krams. Underwater Photography, Michael J. Dugan. Special Effects, Paul K. Lerpae. Costumes, Edith Head. Technical Adviser, Col. Tom Parker. Assistant Director, Robert Goldstein. Editor, Archie Marshek. Songs sung by Elvis: "The Love Machine," "Yoga Is As Yoga Does" (duet with Elsa Lanchester), "Sing, You Children," "You Gotta Stop," "I'll Take Love," "Easy Come, Easy Go." Instrumentals: "Freak Out," "Go-Go Jo." "She's A Machine" was deleted from the film.

Easy Come, Easy Go was also the title of a 1947 movie directed by John Farrow starring Barry Fitzgerald and Diana

Lynn. Frank Faylen, who played opposite Elvis in his screen-test for *The Rainmaker,* appeared in this film.

Easy Come, Easy Go. Title song in the 1967 movie *Easy Come, Easy Go.* The film version has added instrumentation. "Easy Come, Easy Go" was written by Sid Wayne and Ben Weisman and appeared in the Extended Play album "Easy Come, Easy Go" (RCA EPA-4387) and the following Long Playing albums: "C'mon Everybody" (RCA Camden CAL-2518); "C'mon Everybody" (Pickwick CAS-2518); "Double Dynamite" (Pickwick DL2-5001).

Easy Come, Easy Go. RCA EPA-4387. This was a 45 rpm Extended Play album released in May 1967—Elvis's last EP. Songs included—Side 1: "Easy Come, Easy Go," "The Love Machine," "Yoga Is as Yoga Does." Side 2: "You Gotta Stop," "Sing You Children," "I'll Take Love."

(Such An) Easy Question. RCA 47-8585. Released in May 1965 as a 45 rpm single. It reached #11 on *Billboard*'s Hot 100 chart. "It Feels So Right" was on the flip side. Elvis sang "(Such An) Easy Question" in the 1965 movie *Tickle Me.* It was written by Otis Blackwell and Winfield Scott and appeared in the Long Playing album "Pot Luck" (RCA LPM/LSP-2523).

(Such An) Easy Question. RCA 447-0653. Gold Standard Series re-issue of RCA 47-8585.

Ebony Eyes/Honey. Sun 1142. A 45 rpm single released in June 1979 by Orion. It reached #89 on *Billboard*'s Country chart and remained on the chart for six weeks. Orion is a pseudonym used by Jimmy Ellis. The songs sound very much like Elvis. (See: Ellis, Jimmy)

Echoes of Love. Song written by Bob Roberts and Paddy McMains and recorded by Elvis in 1963. "Echoes of Love" appeared in the Long Playing album "Kissin' Cousins" (RCA LPM/LSP-2894).

Eden, Barbara. Female lead (as Rosyln Pierce) in the 1960 movie *Flaming Star.* Barbara Eden was married to actor Michael Ansara. She starred in the TV series "I Dream of Jeannie" (1965/1970).

Edge of Reality. RCA 47-9670. Released in October 1968 as a 45 rpm single. "If I Can Dream" was on the flip side. RCA eliminated its trademark, Nipper, from its label and the color of the label was changed to orange. Elvis sang "Edge of Reality" in the 1968 movie *Live a Little, Love a Little.* Written by Bill Giant, Bernie Baum, and Florence Kaye, "Edge of Reality" appeared in the Long Playing albums "Almost in Love" (RCA Camden CAS-2440) and "Almost in Love" (Pickwick CAS-2440).

Edge of Reality. RCA 447-0668. Gold Standard Series re-issue of RCA 47-9670.

Edmund. One of Elvis's pet dogs.

Ed Sullivan Show, The. Television variety series on which Elvis made three appearances. (September 9, 1956; October 28, 1956; January 6, 1957). He received $50,000 for the three shows.

The first telecast received an 82.6% share of the viewing audience (54 million people). Elvis's performance on that show was broadcast from the CBS studios in Hollywood. Guest host Charles Laughton, in New York City, introduced Elvis. (See: Laughton, Charles; Sullivan, Ed) Contrary to popular opinion, Elvis was televised from the waist up only on his third appearance on "The Ed Sullivan Show" (January 9, 1957). Songs performed on the "Ed Sullivan Show" were: September 9, 1956, "Don't Be Cruel," "Love Me Tender," "Hound Dog." October 28, 1956, "Don't Be Cruel," "Love Me Tender," "Love Me," "Hound Dog." January 6, 1957, "Hound Dog," "Love Me Tender," "Heartbreak Hotel," "Don't Be Cruel," "Too Much," "When My Blue Moon Turns to Gold Again," "Peace in the Valley."

Edwards, Michael. Former boyfriend of Priscilla Presley (1979).

Egan, Richard. Actor who starred in the 1956 movie *Love Me Tender*. Richard Egan starred in the 1962–63 TV series "Empire." After one season the series was canceled and a spin-off called "Redigo" (also starring Richard Egan) took its place. The ratings were so bad that NBC canceled "Redigo" after three months. A few months later, ABC picked up the property and aired new episodes of the original series, "Empire." This was the only time in TV history that a show was canceled, replaced with a spin-off that was also canceled, and then replaced with the original show.

At the February 23, 1972, concert at the Hilton in Las Vegas, it was Richard Egan who stood and began an ovation while Elvis was singing his closing number, "Can't Help Falling in Love."

El. Nickname for Elvis.

El Dorado. Model of Cadillac that Priscilla gave to Elvis as a wedding present (1967).

Electrician. Occupation for which Elvis was studying in 1954.

Eli Cranfield. Name of the fictional character, based on Elvis Presley, in the movie *The Living Legend*. Earl Owensby played Eli Cranfield.

Elliot, Maurice. Vice-president of and spokesman for the Baptist Memorial Hospital in Memphis. He conducted the August 17, 1977, news conference following Elvis's death.

Elliott, Davada "Dee". Maiden name of Elvis's step-mother. (See: Stanley, Davada "Dee")

Ellis Auditorium. Memphis site of Elvis's live concert of February 25, 1961. It was to be Elvis's last live performance until 1968.

El Paso. Song written and recorded by Marty Robbins (Columbia

41511) in 1959. "El Paso" reached #1 on the charts and sold over a million copies. It was the first #1 song to exceed four minutes of playing time. "El Paso" was one of a number of songs of which Elvis sang only a line or two in his live performances in the 1970s.

El Rancho Club. Jackson, Mississippi, nightclub where Elvis first saw Carl Perkins perform in 1954. Elvis and Bob Neal had gone there to see him.

El Toro. Song that Elvis sang in the 1963 movie *Fun In Acapulco.* "El Toro" was written by Bill Giant, Bernie Baum, and Florence Kaye and appeared in the Long Playing album "Fun in Acapulco" (RCA LPM/LSP-2756).

Elvin Pelvin. Character, played by Tom Gilson, who appeared on "The Phil Silvers Show" in 1958 in a satire on Elvis. Elvin Pelvin, whose big hit was "You're Nothin' But a Raccoon," performed at the Silver Slipper Club in Roseville, Kansas. (Mr. Spicer was the club owner.) (See: Phil Silvers Show, The)

ELVIS. Dick Clark Motion Pictures, Inc., 1979. Executive Producer, Dick Clark. Producer/Writer, Anthony Lawrence. Director, John Carpenter. Cast: Elvis Presley/Kurt Russell, Gladys Presley/Shelley Winters, Vernon Presley/Bing Russell, Red West/Robert Gray, Priscilla Presley/Season Hubley, Colonel Tom Parker/Pat Hingle, Bonnie/Melody Anderson, D. J. Fontana/Ed Begley, Jr., Scotty Moore/James Canning, Sam Phillips/Charles Cyphers, Jim Denny/Peter Hobbs, Sonny West/Les Lannom, Bill Black/Elliott Street, Ed Sullivan/Will Jordan, Joe Esposito/Joe Mantegna, Hank Snow/Galen Thompson, Marion Keisker/Ellen Travolta, Natalie Wood/Abi Young, Charlie Hodge/Charlie Hodge, Lisa Marie Presley/Felicia Fenske, Elvis, as a boy/Randy Gray. Director of Photography, Donald M. Morgan. Supervising Producer, Tony Bishop. Casting, Joyce Selznick. Associate Producer, James Ritz. Music Composed and Conducted by Joe Renzetti. Art Directors, Tracy Bousman and James Newp, Supervising Editor, Ron Moler. Set Decorator, Bill Harp. Make-up, Marvin Westmore. Hair Stylist, Ruby Ford. Costume Supervisor, Tony Faso. Production Coordinator, Janet Lee Smith. Assistant to the Producer, Cheri Palmer Kluba. Technical Adviser, Charlie Hodge. Elvis Vocals Sung by, Ronnie McDowell. Elvis Vocals Produced by Felton Jarvis and James Ritz. Executive in Charge of Production, Francis C. LaMaina.

Ronnie McDowell recorded 36 songs for the movie; those sung in the film are as follows: "Mystery Train"—introduction, "Good Rockin' Tonight"—under a tree at high school, "Old Shep"—variety show, "My Happiness"—record cut at the Memphis Recording Service, "That's All Right (Mama)"—Sun recording studio, at home and on car radio, "Blue Moon of Kentucky"—Sun recording studio, "Lawdy, Miss Clawdy"—in concert, "Blue Moon"—Grand Ole Opry audition, "Tutti Frutti"—in concert, "Long Tall Sally"—in concert, "Heartbreak Hotel"—recording session, "Rip It Up"—"Ed Sullivan Show," "Heartbreak Hotel"—scene at Graceland, "Unchained Melody"—to Priscilla in Germany, "Tutti Frutti"—in German beer garden, "Are You Lonesome Tonight"—Elvis's return to Graceland, "Oh Lord, My God"—at piano in Graceland, "Unchained Melody"—at piano in Graceland, "A Fool Such as I"—in concert, "Crying in the Chapel"—in concert, "Pledging My Love"—at a party, "A Fool Such as I"—on record playing at party, "Bosom of Abraham"—at home with his friends, "Suspicious Minds"—at a rehearsal in California, "Until It's Time for You to Go"—as Elvis is at home thinking, "Separate Ways"—as Elvis and Priscilla split, "Sweet Caroline"—sung to Lisa Marie, "Blue Suede Shoes"—in concert at International Hotel, "Dixieland/Battle Hymn of the Republic"—movie in introspect.

Elvis. Name supposedly derived from the Norse word *Alviss*, which means "wise."

Elvis. Subject title of a painting by eccentric pop-culture artist Andy Warhol.

Elvis. Identification name of the middle marker on the ILS (Instrument Landing System) to runway 36R at Memphis airport.

Elvis. A 1977 Elvis tribute record by Tommy Durden on Westbound Records (Westbound 55405).

Elvis. The Hole-in-the-Wall gang's pet dog (1973–74 animated TV series "Butch Cassidy and the Sundance Kids").

Elvis. A 1977 Elvis tribute record by Eddie Karr on Memory Records (Memory 38656).

Elvis. Elvis tribute album by Bobby Hachey, released by London Records (London 5113). The album consists of twelve Elvis songs.

Elvis. Biography of Elvis Presley written by Albert Goldman.

Elvis. RCA LPM-1382. A 33⅓ rpm Long Playing album that was released in October 1956. It reached #1 on *Billboard*'s Hot LP chart. "Elvis" eventually sold over a million copies and received a Gold Disc award from the R.I.A.A. The cover photo on the album was taken by David B. Hecht. Songs included—Side 1: "Rip It Up," "Love Me," "When My Blue Moon Turns to Gold Again," "Long Tall Sally," "First in Line," "Paralyzed." Side 2: "So Glad You're Mine," "Old Shep," "Ready Teddy," "Anyplace Is Paradise," "How's the World Treating You," "How Do You Think I Feel."

Elvis. RCA LSP-1382 (e). This record was the electronically reprocessed stereo re-issue of LPM-1382.

Elvis. RCA APL1-0283. A 33⅓ rpm Long Playing album released in June 1973. It reached #52 on *Billboard*'s Hot LP chart. Songs included—Side 1: "Fool," "Where Do I Go From Here,"

"Love Me, Love the Life I Lead," "It's Still Here," "It's Impossible." Side 2: "(That's What You Get) For Lovin' Me," "Padre," "I'll Take You Home Again Kathleen," "I Will Be True," "Don't Think Twice, It's All Right."

Elvis. RCA DPL2-0056 (e). A 33⅓ rpm Long Playing album released in August 1973. This two-record set was sold exclusively on television. It was not available in stores. When "Elvis" was first released Brookville Records appeared on the cover. In September the label was changed to read: "RCA Special Products." The album was marketed by Brookville Marketing Corporation of New York. "Elvis" sold well over 3 million copies, qualifying for a Platinum Record. Songs included—Side 1: "Hound Dog," "I Want You, I Need You, I Love You," "All Shook Up," "Don't," "I Beg of You." Side 2: "A Big Hunk o' Love," "Love Me," "Stuck on You," "Good Luck Charm," "Return to Sender." Side 3: "Don't Be Cruel," "Loving You," "Jailhouse Rock," "Can't Help Falling in Love," "I Got Stung." Side 4: "(Let Me Be Your) Teddy Bear," "Love Me Tender," "Hard Headed Woman," "It's Now or Never," "Surrender."

Elvis/Daddy's Gone Bye Bye. A 1977 Elvis tribute record by Jenny Nichols on Blue Candle Records (Blue Candle 1525).

Elvis—A Biography. Book written by Jerry Hopkins and first published by Simon and Schuster in 1971. This unauthorized biography of Elvis rates as one of the best books compiled about the man.

Elvis—A Canadian Tribute. RCA KKL1-7065. A 33⅓ rpm Long Playing album released in October 1978. It was originally issued in Canada but was later distributed in the United States. "Elvis—A Canadian Tribute" reached #7 on *Billboard's* Country LP chart and #86 on the Hot LP chart. All songs on the album were written by Canadian composers. Sales of "Elvis—A Canadian Tribute" exceeded 500,000 copies, qualifying it for a Gold Record. Songs included—Side 1: "Jailhouse Rock," "Teddy Bear," "Loving You," "Until It's Time for You to Go," Vancouver Press Conference, "Early Morning Rain." Side 2: "I'm Moving On," "Snowbird," "For Loving Me," "Put Your Hand in the Hand," "Little Darlin'."

Elvis, A Legendary Angel. A 1977 Elvis tribute song by Melody Lloyd on Starr Records (Starr 9277).

Elvis—A Legendary Performer, Volume 1. RCA CPL1-0341. A 33⅓ rpm Long Playing album released in January 1974. It reached #43 on *Billboard's* Hot LP chart. "Elvis—A Legendary Performer, Volume 1" achieved sales of over $1 million, qualifying it for a Gold Record. Songs included: Side 1: "That's All Right," "I Love You Because" (take #2), "Heartbreak Hotel," Excerpt from "Elvis Sails" EP, "Don't Be Cruel," "Love Me," "Tryin' to Get to You" (live-NBC). Side 2: "Love Me Tender," "(There'll Be) Peace in the Valley (For

Me)," Excerpt from "Elvis Sails" EP, "(Now and Then There's) A Fool Such as I," "Tonight's All Right for Love," "Are You Lonesome Tonight" (live-NBC), "Can't Help Falling in Love."

Elvis—A Legendary Performer, Volume 2. RCA CPL1-1349. A 33⅓ rpm Long Paying album released in January 1976. It reached #50 on *Billboard*'s Hot LP chart. "Elvis—A Legendary Performer, Volume 2" achieved sales of over $1 million, qualifying it for a Gold Record. Songs included—Side 1: "Harbor Lights," Interview, 1956, "I Want You, I Need You, I Love You" (take 2), "Blue Suede Shoes" (live-NBC), "Blue Christmas," "Jailhouse Rock," "It's Now or Never." Side 2: "Cane and a High Starched Collar," Presentation of Awards to Elvis, "Blue Hawaii" (live), "Such a Night" (with out-takes), "Baby What You Want Me to Do," "How Great Thou Art," "If I Can Dream."

Elvis—A Legendary Performer, Volume 3. RCA CPL1-3078. A 33⅓ rpm Long Playing album released in November 1978. This album is a limited edition picture disc. Selections are the same as RCA CPL1-3082.

Elvis—A Legendary Performer, Volume 3. RCA CPL-3082. A 33⅓ rpm Long Playing album released in November 1978. It reached #115 on *Billboard*'s Hot LP chart and #16 on the Country chart. Songs included—Side A: "Hound Dog," Excerpts from an interview with Elvis and the Colonel for *TV Guide*, "Danny," "Fame and Fortune," "Frankfurt Special," "Britches," "Crying in the Chapel." Side B: "Surrender," "Guadalajara," "It Hurts Me," "Let Yourself Go," "In the Ghetto," "Let It Be Me (*Je t'Appartiens*)."

Elvis: Aloha from Hawaii. Elvis's TV special telecast to the world via the Intelsat IV Communications satellite at 12:30 P.M. (Honolulu time), January 14, 1974. The one-hour concert from the Honolulu International Center Arena was seen by an estimated 1 billion viewers in forty countries—more than had seen the first moon landing. The concert was a benefit for the Kuiokalani Lee Cancer Fund.

After the audience had left the building, Elvis recorded five more songs for inclusion in the U.S. edition of the TV special which was broadcast by NBC on April 4, 1973. The songs were: "Blue Hawaii"; "Ku-u-i-po"; "No More"; Hawaiian Wedding Song"; "Early Morning Rain." Of those songs, "Ku-u-i-po" and "No More" were not used on the American telecast.

Songs included in both telecasts are as follows: "Also Sprach Zarathustra," "Blue Suede Shoes," "See See Rider," "I'm So Lonesome I Could Cry," "Burning Love," "I Can't Stop Loving You," "Something," "Hound Dog," "You Gave Me a Mountain," "I'll Remember You," "Steamroller Blues," "Long Tall Sally," "What Now My Love," "Whole Lotta Shakin' Goin' On," "Fever," "American Trilogy," "Welcome to My World," "A Big Hunk o' Love," "Suspicious Minds," "Can't Help Fall-

ing in Love," "My Way," "Blue Hawaii" (NBC), "Love Me,"
"Hawaiian Wedding Song" (NBC), "Johnny B. Goode," "Early
Morning Rain" (NBC), "It's Over."

Elvis: Aloha from Hawaii Via Satellite. RCA VPSX-6089. A 33⅓
rpm Long Playing album released in February 1973. It reached
#1 on *Billboard*'s Hot LP chart (for one week, May 5–12).
This two-record album was RCA's first quadradisc album. It
achieved sales of over $1 million, making it the first quadradisc
in the industry to go Gold. "Elvis: Aloha from Hawaii Via
Satellite" was the soundtrack album of Elvis's Hawaii concert
on January 14, 1973. (See: Elvis: Aloha from Hawaii) Songs
included—Side 1: Introduction: "Also Sprach Zarathustra,"
"See See Rider," "Burning Love," "Something," "You Gave Me
a Mountain," "Steamroller Blues." Side 2: "My Way," "Love
Me," "Johnny B. Goode," "It's Over," "Blue Suede Shoes,"
"I'm So Lonesome I Could Cry," "I Can't Stop Loving You,"
"Hound Dog." Side 3: "What Now My Love," "Fever," "Wel-
come to My World," "Suspicious Minds," Introductions by
Elvis. Side 4: "I'll Remember You," Medley: "Long Tall
Sally"/"Whole Lotta Shakin' Goin' On," "An American Trilo-
gy," "A Big Hunk o' Love," "Can't Help Falling in Love."

Elvis: Aloha from Hawaii via Satellite. RCA 2006. A special 33⅓
rpm Extended Play album released in 1973 for jukeboxes.
Songs included—Side 1: "My Way," "What Now, My Love,"
"I'm So Lonesome I Could Cry." Side 2: "Something," "You
Gave Me a Mountain," "I Can't Stop Loving You."

Elvis and His Fans. Book written by Harold Loyd and Lisa De
Angel.

Elvis and Marilyn. Ballad recorded by Leon Russell in 1978.

Elvis and Me. An RCA Extended Play record (RCA EP-4188) by
The Kids. Reference was made to Elvis and several of his songs.

Elvis and the Unmentionables. An Elvis tribute song by Dave
Harris on Town Records.

Elvis Answers Back. A 1956 magazine that included the record
"The Truth About Me" as a part of its cover. (See: Lynchburg
Audio; Rainbow Records; Truth About Me, The)

Elvis as Recorded at Madison Square Garden. RCA LSP-4776. A
33⅓ rpm Long Playing album released in June 1972. It reached
#11 on *Billboard*'s Hot LP chart. "Elvis as Recorded at
Madison Square Garden" included songs that were taped at
Elvis's Madison Square Garden concert on June 10, 1972. It
achieved sales of over $1 million, qualifying it for a Gold
Record. Songs included—Side 1: Introduction: "Also Sprach
Zarathustra," "That's All Right," "Proud Mary," "Never Been
to Spain," "You Don't Have to Say You Love Me," "You've
Lost That Lovin' Feelin'," "Polk Salad Annie," "Love Me,"
"All Shook Up," "Heartbreak Hotel," Medley: "(Let Me Be
Your) Teddy Bear"/"Don't Be Cruel"/"Love Me Tender." Side
2: "The Impossible Dream," Introductions by Elvis, "Hound

Dog," "Suspicious Minds," "For the Good Times," "An American Trilogy," "Funny How Time Slips Away," "I Can't Stop Loving You," "Can't Help Falling in Love."

Elvis as Recorded at Madison Square Garden. RCA SP-33-57. A 33⅓ rpm Long Playing album that was specially banded for radio stations. It contained the same (but longer) selections as RCA LSP-4776.

Elvis—Back in Memphis. RCA LSP-4429. A 33⅓ rpm Long Playing album released in November 1970. "Elvis—Back in Memphis" reached #183 on *Billboard*'s Hot LP chart. This album consisted of sides 3 and 4 of the album "From Memphis to Vegas/From Vegas to Memphis" (RCA LSP-6020). The songs on this album were recorded at the American Sound Studios in Memphis (January 13–23, 1969, and February 17–22, 1969). (See: From Memphis to Vegas/From Vegas to Memphis)

Elvis Blues, The. A 1956 Elvis novelty record by Otto Bash in which reference was made to Elvis and "Baby Let's Play House." It was released by RCA (RCA 6585).

Elvis by Request. RCA LPC-128. This was a special 33⅓ rpm Extended Play album released in April 1961—the only Elvis 33⅓ EP released to the public. LPC stands for Long Playing Compact. It reached #14 on *Billboard*'s Hot 100 chart and sold over a million copies. Songs included—Side 1: "Flaming Star," "Summer Kisses, Winter Tears." Side 2: "Are You Lonesome Tonight," "It's Now or Never."

Elvis' Christmas Album. RCA LOC-1035. A 33⅓ rpm Long Playing album that was released in November 1957. It reached #1 on *Billboard*'s Hot LP chart and remained there for four weeks. A ten-page pamphlet of color photos of Elvis was included with the album. "Elvis' Christmas Album" eventually sold over a million copies and received a Gold Disc award from the R.I.A.A.

Two of the songs on the album, "Silent Night" and "Oh Little Town of Bethlehem," caused a national controversy when several radio stations refused to play them. They thought that Elvis's rock 'n' roll approach to the carols was in extremely bad taste. (See: Priddy, Al; Wittinghill, Dick; Brooks, Allen) Songs on the album included—Side 1: "Santa Claus Is Back in Town," "White Christmas," "Here Comes Santa Claus (Right Down Santa Claus Lane)," "I'll Be Home for Christmas," "Blue Christmas," "Santa Bring My Baby Back (To Me)," Side 2: "Oh Little Town of Bethlehem," "Silent Night," "(There'll Be) Peace in the Valley (For Me)," "I Believe," "Take My Hand, Precious Lord," "It Is No Secret (What God Can Do)."

Elvis Christmas Album. RCA LPM-1951. This record was the monaural re-issue (in November 1958) of LOC-1035. The front cover photo was changed and the back featured four photos of Elvis in the Army.

Elvis' Christmas Album. RCA LSP-1951 (e). This record was the electronically reprocessed stereo re-issue of LPM-1951.

Elvis' Christmas Album. RCA Camden CAL-2428. A 33⅓ rpm Long Playing album released in November 1970. Songs included—Side 1: "Blue Christmas," "Silent Night," "White Christmas," "Santa Claus Is Back in Town," "I'll Be Home for Christmas." Side 2: "If Every Day Was Like Christmas," "Here Comes Santa Claus (Right Down Santa Claus Lane)," "Oh Little Town of Bethlehem," "Santa Bring My Baby Back (To Me)," "Mama Liked the Roses."

Elvis' Christmas Album. Pickwick CAS-2428. A 33⅓ rpm Long Playing album released in December 1975. This album was a re-issue of RCA Camden CAL-2428.

Elvis, Christmas Won't Be Christmas. A 1977 Elvis tribute song by Paul White on Country Jubilee Records (Country Jubilee 0101).

Elvis Classic. Record label on which the 45 rpm version of "Tell Me Pretty Baby" was released in 1978 (EC 5478). See: Red Hots, The; Tell Me Pretty Baby)

Elvis Country. RCA LSP-4460. A 33⅓ rpm Long Playing album released in January 1971. It reached #12 on *Billboard*'s Hot LP chart. The album included a bonus photo of Elvis at the age of three. The song "I Was Born About Ten Thousand Years Ago" was sung briefly at the conclusion of each cut on the album. "Elvis Country" achieved sales of over $1 million, qualifying it for a Gold Record. Songs included—Side 1: "Snowbird," "Tomorrow Never Comes," "Little Cabin on the Hill," "Whole Lotta Shakin' Goin' On," "Funny How Time Slips Away," "I Really Don't Want to Know." Side 2: "There Goes My Everything," "It's Your Baby, You Rock It," "The Fool," "Faded Love," "I Washed My Hands in Muddy Water," "Make the World Go Away."

Elvis' Country Memories. RCA R244069. A two-record album available only to RCA Record Club members. Songs included —Side A: "I'll Hold You in My Heart (Till I Can Hold You in My Arms)," "Welcome to My World" (live), "It Keeps Right on A-Hurtin'," "Release Me (And Let Me Love Again)," "Make the World Go Away." Side B: "Snowbird," "Early Mornin' Rain," "I'm So Lonesome I Could Cry" (live), "Funny How Time Slips Away," "I'm Movin' On." Side C: "Help Me Make It Through the Night," "You Don't Know Me," "How Great Thou Art," "I Washed My Hands in Muddy Water," "I Forgot to Remember to Forget." Side D: "Your Cheatin' Heart," "Baby Let's Play House," "Whole Lotta Shakin' Goin' On," "Gentle on My Mind," "For the Good Times" (live).

Elvis Cover-up, The. Episode of the ABC-TV series "20/20" that was broadcast on September 13, 1979. The show was hosted by Hugh Downs. Geraldo Rivera investigated the death of Elvis and concluded that Elvis had died from an overdose of drugs. (See: Rivera, Geraldo)

Elvis Dollar Bills. One of the many Elvis gimmicks. Dollar bills with Elvis's picture on them were offered at $3.95 each.

Elvis Dreamed and It Came True. A 1977 Elvis tribute song by Don Todd released on Dale Records (Dale 437).

Elvis' Favorite Gospel Songs. A 1977 Elvis tribute album by J.D. Sumner and the Stamps released on QCA Records (QCA 362).

Elvis '57. An Elvis novelty record by Julie Lang on Deluxe Records (Deluxe 6111).

Elvis Forever. A 1977 Elvis tribute song by Jimmy Frey on Philips Records (Philips 6021).

Elvis for Everyone. RCA LPM/LSP-3450. A 33⅓ rpm Long Playing album released in July 1965. It reached #10 on *Billboard*'s Hot LP chart. Songs included—Side 1: "Your Cheatin' Heart," "Summer Kisses, Winter Tears," "Finders Keepers, Losers Weepers," "In My Way," "Tomorrow Night," "Memphis, Tennessee." Side 2: "For the Millionth and the Last Time," "Forget Me Never," "Sound Advice," "Santa Lucia," "I Met Her Today," "When It Rains It Really Pours."

Elvis' 40 Greatest Hits. A 33⅓ rpm Long Playing album released in England. Issued on the Arcade label, "Elvis' 40 Greatest Hits" sold over a million copies in England alone.

Elvis for Xmas. An Elvis novelty record narrated by Mad Milo on which cuts from "Love Me" and "Don't Be Cruel" were included. The record was released by Million Records (Million 20018) in 1957.

Elvis' Golden Records. RCA LPM-1707. A 33⅓ rpm Long Playing album that was released in March 1958. It reached #3 on *Billboard*'s Hot LP chart. "Elvis' Golden Records" received a Gold Disc award from the R.I.A.A. and reportedly sold over a million copies. Songs included—Side 1: "Hound Dog," "Loving You," "All Shook Up," "Heartbreak Hotel," "Jailhouse Rock," "Love Me," "Too Much." Side 2: "Don't Be Cruel," "That's When Your Heartaches Begin," "(Let Me Be Your) Teddy Bear," "Love Me Tender," "Treat Me Nice," "Anyway You Want Me (That's How I Will Be), "I Want You, I Need You, I Love You."

Elvis' Golden Records. RCA LSP-1707 (e). This record was the electronically reprocessed stereo re-issue of LPM-1707.

Elvis' Golden Records, Volume 3. RCA LPM/LSP-2765. A 33⅓ rpm Long Playing album released in September 1963. It reached #4 on *Billboard*'s Hot LP chart. "Elvis' Golden Records, Volume 3" achieved sales of over $1 million, qualifying it for a Gold Record. Songs included—Side 1: "It's Now or Never," "Stuck on You," "Fame and Fortune," "I Gotta Know," "Surrender," "I Feel So Bad." Side 2: "Are You Lonesome Tonight," "(Marie's the Name) His Latest Flame,"

"Little Sister," "Good Luck Charm," "Anything That's Part of You," "She's Not You."

Elvis' Gold Records, Volume 4. RCA LPM/LSP-3921. A 33⅓ rpm Long Playing album released in February 1968. It reached #33 on *Billboard*'s Hot LP chart. "Elvis' Gold Records, Volume 4" was the last of Elvis's monaural albums, except for those albums featuring early material or live cuts. Songs included—Side 1: "Love Letters," "Witchcraft," "It Hurts Me," "What'd I Say," "Please Don't Drag That String Around," "Indescribably Blue." Side 2: "(You're The) Devil in Disguise," "Lonely Man," "A Mess of Blues," "Ask Me," "Ain't That Loving You Baby," "Just Tell Her Jim Said Hello."

Elvis, Goodbye. A 1977 Elvis tribute song by Bobby Freeman on Kimray Records (Kimray 81677).

Elvis Has Left the Building. A 1977 Elvis tribute song by J. D. Sumner on QCA Records (QCA 461).

Elvis: His First and Only Press Conference. One of the cuts that appeared in the Buddah Record album "Current Audio Magazine" (BM-Volume 1). The cut was Elvis's June 1972 Madison Square Garden press conference. Interviews with other people were included on the album. (See: Current Audio Magazine)

Elvis, How Could I Resist. A tribute song to Elvis recorded by the Birds of a Feather on the Amour label in 1977 (Amour 8426).

Elvis in Concert. Title of Elvis's TV special on CBS-TV that aired on October 3, 1977. It consisted of excerpts of his live concerts at Omaha, Nebraska (June 19, 1977), and Rapid City, South Dakota (June 21, 1977).

Elvis in Concert. RCA APL2-2587. A 33⅓ rpm Long Playing album released in November 1977. The album featured songs recorded on tour during June 1977. Sides 1 and 2, plus "Early Morning Rain," were from the CBS-TV special "Elvis in Concert." Sales of "Elvis in Concert" exceeded 500,000 copies, qualifying it for a Gold Record. Songs included—Side A: Elvis's Fans' Comments, 2001 Space Odyssey/Opening Riff, "See See Rider," "That's All Right," "Are You Lonesome Tonight," Medley: "(Let Me Be Your) Teddy Bear"/"Don't Be Cruel," Elvis' Fans' Comments, "You Gave Me a Mountain," "Jailhouse Rock." Side B: Elvis' Fans' Comments, "How Great Thou Art," Elvis' Fans' Comments, "I Really Don't Want to Know," Elvis Introduces His Father, "Hurt," "Hound Dog," "My Way," "Can't Help Falling in Love," Closing Riff, Special Message from Elvis' Father, Vernon Presley. Side C: Medley: "I Got a Woman"/"Amen," Elvis Talks, "Love Me," "If You Love Me (Let Me Know)," Medley: "O Sole Mio" (Sherrill Nielsen solo/"It's Now or Never" (Elvis), "Trying to Get to You." Side D: "Hawaiian Wedding Song," "Fairytale," "Little

Sister," "Early Morning Rain," "What'd I Say," "Johnny B. Goode," "And I Love You So."

Elvis in Concert. Book by John Reggero published in 1979.

Elvis in His Own Words. Title of a 1977 book by Mick Farren and Pearce Marchbank, published by Omnibus Press of New York.

In this book, Elvis recounted many of his own experiences—a number of them inaccurately. Elvis claimed that Pat Boone was chosen over himself to appear at the Grand Ole Opry. In reality, it was on "Arthur Godfrey's Talent Scouts."

Another inaccuracy occurred when Elvis mentioned that the composer of "Bear Cat" had sued the composer of "Hound Dog." Actually, it was the reverse.

Elvis also referred to Col. Tom Parker as Col. Sanders Parkers. (See: Bear Cat)

Elvis in Hollywood. RCA DPL2-0168. A 33⅓ rpm Long Playing album released in January 1976. This two-record set was sold exclusively on television. It was not available in stores. "Elvis in Hollywood" was marketed by Brookville Marketing Corporation of New York. Songs included—Side 1: "Jailhouse Rock," "Rock-a-Hula Baby," "G.I. Blues," "Kissin' Cousins," "Wild in the Country." Side 2: "King Creole," "Blue Hawaii," "Fun in Acapulco," "Follow That Dream," "Girls! Girls! Girls!" Side 3: "Viva Las Vegas," "Bossa Nova Baby," "Flaming Star," "Girl Happy," "Frankie and Johnny." Side 4: "Roustabout," "Spinout," "Double Trouble," "Charro," "They Remind Me Too Much of You."

Elvis in Person at the International Hotel, Las Vegas, Nevada. RCA LSP-4428. A 33⅓ rpm Long Playing album released in November 1970. This album, normally called "Elvis in Person," consisted of sides 1 and 2 of the album "From Memphis to Vegas/From Vegas to Memphis" (RCA LSP-6020). The songs were performed live in Las Vegas from August 22 to 26, 1969. (See: From Memphis to Vegas/From Vegas to Memphis)

Elvis Is a Legend. A tribute song to Elvis recorded in 1977 by B. F. Snow on Dee Bee Records (Dee Bee 20).

Elvis Is Back. RCA LPM/LSP-2231. A 33⅓ rpm Long Playing album that was released in April 1960. It reached #2 on *Billboard*'s Hot LP chart. "Elvis Is Back," according to RCA, had retail sales totaling over $1 million—thus qualifying for a Gold Record. This album was the first by Elvis to be released in true stereo. Phil Spector helped to produce demonstration records of some of the songs included in this album. Songs included—Side 1: "Make Me Know It," "Fever," "The Girl of My Best Friend," "I Will Be Home Again," "Dirty, Dirty Feeling," "Thrill of Your Love." Side 2: "Soldier Boy," "Such a Night," "It Feels So Right," "The Girl Next Door," "Like a Baby," "Reconsider, Baby."

Elvis Is Gone. A 1977 Elvis tribute song by Bob "Li'l Elvis" Harrison on Li'l Elvis World Records (Li'l Elvis World, Inc. 114).

Elvis Is Gone (But Not Forgotten). A 1978 Elvis tribute song by Con Archer on the QCA Record label (QCA 463).

Elvis Is Rocking. A 1960 Elvis novelty record by Roy Hall and the Hunt Sisters. It was released by Fortune Records (Fortune 210).

Elvis Is the King. A 1977 tribute song by Memphis Mill on W.B. Sound Records (W.B. Sound 1621).

Elvis Is the King. A 1977 Elvis tribute song by Louie Fontaine on Emerald Records.

Elvis Leaves Sorrento. An instrumental record in 1961 by the Twisters on Campus Records (Campus 125).

Elvis—Legendary Concert Performances. RCA R244047. A two-record album available only to RCA Record Club members. Songs included—Side A: "Blue Suede Shoes," "Sweet Caroline," "Burning Love," "Runaway," "My Babe." Side B: "Johnny B. Goode," "Yesterday," Medley: "Mystery Train" "Tiger Man," "You Gave Me a Mountain," "Never Been to Spain." Side C: "See See Rider," "Words," "Proud Mary," "Walk a Mile in My Shoes," "Steamroller Blues." Side D: "Polk Salad Annie," "Something," "Let It Be Me (*Je t'Appartiens*)," "The Impossible Dream," "My Way."

Elvis Lives. Broadway show that starred an Elvis look-alike impersonator, Larry Seth.

Elvis: Lonely Star at the Top. A 1977 paperback book written by Hollywood biographer David Hanna. It was published by Leisure Books of New York City.

Elvis' Midget Fan Club. Publicity stunt created by Col. Tom Parker for one of Elvis's concerts in 1957. Parker hired a group of midgets to parade through Memphis.

Elvis Monthly, The. Popular British Elvis Presley fan magazine first published in 1959 by Albert Hand. It is distributed by the official Elvis Presley Fan Club, Worldwide, which was founded in 1956.

Elvis—Now. RCA LSP-4671. A 33⅓ rpm Long Playing album released in February 1972. It reached #43 on *Billboard*'s Hot LP chart. Songs included— Side 1: "Help Me Make It Through the Night," "Miracle of the Rosary," "Hey Jude," "Put Your Hand in the Hand," "Until It's Time for You to Go." Side 2: "We Can Make the Morning," "Early Mornin' Rain," "Sylvia," "Fools Rush In," "I Was Born About Ten Thousand Years Ago."

ELVIS ON TOUR. MGM, 1972. Premiered June 6, 1973 (93 minutes). Elvis's thirty-third movie. Produced, Directed, and Written by Pierre Adidge and Robert Abel. Associate Producer, Sidney Levin. Cast: Elvis Presley, Vernon Presley, Jackie Kahane, James Burton, Charlie Hodge, Ronnie Tutt, Glen Hardin, Jerry Scheff, John Wilkinson, Kathy Westmoreland, J.D. Sumner, The Stamps Quartet, The Sweet Inspirations. Photography, Robert E. Thomas. Music Conductor, Joe Guercio. Montage Supervisor, Martin Scorsese. Elvis's Wardrobe, Bill Schaffer. Editor, Ken Zemke. Songs included: "Johnny B. Goode," "See See Rider," "Polk Salad Annie," "Separate Ways," "Proud Mary," "Never Been to Spain," "Burning Love," "For the Good Times" (backstage), "Don't Be Cruel" (film clip from the "Ed Sullivan Show"), "Ready Teddy" (film clip from the "Ed Sullivan Show"), "That's All Right (Mama)" (Sun Records), "Sweet Sweet Spirit" (backstage by the Stamps), "The Lighthouse" (backstage by the Stamps), "Lead Me, Guide Me" (backstage by Elvis and the Stamps), "Bosom of Abraham" (backstage by Elvis and the Stamps), "Love Me Tender," "Until It's Time for You to Go," "Suspicious Minds," "I, John" (backstage by Elvis and the Stamps), "Bridge Over Troubled Water," "Funny How Time Slips Away," "An American Trilogy," "Mystery Train" (Sun Records), "Suspicious Minds," "I Got a Woman," "A Big Hunk o' Love," "You Gave Me a Mountain," "Sweet Sweet Spirit" (the Stamps), "Lawdy, Miss Clawdy," "Can't Help Falling in Love," "Memories" (over the movie credits). The movie covered a fifteen-day concert tour from Buffalo to Albuquerque. *Elvis on Tour* won a Golden Globe Award for Best Documentary of 1972.

Elvis Perez/Lola. An Elvis novelty record by Lalo Guerrero released by L & M Records (L & M 1000) in 1956. Reference was made to "Hound Dog," "Don't Be Cruel," and "Love Me Tender."

Elvis—Portrait of a Friend. A 1979 book written by Marty Lacker (a Presley aide and friend), Patsy Lacker, and Leslie S. Smith. *Elvis—A Portrait of a Friend* was published by Wimmer Brothers Books.

Elvis Presley. RCA EPA-747. This was a 45 rpm Extended Play album released in March 1956. It reached #24 on *Billboard*'s Hot 100 chart and included the following songs—Side 1: "Blue Suede Shoes," "Tutti Frutti." Side 2: "I Got a Woman," "Just Because."

Elvis Presley. RCA EPA-830. This was a 45 rpm Extended Play album released in September 1956. It reached #55 on *Billboard*'s Hot 100 chart and #6 on the Extended Play chart. Songs included—Side 1: "Shake, Rattle And Roll," "I Love You Because." Side 2: "Blue Moon," "Lawdy, Miss Clawdy."

Elvis Presley. RCA EPB-1254. This was a 45 rpm Extended Play album that contained two records. It was released in March 1956. Songs included—Record 1, Side 1: "Blue Suede Shoes," "I'm Counting on You." Side 4: "I'm Gonna Sit Right Down and Cry (Over You), "I'll Never Let You Go (Little Darlin')." Record 2, Side 2: "I Got a Woman," "One-Sided Love Affair." Side 3: "Tutti Frutti," "Tryin' to Get to You."

Elvis Presley. RCA LPM-1254. A 33⅓ rpm Long Playing album that was released in April 1956. It reached #1 (for ten weeks) on *Billboard*'s Hot LP chart. "Elvis Presley" eventually sold over a million copies and was Elvis's first album release. It received a Gold Disc award from the R.I.A.A. Songs included—Side 1: "Blue Suede Shoes," "I'm Counting on You," "I Got a Woman," "One-Sided Love Affair," "I Love You Because," "Just Because." Side 2: "Tutti Frutti," "Tryin' to Get to You," "I'm Gonna Sit Right Down and Cry (Over You)," "I'll Never Let You Go (Little Darlin')," "Blue Moon," "Money Honey."

Elvis Presley. RCA LSP-1254 (e). This record was the electronically reprocessed stereo re-issue of LPM-1254.

Elvis Presley. RCA SPD-22. This was a two-record, 45 rpm Extended Play album available in late 1956. It had the same songs as EPB-1254 but in a different order. It was never released to the general public; however, you could get it free if you bought a four-speed portable Victrola (model 7EP2) phonograph at the nationally advertised price of $32.95. The Victrolas featured "Presley's autograph stamped in gold on the top cover of extra-strong, scuff-resistant, simulated blue denim cases." The songs on the album included—Record 1, Side 1: "Blue Suede Shoes," "I'm Counting on You." Side 2: "Tutti Frutti," "Tryin' To Get To You." Record 2, Side 3: "I Got a Woman," "One-Sided Love Affair." Side 4: "I'm Gonna Sit Right Down and Cry (Over You)," "I'll Never Let You Go (Little Darlin')."

Elvis Presley. RCA SPD-23. This was a three-record, 45 rpm Extended Play album available in late 1956. It was never released to the public; however, you could get it free if you bought an automatic 45 rpm portable Victrola (model 7EP45) phonograph at the nationally advertised price of $44.95. Songs in the three-record set included—Record 1, Side 1: "Blue Suede Shoes," "I'm Counting on You." Side 2: "I'm Gonna Sit Right Down and Cry (Over You)," "I Got a Woman." Record 2, Side 3: "One-Sided Love Affair," "I'll Never Let You Go (Little Darlin')." Side 4: "Tutti Frutti," "Tryin' to Get to You." Record 3, Side 5: "I Want You, I Need You, I Love You," "Don't Be Cruel." Side 6: "Hound Dog," "My Baby Left Me."

Elvis Presley. A 45 rpm Extended Play bootleg album released by Rockin' Records (Rockin' 45-001). Songs included—Side 1: "I Don't Care If the Sun Don't Shine," "I'll Never Let You Go (Little Darlin')." Side 2: "My Baby Is Gone," "Blue Moon of Kentucky."

Elvis Presley Blues. An Elvis novelty record by Anita Ray and the Nature Boys on Dream Records (Dream 1300). Released in 1956.

Elvis Presley Blues. A 1956 Elvis novelty record by Ivan Gregory and the Blue Notes on G & G Records (G & G 110).

Elvis Presley Boulevard. Name given to a ten-mile section of U. S. Highway 51 South in Memphis. Elvis Presley Boulevard extends through Memphis past Graceland. The north section of U.S. Highway 51 South is known as Bellevue.

Elvis Presley Chapel. Chapel and meditation center built on the grounds of Elvis Presley Park. The chapel was dedicated on August 17, 1979. In attendance were Col. Tom Parker and Kathy Westmoreland.

Elvis Presley Company. Navy company that was never formed but was promised to Elvis by Chief Petty Officer D. U. Stanley if Elvis would enlist in the Navy. Elvis Presley Company was to consist of Memphis boys.

Elvis Presley Convention. Annual worldwide convention first held at the Las Vegas Hilton, September 1–10, 1978.

Elvis Presley Day. Official day of recognition proclaimed in many cities and states: *September 26, 1956*—Elvis appeared at the Mississippi-Alabama Fair and Dairy Show in Tupelo. He returned to the city the $10,000 check he received for the performance. *September 29, 1967*—by proclamation of Tennessee Governor Buford Ellington. *November 11, 1970*—by proclamation of the mayor of Portland, Oregon. *January 8, 1974*—by proclamation of Georgia Governor Jimmy Carter.

Elvis Presley Drive. Present name of the Tupelo, Mississippi street on which Elvis's birthplace is located.

Elvis Presley Enterprises. Company formed in conjunction with Special Products, Inc., to market over 180 Elvis-related items in 1956. The headquarters was at 160 Union Avenue (telephone number: JAckson 6-3667). Some of the items marketed included: Statues, Waste baskets, Bookends, Dolls, Mittens, Lipstick, Scarves, Sneakers, Record cases, Shirts, Jeans, Bracelets, Photo wallets, Polo shirts, Pajamas, Belts, Belt buckles, Handkerchiefs, Billfolds, Handbags, Medallions, Necklaces, Charm bracelets, Perfume, Wristwatches, Hats.

Elvis Presley Enterprises. The company was formed by Elvis Presley and Bob Neal when Neal managed Presley. It was dissolved when Col. Parker became Elvis's manager.

Elvis Presley Enterprises. Memphis football team that Elvis sponsored in the fall of 1963. Elvis also sponsored a baseball team.

Elvis Presley for President. A novelty record by Lou Monte on RCA Records (RCA 6704). The record was released in 1956. "Elvis Presley for President" was written by Norman Henry, Ruth Roberts, and Bill Katz.

Elvis Presley Game, The. Board game marketed in 1957. ("A Party Game for the Tender of Heart. See what the Elvis Presley game predicts for you . . . Love, Romance, Marriage.") The five levels for both players are: Getting To Know Him, Learning To Like Him, Can't Do Without Him, Let's Go Steady, Get the Preacher.

Elvis Presley Medley/Chuck Berry Medley. An Elvis novelty record by Big Wheelie and the Hubcaps. It was released by Scepter Records (Scepter 12375) in 1973.

Elvis Presley Music, Inc. One of several music companies owned by Elvis. Half of the royalties went to Elvis. Elvis Presley Music, Inc., was a subsidiary of Hill and Range and was affiliated with BMI.

Elvis Presley Park. Thirteen-and-a-half-acre park created by the Tupelo (Mississippi) Park and Recreation Department. Tupelo passed a bond issue to buy the land. Elvis Presley Park encompasses Elvis's birthplace. The park contains a swimming pool, a community building, and a chapel.

Elvis Presley Songbook. An Elvis tribute album by the Castaway Strings on Vee Jay Records (Vee Jay 1113). The album contained eleven Elvis songs.

Elvis Presley Speaks. Book written by psychic researcher Hans Holzer, who claims that contact was made with Elvis beyond the grave.

Elvis Presley Story, The. Twelve-hour radio documentary produced by Watermark, Inc., in 1971. "The Elvis Presley Story" was written by Jerry Hopkins; Ron Jacobs was the producer.

Elvis Presley Story, The. Collection of seventy Elvis Presley hit songs on records and tapes released by Candlelite Music. The set which was first sold in 1977, also came with an album of twelve songs titled "Elvis: His Songs of Inspiration."

Elvis Presley Story, The. Paperback book, edited by James Gregory, that was published by Hillman Books in 1960. Dick Clark wrote the introduction.

Elvis Presley Sun Collection, The. RCA Starcall Hy-1001. A 33⅓ rpm Long Playing album released in England in August 1975. RCA released this album in the U. S. as "Elvis—The Sun Sessions (RCA APM1-1675). (See: Elvis—The Sun Sessions)

Elvis Presley Years, The. Movie which was scheduled to be produced by Hal Wallis in 1980.

Elvis Presley Youth Fountain. Memphis-based charity created by Elvis, to which he donated $100,000 yearly. The 1958 address was P.O. Box 331, Tupelo, Mississippi.

Elvis Presley's Golden Hits. A tribute album by Big Ross and the Memphis Sound on Pickwick Records (Pickwick 3292). The album consisted of ten Elvis songs.

Elvis Presley's Sergeant. A 1959 Elvis novelty record released on Key Records (Key 573) by the Bobolinks.

Elvis: Recorded Live on Stage in Memphis. RCA CPL1-0606. A 33⅓ rpm Long Playing album released in June 1974. It reached #33 on *Billboard*'s Hot LP chart. This album contained songs from Elvis's performance at the Mid-South Coliseum in Memphis on March 20, 1974. "Elvis: Recorded Live on Stage in Memphis" was also released in quadradisc.

Elvis: Recorded Live on Stage in Memphis. RCA SP-0606. A 33⅓ rpm Long Playing album that was specially banded for radio stations. It contained the same selections as RCA CPL1-0606.

Elvis Sails. RCA EPA-4325. This was a 45 rpm Extended Play album released in March 1959. It consisted of press interviews with Elvis prior to his departure to West Germany (September 22, 1958). Side 1: Press Interview with Elvis Presley. Side 2: Elvis Presley's Newsreel Interview, Pat Hernon Interviews Elvis.

Elvis Sails. RCA EPA-5157. This record was a Gold Standard Series re-issue of RCA EPA-4325 (April 1961).

Elvis Sings Christmas Songs. RCA EPA-4108. This was a 45 rpm Extended Play album released in November 1957. It reached #2 on *Billboard*'s Extended Play chart. Songs included—Side 1: "Santa Bring My Baby Back (To Me)," "Blue Christmas." Side 2: "Santa Claus Is Back in Town," "I'll Be Home for Christmas."

Elvis Sings Flaming Star. RCA Camden CAS-2304. A 33⅓ rpm Long Playing album released in April 1969. It was a re-issue of "Singer Presents Elvis Singing Flaming Star and Others" (RCA PRS-279). "Elvis Sings Flaming Star" reached #96 on *Billboard*'s Hot LP chart. (See: Singer Presents Elvis Singing Flaming Star and Others)

Elvis Sings Flaming Star. Pickwick CAS-2304. A 33⅓ rpm Long Playing album released in December 1975. It was a re-issue of RCA Camden CAS-2304.

Elvis Sings for Children (And Grownups Too). RCA CPL1-2901. A 33⅓ rpm Long Playing album released in August 1978. The album consisted of previously released material, with the exception of an alternate take of "Big Boots." Songs included—Side A: "(Let Me Be Your) Teddy Bear," "Wooden Heart," "Five Sleepyheads," "Puppet on a String," "Angel," "Old MacDonald." Side B: "How Would You Like to Be," "Cotton Candy Land," "Old Shep," "Big Boots," "Have a Happy."

Elvis Sings Hits from His Movies, Volume 1. RCA Camden CAS-2567. A 33⅓ rpm Long Playing album released in June 1972. It reached #87 on *Billboard*'s Hot LP chart. Songs included: Side 1: "Down by the Riverside and When the Saints Go Marching In," "They Remind Me Too Much of You," "Confidence," "Frankie and Johnny," "Guitar Man." Side 2: "Long Legged Girl (With the Short Dress On)," "You Don't Know Me," "How Would You Like to Be," "Big Boss Man," "Old MacDonald."

Elvis Sings Hits from His Movies, Volume 1. Pickwick CAS-2567. A 33⅓ rpm Long Playing album released in December 1975. It was a re-issue of RCA Camden CAS-2567.

Elvis Sings the Wonderful World of Christmas. RCA LSP-4579. A 33⅓ rpm Long Playing album released in October 1971. Songs included—Side 1: "O Come, All Ye Faithful," "The First

Noel," "On a Snowy Christmas Night," "Winter Wonderland," "The Wonderful World of Christmas," "It Won't Seem Like Christmas (Without You)." Side 2: "I'll Be Home on Christmas Day," "If I Get Home on Christmas Day," "Holly Leaves and Christmas Trees," "Merry Christmas Baby," "Silver Bells."

Elvis Sings the Wonderful World of Christmas. RCA ANL1-1936. A 33⅓ rpm album released in November 1976. This album is a re-issue of RCA LSP-4579 on RCA's Pure Gold label. "Elvis Sings the Wonderful World of Christmas" sold over a million copies, qualifying for a Platinum Record.

Elvis—Standing Room Only. Original title proposed for the 1973 documentary *Elvis on Tour*.

Elvis Stole My Gal. An Elvis novelty song by Huey Long on Fidelity Records (Fidelity 4055).

Elvis Tapes, The. A 33⅓ rpm Long Playing album (Polydor 2912 021) released in 1977. The album consisted of Elvis's press conference in Vancouver, British Columbia, Canada, on August 31, 1957. Canadian disc jockey Red Robinson recorded the press conference, which took place at the Empire Stadium prior to Elvis's concert. (See: Robinson, Red)

ELVIS—THAT'S THE WAY IT IS. MGM, 1970. Premiered San Francisco November 11, 1970 (107 min). Elvis's thirty-second movie. Producer, Herbert F. Soklow. Director, Denis Sanders. Cast: Elvis Presley, James Burton, Charlie Hodge, Ronnie Tutt, Glen Hardin, Jerry Scheff, John Wilkinson, Millie Kirkham, The Imperials, The Sweet Inspirations. Unbilled Guest Appearances: Cary Grant, Sammy Davis, Jr., Juliet Prowse, Dale Robertson, Xavier Cugat, Charo, Norm Crosby. Photography, Lucien Ballard. Music Conductor, Joe Guerico. Elvis's Wardrobe, Bill Belew. Technical Adviser, Col. Tom Parker. Assistant Director, John Wilson. Editor, Henry Berman. Songs included: *In Rehearsal:* "Words," "The Next Step Is Love," "Polk Salad Annie," "Cryin' Time," "That's All Right," "Little Sister," "What'd I Say," "Stranger in the Crowd," "How the Web Was Woven," "Just can't Help Believin'," "You Don't Have to Say You Love Me," "Bridge Over Troubled Water," "Words," "Loving Feeling," "Mary in the Morning." *On Stage:* "Mystery Train"/"Tiger Man," "That's All Right," "I've Lost You," "Patch It Up," "Love Me Tender," "Loving Feeling," "Sweet Caroline," "I Just Can't Help Believin'," "Bridge Over Troubled Water," "Heartbreak Hotel," "One Night," "Blue Suede Shoes," "All Shook Up," "Polk Salad Annie," "Suspicious Minds," "Can't Help Fallin' in Love."

Elvis—That's the Way It Is. RCA LSP-4445. A 33⅓ rpm Long Playing album released in December 1970. It reached #20 on *Billboard*'s Hot LP chart. "Elvis—That's the Way It Is" was the soundtrack of the 1970 documentary of the same name. The songs on the album were recorded at the MGM studios (in Los Angeles), the International Hotel (in Las Vegas), and the Veterans Coliseum (in Phoenix, Arizona). "Elvis—That's the Way It Is" achieved sales of over $1 million, qualifying it for a Gold Record. Songs included—Side 1: "I Just Can't Help Believin'," "Twenty Days and Twenty Nights," "How the Web Was Woven," "Patch It Up," "Mary in the Morning," "You Don't Have to Say You Love Me." Side 2: "You've Lost That Lovin' Feelin'," "I've Lost You," "Just Pretend," "Stranger in the Crowd," "The Next Step Is Love," "Bridge Over Troubled Water."

Elvis the Army Years, 1958–1960. 1978 book by Nick Corvino. A fictionalized recreation of Elvis's experiences during his Army years.

Elvis: The King Lives On. World's best-selling poster in 1978. The year before, the poster didn't even make the top twenty.

Elvis—The Legend Lives. A 1978 book written by Martin A. Grove and published by Manor Books.

Elvis, The Man from Tupelo. A 1977 Elvis tribute song by George Pickard on Bar-Tone Records (Bar-Tone 77169).

Elvis: The Other Sides—Worldwide Gold Award Hits, Volume 2. RCA LPM-6402. A 33⅓ rpm Long Playing album released in August 1971. It reached #120 on *Billboard*'s Hot LP chart. Included inside the four-record album was a color portrait of Elvis and a small piece of his clothing. Songs included—Side 1: "Puppet on a String," "Witchcraft" "Trouble," "Poor Boy," "I Want to Be Free," "Doncha' Think It's Time," "Young Dreams." Side 2: "The Next Step Is Love," "You Don't Have to Say You Love Me," "Paralyzed," "My Wish Came True," "When My Blue Moon Turns to Gold Again," "Lonesome Cowboy." Side 3: "My Baby Left Me," "It Hurts Me," "I Need Your Love Tonight," "Tell Me Why," "Please Don't Drag That String Around," "Young and Beautiful." Side 4: "Hot Dog," "New Orleans," "We're Gonna Move," "Crawfish," "King Creole," "I Believe in the Man in the Sky," "Dixieland Rock." Side 5: "The Wonder of You," "They Remind Me Too Much of You," "Mean Woman Blues," "Lonely Man," "Any Day Now," "Don't Ask Me Why," Side 6: "(Marie's the Name) His Latest Flame," "I Really Don't Want to Know," "(You're So Square) Baby, I Don't Care," "I've Lost You," "Let Me," "Love Me." Side 7: "Got a Lot o' Livin' to Do," "Fame and Fortune," "Rip It Up," "There Goes My Everything," "Lover Doll," "One Night." Side 8: "Just Tell Her Jim Said Hello," "Ask Me," "Patch It Up," "As Long as I Have You," "You'll Think of Me," "Wild in the Country."

Elvis the Pelvis. Nickname conferred upon Elvis by the news media after Elvis was seen dancing while singing.

Elvis—The Sun Sessions. RCA APM1-1675. A 33⅓ rpm Long

Playing album released in March 1976. It reached #48 on *Billboard*'s Hot LP chart. "Elvis—The Sun Sessions" was formerly released in England as "The Elvis Presley Sun Collection" (RCA Starcall Hy-1001). Songs contained in this album were recorded by Elvis between July 1954 and November '55. Songs included—Side 1: "That's All Right," "Blue Moon of Kentucky," "I Don't Care If the Sun Don't Shine," "Good Rockin' Tonight," "Milkcow Blues Boogie," "You're a Heart-breaker," "I'm Left, You're Right, She's Gone," "Baby Let's Play House." Side 2: "Mystery Train," "I Forgot to Remember to Forget," "I'll Never Let You Go (Little Darlin')," "I Love You Because" (take 1), "Tryin' to Get to You," "Blue Moon," "Just Because," "I Love You Because" (take 2).

Elvis'—TV Special. RCA LPM-4088. A 33⅓ rpm Long Playing album released in December 1968. It reached #8 on *Billboard*'s Hot LP chart. "Elvis'—TV Special" featured the soundtrack from the NBC-TV special "Elvis," broadcast on December 3, 1968. The album achieved sales of over $1 million, qualifying it for a Gold Record. Some of the cuts on the album are in stereo. Songs included—Side 1: "Trouble," "Guitar Man," "Lawdy, Miss Clawdy," "Baby What You Want Me to Do," Dialogue, Medley: "Heartbreak Hotel"; "Hotel"; "Hound Dog," "All Shook Up," "Can't Help Falling in Love," "Jailhouse Rock," Dialogue, "Love Me Tender." Side 2: Dialogue, "Where Could I Go But to the Lord," "Up Above My Head," "Saved," Dialogue, "Blue Christmas," Dialogue, "One Night," "Memories," Medley: "Nothingville"; Dialogue; "Big Boss Man"; "Guitar Man"; "Little Egypt"; "Trouble"; "Guitar Man," "If I Can Dream."

Elvis Unique Record Club. Nation's largest supplier of rare Elvis records and memorabilia. The record club is owned and operated by Paul Lichter of Huntingdon Valley, Pennsylvania.

Elvis, Volume 1. RCA EPA-992. This was a 45 rpm Extended Play album released in November 1956. It reached #6 on *Billboard*'s Hot 100 chart and #4 on the Extended Play chart. Songs included—Side 1: "Rip It Up," "Love Me." Side 2: "When My Blue Moon Turns to Gold Again," "Paralyzed."

Elvis, Volume 2. RCA EPA-993. This was a 45 rpm Extended Play album released in December 1956. It reached #47 on *Billboard*'s Hot 100 chart. Songs included—Side 1: "So Glad You're Mine," "Old Shep." Side 2: "Ready Teddy," "Anyplace Is Paradise."

Elvis, We Loved You Tender. Book written by Davada "Dee" Presley, Elvis's step-mother, who divorced Vernon Presley in 1977. She wrote the book with her sons Rick, David, and Billy (and a ghostwriter).

Elvis, We Love You. A 1977 Elvis tribute song by Terry Tiger on Gusto-Starday Records (Gusto-Starday 166).

Elvis, We Miss You Tonight. A 1977 Elvis tribute song by Ron McKee on the American Sound label (American Sound 3090).

Elvis, We're Sorry We Fenced You In. A 1977 Elvis tribute song by Jack Brand on Shane Records (Shane 7101).

Elvis—What Happened? Paperback book written by Red West, Sonny West, and Dave Hebler, which made its first appearance in book stores only four days prior to Elvis's death in 1977.

After Elvis's death, the K-Mart department store chain ordered 2 million copies of *Elvis—What Happened?*—the largest book order in history.

Elvis: Worldwide 50 Gold Award Hits, Volume 1. RCA LPM-6401. A 33⅓ rpm Long Playing album released in August 1970. It reached #45 on *Billboard*'s Hot LP chart. "Elvis: Worldwide 50 Gold Award Hits, Volume 1" was a four-record set that achieved sales of over $1 million, qualifying it for a Gold Record. Songs included—Side 1: "Heartbreak Hotel," "I Was the One," "I Want You, I Need You, I Love You," "Don't Be Cruel," "Hound Dog," "Love Me Tender." Side 2: "Anyway You Want Me (That's How I Will Be)," "Too Much," "Playing for Keeps," "All Shook Up," "That's When Your Heartaches Begin," "Loving You." Side 3: "(Let Me Be Your) Teddy Bear," "Jailhouse Rock," "Treat Me Nice," "I Beg of You," "Don't," "Wear My Ring Around Your Neck," "Hard Headed Woman." Side 4: "I Got Stung," "(Now and Then There's) A Fool Such as I," "A Big Hunk o' Love," "Stuck on You," "A Mess of Blues," "It's Now or Never." Side 5: "I Gotta Know," "Are You Lonesome Tonight," "Surrender," "I Feel So Bad," "Little Sister," "Can't Help Falling in Love." Side 6: "Rock-a-Hula Baby," "Anything That's Part of You," "Good Luck Charm," "She's Not You," "Return to Sender," "Where Do You Come From," "One Broken Heart for Sale." Side 7: "(You're The) Devil in Disguise," "Bossa Nova Baby," "Kissin' Cousins," "Viva Las Vegas," "Ain't That Loving You Baby," "Wooden Heart." Side 8: "Crying in the Chapel," "If I Can Dream," "In the Ghetto," "Suspicious Minds," "Don't Cry, Daddy," "Kentucky Rain," Excerpts from "Elvis Sails" EP.

Elvis: Worldwide Gold Award Hits, Parts 1 and 2. RCA 213690. A special two-record album available only to members of the RCA Record Club. It featured the first four sides of RCA LPM-6401.

Engine House No. 29. Memphis Fire Department engine house located at 2147 Elvis Presley Boulevard. Engine House No. 29 received Joe Esposito's call for help at 2:33 P.M., August 16, 1977.

English Elvis Presley, The. Popular nickname conferred upon British rock 'n' roller Tommy Steele (real name: Tommy Hicks) in 1957.

Enough Rope. Original title announced for the 1960 Twentieth Century-Fox movie *Flaming Star*.

Enterprise, U.S.S. Aircraft carrier that is incorrectly mentioned in several sources as the setting for "The Milton Berle Show" of April 3, 1956. The U.S.S. *Enterprise** is also called the "Big E." Actually, the name of the aircraft carrier used was the U.S.S. *Hancock*.

Entertainer of the Year. Award presented to Elvis in 1974 by Tennessee State Senator LeRoy Johnson.

E.P. Continentals. Early Elvis fan club. The E.P. Continentals was named by Elvis himself after his automobile.

E.P. Express. An Elvis novelty record by Carl Perkins that included references to several Elvis songs. It was released by Mercury Records (Mercury 73690) in 1974.

Erzer, Elie. Hairdresser with whom Priscilla Presley was romantically involved after she left Mike Stone.

Esposito, Joe. Elvis's number-one aide. Esposito and Elvis met while both were in the military. Joe Esposito, who was nicknamed "Diamond Joe," served as Elvis's road manager and bodyguard and also helped Marty Lacker with the bookkeeping. As a member of the Memphis Mafia, he drove the back-up car to the hospital the day Lisa Marie was born (in case the car taking Elvis and Priscilla broke down).

Joe Esposito and Marty Lacker served as best men at Elvis and Priscilla's wedding (May 1, 1967). He was Elvis's highest paid employee. Esposito appeared in three of Elvis's movies: *Kissin' Cousins, Clambake,* and *Stay Away, Joe.* Presently, he is the road manager for the Bee Gees.

Eternal Flame for Elvis. Memphis-based nonprofit organization founded in 1978 by Tony and Donna Russo and Mary Garrett. Nicknamed EFFE, their goal is to build a memorial to Elvis on a two-acre site where the Circle G Ranch is located. The organization is also dedicated to helping the many Elvis fans who come to Memphis from all parts of the world. They are among a small group of people *not* out to make a dollar from the tourists who visit Graceland. The funds used for the memorial are donated by Elvis fans.

Europa. Frankfurt, West Germany, nightclub in which Lili (Juliet Prowse) performed in the 1960 movie *G.I. Blues.*

Evans, Joseph. Memphis probate court judge who handled Elvis Presley's estate upon Elvis's death.

Evans, Marilyn, and Gleaves, Cliff. Reportedly, the audience to the Million-Dollar Session. The two were good friends of Elvis and were present in the Sun studios when the jam session took place.

Evans, Paul. Singer-composer who has recorded two hit records: "Seven Little Girls Sitting in the Back Seat" (Guaranteed 200) in 1959, and "Midnight Special" (Guaranteed 205) in 1960.

---

*The U.S.S. *Enterprise* is also the name of the star ship (identification number: NCC-1701) on the TV series "Star Trek". The new space shuttle is called the *Enterprise.*

Paul Evans composed "Roses Are Red (Epic 9509) for Bobby Vinton in 1962 and has written several TV commercial jingles, including Kent Cigarettes' "Happiness Is."

Paul Evans co-composed several songs that Elvis recorded, including "I Gotta Know," "Something Blue," and "The Next Step Is Love."

Even Elvis. Book by Mary Ann Thornton, published by New Leaf Press, Inc. in 1979.

Everett, Vince. Pseudonym used by Elvis sound-alike Marvin Benefield to record several records, including "Baby, Let's Play House"/"Livin' High" (ABC Paramount 10472) in 1963. The three musicians on the session were Bill Black, Scotty Moore, and D. J. Fontana.

Marvin Benefield chose the name Vince Everett from Elvis's role in the 1957 movie *Jailhouse Rock*. Presently, Benefield is the owner of a nostalgic-record store in London, England.

Everle, Marie. Red Cross nurse who, on January 16, 1959, took blood from Pvt. Elvis Presley. Elvis was in West Germany at the time of this donation.

Everly Brothers. Popular 1950s and '60s country and pop duo. The Everly brothers (Don* and Phil) made their debut on radio when they were eight and six respectively (KMA in Shenandoah, Iowa). Their first hit came in 1957 with "Bye Bye Love" (Cadence 1315). In 1960 the Everly brothers recorded "Let It Be Me" (Cadence 1376). Elvis recorded "Let It Be Me" in February 1970. (See: Cadillac Club)

Eversong, Leny. Female Brazilian singing star who appeared on "The Ed Sullivan Show" on January 6, 1957, as did Elvis.

Everybody Come Aboard. Song that Elvis sang in the 1966 movie *Frankie and Johnny*. "Everybody Come Aboard" was written by Bill Giant, Bernie Baum, and Florence Kaye and appeared in the Long Playing album "Frankie and Johnny" (RCA LPM/LSP-3553).

Everyone Was There/I Took a Dare. Novelty record by Bob Kayli that mentioned Elvis and "Hound Dog" in the lyrics. It was released by Carlton Records (Carlton 482) in 1958.

Ewell Walker. Character, modeled after Elvis and played by Tommy Sands, on the NBC-TV "Kraft Theater" presentation of "The Singing Idol" (January 30, 1957). Sands also played Ewell Walker in the 1958 movie *Sing, Boy, Sing*. (See: Singing Idol, The; Sing, Boy, Sing)

Executive Producer—Elvis Presley. Notation on the Elvis Presley album "Elvis: Recorded Live on Stage in Memphis" (RCA CPL-0606).

Expo '67. World's Fair held in Montreal, Canada, in 1967. At the

---

*Don Everly's wife, Venetia, dated Elvis in 1958. (See: Stevenson, Venetia)

American Spirit Pavilion, the guitar that Elvis used to record "Heartbreak Hotel" and "Hound Dog" was put on display.

EX7-4427. One of Elvis's unlisted telephone numbers* during his life at Graceland. EX stood for EXpress.

Eyes of Texas, The. (See: Yellow Rose of Texas, The)

F

5 lb. Elvis's weight at birth.†

14 Months. Time in prison served by Vince Everett (Elvis) in his one-to-ten-year term for manslaughter in the 1957 movie *Jailhouse Rock*.

$15. Cost of Elvis and Priscilla's marriage license.

42. Age at which Elvis passed away, on August 16, 1977.

46. Age at which Gladys Love Smith Presley died (April 25, 1912– August 14, 1958). Many sources wrongly state that Elvis and his mother both died at the age of 42.

49. Number of cars in Elvis's funeral procession on Thursday, August 18, 1977. It was led by eleven white Cadillacs.

50 feet. Height of cardboard picture of Elvis that was used to advertise his first movie, *Love Me Tender* (1956). It stood in front of the Paramount Theater in New York City.

$450. Price paid for the Presleys' 1942 Lincoln Coupe, which Elvis drove to high school.

462 Alabama Street. Memphis address of the two-story brick apartment building where the Presleys lived (April 1953–late '54) after leaving the apartment at 398 Cypress Ave. They paid fifty dollars per month for rent, plus electric and water. The Presleys' telephone number was 37-4185. Elvis lived at 462 Alabama when he recorded "My Happiness"/"That's When Your Heartaches Begin" at the Memphis Recording Service in the summer of 1953.

Ruth Black, mother of Bill Black, lived at 465 Alabama Street, apartment B.

565 Perugia Way. California address, in Bel-Air, of the oriental-style home that Elvis rented in 1960, after moving from the Beverly Wilshire Hotel. It was the first house that Elvis rented in Hollywood. (He then moved to 1059 Bellagio Road.) The Bel-Air home had previously been owned by Ali Khan and his wife, actress Rita Hayworth.

---

*Elvis gave this number to the FBI under the name of Col. John Burrows of 3764 Highway 51 South, Memphis, Tennessee.
†In comparison, Frank Sinatra weighed thirteen pounds at birth.

572 Poplar Avenue. First Memphis address of the Presleys, after moving from Tupelo, Mississippi. They lived at 572 Poplar from September 12, 1948, to September 20, 1949. The Presleys paid thirty-five dollars per month rent for a one-room apartment. The sixteen-unit apartment building had previously been a large house.

4152 Royal Crest Place. Memphis address of the ranch-style home that Elvis bought for Ginger Alden. The home is located one block behind Graceland.

483473. Serial number on the passport that appeared on the posters that advertised the 1963 movie *Fun in Acapulco*. The posters advertised: "Your Passport to Fun in Acapulco."

53310761. Elvis's Army serial number (1958–60). The number is probably the most well known service number of all time. Other famous serial numbers: Major Glenn Miller (0505273), and Clark Gable (19125047 [enlisted] and 0565390 [officer]).

50,000,000 Elvis Fans Can't Be Wrong—Elvis' Gold Records, Volume 2. RCA LPM-2075. A 33⅓ rpm Long Playing album that was released in December 1959. It reached #31 on *Billboard*'s Hot LP chart. The cover photo showed Elvis wearing his gold lamé suit (See: Lamé Tuxedo). This album received a Gold Disc award from the R.I.A.A. Songs included—Side 1: "I Need Your Love Tonight," "Don't," "Wear My Ring Around Your Neck," "My Wish Came True," "I Got Stung." Side 2: "One Night," "A Big Hunk o' Love," "I Beg of You," "(Now and Then There's) A Fool Such as I," "Doncha Think It's Time."

50,000,000 Elvis Fans Can't Be Wrong—Elvis' Gold Records, Volume 2. RCA LSP-2075 (e). This record was the electronically reprocessed stereo re-issue of RCA LPM-2075.

Fabares, Shelley. Actress and singer who portrayed Valerie in the 1965 movie *Girl Happy*, Cynthia Foxhugh in the 1966 movie *Spinout*, and Dianne Carter in the 1967 movie *Clambake*. On television, Shelley Fabares* starred in "The Donna Reed Show," "The Brian Keith Show," and "The Practice." In 1962 Shelley had a #1 record and million-seller with "Johnny Angel" (Colpix 621). Elvis once stated that Shelley Fabares was his favorite actress of those with whom he had worked.

Fabian. Singer-actor (real name: Fabiano Forte) who resembled Elvis. Fabian was a teen idol of the late 1950s and early '60s. Although many in the music business said he couldn't sing,† Fabian had a number of records on the charts, including his biggest hit—"Tiger" (#3 and a million-seller).

In 1959 Fabian made his movie debut in the movie *Hound-Dog Man* starring Carol Lynley and Arthur O'Connell. Dodie

---

*Shelley Fabares, who is the niece of comedienne Nanette Fabray, later became the wife of record producer Lou Adler.
†Many of his songs were made by splicing various notes that he sang several times over.

Stevens, whose only hit record was "Pink Shoe Laces," also appeared in the film. (See: "Yes I'm Lonesome Tonight")

On December 8, 1960, Elvis and Fabian got together for a friendly chat. While demonstrating karate, Elvis tore his pants. Fabian gave Elvis his pants and kept Elvis's as a souvenir.

Fabian was first considered for the role of Glenn Tyler in the 1961 movie *Wild in the Country*. Elvis eventually received the part.

Factors Etc., Inc. Bear, Delaware, firm that has the exclusive global rights to all Elvis Presley merchandising. It's the largest mass-merchandising company in the world.

Fadal, Eddie. Houston, Texas, friend of Elvis. At Fadal's home, in 1958, Elvis sang a number of songs that Fadal taped. The songs were released in August 1977 on a bootleg album, "Forever Young, Forever Beautiful" (Memphis Flash Records). (See: Forever Young, Forever Beautiful)

Faded Love. Song written by brothers Bob and John Wills and originally recorded by Bob Wills and His Texas Playboys in 1950. In 1963, shortly after her death, Patsy Cline's Decca recording of "Faded Love" (Decca 31522) reached the charts. Elvis recorded "Faded Love" in 1970 and it appeared in the Long Playing album "Elvis Country" (RCA LSP-4460).

Fain, Harry M. Attorney for Elvis who handled the paternity suit brought against Elvis on August 21, 1970, by Patricia Parker. (See: Parker, Patricia)

Fairgrounds Amusement Park. Memphis amusement park, located at the Mid-South Fairgrounds, that Elvis occasionally rented during the early morning hours. Fairgrounds Amusement Park is now called Libertyland. Elvis's favorite ride was the Dodgem cars (bumper cars). The rental of the park cost Elvis $2,500.

Fair Is Moving On, The. RCA 47-9747. Released in June 1969 as a 45 rpm single. "Clean Up Your Own Back Yard" was on the flip side. Written by Flett and Fletcher, "The Fair Is Moving On" appeared in the Long Playing albums "From Memphis to Vegas/From Vegas to Memphis" (RCA LSP-6020) and "Elvis—Back in Memphis" (RCA LSP-4429). On both of those albums the song was listed as "The Fair's Moving On."

Fair Is Moving On, The. RCA 447-0672. Gold Standard Series reissue of RCA 47-9747.

Fairy Tale. Song written by Anita and Bonnie Pointer and originally recorded by the Pointer Sisters in 1974 on the Blue Thumb label. They received a Grammy Award in the category Best Vocal Performance by a Duo or Group. Elvis recorded "Fairy Tale" in 1975 and it appeared in the Long Playing albums "Today" (RCA APL1-1039) and "Elvis in Concert" (RCA APL2-2587).

Fame and Fortune. RCA 47-7740. Released in March 1960 as a 45 rpm single. It reached #17 on *Billboard*'s Hot 100 chart.

"Stuck on You" was on the flip side. "Fame and Fortune" was recorded during Elvis's first recording session (March 20–21, 1960) after his discharge from the Army. It was Elvis's first stereo release. Advance orders exceeded 1 million. Elvis sang "Fame and Fortune" on May 12, 1960, on the ABC-TV program "The Frank Sinatra-Timex Special." Written by Fred Wise and Ben Weisman, "Fame and Fortune" appeared in the Long Playing albums "Elvis' Golden Records, Volume 2" (RCA LPM/LSP-2765), "Elvis: The Other Sides—Worldwide Gold Award Hits, Volume 2" (RCA LPM-6402), and "Elvis—A Legendary Performer, Volume 3" (RCA CPL1-3082).

Fame and Fortune. RCA 447-0637. Gold Standard Series re-issue of RCA 47-7740.

Fame and Fortune. RCA 61-7740. This was a 45 rpm "Living Stereo" single release. "Stuck on You" was on the flip side.

Family Way, The. A 1966 British movie* starring Hayley Mills and her father, John Mills. In the movie, which was scored by Paul McCartney, the Elvis album "His Hand in Mine" can be seen in Jenny Piper's dressing room.

Farewell to the King. Tribute record to Elvis recorded in 1977 by Jimmy Jenkins.

Farmingdale. Hometown of Susie Jessup (Dolores Hart) in the 1957 movie *Loving You.*

Farrell, Glenda. Female lead (as Ma Tatum) in the 1964 movie *Kissin' Cousins.*

Farther Along. Traditional gospel song recorded by Elvis in 1966. Elvis is credited with arranging this number. "Farther Along" appeared in the Long Playing album "How Great Thou Art" (RCA LPM/LSP-3758).

Fastest Guitar Alive, The. A 1967 movie starring Roy Orbison and Sammy Jackson. Elvis was asked to star in *The Fastest Guitar Alive* but Col. Parker nixed the idea.

Faylen, Frank. Veteran actor most widely known as Dobie Gillis's father in the TV series "The Many Loves of Dobie Gillis." Elvis made his screen test with Frank Faylen on April 1, 1956. He went through a few emotions, sang "Blue Suede Shoes," and did a scene from the 1956 movie *The Rainmaker.* Frank Faylen was borrowed by Paramount from the set of the movie *Gunfight at the O.K. Corral.*

Feathers, Charles Arthur. Born June 12, 1932, in Hollow Springs, Mississippi. Charlie Feathers became a Sun recording artist after Elvis left the label in 1955. He was the cowriter (with Stan Kesler) of "I Forgot to Remember to Forget," which Elvis recorded. Feathers, who claims that Elvis's rendition of "Good Rockin' Tonight" was borrowed from him, recorded demos and records for Sun Records, Meteor Records, and Sam Phillips's Holiday Inn Records.

*Originally to be titled *Wedlocked* or *All in Good Time.*

Federal Narcotics Officer Badge. Badge received by Elvis from President Richard M. Nixon. (See: Badges)

Feelings. Song written and recorded by Brazilian song writer Morris Albert in 1975. It reached #1 in Brazil, Chile, and Mexico before being released in the U. S. (RCA PB-10937). "Feelings" was the last song recorded by Elvis. After several takes the song remained incomplete.

Fender, Freddy. Popular Mexican-American country performer. Freddy Fender (real name: Baldemar G. Huerta) chose his name from a popular guitar and amplifier company—Fender. He has recorded many successful songs, including "Wasted Days and Wasted Nights"* and "Before the Last Teardrop Falls." Early in his career Freddy Fender was referred to as the "Be-bop Kid" and the "Mexican Elvis."

Fernwood Records. Record label, founded by Slim Wallace (who previously led a hillbilly band in Memphis called Slim Wallace's Dixie Ramblers), for which Scotty Moore was production chief. It was Moore who selected the song "Tragedy" for Thomas Wayne. The tape was brought over to Sun Records, where Scotty Moore added an echo on Sun's tape-recorder.

Fernwood Records was named for Fernwood Drive, where Jack Clement produced a number of records in Slim Wallace's garage. (See: Wayne, Thomas)

Fetchit, Stepin'. Black character actor whose real name was Lincoln Theodore Monroe Andrew Perry—after four U. S. presidents. He chose the name Stepin' Fetchit from the name of a racehorse that once won him some money. Reportedly, Stepin' Fetchit wrote some songs for Elvis but Col. Parker wouldn't let Elvis use them.

Fever. Song written by John Davenport (a pseudonym for Otis Blackwell†) and Eddie Cooley in 1956. "Fever" was a million-seller for both Little Willie John‡ in 1956, and Peggy Lee (real name: Norma Egstrom) in 1958. Ray Peterson had a version released in 1957 but it was not a big hit. Earl Grant's first success as a singer was with "Fever" in 1959. Elvis sang the song in the 1973 TV special "Elvis: Aloha from Hawaii." "Fever" appeared in the Long Playing albums "Elvis Is Back" (RCA LPM/LSP-2231), "Elvis: Aloha from Hawaii Via Satellite" (RCA VPSX-6089), and "Pure Gold" (RCA ANL1-0971).

Fiedler, Arthur. Conductor of the Boston Pops Orchestra from 1929 to his death in 1979. Arthur Fiedler studied at the Royal

---

*"Wasted Days and Wasted Nights" was first recorded by Freddy Fender in 1959 (released on Imperial). Fender and blues singer Hubbie "Leadbelly" Ledbetter both served time in the Angola State Penitentiary in Louisiana.
†Otis Blackwell took the name from that of his stepfather, John Davenport.
‡Little Willie John (born William J. Woods) died while in Washington State Prison, on May 26, 1968. He was serving a prison term for the murder of railroad employee Kendall Roundtree.

121

Academy of Music in Berlin, Germany. In 1915 he joined the Boston Symphony as a violinist. Fiedler had a million-seller in 1938 with "Jalousie."

Arthur Fiedler and Elvis, who both recorded for RCA Records, had planned, shortly before Elvis's death, to make an album together. (Had this been accomplished, it would have been nothing less than sensational.) Elvis was once invited by Arthur Fiedler to appear with the Boston Pops but was turned down when the orchestra could not afford to pay the fee requested by Colonel Parker.

Field, Eunice. Last reporter to interview Elvis. Eunice Field was also the first person to interview Elvis in Hollywood.

Fike, Lamar. Member of the Memphis Mafia. At 270 pounds, Lamar Fike was the heaviest member of Elvis's entourage. He operated Elvis's lighting system when Elvis appeared in Las Vegas. The German news media dubbed Lamar Fike the "Wrestler."

Finders Keepers, Losers Weepers. Song written by Dory Jones and Ollie Jones and recorded by Elvis in 1963. "Finders Keepers, Losers Weepers" appeared in the Long Playing album "Elvis for Everyone" (RCA LPM/LSP-3450).

Find Out What's Happening. Song that Elvis recorded at the Stax Studios in Memphis in July 1973. "Find Out What's Happening" was written by Jerry Crutchfield and appeared in the Long Playing album "Raised on Rock/For Ol' Times' Sake" (RCA APL1-0388).

Fine Man—That's Different. Words said by Sam Phillips that can be heard at the end of a slow alternate take (unissued) of "Blue Moon of Kentucky."

Finnell, Danny. Original name of the lead character in the 1958 movie *King Creole*. Prior to actually filming the movie, the name was changed to Danny Fisher.

Fire Records. New York record label for which Arthur "Big Boy" Crudup recorded while being financed by Elvis. Elvis had always been a Crudup fan and was aware of the fact that Crudup received very little of the royalties that were rightfully due him as both a composer and a recording artist.

The two records that Crudup recorded for the label were "Rock Me Mama"/"Mean Ole Frisco" (Fire 1501) and "Katie Mae"/"Dig Myself a Hole" (Fire 1502).

Fire Records was one of several labels (Fury, Holiday, Everest, Red Robin, Fling, Vest, and Enjoy) founded by Bobby and Danny Robinson. Buster Brown and Bobby Marchan (previous members of Huey "Piano" Smith's Clowns) recorded for the label. Don Gardner and Dee Dee Ford recorded "TCB (Taking Care of Business)" on the Fire label (Fire 517).

Firestone Tire and Rubber Company. Memphis firm, located at 900 Firestone Blvd., where Bill Black was employed at the same time that Elvis worked for the Crown Electric Company.

First Assembly of God Church. Church that Elvis attended as a child in East Tupelo, Mississippi. The church was located at 206 Adams Street, a block and a half from the Presleys' home. Pastors of the First Assembly of God Church* while the Presleys lived in Tupelo included Edward D. Parks, James F. Ballard, and Frank Smith. The church that Elvis attended still stands, but it was moved several years ago to 909 Beery Street. It now serves as the parsonage.

The Presleys also attended the First Assembly of God Church in Memphis (1085 McLemore).

First in Line. Song written by Aaron Schroeder and Ben Weisman and recorded by Elvis in 1956. "First in Line" was the first song Ben Weisman wrote for Elvis. It appeared in the Extended Play album "Strictly Elvis" (RCA EPA-994) and the Long Playing albums "Elvis" (RCA LPM-1382) and "Elvis" (RCA LSP-1382 [e]).

First Noel, The. Seventeenth-century Christmas carol whose composer is unknown. "The First Noel" was first published in a collection of Christmas carols called *Sandys' Carols* in 1833. "Noel" is a contraction of the phrase "Now All Is Well." Elvis recorded "The First Noel" in 1971 and it appeared in the Long Playing albums "Elvis Sings the Wonderful World of Christmas" (RCA LSP-4597) and "Elvis Sings the Wonderful World of Christmas" (RCA ANL-1936).

First Time Ever I Saw Your Face, The. RCA 74-0672. Released in April 1972 as a 45 rpm single. "An American Trilogy" was on the flip side. "The First Time Ever I Saw Your Face" was written by Ewan McColl† and recorded by Peter, Paul, and Mary in 1965 on their album "See What Tomorrow Brings,"‡ and by the Kingston Trio. Roberta Flack recorded the song in 1971, appearing in her debut album, "First Take." (Elvis recorded the song at virtually the same time, March 15, 1971.) When "The First Time Ever I Saw Your Face" appeared in the 1971 movie *Play Misty for Me*, record dealers were overwhelmed with requests for the song. Atlantic Records released the song in March 1972 and it quickly sold over a million copies. Roberta Flack's "The First Time Ever I Saw Your Face" (Atlantic 2864) won two Grammy Awards: Record of the Year and Song of the Year. Elvis's version did not appear in an album. (See: Play Misty for Me)

Fisher, Eddie. Popular ballad singer of the 1950s for RCA Records. Eddie Fisher was married to Debbie Reynolds (1955–59), Elizabeth Taylor (1959–64), and Connie Stevens (1968–69). Like Elvis, Fisher was drafted into the Army, but he served in the Special Forces.

---

*Country-rock singer Jerry Lee Lewis's parents were members of the First Assembly of God Church in Ferriday, Louisiana.
†Ewan McColl is the brother-in-law of folk-singer Pete Seeger.
‡Another song appeared on the album which Elvis would later record—"Early Mornin' Rain."

In 1951 Eddie Fisher recorded "I'll Hold You in My Heart," which Elvis recorded in 1969.

Fisher, Fred. Popular Tin Pan Alley composer and lyricist. Fisher, who was born in Cologne, Germany, composed such songs as "Peg o' My Heart" and "Chicago (That Toddling Town)." S.Z. Sakall portrayed Fisher in the 1949 movie *Oh, You Beautiful Doll*—the musical biography of Fisher's life.

Elvis recorded, in 1957, "That's When Your Heartaches Begin," which Fred Fisher, William Raskin, and George Brown composed.

Five Sleepy Heads. Song that Elvis recorded for the 1968 movie *Speedway,* but it was cut from the final print of the film. Supposedly, "Five Sleepy Heads" *is* included in the prints in Malaya. "Five Sleepy Heads" was written by Sid Tepper and Roy C. Bennett and appeared in the Long Playing albums "Speedway" (RCA LSP-3989) and "Elvis Sings for Children (And Grownups Too)" (RCA CPL1-2901).

Flaming Heart. Title originally considered for the 1960 movie *Flaming Star.* Another title considered was *Black Star.*

Flaming Lance. Novel by Clair Huffaker on which the 1960 movie *Flaming Star* is based.

Flaming Lance. Title that Elvis used, when referring to the 1960 movie *Flaming Star,* in an interview prior to filming the movie.

Flamingo Hotel. Las Vegas hotel-casino* where Rusty Martin (Ann-Margret) taught swimming and Lucky Jackson (Elvis) worked as a waiter in the 1964 movie *Viva Las Vegas.*

FLAMING STAR. Twentieth Century-Fox, 1960. Premiered December 20, 1960 (101 min). Elvis's sixth movie. Producer, David Weisbart. Director, Don Siegel. Cast: Pacer Burton/Elvis Presley, Roslyn Pierce/Barbara Eden, Clint Burton/Steven Forrest, Neddy Burton/Dolores Del Rio, Pa Burton/John McIntire, Buffalo Horn/Rudolfo Acosta, Dred Pierce/Karl Swenson, Doc Phillips/Ford Rainey, Angus Pierce/Richard Jaeckel, Dorothy Howard/Anne Benton, Tom Howard/L. Q. Jones, Will Howard/Douglas Dick, Jute/Tom Reese, Ph'Sha Anay/Marian Goldina, Dottie Phillips/Barbara Beaird, Mrs. Phillips/Virginia Christine, Indian Brave/Rodd Redwing, Two Moons/Perry Lopez, Bird's Wing/Sharon Bercutt, Townsman/Tom Fadden, The Jordanaires/The Jordanaires. Screenplay, Clair Huffaker and Nunnally Johnson. Photography, Charles G. Clarke. Music, Cyril Mockridge. Conducted by Lionel Newman. Choreography, Josephine Earl. Art Direction, Duncan Cramer and Walter M. Simonds. Set Decoration, Walter M. Scott and Gustav Bernsten. Costumes, Adele

---

*The Flamingo was the first hotel to appear on the famous Las Vegas Strip. It cost $6 million when built in 1946 by gangster Benjamin "Bugsy" Siegel. He named the hotel, which opened on December 26, 1946, after his girlfriend Virginia Hill, whose nickname was Flamingo.

Talmadge. Editor, Hugh S. Fowler. Songs sung by Elvis: "Flaming Star" (title), "A Cane and a High Starched Collar." Red West played an Indian in the film. The screenplay was written for Marlon Brando.

Flaming Star. Title song of the 1960 movie *Flaming Star,* sung by Elvis. In the English LP "Flaming Star and Summer Kisses" some beginning notes are missing. Written by Sid Wayne and Sherman Edwards, "Flaming Star" appeared in the Extended Play album "Elvis by Request" (RCA LPC-128) and the following Long Playing albums: "Singer Presents Elvis Singing Flaming Star and Others" (RCA PRS-279); "Elvis Sings Flaming Star" (RCA Camden CAS-2304); "Elvis Sings Flaming Star" (Pickwick CAS 2304); "Elvis in Hollywood" (RCA DPL2-0168); "Double Dynamite" (Pickwick DL2-5001).

Flaming Star Fan Club. Elvis's Norwegian fan club.

Flatt, Lester. Bluegrass singer and musician. Lester Flatt joined the Grand Ole Opry in 1944 as a member of Bill Monroe's Bluegrass Boys. The following year, Earl Scruggs joined Monroe and, in 1948, Flatt and Scruggs formed their own group. For the next twenty-one years, Flatt and Scruggs were the most popular bluegrass group. Their recording of the theme song for the TV series "The Beverly Hillbillies," called "The Ballad of Jed Clampett," was extremely popular in the pop-music field as well as in the country field.

Lester Flatt, with Bill Monroe, composed "Little Cabin on the Hill," which Elvis recorded in 1970.

Flight 602. Charlie Hodge's singing and dancing group, which appears at many Elvis conventions.

Flint, Elmer and Debra. Dwight, Illinois, couple, who, on June 1, 1978, became the first couple to be married inside the house in which Elvis was born, in Tupelo, Mississippi. Mr. and Mrs. J. C. Grimes served as witnesses.

Flip, Flop, and Fly. Song composed by Charles Calhoun and Lou Willie Turner and originally recorded by Joe Turner in 1955 on Atlantic Records. Turner had a million-seller with the song. Johnnie Ray recorded it for Columbia (Columbia 40471). Elvis sang "Flip, Flop, and Fly" on his third TV appearance on "Stage Show"—February 11, 1956. "Flip, Flop, and Fly" appeared in the Long Playing album "Elvis as Recorded Live on Stage in Memphis" (RCA CPL1-0606).

Flip Records. Non-union subsidiary label of Sun Records. After only four releases, Flip Records was discontinued (in 1956) because there already existed a Flip Records in Los Angeles (whose biggest hit was "A Casual Look" by the Six Teens). Carl Perkins recorded his first record, "Movie Magg"/"Turn Around," on Flip Records of Memphis (Flip 501).

Floor. Code word to inform Elvis and others at concerts that someone was advancing on Elvis in a threatening manner.

Florendo, Dr. Noel. Assistant to Dr. E.E. Muirhead at Elvis's autopsy. He believed that the autopsy revealed "no gross evidence of a heart attack."

Florita, The. Nightclub where Vince Everett (Elvis) applied for a job after getting out of prison in the 1957 movie *Jailhouse Rock*.

Flying Circle G. Second name of Elvis's ranch, the Circle G. It was renamed the Flying Circle G because Elvis discovered that there was a ranch in Texas called the Circle G.

Flying Saucer Goes West/Saucer Serenade. A novelty record by Bill Buchanan and Dickie Goodman that made reference to "General Elvis Presley." It was released on the Luniverse label (Luniverse 108) in 1958.

Flying Saucer, The/Flying Saucer (Part II). Novelty record made in 1956 by Bill Buchanan and Dickie Goodman on the Luniverse label. The record had fifteen excerpts from popular songs, including Elvis's "Heartbreak Hotel" and Carl Perkins's "Blue Suede Shoes."

"The Flying Saucer" (Luniverse 101) was written by Mae Boren Axton and originally released as "Back to Earth."

Flying Saucer (The 2nd). A novelty record by Buchanan and Goodman in which a short excerpt from "All Shook Up" was heard. It was released on the Luniverse label (Luniverse 105).

Flying Windgrens, The. Trapeze team to which Mike Windgren (Elvis) belonged before causing his partner to be seriously injured in the 1963 movie *Fun in Acapulco*.

Flynt, Larry. Publisher of *Hustler* magazine. Larry Flynt purchased Elvis's Tri-Star jet from the Presley estate for $1.1 million in 1978.

Foley, Clyde Julian "Red". One of the founding fathers of country music, he was elected to the Country Music Hall of Fame in 1967. Red Foley was the first major country star to actually record in Nashville* (March 1945 at studio B at radio station WSM). In 1937 he was the first country artist to have a network radio program—"Avalon Time," which costarred Red Skelton.

Red Foley was a veteran of the Grand Ole Opry. In 1955 he moved to network television with "Ozark Jubilee"—a show that he hosted. Foley had a supporting role, as Uncle Cooter, in the ABC-TV series "Mr. Smith Goes to Washington" (1962–63).

One of Red Foley's daughters, Shirley Lee, is married to Pat Boone.

Elvis recorded three songs that Red Foley had previously recorded: "Shake a Hand" (Decca 28839); "Peace in the Valley" (Decca 14573) (the Jordanaires backed both Elvis and Red Foley); "Old Shep" (Decca 46052) (which Foley co-

---

*DeFord Bailey, the first black performer in country music, was probably the first artist, ever, to record in Nashville (October 2, 1928).

composed). "Blue Guitar" and "Tennessee Saturday Night," two unreleased Sun Records by Elvis, were also previously recorded by Red Foley.

In the 1975 movie *Nashville*, Henry Gibson portrayed Haven Hamilton, a character loosely based on Red Foley.

FOLLOW THAT DREAM. United Artists, 1962. Premiered Ocala, Florida, April 11, 1962 (110 min). Elvis's ninth movie. Producer, Davis Weisbart. Director, Gordon Douglas. Cast: Toby Kwimper/Elvis Presley, Pop Kwimper/Arthur O'Connell, Holly Jones/Ann Helm, Alicia Claypoole/Joanna Moore, Carmine/Jack Kruschen, Nick/Simon Oakland, Endicott/Herbert Rudley, Judge/Roland Winters, H. Arthur King/Alan Hewitt, George/Howard McNear, Jack/Frank De Kova, Governor/Harry Holcombe, Eddy Bascombe/Gavin Koon, Teddy Bascombe/Robert Koon, Ariadne Pennington/Pam Ogles, Al/Robert Carricart, Blackie/John Duke. Screenplay, Charles Lederer. Photography, Leo Tover. Music, Hans J. Salter. Art Direction, Malcolm Bert. Set Decoration, Gordon Gurnee and Fred McClean. Assistant Director, Bert Chervin. Editor, William B. Murphy. Songs Sungs by Elvis: "What a Wonderful Life," "I'm Not the Marrying Kind," "Sound Advice," "Follow That Dream," "Angel," "On Top of Old Smokey." Location shots for the film were made near the home of eleven-year-old Tom Petty, who, in 1976, formed the band Tom Petty and the Heartbeats.

Follow That Dream. Title song of the 1962 movie *Follow That Dream.* Written by Fred Wise and Ben Weisman, "Follow That Dream" appeared in the Extended Play album, "Follow That Dream" (RCA EPA-4368) and the following Long Playing albums: "C'mon Everybody" (RCA Camden CAL-2518); "C'mon Everybody" (Pickwick CAS-2518); "Elvis in Hollywood" (RCA DPL2-0168); "Double Dynamite" (Pickwick DL2-5001).

Follow That Dream. RCA EPA-4368. This was a 45 rpm Extended Play album released in May 1962. It reached #15 on *Billboard*'s Hot 100 chart. Songs included—Side 1: "Follow That Dream," "Angel." Side 2: "What a Wonderful Life," "I'm Not the Marrying Kind."

Folsom Prison Blues. Song originally written and recorded by Johnny Cash. Cash got the idea for the song after watching the 1951 movie *Inside the Walls of Folsom* in a movie theater. "Folsom Prison Blues" (Sun 232) was recorded by Cash on July 29, 1955, and became his second Sun Records release (his first release was "Hey, Porter"/"Cry, Cry, Cry"). In 1968 a rerecording of the song (from his album "Johnny Cash at Folsom Prison") did well on the Country and Pop charts (winning a Grammy).

Elvis sang "Folsom Prison Blues" at some of his Las Vegas shows and the song appeared in the bootleg LP "From Hollywood to Vegas."

Fontainebleau Hotel. Miami Beach, Florida, hotel* where Elvis taped "The Frank Sinatra-Timex Special." Elvis taped the ABC-TV program in the Grand Ballroom on March 26, 1960, and it aired on May 12.

Fontana, D. J. (Dominic Joseph). Elvis's drummer from 1955 to '69. Elvis first met D. J. Fontana while appearing at the "Louisiana Hayride" on October 19, 1954. Fontana was the staff drummer for the "Hayride." Previously he had played for radio station KWKH's (Shreveport, Louisiana) studio band.

Popular opinion has it that D. J. Fontana was first heard on "I'm Left, You're Right, She's Gone" and played in Elvis's Sun recordings from that time on. However, he once stated that he did *not* appear on any of Elvis's Sun recordings!

D. J. Fontana left Elvis's band in 1969 to become a session musician in Nashville. D. J. Fontana played drums on Ringo Starr's "Beaucoups of Blues" album. The Jordanaires also appeared in the album (See: Cunningham, Buddy)

Fool. RCA 74-0910. Released in March 1973 as a 45 rpm single. It reached #17 on *Billboard*'s Hot 100 chart and #31 on the Country chart. "Steamroller Blues" was on the flip side. "Fool" was written by Carl Sigman and James Last and appeared in the Long Playing album "Elvis" (RCA APL1-0283).

Fools Fall in Love. RCA 47-9056. Released in January 1967 as a 45 rpm single. "Indescribably Blue" was on the flip side. "Fools Fall in Love" was written by Jerry Leiber and Mike Stoller and originally recorded by the Drifters in 1957 after fifty-six takes (Atlantic 1123). Elvis recorded "Fools Fall in Love" in 1966 and it appeared in the Long Playing albums "I Got Lucky" (RCA Camden CAL-2533), "I Got Lucky" (Pickwick CAS-2533), and "Double Dynamite" (Pickwick DL2-5001).

Fools Fall in Love. RCA 447-0659. Gold Standard Series re-issue of RCA 47-9056.

Fools Rush In (Where Angels Fear to Tread). Song written in 1940 by Johnny Mercer and Rube Bloom. The melody was based on Bloom's "Shangri La." "Fools Rush In" was first popularized by a Glenn Miller recording on the Bluebird label in 1940, also by Frank Sinatra with Tommy Dorsey's orchestra (Victor 26593). Elvis's arrangement of the song was based on Ricky Nelson's (1963), which in turn was based on Brook Benton's. "Fools Rush In" appeared in the Long Playing album "Elvis Now" (RCA LSP-4671).

Fool Such as I, A. RCA 47-7506. Released in March 1959 as a 45 rpm single. It reached #2 on *Billboard*'s Hot 100 chart, #16 on the Rhythm and Blues chart, and #1 in the United Kingdom (for seven weeks, May 2–June 20). The song is correctly titled "(Now and Then There's) A Fool Such as I." The bass singer

---

*Jerry Lewis filmed the 1960 movie *The Bellboy* at the Fontainebleau Hotel.

heard on this song is Ray Walker of the Jordanaires. It sold over a million copies. "I Need Your Love Tonight" was on the flip side. "(Now and Then There's) A Fool Such as I" was written by Bill Trader in 1952 and originally recorded by Hank Snow (RCA 5034) in 1953. Jo Stafford had a bigger hit with the song in 1953 on Columbia Records (Columbia 39930). Elvis recorded "(Now and Then There's) A Fool Such as I" on June 10, 1958, while on leave from the Army. It appeared in the following Long Playing albums: "50,000,000 Elvis Fans Can't Be Wrong—Elvis' Golden Records, Volume 2" (RCA LPM-2075); "50,000,000 Elvis Fans Can't Be Wrong—Elvis' Golden Records, Volume 2" (RCA LSP-2075 [e]); "Elvis: Worldwide 50 Gold Award Hits, Volume 1" (RCA LPM-6401); "Elvis—A Legendary Performer, Volume 1" (RCA CPL1-0341).

Fool Such as I, A. RCA 447-0625. Gold Standard Series re-issue of RCA 47-7506.

Fool, The. Song written by Naomi Ford* and originally recorded by Sanford Clark in 1955 (MCI 1003). When the record was re-issued by Dot Records (Dot 15481) in 1956, it became a big hit, as did a version by the Gallahads (Jubilee 5252). Elvis recorded "The Fool" in 1970 and it appeared in the Long Playing album, "Elvis Country" RCA LSP-4460).

Football. Elvis's favorite sport as stated by him in an interview with Red Robinson on August 31, 1957. (See: Whitehaven High School)

Foote, Mrs. Sophie. Neighbor of the Presley family at the Lauderdale Courts in Memphis.

Forbess, Evan. One of Elvis's close friends at Humes High School. Forbess was nicknamed "Buzzie."

For Elvis. A 1977 Elvis tribute record by Frankie Rich and Nashville East on Texas Records (Texas 1004).

Forest Hill Cemetery. Memphis cemetery, located at 1661 Elvis Presley Blvd., where Elvis and his mother, Gladys Presley, were buried until October 2, 1977. On that date, the bodies were moved to Graceland. Visitors were ruining the grounds at Forest Hill and there was a rumor that Elvis's body might be stolen and held for ransom.

Bill Black, Elvis's bass player in the early years, is buried at Forest Hill.

Forever Young, Forever Beautiful. A 33⅓ rpm Long Playing bootleg album released by Memphis Flash Records in August 1977. It consisted of a number of songs that Eddie Fadal had taped while Elvis was visiting his Houston, Texas, home, in 1958. Songs included—"Happy, Happy Birthday Baby," "Who's Sorry Now," "I Understand," "I Can't Help It (If I'm Still in Love with You)," "Baby Don't Ya Know," "Tomorrow Night,"

---

*On some recordings by other artists, Lee Hazlewood is listed as co-writer.

"Little Darlin'," "Tumbling Tumbleweeds," "Just a Closer Walk with Thee." Some of the songs were sung along with records, some with Anita Wood and some with Elvis playing the piano.

For Every Star That Rises. A 1978 Elvis tribute record by Michael Morguard and Peter McNey.

Forget Me Never. Song that Elvis recorded for the 1961 movie *Wild in the Country*. It was cut from the final release of the film. "Forget Me Never" was written by Fred Wise and Ben Weisman and appeared in the following Long Playing albums: "Elvis for Everyone" (RCA LPM/LSP-3450); "Separate Ways" (RCA Camden CAS-2611); "Separate Ways" (Pickwick CAS-2611).

(That's What You Get) For Lovin' Me. Song written by Gordon Lightfoot in 1964 and first recorded by Peter, Paul, and Mary in the same year (Warner Bros. 5496). Elvis recorded "For Lovin' Me" in 1971 and it appeared in the Long Playing albums "Elvis" (RCA APL1-0283) and "Elvis—A Canadian Tribute" (RCA KKL1-7065).

For LP Fans Only. RCA LPM-1990. A 33⅓ rpm Long Playing album that was released in February 1959. It reached #19 on *Billboard*'s Hot LP chart. "For LP Fans Only" was the first album in history to exclude the performer's name from the outside cover. Songs included—Side 1: "That's All Right," "Lawdy, Miss Clawdy," "Mystery Train," "Playing for Keeps," "Poor Boy." Side 2: "My Baby Left Me," "I Was the One," "Shake, Rattle and Roll," "I'm Left, You're Right, She's Gone," "You're a Heartbreaker."

For LP Fans Only. RCA LSP-1990 (e). This record was the electronically reprocessed stereo re-issue of RCA LPM-1990.

For Ol' Times Sake. RCA APBO-0088. Released in September 1973 as a 45 rpm single. It reached #41 on *Billboard*'s Hot 100 chart and #42 on the Country chart. "Raised on Rock" was on the flip side. "For Ol' Times Sake" was written by Tony Joe White and appeared in the Long Playing album "Raised on Rock/For Ol' Times Sake" (RCA APL1-0388).

Forrest, Steve. Actor who played Clint Burton, Pacer Burton's (Elvis) brother, in the 1960 movie *Flaming Star*.
Steve Forrest has starred in two TV series: "The Baron" and "S.W.A.T."
Steve Forrest's real name is William Forrest Andrews and he is the brother of actor Dana Andrews.

Fortas, Alan. Muscular, 5'11", member of the Memphis Mafia. He was nicknamed "Hog Ears." Alan Fortas's uncle was U. S. Supreme Court Justice Abe Fortas. He served as manager of Elvis's Circle G Ranch. Prior to that, Alan Fortas served as Elvis's bodyguard and took care of travel arrangements. He joined Elvis in 1958.

Fort Chaffee, Arkansas. Army post where Elvis received his Army indoctrination. He received his medical shots, Army fatigues, and took an aptitude test at Fort Chaffee.

Fort Dix, New Jersey. Army post where Elvis was discharged, on March 5, 1960.

For the Good Times. Song written by Kris Kristofferson and originally recorded by Ray Price in 1970 on Columbia Records (Columbia 45178). Elvis recorded "For the Good Times" in 1972 and it appeared in the 1973 documentary *Elvis on Tour.* "For the Good Times" appeared in the Long Playing albums "Elvis as Recorded at Madison Square Garden" (RCA LSP-4776) and "Welcome to My World" (RCA APL1-2274).

For the Heart. RCA PB-10601. Released in March 1976 as a 45 rpm single. It reached #20 on *Billboard*'s Hot 100 chart and #6 on the Country chart. "Hurt" was on the flip side. "For the Heart" was written by Dennis Linde and recorded by Elvis at Graceland on the night of February 5–6, 1976. It appeared in the Long Playing albums "From Elvis Presley Boulevard, Memphis, Tennessee" (RCA APL1-1506) and "Our Memories of Elvis, Volume 2" (RCA (AQL1-3448).

For the Millionth and the Last Time. Song written for Elvis by Sid Tepper and Roy C. Bennett in 1961. "For the Millionth and the Last Time" appeared in the Long Playing album "Elvis for Everyone" (RCA LPM-LSP-3450).

Fort Hood, Texas. Army post where Elvis received his basic training. He was assigned to A Company, Second Medium Tank Battalion, Second Armored Division. Elvis was stationed at Fort Hood from March 28 to September 19, 1958.

Fort Lauderdale Chamber of Commerce. Song that Elvis sang in the 1965 movie *Girl Happy.* Sid Tepper and Roy C. Bennett wrote "Fort Lauderdale Chamber of Commerce." It appeared in the Long Playing album "Girl Happy" (RCA LPM/LSP-3338).

Forty Nina. Stripper (played by Liliane Montevecchi) at the King Creole Club in the 1958 movie *King Creole.* Prior to Danny Fisher's (Elvis) arrival, "Forty" Nina was the club's headliner. She sang "Banana" in one of her performances.

Fountain of Love. Song recorded by Elvis in 1962. "Fountain of Love" was written by Bill Giant and Jeff Lewis and appeared in the Long Playing album "Pot Luck" (RCA LPM/LSP-2523).

Foxx, Redd. Popular black comedian who starred in the TV series "Sanford and Son." Prior to the TV series, Redd Foxx (real name: John Elroy Sanford) was known primarily for his off-color nightclub act and record albums. He was the only entertainer invited to Elvis and Priscilla's wedding breakfast at the Aladdin Hotel on May 1, 1967.

Fraley, Sgt. William. Elvis's drill instructor at Fort Hood, Texas.

Francisco, Dr. Jerry. Memphis and Shelby County (Tennessee) coroner who performed the three-hour autopsy on Elvis, on

August 16, 1977. Dr. Francisco ruled that Elvis's death was the result of coronary arrhythmia—an irregular beating of the heart resulting from hypertensive heart disease.

On October 17, 1977, Dr. Francisco gave a press release in which he stated that Elvis had died of a heart attack—not from drugs.

Frankenstein. An 1860 novel by Mary Wollstonecraft Shelley that was made into numerous movies. Four actors who appeared in Elvis films also appeared in various versions of the Frankenstein movies. The actors and their Elvis films include: Elsa Lanchester (*Easy Come, Easy Go*, 1967); John Carradine (*The Trouble with Girls [And How to Get Into It]*, 1969); Vincent Price (*The Trouble with Girls [And How to Get Into It]*, 1969); and Glenn Strange* (*Jailhouse Rock*, 1957).

Frankenstein of '59/Frankenstein Returns. A 1959 novelty record by Bill Buchanan and Dickie Goodman in which excerpts from two Elvis songs are heard: "One Night" and "I Got Stung." It was released on the Novelty label (Novelty 301).

Frankfurt Special. Song that Elvis sang in the 1960 movie *G.I. Blues*. The film version has additional voices and includes horns. "Frankfurt Special" was written by Sid Wayne and Sherman Edwards and appeared in the Long Playing albums "G.I. Blues" (RCA LPM–LSP-2256) and Elvis—A Legendary Performer, Volume 3" (RCA CPL1-3082).

Frankie and Albert. Original title, in 1888, of the folk ballad "Frankie and Johnny." Director John Huston once traced the song's origin, discovering twenty different versions of the song. In 1929 Huston wrote the stage play *Frankie and Johnny*, scored by actor Sam Jaffe.

FRANKIE and JOHNNY. United Artists, 1966. Premiered Baton Rouge, Louisiana, March 31, 1966 (87 min). Elvis's twentieth movie. Executive Producer, Edward Small. Director, Frederick De Cordova. Cast: Johnny/Elvis Presley, Frankie/Donna Douglas, Nellie Bly/Nancy Kovack, Mitzi/Sue Anne Langdon, Clint Braden/Anthony Eisley, Cully/Harry Morgan, Pet/Audrey Christie, Blackie/Robert Strauss, Wilbur/Jerome Cowan, The Earl Barton Dancers/Wilda Taylor, Larri Thomas, Dee Jay Mattis, Judy Chapman. Associate Producer and Screenplay, Alex Gottlieb. Photography, Jacques Marquette. Music, Fred Karger. Choreography, Earl Barton. Art Direction, Walter Simonds. Set Decoration, Morris Hoffman. Costumes, Gwen Wakeling. Editor, Grant Whytock. Songs Sung by Elvis: "Everybody Come Aboard," "Chesay," "Frankie and Johnny," "What Every Woman Lives For," "Come Along," "Look Out, Broadway," "Beginner's Luck," "Shout It Out," "Hard Luck," "Down by the Riverside"/"When the Saints Go Marching In"

---

*Glenn Strange portrayed Sam O'Brien, the bartender at the Longbranch Saloon, on the TV series "Gunsmoke."

(medley), "Please Don't Stop Loving Me," "Petunia, the Gardener's Daughter" (duet with Donna Douglas).

Frankie and Johnny. RCA 47-8780. Released in March 1966 as a 45 rpm single. It reached #25 on *Billboard*'s Hot 100 chart. "Please Don't Stop Loving Me" was on the flip side. "Frankie and Johnny" was the title song of the 1966 movie of the same name. In the film, Elvis was backed by the chorus that included Sue Ann Langdon, Donna Douglas, and Harry Morgan. "Frankie and Johnny" was a million-seller.

"Frankie and Johnny" was based on a mid-nineteenth-century ballad. In 1904 Hughie Cannon had the first printed version of the song, under the title "He Done Me Wrong." Gene Autry recorded "Frankie and Johnny" in 1929. Years later Sam Cooke recorded the song. Alex Gottlieb, Fred Karger, and Ben Weisman arranged "Frankie and Johnny" for Elvis. Elvis's version appeared in the following Long Playing albums: "Frankie and Johnny" (RCA LPM/LSP-3553); "Elvis Sings Hits from His Movies, Volume 1" (RCA Camden CAS-2567); "Elvis Sings Hits from His Movies, Volume 1" (Pickwick CAS-2567); "Elvis in Hollywood" (RCA DPL2-0168); "Double Dynamite" (Pickwick DL2-5001); "Frankie and Johnny" (Pickwick ACL-7007).

Frankie and Johnny. RCA 447-0656. Gold Standard Series reissue of RCA 47-8780.

Frankie and Johnny. RCA LPM/LSP-3553. A 33⅓ rpm Long Playing album released in April 1966. It reached #20 on *Billboard*'s Hot LP chart. "Frankie and Johnny" featured songs from the 1966 movie of the same name. Songs included—Side 1: "Frankie and Johnny," "Come Along," "Petunia, the Gardener's Daughter," "Chesay," "What Every Woman Lives For," "Look Out, Broadway." Side 2: "Beginner's Luck," "Down by the Riverside/When the Saints Go Marching In," "Shout It Out," "Hard Luck," "Please Don't Stop Loving Me," "Everybody Come Aboard."

Frankie and Johnny. Pickwick ACL-7007. A 33⅓ rpm Long Playing album released in May 1976. This album was *not* a rerelease of RCA LPM/LSP-3553. The songs are not in the same playing order and three songs were deleted. "Frankie and Johnny" featured ten songs from the 1966 movie of the same name. Songs included—Side 1: "Frankie and Johnny," "Come Along," "What Every Woman Lives For," "Hard Luck," "Please Don't Stop Loving Me." Side 2: "Down by the Riverside"/"When the Saints Go Marching In," "Petunia, the Gardener's Daughter," "Beginner's Luck," "Shout It Out."

Frank Sinatra-Timex Special, The. Television show on which Elvis made his first public appearance after being discharged from the Army. It aired on May 12, 1960, on ABC-TV. Elvis sang "Fame and Fortune" and "Stuck on You." He also sang a duet with Sinatra in which Sinatra sang "Love me Tender" and

Elvis sang "Witchcraft" (Sinatra's hit)—both at the same time. Elvis was paid $125,000 for six minutes' work. Also appearing on the TV special were Sammy Davis, Jr., Joey Bishop, Peter Lawford, and Nancy Sinatra.

"The Frank Sinatra-Timex Special" received a 41.5 share of the audience. (See: Fontainebleau Hotel)

Frazier, Dallas. Country singer and composer. When he was twelve years old, Dallas Frazier won a talent contest sponsored by Ferlin Husky. Shortly after, he began touring with Husky.

In 1957 Dallas Frazier composed "Alley Oop" (Lute 5905), which the Hollywood Argyles* recorded in 1960 (it reached #1 and was a million-seller). Elvis recorded three Dallas Frazier songs: "There Goes My Everything"; "Wearin' That Loved-on Look"; and "True Love Travels on a Gravel Road."

Freak Out and Go-Go Jo. Two instrumentals played in the 1967 movie *Easy Come, Easy Go.*

Freberg, Stan. Humorist and recording artist who did cartoon voices for Walt Disney, Warner Bros., Columbia, and Paramount Studios. He also did voices on the TV puppet show "Time for Beany."

In 1950 Stan Freberg signed with Capitol Records and began releasing very successful satire records. In 1953 he had a #1 hit and million-seller with "St. George and the Dragonet" (Capitol 2596)—a parody on the very popular TV series "Dragnet." Freberg recorded a satirical version of "Heartbreak Hotel" (Capitol 3480) in 1956.

Freed, Alan. Extremely popular New York City disc jockey for radio station WINS, who is often credited with coining the phrase *rock 'n' roll.* His career was ruined over the payola scandals of the late 1950s. Alan Freed was portrayed by Tim McIntire in the 1978 movie *American Hot Wax.* Alan Freed was the first DJ in New York City to play Elvis's "Heartbreak Hotel."

Freegate, Texas. Town where Deke Rivers (Elvis) was forbidden to perform in the 1957 movie *Loving You.*

Freeman, Frank. Paramount Studios production chief who sent Elvis's draft board a letter (December 21, 1957) asking for a sixty-day deferment so that Elvis could complete production of *King Creole.* The draft board said that Elvis himself would have to ask for the deferment. He did ask for—and received—the delay.

Friedburg, West Germany. Town north of Frankfurt where Elvis was stationed while in the Army.

Friedman, Sam. Acting city judge in Memphis who presided over the court case involving Elvis and Ed Hopper, a gas station manager. Hopper charged that Elvis assaulted him on October

---

*Gary Paxton, one of the group's members, previously recorded as Flip in the duet Skip and Flip.

18, 1956. Elvis was acquitted and Hopper was fined twenty-five dollars. (See: Hopper, Ed)

From a Jack to a King. Song written and originally recorded by Ned Miller in 1957. In late 1962 "From a Jack to a King" was re-issued on Fabor Records (Fabor 114) and became a million-seller for Miller. Another version was recorded by Wink Martindale. Elvis recorded "From a Jack to a King" at the American Sound Studios in Memphis in January 1969 and it appeared in the Long Playing albums "From Memphis to Vegas/From Vegas to Memphis" (RCA LSP-6020) and "Elvis—Back in Memphis" (RCA LSP-4429).

From Elvis in Memphis. RCA LSP-4155. A 33⅓ rpm Long Playing album that was released in June 1969. It reached #13 on *Billboard*'s Hot LP chart and #1 in the United Kingdom. All songs on this album were recorded at the American Sound Studios in Memphis. "From Elvis in Memphis" received a Gold Disc award from the R.I.A.A. for sales of over $1 million, Songs included—Side 1: "Wearin' That Loved On Look," "Only the Strong Survive," "I'll Hold You in My Heart (Till I Can Hold You in My Arms)," "Long Black Limousine," "It Keeps Right on A-Hurtin'," "I'm Movin' On." Side 2: "Power of My Love," "Gentle on My Mind," "After Loving You," "True Love Travels on a Gravel Road," "Any Day Now," "In the Ghetto."

From Elvis Presley Boulevard, Memphis, Tennessee. RCA APL1-1506. A 33⅓ rpm Long Playing album that was released in May 1976. It reached #1 on *Billboard*'s Country LP chart. This album was also available in Quadrasonic. It received a Gold Disc award from the R.A.I.I. for sales of over $1 million. The songs on "From Elvis Presley Boulevard, Memphis, Tennessee" were recorded at Graceland, February 2-8, 1976. Songs included—Side 1: "Hurt," "Never Again," "Blue Eyes Crying in the Rain," "Danny Boy," "The Last Farewell." Side 2: "For the Heart," "Bitter They Are, Harder They Fall," "Solitaire," "Love Coming Down," "I'll Never Fall in Love Again."

From Graceland to the Promised Land. Merle Haggard's 1977 tribute to Elvis on MCA Records (MCA 40804).

From Hollywood to Vegas. A 33⅓ rpm bootleg album released on the Brookville label. It featured "live" Las Vegas songs and unreleased movie material. Songs included—Side 1: "Loving You" (soundtrack), "Husky Dusky Day" (soundtrack), "On Top of Old Smokey" (soundtrack), "Dainty Little Moonbeams" (soundtrack), "Girls! Girls! Girls!" (soundtrack), "Auralee" (soundtrack), "Signs of the Zodiac" (soundtrack), "Folsom Prison Blues" (Vegas), "I Walk the Line" (Vegas), "Oh Happy Day" (Vegas). Side 2: "I Need Your Loving Every Day" (Vegas), "I Ain't About to Sing" (Vegas), "I Got a Woman" (Vegas), "Amen" (Vegas), "Crying Time" (Vegas), "Lovely Mamie" (soundtrack), "Long Tall Sally" (Vegas),

135

"Flip, Flop, and Fly" (Vegas), "My Boy" (Vegas), "Hound Dog" (Vegas).

From Las Vegas . . . To Niagara Falls. A 33⅓ rpm bootleg two-record album released on the Brookville label. Songs were from the Las Vegas dinner show of September 3, 1973, and the Niagara Falls Concert of June 24, 1974. Songs included—Side 1: "See See Rider," "I Got a Woman," "Amen," "Love Me," "Steamroller Blues," "You Gave Me a Mountain," "Trouble." Side 2: "Love Me Tender," "Fever," "Suspicious Minds," "My Boy," "I Can't Stop Loving You," "Teddy Bear," "Don't Be Cruel," "The First Time Ever I Saw Your Face," "Can't Help Falling in Love." Side 3: "See See Rider," "I Got a Woman," "Love Me," "Trying to Get to You," "All Shook Up," "Love Me Tender," "Hound Dog," "Fever," "Polk Salad Annie." Side 4: "Why Me, Lord," "Suspicious Minds," "I Can't Stop Loving You," "Help Me," "An American Trilogy," "Let Me Be There," "Funny How Time Slips Away," "Big Boss Man," "Teddy Bear," "Don't Be Cruel," "Can't Help Falling in Love."

From Memphis to Vegas/From Vegas to Memphis. RCA LSP-6020. A 33⅓ rpm Long Playing album that was released in November 1969. It reached #12 on *Billboard*'s Hot LP chart. "From Memphis to Vegas/From Vegas to Memphis" was Elvis's first two-record LP. It received a Gold Disc award from the R.I.A.A. for sales of over $1 million. Sides 1 and 2 were recorded "live" in Las Vegas and sides 3 and 4 were recorded in the studio in Memphis. This album was released as two separate albums in November 1970 ("Elvis—Back in Memphis" and "Elvis in Person at the International Hotel, Las Vegas, Nevada"). Songs included—Side 1: "Blue Suede Shoes," "Johnny B. Goode," "All Shook Up," "Are You Lonesome Tonight," "Hound Dog," "I Can't Stop Loving You," "My Babe." Side 2: Medley: "Mystery Train" "Tiger Man," "Words," "In the Ghetto," "Suspicious Minds," "Can't Help Falling in Love." Side 3: "Inherit the Wind," "This Is the Story," "Stranger in My Own Home Town," "A Little Bit of Green," "And the Grass Won't Pay No Mind." Side 4: "Do You Know Who I Am," "From a Jack to a King," "The Fair's Moving On," "You'll Think of Me," "Without Love (There Is Nothing)."

From the Dark, to the Light. A 33⅓ rpm bootleg album released on the Tiger label. It featured songs from Elvis's two documentaries: *Elvis—That's the Way It Is* and *Elvis on Tour*. Side 1: *Elvis—That's the Way It Is.* Side 2: *Elvis on Tour.*

From the Waist Up. A 33⅓ rpm bootleg album released on the Golden Archives label. This album included all the songs performed on the Ed Sullivan shows. Songs were—Side 1: "Don't Be Cruel" (9/9/56), "Love Me Tender" (9/9/56), "Hound Dog" (9/9/56), "Don't Be Cruel" (10/28/56), "Love Me Tender" (10/28/56), "Hound Dog" (10/28/56). Side 2: "Hound Dog" (1/6/57), "Love Me Tender" (1/6/57), "Heartbreak Hotel" (1/6/57), "Don't Be Cruel" (1/6/57), "Peace in the Valley" (1/6/57), "Too Much" (1/6/57), "When My Blue Moon Turns to Gold Again" (1/6/57).

From the Waist Up. The only show on which Elvis was shown from the waist up was his third and final appearance on the "Ed Sullivan Show"—on January 6, 1957—not on all the shows, as is widely believed.

Fruchter, Alf and Jeanette. Family that lived upstairs at 464 Alabama Street at the time the Presleys lived in the lower unit (462 Alabama Street). Alf Fruchter was a rabbi for the Congregation Beth El-Emeth. The Fruchters were good friends of the Presleys and Elvis sometimes used their telephone. Supposedly, it was the Fruchters' telephone number (37-5630) that Marion Keisker wrote down after Elvis recorded "My Happiness"/"That's When Your Heartaches Begin" in the summer of 1953. However, the Presleys *did* have a telephone at the time (37-4185), so that story seems unlikely. Also, Elvis was supposed to have borrowed the Fruchters' phonograph to play his first Sun releases. Friends of Elvis, however, have stated that Elvis *did* have a phonograph. (See: Keisker, Marion)

Fuller, Candy Jo. Grand Island, Nebraska, woman who claims to be the illegitimate daughter of Elvis Presley. Her mother, Terri Taylor, originated the claim. Candy Jo Fuller is a country singer with her husband's band, Dalton Fuller and The Nebraska Playboys. Occasionally she has been billed as "Elvis Presley's secret daughter." Her son Michael is claimed to be Elvis's grandson. (See: Taylor, Terri; Fuller, Michael)

Fuller, Michael. Candy Jo Fuller's son who, it is claimed, is Elvis's grandson. Michael Fuller was born on October 4, 1976. (See: Fuller, Candy Jo; Taylor, Terri)

Fulson, Lowell. Composer of "Reconsider Baby," which Elvis recorded in 1960. In the early 1950s Lowell Fulson and Ray Charles played in the same combo. Fulson recorded "Reconsider Baby" in 1955 (Checker 804).

FUN IN ACAPULCO.* Paramount, 1963. Premiered, Los Angeles November 28, 1963 (98 min). Elvis's thirteenth movie. Producer, Hal B. Wallis. Associate Producer, Paul Nathan. Director, Richard Thorpe. Cast: Mike Windgren/Elvis Presley, Maggie Dauphine/Ursula Andress, Dolores Gomez/Elsa Cardenas, Maximilian/Paul Lukas, Raul Almeido/Larry Domasin, Mareno/Alejandro Rey, José/Robert Carricart, Janie Harkins/Teri Hope, Mr. Harkins/Charles Evans, Dr. John Stevers/Howard McNear, Mrs. Stevers/Mary Treen, Hotel Manager/Alberto Morin, Desk Clerk/Francisco Ortega, Bellboy/Robert De

---

*Fun in Acapulco. Movie that the Beatles went to see at a drive-in theatre in Miami on the evening of February 18, 1964, during their first American tour.

Anda, Telegraph Clerk/Linda Rivera, First Girl/Darlene Tomkins, Second Girl/Linda Rand, Secretary/Adele Palacios, The Jordanaires/The Jordanaires, The Four Amigos/The Four Amigos. Screenplay, Allan Weiss. Photography, Daniel L. Fapp. Music, Joseph J. Lilley. Choreography, Charles O'Curran. Art Direction, Hal Pereira and Walter Tyler. Set Decoration, Sam Comer and Robert Benton. Special Effects, Paul K. Lerpae. Costumes, Edith Head. Technical Adviser, Col. Tom ' Parker. 2nd Unit and Assistant Director, Michael Moore. Editor, Warren Low. Songs sung by Elvis: "Fun in Acapulco," "The Bullfighter Was a Lady," "Vino, Dinero y Amor," "(There's) No Room to Rhumba in a Sports Car," "Mexico" (duet with Larry Domasin), "I Think I'm Gonna Like It Here," "El Toro," "Bossa Nova Baby," "Marguerita," "You Can't Say No in Acapulco." "Guadalajara."

Fun in Acapulco. Title song of the 1963 movie *Fun in Acapulco.* Additional strings were included in the film version. "Fun in Acapulco" was written by Ben Weisman and Sid Wayne and appeared in the Long Playing albums "Fun in Acapulco" (RCA LPM/LSP-2750) and "Elvis in Hollywood" (RCA DPL2-0168).

Fun in Acapulco. RCA LPM/LSP-2756. A 33⅓ rpm Long Playing album that was released in December 1963. It reached #3 on *Billboard*'s Hot LP chart. Elvis received a Gold Record for sales of over $1 million. "Fun in Acapulco" featured songs from the 1963 movie of the same name, plus two bonus songs. Songs included—Side 1: "Fun in Acapulco," "Vino, Dinero y Amor," "Mexico," "El Toro," "Marguerita," "The Bullfighter Was a Lady," "(There's) No Room to Rhumba In a Sports Car." Side 2: "I Think I'm Gonna Like It Here," "Bossa Nova Baby," "You Can't Say No in Acapulco," "Guadalajara," "Love Me Tonight" (bonus), "Slowly But Surely" (bonus).

Funny How Time Slips Away. Song composed by Willie Nelson in 1961 and a hit for Jimmy Elledge on RCA (RCA 7946) in the same year. Joe Hinton's release of "Funny How Time Slips Away," titled "Funny," in 1964, on Back Beat Records, sold over a million copies. Elvis sang "Funny How Time Slips Away" in the 1973 documentary *Elvis on Tour,* and it appeared in the Long Playing albums "Elvis Country" (RCA LSP-4460) and "Elvis as Recorded at Madison Square Garden" (RCA LSP-4776).

Fury at Gunsight Pass. Movie starring Richard Long, David Brian, and Neville Brand. It was shown on the same bill with an appearance by Elvis at Atlanta's Paramount Theatre on Friday, June 22, 1956. Elvis did three shows that day.

G

Gabriel, Kathy. Las Vegas showgirl dated briefly by Elvis in 1956.

Galaxy Hotel. Las Vegas casino where Johnny Tyronne (Elvis) appeared with his Harem of Dancing Jewels from the Near East in the 1965 movie *Harum Scarum*.

Galuan, Tony. San Francisco-area Elvis impersonator.

Gamble, Marvin (Gee Gee), Jr. Member of the Memphis Mafia. Marvin Gamble served as Elvis's valet and chauffeur. He married Elvis's cousin, Patsy Presley.

Gamble, Patsy. Elvis's cousin who became one of his secretaries in 1963 when Pat West quit to have a baby. Patsy, whose maiden name was Presley (her father is Vester Presley), married Marvin Gamble, Elvis's chauffeur and valet. Elvis once bought Patsy Gamble a 1975 blue Pontiac Grand Prix.

Gardner, "Brother" Dave. Comedian and friend of Elvis; he performed as the opening act at some of Elvis's Las Vegas concerts.

Gates of Hawaii. Travel service that Chad Gates (Elvis) and Maile Duval (Joan Blackman) wanted to start after their marriage (1961 movie *Blue Hawaii*).

Gathering of Eagles, A. A 1963 movie starring Rock Hudson and Rod Taylor, about the Strategic Air Command. It was one of Elvis's favorite movies.

Gatorade. Thirst-quencher liked by Elvis. Gatorade is an artificial lemon-lime drink produced by the Stokely-Van Camp Company of Indianapolis, Indiana.

Gautier, Dick. Actor who played the role of Conrad Birdie in the Broadway musical *Bye Bye Birdie*. Dick Gautier is a veteran of four TV series: "Get Smart" (on which he played Hymie, the robot); "Mr. Terrific"; "Here We Go Again"; "When Things Were Rotten." (See: Bye Bye Birdie)

Geissler, Harry. Board chairman of Factors Etc., Inc. In 1977 Harry Geissler bought the merchandising rights to all Elvis products from Vernon Presley and Col. Tom Parker.

Geller, Larry. One of Elvis's personal hair stylists.

General Randall. Confederate general under whom Lt. Vance Reno (Richard Egan) served (1956 movie *Love Me Tender*). The ship on which Elvis sailed to Europe in 1958 was also called the *General Randall* (See: Randall, U.S.S. General)

Geneva Records. First record label for which Vince Everett (Elvis) recorded in the 1957 movie *Jailhouse Rock*. The masters were then sold to Royal Records. The second label for which Vince Everett recorded was Laurel Records, his own.

Gentle on My Mind. Song written and originally recorded by John Hartford in 1967. It appeared on his LP "Earthwords and Music," Glen Campbell had a very successful recording (Capitol 5929) in late 1967. "Gentle on My Mind" received four Grammy Awards: Best Folk Performance; Best Country and Western Recording; Best Country and Western Song; Best Country and Western Solo Vocal Performance—Male.

"Gentle on My Mind" became the theme song of Glen Campbell's TV series, "The Glen Campbell Goodtime Hour" (1969–72).

Elvis recorded "Gentle on My Mind" in 1969 and Ronnie Milsap played piano in the recording. "Gentle on My Mind" appeared in the Long Playing album "From Elvis in Memphis" (RCA LSP-4155).

Gently. Song recorded by Elvis in 1961. "Gently" was written by Murray Wizell and Edward Lisbona and appeared in the Long Playing album "Something for Everybody" (RCA LPM/LSP-2370).

Gentry, Bobbie. Singer-songwriter whose 1967 record "Ode to Billy Joe" was #1 for four weeks and sold over 3 million copies. It was her very first record. Bobby Gentry* (real name: Roberta Streeter) received four Grammy Awards in 1967: Best Solo (Female) Performance; Best Arrangement; Best Contemporary Vocal Performance; Best New Artist. In 1976 "Ode to Billy Joe" was made into a novel and a feature movie. Bobby Gentry, after an unsuccessful marriage to millionaire Bill Harrah, married singer-songwriter Jim Stafford in 1978.

Bobby Gentry was once considered as Elvis's costar in the 1968 movie *The Trouble with Girls (And How to Get Into It)*; instead, Marilyn Mason received the part.

Get Back. Song written by Paul McCartney, though credited as a Lennon-McCartney composition, which The Beatles with Billy Preston recorded in late January of 1969. "Get Back" (Apple 2490) reached #1 on *Billboard*'s Hot 100 chart (for five weeks). It was the first Beatle record to credit another musician on the label. In the 1970 movie, *Let It Be*, "Get Back" was sung by The Beatles on the top of the Apple Studios in London.

At live appearances Elvis sometimes sang "Get Back" in a medley with "Little Sister."

Getlo. Pet Chow, bought in 1957, that was one of the many dogs owned by Elvis. He once flew the dog to Boston for veterinary care when it was ill.

Get Rhythm. Song originally written and recorded by Johnny Cash

---

*Bobby Gentry chose her last name after seeing the 1953 movie *Ruby Gentry* starring Charlton Heston and Jennifer Jones.

in 1956. "Get Rhythm" was on the flip side of "I Walk the Line" (Sun 241). Cash composed "Get Rhythm" for Elvis but Elvis never recorded it.

Ghanem, Elias. Las Vegas physician who treated Elvis when the singer appeared in that city. According to Dr. Ghanem, he "never knew Elvis to take drugs of any kind—only sleeping pills" (quote from ABC-TV's *20/20*.)

Ghidrah, the Three-Headed Monster. A 1965 Japanese science fiction movie that appeared on the same bill with *Harum Scarum* at many theaters.

G.I. BLUES. Paramount, 1960. Premiered October 20, 1960 (104 min). Elvis's fifth movie. Producer, Hal B. Wallis. Associate Producer, Paul Nathan. Director, Norman Taurog. Cast: Tulsa McLean/Elvis Presley, Lili/Juliet Prowse, Cookie/Robert Ivers, Tina/Leticia Roman, Rick/James Douglas, Marla/Sigrid Maier, Sgt. McGraw/Arch Johnson, Jeeter/Mickey Knox, Capt. Hobart/John Hudson, Mac/Ken Becker, Turk/Jeremy Slate, Warren/Beach Dickerson, Mickey/Trent Dolan, Walt/Carl Crow, Papa Mueller/Fred Essler, Harvey/Ronald Starr, Trudy/Erika Peters, Puppet Show Owner/Ludwig Stossel, German Guitarist/Robert Boon, Mrs. Hagermann/Edith Angold, Orchestra Leader/Dick Winslow, Red/Ed Faulkner, Band Leader/Edward Coch, Herr Klugmann/Fred Kruger, Headwaiter/Torben Meyer, First Businessman/Gene Roth, Second Businessman/Roy C. Wright, M. P./Harper Carter, M. P./Tip McClure, Chaplain/Walter Conrad, Dynamite/Edward Stroll Kaffeehouse Manager/William Kaufman, Strolling Girl Singer/Hannarl Melcher, Sergeant/Elisha Matthew "Bitsy" Mott, Jr., Fritzie/Judith Rawlins, Bartender/Blaine Turner, Bargirl/Marianne Gaba, Redhead/Britta Ekman, The Jordanaires/The Jordanaires. Screenplay, Edmund Beloin and Henry Garson. Photography, Loyal Griggs. Music, Joseph J. Lilley. Choreography, Charles O'Curran. Art Direction, Walter Tyler. Set Decoration, Sam Comer and Ray Mayer. Special Effects, John P. Fulton. Costumes, Edith Head. Technical Adviser, Col. Tom Parker. Assistant Director, D. Michael Moore. Editor, Warren Low. Songs Sung by Elvis: "G.I. Blues," "Pocketful of Rainbows," "Blue Suede Shoes" (Played on a juke box), "Didja Ever?", "Tonight Is So Right for Love," "What's She Really Like," "Frankfurt Special," "Shoppin' Around," "Wooden Heart," "Big Boots," "Doin' the Best I Can." This was Elvis's first movie after his discharge.

G.I. Blues. Title song of the 1960 movie *G.I. Blues,* which Elvis sang. "G.I. Blues" was written by Sid Tepper and Roy C. Bennett and appeared in the Long Playing albums "G.I. Blues" (RCA LPM/LSP-2256) and "Elvis in Hollywood" (RCA DPL2-0168).

G.I. Blues. RCA LMP/LSP-2256. A 33⅓ rpm Long Playing album released in October 1960. It reached #1 (for ten weeks) on *Billboard*'s Hot LP chart and remained on the chart longer than any other Presley record—111 weeks. "G.I. Blues" featured songs from the 1960 movie of the same name. It eventually sold over 2 million copies and received a Gold Disc award from the R.I.A.A. Songs included—Side 1: "Tonight Is So Right for Love," "What's She Really Like," "Frankfurt Special," "Wooden Heart," "G.I. Blues." Side 2: "Pocketful of Rainbows," "Shoppin' Around," "Big Boots," "Didja' Ever," "Blue Suede Shoes," "Doin' the Best I Can."

G.I. Blues Babies. Three sets of twins portrayed the role of a single baby in the 1960 movie *G.I. Blues*. They were: Kerry Charles and Terry Earl Ray; David Paul and Donald James Rankin; Donald Clark and David Clark Wise.

Gibson, Don. One of the most prolific of the country music composers. Don Gibson turned professional at the age of fourteen. In 1958 Gibson recorded a two-sided, million-selling hit record for RCA—"Oh Lonesome Me"/"I Can't Stop Loving You" (RCA 7133). Ray Charles recorded "I Can't Stop Loving You" in 1962 and it became the #1 song of the year. Elvis recorded the song on six different occasions, the first being in 1969.

Gibson, Henrietta. Lisa Marie Presley's nursemaid at Graceland.

Gilliland, Homer "Gil". Elvis's personal hairdresser for many years, starting in 1967. Elvis gave Gilliland his $10,000 gold lamé/suit.

Gingerbread. Elvis's pet name for Ginger Alden.

Girl Can't Help It, The. A 1956 Twentieth Century-Fox movie starring Tom Ewell, Jayne Mansfield, and Edmond O'Brien. Julie London, Ray Anthony, Fats Domino, Little Richard, the Platters, Eddie Cochran, and Gene Vincent performed musical numbers in the film. The title song was recorded by Little Richard (Specialty 591). Fats Domino introduced his new release "Blue Monday" in the film. The song was composed by Bobby Troup.* Being the first rock 'n' roll movie to be filmed in color, Elvis was wanted for the film, but when Col. Tom Parker asked for $50,000 to have Elvis sing just one song, the producers of the film felt they could do without Elvis.

GIRL HAPPY. MGM, 1965. Premiered Los Angeles April 14, 1965 (96 min). Elvis's seventeenth movie. Producer, Joe Pasternak. Director, Boris Sagal. Cast: Rusty Wells/Elvis Presley, Valerie/Shelley Fabares, Big Frank/Harold J. Stone, Andy/Gary Crosby, Wilbur/Joby Baker, Sunny Daze/Nita Talbot, Deena/Mary Ann Mobley, Romano/Fabrizio Mioni, Doc/Jimmy Hawkins, Sgt. Benson/Jackie Coogan, Brentwood von Durgenfeld/Peter Brooks, Mr. Penchill/John Fiedler, Betsy/Chris Noel, Laurie/Lyn Eddington, Nancy/Gale Gilmore, Bob-

---

*Bobby Troup and his wife, Julie London, appeared together in the TV series "Emergency," which was produced by London's previous husband, Jack Webb.

bie/Pamela Curran, Linda/Rusty Allen, "Wolf Call" O'Brien/ Norman Grabowski, Bartender/Mike de Anda, Waiter/Olan Soule, Police Captain/Milton Frome, Girl/Beverly Adams, Muscle Boy/Jim Dawson, Garbage Man/Ted Fish, Officer Wilkins/Dick Reeves, Officer Jones/Ralph Lee, The Jordaniares/ The Jordanaires. Screenplay, Harvey Bullock and R. S. Allen. Photography, Philip H. Lathrop. Music, George Stoll. Choreography, David Winters. Art Direction, George W. Davis and Addison Hehr. Set Decoration, Henry Grace and George R. Nelson. Costumes, Don Feld. Editor, Rita Roland. Songs Sung by Elvis: "Girl Happy," "Spring Fever," "Fort Lauderdale Chamber of Commerce," "Startin' Tonight," "Wolf Call," "Do Not Disturb," "Cross My Heart and Hope to Die," "The Meanest Girl in Town," "Do the Clam," "Puppet on a String," "I've Got to Find My Baby." Shelley Fabares and Nita Talbot sang "Read All About It."

Girl Happy. Title song of the 1965 movie *Girl Happy*. The lyrics were changed slightly the second time Elvis sang it. "Girl Happy" was written by Doc Pomus and Norman Meade and appeared in the Long Playing albums "Girl Happy" (RCA LPM/ LSP-3338) and "Elvis in Hollywood" (RCA DPL2-0168).

Girl Happy. RCA LMP/LSP-3338. A 33⅓ rpm album released in April 1965. "Girl Happy" reached #8 on *Billboard*'s Hot LP chart and achieved sales in excess of $1 million, qualifying for a Gold Record. The album contained the songs from the 1963 movie *Girl Happy*, plus one bonus song. Songs included—Side 1: "Girl Happy," "Spring Fever," "Fort Lauderdale Chamber of Commerce," "Startin' Tonight," "Wolf Call," "Do Not Disturb." Side 2: "Cross My Heart and Hope to Die," "The Meanest Girl in Town," "Do the Clam," "Puppet on a String," "I've Got to Find My Baby," "You'll Be Gone" (bonus).

Girl I Left Behind, The. A 1956 movie starring Tab Hunter and Natalie Wood. *The Girl I Left Behind* was on the bill with *Love Me Tender* when it debuted at the Paramount Theater in Brooklyn, New York (November 15, 1956).

Girl I Never Loved, The. Song that Elvis sang in the 1967 movie *Clambake*. The film version has added string instruments. "The Girl I Never Loved" was written by Randy Starr and appeared in the Long Playing album "Clambake" (RCA LPM/LSP-3893).

Girl in Every Port, A. One of the titles considered for the 1962 movie *Girls! Girls! Girls!* Another title considered was *Welcome Aboard*.

Girl Next Door Went A'Walking. Song written by Bill Rice and Thomas Wayne and originally recorded by Wayne in 1959 (Fernwood 122). On the label of Thomas Wayne's record, the title appeared as "Girl Next Door." Elvis recorded the song in 1960 and the title appeared as "The Girl Next Door" on the first pressings of the album "Elvis Is Back." Later pressings listed the title as "Girl Next Door Went A'Walking." Elvis's recording of "Girl Next Door Went A'Walking" appeared on only the one album—"Elvis Is Back" (RCA LPM/LSP-2231).

Girl of Mine. Song recorded by Elvis in 1973. "Girl of Mine" was written by Barry Mason and Les Reed and appeared in the Long Playing albums "Raised on Rock/For Ol' Times Sake" (RCA APL1-0388) and "Our Memories of Elvis" (RCA AQL1-3279).

Girl of My Best Friend, The. Song written by Beverly Ross and Sam Bobrick and originally recorded by Elvis in 1960. Ral Donner, however, had a huge hit with "The Girl of My Best Friend" in early 1961 (Gone 5102). The Donner version sounds so much like Elvis that it's difficult to tell the difference between the two. "The Girl of My Best Friend," by Elvis, appeared in the Long Playing album "Elvis Is Back" (RCA LPM/LSP-2231).

GIRLS! GIRLS! GIRLS! Paramount, 1962. Premiered Honolulu, Hawaii, October 31, 1962 (106 min). Elvis's eleventh movie. Producer, Hal B. Wallis. Associate Producer, Paul Nathan. Director, Norman Taurog. Cast: Ross Carpenter/Elvis Presley, Robin Gantner/Stella Stevens, Laurel Dodge/Laurel Goodwin, Wesley Johnson/Jeremy Slate, Sam/Robert Strauss, Alexander Stavros/Frank Puglia, Mai Ling/Ginny Tiu, Tai Ling/Elizabeth Tiu, Chen Yung/Guy Lee, Kin Yung/Benson Fong, Mme. Yung/Beulah Quo, Mama Stravros/Lili Valenty, Arthur Morgan/Nestor Paiva, Mrs. Morgan/Ann McCrea, Leona Stavros/Barbara Beall, Linda Stavros/Betty Beall, Mr. Peabody/Gavin Gordon, Mrs. Figgor/Mary Treen, Mrs. Dick/Marjorie Bennett, Drunk/Kenneth Becker, Clerk/Richard Collier. Screenplay, Allan Weiss and Edward Anhalt. Photography. Loyal Griggs. Music, Joseph J. Lilley. Choreography; Charles O'Curran. Art Direction, Hal Pereira and Walter Tyler. Set Decoration, Sam Comer and Frank R. McKelvy. Costumes, Edith Head. Assistant Director, D. Michael Moore. Editor, Warren Low. Songs sung by Elvis: "Girls! Girls! Girls!", "A Boy Like Me, A Girl Like You," "I Don't Wanna Be Tied," "Earth Boy" (duet with Ginny and Elizabeth Tiu), "Where Do You Come From," "Return to Sender," "I Don't Want To," "Thanks to the Rolling Sea," "We'll Be Together," "Song of the Shrimp," "The Walls Have Ears," "We're Coming in Loaded," "Because of Love," "Dainty Little Moonbeams." Stella Stevens Sang: "Baby, Baby, Baby," "Never Let Me Go," "The Nearness of You," The Amigos sang: "Mamma."

Girls! Girls! Girls! Title song of the 1962 Elvis movie *Girls! Girls! Girls!* It was performed by Elvis twice in the movie, each time with different lyrics. Still another version with different vocal backing appeared on record. "Girls! Girls! Girls!" was originally recorded by the Coasters in 1962 on Atco Records (Atco 6204). It was written by Jerry Leiber and Mike Stoller and appeared in the Long Playing albums "Girls! Girls! Girls!" (RCA LPM/LSP-2621) and "Elvis in Hollywood" (RCA DPL2-0168).

Girls! Girls! Girls! RCA LPM/LSP-2621. A 33⅓ rpm Long Playing album released in November 1962. It reached #3 on *Billboard*'s Hot LP chart and achieved over $1 million in sales, qualifying for a Gold Record. The album featured the songs from the 1962 movie *Girls! Girls! Girls!* Songs included—Side 1: "Girls! Girls! Girls!," "I Don't Wanna Be Tied," "Where Do You Come From," "I Don't Want To," "We'll Be Together," "A Boy Like Me, A Girl Like You," "Earth Boy." Side 2: "Return to Sender," "Because of Love," "Thanks to the Rolling Sea," "Song of the Shrimp," "The Walls Have Ears," "We're Coming in Loaded."

Give Me More, More, More. Unreleased Elvis Sun recording of October 1954. It appeared on a "Louisiana Hayride" radio transcript.

Give Me the Right. Song written by Fred Wise and Norman Blagman and recorded by Elvis in 1961. "Give Me the Right" appeared in the Long Playing album "Something for Everybody" (RCA LPM/LSP-2370).

Gladys. Name Col. Tom Parker gave to his twenty-six-foot plastic rowboat, which Elvis gave him for his birthday.

Gladys Music, Inc. Music-publishing company owned by Elvis. It was named for Elvis's mother. Gladys Music, Inc., was a subsidiary of Hill and Range. Elvis received 50% of the royalties.

Glaucoma. Disorder of the eye, which Elvis suffered from in later years. It was a severe case of glaucoma that caused singer Ray Charles to go completely blind by age seven.

Gleaves, Cliff. Salaried friend of Elvis. Cliff Gleaves drove Elvis and Dotty Harmony to Kennedy Veterans Hospital in Memphis for Elvis's preinduction physical (January 4, 1957). Later, he traveled to West Germany with Elvis.

Glenn, Darrell. Composer of "Indescribably Blue," which Elvis recorded in 1967. His father, Artie Glenn, wrote "Crying in the Chapel," which Darrell Glenn introduced (Valley 105). Elvis recorded "Crying in the Chapel" in 1960. Elvis thus recorded a song written by a father and later one by his son, as he did with a song written by a mother and later one by her son when he recorded "Heartbreak Hotel" (co-composed by Mae Axton) and "Never Been to Spain" (composed by Hoyt Axton).

Glenn Tyler. Elvis's role (as a writer) in the 1961 movie *Wild in the Country*.

Glick, Captain Leonard. Army doctor who gave Elvis his preinduction physical examination (January 4, 1957).

God Brought the Curtain Down. A 1977 Elvis tribute record by Shiloh on Shane Records (Shane 001).

Go East, Young Man. Song that Elvis sang in the 1965 movie

Harum Scarum. "Go East, Young Man" was written by Bill Giant, Bernie Baum, and Florence Kaye. It appeared in the Long Playing album "Harum Scarum" (RCA LPM/LSP-3468).

Goethestrasse 14. Bad Nauheim, West Germany, address of the four-bedroom house that Elvis, his father, and his grandmother rented during Elvis's stay in the Army. The rent was $800 a month.

Goin' Home. Song that Elvis recorded for the 1968 movie *Stay Away, Joe,* but it was cut from the final print of the film. "Goin' Home" was written by Joy Byers and appeared in the Long Playing album "Speedway" (RCA LSP-3989).

Gold Cadillac. Elvis's favorite custom automobile. The car started as a 1960 Cadillac Series 75 Sedan Limousine, before being tailor-made by famed automobile customizer George Barris. It was painted with diamond-dust gold pearl paint and is valued at $100,000. The Gold Cadillac is presently on display at the Country Music Hall of Fame in Nashville, Tennessee.

Golden Coins. Song that Elvis sang in the 1965 movie *Harum Scarum.* "Golden Coins" was written by Bill Giant, Bernie Baum, and Florence Kaye and appeared in the Long Playing album "Harum Scarum" (RCA LPM/LSP-3468).

Golden Globe Awards. Annual entertainment award given by the Hollywood Foreign Press Association (founded in 1940). The 1972 film *Elvis on Tour* won a Golden Globe Award for Best Documentary. The Golden Globe Awards were established in 1944.

Golden Memories. An Elvis tribute album by Paul Dragon, recorded on Belle Meade Records. Scotty Moore, D. J. Fontana, Bob Moore, and the Jordanaires backed Dragon on the album.

Goldfinger. A 1965 movie starring Sean Connery* as James Bond. Based on Ian Fleming's 1959 novel *Goldfinger,* it was the third James Bond novel to be filmed. *Goldfinger* was one of Elvis's favorite movies. He once stated that he saw the film five times.

Gold Lamé Tuxedo. Suit designed for Elvis in 1957 by Nudie of Hollywood. A photograph of Elvis wearing the gold lamé tuxedo appeared on the cover of the 1959 Long Playing album "50,000,000 Elvis Fans Can't Be Wrong—Elvis' Gold Records, Volume 2." The suit was reported to have been valued at $10,000, though Nudie recently stated that they "made a profit of $9,950 on the suit."

Gold Records. The following is a list of all of Elvis Presley's reported world-wide Gold Records according to the Recording Industry Association of America, RCA, and independent sources. To qualify for a Gold Record, single releases and Extended Play albums must sell over a million units. Long Playing albums must have had over $1 million in sales through

---

*Sean Connery was a contestant in the 1953 Mr. Universe contest, representing Scotland.

December 31, 1974. On January 1, 1975, the criteria for a Gold Record album changed. From that date to the present, an album must sell over 500,000 units. The following records are listed in order of date of release.

1956, Singles: "Heartbreak Hotel," "I Was the One," "I Want You, I Need You, I Love You," "Don't Be Cruel," "Hound Dog," "Love Me Tender," "Any Way You Want Me." Long Playing Albums: "Elvis Presley," "Elvis."

1957, Singles: "Too Much," "Playing for Keeps," "All Shook Up," "That's When Your Heartaches Begin," "(Let Me Be Your) Teddy Bear," "Loving You," "Jailhouse Rock," "Treat Me Nice," "Don't," "I Beg of You." Extended Play Albums: "Jailhouse Rock." Long Playing Albums: "Loving You," "Elvis Christmas Album."

1958, Singles: "Wear My Ring Around Your Neck," "Hard-Headed Woman," "I Got Stung," "One Night." Extended Play Albums: "King Creole, Volume 1." Long Playing Albums: "Elvis Golden Records," "King Creole."

1959, Singles: "(Now And Then There's) a Fool Such as I," "I Need Your Love Tonight," "A Big Hunk o' Love." Long Playing Albums: "50,000,000 Elvis Fans Can't Be Wrong—Elvis Gold Records, Volume 2."

1960, Singles: "Stuck on You," "It's Now or Never," "A Mess of Blues," "Are You Lonesome Tonight," "I Got to Know," "Wooden Heart" (in Europe). Long Playing Albums: "Elvis Is Back," "G.I. Blues," "His Hand in Mine."

1961, Singles: "Surrender," "I Feel So Bad," "Little Sister," "(Marie's the Name) His Latest Flame," "Can't Help Falling in Love," "Rock-A-Hula Baby." Extended Play Albums: "Elvis by Request." Long Playing Albums: "Something for Everybody," "Blue Hawaii."

1962, Singles: "Good Luck Charm," "Anything That's Part of You," "She's Not You," "Return to Sender," "Where Do You Come From." Long Playing Albums: "Pot Luck," "Girls! Girls! Girls!".

1963, Singles: "One Broken Heart for Sale," "(You're the) Devil in Disguise," "Bossa Nova Baby." Long Playing Albums: "Elvis Golden Records, Volume 3," "Fun in Acapulco."

1964, Singles: "Kissin' Cousins," "Viva Las Vegas," "Ain't That Loving You, Baby," "Blue Christmas." Long Playing Albums: "Kissin' Cousins," "Roustabout."

1965, Singles: "Crying in the Chapel," "I'm Yours," "Puppet on a String." Long Playing Albums: "Girl Happy," "Elvis for Everyone."

1966, Singles: "Tell Me Why," "Frankie and Johnny," "Love Letters," "Spinout," "All That I Am," "If Every Day Was Like Christmas." Long Playing Albums: "Paradise, Hawaiian Style."

1967, Singles: "Indescribably Blue," "Big Boss Man." Long Playing Albums: "How Great Thou Art."

147

1968, Singles: "Guitar Man," "Stay Away," "We Call on Him," "Let Yourself Go," "Almost in Love," "If I Can Dream." Long Playing Albums: "Elvis—TV Special."

1969, Singles: "Charro," "His Hand in Mine," "In the Ghetto," "Clean Up Your Own Back Yard," "Suspicious Minds," "Don't Cry, Daddy." Long Playing Albums: "Elvis Sings Flaming Star," "From Elvis in Memphis," "From Memphis to Vegas/From Vegas to Memphis."

1970, Singles: "Kentucky Rain," "The Wonder of You," "Mama Liked the Roses," "I've Lost You," "You Don't Have to Say You Love Me," "Patch It Up," "I Really Don't Want to Know." Long Playing Albums: "On Stage—February, 1970," "Elvis: Worldwide 50 Gold Award Hits, Volume 1," "Elvis—That's the Way It Is."

1971, Singles: "Where Did They Go, Lord," "Only Believe," "I'm Leavin'," "It's Only Love." Long Playing Albums: "Elvis Country," "Elvis Sings the Wonderful World of Christmas."

1972, Singles: "An American Trilogy," "Burning Love," "Separate Ways." Long Playing Albums: "Elvis as Recorded at Madison Square Garden."

1973, Singles: "Raised on Rock." Long Playing Albums: "Elvis: Aloha From Hawaii Via Satellite," "Elvis" (TV mail-order album).

1974, Singles: "Take Good Care Of Her," "It's Midnight." Long Playing Albums: "Elvis—A Legendary Performer, Volume 1."

1975, Singles: "My Boy," "T-R-O-U-B-L-E." Long Playing Albums: "Promised Land," "Pure Gold."

1976, Singles: "Hurt." Long Playing Albums: "Elvis—A Legendary Performer, Volume 2," "From Elvis Presley Boulevard, Memphis, Tennessee."

1977, Singles: "Way Down," "My Way." Long Playing Albums: "Welcome to My World," "Moody Blue," "Elvis in Concert."

Goldsmith's Department Store. Memphis establishment, located at 4545 Poplar Ave., that did the interior decorating at Graceland.

Gone. Song written in 1952 by Smokey Rogers. In 1957 Ferlin Husky recorded "Gone," which was a pop remake of his earlier country recording. "Gone"* (Capitol 3628) reached #4 on *Billboard*'s Hot 100 chart and #1 on the Country chart. The record sold well over a million copies.

Elvis recorded "Gone" in 1955 while at Sun Records, but the song has never been released.

Gone But Not Forgotten. Phrase on one of the two wreaths that Elvis and Col. Parker placed at the U.S.S. Arizona Memorial at Pearl Harbor, Hawaii, on August 15, 1965. The bell-shaped

---

*"Gone" was recorded in the first country session where a modern vocal group and a vibraphone were used.

148

wreath was made of 1,177 carnations—in honor of each man who perished aboard the U.S.S. *Arizona* on December 7, 1941.

Gone with the Wind. A 1939 movie starring Clark Gable, Vivien Leigh, Olivia de Havilland, and Thomas Mitchell. *Gone with the Wind* won ten Oscars, including Best Picture, Best Actress (Vivien Leigh), and Best Supporting Actress (Hattie McDaniel).

Gone with the Wind was shown on television (CBS-TV) for the second time on the evening of February 11, 1979—opposite the ABC-TV movie *Elvis*. It lost out to *Elvis* in the ratings.

In 1977 a survey of 35,000 members of the American Film Institute resulted in *Gone with the Wind* being selected as the top movie of all time.

Ironically, *Gone with the Wind* played at Loew's State Theater the same week in July that Elvis's first record was played on the radio. (See: Elvis; One Flew Over the Cuckoo's Nest)

Gong Show, The. TV variety series hosted by Chuck Barris. (Chuck Barris composed the 1962 hit song "Palisades Park"* and is the son of Harry Barris, a member of Bing Crosby's Rhythm Boys.) On October 18, 1978, "The Gong Show" dedicated the program to Elvis by having Elvis impersonators perform.

Gonna Get Back Home Somehow. Song written by Doc Pomus and Mort Shuman and recorded by Elvis in 1962. "Gonna Get Back Home Somehow" appeared in the Long Playing album "Pot Luck" (RCA LPM/LSP-2523).

Gonna Get Even with Elvis Presley's Sergeant. An Elvis novelty record by Janie Davids and the Four Lettermen, released on Key Records (Key 576) in 1958.

Gonzales and Green Morticians. Mortuary next door to the free clinic in the 1970 movie *Change of Habit*.

Good, Bad, But Beautiful. Song written by Clive Westlake. On July 24, 1973, Elvis's band recorded the instrumental track for "Good, Bad, But Beautiful." Elvis never did record the vocal track.

Goodbye, Bing, Elvis and Guy. A 1977 tribute record to Bing Crosby, Elvis Presley, and Guy Lombardo, recorded by Diana Williams on Little Gem Records (Little Gem 1023).

Goodbye Elvis. A 1977 Elvis tribute record by Jim Whittington on Lew Breyer Records (Lew Breyer Productions 82977).

Goodbye Elvis. A 1977 Elvis tribute record on Topkopi Records by Will Tura (Topkopi 2103 128).

Goodbye Elvis. A 1977 Elvis tribute record by Ron Scott on Arti Bano Records (Arti Bano 1062).

Goodbye Elvis. A 1978 tribute record to Elvis recorded by A Tint of Darkness on Xclusive Records (Xclusive 104).

---

*Recorded by Freddy Cannon on Swan Records (Swan 4106).

Good Bye Elvis. A 1977 French Elvis tribute record by Ringo on Formula 1 Records (Formula 1-49,307)

Goodbye King of Rock 'n' Roll. A 1977 tribute record to Elvis recorded on True Records by Leon Everette (True 107).

Goodbye Mr. Chips. Movie being advertised on the top of the MGM studio tower in the 1972 documentary *Elvis on Tour*. *Goodbye Mr. Chips* was a musical remake of the original 1939 British version. The 1972 version starred Peter O'Toole and Petula Clark.

Good Lovin'. Sun 280. This was Dickey Lee's first Sun release (Sun 280). "Good Lovin'" closely resembled Elvis's version of "Too Much."

Good Luck Charm. RCA 47-7992. Released in February 1962 as a 45 rpm single. It reached #1 on *Billboard*'s Hot 100 chart (for two weeks, April 21–May 5) and #1 in the United Kingdom (for five weeks, May 26–June 30). "Good Luck Charm" sold over a million copies. "Anything That's Part of You" was on the flip side. Written by Aaron Schroeder and Wally Gold, "Good Luck Charm" appeared in the Long Playing albums "Elvis' Golden Records, Volume 3" (RCA LPM/ LSP-2765), "Elvis: Worldwide 50 Gold Award Hits, Volume 1" (RCA LPM-6401), and "Elvis" (RCA DPL2-0056 [e]).

Good Luck Charm. RCA 447-0636. Gold Standard Series re-issue of RCA 47-7992.

Goodman, Diane. Actress who made her movie debut in the 1962 movie *Girls! Girls! Girls!* Diane Goodman was a former Miss Georgia and was once married to actor Russ Tamblyn. Elvis dated Diane Goodman briefly in 1975.

Goodnight Elvis. A 1977 Elvis tribute record by the Teardrops on Laurie Records (Laurie 3660).

Good Rockin' Tonight. Sun 210. Released on September 25, 1954, as a 78 rpm single and a 45 rpm single. It reached #3 on the record charts in Memphis. "I Don't Care If the Sun Don't Shine" was on the flip side. "Good Rockin' Tonight" was written and originally recorded by Roy Brown in 1947 (De-Luxe 1093). Wynonie "Blues" Harris had a more successful version of the song in 1948 (King 4210). Several other artists recorded "Good Rockin' Tonight," including Pat Boone in 1959 (Dot 15888) and Jerry Lee Lewis (Sun).

Good Rockin' Tonight. RCA 20/47-6381. A 78 rpm and a 45 rpm re-issue of the Sun original (Sun 210). "Good Rockin' Tonight" appeared in the Extended Play album "A Touch of Gold, Volume 1" (RCA EPA-5088), and the following Long Playing albums: "A Date with Elvis" (RCA LPM-2011); "A Date with Elvis" (RCA LSP-2011 [e]); "The Elvis Presley Sun Collection" (RCA Starcall Hy-1001); "Elvis—The Sun Sessions" (RCA APM1-1675); "The Sun Years" (Sun 1001).

Good Rockin' Tonight. RCA 447-0602. Gold Standard Series re-issue of RCA 20/47-6381.

Good Rocking Tonight. A 33⅓ rpm bootleg LP released in 1974 on the Bopcat label (Bopcat LP-100). "Good Rocking Tonight" featured various unreleased Sun recordings and alternate takes of released recordings. Side 1 featured cuts by Elvis, with Sam Phillips and Elvis talking between cuts, and side 2 featured cuts by Jerry Lee Lewis, Billy Lee Riley, and Warren Smith. Songs included—Side 1: "Good Rockin' Tonight," "My Baby Is Gone," "I Don't Care If the Sun Don't Shine," "Blue Moon of Kentucky," "I'll Never Let You Go (Little Darlin')," "Mystery Train," "I Forgot to Remember to Forget." Side 2: "The Return of Jerry Lee" (break-in), "Savin' It All For You" (Warren Smith), "Milkshake Mademoiselle" (Jerry Lee Lewis), Jerry and the Lord (Studio Discussion), "Great Balls of Fire" (Jerry Lee Lewis), "Rock With Me Baby" (Billy Riley), "Trouble Bound" (Billy Riley).

Good Time Charlie's Got the Blues. Song written and originally recorded by Danny O'Keefe in 1972 (Signpost 70006). It reached #9 on *Billboard*'s Hot 100 chart. Elvis recorded "Good Time Charlie's Got the Blues" in 1973 and it appeared in the Long Playing album "Good Times" (RCA CPL1-0475).

Good Times. RCA CPL1-0475. A 33⅓ rpm Long Playing album released in March 1974. "Good Times" reached #90 on *Billboard*'s Hot LP chart. Songs included—Side 1: "Take Good Care of Her," "Loving Arms," "I Got a Feelin' in My Body" "If That Isn't Love," "She Wears My Ring." Side 2: "I've Got a Thing About You Baby," "My Boy," "Spanish Eyes," "Talk About the Good Times," "Good Time Charlie's Got the Blues."

Gordon, Gale. Actor who played R. W. Hepworth in the 1968 movie *Speedway*. On radio, Gale Gordon played Flash Gordon and, on TV, he is best known for playing the role of Theodore Mooney on "The Lucy Show."

Got a Lot o' Livin' to Do. Song that Elvis sang in the 1957 movie *Loving You*. The film version of the song appeared in the bootleg LPs "Got a Lot o' Livin' to Do" and "Loving You" (Australian). "Got a Lot o' Livin' to Do" was written by Aaron Schroeder and Ben Weisman and appeared in the Extended Play album "Loving You, Volume 2" (RCA EPA-2-1515) and the following Long Playing albums: "Loving You" (RCA LPM-1515); "Loving You" (RCA LSP-1515 [e]); "Elvis: The Other Sides—Worldwide Gold Award Hits, Volume 2" (RCA LPM-6402).

Got a Lot o' Livin' to Do. A 33⅓ rpm bootleg LP released in 1976 on the Pirate label (Pirate 101). The album was pressed in Los Angeles although the album jacket said Malaysia. Songs included—Side 1: *Jailhouse Rock* Soundtrack. Dick Clark Interviews. Side 2: *Loving You* Soundtrack, Vancouver, British Columbia, Concert and Interview.

Got My Mojo Working. Song written and introduced by Muddy Waters (McKinley Morganfield) in 1957 (Chess 1652). Ann

Cole also recorded the song, as did Jimmy Smith in 1966. "Got My Mojo Working," by Elvis, was a studio jam (paired with "Keep Your Hands Off") on June 5, 1970. It appeared in the Long Playing album "Love Letters from Elvis" (RCA LSP-4530).

Goulet, Robert. Ex-Canadian disc jockey and singer who, for some reason, was disliked by Elvis. In 1974 Presley fired a gun at a television because Goulet was on the screen. At the first Muhammad Ali-Sonny Liston Heavyweight Championship fight, February 25, 1964, Goulet sang "The Star-Spangled Banner," forgetting most of the words of the song. In 1966 Robert Goulet starred in the short-lived TV series "Blue Light."

Graceland. Elvis's Memphis home for the last twenty years of his life. The address was 3764 Elvis Presley Blvd., Memphis, Tennessee 38116. Located in the Memphis suburb of Whitehaven (it was annexed by Memphis in 1969), Graceland was purchased by Elvis in March 1957, from Mrs. Ruth Brown Moore, for $100,000. It was built by Dr. Thomas Moore, Ruth's husband, in the early 1940s and named after Mrs. Moore's aunt—Grace Toof.

The two-story mansion was made of tan Tennessee limestone and originally had twenty-three rooms, including five bedrooms. Elvis painted the mansion blue and gold, which glowed at night. Included in the purchase was 13¾ acres of land.

Prior to Elvis's purchase, Graceland had been used as a church. A portable recording studio was brought to Graceland by RCA on two occasions in 1976—February 2–8 and October 29–31. Some of the songs Elvis recorded there include "Way Down," "Pledging My Love," "Moody Blue," and "Solitaire."

Graceland Fan Club of Memphis. An Elvis fan club headed by Harold Loyd, a cousin of Elvis. Address: Graceland Fan Club, 5100 Poplar Ave./Suite 2612, Memphis, Tn. 38137.

Graceland King, The. A 1977 Elvis tribute record by Mack Fishburn on Sweetwood Records (Sweetwood 8012).

Graham, William. Director of the 1969 movie *Change of Habit*.

Grammy Awards. Annual music awards presented by the National Academy of Recording Arts and Sciences, first presented in 1958.

In 1965 alone, singer-composer Roger Miller won five Grammy Awards and in 1966 he won six more, yet Elvis has won only a total of three: 1967—"How Great Thou Art"—Best Sacred Performance; 1972—"He Touched Me"—Best Inspirational Performance; 1974—"How Great Thou Art"—Best Inspirational Performance.

Grand Ole Opry. Country music show founded by the "Solemn Old Judge" George Hays. It originated on radio station WSM on November 28, 1925, being located at Nashville's Ryman Auditorium between 1942 and 1974.

The last song sung there was "Will the Circle Be Unbroken"

152

on March 15, 1974; after that date the show moved to the new Opryland Auditorium. It was on this radio program on September 25, 1954 that Elvis appeared singing "That's All Right, (Mama)" and "Blue Moon of Kentucky." (See: Denny, Jim; Ryman Auditorium)

Grant, Cary. (Real name: Archibald Leach)* Noted Hollywood actor, now retired, who can be seen as a member of the audience in the 1970 documentary *Elvis—That's the Way It Is.*

Grant, Curry. Airman, based in Weisbaden, West Germany, who first introduced Elvis Presley to Priscilla Beaulieu in 1958.

Gray. Color of Priscilla Beaulieu's eyes.

Gray, Joe. Elvis's stand-in for the 1957 movie *Loving You.*

Great Britain. Country that, contrary to popular opinion, Elvis *did* visit. However, the visit was very short. En route to the United States from West Germany (March 3, 1960), Elvis's transport plane landed at Prestwick Airport in Scotland. Elvis briefly stepped off the plane.

Great Debate, The. An Elvis novelty record that featured a cut from "It's Now or Never." "The Great Debate" was recorded by Ron Cameron on Trey Records (Trey 3013).

Great Escape, The. A 1963 historical World War II movie, starring Steve McQueen and James Garner. *The Great Escape* was one of Elvis's favorite movies.

Greatest Star of All, The. A 1977 Elvis tribute record by Skip Jackson on Alaska Records (Alaska 2010).

Great Southern Hawaiian Fruit Company. Firm owned by Fred Gates (Roland Winters), father of Chad Gates (Elvis), in the 1961 movie *Blue Hawaii.*

Greek Orthodox Church Annuclation. Memphis church, located at 573 Highland N., where, supposedly, Elvis and Ginger Alden were to be married on December 25, 1977.

Green Belt. Rank attained by Priscilla Presley in the art of karate. She was taught by Mike Stone. (See: Stone, Mike)

Green, Green Grass of Home. Classic country song written by Claude "Curly" Putnam, Jr., in 1965 and originally recorded by Porter Wagoner. "Green, Green Grass of Home" has been recorded by several artists, including Ferlin Husky and Jerry Lee Lewis (Smash 2006). Tom Jones, however, is the only performer to have a million-seller with the song (London 59002). He first sang "Green, Green Grass of Home" on a TV program in England in 1965. The response was so terrific that he recorded the song in 1966. It reached #1 in the United Kingdom (for six weeks, December 3, 1966–January 14, 1967) and #11 in the U. S.

Elvis recorded "Green, Green Grass of Home" in 1975 and it

---

*TV host Bert Convy, who was a member of the rock 'n' roll group the Cheers in the 1950s, portrayed Cary Grant in the 1963 movie *Act One.*

appeared in the Long Playing albums "Today" (RCA APL1 1039) and "Our Memories of Elvis, Volume 2" (RCA AQL1-3448).

Green, Leroy, Jr. Schoolmate and friend of Elvis at Milam Junior High in Tupelo, Mississippi. Elvis and Leroy Green, Jr., were two of the poorest children attending the school. Today, Leroy Green, Jr., is a disc jockey at Tupelo radio station WELO.

Greenback Dollar, Watch and Chain/Foolish Heart. Sun. 272. Record released in 1957 by Ray Harris. Popular belief has it that Elvis played piano on both of the songs; however, Ray Harris has stated that the piano player was Charlie Rich.

Greene, Shecky. Comedian who was billed above Elvis at the New Frontier Hotel in Las Vegas (April 23–29, 1956).

Greensboro, North Carolina. Site of concert where Elvis embarrassed Kathy Westmoreland and the Sweet Inspirations on stage by stating that if Kathy didn't like the way he introduced her, she could get off the stage.

Greensleeves. Traditional English folksong supposedly written by King Henry VIII. In 1952 Mantovani (Annunzio Paulo Mantovani) successfully made the charts with "Greensleeves" (London 1171). The melody of "Greensleeves" was used for the Elvis song "Stay Away." In the 1969 movie *The Trouble with Girls (And How to Get Into It)*, "Greensleeves" was used as background music in one scene.

Greenwood, Earl. One of Elvis's Army buddies.

Greg Nolan. Elvis's role (as a playboy photographer) in the 1968 movie *Live a Little, Love a Little.*

Gregory, James. Editor of *Movieland* and *TV Time* magazines. James Gregory also edited the 1960 paperback book *The Elvis Presley Story,* published by Hillman Books.

Grenada. Caribbean island that, in 1979, was the first country to honor Elvis on a postage stamp.

Greyhound. Moving van company trailer into which a Volkswagen drove in the 1967 movie *Double Trouble.* Since the scene was supposed to have been set in Belgium, the presence of the Greyhound van is a blooper.

Grimes, Mrs. J. C. (Oleta). Elvis's homeroom teacher in the fifth grade at Lawhon Grammar School in Tupelo, Mississippi (1945–46).

Grob, Dick. Security chief at Graceland and member of the Memphis Mafia. Dick Grob was previously a fighter pilot in the U.S. Air Force and a sergeant in the Palm Springs, California, Police Department.

Grogan's Gaelic Gardens. Hotel, located in the Catskill Mountain town of Cream Valley, that served as a training camp for boxers in the 1962 movie *Kid Galahad.* Walter Gulick (Elvis) served as a sparring partner at the camp before turning professional. Grogan's Gaelic Gardens was called the "Cradle of Champions Since 1917."

Groom, Arthur. Manager of Loew's State Theater in Memphis who fired Elvis in the summer of 1951. The girl who ran the concession stand gave Elvis free samples and the other usher reported him. Elvis punched him and they were both fired.

Grotto, The. Restaurant in the 1962 movie *Girls! Girls! Girls!*

Gruenwald Hotel. German hotel where Davada "Dee" Stanley met Vernon Presley in 1959. They later married, on July 3, 1960.

Guadalajara. Song that Elvis sang in the 1963 movie *Fun in Acapulco*. Both the Jordanaires and the Amigos sang vocal back-up. "Guadalajara" was written by Pepe Guizar and appeared in the following Long Playing albums: "Fun in Acapulco" (RCA LPM/LSP-2756); "Burning Love and Hits from His Movies, Volume 2" (RCA Camden CAS-2595); "Burning Love and Hits from His Movies, Volume 2" (Pickwick CAS-2595); "Elvis—A Legendary Performer, Volume 3" (RCA CPL1-3082).

Guercio, Joe. Orchestra leader whose twenty-eight-member band backed Elvis on his Las Vegas appearances and many of his concert tours.

Guinness Book of World Records. Book of various records first compiled by Norris and Ross McWhirter* in 1956 under the title of *The Guinness Book of Superlatives*. After *The Holy Bible, The Guinness Book of World Records* is the second-best-selling book in history.

Elvis often read the *Guinness* book and is listed in it as having the most Gold Disc awards for an individual—thirty-eight. Guiness also mentions that Elvis probably has surpassed Bing Crosby as being the most successful recording artist of all time.

Guitar City. Title originally considered for the 1968 movie *Speedway*.

Guitar Man. RCA 47-9425. Released in January 1968 as a 45 rpm single. It reached #43 on *Billboard*'s Hot 100 chart. RCA claims a global million-seller for "Guitar Man." "High Heel Sneakers" was on the flip side. "Guitar Man" was written by Jerry Reed, who played lead guitar in this recording. Elvis sang "Guitar Man" in the 1968 NBC-TV special "Elvis." It appeared in the following Long Playing albums: "Clambake" (RCA LPM/LSP-3893); "Elvis—TV Special" (RCA LPM-4088); "Elvis Sings Hits from His Movies, Volume 1" (RCA Camden CAS-2567); "Elvis Sings Hits from His Movies, Volume 1" (Pickwick CAS-2567).

Guitar Man. RCA 447-0663. Gold Standard Series re-issue of RCA 47-9425.

---

*Norris and Ross McWhirter were twins who were born in London in 1925. Norris is twenty minutes older than Ross. Both brothers joined the British Navy in World War II. That was the first time they had ever been separated. They were reunited when the two ships on which they served collided in the Malta Harbor. Ross McWhirter was killed by terrorists on November 27, 1975.

Guitar That Changed the World, The. An Elvis tribute album by Scotty Moore that included twelve Elvis songs. "The Guitar That Changed the World" was released on Epic Records (Epic 24103).

Gumbo Ya Ya. Title originally considered for the 1962 movie *Girls! Girls! Girls!*

Gunfight at the OK Corral. A 1957 fictionalized movie based on the October 26, 1881, gunfight between the Earp brothers (with Doc Holliday) and the McLaury and Clanton clans. *Gunfight at the OK Corral* starred Burt Lancaster and Kirk Douglas. Leon Uris wrote the screenplay.

Elvis attended a Paramount screening of *Gunfight at the OK Corral*, applauding when producer Hal B. Wallis's name appeared on the credits. (See: Faylen, Frank)

H

Haley, Bill. Country turned rock 'n' roll singer of the mid-1950s who performed many R & B hits with an uptempo country beat. Prior to becoming one of the first rock 'n' roll performers, he headed a country band named the Saddlemen* that played boogie-type country music. In 1953 it was Bill Haley and his Comets who first placed a rock 'n' roll record on the *Billboard* charts with "Crazy, Man, Crazy" on Essex Records (Essex 321). Haley's style and sound were by far ahead of anything any other white artist was doing at the time. In 1951 Haley covered "Rocket 88," which was originally recorded by Jackie Brenston on Chess Records (a Sam Phillips production), Bill Haley and Elvis first met in 1955 at a Cleveland auditorium, then again when Haley was touring Europe in 1959.

Hallyday, Johnny. French entertainer known as the "French Elvis." Johnny Hallyday (real name: Jean Philippe Smet) had a million-seller in 1961 with "Let's Twist Again."

Hamblen, Stuart. Singer and composer of country and gospel songs. He appeared on radio and in a number of western movies. In 1952 Stuart Hamblen ran for President of the U.S. on the Prohibition Party ticket. In 1954 he composed the Rosemary Clooney hit "This Old House." Hamblen is the composer of the songs "Known Only to Him" and "It Is No Secret," recorded by Elvis.

---

*The name of Bill Haley's group began as the Downhomers, then the Four Aces of Western Swing, then the Saddlemen, and finally the Comets.

Hamill, Rev. James E. Pastor of the First Assembly of God Church at 1885 McLemore, Memphis, which the Presleys attended. The Reverend Hamill gave the eulogy at Gladys Presley's funeral.

Hamilton, Bill. Brother of actor George Hamilton, he was a fellow student of Elvis at Humes High School.

Hamilton, Dennis. Driver of the hearse (#25) that took Vernon Presley's body from the Memphis Funeral Home to Graceland on June 28, 1979.

Hamilton, Roy. Popular singer during the 1950s-60s. He died of a stroke at age forty on July 20, 1969. Elvis greatly admired Hamilton's singing ability and style and sang a number of his ballads in the style of Hamilton. The two met at the American Sound Studios in January 1969, just months prior to Hamilton's death. There, Elvis gave Hamilton the song "Angelica" for him to record. Roy Hamilton recorded several songs that Elvis would also record: "Hurt" (Epic), 1954; "You'll Never Walk Alone"* (Epic 9015), 1954; "Unchained Melody" (Epic 9102), 1955; "Without a Song" (Epic 9125), 1955; "Pledging My Love" (Epic 9294), 1958.

Hancock, U.S.S. (CVA-19). Naval aircraft carrier on which Milton Berle's TV show was aired on April 3, 1956. Elvis was the featured guest on the show.

Hand, Albert. Founder in 1959 of the newsletter *Elvis Monthly* originating in Great Britain. He died on April 18, 1972.

Haney, Bill. Elvis impersonator from West Memphis, Arkansas, who resembles Elvis.

Hangout. Racing-oriented nightclub where Steve Grayson (Elvis) and Susan Jacks (Nancy Sinatra) sang in the 1968 movie *Speedway*.

Happy Ending. Song that Elvis sang in the 1963 movie *It Happened at the World's Fair*. The Jordanaires back Elvis on this song. Joan O'Brien sang with Elvis in the film. "Happy Ending" was written by Ben Weisman and Sid Wayne and appeared in the Long Playing albums "It Happened at the World's Fair" (RCA LPM/LSP-2697) and "Mahalo from Elvis" (Pickwick CL-7064).

Happy Happy Birthday Baby. Song written by brother-sister team Gilbert J. Lopez and Margo L. Sylvia in 1952 and originally recorded by the Tune Weavers (Checker 872) in 1957. A version by Elvis of "Happy Happy Birthday Baby" appeared on a bootleg 45 rpm Sun Record (Sun 525) in 1977, backed with "Tweedle Dee."

Hank Snow Jamboree Attractions. Management firm operated by Col. Tom Parker in the mid-1950s. Hank Snow was his fea-

---

*The flip side of "You'll Never Walk Alone" was "I'm Gonna Sit Right Down and Cry (Over You)," which Elvis also recorded.

tured star. For a brief time in 1955, Parker directed Elvis's career while he was still under contract to Bob Neal. Parker made the bookings for Neal.

Hank Tyler. Role played by Memphis Mafia member Bobby "Red" West in the 1961 movie *Wild in the Country*.

Harbor Lights. Song composed by Hugh Williams (real name: Will Groz) and Jimmy Kennedy in 1937 and first popularized by Rudy Vallee in the same year. "Harbor Lights" was revived in 1950 by Sammy Kaye (Columbia 38963), becoming one of the top songs of the year. It sold over a million copies of sheet music and was performed twenty-nine times on the TV series "Your Hit Parade." In 1960 the Platters released "Harbor Lights" (Mercury 71563), reaching #8 on the charts.

"Harbor Lights" was used as the recurring theme song of the 1940 John Ford-directed movie *The Long Voyage Home* starring John Wayne. (The movie was based on the short story by Eugene O'Neill.)

Elvis recorded "Harbor Lights" in 1954 at Sun Records. Sun considered the recording to be of inferior quality and never released it. In 1976, RCA Records released the Sun master on the Long Playing album "Elvis—A Legendary Performer, Volume 2" (RCA CPL1-1349).

Hard Headed Woman. RCA 20/47-7280. Released in June 1958 as a 45 rpm single and a 78 rpm single—the last Presley single to be released as a 78 rpm record. It reached #2 on *Billboard*'s Hot 100 chart, #2 on the Country chart, and #2 on the Rhythm and Blues chart. "Don't Ask Me Why" was on the flip side. Elvis sang "Hard Headed Woman" in the 1958 movie *King Creole*. It sold over a million copies and received a Gold Disc award from the R.I.A.A.—Elvis's first such award, received on August 11, 1958. Written by Claude De Metrius, "Hard Headed Woman" appeared in the Extended Play album "A Touch of Gold, Volume 1" (RCA EPA-5088) and the following Long Playing albums: "King Creole" (RCA LSP-1884 [e]); "Elvis: Worldwide 50 Gold Award Hits, Volume 1" (RCA LPM-6401); "Elvis" (RCA DPL2-0056 [e]).

Hard Headed Woman. RCA 447-0623. Gold Standard Series reissue of RCA 47-7280.

Hardin, Glen. Elvis's piano player (1970–76). Hardin left Elvis to become a member of country singer Emmy Lou Harris's Fallen Angel Band. In the 1960s Glen Hardin was a member of Buddy Holly's old group, the Crickets.

Hard Knocks. Song that Elvis sang in the 1964 movie *Roustabout*. "Hard Knocks" was written by Joy Byers and appeared in the Long Playing album "Roustabout" (RCA LPM/LSP-2999).

Hard Luck. Song that Elvis sang in the 1966 movie *Frankie and Johnny*. "Hard Luck" was written by Sid Wayne and Ben Weisman and appeared in the Long Playing albums "Frankie and Johnny" (RCA LPM/LSP-3553) and "Frankie and Johnny" (Pickwick ACL-7007).

Hardy Shoes. Memphis store on Main Street where Elvis bought his boots. When the manufacturer ceased production of the boots, Elvis bought the pattern.

Harem Holiday. European title of the 1965 movie *Harum Scarum*.

Harem Holiday. Song that Elvis sang in the 1965 movie *Harum Scarum*. Written by Peter Andreoli and Vince Poncia, Jr., "Harem Holiday" appeared in the Long Playing album "Harum Scarum" (RCA LPM/LSP-3468).

Harley-Davidson. Make of motorcycle that Elvis preferred to own and ride.

Harman, Buddy. Second drummer, with D.J. Fontana, in "It's Now or Never" and "The Girl Next Door."

Harmony, Dorothy (Dottie) Blond Las Vegas dancer and singer who accompanied Elvis to his pre-induction Army examination at Kennedy Veterans Hospital in Memphis on January 4, 1957.

Harnbar, Barbara. Girl whom Elvis dated in his youth.

Harra, Johnny. Another Elvis impersonator who looks remarkably like Elvis.

Harris, Becky. Tupelo, Mississippi, first-grader who won first prize at the talent show at the Mississippi-Alabama Fair and Dairy Show on October 3, 1945. She sang "Sentimental Journey"* accompanied on piano. Ten-year-old Elvis Presley won second prize. (See: Mississippi-Alabama Fair and Dairy Show)

Harris, Mrs. Weir. Employee of the Tennessee Employment Security, at 122 Union Avenue, who administered to Elvis the GATB tests (General Aptitude Test Battery) on June 3, 1953.

Harrison, George. Lead guitarist of the Beatles until the group's demise in 1970. Harrison then became a solo performer. As a Beatle, George Harrison composed "Something," a song that Elvis recorded in 1973. George Harrison was once sued for plagiarising the 1963 Ronald Mack composition "He's So Fine" for his 1970 hit "My Sweet Lord."

Hart Brake Hotel. Elvis novelty record by Homer and Jethro on RCA Records (RCA 6542).

Hart, Cheryl. Eleven-year-old Schenectady, New York, girl who was dying of aplastic anemia. She made a request for an autographed photo of Elvis. When Elvis heard about the girl he airmailed a photo to her in the hospital at Albany, New York, signing the photo "To Cheryl, God Bless You, Elvis." Upon receiving the photo, she rallied for a short time, but died two weeks later.

Hart, Dolores. Actress who portrayed Elvis's romantic lead, Nellie,

---

*"Sentimental Journey" was the first million-seller for Doris Day and Les Brown and his orchestra (Columbia 36769) in 1945. It later became Les Brown's theme song.

in the 1958 movie *King Creole*. Elvis also dated Dolores Hart for a brief time. In 1959 Photoplay Magazine printed her article "What It's Like to Kiss Elvis."

HARUM SCARUM. MGM: 1965. Premiered Los Angeles November 24, 1965 (85 min). Elvis's nineteenth movie. Producer, Sam Katzman. Director, Gene Nelson. Cast: Johnny Tyronne/Elvis Presley, Princess Shalimar/Mary Ann Mobley, Aishah/Fran Jeffries, Prince Dragna/Michael Ansara, Zacha/Jay Novello, King Toranshah/Philip Reed, Sinan/Theo Marcuse, Baba/Billy Barty, Mokar/Dirk Harvey, Julna/Jack Costanzo, Captain Herat/Larry Chance, Leilah/Barbara Werle, Emerald/Brenda Benet, Sapphire/Gail Gilmore, Amethyst/Wilda Taylor, Sari/Vicki Malkin, Mustapha/Ryck Rydon, Scarred Bedouin/Richard Reeves, Yussef/Joey Russo, Naja/Suzanne Covington, Princess/Maja Stewart, Noble/Ralph Lee, President/Robert Lamont, Ambassador McCord/Hugh Sanders, Cashier/Judy Durell, Songs Sung by Elvis: "Harem Holiday," "Golden Coins," "Go East, Young Man," "Shake That Tambourine," "Mirage," "Hey Little Girl," "So Close, Yet So Far (From Paradise)," "My Desert Serenade," "Kismet." "Animal Instinct" and "Wisdom of the Ages" were deleted in most prints of the film.

Harum Scarum. RCA LPM/LSP-3468. Released in October 1965 as a 33⅓ rpm Long Playing album. "Harum Scarum" reached #8 on *Billboard*'s Hot LP chart and featured songs from the 1965 movie *Harum Scarum* plus two bonus songs. Songs included—Side 1: "Harem Holiday," "My Desert Serenade," "Go East, Young Man," "Mirage," "Kismet," "Shake That Tambourine." Side 2: "Hey Little Girl," "Golden Coins," "So Close, Yet So Far (From Paradise)," "Animal Instinct" (bonus) "Wisdom of the Ages" (bonus).

Have a Happy. Song that Elvis sang in the 1970 movie *Change of Habit*. "Have a Happy" was written by Ben Weisman, Florence Kaye, and Dolores Fuller and appeared in the following Long Playing albums: "Let's Be Friends" (RCA Camden CAS-2408); "Let's Be Friends" (Pickwick CAS-2408); "Elvis Sings for Children (And Grownups Too)" (RCA CPL1-2901).

Have I Told You Lately That I Love You. Song written by Scott Wiseman and first introduced in 1945 by Lulu Belle and Scotty and first recorded by Foy Willings and the Riders of the Purple Sage (Magestic 6000), followed by a number of artists, including Gene Autry (Columbia 20075). Elvis recorded the song in 1957. Later in 1957, Ricky Nelson cut a version of "Have I Told You Lately That I Love You" that was in the same style as Elvis's version. The Jordanaires sang the same vocal back-up for both versions. "Have I Told You Lately That I Love You" appeared in the Extended Play album "Just for You" (RCA EPA-4041) and the Long Playing albums "Loving You" (RCA LPM-1515) and "Loving You" (RCA LSP-1515 [e]).

Have I Told You Lately That I Love You. RCA 47-7066. A 45 rpm disc jockey "record preview." "Mean Woman Blues" was on the flip side. This is the only time that "Have I Told You Lately That I Love You" appeared on a single release.

Having Fun with Elvis on Stage. RCA CPL1-0818. Released in October 1974 as a 33⅓ rpm Long Playing album, "Having Fun with Elvis on Stage" reached #130 on *Billboard's* Hot LP chart and consisted of dialogue from some of Elvis's concerts. There are no songs in the album. Originally, "Having Fun with Elvis on Stage" was issued on the Boxcar label by Col. Parker and was sold only at Elvis's live concerts.

Hawaii. Setting of the Elvis movies *Blue Hawaii* (1961), *Girls! Girls! Girls!* (1962) (New Orleans was originally considered), and *Paradise—Hawaiian Style* (1966).

Hawaiian Beach Boys. Title originally considered for the 1961 movie *Blue Hawaii*.

Hawaiian Eye. Warner Bros. television series (1959–1963) in which two of the stars would later appear in movies with Elvis. Anthony Eisley (Tracy Steele) played Clint Braden in the 1966 movie *Frankie and Johnny*. Poncie Ponce, who played Kim, the taxicab driver, played Juan Medala in the 1968 movie *Speedway*.

Hawaiian Sunset. Song that Elvis sang in the 1961 movie *Blue Hawaii*. Written by Sid Tepper and Roy C. Bennett, "Hawaiian Sunset" appeared in the Long Playing album "Blue Hawaii" (RCA LPM/LSP-2426).

Hawaiian Village Hotel. Honolulu hotel where Elvis stayed in the penthouse suite during the filming of the 1961 movie *Blue Hawaii*. It was previously the hotel where Cricket Blake* (Connie Stevens) sang on the TV series "Hawaiian Eye."

Hawaiian Wedding Song. Song that Elvis sang in the 1961 movie *Blue Hawaii*. Joan Blackman sang with Elvis toward the end of the song. "Hawaiian Wedding Song" was written in 1926 by Charles E. King, under the title "Ke Kali Nei Ou." In 1958 Al Hoffman and Dick Manning wrote the English lyrics and, in 1959, Andy Williams had a million-seller with "Hawaiian Wedding Song" on Cadence Records (Cadence 1358).

Elvis sang "Hawaiian Wedding Song" in the U. S. edition of the worldwide TV concert "Aloha from Hawaii Via Satellite"; however, the song did not appear in the soundtrack album. It later appeared in the "Mahalo from Elvis" album.

"Hawaiian Wedding Song" appeared in the following Long Playing albums: "Blue Hawaii" (RCA LPM/LSP-2426); "Elvis in Concert" (RCA APL2-2587); "Mahalo from Elvis" (Pickwick CL-7064).

Hayes, Lowell. Elvis's Memphis jeweler, from whom he purchased much of his jewelry.

Hearn, Barbara. Memphis girl whom Elvis dated off· and on for

---

*Cricket's back-up band was that of Arthur Lyman, who in 1959 had a hit with "Taboo" (Hi Fi 550).

years (1950s–60s). Barbara Hearn played a bit part in the 1957 movie *Loving You*.

Heartbreak Hotel. RCA 20/47-6420. Released on January 27, 1956, as a 78 rpm single and a 45 rpm single. It reached #1* on *Billboard*'s Hot 100 chart (for six weeks, May 5–June 16), #1 on the Country chart, and #5 on the Rhythm and Blues chart. "Heartbreak Hotel" was the second record in music history to appear on all three *Billboard* charts (Carl Perkins's "Blue Suede Shoes" was the first). It sold over a million copies. "I Was the One" was on the flip side. Elvis introduced "Heartbreak Hotel" on the Dorsey Brothers "Stage Show" on January 28, 1956. Other TV presentations of "Heartbreak Hotel" included: "Stage Show" (March 17, 1956; March 24, 1956); the "Milton Berle Show" (April 3, 1956); the "Ed Sullivan Show" (January 6, 1957); the NBC-TV special "Elvis" (December 3, 1968). He also sang it in the 1970 documentary *Elvis—That's the Way It Is.* "Heartbreak Hotel" was written by Mae Boren Axton and Tommy Durden. They originally offered the song to the Wilburn Brothers, who turned it down. Tommy Durden, after Elvis's death, donated his royalties to the Heart Association. Elvis recorded "Heartbreak Hotel" on January 10, 1956— his first RCA recording session. ("I Got a Woman" was actually the first song put on tape.) Musicians at the sessions were: Elvis (guitar); Chet Atkins (guitar); Scotty Moore (guitar); Floyd Cramer (piano); Bill Black (bass); D. J. Fontana (drums). "Heartbreak Hotel" appeared in the Extended Play album "Heartbreak Hotel" (RCA EPA-821) and the following Long Playing albums: "Elvis' Golden Records" (RCA LPM-1707); "Elvis' Golden Records" (RCA LSP-1707 [e]); "Elvis-TV Special" (RCA LPM-4088); "Elvis' Worldwide 50 Gold Award Hits, Volume 1" (RCA LPM-6401); "Elvis as Recorded at Madison Square Garden" (RCA LSP-4776); "Elvis—A Legendary Performer, Volume 1" (RCA CPL1-0341).

Heartbreak Hotel. RCA EPA-821. This was a 45 rpm Extended Play album released in May 1956. It reached #75 on *Billboard*'s Hot 100 chart and #5 on the Extended Play chart. Songs included—Side 1: "Heartbreak Hotel," "I Was the One." Side 2: "Money Honey," "I Forgot to Remember to Forget."

Heartbreak Hotel. RCA 447-0605. Gold Standard Series re-issue of RCA 20/47-6420.

Heart of Rome. RCA 47-9998. Released in August 1971 as a 45 rpm single. "I'm Leavin'" was on the flip side. "Heart of Rome" was written by Geoff Stephens, Alan Blaikley, and Ken Howard and appeared in the Long Playing album "Love Letters from Elvis" (RCA LSP-4530)

Heart of Rome. RCA 447-0683. Gold Standard Series re-issue of RCA 47-9998.

*In August 1979, Willie Nelson and Leon Russell had a #1 country hit with "Heartbreak Hotel" (Columbia 3-11023).

Hebler, Dave. Karate champion and bodyguard of Elvis since 1974. Elvis once gave Hebler a $10,000 Mercedes Benz 280SL.

He Is My Everything. Religious song written by Dallas Frazier based on his composition "There Goes My Everything." Elvis recorded "He Is My Everything" in 1971 and it appeared in the Long Playing albums "He Touched Me" (RCA LSP-4690) and "He Walks Beside Me" (RCA AFL1-2772).

He Knows Just What I Need. Religious song written by Mosie Lister and recorded by Elvis in 1960. "He Knows Just What I Need" is sometimes called "Jesus Knows What I Need." It appeared in the Long Playing albums "His Hand in Mine" (RCA LPM/LSP-2328) and "His Hand in Mine" (RCA ANL1-1319). (See: Hess, Jake)

Helden (1914-1918). Steinfurth, Germany, World War I War Memorial that Elvis helped to move to another location while he was a soldier in the U.S. Army.

He Lives. A 1977 Elvis tribute record by Tarry Westley on Chapman Records (Chapman 118).

Heller, Ron. Ex-USC football player who was one of the more experienced men to play on Elvis's football team in the Los Angeles area.

He'll Have to Go. Song written by Joe and Audrey Allison and originally recorded by Jim Reeves (RCA 7643) in 1959. "He'll Have to Go" reached #2 on the charts and sold over 3 million copies. Elvis recorded "He'll Have to Go" in 1976 at Graceland and it appeared in the Long Playing album "Moody Blue" (RCA AFL1-2428).

Hell on Wheels. Motto of the U. S. Army Second Armored Tank Division, with which Elvis served in Germany.

Helm, Anne. Female lead (as Holly Jones) in the 1962 movie *Follow That Dream.*

Help Me. RCA APBO-0280. Released in May 1974 as a 45 rpm single. It reached #6 on *Billboard*'s Hot 100 chart. "If You Talk in Your Sleep" was on the flip side. "Help Me" was written by Larry Gatlin for Elvis and appeared in the Long Playing albums "Elvis Recorded Live on Stage in Memphis" (RCA CPL1-0606) and "Promised Land" (RCA APL1-0873).

Help Me Make It Through the Night. Song written by Kris Kristofferson and originally recorded by Sammi Smith (Mega* 615-0015) in 1971. "Help Me Make It Through the Night" reached #8 on the charts and sold over 2 million copies. It received two Grammy Awards: Best Country Vocal (Female) Performance of 1971 and Best Country Song of 1971. Elvis recorded "Help Me Make It Through the Night" in May 1971 and it appeared in the Long Playing albums "Elvis—Now" (RCA LSP-4671) and "Welcome to My World" (RCA APL1-2274).

---

*"Help Me Make It Through the Night" was the first release on Mega Records.

Henley, Tish. Dr. George Nicopoulus's nurse who served as Elvis's private nurse on his tours.

Herald, The. Humes High School yearbook. The 1953 edition of the yearbook included Elvis's picture along with the following entry: Presley, Elvis Aron. Major: Shop, History, English. Activities: R.O.T.C., Biology Club, English Club, History Club, Speech Club.

Here Comes Santa Claus (Right Down Santa Claus Lane). Christmas song written by Gene Autry and Oakley Haldeman and originally recorded by Autry in 1947. "Here Comes Santa Claus (Right Down Santa Claus Lane)" (Columbia 37942) reached #1 on the charts in December 1947 and sold over a million copies. Elvis recorded "Here Comes Santa Claus (Right Down Santa Claus Lane)" in 1957 and it appeared in the Extended Play album "Christmas with Elvis" (RCA EPA-4340) and the following Long Playing albums: "Elvis' Christmas Album" (RCA LOC-1035); "Elvis' Christmas Album" (RCA LPM-1951); "Elvis' Christmas Album" (RCA LSP-1951 [e]); "Elvis' Christmas Album" (RCA Camden CAL-2428); "Elvis' Christmas Album" (Pickwick CAS-2428); "The Brightest Stars of Christmas" (RCA DLP1-0086).

Here Come the Kwimpers. Title originally considered for the 1967 movie *Follow That Dream*.

Here's to the King. A 1977 Australian Elvis tribute record by Josh Morgan on Fable Records (Fable 310).

Heron, Pat. Reporter who interviewed Elvis in the library of the U.S.S. *General Randall* on September 22, 1958.

Hess, Jake. Leader of the Statesmen Quartet. James Blackwood, leader of another gospel group, the Blackwood Brothers, believes that Elvis borrowed his gospel singing style from Jake Hess. Elvis's style of singing "He Knows Just What I Need" is very similar to a version once recorded by Hess with the Statesmen.

He's Your Uncle, Not Your Dad. Song that Elvis sang in the 1968 movie *Speedway*. The film version has additional voices and instrumentations. "He's Your Uncle, Not Your Dad" was written by Sid Wayne and Ben Weisman and appeared in the Long Play album "Speedway" (RCA LSP-3989).

He Touched Me. RCA 74-0651. Released in March 1972 as a 45 rpm single. "Bosom of Abraham" was on the flip side. This record was first released with a 45 rpm center hole, but it played at 33⅓ rpm. RCA released 10,000 copies before finding the error and recalling the released copies. "He Touched Me" was written by William J. Gaither and appeared in the Long Playing album "He Touched Me" (RCA LSP-4690).

He Touched Me. RCA LSP-4690. Released in April 1972 as a 33⅓ rpm Long Playing album. It reached #79 on *Billboard*'s Hot LP chart. "He Touched Me" won a Grammy Award for Best Inspirational Performance of 1972. Songs included—Side

1: "He Touched Me," "I've Got Confidence," "Amazing Grace," "Seeing Is Believing," "He Is My Everything," "Bosom of Abraham." Side 2: "An Evening Prayer," "Lead Me, Guide Me," "There Is No God But God," "A Thing Called Love," "I, John," "Reach Out to Jesus."

He Walks Beside Me. RCA AFL1-2272. Released in 1978 as a 33⅓ rpm Long Playing album. Songs included—Side 1: "He Is My Everything," "Miracle of the Rosary," "Where Did They Go, Lord," "Somebody Bigger Than You and I," "An Evening Prayer," "Impossible Dream." Side 2: "If I Can Dream," "Padre," "Known Only to Him," "Who Am I," "How Great Thou Art."

Hey, Hey, Hey. Song that Elvis sang in the 1967 movie *Clambake*. "Hey, Hey, Hey" was written by Joy Byers. It appeared in the Long Playing album "Clambake" (RCA LPM/LSP-3893).

Hey Jude. Seven-minute, eleven-second song written by John Lennon and Paul McCartney, originally titled "Hey Jules" (after John Lennon's son, Julian). "Hey Jude" (Apple 2276) was the first 45 rpm record to be released on the Apple Record label. It reached #1 on the charts (for nine weeks, September 28–November 30, 1968) and sold over 7½ million copies. "Hey Jude" has been recorded by several artists, including Tom Jones, Wilson Pickett, and Bing Crosby. Elvis recorded "Hey Jude" in 1969 and it appeared in the Long Playing album "Elvis—Now" (RCA LSP-4691).

Heyland, Anne. Former Miss Texas; Elvis dated her briefly.

Hey, Little Girl. Song that Elvis sang in the 1965 movie *Harum Scarum*. Written by Joy Byers, "Hey, Little Girl" appeared in the Long Playing album "Harum Scarum" (RCA LPM/LSP-3468).

Hey Memphis. Recorded by LaVern Baker in 1961 (Atlantic 2119) as a takeoff on Elvis's "Little Sister." The tune is the same as "Little Sister" although the lyrics have been changed.

Hey, Mr. Presley. Song recorded by Peter de Bree and the Wanderers and by Jimmy Gartin and the Swingers on Fortune Records in 1956. It took the form of a biographical thank-you.

Hezekiah. The Tatum family's hound dog in the 1964 movie *Kissin' Cousins*.

Hibbler, Al. Blind baritone singer who sang with Duke Ellington's band in the 1940-50s. In 1955 he recorded his biggest hit record with *"Unchained Melody"* (from the 1955 movie *Unchained**). In 1977 Elvis recorded "Unchained Melody."

Hickock, Al. Corpus Christie, Texas, disc jockey for radio station KEYS, who in 1956 interviewed Elvis in San Antonio at the

---

*Unchained was one of three movies in which football great Elroy "Crazy Legs" Hirsh appeared. The others were *Crazy Legs* (1953) and *Zero Hour!* (1957).

County Coliseum. The interview was offered on a 78 rpm record only on the KEYS Record label in 1956.

Hickory Log. The meeting place in Memphis for Elvis fans and celebrities since 1976. Located across the street from Graceland (3795 Elvis Presley Blvd.), it was previously called Loeb's Barbecue. It is owned by Hobert and Bonnie Burnette, who enjoy talking to the thousands of Elvis fans.

Hidden Rock. North Carolina town in which Josh Morgan (Elvis) was born (1964 movie *Kissin' Cousins*).

High Heel Sneakers. RCA 47-9425. Released in January 1968 as a 45 rpm single. "Guitar Man" was on the flip side. "High Heel Sneakers" was written by Robert Higgbotham in 1964 and recorded by him under the name of Tommy Tucker (Checker 1067). Using a different spelling, "Hi-Heel Sneakers" reached #11 on the charts. Elvis's version of "High Heel Sneakers" never appeared on an RCA album.

High Heel Sneakers. RCA 447-0663. Gold Standard Series reissue of RCA 47-9425.

High, Milo. Pilot of Elvis's Jet Commander.

High Tension Grove. Dance hall where Glen Tyler (Elvis) took Betty Lee (Millie Perkins) to a dance (1961 movie *Wild in the Country*).

Highway Beverage. Distributor for which Deke Rivers (Elvis) worked in Delville (1957 movie *Loving You*).

Hill, David. Singer/composer who did many Elvis demonstration records for writers because he sounded like Elvis. He also co-composed "That's When Your Heartaches Begin" and "I Got Stung."

Hill and Range Music Company. Publishing company founded by brothers Gene and Julian Aberbach. Elvis became a part owner in the company. Lamar Fike once worked for Hill and Range.

Hillbilly Cat "Live," The. A 1970 bootleg double LP featuring songs from Elvis's 1969 Las Vegas shows. Songs included—Side 1: "That's All Right," "I Got a Woman," "Tiger Man," "Love Me Tender," "I've Lost You," "I Just Can't Help Believin'." Side 2: "You've Lost That Loving Feeling," "Polk Salad Annie," "Johnny B. Goode," "The Wonder of You," "Heartbreak Hotel," "One Night." Side 3: "All Shook Up," "Blue Suede Shoes," "Whole Lotta Shakin' Goin' On," "Hound Dog," "Bridge Over Troubled Water," "Suspicious Minds," "Release Me," "Can't Help Falling in Love." Side 4: "I Got a Woman," "Ave Maria," "Polk Salad Annie," "Heartbreak Hotel," "One Night," "Hound Dog," "When the Snow Falls on the Roses."

Hillbillycat 1954–1974, The, Volume 1. Bootleg LP, released on the Brookville label, that featured songs from two of Elvis's appearances on the "Ed Sullivan Show" and some unreleased RCA material. Songs included—Side 1: "Don't Be Cruel" ("Ed Sullivan Show," September 9, 1956), "Love Me Tender" ("Ed Sullivan Show," September 9, 1956), "Ready Teddy"

("Ed Sullivan Show", September 9, 1956), "Hound Dog" ("Ed Sullivan Show," September 9, 1956), "Don't be Cruel" ("Ed Sullivan Show," October 28, 1956), "Love Me Tender" ("Ed Sullivan Show," October 28, 1956), "Love Me" (Ed Sullivan Show," October 28, 1956). Side 2: "Rags to Riches," "First Time Ever I Saw Your Face," "It's Only Love," "The Sound of Your Cry," "Come What May," "Where Did They Go, Lord," "Let Me."

Hillbilly Cat 101A. A 45 rpm bootleg single release of two of Elvis's songs. The record featured "That's All Right (Mama)" b/w "My Baby's Gone." "My Baby's Gone" was a slower, bluesier version of "I'm Left, You're Right, She's Gone." Credit on the record label was given to "Scotty & Bill."

Hillbilly Cat, The. Name under which Elvis was billed in late 1954 and early '55.

Hillbilly Cat, The. A 45 rpm bootleg Extended Play album released by Rockin' Records (Rockin' 45-002). Songs included— Side 1: "Jailhouse Rock" (soundtrack), "The Truth About Me" (*TV Guide* interview). Side 2: "The Lady Loves Me" (Ann-Margret from *Viva Las Vegas* soundtrack), "Trying to Get to You."

Hi-Lo. Sam Phillips's BMI Publishing Company that owned the publishing rights to *Blue Suede Shoes* and *Mystery Train*, among numerous other Sun songs. On November 22, 1955, Hill and Range Music, owned by brothers Jean and Julian Aberbach, purchased, for $15,000, Hi-Lo Music, from Sam Phillips. "I Forgot to Remember to Forget" was the only Hi-Lo song of which Hill and Range did not acquire full ownership, as Arnold Shaw had previously purchased half of the song's publishing rights.

Hi Records. Memphis record label founded by Joe Cuoghi, on which Bill Black recorded. Willie Mitchell was the label's producer. Recording was done at the Royal Recording Studios, 1320 S. Lauderdale, Memphis. The offices were at Poplar Tunes. The label became a subsidiary of the British-owned London Records.

Hirsch Memorial Coliseum. Location of Elvis's last "Louisiana Hayride" appearance, on December 17, 1955. The performance was a benefit for the Shreveport Y.M.C.A.

His Hand in Mine. RCA 74-0130. Released in April 1969 as a 45 rpm single. "How Great Thou Art" was on the flip side. RCA claims that "His Hand in Mine" sold over a million copies. It appeared in the Long Playing albums "His Hand in Mine" (RCA LPM/LSP-2328) and "His Hand in Mine" (RCA ANL1-1319).

His Hand in Mine. RCA 447-0670. Gold Standard Series re-issue of RCA 74-0130.

His Hand in Mine. RCA LPM/LSP-2328. A 33⅓ rpm Long Play album that was released in December, 1960. It reached #13 on

Billboard's Hot LP chart and had retail sales totaling over $1 million. A Gold Disc award from the R.I.A.A. was presented in 1969. RCA claims that over 500,000 copies of "His Hand in Mine" have been sold. It was Elvis's first religious album. In March 1976 it was deleted from RCA's catalog and re-issued as ANL1-1319. Songs included—Side 1: "His Hand in Mine," "I'm Gonna Walk Dem Golden Stairs," "In My Father's House," "Milky White Way," "Known Only to Him," "I Believe in the Man in the Sky." Side 2: "Joshua Fit the Battle," "He Knows Just What I Need," "Swing Down Sweet Chariot," "Mansion Over the Hilltop," "If We Never Meet Again," "Working on the Building."

His Hand in Mine. RCA ANL1-1319. This 33⅓ rpm Long Playing album is the Pure Gold Series re-issue of the deleted LPM/LSP-2328. It was released in March 1976 and included the same songs as LPM–LSP-2328.

(Marie's the Name) His Latest Flame. RCA 47-7908. Released in August 1961 as a 45 rpm single. It reached #4 on *Billboard*'s Hot 100 chart and #1 in the United Kingdom (for three weeks, November 4–25, 1961). "Little Sister" was on the flip side. "(Marie's the Name) His Latest Flame" sold over a million copies. Written by Doc Pomus and Mort Shuman, (Marie's the Name) His Latest Flame," by Elvis, appeared in the Long Playing albums "Elvis' Golden Records, Volume 3" (RCA LPM/LSP-2765) and "Elvis: The Other Sides—Worldwide Gold Award Hits, Volume 2" (RCA LPM-6402).

(Marie's the Name) His Latest Flame. RCA 447-0634. Gold Standard Series re-issue of RCA 47-7908.

(Elvis) His Legend's Still Alive or It's Great to Have an Idol Part I/ Part II. A 1977 tribute song to Elvis recorded by Ray Hebel on the Encore label (Encore 1775).

Hits Made Famous by Elvis Presley. Elvis tribute album by the Hollyridge Strings on Capitol Records (Capitol ST 2221).

Hits of Elvis and Jim Reeves. Album by the Nashville Singers on Mountain Dew Records (Mountain Dew 7029).

HMV. British record label that released Elvis's records in the United Kingdom until September 30, 1958, after which RCA established their own label. HMV stands for "His Master's Voice" and was a subsidiary of British Decca. Elvis had fourteen singles, two EPs, one ten-inch LP, and two twelve-inch LPs released by HMV.

Hodge, Charlie. Five-foot-three-inch rhythm guitarist, an aide to Elvis. Prior to joining Elvis, Hodge was a member of the Foggy River Boys on Red Foley's TV show, "Ozark Jubilee." He first met Elvis in 1956 during a Red Foley show. The two became good friends while both were in the Army at Fort Hood and again in Germany. They both were on board the U.S.S. *General Randall* enroute to Germany. He supervised the musical aspects of Elvis's life. Charlie Hodge was one of the three witnesses to

Elvis's will. (See: Last Will and Testament) He drove Elvis and Priscilla to Baptist Memorial Hospital the day Lisa Marie was born. At concerts he handed Elvis the silk scarves that Elvis would give to the women in the audience. Charlie Hodge played a barber in the 1967 movie *Clambake*. Charlie Hodge styled Elvis's hair for Elvis's funeral.

Hodges, Eddie. Child actor who played a delivery boy in the 1968 movie *Live a Little, Love a Little*. Hodges played the son of Frank Sinatra in the 1959 movie *A Hole in the Head*. As a contestant on the TV quiz show "Name That Tune" during the early 1960s Hodges won $25,000. (His partner was future astronaut John Glenn.)

Hoffman, Dr. Lester. Dentist whose office is located at 920 Estate Street in Memphis. Elvis and Ginger Alden went to his office to get a cavity filled for Elvis on the last night of his life, August 15–16, 1977.

Holdridge, Cheryl. Child actress who played Julie Foster, Wally's girlfriend, on "Leave It to Beaver." She was a former Mickey Mouse Club Mouseketeer. In 1962 she dated Elvis. Other "famous" Mouseketeers: Cubby O'Brien—became the drummer for the Carpenters. Doreen Tracey—niece of comic Ben Blue. Johnny Crawford—appeared on the TV series "The Rifleman," and became a recording artist. Don Grady—appeared on the TV series "My Three Sons." Bobby Burgess—became lead male dancer on the "Lawrence Welk Show." Paul Peterson—appeared on the "Donna Reed Show"; professional writer-recording artist. Tommy Ivo—became highly successful dragster record holder. Annette Funicello—star of numerous beach-party movies; recording artist; TV commercials. Big Moosketeer Roy Williams—was the designer of the Navy Seabees' and Flying Tigers' insignia.

Holiday Inn. Song sung by Elvis as a spoof of *Heartbreak Hotel*. He sang it on June 23, 1973, at the Nassau Coliseum in Uniondale, Long Island.

Holiday Inn Records. Record label started in 1968 by Sam Phillips and Buddy Cunningham (former Sun Artist). Phillips named the label after the hotel chain that was founded in Memphis in 1952 and named for the 1942 Bing Crosby movie *Holiday Inn.** Phillips had an investment in the hotel chain. Ex-Sun artist Charlie Feathers recorded for the label.

Holloway, Sterling. Actor who played the milkman in the 1968 movie *Live a Little, Love a Little*. Holloway was the first actor drafted into the U. S. Army during World War II. His voice can be heard in the Puppy Chow and Shout commercials.

Holly, Buddy. Popular rock 'n' roll singer (real name: Charles Hardin Holley) of the 1950s. Born in Lubbock, Texas, on

---

*It was in *Holiday Inn* that Bing Crosby first sang "White Christmas," the biggest-selling song of all time.

September 7, 1936, Buddy first met Elvis when Elvis played there at the Cotton Club on October 15, 1955. Buddy, with his friend Bob Montgomery, opened the show. The pair hosted the "Buddy and Bob Show" on KDAV radio.* Buddy recorded the following Elvis songs: "Love Me"; "You're So Square (Baby I Don't Care)"; "Good Rockin' Tonight"; "Blue Suede Shoes"; "Ready Teddy"; "Shake, Rattle and Roll"; "Rip It Up." Buddy Holly was killed in a private plane crash on February 3, 1959, in which Richie Valens (often billed as the next Elvis) and Jiles Perry Richardson (the Big Bopper) were also victims. Waylon Jennings, a member of Holly's Crickets, gave up his seat to Richardson before the flight; Dion, who was offered a ride, decided to take the bus. At Fargo, North Dakota, a local talent named Robert Velline filled in for the now-missing artists. Robert Velline would one day find success as Bobby Vee. Elvis sent a telegram to the Hollys' home in Lubbock, Texas, upon learning about the death of Buddy.

Holly Leaves and Christmas Trees. Christmas song written for Elvis by Red West. Elvis recorded "Holly Leaves and Christmas Trees" in 1971 and it appeared in the Long Playing albums "Elvis Sings the Wonderful World of Christmas" (RCA LSP-4579) and "Elvis Sings the Wonderful World of Christmas" (RCA ANL1-1936).

Hollywood Knickerbocker Hotel. Hotel, located at Ivar Ave. and Hollywood Blvd., at which Elvis and his parents first stayed while he was filming *Love Me Tender*. Elvis rented the entire eleventh floor.

Hollywood or Bust. Movie starring Dean Martin and Jerry Lewis with Anita Ekberg. In the movie a billboard advertising Elvis's appearances at the New Frontier Hotel in Las Vegas in 1956 can be seen in a background scene.

Hollywood Party. Elvis novelty record by Dick Bush on Era Records (Era 1067). Elvis is mentioned in the lyrics.

Hollywood Walk of Fame. Plaques set in cement in Hollywood to commemorate the actors and actresses who made a contribution to the arts of motion pictures, televison, radio, and related fields. Elvis Presley's star is located on Hollywood Blvd. near Highland Ave.

Home Is Where the Heart Is. Song that Elvis sang in the 1962 movie *Kid Galahad*. The movie version is mellower than that released on record. "Home Is Where the Heart Is" was written by Sherman Edwards and Hal David and appeared in the Extended Play album "Kid Galahad" (RCA EPA-4371) and the Long Playing albums "I Got Lucky" (RCA Camden CAL-2533) and "I Got Lucky" (Pickwick CAS-2533).

***

*KDAV (580KC) in 1953 became the first radio station to broadcast nothing but country music. In 1958 Waylon Jennings became a DJ for KDAV prior to joining Buddy Holly's Crickets.

Home Is Where the Heart Is. RCA SP 45-18. Special 45 rpm promotional release. "King of the Whole Wide World" was on the flip side.

Home of the Blues. Ruben Cherry's record store on Beale Street in Memphis, where in the early 1950s Elvis purchased many 78 rpm records by rhythm and blues artists. The name of the store may have inspired Johnny Cash, Lily McAlpin, and Glen Douglas to compose the 1957 Johnny Cash recording of "Home of the Blues" (Sun 279).

Honda 350. Motorcycle that Charlie Rogers (Elvis) rode in the 1964 movie *Roustabout*.

Honolulu International Center. Site of the "Elvis: Aloha from Hawaii" concert on January 14, 1973, which was broadcast around the world via satellite.

Honorary Colonel. Honorary rank conferred upon Elvis in 1961 by the governor of Tennessee.

Hookstratten, E. Gregory. The Presleys' family lawyer who represented Elvis during his divorce proceedings in Los Angeles.

Hookstratten has also represented Dan Rowan, Dick Martin, and Vince Scully.

Hopper, Ed. Memphis filling-station manager whom Elvis was accused of assaulting on October 18, 1956. Elvis had stopped at the station, a crowd gathered, and Hopper told Elvis to move. Witnesses said Hopper then hit Elvis on the back of the head. A fight ensued and 6' 4" Aubry Brown, a second attendant, joined the fight. Elvis was cleared of the charge and both men were fired.

Hopper, Hedda. Hollywood gossip columnist, known for her exotic hats, who once wrote in her column that Elvis was a menace to society and a threat to innocent children. Her son, William Hopper, played Detective Paul Drake on the television series "Perry Mason." He also appeared in the 1955 movie *Rebel Without a Cause.*

Horses. Many of Elvis's horses were boarded in a barn called the "House of Rising Sun" (named after Elvis's favorite horse) at Graceland. At one time or another the following horses were owned by Elvis: Rising Sun (Elvis's favorite), Colonel Midnight (Vernon Presley's horse), Lady, Golden Sun, Scout (same name as Tonto's horse), Flaming Star (named after the movie), Sheba, Thundercloud, El Poco, Beauty (same name as the horse that appeared in the movies *Johnny Guitar* and *Giant*), Traveler (same name as Robert E. Lee's horse), Keno, Buckshot (same name as Wild Bill Hickok's horse on the TV series of the same name), Sun Down, Star Trek, Domino, Mare Ingram (named for the Memphis mayor).

Hot Dog. Song that Elvis sang in the 1957 movie *Loving You.* The film version of "Hot Dog" appeared in the bootleg LPs "Got a Lot o' Livin' to Do" and "Loving You" (Australian). It was written by Jerry Leiber and Mike Stoller and appeared in the Extended Play album "Loving You, Volume 2" (RCA EPA2 -1515) and the following Long Playing albums: "Loving You" (RCA LPM-1515); "Loving You" (RCA LSP-1515 [e]); "Elvis: The Other Sides—Worldwide Gold Award Hits, Volume 2" (RCA LPM-6402).

Hound Dog. RCA 20/47-6604. Released in July 1956 as a 78 rpm single and a 45 rpm single. "Hound Dog" reached #2 on *Billboard*'s Hot 100 chart, #1 on the Country chart, and #1 on the Rhythm and Blues chart. It reached #2 in the United Kingdom. "Don't Be Cruel" was on the flip side. "Hound Dog" b/w "Don't Be Cruel" sold over 9 million copies. "Hound Dog" was written by Jerry Leiber and Mike Stoller in 1952 and originally recorded by Willie Mae "Big Mama" Thornton (Peacock 1612) in 1953. Mama Thornton record labels originally credited the back-up band to Kansas City Bill's Orchestra (although in actuality it was Johnny Otis's band). Tommy Duncan, former lead singer for the Bob Wills Orchestra, also recorded "Hound Dog" (Intro 6071) in 1953. Still another version of "Hound Dog" was recorded in 1953 on Checker Records by John Brim. It was titled "Rattlesnake" (Checker 769). Elvis's version of the song was influenced by Freddie Bell and the Bellboys. (See: Bell, Freddie and the Bellboys) "Hound Dog" was recorded on July 2, 1956, at RCA's New York City studios. It was the very first song on which the Jordanaires sang back-up for Elvis. Elvis sang "Hound Dog" on the following TV programs: "The Milton Berle Show" (June 5, 1956); "The Steve Allen Show" (July 1, 1956); "The Ed Sullivan Show" (September 9, 1956; October 28, 1956; January 6, 1957); "Elvis" (NBC-TV special, December 3, 1968); "Elvis: Aloha from Hawaii" (worldwide, January 14, 1973; NBC-TV, April 3, 1973); "Elvis in Concert" (CBS-TV, October 3, 1977). "Hound Dog" appeared in the following Extended Play albums: "Heartbreak Hotel" (RCA EPA-821); "Elvis Presley" (RCA SPD-23); "The Real Elvis" (RCA EPA-940); "The Real Elvis" (RCA EPA-5120), and the following Long Playing albums: "Elvis' Golden Records" (RCA LPM-1707); "Elvis' Golden Records" (RCA LSP-1707 [e]); "Elvis—TV Special" (RCA LPM-4088); "From Memphis to Vegas"/"From Vegas to Memphis" (RCA LSP-6020); "Elvis in Person" (RCA LSP-4428); "Worldwide 50 Gold Award Hits, Volume 1" (RCA LPM-6401) "Elvis as Recorded at Madison Square Garden" (RCA LSP-4776); "Elvis: Aloha from Hawaii Via Satellite" (RCA VPSX-6089); "Elvis" (RCA DPS2-0056 [e]); "Elvis Recorded Live on Stage in Memphis" (RCA CPL1-0606).

Hound Dog. RCA 447–0608. Gold Standard Series re-issue of RCA 20/47-6604.

Hound Dog Aftershave. One of the hundreds of Elvis-related products manufactured by Factors, Inc.

Hound Dog Man (Play It Again). A 1977 Elvis novelty record by

Lenny Le Blanc on the Big Tree record label (Big Tree 16062).

Hound Dog Man's Gone Home, The. A 1977 Elvis tribute record by Lee and Lowe on Music Mill Records (Music Mill 1011).

Hound Dog Man's Gone Home. A 1977 Elvis tribute record by Arthur Alexander on Music Mill Records (Music Mill 1012).

Hound Dog One. Call sign of the *Lisa Marie* Convair 880 jet.

Hound Dog Two. Call sign of Elvis's Jet Star aircraft.

House of Sand. Song that Elvis sang in the 1966 movie *Paradise, Hawaiian Style*. "House of Sand" had a different beginning in the film. A different take appeared on record. "House of Sand" was written by Bill Giant, Bernie Baum, and Florence Kaye and appeared in the Long Playing album "Paradise, Hawaiian Style" (RCA LPM/LSP-3643).

House That Has Everything, A. Song that Elvis sang in the 1967 movie *Clambake*. The film version had added instrumentation. "A House That Has Everything" was written by Sid Tepper and Roy C. Bennett and appeared in the Long Playing album "Clambake" (RCA LPM/LSP-3893).

Houston, David. Country singer who made his debut on the "Louisiana Hayride" in 1955, playing on the same bill as Elvis. David Houston had a #1 record with "Almost Persuaded" in 1968. He previously recorded a record on the Sun label, "Sherry's Lips"/"Miss Brown" (Sun 403).

Hovatar Alice. Nineteen-year-old Monroe, Louisiana, girl who was killed during an all-night vigil at the gate of Graceland on August 18, 1977—the day of Elvis's funeral. A car driven by Treatise Wheeler III, of Memphis, drove through the crowd, killing Ms. Hovatar and Juanita Joan Johnson. Wheeler was charged with drunk driving and second-degree murder. (See: Baiter, Tammy)

Howard, Edwin. Reporter with the *Memphis Press-Scimitar*. Howard was the first reporter to interview Elvis (on July 27, 1954).

Howard, Frances Humphrey. Sister of the late Hubert Horatio Humphrey, vice-president of the U. S. Frances Howard appeared in the 1967 movie *Clambake*.

How Can You Lose What You Never Had. Song that Elvis recorded for the 1967 movie *Clambake* but was cut from the final print. "How Can You Lose What You Never Had" was written by Sid Wayne and Ben Weisman. It appeared in the Long Playing album "Clambake" (RCA LPM/LSP-3893).

How Do You Think I Feel. Song written by Wayne P. Walker and Webb Pierce and originally recorded by Pierce. Elvis recorded "How Do You Think I Feel" in 1956 and it appeared in the Extended Play album "Strictly Elvis" (RCA EPA-994) and the Long Playing albums "Elvis" (RCA LPM-1382) and "Elvis" (RCA LSP-1382 [e]).

How Great Thou Art. RCA 74-0130. Released in April 1969 as a 45 rpm single. "His Hand in Mine" was on the flip side. "How Great Thou Art"* was written in 1886 by a Swedish minister, the Rev. Carl Boberg, using the title "O Store Gud" ("Oh Great God"). It was translated into German and published in 1907 under the title "Wie Gross Bist Du" ("How Great Thou Art"). English missionary Rev. Stuart K. Hine found a Russian version of the song while in the Ukraine and translated it into English. Elvis sang "How Great Thou Art" on the 1977 CBS-TV special "Elvis in Concert." "How Great Thou Art" appeared in the following Long Playing albums: "How Great Thou Art" (RCA LPM/LSP-3758); "Elvis Recorded Live on Stage in Memphis" (RCA CPL1-0606); "Elvis—A Legendary Performer, Volume 2" (RCA CPL1-1349); "Elvis in Concert" (RCA APL2-2587); "He Walks Beside Me" (RCA AFL1-2772).

How Great Thou Art. RCA 447-0670. Gold Standard Series reissue of RCA 74-0130.

How Great Thou Art. RCA SP-45-162. Special 45 rpm promotional release. "So High" was on the flip side.

How Great Thou Art. RCA LPM/LSP-3758. Released in March 1967 as a 33⅓ rpm Long Playing album. It reached #18 on *Billboard*'s Hot LP chart. "How Great Thou Art" achieved sales of over $1 million, qualifying it for a Gold Record. The album also received Grammy Awards for Best Sacred Performance of 1967 and Best Inspirational Performance of 1974. Songs included—Side 1: "How Great Thou Art," "In the Garden," "Somebody Bigger Than You and I," "Farther Along," "Stand By me," "Without Him." Side 2: "So High," "Where Could I Go But to the Lord," "By and By," "If the Lord Wasn't Walking by My Side," "Run On," "Where No One Stands Alone," "Crying in the Chapel."

How's the World Treating You. Song written by Chet Atkins and Boudleaux Bryant. Elvis recorded "How's the World Treating You" in 1956 and it appeared in the Extended Play album "Strictly Elvis" (RCA EPA-994) and the Long Playing albums "Elvis" (RCA LPM-1382) and "Elvis" (RCA LSP-1382 [e]).

How the Web Was Woven. Song written by Clive Westlake and David Most. Elvis sang "How the Web Was Woven" in the 1970 documentary *Elvis—That's the Way It Is*, and it appeared in the Long Playing album "Elvis—That's the Way It Is" (RCA LSP-4445).

How Would You Like to Be. RCA 47-8950. Released in November 1966 as a 45 rpm single. "If Every Day Was Like Christmas" was on the flip side. Elvis sang "How Would You Like to

*Gospel singer Rev. James Cleveland recorded "How Great Thou Art" on an album for Savoy Records in 1960; the organist on the record was thirteen-year-old Billy Preston.

Be" in the 1963 movie *It Happened at the World's Fair*. It was written by Ben Raleigh and Mark Barman and appeared in the following Long Playing albums: "It Happened at the World's Fair" (RCA LPM/LSP-2697); "Elvis Sings Hits from His Movies, Volume 1" (RCA CAS-2567); "Elvis Sings for Children (And Grownups Too)" (RCA SPL1-2901).

How Would You Like to Be. RCA 447-0681. Gold Standard Series re-issue of RCA 47-8950.

Hugueny, Sharon. Actress whom Elvis dated in 1963. Sharon Hugueny had previously been married to Robert Evans (1961–'62), the head of Paramount Studios.

Humbard, Rev. Rex. Minister in Akron, Ohio and host of "Cathedral of Tomorrow" T.V. series (543 stations) who spoke briefly at Elvis's funeral (August 18, 1977).

Humes High School. Memphis high school, located at 659 N. Manasas Street, that Elvis attended. In 1950 Elvis was a library worker. Elvis graduated from the all-white Humes High* on June 3, 1953. The school is presently used as a junior high. The school was named for Laurence Carl Humes, past president of the Memphis Board of Education (1918–'25). Prior to Humes, the school was named North Side High School.

Humes High Tigers. Name of the Humes High football team. In the fall of 1951 Elvis attended a few practices for the team, and then quit after the coach gave him a hard time about his hair. The coach of the football team was Rube Boyce, Jr.

Hunt, Dr. William R. Physician who delivered Elvis and his still-born brother, Jesse, on January 8, 1935. The birth took place at the Presleys' home.

Hunter, Ivory Joe. Blues singer and composer born in Kirbyville, Texas. He was the seventh of thirteen children. His biggest hits were "I Almost Lost My Mind" (MGM 10578) and "Since I Met You Baby" (Atlantic 1111). Elvis recorded two Ivory Joe Hunter compositions: "My Wish Came True" and "I Need You So." He was the composer of "Ain't That Lovin' You Baby" (with Clyde Otis), which Elvis recorded in 1958. Hunter also recorded demos for Elvis.

Hurt. RCA PB-10601. Released in March 1976 as a 45 rpm single. It reached #20 on *Billboard*'s Hot 100 chart, #6 on the Country chart, and sold over a million copies. "For the Heart" was on the flip side. "Hurt"† was written by Jimmy Craine and Al Jacobs and originally recorded by Roy Hamilton (Epic

---

*Over on the other side of Memphis, Booker T. Jones and Maurie White, future drummer for Ramsey Lewis and leader of Earth, Wind and Fire, respectively, were classmates in the same grade school. Booker T. would later attend Booker T. Washington High, where his father taught math and science. Both Johnny Ace and Rufus Thomas had also previously attended Washington High.
†In 1967 the Italian singer Fausto Leal had a #1 hit and million-seller with "A Chi," Italian for "Hurt." It was released on the Italian RiFi label.

9086) in 1954. In 1961 Timi Yuro had a version of "Hurt" (Liberty 55343) that reached #4 on the charts. "Hurt" appeared in the Long Playing albums "From Elvis Presley Boulevard, Memphis, Tennessee" (RCA APL1-1506) and "Elvis in Concert" (RCA APL2-2587).

Husky Dusky Day. Song that Elvis and Hope Lange sang as a duet in the 1961 movie *Wild in the Country.* "Husky Dusky Day" was never released by RCA in any form, as it was not a complete song.

Hutchins, Will. Actor who played police officer Lt. Tracy Richards in the 1966 movie *Spinout* and Tom Wilson in the 1967 movie *Clambake.* He previously starred in the 1957–60 TV series "Sugarfoot" (titled "Tenderfoot" in Britain). In the movie *Clambake* Elvis sang a duet with Will Hutchins (it's not actually Hutchins's voice that's heard) on "Who Needs Money."

Hutchinson, Ron. Elvis impersonator from England.

Hyland, Brian. Singer who did many demonstration records for composers because he could sound like Elvis. Hyland's previous hits include "Itsy Bitsy Teenie Weenie Yellow Polka Dot Bikini" (Kapp 342) (1960), "Gypsy Woman" (UNI 55240) (1970), and "Sealed with a Kiss" (ABC Paramount 10336) (1962).

I

I Beg of You. RCA 20/47-7510. Released in December 1957 as a 78 rpm single and a 45 rpm single. It reached #8 on *Billboard*'s Hot 100 chart, #2 on the Country chart, and #4 on the Rhythm and Blues chart. "I Beg of You" sold over a million copies. "Don't" was on the flip side. It took Elvis thirty-four takes to get a satisfactory recording of "I Beg of You." It was written by Rose Marie McCoy and Kelly Owens and appeared in the Extended Play album "A Touch of Gold, Volume 1" (RCA EPA-5088) and the following Long Playing albums: "50,000,000 Elvis Fans Can't Be Wrong—Elvis' Gold Records, Volume 2" (RCA LPM-2075); "50,000,000 Elvis Fans Can't Be Wrong—Elvis' Gold Records, Volume 2" (RCA LSP-2075 [e]); "Elvis: Worldwide 50 Gold Award Hits, Volume 1" (RCA LPM-6401); "Elvis" (RCA DPL2-0056 [e]).

I Beg of You. RCA 447-0621. Gold Standard Series re-issue of RCA 20/47-7510.

I Believe. Song written by Ervin Drake, Irvin Graham, Jimmy Shirl, and Al Stillman and introduced by Jane Froman in her TV series, "Jane Froman's U.S.A. Canteen," in 1953. Her recording of "I Believe"* (Capitol 2332) reached #11 on *Billboard*'s Hot 100 chart. Frankie Laine had an even bigger hit with "I Believe" (Columbia 39938) in 1953, reaching #2 and selling over a million copies. Elvis recorded "I Believe" in 1957 and it appeared in the Extended play albums "Peace in the Valley" (RCA EPA-4054) and "Peace in the Valley" (RCA EPA-5121) and the following Long Playing albums: "Elvis' Christmas Album" (RCA LOC-1035); "Elvis' Christmas Album" (RCA LPM-1951); "Elvis' Christmas Album" (RCA LSP-1951 [e]); "You'll Never Walk Alone" (RCA Camden CASX-2472); "You'll Never Walk Alone" (Pickwick CAS-2472).

I Believe in the Man in the Sky. RCA 447-0643. Released in April 1965 as a 45 rpm Gold Standard Series original. "Crying in the Chapel" was on the flip side. "I Believe in the Man in the Sky" was written by Richard Howard and appeared in the following Long Playing albums: "His Hand in Mine" (RCA LPM/LSP-2338); "Elvis: The other Sides—Worldwide Gold Award Hits, Volume 2" (RCA LPM-6402); "His Hand in Mine" (RCA ANL1-1319).

I Can Help. Song written and originally recorded by Billy Swan (Monument 8621) in 1974. "I Can Help" reached #1 on *Billboard*'s Hot 100 chart and sold over a million copies. Elvis recorded "I Can Help" in 1975 and it appeared in the Long Playing albums "Today" (RCA APL1-1039) and "Our Memories of Elvis, Volume 2" (RCA AQL1-3448).

I Can't Stop Loving You. Song written and originally recorded by Don Gibson (RCA 7133) in late 1957. "I Can't Stop Loving You"† by Gibson sold over a million copies, as did Ray Charles's version (ABC Paramont 10330) in 1962. Ray Charles's version was the #1 song of the year in 1962. Elvis sang "I Can't Stop Loving You" in the 1973 TV special "Elvis: Aloha from Hawaii," and it appeared in the following Long Playing albums (all versions were recorded live): "From Memphis to Vegas"/"From Vegas to Memphis" (RCA LSP-6020); "Elvis in Person" (RCA LSP-4428); "Elvis as Recorded at Madison Square Garden" (RCA LSP-4776); "Elvis Recorded Live on Stage in Memphis" (RCA CPL1-0606); "Welcome to My World" (RCA APL1-2274).

I.C. Costume Company. Firm from which Elvis bought his jumpsuits and costumes for his Las Vegas appearances.

I Don't Care If the Sun Don't Shine. Sun 210. Released on September 25, 1954, as a 78 rpm single and a 45 rpm single. "Good Rockin' Tonight" was on the flip side. "I Don't Care If the Sun Don't Shine" was written by Mack David in 1949.

---

*"I Believe" was the first song to become a hit directly because of television exposure.

†The flip side of Don Gibson's "I Can't Stop Loving You" was "Oh Lonesome Me," a two-sided hit for Gibson.

(Marion Keisker added a verse to the song.) Georgia Gibbs had a popular version (Coral 60210) in 1951. Buddy Cunningham played the bongos (actually, it was an empty record box) on Elvis's recording.

I Don't Care If the Sun Don't Shine. RCA 20/47-6381. A 78 rpm and a 45 rpm re-issue of the Sun original (Sun 210). "I Don't Care If the Sun Don't Shine" appeared in the Extended Play album "Any Way You Want Me" (RCA EPA-965) and the following Long Playing albums; "The Elvis Presley Sun Collection" (RCA Starcall Hy-1001); "Elvis—The Sun Sessions" (RCA APM1-1675); "The Sun Years" (Sun 1001).

I Don't Care If the Sun Don't Shine. RCA 447-0602. Gold Standard Series re-issue of RCA 20/47-6381.

I Don't Know It. Original title of "That's All Right (Mama)" when the song's composer, Arthur Crudup, first recorded it, in the 1940s.

I Don't Wanna Be Tied. Song that Elvis sang in the 1962 movie *Girls! Girls! Girls!* It was written by Bill Giant, Bernie Baum, and Florence Kaye and appeared in the Long Playing album "Girls! Girls! Girls!" (RCA LPM/LSP-2621).

I Don't Want Bracelets or Diamonds, I Want Elvis Instead. Christmas novelty song about Elvis recorded by Mary Kaye on Warner Bros. Records.

I Don't Want To. Song that Elvis sang in the 1962 movie *Girls! Girls! Girls!* It was written by Janice Torre and Fred Spielman and appeared in the Long Playing album "Girls! Girls! Girls!" (RCA LPM/LSP-2621).

I Don't Want to be Another Good Luck Charm. Record by Jo that made reference to Elvis. It was released on Capitol Records (Capitol 4745).

I Dreamed I Was Elvis. A novelty record by Sonny Cole and the Rhythm Roamers on the Rollin' Rock label (Rollin' Rock 001).

I Feel So Bad. RCA 47-7880. Released in May 1961 as a 45 rpm single. It reached #5 on *Billboard*'s Hot 100 chart and #15 on the Rhythm and Blues chart. "I Feel So Bad" sold over a million copies. "Wild in the Country" was on the flip side. "I Feel So Bad" was written and originally recorded by Chuck Willis (Okeh 7029) on September 17, 1953. "I Feel So Bad" appeared in the Long Playing albums "Elvis' Golden Records, Volume 3" (RCA LPM/LSP-2765) and "Elvis: Worldwide 50 Gold Award Hits, Volume 1" (RCA LPM-6401).

I Feel So Bad. RCA 447-0631. Gold Standard Series re-issue of RCA 47-7880.

I Feel So Bad. RCA 37-7880. A 33⅓ rpm single release. "Wild in the Country" was on the flip side.

I Feel So Bad. RCA 61-7880. A 45 rpm "Living Stereo" release. "Wild in the Country" was on the flip side.

I Feel That I've Known You Forever. Song that Elvis sang in the

1965 movie *Tickle Me.* "I Feel That I've Known You Forever" was written by Doc Pomus and Alan Jeffries. It was actually recorded three years before the movie was filmed (March 19, 1962). "I Feel That I've Known You Forever" appeared in the Extended Play album "Tickle Me" (RCA EPA-4383) and the Long Playing album "Pot Luck" (RCA LPM/LSP-2523).

If Every Day Was Like Christmas. RCA 47-8950. Released in November 1966 as a 45 rpm single. "How Would You Like to Be" was on the flip side. Some sources indicate that "If Every Day Was Like Christmas" sold over a million copies. It was written by Red West and Glen Spreen and appeared in the Long Playing albums "Elvis' Christmas Album" (RCA Camden CAL-2428) and "Elvis' Christmas Album" (Pickwick CAS-2428).

If Every Day Was Like Christmas. RCA 447-0681. Gold Standard Series re-issue of RCA 47-8950.

If I Can Dream. RCA 47-9670. Released in 1968 as a 45 rpm single. It reached #12 on *Billboard's* Hot 100 chart and sold over a million copies. "Edge of Reality" was on the flip side. "If I Can Dream" was written especially for Elvis's 1968 NBC-TV special by W. Earl Brown. It was the closing song for the special. "If I Can Dream" appeared in the following Long Playing albums: "Elvis—TV Special" (RCA LPM-4088); "Elvis: Worldwide 50 Gold Award Hits, Volume 1" (RCA LPM-6401); "Elvis—A Legendary Performer, Volume 2" (RCA CPL1-1319); "He Walks Beside Me" (RCA AFL1-2772).

If I Can Dream. RCA 447-0668. Gold Standard Series re-issue of RCA 47-9670.

If I Get Home on Christmas Day. Christmas song written by McCaulay and recorded by Elvis in 1971. "If I Get Home on Christmas Day" appeared in the Long Playing albums "Elvis Sings the Wonderful World of Christmas" (RCA LSP-4579) and "Elvis Sings the Wonderful World of Christmas" (RCA ANL1-1936).

If I'm a Fool (For Loving You). Song written by Stan Kesler and recorded by Elvis in 1969 at the American Sound Studios in Memphis. "If I'm a Fool (For Loving You)" appeared in the Long Playing albums "Let's Be Friends" (RCA Camden CAS-2408) and "Let's Be Friends" (Pickwick CAS-2408).

If It Wasn't for Elvis. A 1977 Elvis tribute record by Deke Rivers and the Hansen Brothers. It was released by Paul, Dale, Tom and Ray Records (001).

If I Were You. Song written by Gerald Nelson and recorded by Elvis in 1970. "If I Were You" appeared in the Long Playing album "Love Letters from Elvis" (RCA LSP-4530).

I Forgot to Remember to Forget. Sun 223. Released in August 1955 as a 78 rpm single and a 45 rpm single. It reached #1 on *Billboard's* Country chart and remained on the chart for forty weeks—the longest that any Presley single would remain on the charts. "Mystery Train" was on the flip side. "I Forgot to Remember to Forget" was written by Stanley A. Kesler and Charlie Feathers.

I Forgot to Remember to Forget. RCA 20/47-6383. A 78 rpm single and a 45 rpm re-issue (in November 1955) of the Sun original (Sun 223). "Mystery Train"/"I Forgot to Remember to Forget" was Elvis's first RCA release. "I Forgot to Remember to Forget" appeared in the Extended Play album "Heartbreak Hotel" (RCA EPA-821) and the following Long Playing albums: "A Date with Elvis" (RCA LPM-2011); "A Date with Elvis" (RCA LSP-2011 [e]); "The Elvis Presley Sun Collection" (RCA Starcall Hy-1001); "Elvis—The Sun Sessions" (RCA APM1-1675); "The Sun Years" (Sun 1001).

I Forgot to Remember to Forget You. RCA 447-0600. Gold Standard Series re-issue of RCA 20/47-6383.

If That Isn't Love. Song written by Dottie Rambo and recorded by Elvis in 1973 at the Stax Studios in Memphis. "If That Isn't Love" appeared in the Long Playing album "Good Times" (RCA CPL1-0475).

If the Lord Wasn't Walking By My Side. Gospel song written by Henry Slaughter and recorded by Elvis in 1966. "If the Lord Wasn't Walking By My Side" appeared in the Long Playing album "How Great Thou Art" (RCA LPM/LSP-3758).

If We Never Meet Again. Gospel song written by A.E. Brumley and recorded by Elvis in 1960. "If We Never Meet Again" appeared in the Long Playing albums "His Hand in Mine" (RCA LPM/LSP-2328) and "His Hand in Mine" (RCA ANL1-1319).

If You Don't Come Back. Song written by Jerry Leiber and Mike Stoller and originally recorded by the Drifters (Atlantic 2191) in 1963. Elvis recorded "If You Don't Come Back" in 1973 at the Stax Studios in Memphis. It appeared in the Long Playing album "Raised on Rock"/"For Ol' Times Sake" (RCA APL1-0388).

If You Don't Know. Record by George Hamilton that mentioned Elvis in the lyrics. "If You Don't Know" was on the flip side of his hit record "A Rose and a Baby Ruth." It was released by ABC Records (ABC Paramount 9765) in 1956.

If You Love Me (Let Me Know). Song written by John Rostill and originally recorded by Olivia Newton-John in 1974. "If You Love Me (Let Me Know)" (MCA 40209) reached #5 on *Billboard*'s Hot 100 chart and sold over a million copies. Elvis recorded "If You Love Me (Let Me Know)" in 1977 and it appeared in the Long Playing album "Moody Blue" (RCA AFL1-2428).

If You Talk in Your Sleep. RCA APBO-0280. Released in May 1974 as a 45 rpm single. It reached #17 on *Billboard*'s Hot 100 chart and #6 on the Country chart. "Help Me" was on the flip side. "If You Talk in Your Sleep" was written by Red

West and Johnny Christopher and appeared in the Long Playing album "Promised Land" (RCA APL1-0873).

If You Talk in Your Sleep. RCA 6PB-10157. Gold Standard Series original that was released in January 1975. Though "If You Talk in Your Sleep" had been released as a single previously (RCA APBO-0280), this Gold Standard Series issue had a different flip side, "Raised on Rock," making it a different record.

If You Think I Don't Need You. Song that Elvis sang in the 1964 movie *Viva Las Vegas.* "If You Think I Don't Need You" was written by Red West and Joe Cooper and appeared in the Extended Play album "Viva Las Vegas" (RCA EPA-4382) and the following Long Playing albums: "I Got Lucky" (RCA Camden CAL-2533); "I Got Lucky" (Pickwick CAS-2533); "Double Dynamite" (Pickwick DLC-5001).

I Got a Feelin' in My Body. RCA PB-11679. Released in August 1979 as a 45 rpm single. It reached #6 on *Billboard*'s Hot Country chart. "There's a Honky Tonk Angel (Who Will Take Me In)" was on the flip side. "I Got a Feelin' in My Body" was written by Dennis Linde and appeared in the Long Playing albums "Good Times" (RCA CPL1-0475) and "Our Memories of Elvis, Volume 2" (RCA AQL1-3448).

I Got a Sweetie. Title used in place of "I Got a Woman" on Elvis albums released in Great Britain in 1956.

I Got a Woman. RCA 20/47-6637. Released in September 1956 as a 78 rpm single and a 45 rpm single. "I'm Counting on You" was on the flip side. "I Got a Woman" (under the original title, "I've Got A Woman") was written and originally recorded by Ray Charles at radio station WGST in Atlanta on the grounds of Georgia Tech (Atlantic 1050) in 1954. Ray Charles had based the song on the gospel tune "My Jesus Is All the World I Need." It was the first song that Elvis recorded with RCA (January 10, 1956). Elvis sang "I Got a Woman" on his third "Stage Show" appearance (February 11, 1956) and in the 1972 documentary *Elvis on Tour.* In Great Britain "I Got a Woman" was released as "I Got a Sweetie." It appeared in the following Extended Play albums: "Elvis Presley" (RCA EPA-247); "Elvis Presley" (RCA EPB-1254); "Elvis Presley" (RCA SPD-22); "Elvis Presley" (RCA SPD-23); and the following Long Playing albums: "Elvis Presley" (RCA LPM-1254); "Elvis Presley" (RCA LSP-1254 [e]); "Elvis Recorded Live on Stage in Memphis" (RCA CPL1-0606); "Pure Gold" (RCA ANL1-0971).

I Got a Woman. RCA 447-0610. Gold Standard Series re-issue of RCA 20/47-6637.

I Got a Woman. RCA 47-6689. A 45 rpm disc jockey "record preview." "Money Honey" was on the flip side. On the regular release, RCA 20/47-6637, "I'm Counting on You" was on the flip side.

I Got Lucky. Song that Elvis sang in the 1962 movie *Kid Galahad*. Written by Dolores Fuller, Fred Wise, and Ben Weisman, "I Got Lucky" appeared in the Extended Play album "Kid Galahad" (RCA EPA-4371) and the Long Playing albums "I Got Lucky" (RCA Camden CAL-2533) and "I Got Lucky" (Pickwick CAS-2533).

I Got Lucky. Camden CAL-2533. A 33⅓ rpm Long Playing album released in November 1971. It reached #104 on *Billboard*'s Hot LP chart. Songs included—Side 1: "I Got Lucky," "What a Wonderful Life," "I Need Somebody to Lean On," "Yoga Is as Yoga Does," "Riding the Rainbow." Side 2: "Fools Fall in Love," "The Love Machine," "Home Is Where the Heart Is," "You Gotta Stop," "If You Think I Don't Need You."

I Got Lucky. Pickwick CAS-2533. A 33⅓ rpm Long Playing album that was a re-issue of RCA Camden Cal-2533. "I Got Lucky" was released in December 1975.

I Got Stung. RCA 47-7410. Released in October 1958 as a 78 rpm single and a 45 rpm single. It reached #8 on *Billboard*'s Hot 100 chart and #1 in the United Kingdom (for five weeks, January 24–February 22, 1959). "I Got Stung" sold over a million copies. "One Night" was on the flip side. Written by Aaron Schroeder and David Hill, "I Got Stung" appeared in the following Long Playing albums: "50,000,000 Elvis Fans Can't Be Wrong—Elvis' Gold Records, Volume 2" (RCA LPM-2075); "50,000,000 Elvis Fans Can't Be Wrong—Elvis' Gold Records, Volume 2" (RCA LSP-2075 [e]); "Elvis: Worldwide 50 Gold Award Hits, Volume 1" (RCA LPM-6401); "Elvis" (RCA DPL2-0056 [e]).

I Got Stung. RCA 447-0624. Gold Standard Series re-issue of RCA 47-7410.

I Gotta Know. RCA 47-7810. Released in November 1960 as a 45 rpm single. It reached #20 on *Billboard*'s Hot 100 chart and sold over a million copies. "Are You Lonesome Tonight" was on the flip side. Written by Paul Evans and Matt Williams, "I Gotta Know" appeared in the Long Playing albums "Elvis' Golden Records, Volume 3" (RCA LPM/LSP-2765) and "Elvis: Worldwide Gold Award Hits, Volume 1" (RCA LPM-6401).

I Gotta Know. RCA 447-0629. Gold Standard Series re-issue of RCA 47-7810.

I Gotta Know. RCA 61-7810. A 45 rpm "Living Stereo" release. "Are You Lonesome Tonight" was on the flip side.

I, John. Gospel song written by William Johnson, George McFadden, and Ted Brooks. Elvis recorded "I, John" in 1971 and sang it with the Stamps (backstage) in the 1972 documentary *Elvis on Tour*. "I, John" appeared in the Long Playing album "He Touched Me" (RCA LSP-4690).

I Just Can't Help Believin'. Song written by Barry Mann and

Cynthia Weil and originally recorded by B. J. Thomas (Scepter 12283) in 1970. Elvis sang "I Just Can't Help Believin' " in the 1970 documentary *Elvis—That's the Way It is,* and it appeared in the Long Playing album "Elvis—That's the Way It Is" (RCA LSP-4445).

I Just Wanted to Know. A 1978 Elvis tribute record by Ronnie McDowell and the Jordanaires on Scorpion Records (Scorpion 0553).

I'll Be Back. Song that Elvis sang in the 1966 movie *Spinout.* The film version has added instrumentation and is longer than that on record. "I'll Be Back" was written by Sid Wayne and Ben Weisman and appeared in the Long Playing album "Spinout" (RCA LPM/LSP-3702).

I'll Be Home for Christmas. Christmas song written by Walter Kent, Kim Gannon, and Buck Ram and originally recorded by Bing Crosby in 1943. Crosby's record reached #3 on the charts and sold over a million copies. Elvis recorded "I'll Be Home for Christmas" in 1957 and it appeared in the Extended Play album "Elvis Sings Christmas Songs" (RCA EPA-4108) and the following Long Playing albums: "Elvis' Christmas Album" (RCA LOC-1035); "Elvis' Christmas Album" (RCA LPM-1951); "Elvis' Christmas Album" (RCA LSP-1951 [e]); "Elvis' Christmas Album" (RCA Camden CAL-2428); "Elvis' Christmas Album" (RCA CAS-2428).

I'll Be Home on Christmas Day. Christmas song written by Michael Jarrett and recorded by Elvis in 1971. "I'll Be Home on Christmas Day" appeared in the Long Playing albums "Elvis Sings the Wonderful World of Christmas" (RCA LSP-4569) and "Elvis Sings the Wonderful World of Christmas" (RCA ANL1-1936).

I'll Be There (If Ever You Want Me). Song written by Gabbard and Price and originally recorded by Bobby Darin (Atco 6167) in 1960. Tony Orlando recorded "I'll Be There (If You Ever Want Me)" (Epic 9622) in 1963. It wasn't until 1964 that a successful version of the song was recorded by Gerry and the Pacemakers (Laurie 3279). It reached #14 on *Billboard*'s Hot 100 chart. Elvis recorded "I'll Be There (If Ever You Want Me)" in 1969 at the American Sound Studios in Memphis. It appeared in the following Long Playing albums: "Let's Be Friends" (RCA Camden CAS-2408); "Let's Be Friends" (Pickwick CAS-2408); "Double Dynamite" (Pickwick DL2-5001).

I'll Hold You in My Heart (Till I Can Hold You in My Arms). Country song written by Eddy Arnold, Hal Horton, and Tommy Dilbeck and originally recorded by Eddy Arnold (RCA 2332) in 1947. It eventually sold over a million copies. Elvis recorded "I'll Hold You in My Heart (Till I Can Hold You in My Arms)" at the American Sound Studios in Memphis in 1969. It appeared in the Long Playing album "From Elvis in Memphis" (RCA LSP-4155).

I'll Never Fall in Love Again. Song written by Jim Currie and Lonnie Donegan and originally recorded by Tom Jones in 1967. "I'll Never Fall in Love Again" (London 59003) was re-issued in 1969, reaching #6 on *Billboard*'s Hot 100 chart; it sold over a million copies. Elvis recorded "I'll Never Fall in Love Again" at Graceland in 1976 and it appeared in the Long Playing album "From Elvis Presley Boulevard, Memphis, Tennessee" (RCA APL1-1506).

I'll Never Know. Song written by Fred Karger, Ben Weisman, and Sid Wayne and recorded by Elvis in 1970. "I'll Never Know" appeared in the Long Playing album "Love Letters from Elvis" (RCA LSP-4530).

I'll Never Let You Go (Little Darlin'). RCA 20/47-6638. Released in September 1956 as a 78 rpm single and a 45 rpm single. "I'm Gonna Sit Right Down and Cry (Over You)" was on the flip side. Elvis recorded "I'll Never Let You Go (Little Darlin') at the Sun studios in January 1955. It was written and originally recorded by Jimmy Wakeley (Decca 5973). "I'll Never Let You Go (Little Darlin')" appeared in the following Extended Play albums: "Elvis Presley" (RCA EPB-1254); "Elvis Presley" (RCA SPD-22); "Elvis Presley" (RCA SPD-23); and the following Long Playing albums: "Elvis Presley" (RCA LPM-1254); "Elvis Presley" (RCA LSP-1254 [e]); "The Elvis Presley Sun Collection" (RCA Starcall Hy-1001); "Elvis—The Sun Sessions" (RCA APM1-1675).

I'll Never Let You Go (Little Darlin'). RCA 447-0611. Gold Standard Series re-issue of RCA 20/47-6638.

I'll Never Stand in Your Way. Song written by Fred Rose and Clint Horner in 1941. Joni James had a hit with "I'll Never Stand In Your Way" (MGM 11606) in the early 1950s. On January 4, 1954, Elvis recorded "I'll Never Stand in Your Way" at the Memphis Recording Service, along with "Casual Love Affair." The two songs were recorded on a ten-inch acetate and cost four dollars. (See: Keisker, Marion; Memphis Recording Service; Phillips, Sam)

I'll Remember You. Song written by Hawaiian composer Kuiokalani Lee. Elvis sang "I'll Remember You" in the 1973 TV special "Elvis: Aloha from Hawaii." It appeared in the Long Playing albums "Spinout" and "Elvis' Aloha from Hawaii Via Satellite" (RCA VPSX-6089).

I'll Take Love. Song that Elvis sang in the 1967 movie *Easy Come, Easy Go.* Written by Dolores Fuller and Mike Barkan, "I'll Take Love" appeared in the Extended Play album "Easy Come, Easy Go" (RCA EPA-4387) and the Long Playing albums "C'mon Everybody" (RCA Camden CAL-2518) and "C'mon Everybody" (Pickwick CAS-2518).

I'll Take You Home Again, Kathleen. Song written by Thomas P. Westendorf in 1876. It was based on the popular ballad "Barney, Take Me Home Again." I'll Take You Home Again,

Kathleen" was the theme song of the radio series "Orphans of Divorce." Through the years it has been recorded by several artists, including Dean Hudson (Okeh 1671) and Bradley Kincaid* (Bluebird 5569). Elvis recorded "I'll Take You Home Again, Kathleen" in 1974 and it appeared in the Long Playing album "Elvis" (RCA APL1-0283).

I'll Wait Forever. Song recorded in 1958 by Anita Wood—Elvis's girlfriend at the time. Recorded on the Sun label (Sun 361), "I'll Wait Forever" concerned Elvis's induction into the Army and Anita Wood pledging to "wait forever" for his return.

I Love Only One Girl. Song that Elvis sang in the 1967 movie *Double Trouble.* The film version is longer and has added instrumentation. Written by Sid Tepper and Roy C. Bennett, "I Love Only One Girl" appeared in the following Long Playing albums: "Double Trouble" (RCA LPM-LSP-3787); "Burning Love and Hits from His Movies, Volume 2" (RCA Camden CAS-2595); "Burning Love and Hits from His Movies, Volume 2" (Pickwick CAS-2595).

I Love You Because. RCA 20/47-6639. Released in September 1956 as a 78 rpm single and a 45 rpm single. "Tryin' to Get to You" was on the flip side. "I Love You Because" was written and originally recorded by Leon Payne (Capitol 40238) in 1949. Al Martino had a big hit with the song in 1963 (Capitol 4930), as did Jim Reeves (RCA 10557) in 1964, Reeves's version sold over a million copies. "I Love You Because" was the first song Elvis sang at a commercial recording session—July 5, 1954. It appeared in the Extended Play album "Elvis Presley" (RCA EPA-830) and the following Long Playing albums: "Elvis Presley" (RCA LPM-1254); "Elvis Presley" (RCA LSP-1254 [e]); "Elvis—A Legendary Performer, Volume 1" (RCA CPL1-0341); "The Elvis Presley Sun Collection" (RCA Starcall Hy-1001); "Elvis—The Sun Sessions" (RCA APM1-1675); "The Sun Years" (Sun 1001).

I Love You Because. RCA 447-0612. Gold Standard Series reissue of RCA 20/47-6639.

I'm Comin' Home. Song written by Charlie Rich for Carl Mann (Phillips International 3555) in 1960. Elvis recorded "I'm Coming Home" in 1961 using Carl Mann's phrasing. (Floyd Cramer copied the piano-playing from Mann's recording.) "I'm Coming Home" appeared in the Long Playing album "Something for Everybody" (RCA LPM/LSP-2370).

I'm Counting on You. RCA 20/47-0637. Released in September 1956 as a 78 rpm single and a 45 rpm single. "I Got a Woman" was on the flip side. Elvis recorded "I'm Counting on You" on January 11, 1956. It was written by Don Robertson and

---

*Bradley Kincaid was a regular member of the "Grand Ole Opry." On the "Opry" he was billed as the Kentucky Mountain Boy with His Houn' Dog Guitar.

appeared in the Extended Play albums "Elvis Presley" (RCA EPB-1254), (RCA SPD-22) and "Elvis Presley" (RCA SPD-23), and the Long Playing albums "Elvis Presley" (RCA LPM-1254) and "Elvis Presley" (RCA LSP-1254 [e]).

I'm Counting on You. RCA 447-0610. Gold Standard Series re-issue of RCA 20/47-0637.

I'm Counting on You. RCA 47-6492. A 45 rpm disc jockey "record preview." "Blue Suede Shoes" was on the flip side. On the regular release, RCA 20/47-0637, "I Got a Woman" was on the flip side.

I Met Her Today. Song written by Don Robertson and Hal Blair and recorded by Elvis in 1961. "I Met Her Today" appeared in the following Long Playing albums: "Elvis for Everyone" (RCA LPM/LSP-3450); "Separate Ways" (RCA Camden CAS-2611); "Separate Ways" (Pickwick CAS-2611).

I'm Falling in Love Tonight. Song that Elvis sang in the 1963 movie *It Happened at the World's Fair*. The Mello Men back Elvis on this song. "I'm Falling in Love Tonight" was written by Don Robertson and appeared in the Long Playing album "It Happened at the World's Fair" (RCA LPM/LSP-2697).

I'm Gonna Sit Right Down and Cry (Over You). RCA 20/47-6638. Released in September 1956 as a 78 rpm single and a 45 rpm single. "I'll Never Let You Go (Little Darlin')" was on the flip side. "I'm Gonna Sit Right Down and Cry (Over You)" was written by Joe Thomas and Howard Biggs and appeared in the following Extended Play albums: "Elvis Presley" (RCA EPB-1254) "Elvis Presley" (RCA SPD-22); "Elvis Presley" (RCA SPD-23); and the Long Playing albums "Elvis Presley" (RCA LPM-1254) and "Elvis Presley" (RCA LSP-1254 [e]).

I'm Gonna Sit Right Down and Cry (Over You). RCA 447-0611. Gold Standard Series re-issue of RCA 20/47-6638.

I'm Gonna Walk Dem Golden Stairs. Spiritual recorded by Elvis in 1960. "I'm Gonna Walk Dem Golden Stairs" appeared in the Long Playing albums "His Hand in Mine" (RCA LPM/LSP-2328) and "His Hand in Mine" (RCA ANL1-1319).

I'm Hanging Up My Rifle. Answer record by Bobby Bare to his own record "All American Boy" recorded on Fraternity Records (Fraternity 861) in 1959.

I'm in Love with Elvis Presley. A 1956 novelty record about Elvis by Virginia Lowe on Melba Records (Melba 107).

I Miss You. Song written by Donnie Sumner and recorded by Elvis at his Palm Springs, California, home on September 24, 1973. "I Miss You" appeared in the Long Playing album "Raised on Rock"/"For Ol' Times Sake" (RCA APL1-0388).

I'm Leavin'. RCA 47-9998. Released in August 1971 as a 45 rpm single. It reached #36 on *Billboard*'s Hot 100 chart and reportedly sold over a million copies globally. "Heart of Rome" was on the flip side. "I'm Leavin'" was written by Michael Jarrett and Sonny Charles and never appeared in an album.

I'm Leavin'. RCA 447-0683. Gold Standard Series re-issue of RCA 47-9998.

I'm Leaving It Up to You. Song written and originally recorded by Don "Sugarcane" Harris and Dewey Terry (Don and Dewey) in 1957. Dale and Grace (Dale Houston and Grace Broussard) recorded "I'm Leaving It Up to You" in 1963 (Montel 921; then, Michelle 921). It reached #1 for two weeks (November 23–December 7) and sold over a million copies. Elvis sang "I'm Leaving It Up to You" in 1971 in Las Vegas. It was never recorded by RCA; however, it *did* appear on a bootleg Extended Play album by Vegas Records (Vegas 45002).

I'm Left, You're Right, She's Gone. Sun 217. Released on April 1, 1955, as a 78 rpm single and a 45 rpm single. "Baby, Let's Play House" was on the flip side. "I'm Left, You're Right, She's Gone" was written by Stanley Kesler and William Taylor, based on a Campbell's Soup jingle.

I'm Left, You're Right, She's Gone. RCA 20/47-6383. A 78 rpm and a 45 rpm re-issue of the Sun original (Sun 217). "I'm Left, You're Right, She's Gone" appeared in the Extended Play album "Anyway You Want Me" (RCA EPA-965) and the following Long Playing albums: "For LP Fans Only" (RCA LPM-1990); "For LP Fans Only" (RCA LSP-1990 [e]); "The Elvis Presley Sun Collection" (RCA Starcall Hy-1001); "Elvis —The Sun Sessions" (RCA APM1-1675); "The Sun Years" (Sun 1001).

I'm Left, You're Right, She's Gone. RCA 447-0604. Gold Standard Series re-issue of RCA 20/47-6383.

I'm Lonesome for Elvis. An Elvis tribute song by Jerry Webb.

Immaculate Conception. Catholic school, 1725 Central Ave., in Memphis, attended by Priscilla Beaulieu while living with Elvis's parents. She enrolled there January 1962, at age seventeen, and was graduated on June 14, 1963. The principal was Sister Mary Adrian.

I'm Moving On. RCA 50476. Released in 1978 as a 45 rpm single. "I'm Movin' On" was released on gold vinyl. "Little Darlin'" was on the flip side. "I'm Moving On" was written in 1945 by Clarence Eugene "Hank" Snow but not recorded by him until 1950 (RCA 0328). Steve Sholes of RCA didn't want Snow to record the song. "I'm Movin' On" holds the record for occupying the #1 position on *Billboard*'s charts—twenty-one straight weeks. It was in the top ten for sixty weeks. Hank Snow once recorded a follow-up record titled "I'm Still Movin' On" (RCA 1068). In 1959 Ray Charles recorded a version of "I'm Moving On"* (Atlantic 2043). Elvis's version of "I'm Movin' On" appeared in the Long Playing albums "From Elvis in Memphis"

---

*The flip side of Ray Charles's record was a blues song called "I Believe to My Soul," in which Charles dubbed in all the voices of a female chorus.

(RCA LSP-4155) and "Elvis—A Canadian Tribute" (RCA KKL1-7065).

I'm Not the Marrying Kind. Song that Elvis sang in the 1962 movie *Follow That Dream.* "I'm Not the Marrying Kind" was written by Hal David and Sherman Edwards and appeared in the Extended Play album "Follow That Dream" (RCA EPA-4368) and the Long Playing albums "C'mon Everybody" (RCA Camden CAL-2518) and "C'mon Everybody" (Pickwick CAS-2518).

Imperial Quartet, The. One of several vocal groups that backed Elvis during his career. In 1969 the Imperial Quartet consisted of Jake Hess, Jim Murray, Gary McSpadded, and Armand Morales. In 1970 the group consisted of Terry Blackwood, Joe Moskeo, Armand Horules, and Tim Murray.

Impossible Dream, The. Song written by Joe Darion and Mitch Leigh in 1965 and introduced in the musical *Man of La Mancha* by Richard Kiley. "The Impossible Dream" was subtitled "The Quest." Elvis recorded "The Impossible Dream" in 1972 and it appeared in the Long Playing albums "Elvis As Recorded at Madison Square Garden" (RCA LSP-4776) and "He Walks Beside Me" (RCA AFL1-2772).

I'm So Lonesome I Could Cry. Country song written and originally recorded by Hank Williams (MGM 10560) in 1949. B.J. Thomas with the Triumphs had a million-seller with "I'm So Lonesome I Could Cry" (Scepter 12129) in 1966. It was B.J. Thomas's first successful recording. Elvis sang "I'm So Lonesome I Could Cry" in the 1973 TV special "Elvis: Aloha from Hawaii," saying it was the saddest song he ever heard. It appeared in the Long Playing albums "Elvis: Aloha from Hawaii Via Satellite" (RCA VPSX-6089) and "Welcome to My World" (RCA APL1-2274).

I'm Yours. RCA 47-8657. Released in August 1965 as a 45 rpm single. It reached #11 on *Billboard*'s Hot 100 chart. "'I'm Yours" reportedly sold over a million copies globally. "(It's A) Long Lonely Highway" was on the flip side. Elvis sang "I'm Yours" in the 1965 movie *Tickle Me.* The album cut of the song had narration, while the single release didn't. Written by Don Robertson and Hal Blair, "I'm Yours" appeared in the Long Playing album "Pot Luck" (RCA LPM/LSP-2523).

I'm Yours. RCA 447-8654. Gold Standard Series re-issue of RCA 47-8657.

Indescribably Blue. RCA 47-9056. Released in January 1967 as a 45 rpm single. It reached #33 on *Billboard*'s Hot 100 chart. "Fools Fall in Love" was on the flip side. "Indescribably Blue" was written by Darrell Glenn and appeared in the Long Playing album "Elvis' Gold Records, Volume 4" (RCA LPM/LSP-3921).

Indescribably Blue. RCA 447-0659. Gold Standard Series re-issue of RCA 47-9056.

I Need Somebody to Lean On. Song that Elvis sang in the 1964 movie *Viva Las Vegas.* "I Need Somebody to Lean On" was written by Doc Pomus and Mort Shuman and appeared in the Extended Play album "Viva Las Vegas" (RCA EPA-4382) and the Long Playing albums "I Got Lucky" (RCA Camden CAL-2533) and "I Got Lucky" (Pickwick CAS-2533).

I Need Your Love Tonight. RCA 47-7506. Released in March 1959 as a 45 rpm single. It reached #4 on *Billboard*'s Hot 100 chart and sold over a million copies. "A Fool Such as I" was on the flip side. "I Need Your Love Tonight" was written by Sid Wayne and Bix Reichner and appeared in the following Long Playing albums: "50,000,000 Elvis Fans Can't Be Wrong —Elvis' Gold Records, Volume 2" (RCA LPM-2075) "50,000,000 Elvis Fans Can't Be Wrong—Elvis' Gold Records, Volume 2" (RCA LSP-2075 [e]); "Elvis: The Other Sides— Worldwide Gold Award Hits, Volume 2" (RCA LPM-6402).

I Need Your Love Tonight. RCA 447-0625. Gold Standard Series re-issue of RCA 47-7506.

I Need Your Loving (Every Day). Song originally recorded by Don Gardner and Dee Dee Ford on Fire Records in 1962. Elvis sang "I Need Your Loving (Every Day)" at a few of his Las Vegas appearances. RCA has never released the song; however, it did appear on the bootleg album "From Hollywood to Vegas."

I Need You So. Song written and originally recorded by Ivory Joe Hunter (MGM 10663) in 1950. Elvis recorded "I Need You So" in 1957 and it appeared in the Extended Play album "Just For You" (RCA EPA-4041) and the Long Playing albums "Loving You" (RCA LPM-1515) and "Loving You" (RCA LSP-1515 [e]).

I Never Had It So Good. Song that Elvis may have recorded for the 1964 movie *Roustabout.* It may have been an alternate song for the scene in which "One Track Heart" was used. Another theory is that "I Never Had It So Good" was the original title of "It's a Wonderful World."

Inherit the Wind. Song written by Eddie Rabbitt and recorded by Elvis at the American Sound Studios in Memphis in 1969. "Inherit the Wind" appeared in the Long Playing albums "From Memphis to Vegas"/"From Vegas to Memphis" (RCA LSP-6020) and "Elvis—Back in Memphis" (RCA LSP-4429).

Ink Spots. Easy-listening quartet from the 1930s. The group's theme song was "If I Didn't Care." The members were Orville "Hoppy" Jones. Ivory "Deek" Watson, Charlie Fuqua, and Bill Kenny (there have been others). The group split into two factions in 1952. Elvis enjoyed listening to the Ink Spots. When he recorded the acetate "My Happiness" and "That's When Your Heartaches Begin" he was recording two Ink Spot songs. Bill Kenny, who served as the group's lead singer for years,

189

composed "There Is No God But God," which Elvis recorded in 1971.

In My Dreams. Unreleased song that Elvis may have recorded on acetate only, for RCA Victor.

In My Father's House (Are Many Mansions). Gospel song written by Aileene Hanks and recorded by Elvis in 1960. "In My Father's House (Are Many Mansions)" appeared in the Long Playing albums "His Hand in Mine" (RCA LPM/LSP-2328) and "His Hand in Mine" (RCA ANL1-1319).

In My Harem. Title originally considered for the 1965 movie *Harum Scarum*. Another title considered was *Harem Holiday*, which was used when the film was released in England.

In My Way. An Elvis tribute narration by Dave Kaye. It was released by Decca Records (England).

In My Way. Song that Elvis sang in the 1961 movie *Wild in the Country*. "In My Way" was written by Fred Wise and Ben Weisman and appeared in the following Long Playing albums: "Elvis for Everyone" (RCA LPM/LSP-3450); "Separate Ways" (RCA Camden CAS-2611); "Separate Ways" (Pickwick CAS-2611).

Inscription on Elvis's Grave. By Vernon Presley.

> He was a precious gift from God
> We cherished and loved dearly
>
> He had God-given talent that he shared
> with the world and without a doubt
> He became most widely acclaimed
> capturing the hearts of young and old alike
>
> He was admired not only as an entertainer
> But as the great humanitarian that he was
> For his generosity and his kind feeling
> For his fellow man
>
> He revolutionalized the field of music and
> Received its highest award
>
> He became a living legend in his own time
> Earning the respect and love of millions
>
> God saw that he needed some rest and
> called him home to be with him
>
> We miss you, Son and Daddy. I thank God
> that he gave us you as our son.

Inside Elvis. Book about Elvis written by Ed Parker, published by Rampart House, Ltd., in 1978.

Intelsat IV. Communications satellite used to transmit the 1973 TV special "Elvis: Aloha from Hawaii." The special was seen by an estimated 1 billion viewers.

International Hotel. (See: Las Vegas International Hotel)

International Kenpo Karate Association (IKKA). Emblem that Elvis had affixed to his guitar. The emblem was on the guitar he used in the 1973 TV special "Elvis: Aloha from Hawaii."

In the Garden. Hymn written by C.A. Miles and recorded by Elvis in 1966. "In the Garden" appeared in the Long Playing album "How Great Thou Art" (RCA LPM/LSP-3758)

In the Ghetto. RCA 47-9741. Released in April 1969 as a 45 rpm single. It reached #3 on *Billboard*'s Hot 100 chart, #60 on the Country chart, and #2 in the United Kingdom. "In the Ghetto" sold over a million copies. "Any Day Now" was on the flip side. "In the Ghetto" was written by Mac Davis and was first offered to Bill Medley (of the Righteous Brothers) and Sammy Davis, Jr. Originally, "In the Ghetto" had a subtitle—"The Vicious Circle"—but RCA was granted permission to release it without the subtitle. "In the Ghetto" appeared in the following Long Playing albums: "From Elvis in Memphis" (RCA LSP-4155); "From Memphis to Vegas/From Vegas to Memphis" (RCA LSP-6020); "Elvis in Person" (RCA LSP-4428); "Elvis: Worldwide 50 Gold Award Hits, Volume 1" (RCA LPM-6401); "Pure Gold" (RCA ANL1-0971); "Elvis—A Legendary Performer, Volume 3" (RCA CPL1-3082).

In the Ghetto. RCA 447-0671. Gold Standard Series re-issue of RCA 47-9741.

In Your Arms. Song written by Aaron Schroeder and Wally Gold and recorded by Elvis in 1961. "In Your Arms" appeared in the Long Playing album "Something for Everybody" (RCA LPM/LSP-2370).

I Really Don't Want to Know. RCA 47-9960. Released in December 1970 as a 45 rpm single. It reached #21 on *Billboard*'s Hot 100 chart and #9 on the Country chart. "I Really Don't Want to Know" was credited with selling over a million copies. "There Goes My Everything" was on the flip side. Elvis sang "I Really Don't Want to Know" in the 1977 CBS-TV special "Elvis in Concert." "I Really Don't Want to Know" was written by Don Robertson and Howard Barnes and originally recorded by Eddy Arnold (RCA 5525) in 1953. Tommy Edwards had a successful recording of the song (MGM 12890) in 1960. Elvis's version of "I Really Don't Want to Know" appeared in the following Long Playing albums: "Elvis Country" (RCA LSP-4460); "Elvis: The Other Sides—Worldwide Gold Award Hits, Volume 2" (RCA LPM-6402); "Welcome to My World" (RCA APL1-2274); "Elvis in Concert" (RCA APL1-2587).

I Really Don't Want to Know. RCA 447-0679. Gold Standard Series re-issue of RCA 47-9960.

Ireland, John. Veteran actor who played Phil Macy in the 1961 movie *Wild in the Country*. John Ireland had been married to actress Joanne Dru (sister of TV host Peter Marshall, who is the father of major league baseball player Peter La Cock). John Ireland is the brother of comedian Tommy Noonan.

I Remember Elvis. A 1977 Elvis tribute record by Roy Williams on WB Country Sound Records (WB Country Sound 7700).

I Remember Elvis Presley. A 1978 Elvis tribute record by Danny Mirror on Poker Records (Poker 15023).

I Saw Elvis Presley Last Night. A 1969 Elvis tribute record by Gary Lewis* and the Playboys (Liberty 56114).

I Sing This Song for Elvis. A 1977 Elvis tribute record by Terry Lee on Mercury Records (Mercury 6198).

Is It So Strange. Country song written and originally recorded by Faron Young. Elvis recorded "Is It So Strange" in 1957 and it appeared in the Extended Play album "Just for You" (RCA EPA-4041) and the following Long Playing albums: "A Date with Elvis" (RCA LPM-2011); "A Date with Elvis" (RCA LSP-2011) "Separate Ways" (RCA Camden CAS-2611); "Separate Ways" (Pickwick CAS-2611).

Island of Golden Dreams. (a.k.a. "My Isle of Golden Dreams")† One of the many songs sung by Elvis, Jerry Lee Lewis, and Carl Perkins during the Million Dollar Session. (See: Million Dollar Session)

Island of Love (Kauai). Song that Elvis sang in the 1961 movie *Blue Hawaii*. The film version has female vocal back-up. "Island of Love (Kauai)" was written by Sid Tepper and Roy C. Bennett and appeared in the Long Playing album "Blue Hawaii" (RCA LPM/LSP-2426).

I Slipped, I Stumbled, I Fell. Song that Elvis sang in the 1961 movie *Wild in the Country*. The film version is slower than the record version and is not a complete song. Written by Fred Wise and Ben Weisman, "I Slipped, I Stumbled, I Fell" appeared in the following Long Playing albums: "Something for Everybody" (RCA LPM/LSP-2370); "Separate Ways" (RCA Camden CAS-2611); "Separate Ways" (Pickwick CAS-2611).

It Ain't No Big Thing (But It's Growing). Song written by Merritt, Joy, and Hall and recorded by Elvis in 1970. "It Ain't No Big Thing (But It's Growing)" appeared in the Long Playing album "Love Letters from Elvis" (RCA LSP-4530).

It Feels So Right. RCA 47-8585. Released in May 1965 as a 45 rpm single. It reached #55 on *Billboard*'s Hot 100 chart. "(Such An) Easy Question" was on the flip side. Elvis sang "It Feels So Right" in the 1965 movie *Tickle Me*. Written by Fred Wise and Ben Weisman, it appeared in the Long Playing album "Elvis Is Back" (RCA LPM/LSP-2231).

---

*Gary Lewis is the son of comedian Jerry Lewis.
†In an interview Bing Crosby once stated that of all the songs he had recorded, his favorite was "My Isle of Golden Dreams."

It Feels So Right. RCA 447-0653. Gold Standard Series re-issue of RCA 47-8585.

IT HAPPENED AT THE WORLD'S FAIR. MGM, 1963. Premiered Los Angeles April 3, 1963 (105 min). Elvis's twelfth movie. Producer, Ted Richmond. Director, Norman Taurog. Cast: Mike Edwards/Elvis Presley, Diane Warren/Joan O'Brien, Danny Burke/Gary Lockwood, Sue-Lin/Vicky Tiu, Vince Bradley/H. M. Wynant, Miss Steuben/Edith Atwater, Barney Thatcher/Guy Raymond, Miss Ettinger/Dorothy Green, Mechanic/William Wood, Foreman/Robert B. Williams, Mr. Johnson/Olan Soule, Mrs. Johnson/Jacqueline De Witt, Charlie/John Day, Fred/Robert "Red" West, June/Sandra Giles, Rita/Evelyn Dutton, Redhead/Linda Humble, Boy/Kurt Russell,* The Jordanaires/The Jordanaires, The Mello Men/The Mello Men, Screenplay, Si Rose and Seamon Jacobs. Photography, Joseph Ruttenberg. Music, Leith Stevens. Choreography, Jack Baker. Art direction, George W. Davis and Preston Ames. Assistant Director, Al Jennings. Editor, Fredric Steinkamp. Songs sung by Elvis: "I'm Falling in Love Tonight," "Cotton Candy Land," "Relax," "A World of Our Own," "How Would You Like to Be," "Take Me to the Fair," "Beyond the Bend," "They Remind Me Too Much of You," "One Broken Heart for Sale," "Happy Ending" (Duet with Joan O'Brien), "How Would You Like to Be" (Duet with Vicky Tiu).

It Happened at the World's Fair. RCA LPM/LSP-2697. A 33⅓ rpm Long Playing album released in April 1963. It reached #4 on *Billboard*'s Hot LP chart. "It Happened at the World's Fair" featured songs from the 1963 movie of the same name. Songs included—Side 1: "Beyond the Bend," "Relax," "Take Me to the Fair," "They Remind Me Too Much of You," "One Broken Heart for Sale." Side 2: "I'm Falling in Love Tonight," "Cotton Candy Land," "A World of Our Own," "How Would You Like to Be," "Happy Ending."

I Think I'm Gonna Like It Here. Song that Elvis sang in the 1963 movie *Fun in Acapulco*. The film version differs slightly from the record version because of Elvis's delivery. "I Think I'm Gonna Like It Here" was written by Don Robertson and Hal Blair and appeared in the Long Playing album "Fun in Acapulco" (RCA LPM/LSP-2756).

It Hurts Me. RCA 47-8307. Released in February 1964 as a 45 rpm single. It reached #29 on *Billboard*'s Hot 100 chart. "Kissin' Cousins" was on the flip side. Elvis recorded "It Hurts Me" for the "Guitar Man" segment of the 1968 NBC-TV special "Elvis," but it was cut from the program because of time. "It Hurts Me" was written by Joy Byers and appeared in the following Long Playing albums: "Elvis' Gold Records,

*Kurt Russell would sixteen years later portray Elvis in the 1979 ABC televison movie *Elvis*.

Volume 4" (RCA LPM/LSP-3921); "Elvis: The Other Sides—
Worldwide Gold Award Hits, Volume 2" (RCA LPM-6402);
"Elvis—A Legendary Performer, Volume 3" (RCA CPL1-
3082).

It Hurts Me. RCA 447-0664. Gold Standard Series re-issue of
RCA 47-8307.

It Is No Secret (What God Can Do). Hymn written and original-
ly recorded by Stuart Hamblen (Columbia 20724) in 1950.
(He wrote it in seventeen minutes.) Elvis recorded "It Is No
Secret (What God Can Do)" in 1957 and it appeared in the
Extended Play albums "Peace in the Valley" (RCA EPA-4054)
and "Peace in the Valley" (RCA EPA-5121) and the following
Long Playing albums: "Elvis' Christmas Album" (RCA LOC-
1035); "Elvis' Christmas Album" RCA LPM-1951); "Elvis'
Christmas Album" (RCA LSP-1951 [e]); "You'll Never Walk
Alone" (RCA Camden CALX-2472); "You'll Never Walk
Alone" (Pickwick CAS-2472).

It Keeps Right on A-Hurtin'. Song written and originally recorded
by Johnny Tillotson (Cadence 1418) in 1962. It reached #3
on *Billboard*'s Hot 100 chart. Elvis recorded "It Keeps Right on
A-Hurtin' " in 1969 at the American Sound Studios in Memphis. It appeared in the Long Playing album "From Elvis in
Memphis" (RCA LSP-4155).

Ito Eats. Song that Elvis sang in the 1961 movie *Blue Hawaii*.
"Ito Eats" was written by Sid Tepper and Roy C. Bennett and
appeared in the Long Playing album "Blue Hawaii" (RCA
LPM/LSP-2426).

It's a Matter of Time. RCA 74-0769. Released in August 1972 as
a 45 rpm single. It reached #10 on *Billboard*'s Country chart.
"Burning Love" was on the flip side. "It's a Matter of Time"
was written by Clive Westlake and appeared in the following
Long Playing albums: "Burning Love and Hits from His Movies, Volume 2" (RCA Camden CAS-2595); "Burning Love
and Hits from His Movies, Volume 2" (Pickwick CAS-3595);
"Double Dynamite" (Pickwick DL2-5001).

It's a Sin. Country song written by Fred Rose and Zeb Turner
and originally recorded by Eddy Arnold (RCA 20-2241) in
1947. "It's a Sin" was Eddy Arnold's first successful recording.
Elvis recorded "It's a Sin" in 1961 and it appeared in the Long
Playing album "Something for Everybody" (RCA LPM/LSP-
2370).

It's a Wonderful World. Song that Elvis sang in the 1964 movie
Roustabout. "It's a Wonderful World" is rumored to have
originally been titled "I Never Had It So Good." Though it was
not finally nominated for an Academy Award, "It's a Wonderful World" was considered in the preliminary. It was the only
Elvis song considered for an Oscar nomination. It was written
by Sid Tepper and Roy C. Bennett and appeared in the Long
Playing album "Roustabout" (RCA LPM/LSP-2999).

It's Carnival Time. Song that Elvis sang in the 1964 movie *Roustabout*. The film version differs from that on record in the phrasing and the backing. "It's Carnival Time" was written by Ben Weisman and Sid Wayne and appeared in the Long Playing album "Roustabout" (RCA LPM/LSP-2999).

It's Easy for You. Song written by Webber and Rice and recorded by Elvis at Graceland in 1976. "It's Easy for You" appeared in the Long Playing album "Moody Blue" (RCA AFL1-2428).

It's Impossible. Song written by Sid Wayne and Armando Manzanero* and popularized by Perry Como in 1970. "It's Impossible" reached #10 on *Billboard*'s Hot 100 chart and was a million-seller. The original title of the song was "Somos Novios." Elvis recorded "It's Impossible" in 1972 and it appeared in the Long Playing albums "Elvis" (RCA APL1-0283) and "Pure Gold" (RCA ANL1-0971).

It's Midnight. RCA PB-10074. Released in October 1974 as a 45 rpm single. It reached #9 on *Billboard*'s Hit 100 chart. "It's Midnight" reportedly sold over a million copies. "Promised Land" was on the flip side. Written by Billy Edd Wheeler and Jerry Chesnut, "It's Midnight" appeared in the Long Playing albums "Promised Land" (RCA APL1-0873) and "Our Memories of Elvis" (RCA AQL1-3279).

It's Midnight. RCA GB-10488. Gold Standard Series re-issue of RCA PB-10074.

It's Now or Never. RCA 47-7777. Released in July 1960 as a 45 rpm single. It reached #1 on *Billboard*'s Hot 100 chart (for five weeks, August 15–September 19) and #7 on the Country chart. "It's Now or Never" reached #1 in the United Kingdom (for eight weeks, October 30–December 25, the longest any Presley single was #1 in the United Kingdom). "A Mess of Blues" was on the flip side. In the United Kingdom it was "Make Me Know It." Worldwide sales of "It's Now or Never" are numbered at over 22 million copies. In the first three weeks after release, it sold 1¼ million copies. *Billboard* named it the vocal single of 1960. "It's Now or Never" was based on the Italian song "O Sole Mio," written by G. Capurro and Eduardo Di Capua in 1901. Through the years, "O Sole Mio" has been recorded by several artists, including Jan Pearce and Tony Martin (who had a contemporary version called "There's No Tomorrow"). Aaron Schroeder and Wally Gold added new lyrics to the old standard. "It's Now or Never" appeared in the Extended Play album "Elvis By Request" (RCA LPC-128) and the following Long Playing albums: "Elvis' Golden Records, Volume 3" (RCA LPM/LSP-2765); "Elvis: Worldwide 50 Gold Award Hits, Volume 1" (RCA LPM-6401); "Elvis" (RCA DPL2-0056 [e]); "Elvis—A Legendary Performer, Vol-

---

*Armando Manzanero was RCA's first Mexican artist to exceed $1 million in sales of his records.

195

ume 2" (RCA CPL1-1349); "Elvis in Concert" (RCA APL2-2587). (See: O Sole Mio)

It's Now or Never. RCA 447-0628. Gold Standard Series re-issue of RCA 47-7777.

It's Now or Never. RCA 61-7777. A 45 rpm "Living Stereo" single. "A Mess of Blues" was on the flip side.

It's Only Love. RCA 48-1017. Released in October 1971 as a 45 rpm single, the only Presley single to be released with a "48" prefix. It reached #51 on *Billboard's* Hot 100 chart and reportedly sold over a million copies globally. "The Sound of Your Cry" was on the flip side. "It's Only Love" was written by Mark James and Steve Tyrell Taylor and never appeared in a Long Playing album.

It's Only Love. RCA 447-0684. Gold Standard Series re-issue of RCA 48-1017.

It's Over. Song written and originally recorded by Jimmie Rodgers in 1966. Elvis sang "It's Over" in the 1973 TV special "Elvis: Aloha from Hawaii." It appeared in the Long Playing album "Elvis: Aloha from Hawaii Via Satellite" (RCA VPSX-6089).

It's Still Here. Song written by Ivory Joe Hunter and recorded by Elvis in 1971. "It's Still Here" appeared in the Long Playing album "Elvis" (RCA APL1-0283).

It's Your Baby, You Rock It. Song written by Shirl Milete and Nora Fowler and recorded by Elvis in 1970. "It's Your Baby, You Rock It" appeared in the Long Playing album "Elvis Country" (RCA LSP-4460).

It Won't Be Long. Song that Elvis recorded for the 1967 movie *Double Trouble,* but which was cut from the final print of the film. "It Won't Be Long" was written by Sid Wayne and Ben Weisman and appeared in the Long Playing album "Double Trouble" (RCA LPM/LSP-3787).

It Won't Happen to Me. A 1961 record by Jerry Lee Lewis that mentioned Elvis, Ricky Nelson, and Jackie Wilson in the lyrics. It was released by Sun Records (Sun 364).

It Won't Seem Like Christmas (Without You). Christmas song written by Balthrop and recorded by Elvis in 1971. "It Won't Seem Like Christmas (Without You)" appeared in the Long Playing albums "Elvis Sings the Wonderful World of Christmas" (RCA LSP-4579) and "Elvis Sings the Wonderful World of Christmas" (RCA ANL1-1936).

I've Got a Thing About You, Baby. RCA APBO-0196. Released in January 1974 as a 45 rpm single. It reached #39 on *Billboard's* Hot 100 chart and #4 on the Country chart. "Take Good Care of Her" was on the flip side. "I've Got a Thing About You, Baby" was written by Tony Joe White and recorded by Elvis at the Stax Studios in Memphis in 1973. It appeared in the Long Playing album "Good Times" (RCA CPL1-0475).

196

I've Got a Thing About You, Baby. RCA GB-10485. Gold Standard Series re-issue of RCA APBO-0196.

I've Got Confidence. Gospel song written by Andrae Crouch and recorded by Elvis in 1971. "I've Got Confidence" appeared in the Long Playing album "He Touched Me" (RCA LSP-4690).

I've Got to Find My Baby. Song that Elvis sang in the 1965 movie *Girl Happy.* "I've Got to Find My Baby" was written by Joy Byers and appeared in the Long Playing album "Girl Happy" (RCA LPM/LSP-3338).

I've Lost You. RCA 47-9873. Released in July 1970 as a 45 rpm single. It reached #32 on *Billboard*'s Hot 100 chart and #57 on the Country chart. "I've Lost You" reportedly sold over a million copies. "The Next Stop Is Love" was on the flip side. Elvis sang "I've Lost You" in the 1970 documentary *Elvis—That's The Way It Is.* Written by Ken Howard and Alan Blaickley, "I've Lost You" appeared in the Long Playing albums "Elvis—That's The Way It Is" (RCA LSP-4445) and "Elvis: The Other Sides—Worldwide Gold Award Hits, Volume 2" (RCA LPM-6402).

I've Lost You. RCA 447-0677. Gold Standard Series re-issue of RCA 47-9873.

I Walk the Line. Song written and originally recorded by Johnny Cash (Sun 241) in 1956. Johnny Cash originally wrote "I Walk the Line" as a ballad but Sam Phillips of Sun Records thought that it sounded better at a faster tempo and released it that way. Elvis sang "I Walk the Line" at some of his Las Vegas and Lake Tahoe shows. RCA never recorded "I Walk the Line," but a portion of it did appear on a bootleg album, "To Know Him Is to Love Him."

I Wanna Spend Christmas with Elvis. A 1956 Elvis novelty record by Marlene Paula on Regent Records (Regent 7506).

I Want Elvis for Christmas. A 1956 Elvis novelty record by the Holly Twins on Liberty Records (Liberty 55048).

I Want It That Way. Unreleased song that Elvis recorded on acetate only.

I Want to Be Free. Song that Elvis sang in the 1957 movie *Jailhouse Rock.* Written by Jerry Leiber and Mike Stoller, "I Want to Be Free" appeared in the Extended Play album "Jailhouse Rock" (RCA EPA-4114) and the following Long Playing albums: "A Date with Elvis" (RCA LPM-2011); "A Date with Elvis" (RCA LSP-2011 [e]); "Elvis: The Other Sides—Worldwide Gold Award Hits, Volume 2" (RCA LPM-6402).

I Want to Spend Christmas with Elvis. Novelty record by Little "Lambsie" Penn on Atco Records (Atco 6082).

I Want You, I Need You, I Love You. RCA 20/47-6540. Released in May 1956 as a 78 rpm single and a 45 rpm single. It reached #3 on *Billboard*'s Hot 100 chart, #1 on the Country chart, and #10 on the Rhythm and Blues chart. "I Want You, I Need You, I Love You" sold over a million copies. "My Baby Left Me" was on the flip side. Elvis sang "I Want You, I Need You, I Love You" on his second appearance on the "Milton Berle Show" (June 5, 1956) and on the "Steve Allen Show" (July 1, 1956). An alternate take where Elvis rearranged the lyrics ("I Need You, I Want You, I Love You") appeared in the Long Playing album "Elvis—A Legendary Performer, Volume 2." Written by Maurice Mysels and Ira Kosloff, "I Want You, I Need You, I Love You" appeared in the following Extended Play albums: "The Real Elvis" (RCA EPA-940); "The Real Elvis" (RCA EPA-5120); "Elvis Presley" RCA SPD-23); and the following Long Playing albums: "Elvis' Golden Records" (RCA LPM-1707); "Elvis' Golden Records" (RCA LSP-1707 [e]); "Elvis: Worldwide 50 Gold Award Hits, Volume 1" (RCA LPM-6401); "Elvis" (RCA DPL2-0056 [e]); "Elvis—A Legendary Performer, Volume 2" (RCA CPL1-1349).

I Want You, I Need You, I Love You. RCA 447-0607. Gold Standard Series re-issue of RCA 20/47-6540.

I Want You with Me. Song written by Woody Harris and recorded by Elvis in 1961. "I Want You with Me" appeared in the Long Playing album "Something for Everybody" (RCA LPM/LSP-2370).

I Was Born About Ten Thousand Years Ago. Country song of which Elvis arranged excerpts. "I Was Born Ten Thousand Years Ago" appeared after every song in the Long Playing album "Elvis Country" (RCA LSP-4460). The entire song appeared in the Long Playing album "Elvis—Now" (RCA LSP-4671).

I Washed My Hands in Muddy Water. Song written by Joe Babcock and originally recorded by Stonewall Jackson (Columbia 43197) in 1964. Elvis recorded "I Washed My Hands in Muddy Water" in 1970 and it appeared in the Long Playing album "Elvis Country" (RCA LSP-4460).

I Was the One. RCA 20/47-6420. Released on January 27, 1956, as a 78 rpm single and a 45 rpm single. It reached #23 on *Billboard*'s Hot 100 chart and sold over a million copies. "Heartbreak Hotel" was on the flip side. Elvis sang "I Was the One" on his second appearance on "Stage Show" (February 4, 1956). "Heartbreak Hotel"/"I Was the One" was the first RCA release of new material. "I Was the One" was written by Aaron Schroeder, Claude DeMetrius, Hal Blair, and Bill Pepper and appeared in the Extended Play album "Heartbreak Hotel" (RCA EPA-821) and the following Long Playing albums: "For LP Fans Only" (RCA LPM-1990); "For LP Fans Only" (RCA LSP-1990 [e]); "Elvis: Worldwide 50 Gold Awards, Volume 1" (RCA LPM-6401).

I Was the One. RCA 447-0605. Gold Standard Series re-issue of RCA 20/47-6420.

I Will Be Home Again. Song written by Bennie Benjamin, Raymond Leveen, and Lou Singer and recorded by Elvis in 1960. "I Will Be Home Again" appeared in the Long Playing album "Elvis Is Back" (RCA LPM/LSP-2231).

I Will Be True. Song written and originally recorded by Ivory Joe Hunter (MGM 11195) in 1952. Elvis recorded "I Will Be True" in 1971 and it appeared in the Long Playing album "Elvis" (RCA APL1-0283).

I Will Rock 'n' Roll with You. A 1978 record by Johnny Cash reminiscing about his days with Sun Records. He mentioned other Sun artists such as Billy Riley, Charlie Rich, Carl Perkins, Jerry Lee Lewis, Roy Orbison, Elvis Presley, Sam Phillips, and Jack Clement.

I Won't Be Rockin' Tonight. Answer record by Jean Chapel to Elvis's "Good Rockin' Tonight," released in 1956 on Sun Records (Sun 244).

I Won't Have to Cross Jordan Alone. One of Elvis's favorite gospel songs. He sang "I Won't Have to Cross Jordan Alone" during the Million Dollar Session of December 4, 1956. (See: Million Dollar Session)

J

Jackson, Pee Wee. One of the many gardeners employed at Graceland.

JAckson 7-7197: Telephone number of Sun Records in the mid-1950s.

Jacksonville, Florida. Site of a Hank Snow All Star Jamboree concert on May 13, 1955. It was at this performance that a crowd first caused a riot at an Elvis Presley concert. There was so much excitement that Elvis got his clothes torn off by some of the more emotional females in the audience. A local Jacksonville disc jockey named Johnny Tillotson (the future singing star) was in attendance at this concert. Other performers on stage included Hank Snow, Slim Whitman, Faron Young, the Davis Sisters (Skeeter and Bee Jay),* the Carter Sisters, and the Wilburn brothers.

---

*In reality, the Davis Sisters were not related. Skeeter's real name is Mary Frances Penick and Bee Jay's real name was Betty Jack Davis. Betty was killed in an automobile accident in August 1953.

Jack Valentine. Spy story that was to be made into a movie starring Elvis. Although the project was announced in 1968, it was scrapped.

Jacobs, Little Walter. Chess Records artist (born: Marion Walter Jacobs) known simply as Little Walter (And His Jukes*). He originally recorded the song "My Babe" in 1955 (Checker 811). Elvis recorded "My Babe" in August 1969.

JAILHOUSE ROCK. MGM, 1957. Premiered October 21, 1957 (96 min.) Elvis's third movie. Producer, Pandro S. Berman. Associate Producer, Katherine Hereford. Director, Richard Thorpe. Cast: Vince Everett/Elvis Presley, Peggy Van Alden/Judy Tyler, Hank Houghton/Mickey Shaughnessy, Mr. Shores/Vaughn Taylor, Sherry Wilson/Jennifer Holden, Teddy Talbot/Dean Jones, Laury Jackson/Anne Neyland, Prof. August Van Alden/Grandon Rhodes, Mrs. Van Alden/Katherine Warren, Mickey Alba/Don Burnett, Jake the Bartender/George Cisar, Warden/Hugh Sanders, Convict/Glenn Strange, Convict/John Indrisano, Bardeman/Robert Bice, Sam Brewster/Percy Helton, Jack Lease/Peter Adams, Studio Head/William Forrest, Paymaster/Dan White, Dotty/Robin Raymond, Ken/John Day, Judge/S. John Launer, Cleaning Woman/Elizabeth Slifer, Stripper/Gloria Paul, Bartender/Fred Colby, Shorty/Walter Johnson, Drunk/Frank Kreig, Record Distributor/William Tannen, Recording Engineer/Wilson Wood, TV Director/Tom McKee, Photographer/Donald Kerr, Drummond/Carl Milletaire, Surgeon/Francis DeSales, Hotel Clerk/Harry Hines, Extra in Café/Dorothy Abbott, The Jordanaires/The Jordanaires. Screenplay, Guy Trosper. Photography, Robert Bronner. Music, Jeff Alexander. Art Direction, William A. Hornung and Randall Duell. Set Decoration, Henry Grace and Keogh Gleason. Special Effects, A. Arnold Gillespie. Technical Adviser, Col. Tom Parker. Assistant Director, Robert E. Relyea. Editor, Ralph E. Winters. Songs sung by Elvis: "Jailhouse Rock," "Baby, I Don't Care," "Treat Me Nice," "Young and Beautiful," "I Wanna Be Free," "Don't Leave Me Now." Mickey Shaughnessy sang "One More Day." First movie to credit Thomas Parker as technical adviser.

Jailhouse Rock. RCA 20/47-7035. Released in September 1957 as a 78 rpm single and a 45 rpm single. It reached #1 on *Billboard*'s Hot 100 chart (for six weeks, November 14–December 9), #1 on the Country chart, and #1 on the Rhythm and Blues chart. "Jailhouse Rock" also reached #1 in the United Kingdom (for three weeks, January 24–February 14, 1958). It was a million-seller. "Treat Me Nice" was on the flip side. "Jailhouse Rock" was written by Jerry Leiber and Mike Stoller for the big production number in the 1957 movie of the

---

*Originally named the Night Cats.

same name. Contrary to popular belief, Mike Stoller did not play piano in the film* or record versions of the song. Dudley Brooks was the pianist. In addition to the movie, Elvis sang "Jailhouse Rock" in the 1968 NBC-TV special "Elvis" and in the 1977 CBS-TV special "Elvis in Concert." "Jailhouse Rock" appeared in the Extended Play album "Jailhouse Rock" (RCA EPA-4114) and the following Long Playing albums: "Elvis' Golden Records" (RCA LPM-1707); "Elvis' Golden Records" (RCA LSP-1707 [e]); "Elvis—TV Special" (RCA LPM-4088); "Elvis: Worldwide 50 Gold Award Hits, Volume 1" (RCA LPM-6401); "Elvis" (RCA DPL2-0056 [e]); "Elvis Recorded Live on Stage in Memphis" (RCA CPL1-0606); "Pure Gold" (RCA ANL1-0971); "Elvis in Hollywood" (RCA DPL2-0168); "Elvis—A Legendary Performer, Volume 2" (RCA CPL1-1349); "Elvis in Concert" (RCA APL2-2587).

Jailhouse Rock. RCA 447-0619. Gold Standard Series re-issue of RCA 47-7035.

Jailhouse Rock. RCA EPA-4114. This was a 45 rpm Extended Play album released in November 1957. It reached #1 on *Billboard*'s Extended Play chart and sold over a million copies—Elvis's biggest-selling EP. Songs included—Side 1: "Jailhouse Rock," "Young and Beautiful." Side 2: "I Want to Be Free," "Don't Leave Me Now," "(You're So Square) Baby I Don't Care."

Jambalaya (On the Bayou). Million-selling song on MGM Records (MGM 11283) for Hank Williams in 1953. Jo Stafford also had a million-seller with "Jambalaya (On the Bayou)" (Columbia 39838), which Hank Williams wrote. Elvis once sang a few lines of "Jambalaya (On the Bayou)" at a concert, but he never recorded it. *Jambalaya* was one of the titles considered for the 1962 movie *Girls! Girls! Girls!*

James Dean Story, The. Film project discussed in 1956 for which Elvis wanted to play the lead role. The film was finally released as a documentary in 1957, narrated by Martin Gable.

Janis Martin and Elvis Presley. RCA T-31-077. A ten-inch 33⅓ rpm Long Playing album released in South Africa. Janis Martin had five songs on the album and Elvis had five. This record has been valued at over $1,200. Songs included: Side 1: "Ooby Dooby" (Janis Martin). "I'm Left, You're Right, She's Gone" (Elvis), "One More Year to Go" (Janis Martin), "You're a Heartbreaker" (Elvis), "I Forgot to Remember to Forget" (Elvis). Side 2: "My Boy Elvis" (Janis Martin), "All Right, Baby' (Janis Martin), "Mystery Train" (Elvis), "Will You, Will Yum" (Janis Martin), "Baby, Let's Play House" (Elvis).

January 8, 1935. Birthdate of Elvis Aaron Presley. Others who

---

*Stoller *did* make a cameo appearance as the piano player while Elvis sang "Jailhouse Rock" but it wasn't his playing that was heard.

were born on January 8 are: José Ferrer (1909), Shirley Bassy (1937), Yvette Mimieux (1939), "Little" Anthony Gourdine (1941), Jimmy Page (1944), David Bowie* (1941).

Jarvis, Felton. Elvis's producer at RCA since 1966. He assumed Chet Atkins's job. In addition to Elvis, Jarvis produced records for Lloyd Price, Fats Domino, Tommy Roe, and Gladys Knight and the Pips. With James Fitz, he produced Ronnie McDowell's songs in the 1979 TV movie *Elvis*.

In 1959, Felton Jarvis recorded "Don't Knock Elvis" on Viva Records. (Viva 1001)

Jasmine. Elvis's favorite flower. Jasmine is the main ingredient of many perfumes and the essence sells for $4,090 a pound.

Jaycees Award. (See: Ten Outstanding Young Men of America)

Jenkins, Mary. Black cook at Graceland for fourteen years. Elvis once bought her a new house.

Jenner, Bruce. Decathlon winner in the 1976 Olympic Games. In late 1979 and 1980, Bruce Jenner was the steady boyfriend of Linda Thompson.

Jennings, Waylon. Disc jockey for Lubbock, Texas, radio station KDAV, who joined Buddy Holly's Crickets after Holly had bought him his first bass guitar. Jennings gave up his seat to the Big Bopper the night Buddy Holly died. In the late 1960s Waylon Jennings became a very successful country artist. In the 1970s he and veteran musician Willie Nelson teamed up to become known as the Outlaws. In 1973 Waylon Jennings and Billy Joe Shaver composed "You Asked Me To," which Elvis recorded in 1973. (See: Holly, Buddy)

Jerry Lewis Telethon. Annual (since 1966) Labor Day telethon, hosted by Jerry Lewis, to raise money for the Muscular Dystrophy Association. Elvis donated $5,000 on August 31, 1975, while he was in the hospital.

Jesse Wade. Elvis's role (as a reformed outlaw) in the 1969 movie *Charro!*

Jesus Knows What I Need. Title sometimes used for the gospel song "He Knows Just What I Need." (See: He Knows Just What I Need)

Jewish Community Center. Memphis recreation center, located at 6560 Poplar Ave., where Elvis played racquetball prior to building his own court.

Jim. Name of the singer in Elvis's version of "Old Shep." Elvis again referred to himself as Jim in the song "Just Tell Her Jim Said Hello."

Jim Dandy. Title originally considered for the 1966 movie *Spinout*. Another title considered was *Never Say Yes*.

Jimmie Rodgers Memorial Day Celebration. Concert held Thursday, May 26, 1955, at the Junior College Stadium in Meridian, Mississippi. Named after country music great Jimmie Rodgers,

---

*David Bowie, born David Robert Jones, had to change his name since there was already another singer named David Jones, who was a member of the Monkees.

the third annual celebration was hosted by Horace Logan of the "Louisiana Hayride." It featured Jim Reeves, Dizzy Dean, Elvis Presley, and Johnny, the Philip Morris cigarette page boy. (See: Johnny) Elvis sang "I'm Left, Your're Right, She's Gone" and "Baby, Let's Play House."

Jimmy Curry. Role in the 1956 movie *The Rainmaker* for which Elvis auditioned. The part went to Earl Holliman. Interestingly, Yvonne Lime appeared as Jimmy Curry's girlfriend Snooky McGuire. She would later appear with Elvis in *Loving You* (1957).

Jodie Tatum. One of the two roles played by Elvis in the 1964 movie *Kissin' Cousins*. Jody was the blond look-alike cousin of Josh Morgan (Elvis's other role).

Jo Haynes School of Dancing. Memphis dancing school, located at 4679 Highway 51 South, where Priscilla Beaulieu studied ballet.

John, Elton Hercules. Popular piano player and singer of the 1970s. Elton John (real name: Reginald Dwight) chose the name Elton from Elton Dean, a member of his early band, Bluesology, and the name John from Long John Baldry, the leader of a soul band for which he had played.

Elton John was the first white performer to appear in the TV series "Soul Train." Neil Sedaka* made his successful recording comeback of the 1970s on John's record label, Rocket Records.

Elton John was Lisa Marie Presley's favorite rock singer. Elvis arranged for the two to meet on Lisa Marie's birthday in 1975 (February 1).

The first record that Elton John can remember his mother bringing home was "Hound Dog" by Elvis Presley.

At the June 26, 1976, Elvis concert at Largo, Maryland, Elton John was one of the members of the audience.

John Brown's Body. Song on which "The Battle Hymn of the Republic" was based. "John Brown's Body" was originally titled "Say Brothers, Will You Meet Me." John Brown, the subject of the song, was a descendent of Peter Brown, who came to the New World on the *Mayflower*. (See: An American Trilogy)

John Burrows. Code name used by Elvis for receiving personal mail or telephone calls. Sometimes he used John Burrows, Jr. Elvis also used the alias of Dr. John Carpenter.

John Carpenter. Role played by Elvis (as a ghetto doctor) in the 1969 movie *Change of Habit*. Elvis used the name Dr. John Carpenter when making airline reservations.

By a strange coincidence, John Carpenter is the actual name of the man who directed the 1979 TV movie *Elvis*.

Johnny. Philip Morris cigarette bellboy played by Johnny Roven-

---

*Elton John sang duet with Neil Sedaka on "Bad Blood."

tini, a 49-pound, 47-inch midget (Sometimes the part was played by Freddy Douglas.) Johnny would yell, "Call for Philip Mor-rees" in the radio and TV advertisements. The musical theme of the commercials was "On the Trail" from Ferde Grofé's "Grand Canyon Suite."

Johnny and Elvis appeared on the same bill at the Jimmie Rodgers Memorial Day Celebration, in Meridian, Mississippi, on May 26, 1955. (See: Jimmie Rodgers Memorial Day Celebration)

Johnny B. Goode. Million-selling song written and originally recorded by Chuck Berry (Chess 1691).* "Johnny B. Goode" is said to be a musical biography of Berry. Elvis sang it in the 1972 documentary *Elvis on Tour,* in the 1973 TV special "Elvis: Aloha from Hawaii," and in the 1977 TV special "Elvis in Concert." "Johnny B. Goode" appeared in the following Long Playing albums: "From Memphis to Vegas/From Vegas to Memphis" (RCA LSP-6020); "Elvis in Person" (RCA LSP-4428); "Elvis: Aloha from Hawaii Via Satellite" (RCA VPSX-6089); "Elvis in Concert" (RCA APL2-2587).

Johnny Tyrrone. Role played by Elvis (as a Hollywood actor and singer) in the 1965 movie *Harum Scarum.*

Johnson, Blake. Hairdresser who owned Blake's Coiffure. At the suggestion of Gladys Tipler (wife of James Tipler, the owner of Crown Electric), Elvis had his hair trimmed on several occasions at Blake's Coiffure. He was working at Crown Electric at the time (1953–54).

Johnson, Francis. Elvis's first sergeant at Fort Chaffee, Arkansas, during Army indoctrination. (See: Fort Chaffee, Arkansas)

Johnson, Juanita Joan. Monroe, Louisiana, girl who was killed during an all-night vigil at the gate of Graceland on August 18, 1977—the day of Elvis's funeral. A car driven by Treatise Wheeler III, of Memphis, swung through the crowd, instantly killing her and Alice Hovatar. Wheeler was charged with drunk driving and second-degree murder. (See: Baiter, Tammy)

Johnson, Lyndon Baines. Thirty-sixth president of the U. S. (from 2:30 P.M., C.S.T., November 22, 1963, to 12:00 P.M., E.S.T., January 20, 1969). All members of President Johnson's immediate family shared the initials L.B.J. (Lady Bird Johnson; Lucy Baines Johnson; Lynda Bird Johnson). Lyndon Johnson once visited Elvis on the set of the 1966 movie *Spinout.*

Johnson, Nick. Kentucky state representative from Harlan, Kentucky, who resigned from his draft board because Elvis received a sixty-day deferment in January 1958. He was quoted as saying, "I cannot conscientiously ask any mountain boy to serve the same country unless afforded the same treatment as Presley."

---

*In 1961 Chuck Berry recorded a sequal record on Chess titled "Bye Bye Johnny" (Chess 1754).

Johnson, Rafer. Black athlete and actor who portrayed Davis in the 1961 movie *Wild in the Country*. Rafer Johnson won the 1960 Olympic Decathlon. In 1968 he and former football player Roosevelt Grier served as Robert F. Kennedy's bodyguards. When Kennedy was shot, on June 5, 1968, at the Ambassador Hotel in Los Angeles, he and Grier disarmed Sirhan Bishara Sirhan. Kennedy died early the next day.

Johnson, Susan. One of Elvis's teachers at Humes High School in Memphis.

Jones, Carolyn. Actress who portrayed Ronnie in the 1958 movie *King Creole*. Carolyn Jones later portrayed Morticia Addams in the TV series "The Addams Family." In 1977 she played the role of Mrs. Moore in the TV production of "Roots."

Jones, Ira. Army master sergeant who was Elvis's platoon sergeant in Friedberg, West Germany. Elvis chauffeured for him.

Jones, Thomas S. Army lt. colonel who gave Elvis his orders promoting him to sergeant in January 1960. Elvis received a $22.94 raise.

Jones, Tom. Popular Welsh singer (real name: Thomas Jones Woodward) whose powerful voice and vitality remind one of Elvis. Tom Jones and actor Richard Burton were both born in the South Wales village of Pontypridd.

When Tom Jones appeared at the Flamingo Hotel in Las Vegas in 1968, Elvis and Priscilla drove there to see his act. Elvis personally visited him backstage—their first meeting. Later, Elvis gave Tom Jones a TCB medallion, which Jones now wears. In the 1970 documentary *Elvis—That's the Way It is,* Tom Jones sent Elvis a note, which Elvis read: "Here's hoping you have a very successful opening and break both legs—Tom Jones." Elvis recorded two Tom Jones hits, "I'll Never Fall in Love Again" (1976) and "Without Love" (1969). Both artists recorded versions of "Green Green Grass of Home"; "Any Day Now"; "Yesterday"; "Hey Jude"; "Polk Salad Annie"; "Proud Mary"; "You've Lost That Lovin' Feelin' "); "The Impossible Dream."

Jones, Ulysses S., Jr. (See: Crosby, Charlie)

Jordanaires, The. Gospel and country vocal group with whom Elvis recorded. Formed in Springfield, Missouri, in 1948, the Jordanaires originally included Gordon Stoker (1st tenor), Neal Matthews* (2nd tenor), Hoyt Hawkins (baritone), and Hugh Jarrett (bass). Elvis met the Jordanaires when he appeared on the "Grand Ole Opry." Their first recording session with Elvis occurred on July 2, 1956, producing the songs "Hound Dog," "Don't Be Cruel," and "Any Way You Want Me." Beginning with the recording session of June 10–11, 1958, Ray Walker replaced Hugh Jarrett. Songs produced during that session include "I Need Your Love Tonight"; "A Big Hunk o' Love";

---

*Neal Matthews taught Ricky Nelson to play the guitar.

"Ain't That Loving You, Baby"; "A Fool Such As I"; "I Got Stung."

While attending David Lipscomb High, Ray Walker sang in a quartet with fellow student Pat Boone.

In 1956 the Jordaniares won on the "Arthur Godfrey's Talent Scouts" TV series.

Through the years, the Jordanaires have backed up a number of performers. Among them are: Ricky Nelson;* Marty Robbins; Kitty Wells; Tennessee Ernie Ford; Don Gibson; Connie Francis; Johnny Horton. Specifically, they have provided vocal accompaniment on Jimmy Dean's "Big Bad John," Marie Osmond's 1973 hit "Paper Roses" (which was produced by Sonny James), and Merle Haggard's 1977 album "From Graceland To The Promised Land." The Jordanaires also provided the backup to Ronnie McDowell's singing in the 1979 TV movie *Elvis.*† The group has sung for other record companies under the pseudonyms of the Stephen Scott Singers, the Merry Melody Singers, and the Milestone Singers. In 1958, the Jordanaires appeared in the Paramount movie *Country Music Holiday* starring Rocky Graziano, Zsa Zsa Gabor,‡ Ferlin Husky, Faron Young, Oscar and Lonzo, and others.

Jordan, Will. Comedian who portrayed TV host Ed Sullivan in the 1979 TV movie *Elvis.* He also portrayed Sullivan in the Broadway play *Elvis—The Legend Lives* and the movies *The Buddy Holly Story* (1978) and *I Want to Hold Your Hand* (1978).

Joseph. Rooster on Susan Jessup's (Dolores Hart) parents' farm in Farmingdale in the 1957 movie *Loving You.*

Joseph, Carolyn. Stephens College (Columbia, Missouri) student whom Elvis dated in the late 1950s.

Josh Morgan. One of two roles played by Elvis in the 1964 movie *Kissin' Cousins.* Josh was the black-haired look-alike cousin of Jodie Tatum (Elvis's other role).

Joshua Fit the Battle. RCA 447-0651. Released in February 1966 as a 45 rpm Gold Standard Series Original. "Joshua Fit the Battle" was recorded on October 31, 1960. "Known Only to Him" was on the flip side. A traditional gospel song, "Joshua Fit the Battle" appeared in the Long Playing albums "His Hand in Mine" (RCA LPM/LSP-2328) and "His Hand in Mine" (RCA ANL1-1319).

Juanico, June. Auburn-haired, blue-eyed receptionist from Biloxi, Mississippi, whom Elvis dated in 1955 and '56. June Juanico met Elvis after a concert in Biloxi in 1955.

---

*The Jordanaires can be heard on some of Nelson's biggest hits, "Believe What You Say", "Lonesome Town" and "Poor Little Fool."
†On the soundtrack album they are credited as the Jordanairs (*sic*).
‡In 1936, Zsa Zsa Gabor won the title of Miss Hungary, but she was disqualified when it was revealed that she was only sixteen years old.

Judd Records. Record company begun by Judd Phillips in the summer of 1958 in Sheffield, Alabama. He and his brother, Sam, had previously dissolved their partnership. The biggest hit on Judd was "Rockin' Little Angel" by Elvis-sound-alike Ray Smith in 1960 (Judd 1016). Judd Records was the original label on which Tommy Roe and the Satins recorded "Sheila" in 1960. Judd was sold to NRC Records in 1960. (See: Phillips, Sam; Sun Records)

Judy. Song recorded by Rudy Grazell (Sun 290) and produced by Roy Orbison, in which Elvis's name is mentioned.

Judy. RCA 47-9287. Released in August 1967 as a 45 rpm single. It reached #78 on *Billboard*'s Hot 100 chart. "There's Always Me" was on the flip side. Elvis recorded "Judy" on March 13, 1961. It was written and originally recorded by Teddy Redell (Atco 6162). "Judy" appeared in the Long Playing album. "Something for Everybody" (RCA LPM/LSP-2370).

Judy. RCA 447-0661. Gold Standard Series re-issue of RCA 47-9287.

July 26, 1969. Opening date in the 1979 TV movie *Elvis*.

June Taylor Dancers, The. Female dancers on several of Jackie Gleason's variety series. Gleason's third wife, Marilyn, is June Taylor's sister. The June Taylor Dancers were regulars on "Stage Show"—the TV series on which Elvis made his national TV debut. (See: Stage Show)

Just a Closer Walk with Thee. Traditional gospel hymn with which Red Foley had a million-seller in 1950 (Decca 14505). Foley was backed by the Jordanaires on the recording. In 1958, at the home of Eddie Fadal in Houston, Texas, Elvis sang "Just a Closer Walk with Thee," accompanying himself on piano. The song appeared on the bootleg LP "Forever Young, Forever Beautiful."

Just a Country Boy. A 1978 Elvis tribute record by Frankie Allen on the Rockfield label. (Rockfield 36337).

Just a Little Bit. One of the songs Elvis recorded at Stax Studios in Memphis on July 22, 1973. "Just a Little Bit" was written by John Thornton, Piney Brown, Ralph Bass, and Earl Washington and appeared in the Long Playing album "Raised on Rock/For Ol' Times Sake" (RCA APL1-0388).

Just Because. RCA 20/47-6640. Released in September 1956 as a 78 rpm single and a 45 rpm single. "Just Because" was recorded by Elvis in September 1954, while he was still with Sun Records. "Blue Moon" was on the flip side. "Just Because" was written by Bob Shelton, Joe Shelton, and Sid Robin in 1937 and was first recorded by Dick Stabile (Decca 716).* "Just Because" appeared in the Extended Play album "Elvis Presley" (RCA EPA-747) and the following Long Playing albums; "Elvis

---

*Roland "Bunny" Berigan played in the record.

Presley" (RCA LPM-1254); "Elvis Presley" (RCA LSP-1254 [e]); "The Elvis Presley Sun Collection" (RCA Starcall Hy-1001); "Elvis—The Sun Sessions" (RCA APM1-1675).

Just Because. RCA 447-0613. Gold Standard Series re-issue of RCA 47-6640.

Just Call Me Lonesome. Song that Rex Griffin wrote and recorded in the 1940s. Red Foley recorded a version on Decca Records (Decca 29626). Elvis recorded "Just Call Me Lonesome" in 1967 and it appeared in the Long Playing album "Clambake" (RCA LPM/LSP-3893).

Just for Old Time's Sake. Song written for Elvis by Sid Tepper and Roy C. Bennett in 1962. "Just for Old Time's Sake" appeared in the Long Playing album "Pot Luck" (RCA LPM/LSP-2523).

Just for You. RCA EPA-4041. This was a 45 rpm Extended Play album released in September 1957. It reached #2 on *Billboard*'s Extended Play chart. Songs included—Side 1: "I Need You So," "Have I Told You Lately That I Love You." Side 2: "Blueberry Hill," "Is It So Strange."

Just Pretend. Song written by Doug Flett and Guy Fletcher that Elvis recorded in June 1970. "Just Pretend" appeared in the Long Playing album "Elvis—That's the Way It Is" (RCA LSP-4445).

Just Tell Her Jim Said Hello. RCA 47-8041. Released in July 1962 as a 45 rpm single. It reached #55 on *Billboard*'s Hot 100 chart. "She's Not You" was on the flip side. "Just Tell Her Jim Said Hello" was written by Jerry Leiber and Mike Stoller and appeared in the Long Playing albums "Elvis' Gold Records, Volume 4" (RCA LPM/LSP-3921) and "Elvis: The Other Sides—Worldwide 50 Gold Award Hits, Volume 2" (RCA LPM-6402).

Just Tell Her Jim Said Hello. RCA 447-0637. Gold Standard Series re-issue of RCA 47-8041.

Just Tell Him Jane Said Hello. Answer record to "Just Tell Her Jim Said Hello," by Gerri Granger on Big Top Records (Big Top 3150) in 1963.

K

Kaempfert, Bert. Musical producer, composer, arranger, and orchestra leader for Polydor Records of West Germany. In 1961 Kaempfert had a #1 record and million-seller with "Wonderland by Night" (Decca 31141). He was the first man to record the Beatles when in 1961 he hired them to back Tony Sheridan on Sheridan's recording of "My Bonnie"/"When the

Saints go Marching In" (Polydor 24 673).* In 1965 Bert Kaempfert, Charles Singleton, and Eddie Snyder wrote "Spanish Eyes," which Elvis recorded in December 1973.

Kahane, Jackie. Comedian who was the opening act for many of Elvis's live performances. Jackie Kahane had previously worked with Wayne Newton and he was selected by Col. Parker because of his clever jokes. He was once booed off stage at Madison Square Garden by the audience, which was impatient to see and hear Elvis. Jackie Kahane delivered the eulogy at Elvis's funeral.

Kahuna. Elvis's nickname for Ed Parker. *Kahuna* is Hawaiian for "high priest."

Kanter, Hal. Director of Elvis's 1957 movie *Loving You*.

Kantor, Dr. Edward. Beverly Hills ear, nose, and throat specialist who tended to Elvis for fifteen years.

Kapoo. Kin Yung's (Benson Fong) weather-forecasting cat (white spots in his eyes mean rain) in the 1962 movie *Girls! Girls! Girls!*

Karate. Elvis's hobby for over eighteen years. He held an eighth-degree black belt. Elvis studied Tae Kwan Do from Kang Rhee and Kempo from Ed Parker. While practicing on September 16, 1974, he broke his wrist—his only serious accident.

Karate. Name of Elvis's boat. *Karate* had a hull designed by Glaspar and a 50-hp Johnson outboard motor.

Karate Nicknames. Nicknames conferred upon Elvis and his friends at Kang Rhee's Karate School: Elvis—"Tiger Man," Red West—"Mr. Dragon," Sonny West—"Mr. Eagle," Charlie Hodge—"Mr. Cobra," Lamar Fike—"Mr. Bull."

Karlson, Phil. Director of Elvis's 1962 movie *Kid Galahad*.

Katz Drug Store. Store, located in the Airways Shopping Center at 2256 Lamar Ave., where, on September 9, 1954, Elvis, Scotty, and Bill played for the store's grand opening. They played from the back of a flatbed truck† that store manager Peter Morton had rented for the occasion. Elvis, Scotty, and Bill received sixty-five dollars for their performance. Katz Drug Store is now known as Scagg's.

Katzman, Sam. Hollywood film producer who is nicknamed "Jungle Jim" and "King of the Quickies." Katzman produced two Elvis movies: *Kissin' Cousins* (1964) and *Harum Scarum* (1965).

KCA Record Company. Record label on which Guy Lambert (Elvis) recorded the song "Could I Fall in Love" in the 1967 movie *Double Trouble*.

------

*When record dealer Brian Epstein began getting requests for the German record in his store in Liverpool (the first was from eighteen-year-old Raymond Jones at 3:00 P.M., Saturday, October 28, 1961) he sought out the Beatles. After seeing them, he became convinced that they had tremendous potential. He soon became the Beatles' manager and persuaded Polydor to release "My Bonnie" in England.

†John Lennon and his group, the Quarrymen, made their professional debut in 1957 playing from the back of a flatbed lorry (truck) in Liverpool.

Keep Your Hands Off Her. Song that Elvis recorded on June 5, 1970. It was a medley with "Got My Mojo Working." "Got My Mojo Working"/"Keep Your Hands Off Her" was not meant to be recorded—it was a studio jam. The voices, horns, and strings were overdubbed later. "Keep Your Hands Off Her" doesn't appear by itself on any RCA release.

Kefauver, Estes. United States senator from Tennessee who, in March 1960, placed a tribute to Elvis into the Congressional Record.

Keisker, Marion. Secretary to Sam Phillips at the Memphis Recording Service and Sun Records in the 1950s. Marion Keisker once held the title of Miss Radio of Memphis. She was present when Elvis entered the Memphis Recording Service to cut "My Happiness" and "That's When Your Heartaches Begin," on acetate, in the summer of 1953. Marion Keisker asked Elvis who he sounded like and received the reply: "I don't sound like nobody." It was Marion Keisker's foresight to have turned on the master tape-recorder while Elvis was singing and then to ask him for his address and phone number. Because of this act, Marion Keisker should rightfuly be given credit for discovering Elvis Presley. (This does not in the least take away from Sam Phillips's foresight and patience in developing Elvis. Surely Sam Phillips can be considered a genius in the history of rock music.) Marion Keisker even contributed a verse to the song "I Don't Care If the Sun Don't Shine," which Elvis recorded in September 1954. Miss Keisker became an Air Force captain at the same time that Elvis was in the service. The two met in Germany while she was working with the Armed Forces Television Network as an assistant manager. In the 1979 TV movie *Elvis*. Marion Keisker was portrayed by Ellen Travolta, the elder sister of John Travolta. (See: Memphis Recording Service)

Kelly, Grace. Oscar-winning actress who is presently Princess Grace of Monaco, having married Prince Ranier in 1956. Grace Kelly was born in Philadelphia in 1929.* She began her movie career in 1951 with *Fourteen Hours* and ended it in 1956 with *High Society*. Although she made only twelve films, Grace Kelly did win an Academy Award for Best Actress in 1954 for her portrayal of Georgie Elgin in the movie *The Country Girl.*

In 1956 Grace Kelly teamed with Bing Crosby to record the song, "True Love" (Capitol 3507), which was from their movie *High Society*. "True Love" reached #4 on the charts and sold over a million copies.

Elvis recorded "True Love" on February 23, 1957.

---

*Grace Kelly's father, John B. Kelly, won three Gold Medals in the Olympics for rowing. He won the Sculls in 1920 and Double Sculls in 1920 and '24. His cousin, Paul V. Costello, won the double Sculls in 1920, '24, and '28.

Kennedy, Caroline. Daughter of the late President John Fitzgerald Kennedy and Jacqueline Kennedy Onassis. Caroline was one of the photo journalists who covered Elvis's funeral.

Like Lisa Marie, Caroline also had an aircraft named after her—*Caroline* (*Air Force One*, a Boeing 707 [AF 26000 and 27000])—while her father was president.

Kennedy, Jerry. Captain on the Denver vice squad to whom Elvis gave a new 1976 Lincoln Continental Mark IV on January 14, 1976. Kennedy was given the automobile because of his previous assistance to Elvis as a security guard. Elvis was vacationing in Vail, Colorado, at the time. (See: Starkey, Gerald; Kumpf Lincoln-Mercury)

Kennedy Veterans Hospital. Memphis facility, located at 1030 Jefferson Ave., where Elvis underwent his preinduction physical on January 4, 1957. When he was inducted into the Army on March 24, 1958, Elvis signed his loyalty oath and took his mental examinations and blood tests at the Kennedy Veterans Hospital. Early in the summer of 1954, shortly after recording "That's All Right (Mama)" and "Blue Moon of Kentucky," Elvis performed at the hospital.

Kentucky Rain. RCA 47-9791. Released in January 1970 as a 45 rpm single. It reached #16 on *Billboard*'s Hot 100 chart and #31 on the Country chart. "Kentucky Rain" was written for Elvis by Eddie Rabbitt and Dick Heard and sold over a million copies. "My Little Friend" appeared on the flip side. "Kentucky Rain" appeared in the long playing albums "Elvis: Worldwide 50 Gold Award Hits, Volume 1" (RCA LPM-6401) and "Pure Gold" (RCA ANL1-0971).

Kentucky Rain. RCA 447-0675. Gold Standard Series re-issue of RCA 47-9791.

Kesler, Stanley A. Steel guitarist on many Sun recordings in the 1950s. Stan Kesler toured with Elvis in 1954 and 1955. He composed three songs that Elvis recorded: "I'm Left, You're Right, She's Gone" (cowritten with Bill Taylor*); "I Forgot to Remember to Forget" (cowritten with Charlie Feathers); and "Playing for Keeps."

KID GALAHAD. United Artist; 1962. Premiered Atlanta, Georgia, August 1, 1962 (95 min). Elvis's tenth movie. Producer, David Weisbart. Director, Phil Karlson. Cast: Walter Gulick/Elvis Presley, Willy Grogan/Gig Young, Dolly Fletcher/Lola Albright, Rose Grogan/Joan Blackman, Lew Nyack/Charles Bronson, Joie Shakes/Michael Dante, Zimmerman/Judson Pratt, Sperling/George Mitchell, Father Higgins/Liam Redmond, Ralphie/Jeffrey Morris, Promoter/Roy Roberts, Pete Prohosko/Ralph Moody, Ramon "Sugar Boy" Romero/Ramon De La Fuente, Romero's Manager/Frank Gerstle, Romero's

---

*Stan Kesler and Bill Taylor both played at the Cotton Club in West Memphis in the early 1950s with Clyde Leoppard's Snearly Ranch Boys.

Trainer/George J. Lewis. Screenplay, William Fay. Photography, Gurnett Guffey. Music, Jeff Alexander. Art Direction, Cary Odell. Set Decoration, Edward G. Boyle. Special Effects, Milt Rice. Costumes, Bert Henrikson and Irene Caine. Assistant Director, Jerome M. Siegel. Editor, Stuart Gilmore. Songs Sung by Elvis: "King of the Whole Wide World," "A Whistling Tune," "This Is Living," "Riding the Rainbow," "Home Is Where the Heart Is," "I Got Lucky." Sonny West played an extra in the movie. The movie is from the 1936 novel by Francis Wallace, *Kid Galahad*, which was previously filmed by Warner Bros. in 1937, starring Edward G. Robinson, Bette Davis, Humphrey Bogart, and Wayne Morris as Ward Guisenberry (Morris and Elvis played the same role).

Kid Galahad. RCA EPA-4371. This was a 45 rpm Extended Play album released in September 1962. It reached #30 on *Billboard*'s Hot 100 chart. Songs included—Side 1: "King of the Whole Wide World," "This is Living," "Riding the Rainbow." Side 2: "Home Is Where the Heart Is," "I Got Lucky," "A Whistling Tune."

Killeen, Texas. Town close to Fort Hood, where Elvis lived while receiving his Army basic training in 1958. Soon after arriving in Fort Hood, Elvis moved off base to Killeen—first renting a three-bedroom trailer and then a three-bedroom house.

Kilohana. Tuna boat skippered by Ross Carpenter (Elvis) in the 1962 movie *Girls! Girls! Girls!*. Call letters of the boat were WY 2768.

King, B.B. Blues singer, nicknamed "King of the Blues," who was born Riley B. King, on September 16, 1925, in Indianola, Mississippi. B.B. King was a disc jockey at Memphis radio station WDIA when he received his nickname "Blues Boy," given to him by station manager Don Kern. He recorded for Sun Records prior to Elvis. B.B. King claimed to have known Elvis before Elvis became a successful singer. Elvis watched King play at a club on Beale Street. Elvis and B.B. King appeared together at the WDIA Goodwill Review in December 1956.

King, The. Title conferred upon two entertainers—actor Clark Gable and singer Elvis Presley. When both men died, the news media publicized "The King is Dead."

On Sunday, February 11, 1979, the TV movie *Elvis*, on ABC, received a higher rating than *Gone With the Wind*, on CBS.

King Cotton. West Coast brand of bacon that Elvis especially liked.

King Creole. New Orleans nightclub, located on Bourbon Street, owned by Charlie LeGrand in the 1958 movie *King Creole*. Danny Fisher (Elvis) performed at the club.

KING CREOLE. Paramount, 1958. Premiered June 4, 1958 (115 min). Elvis's fourth movie. Producer, Hal B. Wallis. Associate

Producer, Paul Nathan. Director, Michael Curtiz. Cast: Danny Fisher/Elvis Presley, Bonnie/Carolyn Jones, Nellie/Dolores Hart, Mr. Fisher/Dean Jagger, Maxie Fields/Walter Matthau, "Forty" Nina/Lilliane Montevecchi, Shark/Vic Morrow, Mimi Fisher/Jan Shepard, Charlie LeGrand/Paul Stewart, Mr. Evans/Raymond Bailey, Chorus Girl/Ziva Rodann, Desk Clerk/Ned Glass, Doorman/Candy Candido, Girl/Lilyan Chauvin, Old Man/Franklyn Farnum, Old Woman/Minta Durfee, Old Woman/Hazel "Sonny" Boyne, The Jordanaire/The Jordanaires. Screenplay, Herbert Baker and Michael V. Gazzo. Photography, Russell Harlan. Music, Walter Scharf. Choreography, Charles O'Curran. Art Direction, Hal Pereira and Joseph MacMillan Johnson. Set Decoration, Sam Comer and Frank McKelvy. Special Effects, John P. Fulton. Costumes, Edith Head. Technical Adviser, Col. Tom Parker. Assistant Director, D. Michael Moore. Editor, Warren Low. Songs sung by Elvis: "King Creole," "Hard Headed Woman," "As Long as I Have You," "Trouble," "Dixieland Rock," "Don't Ask Me Why," "Lover Doll," "Crawfish" (sung with Kitty White), "Young Dreams," "Steadfast, Loyal and True," "New Orleans," "Turtles, Berries and Gumbo" (sung by black street vendors). "Banana" (sung by Lilliane Montevecchi). It was while filming this movie that Elvis was drafted into the Army. Elvis claimed this as his favorite movie role. It was the first Elvis movie to be shot on location.

King Creole. Title song of the 1958 movie *King Creole*. It was written by Jerry Leiber and Mike Stoller and appeared in the Extended Play albums "King Creole, Volume 1" (RCA EPA-4319) and "King Creole, Volume 1" (RCA EPA-5122) and the following Long Playing albums: "King Creole" (RCA LPM-1884); "King Creole" (RCA LSP-1884 [e]); "Elvis: The Other Sides—Worldwide Gold Award Hits, Volume 2" (RCA LPM-6402); "Elvis in Hollywood" (RCA DPL2-0168).

King Creole. RCA LPM-1884. A 33⅓ rpm Long Playing album that was released in August 1958. It reached #2 on *Billboard*'s Hot LP chart. "King Creole" featured the songs from the 1958 movie of the same name. RCA claims that this album sold over a million copies. Songs included—Side 1: "King Creole," "As Long as I Have You," "Hard Headed Woman," "Trouble," "Dixieland Rock." Side 2: "Don't Ask Me Why," "Lover Doll," "Crawfish," "Young Dreams," "Steadfast, Loyal and True," "New Orleans."

King Creole. RCA LSP-1884 (e). This record was the electronically reprocessed stereo re-issue of LPM-1884

King Creole, Volume 1. RCA EPA-4319. This was a 45 rpm Extended Play album released in October 1958. It reached #1 on *Billboard*'s Extended Play chart and sold over a million copies. Songs included—Side 1: "King Creole," "New Orleans." Side 2: "As Long as I Have You," "Lover Doll."

King Creole, Volume 1. RCA EPA-5122. This record was a Gold Standard Series re-issue of RCA EPA-4319 (April 1961).

King Creole, Volume 2. RCA EPA-4321. This was a 45 rpm Extended Play album released in October 1958. It reached #1 on *Billboard*'s Extended Play chart. Songs included—Side 1: "Trouble," "Young Dreams." Side 2: "Crawfish," "Dixieland Rock."

King Does the King's Thing, The. An Elvis tribute album by Albert King that was recorded on Stax Records (Stax STS 2015).

Kingfisher. Charter fishing boat skippered by Ross Carpenter (Elvis) in the 1962 movie *Girls! Girls! Girls!*. Ross later bought the sailboat *Westwind*.

King Is Coming Back, The. A 1959 Elvis novelty song by Billy and Eddie on Top Rank Records (Top Rank 2017). The song was about Elvis's discharge from the Army.

King Is Dead, The. Headlines in many of the world's newspapers following Elvis's death, including the Paris edition of *L'Humanité*—the Communist Party newspaper.

King Is Dead, The. Line that Gary Crosby said to Elvis in the 1962 movie *Girls! Girls! Girls!*.

King Is Dead—Elvis Presley, The. A 1977 book written by Martin A. Grove and published by Manor Books.

King Is Free (Love Me), The. A 1977 Elvis tribute record by Bruce Channel and Major Bill Smith on LeCam Records (LeCam 7277). Smith did a recitation over Channel's singing of "Love Me." The recitation was written by Dean Charles, Dr. James Wakefield Burke, and Major Bill Smith.

King Is Gone, The. A 1977 Elvis tribute record by Johnny Farago on Concorde Records (Concorde 18).

King Is Gone, The. (Scorpion 135) Ronnie McDowell's tribute record to Elvis. "The King Is Gone" was written by McDowell and Lee Morgan the night of Elvis's death and became the fastest-selling record of 1977. It became a million-seller just five days after its release.

King of Blue Suede Shoes, The. A 1977 Elvis tribute record by Rick Saucedo on Eclipse Records (Eclipse 1732).

King of Hearts. Award presented to Elvis by the March of Dimes on April 28, 1956.

King of Rock and Roll. A 1977 Elvis tribute record by Jim Camilli.

King of Rock 'n' Roll. Title conferred on Elvis by the press and his millions of fans.

King of Rock 'n' Roll, The. $10-million movie which remains unreleased. The screenplay was written by George Klein. Sol Swimmer and Bill Cash produced *The King of Rock 'n' Roll*. Considered for the role of Elvis were John Travolta, Lee Majors, Kris Kristofferson, and Warren Beatty.

King of Swoon. One of the many nicknames bestowed upon Elvis by the press.

King of the Whole Wide World. Song that Elvis sang in the 1962 movie *Kid Galahad*. The movie version has added string instruments. "King of the Whole Wide World" was written by Ruth Batchelor and Bob Roberts and appeared in the Extended Play album "Kid Galahad" (RCA EPA-4371) and the Long Playing albums "C'mon Everybody" (RCA Camden CAL-2518) and "C'mon Everybody" (Pickwick CAS-2518).

King of the Whole Wide World. RCA SP-45-18. Special 45 rpm promotional release. "Home Is Where the Heart Is" was on the flip side.

King of Western Bop, The. Nickname of Elvis in 1955 because his music was a cross between country and rhythm and blues. The style cannot be credited to Elvis alone. Others, such as Carl Perkins, were singing in that style.

King's Country, The. An Elvis novelty record by Jerry Jay released in 1966 by Quality Records (Quality 201).

King's Court. Name given to the social gatherings of Elvis and his friends.

Kingsley, James. Staff reporter for the *Memphis Commercial Appeal* newspaper. Kingsley is said to have been the reporter closest to Elvis.

Kingsley, James. Hollywood stuntman who, prior to going into films, was employed by Elvis as a bodyguard.

Kiowa. The tribe to which Pacer Burton's (Elvis) mother belonged in the 1960 movie *Flaming Star*. His mother was a full-blooded Kiowa and his father was white, making Pacer a half-breed.

Kirkham, Mildred. Back-up singer for Elvis in many recordings and live performances in the 1960s and '70s. On occasion, Millie Kirkham and Dolores Dinning sang with the Jordanaires.

Kirsch, Jack. Pharmacist at the Prescription House, located at 1247 Madison Ave., Memphis, who filled Dr. George Nichopoulos's prescriptions for Elvis. Over a seven-month period Jack Kirsch prepared 5,684 pills for Elvis.

Kismet. Song that Elvis sang in the 1965 movie *Harum Scarum*. This is not to be confused with the 1953 play *Kismet*. Written by Sid Tepper and Roy C. Bennett, "Kismet" appeared in the Long Playing album "Harum Scarum" (RCA LPM/LSP-3468).

KISSIN' COUSINS. MGM, 1964. Premiered Phoenix, Arizona, March 6, 1964 (96 min). Elvis's fourteenth movie. Producer, Sam Katzman. Director, Gene Nelson. Cast: Josh Morgan, Jodie Tatum/Elvis Presley, Pappy Tatum/Arthur O'Connell, Ma Tatum/Glenda Farrell, Capt. Robert Salbo/Jack Albertson, Selena Tatum/Pam Austin, Midge/Cynthia Pepper, Azalea Tatum/Yvonne Craig, Gen. Alvin Danford/Donald Woods, M/Sgt. William George Bailey/Tommy Farrell, Trudy/Beverly Powers, Dixie/Hortense Petra, General's Aide/Robert Stone, Mike/Joseph Esposito, Loraine/Maureen Reagan, Jonesy/Joan Staley, Gen. Sam Kruger/Robert Carson. Screenplay, Gerald Drayson Adams and Gene Nelson. Photography, Ellis W. Carter. Music,

Fred Karger. Choreography, Hal Belfer. Art Direction, George W. Davis and Eddie Imazu. Set Decoration, Henry Grace and Budd S. Friend. Technical Adviser, Col. Tom Parker. Assistant Director, Eli Dunn. Editor, Ben Lewis. Songs Sung by Elvis: "Kissin' Cousins," "Once Is Enough," "One Boy, Two Little Girls," "Smokey Mountain Boy," "There's Gold in the Mountains," "Tender Feeling," "Catchin' on Fast," "Barefoot Ballad," "Kissin' Cousins No. 2." Glenda Farrell sang "Pappy, Won't You Please Come Home." "Anyone (Could Fall in Love with You)" was cut from the film.

Kissin' Cousins. RCA 47-8307. Released in February 1964 as a 45 rpm single. It reached #12 on *Billboard*'s Hot 100 chart. "Kissin' Cousins" was written by Fred Wise and Randy Starr and was a million-seller. "It Hurts Me" was on the flip side. "Kissin' Cousins" was the title song of the 1964 movie of the same name. "Kissin' Cousins (No. 2)" is a completely different song. "Kissin' Cousins" appeared in the following Long Playing albums: "Kissin' Cousins" (RCA LPM/LSP-2894); "Elvis: Worldwide 50 Gold Award Hits, Volume 1" (RCA LPM-6401); "Elvis in Hollywood" (RCA DPL2-0168).

Kissin' Cousins. RCA 447-0644. Gold Standard Series re-issue of RCA 47-8307.

Kissin' Cousins. RCA LSP/LPM-2894. A 33⅓ rpm Long Playing album that was released in March 1964. It reached #6 on *Billboard*'s Hot LP chart. "Kissin' Cousins" featured songs from the 1964 movie of the same name, plus three bonus songs. Songs included—Side 1: "Kissin' Cousins (No. 2)", "Smokey Mountain Boy," "There's Gold in the Mountains," "One Boy, Two Little Girls," "Catchin' on Fast," "Tender Feeling." Side 2: "Anyone (Could Fall in Love with You)" (bonus), "Barefoot Ballad," "Once Is Enough," "Kissin' Cousins," "Echoes of Love" (bonus), "(It's A) Long, Lonely Highway" (bonus).

Kissin' Cousins (No. 2). Song that Elvis sang in the 1964 movie *Kissin' Cousins*. This is a completely different version from the "Kissin' Cousins" that was released as a single. "Kissin' Cousins (No. 2)" was written by Bill Giant, Bernie Baum, and Florence Kaye and appeared in the Long Playing album "Kissin' Cousins" (RCA LPM/LSP-2894).

Kiss Me Quick. RCA 447-0639. Released in April 1964 as a 45 rpm single—the first original Gold Standard Series issue. It reached #34 on *Billboard*'s Hot 100 chart. "Suspicion" was on the flip side. A different version of "Kiss Me Quick" appeared in the foreign EP "Elvis Presley." One of the stereo channels, with the Jordanaires on it, was omitted. "Kiss Me Quick" was written by Doc Pomus and Mort Shuman and appeared in the Long Playing album "Pot Luck" (RCA LPM/LSP-2523). The Beatles once rated the song when they were contestants on the British TV series "Juke Box Jury" in 1964.

Kiss My Firm But Pliant Lips. Novel, by Dan Greenberg, on which the 1968 movie *Live a Little, Love a Little* is based.

Klein, George. Disc jockey for Memphis radio station WHBQ. Elvis met George Klein while he was attending Humes High School and they soon became very close friends. Klein was president of Elvis's senior class. In 1961 Klein cut one record for Sun, titled "U.T. Party" (Sun 358). George Klein had bit parts in the Elvis movies *Frankie and Johnny* and *Double Trouble*. His disc jockey voice is heard in the 1972 documentary, *Elvis on Tour*. When George got married, Elvis was his best man. The screenplay for the 1979 movie *The King of Rock 'n' Roll* was written by George Klein. George Klein's wife Barbara once worked for Dr. George Nichopoulos.

Known Only to Him. RCA 447-0651. Released in February 1966 as a 45 rpm Gold Standard Series original. "Joshua Fit the Battle" was on the flip side. Written by Stuart Hamblen, "Known Only to Him" appeared in the following Long Playing albums: "His Hand in Mine" (RCA LPM/LSP-2328); "His Hand in Mine" (RCA ANL1-1319); "He Walks Beside Me" (RCA AFL1-2772).

Kristofferson, Kris. Singer-songwriter whose first professional job with Columbia Records was cleaning their Nashville studios. Kristofferson is the son of a retired Air Force general. He was class president in high school, played football, and was an honor student. He attended Oxford University as a Rhodes Scholar. Kristofferson has authored several books and has won a contest for a short story sponsored by the *Atlantic Monthly*. He has been a Golden Gloves boxer, attended jump school in the Army, and flew helicopters in Vietnam as an Army captain. After stints as a janitor and a civilian helicopter pilot, Kristofferson wrote "Me and Bobby McGhee," which Roger Miller (Smash 2230) and Janis Joplin (Columbia 45314) recorded. Soon, he signed a recording contract with Monument Records. In addition to his music career, Kris Kristofferson began a movie career in the early 1970s. In 1976 he costarred with Barbra Streisand in *A Star Is Born*—a movie for which he wrote many of the songs. Elvis recorded three Kris Kristofferson songs: "Help Me Make It Through the Night"; "Why Me Lord"; and "For the Good Times."

KTED. Freegate, Texas, television station that filmed the national TV program featuring rock 'n' roll star Deke Rivers in the 1957 movie *Loving You*.

Kuiokalani Lee Cancer Fund. Charity named for Hawaiian composer Kuiokalani Lee, who died of cancer. Elvis's TV special "Aloha from Hawaii" was a benefit for the cancer fund. Kuiokalani Lee composed "I'll Remember You," which Elvis sang during the benefit concert. Earlier, in 1966, Elvis recorded the song. (See: Elvis: Aloha from Hawaii)

Kumpf Lincoln-Mercury. Denver car dealership, located at 869 Broadway, from which Elvis purchased five cars (totaling

$70,000) for friends on January 14, 1976. Elvis was vacationing in Vail, Colorado, at the time. (See: Kennedy, Jerry; Starkey, Gerald)

Ku-u-i-po. Song that Elvis sang in the 1961 movie *Blue Hawaii*. The film version had female vocal back-up.

"Ku-u-i-po" was recorded by Elvis for—but did not appear in—the U. S. edition of the worldwide TV concert "Aloha from Hawaii." The song did not appear in the soundtrack album from the TV broadcast, but it was included in the "Mahalo from Elvis" album.

"Ku-u-i-po" means "Hawaiian sweetheart" and was written by George Weiss, Hugo Peretti, and Luigi Creatore.* It appeared in the Long Playing albums "Blue Hawaii" (RCA LPM/LSP-2426) and "Mahalo from Elvis" (Pickwick ACL-7064).

KWKH. Shreveport, Louisiana, radio station that aired the "Louisiana Hayride." Elvis performed and did commercials for the station in 1955. (See: Louisiana Hayride)

L

Lacker, Marty. Member of the Memphis Mafia 1960–67. He served as Elvis's personal bookkeeper and secretary. Marty Lacker was Elvis's best man (along with Joe Esposito) at his wedding. In 1979 he coauthored the book *Elvis: Portrait of a Friend.*

Lacker, Marty and Esposito, Joe. Two witnesses who signed Elvis and Priscilla's marriage license.

Lady Loves Me, The. Song that Elvis and Ann-Margret sang, as a duet, in the 1964 movie *Viva Las Vegas*. Ann-Margret requested that "The Lady Loves Me" not be released by RCA on record. It does, however, appear on a French bootleg LP, "Trouble in Vegas," and several other bootleg LPs and EPs.

Lance and the Spirits. Group which played the house band at the Hangout in the 1968 movie *Speedway*.

Lanchester, Elsa. Theater and movie actress who played Madame Neherina in the 1967 movie *Easy Come, Easy Go*. Elsa Lanchester was married to actor Charles Laughton, who introduced Elvis Presley on "The Ed Sullivan Show" on September 9, 1956. (See: Laughton, Charles; Frankenstein)

Lane, Jocelyn. Actress who costarred with Elvis in the 1965 movie *Tickle Me*. She became a princess when she married into British royalty in 1971. She first appeared in films at the age of

---

*In 1957 Hugo and Luigi purchased Roulette Records from George Goldner.

six. While Miss Lane was filming *Tickle Me* for Allied Artists, she was under contract to Universal.

Langdon, Sue Ann. Actress who appeared in the Elvis movies *Roustabout* (1964), as Madame Mijanou, and *Frankie and Johnny* (1966), as Mitzi.

Lange, Hope. Female lead, as Irene Sperry, in the 1961 movie *Wild in the Country*, along with Tuesday Weld and Millie Perkins.

Lansbury, Angela. Actress who played Sarah Lee Gates in the 1961 movie *Blue Hawaii*. Angela Lansbury's grandfather George Lansbury was the leader of the British Labour Party from 1931 to 1935.

Lansky, Bernard. Co-owner of Lansky's Clothing Emporium in Memphis. In 1956 Elvis traded Lansky his Messerschmidt for clothes. (See: Messerschmidt)

Lansky Brothers. Memphis men's clothing store, established in 1939 as an Army surplus store by Bernard and Guy Lansky, located at 126 Beale Street. They specialized in loud clothing, i.e. yellow suits, pink sports coats, and white shoes. The store catered mainly to black patrons, including Rufus Thomas and Junior Parker. Elvis first stopped there in 1952 and bought clothes from Lansky's for many years. Many of the Sun recording artists—Sonny Burgess, Billy Riley, Charlie Feathers, Roy Orbison, and Bill Justice—bought their clothes at Lansky's. Lansky Brothers provided the suits for both Elvis and Vernon Presley's pall-bearers at their funerals.

La Paloma. Song that Elvis recorded for the 1961 movie *Blue Hawaii* but which was cut from the final print of the film. Some sources state that "La Paloma" was another name for "No More," which did appear in the film. "La Paloma" is not available on record.

Last Farewell, The. Song written by Roger Whittaker and R.A. Webster and originally recorded by Roger Whittaker (RCA 10494) in 1975. Elvis recorded "The Last Farewell" at Graceland in 1976 and it appeared in the Long Playing album "From Elvis Presley Boulevard, Memphis, Tennessee" (RCA APL1-1506).

Last Farewell, The. A 33⅓ rpm bootleg album on E.P. Records that contained Elvis's complete ninety-minute concert at the Market Square Arena in Indianapolis, Indiana (June 26, 1977). Songs included—Side 1: "2001 Space Odyssey," "C. C. Rider," "I Got a Woman," "Amen," "Love Me," "Fairy Tale." Side 2: "You Gave Me a Mountain," "Jailhouse Rock," "O Sole Mio," "It's Now or Never," "Little Sister," "Teddy Bear," "Don't Be Cruel," "Release Me," "I Can't Stop Loving You." Side 3: "Bridge Over Troubled Water," Introduction of the Backing Vocals, "Early Morning Rain," "What'd I Say," "Johnny B. Goode," TCB Band Theme, "Blues A La Scheff," "Two Miles Pike." Side 4: "I Really Don't Want to Know," "Bobby's

Choice," "Jazzing in Vegas," "Hurt," "Hound Dog," Introduction, "Can't Help Falling in Love," "Closing Vamp."

Lastfogel, Abe. Top executive of the William Morris Agency and Elvis's personal agent.

Last Photograph. Rare photograph of Elvis lying in his open coffin, taken by two of Elvis's close friends. The *National Enquirer*, which owns the exclusive rights to the photograph, ran the picture on the cover of its September 6, 1977, issue, selling out in record time.

Because of the hairstyle* in the picture, many Elvis fans believe the picture to be phony.

Last Will and Testament. Elvis's thirteen-page will, dated March 3, 1977, and witnessed by Charles Hodge, Ginger Alden, and Ann Dewey Smith (wife of the attorney). Copies of Elvis's will were being hawked in Memphis for four dollars each.

Las Vegas Hilton. New name (since 1971) of the International Hotel in Las Vegas. Elvis made three appearances under the hotel's original name (1969–70) and appeared there on thirteen separate occasions under the new name (1971–76).

Las Vegas International Hotel. Resort hotel (first major hotel built off the famous Strip) where, on July 31, 1969, Elvis began his comeback with a live concert. He earned $1 million for his four-week appearance. The hotel has been called the Las Vegas Hilton since 1971.

Lauderdale Courts. Federally funded housing project at 185 Winchester Street in Memphis; the Presleys resided, for thirty-five dollars a month rent, in one of the 433 units. (See: 185 Winchester)

Laughton, Charles. Actor who substituted for Ed Sullivan on TV's "The Ed Sullivan Show" on September 9, 1956, the evening Elvis made his first appearance on the series. Laughton also gave a recitation of Shakespeare during the show. Laughton had previously made his TV debut on Sullivan's "Toast of the Town" in 1949, reciting *The Burning Fiery Furnace* from the Book of Daniel.

Laurel Records. Second record label for which Vince Everett (Elvis) recorded in the 1957 movie *Jailhouse Rock*. He co-owned the label. (See: Geneva Records; Royal Records)

Laurel Records 101. Release of "Treat Me Nice" by Vince Everett (Elvis) in the 1957 movie *Jailhouse Rock*.

Laurence, Douglas. Producer of the following Elvis movies: *Live a Little, Love a Little* (1968 MGM), *Spinout* (1960 MGM), and *Stay Away, Joe* (1968 MGM).

Laven, Arnold; Gardner, Arthur; Levy, Jules. Producers of the 1967 United Artists movie *Clambake*.

Law Enforcement. Police-accessories store in Memphis, owned by Charles Church, where Elvis bought his guns.

---

*Similar to the one he wore when he got out of the Army.

Lawdy, Miss Clawdy. RCA 20/47-6642. Released in September of 1956 as a 78 rpm single and a 45 rpm single. "Shake, Rattle, and Roll" was on the flip side. "Lawdy, Miss Clawdy"* was written and originally recorded by Lloyd Price (Specialty 428) in 1952. Cliff Richard's first demo record sent out to British record companies was "Lawdy Miss Clawdy" b/w "Breathless." Elvis sang "Lawdy, Miss Clawdy" in the 1968 NBC-TV special "Elvis" and the 1972 documentary *Elvis on Tour*. In the 1969 movie *Change of Habit*, Dr. John Carpenter (Elvis) played the song on the piano. "Lawdy, Miss Clawdy" appeared in the Extended Play album "Elvis Presley" (RCA EPA-830) and the following Long Playing albums: "For LP Fans Only" (RCA LPM-1990); "For LP Fans Only" (RCA LSP-1990 [e]); "Elvis —TV Special" (RCA LPM-4088); "Elvis Recorded Live on Stage in Memphis" (RCA CPL1-0606).

Lawdy, Miss Clawdy. RCA 447-0615. Gold Standard Series reissue of RCA 20/47-6642.

Lawhon Elementary. Grammar school attended by Elvis in East Tupelo, Mississippi.

Lawrence of Arabia. A 1962 movie based on the life of Thomas Edward Lawrence (1888–1935), starring Peter O'Toole which won an Academy Award for Best Picture. *Lawrence of Arabia* was one of Elvis's favorite movies.

L.C. Humes High School. (See: Humes High School)

Lead Me, Guide Me. Gospel song written by Doris Akers and recorded by Elvis in 1971. Elvis sang "Lead Me, Guide Me" in a duet with the Stamps backstage in the 1972 documentary *Elvis on Tour*. It appeared in the Long Playing Album "He Touched Me" (RCA LSP-4690).

Leaf on a Tree. Song that Elvis sang to his class on his last day at Milam Jr. High, the day before he left with his parents to move to Memphis in the fall of 1948.

Leave My Sideburns Be. Novelty song recorded in late 1956 by Steve Schickel, a disc jockey for radio station WGN in Chicago. The song was inspired by the false report in *Billboard* magazine that Elvis was going to be inducted into the Army.

Leave My Woman Alone. Song that Elvis recorded for the 1967 movie *Easy Come, Easy Go,* but it was not used. "Leave My Woman Alone" has never been released in any form.

Lee, Dickie. Memphis-born singer (real name: Dickie Lipscomb) who had the hit "Patches"† in 1962. Dickie Lee, a former Golden Gloves Champion, composed "She Thinks I Still Care," which Elvis recorded in 1976. Dickie Lee was a personal friend of Elvis and visited Graceland on a number of occasions. Dickie Lee's band was called the Collegiates, and his first Sun

---

*In Lloyd Price's version of "Lawdy, Miss Clawdy," Fats Domino played piano.
†Produced by Jack Clement.

release, "Good Lovin'" (Sun 280), closely resembled Elvis's version of "Too Much."

Lee, Peggy. Singer of the 1940s–50s. She composed the theme music for the 1954 movie *Johnny Guitar* and the 1960 movie *The Time Machine*. Peggy Lee replaced Elvis as headliner at the Las Vegas Hilton Hotel on August 23, 1976, when Elvis became ill (Elvis returned to Memphis, where he was hospitalized at the Baptist Hospital). Bill Cosby and Roy Clark were billed for the remainder of the Presley engagement. Peggy Lee recorded a hit version of "Fever" in 1958. Elvis recorded "Fever" in 1960.

LeGault, Lance. Louisiana blues singer and double for Elvis in his movies from 1960 to 1968. Lance LeGault was also assistant choreographer in the films. A blooper occurred in the 1963 movie *Kissin' Cousins* in which Elvis played twins. When both the twins were on the screen, LeGault would be the twin with his back to the camera. In the final scene of the movie, LeGault could be seen looking straight into the camera. Director Sam Katzman didn't think anyone would notice.

Legend Lives, The. A 1978 Broadway show at the Palace Theatre that starred Rick Saucedo. Pomus and Foster composed the music. Kathy Westmoreland and the Jordanaires sang vocal back-up for Saucedo in the show. The play lasted only two months. Not far away, at the Winter Garden Theatre, *Beatlemania* was featured at the same time.

Legend Lives On, The. A 33⅓ rpm bootleg LP released in 1977 on the Presley Collector Series label (PCS 1001). It featured live material from Las Vegas. Songs included—Side 1: Dialogue, "Yesterday"/"Hey Jude," "Happy Birthday" (To James Burton), "In the Ghetto," "Suspicious Minds." Side 2: "What'd I Say," "Can't Help Falling in Love," "It's Over," "A Big Hunk o' Love," "It's Impossible," "The Impossible Dream," "Bridge Over Troubled Water."

Legend Lives On, The. Tribute record by Rick Saucedo on Fraternity Records (Fraternity 3416). D.J. Fontana and the Jordanaires provided part of the backing.

Legend of Elvis Presley, The. A 1977 Elvis tribute record by Dub Crouch on Professional Artist Records (Professional Artists 774588).

Legend of a King, The. A 1977 Elvis tribute record by Warren Jacks on Paper Dragon Records (Paper Dragon 5083).

Leiber and Stoller. Prolific songwriting team of Jerry Leiber and Mike Stoller. The pair composed songs for many artists, beginning in 1952. They included: "Kansas City"; "Down in Mexico"; "Searchin'"; "Yakety-Yak"; "Poison Ivy"; "Charlie Brown"; "Black Denim Trousers and Motorcycle Boots"; "Love Potion #9"; "On Broadway"; "Ruby Baby"; "I Am Woman." Those compositions of Leiber and Stoller that Elvis recorded were: "Jailhouse Rock"; "Girls! Girls! Girls!"; "Bossa Nova Baby";

"Loving You"; "Treat Me Nice"; "Love Me"; "Trouble"; "Just Tell Her Jim Said Hello"; "Dirty Dirty Feelin'"; "Santa Claus Is Back in Town"; "(You're So Square) Baby I Don't Care"; "Hound Dog"; "Little Egypt"; "Saved"; "Hot Dog"; "She's Not You." Mike Stoller appeared in the 1957 movie *Jailhouse Rock*, playing piano for Vince Everett's (Elvis) band. On July 26, 1956, Mike Stoller, along with actress Ruth Roman and Cary Grant's third wife, Betsy Drake, were on board the Italian liner *Andrea Doria* when it was rammed by the Swedish liner *Stockholm* off Nantucket. The *Andrea Doria* sank.

Lennon, John and Dylan, Bob. Two rock superstars who attended Elvis's concert at Madison Square Garden in New York on June 10, 1972.

Lepley, (Sleepy Eyed) John. Memphis disc jockey who booked the Eagles Nest ballroom, where Elvis made some of his first professional appearances in early 1954, earning ten dollars a night. He tried to become Elvis's manager, but Scotty Moore beat him to it. (See: Moore, Scotty) Lepley was one of the first disc jockeys to play "Blue Moon of Kentucky," the country side of "That's All Right (Mama)," in July 1954 on station WHHM. (See: WHHM)

Let It Be Me. Song written by Mann Curtis, Pierre Delanoe, and Gilbert Becaud under the French title "Je t'Appartiens." "Let It Be Me" was introduced by Gilbert Becaud in France in 1955 and first presented to American audiences by Jill Corey in an episode of the TV series "Climax" in 1957. Jill Corey (real name: Norma Jean Speranza) first recorded "Let It Be Me" (Columbia 40878) in 1957, but it wasn't until the Everly Brothers (Cadence 1376) recorded the song in 1960 that it became popular. Elvis recorded "Let It Be Me" in 1970 and it appeared in the Long Playing albums "On Stage—February, 1970" (RCA LSP-4362) and "Elvis—A Legendary Performer, Volume 3" (RCA CPL1-3082).

Let Me. Song that Elvis sang in the 1956 movie *Love Me Tender*. The film version has girls screaming and hands clapping. Though Elvis and Vera Matson are credited with writing "Let Me," Ken Darby was actually the composer. (See: Darby, Ken) "Let Me" appeared in the Extended Play album "Love Me Tender" (RCA EPA-4006) and the Long Playing album "Elvis: The Other Sides—Worldwide Gold Award Hits, Volume 2" (RCA LPM-6402).

Let Me Be There. Song written by John Rostill* and originally recorded by Olivia Newton-John (MCA 40101) in 1973. "Let Me Be There" sold over a million copies and won a Grammy Award for Ms. Newton-John as Best Female Country Vocal of 1973. Elvis recorded "Let Me Be There" in 1974 and it appeared in the Long Playing albums "Elvis Recorded Live on

---

*John Rostill is an ex-member of the English group the Shadows.

Stage in Memphis (RCA CPL1-0606) and "Moody Blue" (RCA AFL1-2428).

Let Me Be There (Mono)/Let Me Be There (Stereo). RCA JH-10951. A 45 rpm special promotional release in 1977. The publisher of "Let Me Be There," Al Gallico, had RCA press 2,000 copies of this record to distribute to radio stations. Gallica wanted to force the release of "Let Me Be There" by RCA.

Let Me Call You Sweetheart. Ballad written by Beth Slater Whitson and Leo Friedman in 1910. "Let Me Call You Sweetheart"* was one of many songs played at Elvis and Priscilla's wedding reception at Graceland on May 29, 1967.

Let's Be Friends. Song that was originally scheduled to be in the 1970 movie *Change of Habit*. It was cut from the film. "Let's Be Friends" was written by Arnold, Morrow, and Martin and appeared in the Long Playing albums "Let's Be Friends" (RCA Camden CAS-2408) and "Let's Be Friends" (Pickwick CAS-2408).

Let's Be Friends. RCA Camden CAS-2408. A 33⅓ rpm Long Playing album released in April 1970. "Let's Be Friends" reached #105 on *Billboard*'s Hot LP chart. Songs included— Side 1: "Stay Away, Joe," "If I'm a Fool (For Loving You)," "Let's Be Friends," "Let's Forget About the Stars," "Mama." Side 2: "I'll Be There (If Ever You Want Me)," "Almost," "Change of Habit," "Have a Happy."

Let's Be Friends. Pickwick CAS-2408. A 33⅓ rpm Long Playing album that was a re-issue of RCA Camden CAS-2408.

Let's Forget About the Stars. Song written by Al Owens and recorded by Elvis in 1969. "Let's Forget About the Stars" appeared in the Long Playing albums "Let's Be Friends" (RCA Camden CAS-2408) and "Let's Be Friends" (Pickwick CAS-2408).

Let's Live a Little. Song that Elvis recorded for the 1968 movie *Live a Little, Love a Little,* but it was cut from the final print of the film.

Letter to Elvis, A. A 1977 Elvis tribute record by Odie Palmer on Little Gem Records (Little Gem 1020).

Let Us Pray. Song that Elvis sang in the 1970 movie *Change of Habit.* "Let Us Pray" was written by Ben Weisman and Buddy Kaye and appeared in the Long Playing albums "You'll Never Walk Alone" (RCA Camden CALX-2472) and "You'll Never Walk Alone" (Pickwick CAS-2472).

Let Yourself Go. RCA 47-9547. Released in May 1968 as a 45 rpm single. It reached #71 on *Billboard*'s hot 100 chart. "Let Yourself Go" reportedly sold over a million copies. "Your Time Hasn't Come Yet, Baby" was on the flip side. Elvis sang

---

*"Let Me Call You Sweetheart" was the first song published by music publisher Harold Rossiter.

"Let Yourself Go" in the 1968 movie *Speedway* and recorded it for the 1968 NBC-TV special "Elvis." The song was sung in a bordello scene, which was cut from the telecast. "Let Yourself Go" was written by Joy Byers and appeared in the Long Playing albums "Speedway" (RCA LSP-3989) and "Elvis—A Legendary Performer, Volume 3" (RCA CPL1-3082).

Let Yourself Go. RCA 447-0666. Gold Standard Series re-issue of RCA 47-9547.

Levitch, Harry. Memphis jeweler, Harry Levitch Jewelers, 159 Union Ave., from whom Elvis bought Priscilla's wedding ring in 1967. It was a $4,000 three-karat diamond ring surrounded by twenty smaller diamonds.

Lewis, George. One of the guards employed to protect Graceland.

Lewis, Jerry Lee. Country/rock singer born in Ferriday, Louisiana, September 29, 1935. In his youth he listened to many Al Jolson records (he still has a large collection). He went to Memphis in 1956 in order to record for the Sun label. His first release was "Crazy Arms" (Sun 259) in 1957. His biggest hit record came in 1957. It was a song that Sam Phillips insisted he record, against Lewis's argument that it had suggestive lyrics. "Whole Lotta Shakin' Goin' On"* (Sun 267) was recorded in only one take. Lewis was billed as Jerry Lee Lewis and his Pumping Piano. Lewis, who was nicknamed the "Killer", became the only guest to appear on "American Bandstand" who sang live rather than lip-sync to his records. He made his national debut on the "Steve Allen Show," later naming one of his sons Steve Allen Lewis (the boy drowned in the family pool in 1962). Jerry Lee Lewis's career as a rock 'n' roll artist was ruined when in 1958 he married his thirteen-year-old third cousin, Myra Brown. In 1960 he cut an instrumental on the Phillips International label, "In the Mood"/"I Get the Blues When It Rains" (Phillips 3559) under the name Hawk. Lewis was one of the participants in the famed Million Dollar Session. Lewis left Sun Records on September 29, 1963, to record for Mercury's subsidiary label Smash, then run by Shelby Singleton. In December 1976 Lewis was arrested for shooting a gun outside the gates of Graceland in the early morning hours, when he was refused permission to see Elvis. Lewis was a patient of Dr. George Nichopoulos, from whom Lewis could obtain prescriptions for vast amounts of legal pills. Jerry Lee Lewis has been successful in both the rock and the country fields. Country artist Mickey Gilley, the owner of the world's largest nightclub, is the cousin of Jerry Lee Lewis. Jerry Lee Lewis and Elvis Presley were not Sun Record artists at the same time (See: Million Dollar Session)

Lewis, Paulette Shafer. One of a number of secretaries at Graceland.

---

*John Lennon called it the greatest rock 'n' roll song ever written.

Lewis, Sammy. Producer at the New Frontier Hotel in Las Vegas who signed Elvis for his first Las Vegas performance, April 23–29, 1956.

Lewis, Smiley. R & B artist (1920–65) of the early 1950s (real name: Overton Amos Lemons). Fats Domino covered his 1954 hit "Blue Monday"; Gale Storm covered his 1955 hit "I Hear You Knockin' "; Elvis covered his 1956 hit "One Night" (Lewis's version was originally titled "One Night of Sin").

Lewis Boogie. A 1958 Jerry Lee Lewis Sun recording (Sun 301) in which he made reference to "Memphis" and "Presley Boy You Ain't Nothin' But a Hound."

Liberace. Now legal name of millionaire pianist Wladziu Valentino Liberace. (Lee is his nickname). Elvis and Liberace appeared in Las Vegas together in 1956. Liberace and his brother George went backstage to meet Elvis at the New Frontier, where Elvis got Liberace's autograph to give to his mother. Photos of the two meeting were published in many magazines.

Libertyland. Memphis amusement park, on East Parkway, previously called Fairgrounds Amusement Park and rented by Elvis for $14,000 on August 7, 1977, from 1:15 A.M. until dawn as a present for Lisa Marie.

Lichter, Paul. President of the Elvis Unique Record Club and the Memphis Flash Record label, in suburban Philadelphia. He acquired Elvis's red "Burning Love" jumpsuit by donating $5,000 and a rare Elvis Sun Record to a Cerebral Palsy Telethon in March 1974 in Nashville.

Lido, The. Paris nightclub where Elvis once appeared on stage as an unplanned act while he was stationed overseas (1958–60). (On May 29, 1979, Shirley MacLaine and Tom Jones hosted a TV special "From the Lido De Paris.")

Life. RCA 47-9985. Released in May 1971 as a 45 rpm single. It reached #53 on *Billboard*'s Hot 100 chart and #34 on the Country chart. "Only Believe" was on the flip side. "Life" was written by Shirl Milete and appeared in the Long Playing album "Love Letters from Elvis" (RCA LSP-4530).

Life. RCA 447-0682. Gold Standard Series re-issue of RCA 47-9985.

Life of Elvis, The. Book by Sean Shaver and Hal Noland.

Life of Elvis, The. A 1977 Elvis tribute record by Pam Cassidy and Cindy Watson on the Moon Record label (Moon 1003).

Life Magazine. First national magazine to do a feature story on Elvis. They interviewed him in Amarillo, Texas, in 1956.

Lightfoot, Gordon. Canadian-born singer and composer. He wrote "Early Mornin' Rain" and "For Lovin' Me," both of which were originally recorded by Peter, Paul and Mary. Elvis recorded both songs years later, on March 15, 1971. In 1974, when Lightfoot divorced his wife, he made the largest alimony settlement in Canada's history. She received both children, a $220,000 house, $150,000 in cash, and $4,500 a month.

Like a Baby. Song written by Jesse Stone and recorded by James Brown (King 5710) in 1963. Elvis recorded "Like a Baby" in 1960 and it appeared in the Long Playing album "Elvis Is Back" (RCA LPM/LSP-2231).

Lime, Yvonne. Hollywood actress whom Elvis dated in 1957. He met her on the set of *Loving You*. On television, Yvonne Lime was a regular on three series: "Father Knows Best" (As Dottie Snow, Betty's friend); "The Many Loves of Dobie Gillis" (as Melissa Frame); "Happy" (as Sally Day).

Linde, Dennis. Abilene, Texas, composer and occasional bass guitarist in Elvis's recording band in the 1970s. He composed "For the Heart," "Burning Love," and "I Got a Feelin' in My Body," which were recorded by Elvis.

Lipstick. Elvis-related product sold in the 1950s, each tube costing a dollar. The colors were Tender Pink, Heartbreak Pink, Love-ya Fuchia, Hound Dog Orange, Tutti Frutti Red, and Cruel Red.

Lisa Marie. Elvis Presley's custom blue-and-white Convair 880 jet (N880EP), bought at a price of $1.2 million in November 1975. Named for his daughter, the jet required a crew of four, including the stewardess. It was characterized by the letters TCB (Taking Care of Business) and a lightning bolt in gold on the tail section under an American flag. The crew were Elwood David (captain), Ron Strauss (copilot), and Jim Manny (flight engineer). The *Lisa Marie* had a queen-size bed costing $13,000.

Little Baby Bunting. Linda Thompson's nickname for Elvis Presley.

Littlebit. Name of toy French poodle that Elvis gave Anita Wood for Christmas in 1958.

Little Bit of Green, A. Song written by Arnold, Morrow, and Martin and recorded by Elvis in 1969 at the American Sound Studios in Memphis. "A Little Bit of Green" appeared in the Long Playing albums "From Memphis to Vegas"/"From Vegas to Memphis" (RCA LSP-6020) and "Elvis—Back in Memphis" (RCA LSP-4429).

Little Cabin on the Hill. Song written by Bill Monroe and Lester Flatt and originally recorded by Bill Monroe's Bluegrass Boys (Columbia 20459) in 1949. Elvis recorded "Little Cabin on the Hill" in 1970 and it appeared in the Long Playing album "Elvis Country" (RCA LSP-4460).

Little Darlin'. RCA 50476. Released in 1978 in Canada as a 45 rpm single. "Little Darlin' " was released on gold vinyl. "I'm Movin' On" was on the flip side. "Little Darlin' " was composed by Maurice Williams and originally recorded by the Gladiolas (Excello 2101) in 1957. The Diamonds had a #2 hit and million-seller with "Little Darlin' " (Mercury 71060) later in 1957. Elvis's version of "Little Darlin' " appeared in the Long Playing albums "Moody Blue" (RCA AFL1-2428) and "Elvis —A Canadian Tribute" (RCA KKL1-7065).

Little Egypt. Song that Elvis sang in the 1964 movie *Roustabout*.

There is additional instrumentation in the film version. The Coasters originally recorded "Little Egypt" in 1961 (Atco 6192). Written by Jerry Leiber and Mike Stoller, "Little Egypt" appeared in the Long Playing albums "Roustabout" (RCA LPM/LSP-2999) and "Elvis—TV Special" (RCA LPM-4088).

Little Girl. Unreleased song that Elvis recorded on acetate only.

Little Less Conversation, A. RCA 47-9610. Released in September 1968 as a 45 rpm single. It reached #63 on *Billboard*'s Hot 100 chart. "Almost in Love" was on the flip side. Elvis sang "A Little Less Conversation" in the 1968 movie *Live a Little, Love a Little*. It was written by Billy Strange and Mac Davis and appeared in the Long Playing albums "Almost in Love" (RCA Camden CAS-2440) and "Almost in Love" (Pickwick CAS-2440).

Little Less Conversation, A. RCA 447-0667. Gold Standard Series re-issue of RCA 47-9610.

Little Sister. RCA 47-7908. Released in August 1961 as a 45 rpm single. It reached #5 on *Billboard*'s Hot 100 chart. "Little Sister" sold over a million copies. "(Marie's the Name) His Latest Flame" was on the flip side. Elvis sang "Little Sister" in the 1970 documentary *Elvis—That's the Way It Is*. In 1961 LaVerne Baker recorded "Hey, Memphis" (Atlantic 2119), which used the same melody as "Little Sister." Written by Doc Pomus and Mort Shuman, "Little Sister" appeared in the following Long Playing albums: "Elvis' Golden Records, Volume 3" (RCA LPM/LSP-2765); "Elvis: Worldwide 50 Gold Award Hits, Volume 1" (RCA LPM-6401); "Elvis in Concert" (RCA SPL2-2587).

Little Sister. RCA 447-0634. Gold Standard Series re-issue of RCA 47-7908.

LIVE A LITTLE, LOVE A LITTLE. MGM, 1968. Premiered Los Angeles October 23, 1968 (89 min). Elvis's twenty-eighth movie. Producer, Douglas Laurence. Director, Norman Taurog. Cast: Greg/Elvis Presley, Bernice/Michele Carey, Mike Landsdown/Don Porter, Penlow/Rudy Vallee, Harry/Dick Sargent, Milkman/Sterling Holloway, Ellen/Celeste Yarnell, Delivery Boy/Eddie Hodges, Robbie's Mother/Joan Shawlee, Receptionist/Emily Banks, Art Director/Michael Keller, 1st Secretary/Merri Ashley, 2d Secretary/Phyllis Davis, Perfume Model/Ursula Menzel, Model No. 1/Susan Shute, Model No. 2/Edie Baskin, Model No. 3/Gabrielle, Model No. 4/Giny Kaneen, Mermaid/Susan Henning, 1st Motorcycle Cop/Morgan Windbell, 2d Motorcycle Cop/Benjie Nacroft. Screenplay, Michael A. Hoey and Dan Greenburg. Photograhy, Fred Koenekamp. Music, Billy Strange. Choregraphy, Jack Regas and Jack Baker. Art Direction, George W. Davis and Preston Ames. Set Decoration, Henry Grace and Don Greenwood, Jr. Assistant Director, Al Shenberg. Editor, John McSweeney. Songs Sung by Elvis: "A

Little Less Conversation," "Almost In Love," "Edge of Reality," "Wonderful World." The movie was never released in Britain. Vernon Presley played in a nonspeaking role sitting at a table.

Live Experience in Vegas ... February, 1971. A 33⅓ rpm bootleg album released on the Bonthand label. The album was made in Canada, although the cover stated that it was made in Holland. Songs included—Side 1: "That's All Right," "I Got a Woman," "Jailhouse Rock," "Love Me," "Mystery Train," "Tiger Man," "Polk Salad Annie," "Sweet Caroline," "You've Lost That Loving Feeling," "Something," Side 2: "How Great Thou Art," "Don't Be Cruel," "Heartbreak Hotel," "Blue Suede Shoes," "Little Sister," "Get Back," "Now or Never," "Hound Dog," "The Impossible Dream," "Johnny B. Goode."

Living Stereo. Trademark for RCA Victor Stereo recordings. The first Elvis release in "Living Stereo" was on the October 1958 "Christmas Sampler" (RCA Victor SPS 33-54) sent to disc jockeys. The album had Christmas songs by various RCA Victor artists. However, Elvis's song "Blue Christmas" was in monaural (the only one on the record).

Livingston, Jay. Composer of many popular songs with Ray Evans ("To Each His Own"; "Tammy"; "Mona Lisa"; etc.); also theme songs for the TV series "Mr. Lucky" and "Mr. Ed." Jay Livingston is the coauthor (with lyricist Ray Evans) of "Silver Bells," which Elvis recorded in 1971.

Locke, Dixie. Girlfriend of Elvis during his high-school days. They both attended the First Assembly of God Church at 1885 McLemore in Memphis. Dixie Locke first met Elvis in the winter of early 1953 and dated him steadily until late '55. The two attended the Southside High School prom together, double-dating with Gene Smith and his date, Betty. Dixie Locke became the president of the first Elvis Presley fan club. The popular photograph of Elvis's prom night is actually Dixie Locke's prom in 1954.

Locklin, Hank. Country-western singer who in his youth leaned toward becoming an Irish tenor. Hank Locklin appeared on the same bill as Elvis at the Big D Jamboree Sportatorium (Dallas, Texas) on April 16, 1955.

Lockname, Rich. Elvis impersonator from Carlsbad, New Mexico.

Loew's Palace Theatre. Memphis theater that is incorrectly pointed out by some tours as the theater where Elvis worked. Elvis worked at the Lowe's State, which no longer exists. In 1951 Bobby "Blue" Bland won first prize at Lowe's Palace in an amateur show.

Loew's State Theatre. Memphis movie theater (152 S. Main) managed by Arthur Groom, where Elvis worked as an usher during high school for $12.75 a week. His hours were 5:00–10:00 weeknights. It is also the theater where *Jailhouse Rock* (MGM

229

1957) premiered, on October 21, 1957. The late comedian Freddie Prinze was himself an usher at New York City's Lowe's Theater (the theater no longer exists).

Lonely Blue Boy. Hit record (MGM 12857) by Conway Twitty in 1960. It was a million-seller and reached #6 on *Billboard*'s Hot 100 chart. Twitty's group the Lonely Blue Boys obtained their name from the song's title. "Lonely Blue Boy" was originally titled "Danny," written by Fred Wise and Ben Weisman and recorded by Elvis for the 1958 movie *King Creole*. "Danny" was not used in the film and the song didn't surface until 1978, when it appeared in the Elvis album "Elvis—A Legendary Performer, Volume 3."

Lonely Man. RCA 47-7850. Released in February 1961 as a 45 rpm single. It reached #32 on *Billboard*'s Hot 100 chart. "Surrender" was on the flip side. Elvis recorded "Lonely Man" for the 1961 movie *Wild in the Country*, but it was cut from the film. "Lonely Man" was written by Bennie Benjamin and Sol Marcus and appeared in the Long Playing albums "Elvis' Gold Records, Volume 4" (RCA LPM/LSP-3921) and "Elvis: The Other Sides—Worldwide Gold Award Hits, Volume 2" (RCA LPM-6402).

Lonely Man. RCA 447-0630. Gold Standard Series re-issue of RCA 47-7850.

Lonely Man. RCA 37-7850. A 33⅓ rpm single release—the first release by RCA. "Surrender" was on the flip side.

Lonely Man. RCA 61-7850. A 45 rpm "Living Stereo" release. "Surrender" was on the flip side.

Lonely Man. RCA 68-7850. A 33⅓ rpm "Living Stereo" single—the only one by Elvis released by RCA. "Surrender" was on the flip side.

Lonesome Cowboy. Song that Elvis sang in the 1957 movie *Loving You*. The film version of "Lonesome Cowboy" appeared in the bootleg LPs "Got a Lot o' Livin' to Do" and "Loving You" (Australian). It was written by Sid Tepper and Roy C. Bennett and appeared in the Extended Play album "Loving You, Volume 2" (RCA EPA2-1515) and the following Long Playing albums: "Loving You" (RCA LPM-1515); "Loving You" (RCA LSP-1515 [e]); "Elvis: The Other Sides—Worldwide Gold Award Hits, Volume 2" (RCA LPM-6402).

Lonesome Cowboy, The. Title originally considered for the 1957 Elvis movie *Loving You*. Another title considered was *Something for the Girls*.

Long, Steve. Elvis impersonator.

Long Black Limousine. Song written by Vern Stovall and Bobby George in 1962 and recorded by Elvis in 1969 at the American Sound Studios in Memphis. "Long Black Limousine" appeared in the Long Playing album "From Elvis in Memphis" (RCA LSP-4155).

Long Legged Girl (With the Short Dress On). RCA 47-9115. Re-

230

leased in May 1967 as a 45 rpm single. It reached #63 on *Billboard*'s Hot 100 chart. "That's Someone You Never Forget" was on the flip side. Elvis sang "Long Legged Girl (With the Short Dress On)" in the 1967 movie *Double Trouble*. It was written by J. Leslie McFarland and Winfield Scott and appeared in the following Long Playing albums: "Double Trouble" (RCA LPM–LSP-3787); "Almost in Love" (RCA Camden CAS-2440); "Almost in Love" (Pickwick CAS-2440); "Elvis Sings Hits from His Movies, Volume 1" (RCA Camden CAS-2567); "Elvis Sings Hits from His Movies, Volume 1" (Pickwick CAS-2567).

Long Legged Girl (With the Short Dress On). RCA 447-0660. Gold Standard Series re-issue of RCA 47-9115.

(It's A) Long Lonely Highway. RCA 47-8657. Released in August 1965 as a 45 rpm single. "I'm Yours" was on the flip side. Elvis sang "(It's A) Long Lonely Highway" in the 1965 movie *Tickle Me*. Written by Doc Pomus and Mort Shuman, "(It's A) Long Lonely Highway" appeared in the Long Playing album "Kissin' Cousins" (RCA LPM–LSP-2894).

(It's A) Long Lonely Highway. RCA 447-0654. Gold Standard Series re-issue of RCA 47-8657.

Long Tall Sally. Song originally titled "The Thing," then "Bald-Headed Sally," written by Enotris Johnson*, Robert "Bumps" Blackwell and Richard Penniman and originally recorded by Little Richard (Specialty 572) in 1956. Richard Penniman (Little Richard) claimed to have written the song in a Greyhound bus depot in Macon, Georgia. "Long Tall Sally"† reached #13 on *Billboard*'s Hot 100 chart and sold over a million copies. Elvis recorded "Long Tall Sally" in 1956 and sang it in the 1973 TV special "Elvis: Aloha from Hawaii." It appeared in the Extended Play album "Strictly Elvis" (RCA EPA-994) and the following Long Playing albums: "Elvis" (RCA LPM-1382); "Elvis" (RCA LSP-1382 [e]); "Elvis: Aloha from Hawaii Via Satellite" (RCA VPSX-6089); "Elvis Recorded Live on Stage in Memphis" (RCA CPL1-0606).

Lonnie Beale. Role played by Elvis (as a rodeo star) in the 1965 movie *Tickle Me*.

Look Magazine. Popular weekly magazine on whose cover Elvis appeared on May 4, 1971.

Look Out, Broadway. Song that Elvis sang in the 1966 movie *Frankie and Johnny*. "Look Out, Broadway" was written by Fred Wise and Randy Starr and appeared in the Long Playing album "Frankie and Johnny" (RCA LPM/LSP-3553).

Los Angeles Indian Tribal Council. In December 1960 Elvis was inducted into the council by Chief Wah-Nee-Ota. This was in

---

*On the 1956 album "Elvis," only Enotris Johnson was credited as composer.

†"Long Tall Sally" (Cameo 308) was the Kinks' first hit record (1964).

recognition of his "constructive portrayal of a man of Indian blood." Elvis had just starred in the movie *Flaming Star*.

Los Angeles Residences of Elvis. 565 Perugia Way—1960–63, 1059 Bellagio—1963, 565 Perugia Way—1963–late '65, 10550 Rocca Place—late 1965–May 7, 1967, 1174 Hillcrest—May 7, 1967–late 1967, 144 Monovale—late 1967–unknown.

Lost Country, The. Novel by J.R. Salamanca on which the 1961 movie *Wild in the Country* was based.

Louise, Tina. Actress best known for her portrayal of Ginger Grant in the TV series "Gilligan's Island." Tina Louise covered Elvis's Army homecoming on radio, on March 3, 1960, for the Mutual Broadcasting Network.*

Louisiana Hayride. Country music program broadcast on Saturday nights from eight to eleven o'clock on Shreveport, Louisiana, radio station KWKH (began April 3, 1948). It is sometimes referred to as the "Junior Grand Ole Opry." Elvis became a regular on the show from October 16, 1954, to December 17, 1955. Frank Page was the man who introduced Elvis to the audience that first night. Elvis also made an appearance on the TV version of the "Louisiana Hayride" on March 5, 1955. (This was his first television appearance that can be documented—it was broadcast regionally.) His "Stage Show" appearance in 1956 was his first *national* TV exposure. Elvis signed a year's contract to appear on the show for $18 a night. Bill Black and Scotty Moore were each paid $12. During the last six months of the show, Elvis paid $400 a night *not* to appear. Many artists appeared on the same bill as Elvis on those "Hayride" shows. They included: Slim Whitman, who urged the "Hayride" to sign Elvis; Johnny Horton; Jim Reeves; David Houston, who was also a Sun artist, who made his debut on the "Louisiana Hayride." Hank Williams appeared on the show from August 7, 1948, to June 3, 1949, and again from September 4, 1952, until his death.

Love, American Style. ABC-TV network program containing comedy vignettes about love. The episodes aired from 1969 to '74. Reportedly, this was one of Elvis's favorite television shows. (One of the spin-offs of the series is "Happy Days.")

Love, Darlene. Member of the Blossoms vocal group, which sang back-up for Elvis. Darlene Love sang lead for the Crystals on their #1 hit "He's a Rebel" (Philles 106) in 1962 and joined Bob B. Soxx and the Blue Jeans a few days later to record "Zip-A-Dee-Doo-Dah" (Philles 107). (See: The Blossoms) Darlene Love, born Darlene Wright, is the sister of Edna Wright of the Honey Cones.

Love Coming Down. Song written by Jerry Chestnut and recorded

---

*The Mutual Broadcasting Network was created from the three-station radio network that originally broadcast "The Lone Ranger" series (WGN, Chicago; WOR, Newark, New Jersey; and the originating station, WXYZ, Detroit).

by Elvis in 1976 at Graceland. "Love Coming Down" appeared in the Long Playing album "From Elvis Presley Boulevard, Memphis, Tennessee" (RCA APL1-1506).

Love Him Tender, Sweet Jesus. A 1977 Elvis tribute record by David Price on Rice Records (Rice 5075).

Love in Las Vegas. British title of the 1964 Elvis movie *Viva Las Vegas*.

Love Is for Lovers. Song that Elvis recorded for the 1962 movie *Kid Galahad*, but it was cut from the final print. "Love Is for Lovers" was written by Ruth Batchelor and Sharon Silbert and is not available on record.

Love Letters. RCA 47-8870. Released in June 1966 as a 45 rpm single. It reached #19 on *Billboard*'s Hot 100 chart and reportedly sold over a million copies. "Come What May" was on the flip side. "Love Letters" was written by Edward Heyman and Victor Young as the theme song of the 1945 movie of the same name, starring Joseph Cotton and Jennifer Jones. In 1962 Ketty Lester had a #5 hit and million-seller with "Love Letters." Her piano player was Lincoln Mayorga a former member of the Piltdown Men (Era 3068). Elvis's version appeared in the Long Playing albums "Elvis Gold Records, Volume 4" (RCA LPM/LSP-3921) and "Love Letters from Elvis" (RCA LSP-4530).

Love Letters. RCA 447-0657. Gold Standard Series re-issue of RCA 47-8870.

Love Letters from Elvis. RCA LSP-4530. Released in June 1971 as a 33⅓ rpm Long Playing album. "Love Letters from Elvis" reached #33 on *Billboard*'s Hot LP chart. On the original album jacket the words "Love Letters From" appeared on one line. The re-issue had the words on two lines. Songs included—Side 1: "Love Letters," "When I'm Over You," "If I Were You," "Got My Mojo Working," "Heart of Rome." Side 2: "Only Believe," "This Is Our Dance," "Cindy, Cindy," "I'll Never Know," "It Ain't No Big Thing (But It's Growing)," "Life."

Love Letters to Elvis. Book of letters written to Elvis by his fans, compiled by Bill Adler, who also compiled the book *Love Letters to the Monkees*.

Lovely Mamie. Song that Elvis sang in the 1968 movie *Stay Away, Joe*. The song lasted fifteen seconds and Elvis sang it with only guitar accompaniment. "Lovely Mamie" has never been released by RCA; however, it does appear in the bootleg LP "From Hollywood to Vegas," released on the Brookville label.

Love Machine, The. Song that Elvis sang in the 1967 movie *Easy Come, Easy Go*. "The Love Machine" was was written by Gerald Nelson, Fred Burch, and Chuck Taylor. It appeared in the Extended Play album "Easy Come, Easy Go" (RCA EPA-4387) and the Long Playing albums "I Got Lucky" (RCA Camden CAL-2355) and "I Got Lucky" (Pickwick CAS-2355).

233

Love Me. Song written by Jerry Leiber and Mike Stoller and originally recorded by Willie and Ruth (Spark 105) in 1954. Georgia Gibbs also recorded "Love Me" (Mercury 70473) in 1954. Leiber and Stoller claimed that "Love Me" was the worst song they ever wrote. In 1956 Elvis recorded "Love Me." He sang it in his second appearance on the "Ed Sullivan Show" (October 28, 1956) and in the 1973 TV special "Elvis: Aloha from Hawaii." "Love Me" was the only song by Elvis, never released as a single, to reach the singles' chart. It was the lead song in an Extended Play album ("Elvis, Volume 1") and, as such, reached #6 on *Billboard*'s Hot 100 chart. "Love Me" appeared in the Extended Play albums "Elvis, Volume 1" (RCA EPA-992) and "Perfect for Parties Highlight Album" (RCA SPA7-37) and the following Long Playing albums: "Elvis" (RCA LPM-1382); "Elvis" (RCA LSP-1382 [e]); "Elvis' Golden Records" (RCA LPM-1707); "Elvis' Golden Records" (RCA LSP-1707 [e]); "Elvis: The Other Sides—Worldwide Gold Award Hits, Volume 2" (RCA LPM-6402); "Elvis as Recorded at Madison Square Garden" (RCA LSP-4776); "Elvis: Aloha from Hawaii Via Satellite" (RCA VPSX-6089); "Elvis" (RCA DPL2-0056); "Elvis—A Legendary Performer, Volume 1" (RCA CPL1-0341); "Elvis Recorded Live on Stage in Memphis" (RCA CPL1-0606).

Love Me, Love the Life I Lead. Song written by Macaulay and Greenaway and recorded by Elvis in 1971. "Love Me, Love the Life I Lead" appeared in the Long Playing album "Elvis" (RCA APL1-0283).

LOVE ME TENDER. Twentieth Century-Fox, 1956. Premiered New York City November 16, 1956 (89 min). Elvis's first movie. Producer, David Weisbart. Director, Robert D. Webb. Cast: Vance Reno/Richard Egan, Cathy/Debra Paget, Clint Reno/Elvis Presley, Siringo/Robert Middleton, Brett Reno/William Campbell, Mike Gavin/Neville Brand, The Mother/ Mildred Dunnock, Maj. Kincaid/Bruce Bennett, Ray Reno/James Drury, Ed Galt/Russ Conway, Kelso/Ken Clark, Davis/Barry Coe, Fleming/L.Q. Jones, Jethro/Paul Burns, Train Conductor/Jerry Sheldon, Storekeeper/James Stone, Auctioneer/Ed Mundy, First Soldier/Joe Di Reda, Station Agent/Bobby Rose, Paymaster/Tom Greenway, Maj. Harris/Jay Jostyn, Second Conductor/Steve Darrell. Screenplay, Robert Buckner. Photography, Leo Tover. Music, Lionel Newman. Songs, Elvis Presley and Vera Matson. Art Direction, Lyle R. Wheeler and Maurice Ransford. Set Decoration, Walter M. Scott and Fay Babcock. Special Effects, Ray Kellogg. Costumes, Mary Wills. Assistant Director, Stanley Hough. Editor, Hugh S. Fowler. Songs sung by Elvis: "Love Me Tender," "Let Me," "Poor Boy," "We're Gonna Move." The film cost less than $1 million but grossed over $5 million. First released in Britain in 1957, it was the first Elvis movie to be shown on television (December 11, 1963).

The cost of the movie was recovered in three days after its debut.

Love Me Tender. RCA 20/40-6643. Released in September 1956 as a 78 rpm single and a 45 rpm single. It reached #1 on *Billboard*'s Hot 100 chart (for four weeks, November 17–December 8 and December 22–29), #3 on the Country chart, and #4 on the Rhythm and Blues chart. "Love Me Tender" had an *advance* sale of over a million copies—the first known record to do so. "Any Way You Want Me" was on the flip side. Elvis sang "Love Me Tender" in the following: the 1956 movie of the same name; all three appearances on "The Ed Sullivan Show"; "The Frank Sinatra-Timex Special" (he sang just the ending); the 1968 NBC-TV special "Elvis"; the 1970 documentary *Elvis —That's the Way It Is;* the 1972 documentary *Elvis on Tour*. "Love Me Tender" was the first song by Elvis that Priscilla Beaulieu ever heard, becoming her favorite ballad. The song was composed by Ken Darby (based on the 1861 ballad "Aura Lee") for the 1956 movie of the same name, but it was credited to Vera Matson and Elvis. The Ken Darby Trio provided the vocal back-up. The film version of "Love Me Tender" had one extra verse. "Love Me Tender" appeared in the Extended Play album "Love Me Tender" (RCA EPA-4006) and the following Long Playing albums: "Elvis' Golden Records" (RCA LPM-1707); "Elvis' Golden Records" (RCA LSP-1707 [e]); "Elvis—TV Special" (RCA LPM-4088); "Elvis: Worldwide 50 Gold Award Hits, Volume 1" (RCA LPM-6401); "Elvis as Recorded at Madison Square Garden" (RCA LSP-4776); "Elvis" (RCA DPL2-0056 [e]); "Elvis—A Legendary Performer, Volume 1" (RCA CPL1-9341); "Pure Gold" (RCA ANL1-0971).

Love Me Tender. RCA 447-0610. Gold Standard Series re-issue of RCA 20/47-6643.

Love Me Tender. RCA EPA-4006. This was a 45 rpm Extended Play album released in December 1956. It reached #35 on *Billboard*'s Hot 100 chart and #10 on the Extended Play chart. All the songs in the 1956 movie *Love Me Tender* were included. Side 1—"Love Me Tender"; "Let Me." Side 2—"Poor Boy"; "We're Gonna Move."

Love Me Tender. Song that received much air play in December 1978. The tape was an excellent splicing of Elvis's 1956 version and Linda Ronstadt's 1978 updated version from her album "Living in the U. S. A." The tape was created by Ray Quinn, the program manager for radio station WCBM in Baltimore. Although demand grew for the tape, no copies were legally made available to the public.

Love Me Tender. Name of candy created in 1956. One unwrapped bar is worth up to seventy-five dollars today.

Love Me Tender Perfume. One of the hundreds of Elvis-related products manufactured by Factors, Inc.

Love Me Tonight. Song written by Don Robertson for Elvis and recorded by Elvis in 1963. "Love Me Tonight" appeared in the Long Playing album "Fun in Acapulco" (RCA LPM/LSP-2756).

Love My Baby. A 1953 record by Junior Parker on Sun Records (Sun 192). A guitar riff was borrowed by Scotty Moore from "Love My Baby" to be heard in "Mystery Train."

Lover Doll. Song from the 1958 movie *King Creole*. Elvis (as Danny Fisher) sang "Lover Doll" to divert attention while Shark (Vic Morrow) and his pals shoplifted at a five-and-dime store. The LP version of "Lover Doll" is longer than the EP version. Also, the Jordanaires appear in the LP and not in the EP. Backed with "Young and Beautiful," "Lover Doll" was released as a single in Europe. "Lover Doll" was written by Sid Wayne and Abner Silver and appeared in the Extended Play albums "King Creole, Volume 1" (RCA EPA-4319) and "King Creole, Volume 1" (RCA EPA-5122) and the following Long Playing albums: "King Creole" (RCA LPM-1884); "King Creole" (RCA LSP-1884 [e]); "Elvis: The Other Sides—Worldwide Gold Award Hits, Volume 2" (RCA LPM-6402).

Love Song of the Year. Song written by Chris Christian and recorded by Elvis in 1973 at the Stax Studios in Memphis. "Love Song of the Year" appeared in the Long Playing album "Promised Land" (RCA APL1-0873).

Loving Arms. Song written by Tom Jans and originally recorded by Dobie Gray in July 1973 (MCA 40100). Elvis recorded it in 1973 at the Stax Studios in Memphis. "Loving Arms" appeared in the Long Playing album, "Good Times" (RCA CPL1-0475).

Loving Arms. RCA 2458EX. A 1974 45 rpm special release. "My Boy" was on the flip side.

LOVING YOU. Paramount, 1957. Premiered July 9, 1957 (101 min). Elvis's second movie. Producer, Hal B. Wallis. Associate Producer, Paul Nathan. Director, Hal Kantor. Cast: Deke Rivers/Elvis Presley, Glenda Markle/Lizabeth Scott, Walker "Tex" Warner/Wendell Corey, Susan Jessup/Dolores Hart, Carl Meade/James Gleason, Skeeter/Paul Smith, Wayne/Ken Becker, Daisy/Jana Lund, Tallman/Ralph Dumke, Sally/Yvonne Lime, Teddy/Skip Young, Harry Tayler/Vernon Rich, Castle/David Cameron, Mrs. Gunderson/Grace Hayle, Mack/Dick Ryan, O'Shea/Steve Pendleton, Grew/Sydney Chatton, TV Announcer/Jack Latham, Mr. Jessup/William Forrest, Mrs. Jessup/Irene Tedrow, Lieutenant/Hal K. Dawson, Woman/Madge Blake, Editor/Joe Forte, Woman/Almira Sessions, Waitress/Karen Scott, Glenn/Beach Dickerson, Candy/Gail Lund, Mayor/Harry Cheshire, Buzz/Timothy Butler, Girl/Myrna Fahey, Sorority Girl/Sue England, The Jordanaires/The Jordanaires, Woman in Audience/Gladys Presley, Man in Audience/Vernon Presley. Screenplay, Herbert Baker.

Photography, Charles Lang, Jr. Music, Walter Scharf. Choreography, Charles O'Curran. Art Direction, Hal Pereira and Albert Nozaki. Set Decoration, Sam Comer and Frank McKelvy. Special Effects, John P. Fulton. Costumes, Edith Head. Technical Adviser, Col. Tom Parker. Editor, Howard Smith. Songs sung by Elvis: "(Let Me Be Your) Teddy Bear," Got a Lot o' Livin' to Do," "Loving You," "Lonesome Cowboy," "Hot Dog," "Mean Woman Blues," "(Let's Have A) Party." Dolores Hart sang "Detour" and "The Yellow Rose." Instrumental: "Candy Kisses." In the film, Elvis's parents, Vernon and Gladys Presley, appear in an audience as extras. They can be seen as Elvis is singing "Got a Lot of Livin' to Do".

Loving You. RCA 20/47-7000. Released in June 1957 as a 78 rpm single and a 45 rpm single. It reached #28 on *Billboard*'s Hot 100 chart and #1 on the Rhythm and Blues chart. "Loving You" sold over a million copies. "(Let Me Be Your) Teddy Bear" was on the flip side. Elvis sang "Loving You" in the 1957 movie of the same name. A fast version of the song appeared in the bootleg album "Got a Lot o' Livin' to Do." It took Elvis forty takes to get an acceptable recording of the song. "Loving You" was written for Elvis by Jerry Leiber and Mike Stoller and appeared in the Extended Play album "Loving You, Volume 1" (RCA EPA1-1515) and the following Long Playing albums: "Loving You" (RCA LPM-1515); "Loving You" (RCA LSP-1515 [e]); "Elvis' Golden Records" (RCA LPM-1707); "Elvis' Golden Records" (RCA LSP-1707 [e]); "Elvis: Worldwide 50 Gold Award Hits, Volume 1" (RCA LPM-6401); "Elvis" (RCA DPL2-0056 [e]); "Pure Gold" (RCA ANL1-0971); "Elvis—A Canadian Tribute" (RCA KKL1-7065).

Loving You. RCA 447-0620. Gold Standard Series re-issue of RCA 20/47-7000.

Loving You. RCA LPM-1515. A 33⅓ rpm Long Playing album that was released in July 1957. It reached #1 on *Billboard*'s Hot LP chart. "Loving You" included songs from the 1957 movie of the same name on side 1 and bonus songs that weren't in the movie on side 2. The "Loving You" album received a Gold Disc award from the R.I.A.A. and, according to RCA, has sold over a million copies. Songs included—Side 1: "Mean Woman Blues," "(Let Me Be Your) Teddy Bear," "Loving You," "Got a Lot o' Livin' to Do," "Lonesome Cowboy," "Hot Dog," "Party." Side 2: "Blueberry Hill," "True Love," "Don't Leave Me Now," "Have I Told You Lately That I Love You," "I Need You So."

Loving You. RCA LSP-1515 (e). This record was the electronically reprocessed stereo re-issue of RCA LPM-1515.

Loving You, Volume 1. RCA EPA1-1515. This was a 45 rpm Extended Play album released in June 1957. It reached #1 on

Billboard's Extended Play chart. Songs included—Side 1: "Loving You," "Party." Side 2: "(Let Me Be Your) Teddy Bear," "True Love."

Loving You, Volume 2. RCA EPA2-1515. This was a 45 rpm Extended Play album released in June 1957. It reached #4 on *Billboard's* Extended Play chart. Songs included—Side 1: "Lonesome Cowboy," "Hot Dog." Side 2: "Mean Woman Blues," "Got a Lot o' Livin' to Do."

Lowbridge, Kentucky. Town in which Walter Gulick (Elvis) grew up in the 1962 movie *Kid Galahad.*

Loyd, Harold. Night-shift gate guard at Graceland. Harold Loyd was Elvis's first cousin.

Loyd, Robert. Security guard at Graceland. Son of Harold Loyd, it was he who called the Memphis police at 3:07 A.M. on November 23, 1976, when Jerry Lee Lewis was making threats with his .38 Derringer outside of Graceland. Patrolman B. J. Kirkpatrick arrested Lewis. Memphis judge Albert Boyd found Jerry Lee not guilty.

Lubbock, Texas. Hometown of Buddy Holly, Mac Davis, and Waylon Jennings. Location of 1955 concert headed by Marty Robbins and Elvis Presley in the Cotton Club dance hall. Two local musicians named Buddy and Bob opened the performance. Buddy's full name was Buddy Holly and Bob's was Bob Montgomery. Thus two legendary performers played on the same stage that night—Buddy Holly and Elvis Presley. After this performance was over, Jim Denny of Decca Records approached Buddy Holly with an offer to record for his label. One of the enthused spectators watching the show was a young lad named Scott "Mac" Davis, who would one day compose songs for Elvis.

Lucky Jackson. Elvis's role as a racecar driver in the 1964 movie *Viva Las Vegas.*

Lucky Strike Guest Time. Featured segment on the "Louisiana Hayride" that introduced a new artist each week. Elvis Presley appeared on the segment on October 19, 1954. Introduced by Frank Page, this was Elvis's first appearance on the show.

Lunarkand. Arab country to which Johnny Tyronne (Elvis) traveled as a guest of King Toranshah in the 1965 movie *Harum Scarum.*

Lund, Jana. Actress whom Elvis dated in 1957 while filming *Jailhouse Rock.*

Lynchburg Audio. Lynchburg, Virginia, company that produced a 45 rpm, seven-inch, plastic record called "The Truth About Me." The record, which came with either a black or a blue label, was inserted into the pages of a 1956 issue of *Teen Parade* magazine. It was released "By Arrangement with RCA Victor Records." (See: Rainbow Records)

M

MacArthur Park. Song composed by Jimmy Webb and recorded by Richard Harris (Dunhill 4132) in 1968. "MacArthur Park" sold over a million copies. In 1979 Donna Summer also had a popular version (Casablanca 5939). Elvis sang a comedy version of "MacArthur Park" during the taping of the 1968 NBC-TV special (June 27, 1968).

Madison, Tennessee. Town, just north of Memphis, where Col. Tom Parker makes his home. Also, it is the headquarters of his national business operations. In 1955 he used the address: Box 417, Madison, Tenn.

Madison Square Garden. Site of June 9–11, 1972, New York City concerts by Elvis Presley. During the concerts, Elvis broke the Garden's attendance record, with 80,000 people.

Magical Rockin' Sound Of Elvis Presley, The. Ten-inch bootleg album on the Jubilee label made in Canada, though credited to Cambodia. Songs included—Side 1: "First In Line," "I Got A Woman," "Is It So Strange," "I Want To be Free," "Trouble," "Lover Doll," "Crawfish." Side 2: "I Love You Because," "I Want You, I Need You, I Love You," "Dixieland Rock," "Don't Leave Me Now," "I'm Gonna Sit Right Down And Cry (Over You)," "Young And Beautiful," "Any Way You Want Me (That's How I Will Be)."

Magnani, Anna. Actress who won an Academy Award for Best Actress in 1955 for her performance in *The Rose Tattoo*. Thomas Lanier "Tennessee" Williams wrote *The Rose Tattoo* for her. Anna Magnani had just finished filming *Wild Is the Wind* (1957) when Paramount gave her dressing room to Elvis. Elvis was to begin filming *King Creole*.

Mahalo from Elvis. Pickwick ACL-7064. A 33⅓ rpm Long Playing album released in September 1978. The songs on side 1 of "Mahalo from Elvis" were recorded on January 14, 1973, for inclusion in the NBC-TV special "Elvis: Aloha from Hawaii." Side 2 contained five previously recorded songs from Elvis's movies. Songs included—Side 1: "Blue Hawaii," "Early Mornin' Rain," "Hawaiian Wedding Song," "Ku-u-i-po," "No More." Side 2: "Relax," "Baby, If You'll Give Me All of Your Love," "One Broken Heart for Sale," "So Close, Yet So Far (From Paradise)," "Happy Ending."

Make Me Know It. Song written by Otis Blackwell and recorded by Elvis on March 20, 1960. "Make Me Know It" was Elvis's first recording after being discharged from the Army. It appeared in the Long Playing album "Elvis Is Back" (RCA LPM/LSP-2231).

Make the World Go Away. Song written by Hank Cochran and originally recorded by Eddy Arnold (RCA 8679) in 1965. "Make the World Go Away" reached #8 on *Billboard*'s Hot 100 chart. Elvis recorded "Make the World Go Away" in 1970 and it appeared in the Long Playing albums "Elvis Country" (RCA LSP-4460) and "Welcome to My World" (RCA APL1-2274).

Malaguena. Song that Elvis recorded for the 1963 movie *Fun in Acapulco*, but it was cut from the final print. "Malaguena" is not available on record.

Malco Theatres, Inc. Memphis theater corporation (89 Beale Street). Paul Shafer, a Malco executive, supplied Elvis with movies for his private parties.

   *Let's Rock,** the movie debut of Memphis disc jockey Wink Martindale, had its world premiere at the Malco Theater in 1958.

Mama. Song that Elvis recorded for the 1962 movie *Girls! Girls! Girls!*, but it was cut from the final print. The Amigos, however, did sing "Mama" in the movie. Written by Charles O'Curran and Dudley Brooks, Elvis's version of "Mama" appeared in the following Long Playing albums: "Let's Be Friends" (RCA Camden CAS-2408); "Let's Be Friends" (Pickwick CAS-2408); "Double Dynamite" (Pickwick DL2-5001).

Mama Liked the Roses. RCA 47-9835. Released in May 1970 as a 45 rpm single. It reached #9 on *Billboard*'s Hot 100 chart. "The Wonder of You" was on the flip side. "Mama Liked the Roses" was written by Johnny Christopher and sold over a million copies. It appeared in the Long Playing albums "Elvis' Christmas Album" (RCA Camden CAL-2428) and "Elvis' Christmas Album" (Pickwick CAS-2428).

Mama Liked the Roses. RCA 447-0676. Gold Standard Series reissue of RCA 47-9835.

MAmmoth 6-2480. Telephone number of the Size Pet Shop radio commercial for dog food. The commercial was read over Vince Everett's (Elvis) singing of his first release, "Treat Me Nice," in the 1957 movie *Jailhouse Rock*.

Manhattan Club. Memphis nightclub, located on Bellevue Ave., that Elvis rented for a New Year's Eve party. Rufus Thomas was the house performer at the time.

Mann, Barry and Weil, Cynthia. Songwriting team originally with Aldon Music (Al Nevins and Don Kirshner). They composed hit records for the Crystals, Paul Revere and the Raiders, Paul Peterson, and the Righteous Brothers. They were the composers

---

*Also known under the title *Keep It Cool*.

240

of two of the Elvis songs "You've Lost that Loving Feeling" and "I Just Can't Help Believin'." In 1961 Barry Mann recorded "Who Put the Bomp" (ABC Paramount 10237).

Mann, Kal and Lowe, Bernie. Music composers who founded Cameo-Parkway Records in Philadelphia in 1956. They composed the Elvis hit "Teddy Bear." Previously, they wrote the 1956 Pat Boone hit "Remember You're Mine" (Dot 15602). The two men composed "Butterfly" for Charlie Gracie (Cameo 105) in 1956 under the pseudonym Anthony September.

Manning, James. Flight engineer of Elvis's Convair 880 jet; reportedly he earned $39,000 a year.

Man of La Mancha. Musical play and (1972) movie directed by Arthur Hiller, based on Cervantes' 1605–15 novel, *Don Quixote*. The play's theme song, "The Impossible Dream" (The Quest), composed by Joe Darion and Mitch Leigh, was recorded by Elvis in 1972.

Mansfield, Rex. Friend of Elvis in the Army in Germany. Elvis practiced his karate with Mansfield.

Mansion Over the Hilltop. Gospel song written by Ira Stamphill and recorded by Red Foley in the late 1940s (Decca 28694). "Mansion Over the Hilltop," recorded by Elvis in October 1960, appeared in the Long Playing albums, "His Hand in Mine" (RCA LPM/LSP-2328) and "His Hand in Mine" (RCA ANL1-1319).

Many Loves of Dobie Gillis, The. Popular CBS-TV series (1959–63) starring Dwayne Hickman, Bob Denver, Tuesday Weld, Frank Faylen, Doris Packer, and William Schallert. Tuesday Weld costarred with Elvis in *Wild in the Country* (1961), Doris Packer appeared in *Paradise—Hawaiian Style* (1966), and William Schallert had a role in *Speedway* (1968). Frank Faylen appeared with Elvis in his screen test in 1956. (See: Weld, Tuesday; Faylen, Frank)

Marchin' Elvis. Song recorded in 1958 by the Greats on Ebb Records (Ebb 145). Title was in reference to Elvis's induction into the Army.

March of Dimes Galaxy of Stars. Extremely rare promotional record. Elvis was one of several stars on this 16-inch disc. In addition to a promotional announcement for the March of Dimes, Elvis sang "Love Me Tender." The record was to be destroyed after being used January 2–21, 1957.

March of Dimes Presents Elvis. Title of a promotional 45 rpm release.

Mare Ingram. One of the horses Elvis boarded at the Circle G. The horse was named for William B. Ingram, who was the mayor of Memphis at the time.

Marg, Hal. Vice-president at RCA Victor who, in 1956, presented Elvis with his Gold Record for "Heartbreak Hotel."

Marguerita. Song that Elvis sang in the 1963 movie *Fun in*

Acapulco. "Marguerita" was written for Elvis by Don Robertson and appeared in the Long Playing album "Fun in Acapulco" (RCA LPM/LSP-2756).

Market Square Arena. Indianapolis, Indiana, auditorium where, on June 26, 1977, Elvis gave his last live concert. (See: Last Farewell, The)

Mar-Keys. Instrumental group who recorded their first hit, "Last Night," in 1961 on the Satellite Record label (name later changed to Stax Records). Two of the group's members were Donald "Duck" Dunn (bass guitar) and Steve Crooper (guitar), who left the group to join with Booker T. and the MG's (Memphis Group). The horn section later became the Memphis Horns, who played in the Elvis recording sessions at the American Sound Studios in Memphis from February 17 to 22, 1969.

Marl Metal Manufacturing Company. Memphis firm where Elvis worked briefly (208 Georgia Ave.), for a dollar an hour for two months, starting in September 1952. The company manufactured dinettes. He worked a full shift from 3:00 P.M. to 11:30 P.M. When he began to fall asleep in class, his parents made him quit.

Marl stood for *M*oris, *A*lbert, *R*obert, and *L*ouis Bozoff—the brothers who owned the company. Elvis was hired by Robert Bozoff to work in the fabricating division.

Marmann, Elsie. Elvis's eighth-grade music teacher at Humes High School.

Marquett, Robert Stephen. Young polio victim with whom Elvis posed, while as a private in the Army, in order to launch the March of Dimes drive. He was one of a number of children with whom Elvis posed.

The March of Dimes is a campaign of the National Foundation of Infantile Paralysis to raise money for polio victims. The foundation was founded on January 3, 1938, by President Franklin D. Roosevelt. The phrase *March of Dimes* was coined by comedian Eddie Cantor.

Martin, Dean. Straight man of comedy team Martin and Lewis (Jerry Lewis). After the pair split in 1956* Dean became a successful recording artist. Dean Martin was one of Elvis Presley's singing idols in the early 1950s.

Martin, Dino. Son of singer/actor Dean Martin. The elder Martin took his son to Paramount Studios in 1957 to meet Elvis.

Later (1965) Dino formed the rock band Dino, Desi, and Billy (Desi Arnaz, Jr., and William Hinsche). The trio was discovered by Frank Sinatra, who signed them to his record label, Reprise Records.

---

*After the comedians split they did not see each other again for twenty years, when Frank Sinatra surprised Lewis on September 5, 1976, at one of Lewis's telethons in Las Vegas by bringing Martin on stage. There, the twenty-year-old feud died.

Dino Martin was once ranked #250 in World Tennis. Also, he was drafted by the Portland Storm in the World Football League, but he never played.

Martin, Freddy. Popular bandleader of the 1940s, whose theme song, "Tonight We Love" (Bluebird 11211) based on Tchaikovsky's Piano Concerto No. 1, became a huge hit. Merv Griffin was once a vocalist for his band. Freddy Martin was the featured performer at the New Frontier Hotel in Las Vegas when Elvis appeared there in 1956.

Martindale, Wink. Country singer (real name: Winston Conrad Martindale), also called Win Martindale, and TV game show host ("Gambit"; "How's Your Mother-in-Law?"; "Can You Top This?"; "Dream Girl"; "What's This Song"; "Words and Music"; "Tic Tac Dough").

On Memphis WHBQ-TV's "Dance Party," Wink Martindale interviewed Elvis in 1957. Martindale joined WHBQ on April 20, 1953. He made his movie debut in the 1958 rock 'n' roll movie *Keep It Cool*. In 1959 Wink Martindale recorded the hit record "Deck of Cards" (Dot 15968). He also recorded a version of "From a Jack to a King," which Elvis recorded in January 1969.

Martini Club. Tavern across the street from the King Creole Club in the 1958 movie *King Creole*.

Marx, Groucho. Comedian member of the famed Marx Brothers. Born Julius Marx, on October 2, 1895 (same day as comedian William "Bud" Abbott), he died on August 19, 1977, three days after Elvis's death. He was one of the many celebrities who died shortly after Elvis. (See: Mostel, Samuel "Zero"; Cabot, Sebastian)

Mary in the Morning. Song written by Johnny Cymbal and Michael Rashkow and originally recorded by Al Martino (Capitol 5904) in 1967. Elvis recorded "Mary in the Morning" in 1970 and sang it in the documentary *Elvis—That's the Way It Is*. "Mary in the Morning" appeared in the Long Playing album "Elvis—That's the Way It Is" (RCA LSP-4445).

Mary Jane Hamilton. Fifteen-year-old girl from Riverport who wrote Deke Rivers (Elvis) a fan letter giving her measurements as 33-25-36, her eyes as blue, and her phone number as LOckwood 4357 (1957 movie *Jailhouse Rock*).

Mason, Marlyn. Female lead, as Charlene, in the 1969 movie *The Trouble with Girls (And How to Get Into It)*.

Matilda. Skeeter's (Paul Smith) parakeet in the 1957 movie *Loving You*.

Matson, Vera. Listed composer with Elvis on "Love Me Tender," "We're Gonna Move," and "Poor Boy." Vera Matson is the wife of Ken Darby, who in actuality composed the songs.

Matthau, Walter. Actor who played Maxie Fields in the 1958 movie *King Creole*. Walter Matthau's father, Melas Matus-

243

chanskayasky, had been a Catholic priest in czarist Russia prior to marrying.

Mawn, (Captain) John. Public information director at Fort Chaffee, Arkansas, where Elvis was indoctrinated.

McClellan, Lou. Purchaser of Elvis's Circle G Ranch, for a $440,100 note carried by Elvis, with plans to turn it into a gun club. Because of troubles in getting a permit for the gun club, McClellan had to put the ranch up for auction, and Elvis bought it back.

McDowell, Ronnie. Country artist and Elvis sound-alike who recorded the tribute record "The King Is Gone." (See: King Is Gone, The) Ronnie McDowell recorded the vocals used in the 1979 TV movie *Elvis.* Ronnie McDowell first saw Elvis in the 1958 movie *King Creole.*

McGarrity, Bonya. One of Elvis's personal secretaries.

McGregor, Mike. One of Elvis's groundskeepers and handymen at Graceland. He also attended to Elvis's horses.

McGuire Air Force Base. Air Force facility in New Jersey where Elvis's plane landed in a snowstorm on his return home from his European assignment, March 3, 1960. (Actress Constance Bennett's husband, Brigadier General Theron "John" Coulter, whom she married in 1946, later became commander of McGuire Air Force Base.)

McIntyre, Sgt. Robert. R.O.T.C. instructor at Humes High School while Elvis was a student there.

McMahon, Mike. Business associate of Elvis. He also played racquet ball with Elvis at Graceland.

McNulty, Donald Leslie. Australian man who legally changed his name to Elvis Presley. Donald decided to change his name after seeing Elvis in the 1960 movie *G.I. Blues;* he further decided that he looked like Elvis. He also named his son Elvis.

Meanest Girl in Town, The. Song that Elvis sang in the 1965 movie *Girl Happy.* "The Meanest Girl in Town" was written by Joy Byers and appeared in the Long Playing album "Girl Happy" (RCA LPM/LSP-3338).

Mean Woman Blues. Song that Elvis sang in the 1957 movie *Loving You.* It was written by Claude de Metrius. Roy Orbison had a hit (#5) with "Mean Woman Blues" (Monument 824) in 1963. Jerry Lee Lewis had an Extended Play album (Sun 107) that included "Mean Woman Blues." "Mean Woman Blues" appeared in the Extended Play album "Loving You, Volume 2" (RCA EPA2-1515) and the following Long Playing albums: "Loving You" (RCA LPM-1515); "Loving You" (RCA LSP-1515 [e]); "Elvis: The Other Sides—Worldwide Gold Award Hits, Volume 2" (RCA LPM-6402).

Mean Woman Blues. RCA 47-7066. A 45 rpm disc jockey "record preview." "Have I Told You Lately That I Love You" was on the flip side. This is the only time that "Mean Woman Blues" was released as a single.

Medals. During Elvis's Army career he was awarded two medals for expert marksmanship—one for rifle and pistol, the other for sharpshooter with a carbine.

Meditation Gardens. Gravesite of both Elvis and his mother, Gladys Presley, at Graceland since October 2, 1977 (it was built in 1966).

Medley, Bill. Former member of the Righteous Brothers, who along with Sammy Davis, Jr., was first offered "In the Ghetto" prior to Elvis recording it. Unlike Davis, Medley turned it down.

Elvis once interrupted a Bill Medley performance in Las Vegas by walking across the stage as a joke.

Mello Man. Vocal group that backed Elvis on the 1963 song "One Broken Heart for Sale." "They Remind Me Too Much of You" was on the flip side. This was the only single in which the group appeared. The group appeared in the 1963 movie *It Happened at the World's Fair*.

Memories. RCA 47-9731. Released in March 1969 as a 45 rpm single. It reached #37 on *Billboard*'s Hot 100 chart and #56 on the Country chart. "Charro" was on the flip side. Elvis sang "Memories" in the 1968 NBC-TV special "Elvis" and the 1972 documentary *Elvis on Tour*. Written by Billy Strange and Mac Davis, "Memories" appeared in the Long Playing album "Elvis —TV Special" (RCA LPM-4088).

Memories. RCA 447-0669. Gold Standard Series re-issues of RCA 47-9731.

Memories of the King. A 1977 Elvis tribute record by Elvis Wade on Memory Records (Memory 244).

Memory Revival. Song for which only an instrumental track exists. It was recorded on February 22, 1969, at American Sound Studios in Memphis. Elvis never did record a vocal track for "Memory Revival."

Memphian Theatre. One of the Memphis theaters (51 S. Cooper) rented by Elvis for his private movie showings.

Memphis Funeral Home. Mortuary, at 1177 Union Ave. in Memphis, that handled Elvis's funeral and later Vernon Presley's. (See: National Funeral Home) The Memphis Funeral Home also handled Bill Black's funeral.

Memphis Housing Authority. Memphis-based organization that provided federally funded housing for people with small incomes. (See: Richardson, Jane)

Memphis Mafia. Close friends, associates, and employees of Elvis as coined by the news media, much like Frank Sinatra's Rat Pack and Humphrey Bogart's Holmby Hills Rat Pack of the 1950s. Since there were so many people Elvis came into contact with, a precise list would be impossible. Here is a partial list of the members: Alan Fortas, Sonny West, Charlie Hodge, Bobby "Red" West, Gene Smith, Billy Smith, Marty Lacker, Joe Esposito, Lamar Fike, Ray Sitton, Marvin Gamble, Patsy Gamble, Bitsy Mott, Louis Harris, George Klein, Jimmy Kingsley, Cliff Gleaves, Larry Geller, Jerry Schilling.

Memphis Pool and Landscaping Company. Memphis firm at 6620 Highway 70 that took care of the Graceland swimming pool.

Memphis Recording Service. Recording studio, at 706 Union Ave. (telephone; JAckson 7-7197), begun by Sam Phillips in 1950. For four dollars a person could record a two-sided acetate at the studio. The motto of the firm was: "We Record Anything—Anywhere—Anytime." Elvis came to the Memphis Recording Service in the summer of 1953 (the exact date is unknown) and, after talking to Marion Keisker, recorded two songs: "My Happiness" and "That's When Your Heartache Began." Elvis returned to the Memphis Recording Service on January 4, 1954, to record two more songs: "I'll Never Stand in Your Way" and "Casual Love Affair." He again paid four dollars, but this time the studio's owner, Sam Phillips, was there (Marion Keisker was not present). The Memphis Recording Service was also the home of Sun Records. (See: Sun Records; Phillips, Sam; Keisker, Marion)

Memphis Residences of Elvis. 571 Poplar Ave. (September 12, 1948–September 20, 1949), 185 Winchester Street (September 20, 1949–January 7, 1953), 398 Cypress Street (January 7, 1953–April 1953), 462 Alabama Street (April 1953–late 1954), 2414 Lamar Ave. (late 1954–mid-1955), 1414 Getwell Street (mid-1955–April 1956), 1034 Audubon Drive (April 1956–March 1957), 3764 Elvis Presley Blvd. (March 1957–August 16, 1977).

Memphis Sound—Elvis Presley's Golden Hits, The. Elvis tribute album by Big Ross on Pickwick Records.

Memphis, Tennessee. Song written and originally recorded by Chuck Berry (Bo Diddley played rhythm guitar). (Chess 1729) in 1959. Chuck Berry sang "Memphis, Tennessee" (also known as "Memphis") in the 1959 movie *Go, Johnny, Go,* in which several other artists performed, including Eddie Cochran, Jimmy Clanton, Jackie Wilson, Ritchie Valens*, the Flamingos, the Cadillacs, Harvey and the Moonglows, and Jo-Ann Campbell. Several other artists have recorded "Memphis, Tennessee," including Lonnie Mack (Fraternity 906) in 1963 and Johnny Rivers (Imperial 66032) in 1964. It was a British hit for Dave Berry and the Cruisers in 1963. (Born David Grundy, he adopted Chuck Berry's last name, his singing idol.)

Elvis recorded "Memphis, Tennessee" in 1963 and it appeared in the Long Playing album "Elvis for Everyone" (RCA LPM/LSP-3450).

Mercedes-Benz. Sedan automobile owned by Elvis while he was stationed in Germany.

Mercer, Johnny. Songwriter of dozens of classic songs, such as

---

*Only movie appearance of Ritchie Valens.

"That Old Black Magic" (with Jerome Kern), "Satin Doll" (with Duke Ellington), and "Moon River" (with Henry Mancini). He cowrote (with Rube Bloom) "Fools Rush In," which Elvis recorded in 1971. In 1942 Johnny Mercer and Buddy de Sylva, with the administration of Glenn E. Wallichs, founded Capitol Records. (It was Capitol that first turned down the U.S. distribution rights to the Beatles.)

Mercury Records. Chicago record label, founded in 1946, that unsuccessfully bid $10,000 for Elvis in 1955.

Merry Christmas Baby. RCA 74-0572. Released in November 1971 as a 45 rpm single. "O Come All Ye Faithful" was on the flip side. "Merry Christmas Baby" was written by Lou Baxter and Johnny Moore and originally recorded by Johnny Moore's Three Blazers (Exclusive 254) in 1947. The record was reissued in 1949 (Jubilee 5017) and again in 1951 (Swing Time 238). Charles Brown (Aladdin 3348), in 1956, and Chuck Berry (Chess 1716), in 1958, also had hit versions of "Merry Christmas Baby."

Elvis's version of "Merry Christmas Baby" appeared in the Long Playing albums "Elvis Sings the Wonderful World of Christmas" (RCA LSP-4579) and "Elvis Sings the Wonderful World of Christmas" (RCA ANL1-1936).

Messerschmitt. Red and black German automobile purchased by Elvis on March 24, 1956. It weighed 3,600 pounds. Its I.D. number was 56007 and its title number was 4447521. In 1957 Elvis gave the three-wheeled car to clothing-store owner Bernard Lansky, in exchange for selecting a wardrobe from his store.

Mess of Blues, A. RCA 47-7777. Released in July 1960 as a 45 rpm single. It reached #32 on *Billboard*'s Hot 100 chart and sold over a million copies. "It's Now or Never" appeared on the flip side. "A Mess of Blues" was written by Doc Pomus and Mort Shuman and appeared in the Long Playing albums "Elvis' Gold Records, Volume 4" (RCA LPM/LSP-3921) and "Elvis: Worldwide 50 Gold Award Hits, Volume 1" (RCA LPM-6401).

Mess of Blues, A. RCA 447-0628. Gold Standard Series re-issue of RCA 47-7777.

Mess of Blues, A. RCA 61-7777. A 45 rpm "Living Stereo" release. "It's Now or Never" was on the flip side.

Metheny, Captain Arlie. Public information officer at Fort Chaffee, Arkansas, where Elvis was indoctrinated prior to being assigned to Fort Hood, Texas, for his basic training in 1958.

Methodist Church. Nashville church at 1525 McGavock Street, where on January 10, 1956, Elvis recorded "Heartbreak Hotel." RCA Victor used the facility as a recording studio that day. The first record recorded at the session was "I Got a Woman."

Methodist Hospital. Memphis medical facility, at 1265 Union Ave., where Gladys Love Presley died of a heart attack on August

247

14, 1958. She had been sequestered in room 688 (See: Presley, Gladys)

Mexico. Song that Elvis sang in the 1963 movie *Fun in Acapulco*. In the movie, Larry Domasin sang a duet with Elvis. The film version of "Mexico" has a different background and a dialogue that's not included in the record version. It was written by Sid Tepper and Roy C Bennett and appeared in the Long Playing album "Fun in Acapulco" (RCA LPM/LSP-2765).

Meyer, Alan. Billed as "Alan," this ex-NASA engineer is the highest paid of all the Elvis imitators, receiving $50,000 a week in Las Vegas. He began impersonating Elvis in 1974 and has a sound very close to that of Elvis in his early years.

Meyer, Dr. David. Elvis's eye doctor, whose Memphis offices are located at 909 Ridgeway Loop Road.

MGM. Metro-Goldwyn-Meyer picture studios in Los Angeles, where Elvis became the first person to be given two dressing rooms by the studio.

Mickey Alba. Geneva Records artist who covered Vince Everett's (Elvis) unreleased version of "Don't Leave Me Now" in the 1957 movie *Jailhouse Rock*.

Mickey Mouse Club March. Short song* Elvis sang after he had just sung "Young and Beautiful" and "Happy Birthday" to a fan named Karen at a live performance on May 30, 1976, in Odessa, Texas.

Midnight Cowboy. Only X-rated movie ever to win an Oscar for Best Picture (1969). The role of Joe Buck, played by Jon Voight,† was first offered to Elvis. Bob Dylan originally composed "Lay Lady Lay" for the movie, but Harry Nillson's "Everybody's Talking" was chosen instead.

Mid-South Coliseum. Previous name of the Elvis Presley Coliseum. The name was changed by Memphis Mayor William B. Ingram, Jr., on January 4, 1967.

Mid-South Hospital. Memphis facility where, on June 18, 1975, Elvis underwent a face lift.

Mike Edwards. Elvis's role in the 1963 movie *It Happened at the World's Fair*.

Mike McCoy. Elvis's role in the 1966 movie, *Spinout*.

Mike Windgren. Elvis's role (as a former trapeze artist) in the 1963 movie *Fun in Acapulco*.

Milam Junior High School. Junior high school located at the corner of Gloster and Jefferson in Tupelo. Elvis briefly attended the school before moving to Memphis in 1948.

Military Ocean Terminal. Elvis's port of embarkation, located in Brooklyn, New York, from which he left the States on September 22, 1958. The Army band played "All Shook Up," "Hound

---

*The song was composed by Jimmie Dodd, host of the TV series "The Mickey Mouse Club."
†Jon Voight's brother is musician Chip Taylor.

Dog," "Don't Be Cruel," "Tutti Frutti," "Dixie," and "Sentimental Journey" in military fashion.

The interview with Elvis, in which the press asked questions, was made there and later incorporated in the 1958 EP "Elvis Sails." (See: Elvis Sails)

Miller, Mitch. Head A & R man for Columbia Records during the 1950s. Born in Rochester, New York, in 1911, Miller did not like rock 'n' roll music. (Because of Miller, Columbia Records was the last major label to record rock artists.) Columbia's first rock group was Paul Revere and the Raiders, who joined the label in 1965. In 1950 Frank Sinatra left the Columbia Records label because Mitch Miller gave him such poor material to record. The song that broke the camel's back was a duet with the sexy Dagmar titled "Mama Barks." Sinatra left Columbia for the Capitol label. Mitch Miller's first "Sing Along with Mitch" record album debuted at the same time as the short-lived TV series "Sing Along" (June–July 1958). The show was hosted by Jim Lowe. In December 1958 Miller had three "Sing Alongs" albums in the top five (#1, #2, and #5). For a time, Miller showed interest in obtaining Elvis for the Columbia label, but when Bob Neal told Mitch that the bid was now up to $18,000, Miller said: "Oh, forget it, nobody's worth that much." (See: Call from Mitch Miller, A)

Milkcow Blues Boogie. Sun 215. Released on January 8, 1955, as a 78 rpm single and a 45 rpm single. "You're a Heartbreaker" was on the flip side. "Milkcow Blues Boogie" was written and originally recorded by James "Kokomo" Arnold in 1935 under the title "Milk Cow Blues" (Decca 7029). "Milk Cow Blues" has been recorded by several artists through the years, including Johnnie Lee Wills (Decca 5985) in 1941, Moon Mullican, as "New Milk Cow Blues" (King 607), in 1946, and Bob Crosby (Decca 1962).

Milkcow Blues Boogie. RCA 20/47-6382. A 78 rpm and a 45 rpm re-issue of the Sun original (Sun 215), released in November 1955. "Milkcow Blues Boogie" appeared in the following Long Playing albums: "A Date with Elvis" (RCA LPM-2011); "A Date with Elvis" (RCA LSP-2011 [e]); "The Elvis Presley Sun Collection" (RCA Starcall Hy-1001); "Elvis—The Sun Sessions" (RCA APM1-1675); "The Sun Years" (Sun 1001).

Milkcow Blues. RCA 447-0603. Gold Standard Series re-issue of RCA 20/47-6382.

Milky White Way. RCA 447-0652. Released in February 1966 as a 45 rpm Gold Standard Series original. "Swing Down Sweet Chariot" was on the flip side. "Milky White Way" was a gospel standard (recorded in 1948 by the gospel group the Trumpeteers on Score Records [Score 5001]) that Elvis arranged. It appeared in the Long Playing albums "His Hand in Mine" (RCA LPM/LSP-2328) and "His Hand in Mine" (RCA ANL1-1319).

Miller, Sandy. Vernon Presley's nurse who attended to him at the time of his heart attack in 1979.

Million-Dollar Session. Impromptu recording session on December 4, 1956, at the Sun Studios in Memphis. Those in attendance were: Johnny Cash—guitar and vocal; Carl Perkins—guitar and vocal; Jerry Lee Lewis—piano and vocal; Elvis—piano and vocal. Elvis, who was then an RCA Victor artist, had stopped by the studio to say hello to everyone.

As this was not a recording session, there was much joking, laughing, and talking by the group. Sun producer and engineer Jack Clement had the foresight to tape the session. Today the tapes are owned by Shelby Singleton, the present owner of Sun International.

The following songs were recorded during the Million Dollar Session: "Big Boss Man"; "Blueberry Hill"; "I Won't Have to Cross the Jordan Alone"; "Island of Golden Dreams"; "The Old Rugged Cross"; "Peace in the Valley." Shelby Singleton planned to release the first volume on December 15, 1977, but a suit brought by RCA Victor and later by Johnny Cash halted its release. Volume 1 (Sun 1008) was to have been thirty-two minutes long and would have featured the following songs: "Have a Little Talk with Jesus," "Walk That Lonesome Valley," "I Shall Not Be Moved," "Down by the Riverside," "Will the Circle Be Unbroken," "I Was There When It Happened."

Milton Berle Show, The. NBC-TV variety series on which Elvis made two guest appearances in 1956 (April 3 and June 5). Elvis was paid $5,000 for each appearance. The April 3 show was telecast from the deck of the U.S.S. *Hancock*. Songs performed were: (April 3) "Heartbreak Hotel"; "Money Honey"; "Blue Suede Shoes"; (June 5) "Hound Dog"; "I Want You, I Need You, I Love You."

Mine. Song written by Sid Tepper and Roy C. Bennett and recorded by Elvis in 1967. "Mine" appeared in the Long Playing album "Speedway" (RCA LSP-3989).

Miracle of the Rosary. Song written by Lee Denson in 1971 and recorded by Elvis in the same year. "Miracle of the Rosary" appeared in the Long Playing albums "Elvis—Now" (RCA LSP-4671) and "He Walks Beside Me" (RCA AFL1-2772).

Mirage. Song that Elvis sang in the 1965 movie *Harum Scarum*. "Mirage" was written by Bill Giant, Bernie Baum, and Florence Kaye and appeared in the Long Playing album "Harum Scarum" (RCA LPM/LSP-3468).

Miss Beverly Hills. Movie credit given to the actress who played Mary Ann in the 1968 movie *Speedway*. In the movie credits, her real name was not mentioned.

Miss Charlotte Speedway 100. Beauty contest winner who presented Steve Grayson (Elvis) his trophy for winning the stock-car race in the 1968 movie *Speedway*. Her name was Mary Ann Ashman (played by Miss Beverly Hills).

Mississippi-Alabama Fair and Dairy Show. Annual fair in Tupelo, Mississippi, founded in 1904 as the Lee County Fair.

On October 3, 1945, J. D. Cole, principal of the Lawhon Grammar School, entered Elvis in the annual talent contest sponsored by WELO radio. Elvis won second prize, singing "Old Shep." He received five dollars and free admission to all the amusement rides. This was Elvis's first public appearance and, since the talent show was broadcast by WELO, his first radio appearance. The two featured performers at the fair that year were Minnie Pearl and Pee Wee King. Elvis returned on September 27, 1957, to perform before the hometown people, donating his $10,000 fee to the town of Tupelo. (See: Harris, Becky; Cole, J.D.; WELO)

Mister, Will You Marry Me. Title originally considered for the 1963 MGM movie *It Happened at the World's Fair*. Prior to the film's final title, it was changed to *Take Me to the Fair*.

Mobley, Mary Ann. Miss America 1959 (representing Mississippi). Mary Ann Mobley played Princess Shalimar in the 1965 movie *Harum Scarum* and Deena in the 1965 movie *Girl Happy*.

Money Honey. RCA 20/47-6641. Released in September 1956 as a 78 rpm single and a 45 rpm single. "One-Sided Love Affair" was on the flip side. "Money Honey" was written by Jesse Stone and originally recorded by Clyde McPhatter and the Drifters (Atlantic 1006) in 1953. Elvis sang "Money Honey" on "Stage Show" (March 24, 1956) and on "The Milton Berle Show" (April 3, 1956). It appeared in the Extended Play album "Heartbreak Hotel" (RCA EPA-821) and the Long Playing albums "Elvis Presley" (RCA LPM-1254) and "Elvis Presley" (RCA LSP-1254 [e]).

Money Honey. RCA 47-6689. A 45 rpm disc jockey "record preview." "I Got a Woman" was on the flip side. On the regular release, RCA 20/47-6641, "One-Sided Love Affair" was on the flip side.

Monologue L.P., The. A 33⅓ rpm bootleg album on the Bullet label. The album consisted of some of Elvis's opening-night songs at the International Hotel in Las Vegas on July 26, 1969. Also included was a five-minute monologue by Elvis about his career. Selections included—Side 1: The King Talks About His Career, "Jailhouse Rock," "Don't Be Cruel," "Memories," "Lawdy, Miss Clawdy," "Until It's Time for You to Go," "Oh Happy Day," "Sweet Inspiration," "More." Side 2: "Hey, Jude," "What Now," "Are You Laughing Tonight," "I, John," "Baby, What You Want Me to Do," "I'm Leaving," "What'd I Say."

Monopoly and Scrabble. Elvis's favorite board games. Monopoly was created in 1933 by Charles Darrow. Parker Brothers, the manufacturer of Monopoly, prints more money than the U. S. mint.

Scrabble is produced by Sel Right. The words *Elvis Presley* total twenty points in Scrabble.

251

Monroe, Bill. Country bluegrass fiddler and singer called the "Father of Bluegrass." In 1970 Bill Monroe was elected to the Country Music Hall of Fame. Monroe was the composer of two songs that Elvis recorded: "Blue Moon of Kentucky" (1954) and "Little Cabin on the Hill" (1970).

Montenegro, Hugo. Orchestra leader who scored the 1969 movie *Charro!* He previously scored the Clint Eastwood Italian westerns. In 1968 Hugo Montenegro had a #2 hit record (#1 in England) with "The Good, the Bad and the Ugly,"

Monte's Catering Service. Memphis firm, located at 3788 Summer Ave., that provided the food for Elvis and Priscilla's Memphis wedding reception.

Montgomery, Larry. Tupelo police officer who sang the National Anthem at the dedication of the Elvis Presley Memorial Chapel in Tupelo, Mississippi, August 17, 1979.

Montgomery Ward. Store where Deke Rivers (Elvis) bought his blue shirt in the 1957 movie *Loving You.* He referred to the store as "Monkey Wards."*

Moody Blue. RCA PB-10857. Released in December 1976 as a 45 rpm single. It reached #31 on *Billboard*'s Hot 100 chart and #2 on the Easy Listening chart. "She Thinks I Still Care" was on the flip side. "Moody Blues" was written by Mark James and recorded by Elvis at Graceland on the night of February 4–5, 1976. Five copies of "Moody Blue" were pressed on translucent blue plastic. The song appeared in the Long Playing album "Moody Blue" (RCA AFL1-2428).

Moody Blue. RCA AFL1-2428. Released in June 1977 as a 33⅓ rpm Long Playing album. It reached #3 on *Billboard*'s Hot LP chart and #1 on the Hot Country LP chart. The first pressing of "Moody Blue" was on translucent blue plastic (250,000 copies). RCA pressed its one-billionth record while pressing "Moody Blue." The album sold over a million copies, making it a Platinum Record. Songs included—Side 1: "Unchained Melody," "If You Love Me (Let Me Know)," "Little Darlin'," "He'll Have to Go," "Let Me Be There." Side 2: "Way Down," "Pledging My Love," "Moody Blue," "She Thinks I Still Care," "It's Easy for You."

Moonlight Swim. Song that Elvis sang in the 1961 movie *Blue Hawaii.* "Moonlight Swim" was earlier recorded by actor Tony Perkins (RCA 7020) and by Nick Noble (Mercury 71169) in 1957. It was written by Sylvia Dee and Ben Weisman and appeared in the Long Playing album "Blue Hawaii" (RCA LPM/LSP-2426).

Moore, Bob. Bass guitarist and popular Nashville session musician who played in a number of Elvis's recording sessions. In 1961

---

*Actor Gregory Peck once modeled for the 1940 Montgomery Ward catalog.

Bob Moore had a hit instrumental titled "Mexico." He also composed the theme for the TV series "My Three Sons."

Moore, Joanna. Actress who played Alicia Claypool in the 1962 movie *Follow That Dream*. Miss Moore is the mother of Tatum O'Neal, the youngest* person to win an Academy Award (Best Supporting Actress in 1973 for her role of Addie Loggins in *Paper Moon*).

Moore, Michael. Director of the 1965 movie *Paradise—Hawaiian Style*.

Moore, Robbie. Woman who sued Elvis because she objected to having her picture taken with him in 1956. Elvis gave Miss Moore $5,000 as an out-of-court settlement in October 1956.

Moore, III, Winfield Scott (Scotty). Lead guitarist who backed Elvis Presley from his first recording sessions in July of 1954, through June of 1968.

Scotty Moore was a member in 1954, along with Bill Black, of Doug Poindexter's Starlight Wranglers, a country band that performed in the Memphis area. While a member of the Starlight Wranglers, Moore was asked by Sam Phillips to invite Elvis over to his (Moore's) apartment to rehearse a few songs. On Sunday, July 4, 1954, Elvis went to Scotty Moore's apartment. Later that afternoon Bill Black arrived. Some of the songs they rehearsed were "I Don't Hurt Anymore," "I Apologize," and "I Don't Really Want To Know".

The next evening, July 5, Elvis, Scotty, and Bill recorded "That's All Right (Mama)" at the Sun Studios. The full sound they created was so good that Sam Phillips didn't bother to add any additional instrumentation.

On July 12, 1954, a week after the first Sun recording sessions, Scotty Moore became Elvis's first manager when Elvis and Scotty signed a one-page contract giving Moore a ten percent commission on all of the bookings he made. Elvis's parents also signed the document because he was not yet twenty-one. When Moore found that he could no longer act as both musician and manager, he allowed Elvis to void the contract, thus allowing him to sign with Bob Neal.

For a brief time Elvis, Scotty, and Bill were known as the Blue Moon Boys.

In 1958 Scotty Moore and Bill Black split with Elvis because they didn't like the salary they were receiving. (They received a flat fee—no royalties.) Though Bill Black never did record with Elvis again, Moore did go back to Elvis in 1960. During his two-year hiatus, Moore produced some Jerry Lee Lewis recording sessions. Some of the songs included "Sweet Little Sixteen," "Good Rockin' Tonight," "Hello, Josephine," and "Be-Bop-A-Lula."

---

*George Burns was the oldest person to win an Oscar. He won Best Supporting Actor in 1975 for his portrayal of Al Lewis in *The Sunshine Boys*. Burns was eighty-three.

Although Sam Phillips is given credit for developing Elvis Presley's talent in the early years (and rightly so!), Scotty Moore hasn't received much acknowledgment. Scotty Moore, perhaps more than anyone, must be given credit for creating the driving guitar sound that became known as the "Elvis Presley sound."

Today Scotty Moore is a record producer in Nashville.

Moreno, Rita. Academy Award winning actress nicknamed the "Puerto Rican Bombshell." Rita Moreno won her Oscar in 1961 for her role of Anita in *West Side Story*. Rita Moreno is the only artist to have won an Oscar, a Tony, a Grammy, and an Emmy. Elvis dated Ms. Moreno in 1957 while he was filming *Loving You.* He once took her to the Moulin Rouge in Los Angeles to see Dean Martin.

Morris, Bobby. Musical conductor for Elvis at the International Hotel in Las Vegas in 1969.

Morris, William. Shelby County, Tennessee, sheriff to whom Elvis gave a Mercedes-Benz automobile. He later became mayor of Shelby County.

Mostel, Samuel "Zero". Comedian who died on September 8, 1977—three weeks after Elvis passed away. Mostel acquired his nickname in elementary school because his shyness prevented him from answering many of the teacher's questions. He was one of several people who died around the time of Elvis's death. (See: Marx, Groucho; Cabot, Sebastian)

Mother Is a Freshman. Speech play presented by the Thespian Club in Elvis's senior year (1952–53) at Humes High School.

Mother's Tea House. Espresso café where Charlie Rogers (Elvis) sang at the beginning of the 1964 movie *Roustabout.*

Motion Picture Relief Fund. Organization to help retired actors and actresses, founded in 1923 by actor Jean Hersholt (Joseph Schenck was its first President). Elvis once contributed $50,000 to the M.P.R.F. The check, given to President George L. Bagnell, was the largest contribution to the fund.

Moulin Rouge. West German nightclub managed by a Mr. Schumann, who, with Elvis, sang, in jest, "O Sole Mio"—until Elvis was advised that he wasn't supposed to sing in public.

Mountain Maiden's Breath. Nickname for Ma Tatum's (Glenda Farrell) moonshine in the 1964 movie *Kissin' Cousins.*

Mountain Valley. Brand of mineral water liked by Elvis.

Movie Bloopers. The following bloopers occurred in Elvis's movies: *Love Me Tender*—A set of drums was used in a movie that was set in 1865. *Double Trouble*—A Greyhound moving van is seen in a scene taking place in Brussels, Belgium. *Clambake* —The setting is Miami, Florida, yet the mountains of California can be seen in the background. *The Trouble with Girls (And How To Get Into It)*—The movie is set in 1927, yet Elvis has a plastic football helmet.

Movies. Movies in which Elvis appeared: 1. *Love Me Tender* (1956) —Clint Reno. 2. *Loving You* (1957)—Deke Rivers (Jim Tompkins). 3. *Jailhouse Rock* (1957)—Vince Everett. 4. *King Creole* (1958)—Danny Fisher. 5. *G.I. Blues* (1960)—Tulsa McLean. 6. *Flaming Star* (1960)—Pacer Burton. 7. *Wild in the Country* (1961)—Glenn Tyler. 8. *Blue Hawaii* (1961)— Chad Gates. 9. *Follow That Dream* (1961)—Tony Kwimper. 10. *Kid Galahad* (1962)—Walter Gulick. 11. *Girls! Girls! Girls!* 1962)—Ross Carpenter. 12. *It Happened at the World's Fair* (1963)—Mike Edwards. 13. *Fun in Acapulco* (1963)— Mike Windgren. 14. *Kissin' Cousins* (1964)—Josh Morgan/ Jodie Tatum. 15. *Viva Las Vegas* (1964)—Lucky Jackson. 16. *Roustabout* (1964)—Charlie Rogers. 17. *Girl Happy* (1965)—Rusty Wells. 18. *Tickle Me* (1965)—Lonnie Beale. 19. *Harum Scarum* (1965)—Johnny Tyronne. 20. *Frankie and Johnny* (1966)—Johnny. 21. *Paradise—Hawaiian Style* (1966) —Rick Richards. 22. *Spinout* (1966)—Mike McCoy. 23. *Easy Come, Easy Go.* (1967)—Ted Jackson. 24. *Double Trouble* (1967)—Guy Lambert. 25. *Clambake* (1967)—Scott Heywood. 26. *Stay Away Joe* (1968)—Joe Lightcloud. 27. *Speedway* (1968)—Steve Grayson. 28. *Live a Little, Love a Little* (1968) Greg Nolan. 29. *Charro!* (1968)—Jesse Wade. 30. *The Trouble with Girls* (*And How To Get Into It*) (1969)—Walter Hale. 31. *Change of Habit* (1969)—Dr. John Carpenter. 32. *Elvis—That's the Way It Is* (1970). 33. *Elvis on Tour* (1972).

Mr. Haney. Character played by Pat Buttram on the 1965–71 CBS-TV series "Green Acres." Pat Buttram patterned Mr. Haney's character after Col. Tom Parker, whom Buttram had met years before.

Mr. Rock 'n' Roll. A 45 rpm Extended Play bootleg album on the Pelvis label. Songs included—Side 1: "Fame and Fortune," "Stuck on You." Side 2: "The Truth About Me" (interview) 1972 Madison Square Garden Press Conference.

Mr. Safety. Award Elvis won for safe driving while a student in high school.

Mr. Songman. RCA PB-10278. Released in April 1975 as a 45 rpm single. "T-R-O-U-B-L-E" was on the flip side. "Mr. Songman" was written by Donnie Sumner and appeared in the Long Playing album "Promised Land" (RCA APL1-0873).

Mr. Songman. RCA GB-10487. Gold Standard Series re-issue of RCA PB-10278.

Muffin. Great Pyrenees dog with white hair that Elvis had as a pet at Graceland. Muffin was injured at obedience school and had to be put to sleep.

Murray, Anne. Canadian singer who holds the distinction of being the first Canadian female to have a million-seller ("Snowbird" in 1970). Anne Murray's Gold Record was presented to her on the syndicated TV series "The Merv Griffin Show" on November 10, 1970. Anne Murray, Gordon Lightfoot, Wilf Carter, and Hank Snow all hail from Nova Scotia, Canada. Elvis recorded "Snowbird" in September 1970.

Music Gate. Name given to the wrought-iron front gates at Graceland. They were built in 1957 by Doors, Inc.

Music Sales. Memphis firm, located at 117 Union Ave., that distributed Sun records locally in the 1950s.

Muss I Denn Zum Stadtele Naus. Old German folk song on which "Wooden Heart" is based.

My Babe. Adaptation of the gospel tune "This Train," written by Willie Dixon and Charles Stone and originally recorded by Little Walter Jacobs (Checker 811) in 1955. Elvis recorded "My Babe" in 1969 and it appeared in the Long Playing albums "From Memphis to Vegas/From Vegas to Memphis" (RCA LSP-6020) and "Elvis in Person" (RCA LSP-4428).

My Baby Left Me. RCA 20/47-6540. Released in May 1956 as a 78 rpm single and a 45 rpm single. It reached #31 on *Billboard*'s Hot 100 chart and #1 on the Country chart. "I Want You, I Need You, I Love You" was on the flip side. "My Baby Left Me" was written and originally recorded by Arthur Crudup (RCA 130-284) in 1950. Elvis's version of "My Baby Left Me" appeared in the following Extended Play albums: "The Real Elvis" (RCA EPA-940); "The Real Elvis" (RCA EPA-5120); "Elvis Presley" (RCA SPD-23); and the following Long Playing albums: "For LP Fans Only" (RCA LPM-1990); "For LP Fans Only" (RCA LSP-1990 [e]); "Elvis: The Other Sides—Worldwide Gold Award Hits, Volume 2" (RCA LPM-6402); "Elvis Recorded Live on Stage in Memphis" (RCA CPL1-0606).

My Baby Left Me. RCA 447-0607. Gold Standard Series re-issue of RCA 20/47-6540.

My Baby's Crazy 'Bout Elvis. A 1957 Elvis novelty song by Billy Boyle on Decca Records (Decca 11503).

My Baby's Gone. Slower and bluesier version of "I'm Left, You're Right, She's Gone." "My Baby's Gone" (a.k.a. "My Baby Is Gone") has never been released by Sun or by RCA. It can be found on the bootleg LP "Good Rockin' Tonight" and several bootleg single releases.

My Boy. RCA PB-10191. Released in January 1975 as a 45 rpm single. It reached #20 on *Billboard*'s Hot 100 chart and #14 on the Country chart. "Thinking About You" was on the flip side. "My Boy" was written by Claude Francis and Jean-Pierre Boutayre (English words by Bill Martin and Phil Coulter) and originally recorded by actor Richard Harris in 1971. It appeared in the Long Playing albums "Good Times" (RCA CPL1-0475) and "Our Memories of Elvis" (RCA AQL1-3279).

My Boy. RCA GB-10489. Gold Standard Series re-issue of RCA PB-10191.

My Boy. RCA 2458 EX. A 1974 45 rpm special release. "Loving

Arms" was on the flip side. On the 1975 regular release, "Thinking About You" was on the flip side.

My Boy Elvis. Song recorded by Janis Martin, a South African singer, and released on RCA Records (RCA 6652) in 1956. The lyrics contained the titles of Elvis's first few singles.

My Darling Ginger. A 1978 Elvis novelty record by Jimmy Luke and Bruce Channell on LeCam Records, sung to the tune of "Since I Met You, Baby" (LeCam 512).

My Desert Serenade. Song that Elvis sang in the 1965 movie *Harum Scarum*. "My Desert Serenade" was written by Stan Gelber and appeared in the Long Playing album "Harum Scarum" (RCA LPM/LSP-3468).

My Friend Elvis. A 1977 Elvis tribute record by the Hanson Brothers on AAA-Aron Records (AAA-Aron 001).

My Happiness. Song written by Betty Peterson and Borney Bergantine, which became million-sellers for John and Sandra Steele and the Pied Pipers in 1948. Connie Francis also had a million-seller with "My Happiness" (MGM 2738) in 1959. "My Happiness" was the first song Elvis ever recorded. He recorded it at the Memphis Recording Service in the summer of 1953. Elvis's version of "My Happiness" was based on the Ink Spots' recording. (See: Keisker, Marion; Memphis Recording Service; That's When Your Heartaches Begin)

My Heart's Content (Goodbye from the King). A 1977 Elvis tribute record by Wilguis J. C. Raynor on RTF Records (RTF 101).

My Heavenly Father. Song that Kathy Westmoreland sang at a number of Elvis's concerts. She sang "My Heavenly Father" at Elvis's funeral (August 18, 1977) and later at the dedication of the Elvis Presley Memorial Chapel (August 17, 1979).

My Little Friend. RCA 47-9791. Released in January 1970 as a 45 rpm single. "Kentucky Rain" was on the flip side. "My Little Friend" was written by Shirl Milete and appeared in the Long Playing albums "Almost in Love" (RCA Camden CAS-2440) and "Almost in Love" (Pickwick CAS-2440).

My Little Friend. RCA 447-0675. Gold Standard Series re-issue of RCA 47-9791.

My Little Girl's Prayer (For Elvis). A 1977 Elvis tribute record by Kelly Leroux on King's International Records (King's International 5099).

My Old Kentucky Home. Official state song of Kentucky, which is played prior to the start of the annual Kentucky Derby horse race at Churchill Downs in Louisville. "My Old Kentucky Home" was written by Stephen Foster in 1853 in Bardstown, Kentucky, while he was visiting a cousin. The song was introduced by Ed Christy's Minstrels.

In the 1969 movie *The Trouble With Girls (And How To Get Into It)*, "My Old Kentucky Home" was sung by a group of college boys. (See: "Boola Boola"; "Eyes Of Texas, The"; "On Wisconsin")

Mystery Train. Sun 223. Released in August 1955 as a 78 rpm single and a 45 rpm single. It reached #1 on *Billboard*'s Country chart—the first Presley single to reach #1 on any national chart. "I Forgot to Remember to Forget" was on the flip side. Elvis sang "Mystery Train" in the 1970 documentary *Elvis—That's the Way It Is* and the 1972 documentary *Elvis on Tour*. "Mystery Train" was written by Herman "Little Junior" Parker and Sam Phillips and was first recorded by Parker (Sun 192) in 1953. (The record label credited "Little Junior's Blue Flames.") While Parker had a "bluesy" version, Elvis's rendition was faster and more exciting. Credit should be given to Elvis, Scotty Moore, and Bill Black for indeed creating a new sound. A sound that wasn't rhythm and blues, country, or even rock-a-billy, it was Elvis singing pure, basic rock 'n' roll.

Mystery Train. RCA 20/47-6357. A 78 rpm and 45 rpm re-issue of the Sun original. "Mystery Train"/"I Forgot to Remember to Forget" was Elvis's first RCA release. "Mystery Train" appeared in the Extended Play album "Any Way You Want Me" (RCA EPA-965) and the following Long Playing albums: "For LP Fans Only" (RCA LPM-1990); "For LP Fans Only" (RCA LSP-1990 [e]); "From Memphis to Vegas/From Vegas to Memphis" (RCA LSP-6020); "Elvis in Person" (RCA LSP-4428); "The Elvis Presley Sun Sessions" (RCA Starcall Hy-1001); "Elvis—The Sun Sessions" RCA APM1-1675); "The Sun Years" (Sun 1001).

Mystery Train. RCA 447-0600. Gold Standard Series re-issue of RCA 20/47-6357.

My Way. RCA PB-11165. Released in 1977 as a 45 rpm single. "America the Beautiful" was on the flip side. "My Way" sold over a million copies. It was written by Gilles Thibault, Clyde Francois, and Jacques Revaux in 1967 under the French title "Comme d'habitude." Paul Anka added English lyrics in 1969 and Frank Sinatra had a million-seller with the song (Reprise 734). Sinatra's recording remained on the British charts for 122 straight weeks—a British record. Elvis sang "My Way" in the 1973 TV special "Elvis: Aloha from Hawaii." It appeared in the Long Playing albums "Elvis: Aloha from Hawaii Via Satellite" (RCA VPSX-6089) and "Elvis—A Canadian Tribute" (RCA KKL1-7065).

My Wish Came True. RCA 47-7600. Released in June 1959 as a 45 rpm single. It reached #12 on *Billboard*'s Hot 100 chart and #15 on the Rhythm and Blues chart. "A Big Hunk o' Love" was on the flip side. "My Wish Came True" was written by Ivory Joe Hunter and appeared in the following Long Playing albums: "50,000,000 Elvis Can't Be Wrong—Elvis' Golden Records, Volume 2" (RCA LPM-2075); "50,000,000 Elvis Fans Can't Be Wrong—Elvis' Golden Records, Volume 2" (RCA LSP-2075 [e]); "Elvis: The Other Sides—Worldwide Gold Award Hits, Volume 2" (RCA LPM-6402).

My Wish Came True. RCA 447-0626. Gold Standard Series reissue of RCA 47-7600.

N

9. Number on the side of the borrowed 1966 blue Shelby Cobra that Mike McCoy (Elvis) drove to victory in the 1966 movie *Spinout.*

19 Elvis Presley Great Hits. A 33⅓ rpm bootleg album released in England on the Rex label. Songs included—Side 1: "I Just Can't Help Believin'," "Love Me Tender," "I Gotta Know," "Surrender," "Are You Lonesome Tonight," "Little Sister," "Good Luck Charm," "In the Ghetto," "The Wonder of You." Side 2: "Don't Be Cruel," "One Night," "It's Now or Never," "Jailhouse Rock," "No More," "Moonlight Swim," "King Creole," "Kiss Me Quick," "Life," "(You're The) Devil in Disguise."

91%. Elvis's peak tax bracket.

97th General Hospital. U. S. Army hospital in West Germany where Elvis was hospitalized for tonsillitis.

1935. Birth year of Elvis and the following celebrities: Woody Allen (December 1), Carol Burnett (April 26), Steve Lawrence (July 8), Johnny Mathis (September 30), Lee Remick (December 14).

1939 Plymouth. Green automobile that Vernon Presley owned when he, Gladys, and Elvis moved to Memphis from Tupelo on September 12, 1948.

1942 Lincoln Coupe. Automobile that Elvis drove during high school. It cost $450.

1955 Sun Days. Album featuring outtakes by Elvis Presley, Johnny Cash, Charlie Rich, Roy Orbison, Jerry Lee Lewis, and Carl Perkins on Sun Records (Sun 1009), which Shelby Singleton planned to release on December 15, 1977, until a lawsuit filed by RCA Victor halted the release (see: Million Dollar Session).

1975 Cadillac Coupe DeVille. Gold-colored Cadillac that Elvis gave to Vester Presley in 1975.

97887711. Army serial number of Captain Robert Jason Salbo (Jack Albertson) in the 1964 movie *Kissin' Cousins.*

N777EP. U. S. registration number of Elvis's Jet Commander aircraft.

N880EP. U. S. registration number of Elvis's Convair 880 jet aircraft. N = November (U. S. Registration letter), 880 = Convair 880, EP = Elvis Presley.

N53328. Registration number of Danny Kohana's (James Shigeta) helicopter in the 1966 movie *Paradise—Hawaiian Style*.

N73202. Registration number of Rick Richard's (Elvis) helicopter in the 1966 movie *Paradise—Hawaiian Style*.

Nadel, Arthur. Director of the 1967 movie *Clambake*.

Nash, W.S. Pharmacist at Baptist Memorial Hospital in Memphis who made out Dr. George Nichopoulos's last prescription for Elvis the day before Elvis's death.

NAshville 8-2858. Col. Parker's telephone number in Madison, Tennessee, during the 1950s.

Nashville Outtakes and Early Interviews. A 33⅓ rpm bootleg album on the Wizardo label. Songs included—Side 1: "Good Rockin' Tonight," "My Baby Is Gone," "I Don't Care If the Sun Don't Shine," "Blue Moon of Kentucky," "I'll Never Let You Go (Little Darlin')," "Mystery Train," "I Forgot to Remember to Forget." Side 2: "Hey, Jude," "What Now, My Love," "Are You Laughing Tonight," "I John," "Baby, What You Want Me to Do," "I'm Leaving," "What'd I Say."

Nassau Coliseum. Uniondale, New York, concert site where, on July 19, 1975, Elvis played the piano in public for the first time. He sang "You'll Never Walk Alone" as he played.

Elvis was to have appeared at the Nassau Coliseum on August 22, 1977. Those who hold tickets to that concert have until 1983 to redeem their now-valuable tickets.

National Bank of Commerce. Memphis, Tennessee, banking institution with which Elvis had a checking account. Sam C. Phillips (at least in the 1950s) also banked at the National Bank of Commerce.

National Funeral Home. Memphis mortuary, located at 1177 Union Ave., that handled the funeral services of Gladys Presley in August 1958. The facility was then affiliated with National Life and Burial Insurance. In 1962 National changed its name to the Memphis Funeral Home. (See: Memphis Funeral Home)

Neal, Bob. (Robert Neal Hopgood) Born in the Belgian Congo in 1917, Bob Neal moved to the U.S. in 1930, becoming a disc jockey for WMPS in Memphis during the 1940s. In 1952 he became a promoting agent, establishing the Memphis Promotions Agency. From January 1, 1955 to March 15, 1956, he served as Elvis's second manager, collecting fifteen percent of Elvis's earnings. In 1956, with the partnership of Sam Phillips, Neal founded Stars Incorporated (suite 1916 Sterick Bldg.), in Memphis, to handle recording artists. In 1958 Bob Neal became Johnny Cash's first manager. Bob Neal also has handled Jerry Lee Lewis, Carl Perkins, Roy Orbison, Conway Twitty, Warren Smith, Sonny James, Lynn Anderson, Stonewall Jackson, Bobby Helms, Nat Stuckey, and others.

Nearness of You, The. Song that Robin Ganter (Stella Stevens) sang in the 1962 Elvis movie *Girls! Girls! Girls!* It was written by Ned Washington and Hoagy Carmichael in 1940. Gladys Swarthout introduced "The Nearness of You" in the Paramount movie *Romance in the Dark*. Glenn Miller had a popular recording of the song on the Bluebird label.

Neely, Richard. Davada "Dee" Stanley's brother. Richard Neely was Vernon Presley's best man when Vernon married Dee. The wedding took place at Neely's Huntsville, Alabama, home on July 3, 1960.

Nelson, Gene. Director (real name: Eugene Berg) of the 1964 movie *Kissin' Cousins* and the 1965 movie *Harum Scarum*. From 1938 to 1950 Nelson was an actor.

Nelson, Jimmy. Ventriloquist who, with his dummies Danny O'Day and Farfel, advertised Nestle's Quick on the TV series "Stage Show" on March 17, 1956. Elvis appeared on that show—his fifth of six appearances.

Nelson, Ricky. Youngest son of Ozzie* and Harriet Nelson. He was born Eric Hilliard Nelson, on May 8, 1940. Ricky became popular by appearing on the TV series "The Adventures of Ozzie and Harriet." He and his brother David first sang in public when they sang "The Lord's Prayer" for a Sunday School program. Ricky had made his movie debut in the 1951 movie *The Story of Three Loves*.† As a teenager, in early 1951, he began singing on his parent's TV show. He first sang the Fats Domino hit "I'm Walking" on an episode in early 1957. On another episode Ricky Nelson attended a costume party dressed like Elvis Presley. There he sang a few lines of "Love Me Tender." Over 10,000 letters were received from television viewers asking to hear more of Ricky singing. His father, Ozzie, then set him up with his first recording company, Verve Records, where he recorded his first hit, "A Teenager's Romance" backed with "I'm Walking" (Verve 10047). By mid-1957 Ricky Nelson was established as a recording artist, with Johnny and Dorsey Burnette and Gene Pitney writing his hit songs. James Burton was the guitar player whose licks gave Nelson's songs their distinctive style, and the Jordanaires provided his vocal back-up. Burton would later become a session musician for Elvis Presley. Ricky married football great Tom Harmon's daughter Kristen. In 1970 Rick Nelson formed the Stone Canyon Band, having a hit record, "Garden Party" (Decca 32980), which was an autobiographical account of an incident that occurred to him at Madison Square Garden in 1972, where he was booed off stage for not singing some of his old hits.

Nelson, Willie. Country composer and singer, nicknamed the "Red

---

*Ozzie (Oswald) Nelson. At age thirteen Ozzie was the youngest Eagle Scout in the U. S. He was also a Rutgers honor student.
†He is often credited as having debuted in the 1959 John Wayne movie *Rio Bravo*, but that was his third movie appearance. His second movie was *Here Come the Nelsons* (1952).

Headed Stranger." He composed a number of classic country hits including "Crazy," "Hello Walls" (cowriter), and "Touch Me." Willie also composed "Funny How Time Slips Away," which Elvis recorded. Willie Nelson and Leon Russell recorded "Heartbreak Hotel" as a rocker in 1979.

Nesbitt's. Brand of orange soda preferred by Elvis.

Neutrogena. Brand of soap that Elvis preferred.

Never Again. Song that Elvis recorded at Graceland on the night of February 6–7, 1976. "Never Again was written by Billy Edd Wheeler and Jerry Chesnut and appeared in the Long Playing albums "From Elvis Presley Boulevard, Memphis, Tennessee" (RCA APL1-1506) and "Our Memories of Elvis" (RCA AQL1-3279).

Never Been to Spain. Song that Elvis sang in the 1972 documentary *Elvis on Tour*. "Never Been to Spain" was written by Hoyt Axton and was a 1972 hit for Three Dog Night (Dunhill 4299). Originally, Elvis's version was scheduled to appear in the "Standing Room Only" album, but the album was never released. "Never Been to Spain" did appear in the Long Playing album "Elvis as Recorded at Madison Square Garden" (RCA LSP-4776).

Never Ending. RCA 47-8400. Released in July 1964 as a 45 rpm single. "Such a Night" was on the flip side. "Never Ending" was written by Buddy Kaye and Philip Springer and appeared in the Long Playing album "Double Trouble" (RCA LPM/LSP-3787).

Never Ending. RCA 447-0645. Gold Standard Series re-issue of RCA 47-8400.

Never Let Me Go. Song that Robin Ganter (Stella Stevens) sang in the 1962 Elvis movie *Girls! Girls! Girls!*. "Never Let Me Go" was written by Jay Livingston and Ray Evans in 1956 and was introduced by Nat "King" Cole in the Paramount movie *The Scarlet Hours*.

Never Say Yes. Song that Elvis sang in the 1966 movie *Spinout*. "Never Say Yes" was written by Doc Pomus and Mort Shuman and appeared in the Long Playing album "Spinout" (RCA LPM/LSP-3702).

Never Say Yes. Title originally considered for the 1966 movie *Spinout*.

New Angel Tonight. Song that was released by Red River Dave in 1958, shortly after Gladys Presley's death. "New Angel Tonight" alluded to Mrs. Presley.

New Frontier Hotel. Hotel where Elvis made his first Las Vegas appearance, April 23–29, 1956. The New Frontier's manager, Sammy Lewis, signed Elvis for two weeks at $7,500 per week. Elvis was advertised as the "Atomic Powered Singer." The featured act on the bill was the Freddie Martin Orchestra. Comedian Shecky Greene was also on the bill. Due to the poor reception, Col. Parker and the New Frontier ended Elvis's engagement after only one week.

On January 15, 1970, Diana Ross* gave her final performance with the Supremes at the Frontier Hotel (the "New" had been dropped from the name). Ironically, the trio's last song together was "Someday We'll Be Together," which had topped the charts three weeks earlier.

New Gladiators, The. Uncompleted 1974 karate documentary in which Elvis appeared. Produced by George Waite, the film has never been released. Supposedly, Elvis gave financial backing to the film and was to have narrated it.

New Morning. A Bob Dylan tribute album to Elvis on Columbia Records (Columbia 30290), released in October 1971.

New Orleans. Song that Elvis sang in the 1958 movie *King Creole.* "New Orleans" was written by Sid Tepper and Roy C. Bennett and appeared in the Extended Play albums "King Creole, Volume 1" (RCA EPA-4319) and "King Creole, Volume 1" (RCA EPA-5122) and the following Long Playing albums: "King Creole" (RCA LPM-1884); "King Creole" RCA LSP-1884 [e]); "Elvis: The Other Sides—Worldwide Gold Award Hits, Volume 2" (RCA LPM-6402).

New Orthophonic. High Fidelity recording process first introduced by RCA Records in the mid-1950s. Elvis's first albums were produced using this process.

New Plaza. Run-down hotel alluded to by Robin Ganter (Stella Stevens) in the 1962 movie *Girls! Girls! Girls!*. Robin falsely told Ross Carpenter (Elvis) that she lived at the New Plaza.

New Star in Heaven, A. A 1977 Elvis tribute record by Wally Fowler on Dove Records (Dove 2177). (See: Pricilla)

Newton-John, Olivia. Popular Australian singer who has gained fame in both rock and country music. Born on September 26, 1947, the same day as country artist Lynn Anderson, she is the granddaughter of Cambridge University professor Max Born, who won the Nobel Prize in 1954. Olivia Newton-John had a hit in late 1973 with "Let Me Be There" (MCA 40101), which Elvis recorded in 1974.

Newton, Wayne. Popular singer who is, reportedly, the highest-paid performer in Las Vegas. Wayne Newton made his TV debut on "The Jackie Gleason Show" in September 1962. Shortly after, Bobby Darin signed him to Capitol Records and produced Newton's first record, "Heart" (Capitol 4920). In 1972 Wayne Newton was the first artist signed by the Chelsea label. His first million-seller, "Daddy, Don't You Walk So Fast," was also Chelsea's first million-seller.

Wayne Newton purchased Elvis's Jet Commander aircraft for

---

*When Diana Ross left the Supremes, she was replaced by Jean Terrell, the sister of Heavyweight boxer Ernie Terrell.

$300,000. As a part of his stage show, Newton does an Elvis impersonation. On the album "Elvis in Concert" Elvis introduced himself to his audience in Rapid City, South Dakota, as Wayne Newton.

Next Step Is Love, The. RCA 47-9873. Released in July 1970 as a 45 rpm single. It reached #32 on *Billboard*'s Hot 100 chart and #51 on the Country chart. "I've Lost You" was on the flip side. Elvis sang "The Next Step Is Love" in the 1970 documentary *Elvis—That's the Way It Is.* Written by Paul Evans and Paul Parnes, "The Next Step Is Love" appeared in the Long Playing albums "Elvis—That's the Way It Is" (RCA LSP-4445) and "Elvis: The Other Sides—Worldwide Gold Award Hits, Volume 2" (RCA LPM-6402).

Next Step Is Love, The. RCA 447-0677. Gold Standard Series reissue of RCA 47-9873.

Neyland, Anne. Elvis's costar in the 1957 movie *Jailhouse Rock.* Elvis dated Anne Neyland briefly in 1957.

Nicholson, Pauline. Cook and maid at Graceland for fifteen years. Elvis once gave her a new 1964 Buick LeSabre.

Nichopoulos, George C. Personal physician of Elvis and his family. George Nichopoulos, nicknamed Doctor Nick, was attending to Elvis at the time of the star's death. Nichopoulos's offices were located at 1734 Madison Ave. in downtown Memphis. For years he and his wife, Edna, were close friends of both the Presleys and the members of the Memphis Mafia. He even introduced Elvis to the sport of racquetball. Nichopoulos invested in a number of projects around the Memphis area, one of which was a medical building at 1750 Madison Ave. He and his wife were heavily indebted to Elvis for loans granted to them by Elvis (estimated at over $300,000). Dr. Nichopoulos prescribed large amounts of drugs to sixteen of his patients, including Marty Lacker and Jerry Lee Lewis. Between January 20 and August 16, 1977, he prescribed to Elvis 5,684 narcotic and amphetamine pills (an average of 25 per day). Elvis filled nine different prescriptions the day before he died.

Dr. George Nichopoulos was a pallbearer at Elvis's funeral. In September 1979 he was charged by the Tennessee Board of Medical Examiners with "indiscriminately prescribing 5,300 pills and vials for Elvis in the seven months before his death."

Nicknames. Some of Elvis's nicknames included: Big E; Big El; the Chief; Crazy; E; El; Elvis the Pelvis; Elvis the Pretzel; the Hillbilly Cat; the King; the King of Rock 'n' Roll; the King of Western Bop; Mr. Wiggle and Shake; Sir Swivel Hips; Tiger Man; Wiggle Hips; Memphis Flash; and others.

Nielson, Sherril. Back-up vocalist for Elvis at many of his live performances. Sherril Nielson sang duet with Elvis on "Spanish Eyes" when it was sung at his concerts. Nielson also sang a solo of "O Sole Mio" prior to Elvis singing "It's Now or Never" at live concerts.

Night Life. Song that Elvis recorded for the 1964 movie *Viva Las Vegas*. It was cut from the final print of the film. "Night Life" was written by Bill Giant, Bernie Baum, and Florence Kaye and appeared in the following Long Playing albums: "Singer Presents Elvis Singing Flaming Star and Others" (RCA PRS-279); "Elvis Sings Flaming Star" (RCA Camden CAS-2304); "Elvis Sings Flaming Star" (Pickwick CAS-2304).

Night Rider. Song that Elvis sang in the 1965 movie *Tickle Me*. It was written by Doc Pomus and Mort Shuman. "Night Rider" appeared in the Extended Play album "Tickle Me" (RCA EPA-4383) and the Long Playing album "Pot Luck" (RCA LPM..LSP-2523).

Nipper. RCA Victor dog in the trademark "His Master's Voice." Nipper was born in Bristol, England, in 1884, and died in 1895. The original painting of Nipper was by his second master, Francis Barroud. He was first the symbol of the Gramophone Company, then the Victor Talking Machine Company, and, finally, RCA Victor in 1929. The phonograph shown in the trademark painting is a 1905 Victor Gold Medal.

Elvis wrestled with a paper-mâché Nipper at the Pan Pacific concerts, October 28–29, 1957. At the U.S.S. *Arizona* benefit concert in Honolulu, March 25, 1961, Elvis sang to a statue of Nipper.

Nixon, Richard M. Thirty-seventh President of the United States. During his campaign, President Nixon used the same F-28 jet aircraft used by Elvis on his 1971 tour.

No More. Song that Elvis sang in the 1961 movie *Blue Hawaii*. "No More" was recorded by Elvis for—but did not appear in—the U. S. edition of the worldwide TV concert "Elvis: Aloha from Hawaii." The song did not appear in the soundtrack album from the TV broadcast, but it was included in the "Mahalo from Elvis" album.

"No More" was written by Don Robertson and Hal Blair and appeared in the Long Playing albums "Blue Hawaii" (RCA LPM/LSP-2426) and "Mahalo from Elvis" (Pickwick ACL-7064).

Noone, Peter. Lead singer of the British group Herman's Hermits. Peter Noone interviewed Elvis in a live conference at the Polynesian Cultural Center in Hawaii. In the interview Peter asked Elvis when he was coming to England.

(There's) No Room to Rhumba in a Sports Car. Song that Elvis sang in the 1963 movie *Fun in Acapulco*. "(There's) No Room to Rhumba in a Sports Car" was written by Fred Wise and Dick Manning and appeared in the Long Playing album "Fun in Acapulco" (RCA LPM/LSP-2756).

Nothingville. Song that Elvis sang in the 1968 NBC-TV special "Elvis." "Nothingville" was written by Billy Strange and Mac Davis and appeared in the Long Playing album "Elvis—TV Special" (RCA LPM-4088).

No Time for Sergeants. A 1958 movie, starring Andy Griffith as Private Will Stockdale, which Elvis watched in 1958 at the Waco Theater in Waco, Texas. Elvis went to the movie with Anita Wood and Ed Fadal. Elvis's friend Nick Adams appeared in the movie as Will Stockdale's friend Ben. At the same time, *King Creole* was playing at the Orpheum Theater in Waco.

Not Mine But Thy Will Be Done. Words on the front of Gladys Presley's grave marker.

Novarese, Leticia (Leticia Roman). Actress whom Elvis dated in 1960.

Nudie's Rodeo Tailors. Hollywood clothes-designer firm that created Elvis's $10,000 gold lamé tuxedo. Nudie also created a $7,500 suit for Alan Meyer, one of the Elvis imitators.

Number One Records. Elvis had fourteen singles that reached #1 in *Billboard*'s Hot 100 chart. They were: "Heartbreak Hotel" (May 5–June 16, 1956—6 weeks), "Don't Be Cruel" (September 15–November 3, 1956–7 weeks) "Love Me Tender" (November 17–December 8, 1956, and December 22–29, 1956—4 weeks), "All Shook Up" (April 20–June 15, 1957—8 weeks), "Teddy Bear" (July 15–September 2, 1957—7 weeks), "Jailhouse Rock" (November 4–December 9, 1957—6 weeks), "Don't" (March 10–17, 1958—1 week), "A Big Hunk o' Love" (August 10–24, 1959—2 weeks), "Stuck on You" (April 25–May 23, 1960—4 weeks), "It's Now or Never" (August 15–September 19, 1960—5 weeks), "Are You Lonesome Tonight" (November 28, 1960–January 9, 1961—"Surrender" (March 20–April 3, 1961—2 weeks), "Good Luck Charm" (April 21–May 5, 1962—2 weeks), "Suspicious Minds" (November 1–8, 1969—1 week).

O

O11-143875. Elvis's checking account number with the National Bank of Commerce in Memphis. Elvis signed his checks "E. A. Presley."

1-CF652. Tennessee license plate number of the white Cadillac hearse (#25) that carried Elvis's body from Graceland to Forest Hill Cemetery (August 18, 1977).

1+2=½. Three-piece combo that backed Mike McCoy (Elvis) in the 1966 movie *Spinout*. The drummer was a female named Les (Deborah Walley).

$109.54. Amount of Elvis's monthly pay upon his discharge from the Army, May 5, 1960.

110–97. Final score of the football game in which Walter Hale (Elvis) played in the 1969 movie *The Trouble with Girls* (*And How To Get Into It*).

136 Bay Street, Apartment 3. Home address of Laurel Dodge (Laurel Goodwin) in the 1962 movie *Girls! Girls! Girls!*.

144 Monovale. Address of Elvis's home in Holmby Hills, California, bought for $400,000. Elvis and Priscilla moved there from 1174 Hillcrest in late 1967.

185 Lbs. Elvis's weight at his Army induction. Upon his discharge, Elvis's weight was down to 170 pounds.

185 Winchester Street. Memphis address of the Lauderdale Courts, where, on September 20, 1949, the Presleys moved into a two-bedroom, ground-floor apartment (#328). They moved there from 572 Poplar Street. Their telephone number was 37-4185. The monthly rent in the federally funded, 433-unit housing project was thirty-five dollars. On January 7, 1953, the family moved to 398 Cypress. Bill Black's mother, Mrs. Ruby Black, also lived in the housing complex.

1010. Number on the train engine that brought the Chautauqua group to Radford Center, Iowa, in the 1969 movie *The Trouble with Girls* (*And How To Get Into It*).

1034 Audubon Drive. Memphis address of the home Elvis bought, for $40,000, in April 1956. He added a swimming pool to the back yard. The Presleys' telephone number was unlisted. The green and white ranch-style home sold for $55,000 in March 1957. Elvis and his parents then moved to Graceland.

1059 Bellagio Road. Address of the Mediterranean-style home in Bel-Air that Elvis rented after moving from the home at 565 Perugia Way. Elvis next moved to 10550 Rocca Place in Bel-Air.

1,087. Number of photographs of Elvis that sisters Graylee and Sharyn Davolt had hanging on their bedroom wall in their Memphis home in 1957. A photograph of their bedroom has appeared in most Elvis fan magazines.

1103 Imports. Wholesale division of the Nevada Diamond Exchange, located in the Thunderbird Hotel in Las Vegas. In November and December 1976, Elvis spent $23,702 on jewelry from 1103 Imports.

1174 Hillcrest Road. Multi-level French Regency house in the Trousdale Estates near Los Angeles, purchased by Elvis for $400,000 on May 7, 1967. Elvis and Priscilla moved to 144 Monovale in Holmby Hills in late 1967.

$1,250. Salary paid to Elvis for each of his six appearances on the Dorsey Brothers' "Stage Show" TV series.

1313. Number on all the cell doors in the "Jailhouse Rock" musical routine in the 1957 movie *Jailhouse Rock*.

1414 Getwell. Memphis address of the home in which the Presleys lived from mid-1955 to April 1956. Their telephone number at that address was 48-4921. Prior to 1414 Getwell, the Presleys lived at 2414 Lamar Ave. In April 1956 they bought a home at 1034 Audubon Drive.

1525 McGavock Street. Address of the converted studio in Nashville that RCA rented from the Methodist Church in the mid-1950s. The studio was owned by the Methodist TV, Radio, and Film Commission. Elvis's first RCA recording session, on January 10, 1956, was held at the 1525 McGavock Street studio.

1734 Madison Avenue. Memphis address of Dr. George Nichopoulos's office.

1750 Madison Avenue. Memphis address of the $5.5 million medical building in which Dr. George Nichopoulos was an investor in 1977. The investment was a failure.

1850 Dolan Road. Memphis address of Vernon Presley's home. The ranch-style home, situated adjacent to Graceland, was bought in 1978 by Hobart and Bonnie Burnette. (See: Hickory Log)

10550 Rocca Place. Address of the third home in Bel-Air that Elvis rented. The modern ranch-style home was rented from late 1965 to mid-1967. Elvis moved to 10550 Rocca Place from 1059 Bellagio Road.

$75,000. Yearly salary that Elvis was paying his father Vernon Presley at the time of Elvis's death.

$145,000. Amount of money that Steve Grayson (Elvis) owed the I.R.S. in back taxes in the 1968 movie *Speedway*.

$1,055,173.69. Amount of money Elvis had in his checking account at the National Bank of Commerce in Memphis at the time of his death.

$1,434,536.51. Amount filed in a claim by the National Bank of Commerce against the Presley estate. The claim was filed on February 18, 1978, and the amount was for the balance owed on three notes signed by Elvis.

$150,000,000. Reportedly, the amount grossed at the box office for Elvis's thirty-one movies and two documentaries.

1,000,000,000. Number of estimated TV viewers of the "Aloha from Hawaii" TV special—one of every four people on earth. (See: Elvis: Aloha from Hawaii)

O. Elvis's blood type.

Oakie Boogie. Unreleased Sun recording by Elvis.

Obey. Word intentionally left out of Elvis and Priscilla's wedding ceremony.

O'Brien, Jim. One of Col. Tom Parker's assistants.

O'Brien, Joan. Female lead (as Diane Warren) in the 1963 movie *It Happened at the World's Fair*.

Ocean. Vocal quintet from London, Ontario, Canada, who recorded mostly songs by Canadian composers. In 1971 Ocean had a million-seller with "Put Your Hand in the Hand (Of the Man from Galilee)," which Elvis recorded later in the year.

O Come, All Ye Faithful. RCA 74-0572. Released in November 1971 as a 45 rpm single. "Merry Christmas, Baby" was on the flip side. "O Come, All Ye Faithful" was written in France in the mid-1700s under the title "Adeste Fidelis." The composers are unknown. It was first published in England in John F. Wade's volume *Cantus Diversi* (1751). In 1841 Frederick Oakley (1802–80) translated the Latin words into English.

"O Come, All Ye Faithful" appeared in the Long Playing albums "Elvis Sings the Wonderful World of Christmas" (RCA LSP-4579) and "Elvis Sings the Wonderful World of Christmas" (RCA ANLI-1936).

Odd. One-word reply by Beatle Paul McCartney when asked by reporters of his impression of Elvis. (The Fab Four had just finished visiting Elvis on August 27, 1965.)

Oddfellows (Independent Order of). Friendly society, founded in 1810, with lodges throughout the world. Elvis belonged to an Oddfellows group while attending L. C. Humes High School.

Official Elvis Presley Fan Club of Great Britain, Worldwide. The world's oldest established Elvis fan club. It was founded in 1956 by Jeannie Seward. The club's address is; Box 4, Leicester, England.

Oh Baby Babe. Song credited to Johnny Burnette, Dorsey Burnette, Paul Burlison, and Al Mortimer as composers, recorded May 7, 1956, by the Johnny Burnette Trio on Coral Records (Coral 61675). The song's tune is an exact copy (even some of the original lyrics are repeated) of the Elvis-recorded song "Baby Let's Play House," composed by Arthur Gunter.

Oh Elvis. An Elvis novelty record by Reed Harper and the 3 Notes on the Pyramid label (Pyramid 4012).

Oh Happy Day. Song popularized by the Edwin Hawkins Singers in 1969 on Pavillion Records. Dorothy Morrison sang lead in that recording. Elvis sang "Oh Happy Day" at some of his Las Vegas concerts. It appeared in the bootleg LP "From Hollywood to Vegas."

Oh, How I Miss You Tonight. Answer record by Jeanne Black on Capitol Records (Capitol 4492), released in 1960 in response to Elvis's song "Are You Lonesome Tonight."

Oh, It Was Elvis. An Elvis novelty record by Carmella Rosella on the Nancy label (Nancy 1004) in 1961.

Oh Yes He's Gone. A 1977 Elvis tribute record by Tom Holbrook on Hillside Records (Hillside 08).

Okay, I Won't. Last words spoken by Elvis before he died, on August 16, 1977. They were spoken in response to Ginger Alden's statement (as Elvis was going into the bathroom with a book): "Don't fall asleep."

Okinawa. Pacific island on which Walter Gulick (Elvis) was stationed while working in the motor pool with the Army in the 1962 movie *Kid Galahad.*

Old Gold. A 45 rpm Extended Play bootleg album released on the

Pelvis label (Pelvis PR EP-2001). Songs included: Side 1: "The Truth About Me" (interview), "The Lady Loves Me." Side 2: "My Baby's Gone," "Jailhouse Rock."

Old MacDonald. Children's song that Elvis sang in the 1967 movie *Double Trouble.* Randy Starr arranged the song for Elvis. "Old MacDonald" appeared in the following Long Playing albums: "Double Trouble" (RCA LPM/LPS-3787); "Elvis Sings Hits from His Movies, Volume 1" (RCA Camden CAS-2567); "Elvis Sings Hits from His Movies, Volume 1" (Pickwick CAS-2567); "Elvis Sings for Children (And Grownups Too)" (RCA CLP1-2901).

Old Rugged Cross, The. Gospel hymn written by the Rev. George Bernard (1873–1958) in 1913. "The Old Rugged Cross" was one of the songs that Elvis sang in the Million Dollar Session (December 4, 1956). (See: Million Dollar Session)

Old Saltillo Road. East Tupelo, Mississippi, road on which the Presleys' two-room, wood-frame house was located.

Old Shep. Country song written by Red Foley and Willis Arthur in 1933. Red Foley wrote the song about his dog, a German shepherd named Hoover, who had been poisoned. The song was originally recorded by Red Foley in 1940. Elvis sang "Old Shep" at the 1945 Mississippi-Alabama Fair and Dairy Show— his first public appearance. He also sang it at the Humes High talent show during his senior year. Elvis recorded "Old Shep" in 1956 and played piano on the cut. A completely different take appeared in some copies of the European LP "Rock and Roll No. 2" (HMVV-1105). It appeared in the Extended Play album "Elvis, Volume 2" (RCA EPA-993) and the following Long Playing albums: "Elvis" (RCA LPM-1382); "Elvis" (RCA LSP-1382 [e]); "Separate Ways" (RCA Camden CAS-2611); "Separate Ways" (Pickwick CAS-2611); "Double Dynamite" (Pickwick DL2-5001); "Elvis Sings for Children (And Grownups Too)" (RCA CPL1-2901).

Old Shep. RCA CR-15. Special disc jockey 45 rpm single. The one-sided record was sent to radio stations to promote the album "Elvis."

Old Soldiers Never Die. Classic farewell address given by General Douglas MacArthur before the House of Representatives on April 19, 1952. Elvis was so impressed by the speech that he memorized it while in high school. By coincidence, "Old Soldiers Never Die" is the song on the flip side of Red Foley's second release of "Peace in the Valley."

O Little Town of Bethlehem. Popular Christmas carol written by Phillips Brooks and Lewis H. Redner in 1868.

Phillips Brooks, pastor of the Holy Trinity Church in Phila-delphia, visited Jerusalem and Bethlehem in December 1865. Three years later, the impressions of Bethlehem remained clear in Brooks's mind. In early December 1868, he wrote a five-stanza poem (modern hymnals omit the third stanza) about

Bethlehem. Brooks asked his church organist and Sunday-school superintendent, Lewis Redner, to write music to the poem. Redner wrote the music on the night of December 26–27, 1868. That Sunday morning (the 27th), "O Little Town of Bethlehem" was sung for the first time, by a chorus comprised of six Sunday-school teachers and thirty-six children. Originally, Phillips Brooks called his Christmas carol "St. Louis"—a different spelling of Lewis Redner's first name.

Elvis recorded "Oh Little Town of Bethlehem" in 1957. It appeared in the Extended Play album "Christmas with Elvis" (RCA EPA-4340) and the following Long Playing albums: "Elvis' Christmas Album" (RCA LOC-1035); "Elvis' Christmas Album" (RCA LPM-1951); "Elvis' Christmas Album" (RCA LPM-1951 [e]); "Elvis' Christmas Album" (RCA Camden CAL-2428); "Elvis' Christmas Album" (Pickwick CAS-2428).

Olson, Ann-Margret. Beautiful and talented singer, dancer, and actress, born March 28, 1942, in Sweden. She was discovered by George Burns while performing with a combo named the Suttletones at the Dunes Hotel in Las Vegas. Ann-Margret made her national TV debut on "The Jack Benny Show." She made her movie debut in *Pocketful of Miracles* (1961) and her record debut on RCA Victor with "Lost Love"/"I Ain't Got Nobody" (1961). Elvis and Ann-Margret had a very close relationship for a while. Ever since filming *Viva Las Vegas* together (Ann-Margret played Rusty Martin in the 1964 film), Elvis sent a large flower arrangement in the shape of a guitar whenever she opened an engagement. She appeared in the 1963 movie "Bye Bye Birdie." In 1962 Ann-Margret recorded "Heartbreak Hotel" on the flip side of "Moon River" (RCA Victor). In *Viva Las Vegas* she sang "The Lady Loves Me" and "C'mon Everybody" in duet with Elvis. She also sang "My Rival" and "Appreciation" in the film.

In 1972 Ann-Margret was nominated for an Oscar for *Carnal Knowledge*. In September 1972 she fell twenty-two feet off the stage at the Sahara Tahoe Hotel, breaking her jaw and fracturing her left arm, along with a brain concussion. After her recovery she underwent plastic surgery that made her as beautiful as ever.

Ann-Margret and her husband, Roger Smith, attended Elvis's funeral. Early in her career Ann-Margret had been referred to as the female Elvis, but that waned when she failed to pursue a career as a rock 'n' roll singer.

On a Snowy Christmas Night. Christmas song, written by Stanley A. Gelber, which Elvis recorded in 1971. "On a Snowy Christmas Night" appeared in the Long Playing albums "Elvis Sings the Wonderful World of Christmas" (RCA LSP-4579) and "Elvis Sings the Wonderful World of Christmas" (RCA ANL1-1936).

Onassis, Jacqueline Bouvier Kennedy. Former first lady (January

20, 1961–November 22, 1963) who paid her last respects to Elvis when she visited Graceland on August 17, 1977. Mrs. Onassis's daughter, Caroline Kennedy, accompanied her.

Jackie Onassis is the most photographed woman in history. Elvis was the most photographed man.

On Campus/Mambo Suzie. A novelty record by Dickie Goodman on the Cotique label (Cotique 158). A segment of Elvis's version of "In the Ghetto" appeared on the record.

Once Is Enough. Song that Elvis sang in the 1964 movie *Kissin' Cousins*. "Once Is Enough" was written by Sid Tepper and Roy C. Bennett and appeared in the Long Playing album "Kissin' Cousins" (RCA LPM/LSP-2894).

O'Neal, Doris. One of the secretaries employed at Graceland.

One Boy, Two Little Girls. Song that Elvis sang in the 1964 movie *Kissin' Cousins*. "One Boy, Two Little Girls" was written by Bill Giant, Bernie Baum, and Florence Kaye and appeared in the Long Playing album "Kissin' Cousins" (RCA LPM/LSP-2894).

One Broken Heart for Sale. RCA 47-8134. Released in January 1963 as a 45 rpm single. It reached #11 on *Billboard*'s Hot 100 chart and #21 on the Rhythm and Blues chart. "One Broken Heart for Sale" sold over a million copies. "They Remind Me Too Much of You" was on the flip side. "Elvis sang "One Broken Heart for Sale" in the 1963 movie *It Happened at the World's Fair*. The film version had an extra verse:

"Hey cupid, where are you, my heart is growing sadder.
That girl rejected me, just when I thought I had her."

"One Broken Heart for Sale" was written by Otis Blackwell and Winfield Scott and appeared in the following Long Playing albums: "It Happened at the World's Fair" (RCA LPM/LSP-2697); "Elvis: Worldwide 50 Gold Award Hits, Volume 1" (RCA LPM-6401); "Mahalo from Elvis" (Pickwick ACL-7064).

One Broken Heart for Sale. RCA 447-0640. Gold Standard Series re-issue of RCA 47-8134.

One Flew Over the Cuckoo's Nest. A 1975 Oscar-winning movie based on Ken Kesey's novel about patients in a mental hospital. Produced by Michael Douglas,* *One Flew Over the Cuckoo's Nest* is one of only two movies to win the top five Academy Awards: Best Picture; Best Actor (Jack Nicholson); Best Actress (Louise Fletcher); Best Director (Milos Forman); Best Screenplay (Laurence Haubman and Bo Goldman). The other movie to accomplish the feat was *It Happened One Night* (1934).

On February 11, 1979, *One Flew Over the Cuckoo's Nest*

---

*Son of actor Kirk Douglas (real name: Issor Danielovitch Demsky).

aired on NBC-TV opposite the ABC-TV telecast of *Elvis*. CBS-TV aired the movie *Gone with the Wind*. (See: Elvis; Gone With the Wind)

O'Neill, Jimmy. Host of the ABC-TV show "Shindig" in the mid-1960s. Jimmy O'Neill was a friend of Elvis and double-dated with him a few times. Elvis was dating Jackie DeShannon at the time. O'Neill's first wife was songwriter Sharon Sheeley.* (See: Shindig; DeShannon, Jackie)

One More Day. Song that Hunk Houghton (Mickey Shaughnessy) sang in the 1957 movie *Jailhouse Rock*. Hunk was a cellmate of Vince Everett (Elvis). "One More Day" has never been released by RCA.

One More Jelly Doughnut. Uncomplimentary novelty record about Elvis's eating habits. It was released in 1976 by Rick Dees and His Cast of Idiots on RSO Records (RSO 870). Upon Elvis's sudden death, the record was quickly taken off the market.

One Night. RCA 47-7410. Released in October 1958 as a 45 rpm single. "One Night" reached #4 on *Billboard*'s Hot 100 chart, #24 on the Country chart, and #10 on the Rhythm and Blues chart. It reached #1 in the United Kingdom (for five weeks, January 24–February 22, 1958). "I Got Stung" was on the flip side. "One Night" sold over a million copies. It was written by Dave Bartholomew and Pearl King and originally recorded as "One Night of Sin" by Smiley Lewis in 1956. Elvis's version used slightly different words. Elvis sang "One Night" in the 1968 TV special "Elvis" and the 1970 documentary *Elvis—That's the Way It Is*. It appeared in the Extended Play album "A Touch of Gold, Volume 2" (RCA EPA-5101) and the following Long Playing albums: "50,000,000 Elvis Fans Can't Be Wrong—Elvis' Gold Records, Volume 2" (RCA LPM-2075); "50,000,000 Elvis Fans Can't Be Wrong—Elvis' Gold Records, Volume 2" (RCA LSP-2075 [e]); "Elvis—TV Special" (RCA LPM-4088); "Elvis: The Other Sides—Worldwide 50 Gold Award Hits, Volume 2" (RCA LPM-6402).

One Night. RCA 447-0624. Gold Standard Series re-issue of RCA 47-7410.

One-Sided Love Affair. RCA 20/47-6641. Released in September 1956 as a 78 rpm single and a 45 rpm single. "Money Honey" was on the flip side. "One-Sided Love Affair" was a country song written by Bill Campbell. Elvis recorded the song in 1956 and it appeared in the following Extended Play albums: "Elvis Presley" (RCA EPB-1254); "Elvis Presley" (RCA SPD-22); "Elvis Presley" (RCA-SPD-23); and the Long Playing albums "Elvis Presley" (RCA LPM-1254) and "Elvis Presley" (RCA LSP-1254 [e]).

---

*Sharon Sheeley was the composer of Ricky Nelson's 1958 hit, "Poor Little Fool" (Imperial 5528). She was the fiancée of singer Eddie Cochran when he was killed in a London taxicab accident on April 17, 1960. Singer Gene Vincent was injured in that accident.

One-Sided Love Affair. RCA 447-0614. Gold Standard Series re-issue of RCA 20/47-6641.

One-Sided Love Affair. RCA 47-6466. Special 45 rpm disc jockey preview. "Tutti Frutti" was on the flip side.

One Track Heart. Song that Elvis sang in the 1964 movie *Roustabout.* "One Track Heart" was written by Bill Giant, Bernie Baum, and Florence Kaye and appeared in the Long Playing album "Roustabout" (RCA LPM/LSP-2999).

One Track Heart. RCA SP-45-139. Special 45 rpm promotional release. "Roustabout" was on the flip side.

Only Believe. RCA 47-9985. Released in May 1971 as a 45 rpm single. It reached #53 on *Billboard*'s Hot 100 chart. "Life" was on the flip side. Written by Paul Rader, "Only Believe" appeared in the Long Playing album "Love Letters from Elvis" (RCA LSP-4530).

Only Believe. RCA 447-0682. Gold Standard Series re-issue of RCA 47-9985.

Only Girl in Town, The. Title originally considered for the 1964 movie *Viva Las Vegas.*

Only the Lonely. Song written and originally recorded by Roy Orbison. He cowrote the song with Joe Melson. "Only the Lonely" (Monument 421) (1960) reached #2 on *Billboard*'s Hot 100 chart and became Orbison's first million-seller.

On the way to Nashville to record "Only the Lonely," Orbison and Melson stopped in Memphis to see if Elvis wanted to record it. Elvis was asleep when they arrived, so he lost the opportunity to have perhaps another million-seller. When Orbison and Melson arrived in Nashville, they offered "Only the Lonely" to the Everly Brothers, who declined it. So, by default, Roy Orbison had his first giant hit.

Only the Strong Survive. Song written by Jerry Butler, Kenny Gamble, and Leon Huff and originally recorded by Butler in 1969. Butler's recording, on Mercury Records, reached #4 on *Billboard*'s Hot 100 chart and sold over a million copies. Elvis recorded "Only the Strong Survive" in 1969 and it appeared in the Long Playing album "From Elvis in Memphis" (RCA LSP-4155).

On Stage—February, 1970. RCA LSP-4362. A 33⅓ rpm Long Playing album released in June 1970. It reached #13 on *Billboard*'s Hot LP chart. "On Stage—February, 1970" was recorded at the Las Vegas International Hotel and received a Gold Record for sales exceeding $1 million. This album didn't have Elvis's name on the front or back of the album jacket—the second album so distinguished ("For LP Fans Only" was the first). Songs included—Side 1: "See See Rider," "Release Me (And Let Me Love Again)," "Sweet Caroline," "Runaway," "The Wonder of You." Side 2: "Polk Salad Annie," "Yesterday," "Proud Mary," "Walk a Mile in My Shoes," "Let It Be Me."

On Stage in the U.S.A. A 33⅓ rpm bootleg album released on the Wizardo label (WRMB 304).

On Top of Old Smokey. American southern highlands folk song. The composer is unknown.* In 1951 the Weavers (with an arrangement by Pete Seeger) had a million-seller on Decca Records (Decca 27515) with "On Top of Old Smokey." Gene Autry sang it in the 1951 movie *Valley of Fire.*

Elvis sang about ten seconds of "On Top of Old Smokey" in the 1962 movie *Follow That Dream.*

On Wisconsin. University of Wisconsin football fight song written in 1909 by Carl Beck and W.T. Purdy. "On Wisconsin"† is also the official state song of Wisconsin. "On Wisconsin" was one of several college fight songs sung by the collegiate quartet in the 1969 movie *The Trouble with Girls (And How To Get Into It).*

Operation Elvis. The Army's program for handling Elvis while he was in the Armed Forces (March 24, 1958–March 5, 1960).

Operation Elvis. A 1960 book, by Alan Levy, about Elvis's military career.

Orange Bowl International Power Boat Regatta. Boat race won by Scott Heywood (Elvis) in the 1967 movie *Clambake.* Actual race footage was incorporated into the film.

Orbison, Roy K. Popular early 1960s ballad singer and contemporary of Elvis. Roy Orbison began his recording career while a student at North Texas State University. In 1956 Orbison and his band the Teen Kings‡ (originally named the Wink Westerners), recorded "Ooby Dooby" at their own expense at Norman Petty's studio in Clovis, New Mexico. The release, on JEW-EL Records (JEW-EL 101),§ was not successful; however, upon the insistence of Johnny Cash, Orbison sent Sam Phillips (of Sun Records) a copy of "Ooby Dooby." Phillips liked the record and had Orbison re-record a slightly different version of it on his own Sun label (Sun 242). The flip side of "Ooby Dooby" on the JEW-EL label was "Trying to Get to You,‖ which Elvis recorded in 1955.

In 1958 the Everly Brothers recorded an Orbison composition titled "Claudette," named after Orbison's wife. (Claudette was killed in a motorcycle accident in 1965.)

---

*Musicologists John A. Lomax and Alan Lomax adapted and arranged a version titled "Old Smoky."

†Actor Dick Powell once recorded "On Wisconsin"/"The Eyes of Texas" (Decca 2013), both of which were sung in *The Trouble with Girls (And How To Get Into It).*

‡The members of the Teen Kings were: Billy Ellis; Jack Kennelly; James Morrow; Johnny "Peanuts" Wilson.

§Today the record is a collector's item and a single copy may sell for $200.

‖When Imperial Records bought the master of "Ooby Dooby" and "Trying to Get to You" from JEW-EL, they did an unexplained thing with the "Trying to Get to You" side of the record. Imperial released the song by the Teen Kings on the flip side of "So Long, Good Luck And Goodbye" by Weldon Rogers (Imperial 5457) and credited both sides of the record to Weldon Rogers.

Like Elvis, Roy Orbison went to RCA after Sun, but he stayed with RCA for only one year (1958). He came into national prominence in 1960 with his first million-seller, "Only the Lonely," on Monument Records. Roy Orbison was Elvis's chief rival from 1960 to '64, having several hits. Singer Bobby Goldsboro was once a member of his back-up group, the Candymen.*

Between May and June 1963, Roy Orbison toured England with an up-and-coming British group called the Beatles—making Orbison the only artist to have toured with both Elvis Presley and the Beatles.

Elvis greatly admired Roy Orbison's singing. Elvis's hairstyle was combed much like Orbison's—even to the point of dying his hair black.

Roy Orbison composed and recorded several songs for the movie *The Living Legend*. (See: Boone, Pat; Living Legend, The; Only the Lonely)

Order of Little Sisters of Mary. Convent to which Sister Michelle (Mary Tyler Moore) belonged in the 1969 movie *Change of Habit*.

Orioles, The. Popular rhythm and blues group of the late 1940s and early 50s'. All of the members were from Baltimore, Maryland. The Orioles, with lead singer Sonny Til (real name: Earlington Tilghman), began in the mid-1940s under the name the Vibranaires. In early 1948 the Vibranaires changed their name to the Orioles (after the Maryland state bird) and appeared on "Arthur Godfrey's Talent Scouts." Singing "Barbara Lee," they lost in the competition.† However, Godfrey liked the Orioles and added them to his daytime program. There they received much national exposure.

In 1958 the Orioles recorded "Crying in the Chapel"‡ (Jubilee 5122), which quickly became a million-seller for them. Elvis recorded "Crying in the Chapel" in 1960.

Orion. Pseudonym for singer Jimmy Ellis. (See: Ellis, Jimmy)

Orion. Sun 1012. A 33⅓ rpm Long Playing album released in 1979. The singer is a mysterious, masked character known only as "Orion Eckley Darnell." From the cryptic album notes, one is led to believe that the singer is actually Elvis. The "mysterious" artist is in actuality *Elvis sound-a-like* Jimmy Ellis. A 45 rpm single release (Sun 1142), composed of two songs from the album ("Ebony Eyes" and "Honey"), reached #89 on *Billboard*'s Country chart in July 1979. Songs in the album included—Side 1: "Honey," "Lover Please," "Got You on My Mind," "Mona Lisa," "Before the Next Teardrop Falls." Side 2:

---

*Several members of the Candymen are today performing as the Atlanta Rhythm Section; others are with B.J. Thomas's band Beverteeth.
†They lost to blind pianist George Shearing.
‡Years later Sonny Til and the Orioles recorded "Back in the Chapel Again (Parker 213).

"Ebony Eyes," "Washing Machine," "Baby, I Still Love You," "You Can Have Her," "Lonesome Angel."

O Sole Mio. Italian song, composed in 1901 by G. Capurro and Eduardo DiCapua, on which "It's Now or Never" is based. "O Sole Mio" sung by Sherill Nielson can be found on the Long Playing album "Elvis in Concert" (RCA APL2-2587). (See: It's Now or Never)

Otis, Clyde. First black A & R executive for a major record company (Mercury) in the 1950s. Clyde Otis cowrote (with Willie Dixon) "Doncha' Think It's Time," which Elvis recorded in 1958. He cowrote (with Ivory Joe Hunter) "Ain't That Loving You, Baby," which Elvis recorded in 1958 (released as a single in 1964). Timi Yuro's original version of "Hurt" (Liberty 55343) (1961) was produced by Clyde Otis. "Hurt" was recorded by Elvis in February 1976.

Otis, Johnny. West Coast white blues singer and musician who appeared on various labels since 1950. His biggest hit record, "Willie and the Hand Jive," came in 1958 (Capitol 3966).

In 1953, when one of Otis's discoveries, Willie Mae Thornton, recorded "Hound Dog" on Peacock records (Peacock 1612), the song was credited to Johnny Otis, who claimed to have co-written the song. The song was rightfully credited to Jerry Leiber and Mike Stoller on the Elvis version of the song. Leiber and Stoller had to go to court in order to receive their writers' royalties for the Thornton version of "Hound Dog." Thorton had toured with Otis and it was Otis who had produced her version of "Hound Dog." It was also Otis and his orchestra who backed Johnny Ace's "Pledging My Love" (Otis also produced the record).

Our Memories of Elvis. RCA AQL1-3279. A 33⅓ rpm Long Playing album released in February 1979. "Our Memories of Elvis" reached #28 on *Billboard*'s Hot Country LP chart. All songs on the album are without overdubbing by RCA—Elvis is heard just as he was in the recording studio. Songs included— Side 1: "Are You Sincere," "It's Midnight," "My Boy," "Girl of Mine," "Take Good Care of Her," "I'll Never Fall in Love Again." Side 2: "Your Love's Been a Long Time Coming," "Spanish Eyes," "Never Again," "She Thinks I Still Care," "Solitaire."

Our Memories of Elvis, Volume 2. RCA AQL1-3448. A 33⅓ rpm Long Playing album released in August 1979. It reached #157 on *Billboard*'s Hot LP chart and #12 on the Hot Country LP chart. Songs included—Side 1: "I Got a Feelin' in My Body," "Green, Green Grass of Home," "For the Heart," "She Wears My Ring," "I Can Help," "Way Down." Side 2: "There's a Honky Tonk Angel," "Find Out What's Happening," "Thinking About You," "Don't Think Twice, It's All Right."

Overton Park Shell. Memphis outdoor auditorium where, on July 30, 1954, Elvis made his first appearance before a concert audience. Bob Neal promoted the concert. Elvis sang "That's All Right (Mama)" and "Blue Moon of Kentucky." Headlining the show were Slim Whitman, Billy Walker, and the Louvin Brothers (Ira and Charlie).

On August 10, 1954, Elvis made an unbilled appearance at the Overton Park Shell. Slim Whitman and Carl Smith were the headliners for the two shows—one in the afternoon and one in the evening. In the afternoon, Elvis sang "Old Shep" and "That's When Your Heartaches Begin" and received very little response. His reception in the evening was overwhelming—so much so that Webb Pierce declined to perform. "Good Rockin' Tonight" and "That's All Right (Mama)" were sung by Elvis that evening.

In the summer of 1955, Elvis was the featured artist at the Overton Park Shell. At this concert, Johnny Cash and the Tennessee Two made their first concert appearance, singing "Cry, Cry, Cry" and "Hey, Porter."

P

Pablo Cruise. San Francisco rock group who broke Elvis's attendance record at the Sahara-Tahoe Hotel in Las Vegas in 1979.

Pacer Burton. Elvis's role in the 1960 movie *Flaming Star*. Marlon Brando was originally considered for the part.

Pacific War Memorial Commission. (See: Arizona, U.S.S.; Bloch Arena)

Padre. Song written by French composer Jacques Larue and Alain Romans in 1957. English lyrics to "Padre" were written by Paul Francis Webster in 1958. Lola Dee first recorded "Padre" in the U.S., but Toni Arden had a million-seller with it later in 1958 (Decca 30628)

Elvis recorded "Padre" in 1971 and it appeared in the Long Playing albums "Elvis" (RCA APL1-0283) and "He Walks Beside Me" (RCA AFL-2772).

Page, Patti. One of Elvis's two favorite female vocalists (the other was Kay Starr), as stated by him in Red Robinson's Vancouver, British Columbia, interview on August 31, 1957. Patti Page (real name: Clara Ann Fowler*) received her stage name from her radio sponsor, the Page Milk Company. Her biggest

---

*As a young girl Clara Ann Fowler baby-sat for Mark Dinning. In 1960 Mark Dinning had a #1 hit and million-seller with "Teen Angel" (MGM 1284). "Teen Angel" was banned from British radio.

hit, "The Tennessee Waltz" (Mercury 5534), came in 1950. "The Tennessee Waltz" is the biggest-selling song of all time by a female singer (over 10 million copies sold). Frank Sinatra was offered the song but turned it down.

Paget, Debra. Female lead (as Cathy) in the 1956 movie *Love Me Tender*. It was Debra Paget who gave Elvis his first screen kiss.

Painters Union Local 49. Memphis AFL-CIO union that picketed Graceland in May of 1957 because a non-union painting contractor, C. W. Nichols, had been hired to paint the mansion.

Pajamas. Elvis owned twenty pairs of pajamas at the time of his death. When he died, he was wearing pajamas with a blue top and yellow bottoms.

Palm Springs. California location where Elvis and Priscilla spent their honeymoon in May 1967.

Col. Tom Parker's California home is in Palm Springs.

Panhandle Kid. Cowboy whom Lonnie Beale (Elvis) became in a dream sequence in the 1965 movie *Tickle Me*.

Paradise Cove. Nightclub in the 1962 movie *Girls! Girls! Girls!*.

PARADISE—HAWAIIAN STYLE. Paramount, 1966. Premiered New York City June 15, 1966 (91 min). Elvis's twenty-first movie. Producer, Hal B. Wallis. Associate Producer, Paul Nathan. Director, Michael Moore. Cast: Rick Richards/Elvis Presley, Judy Hudson/Suzanna Leigh, Danny Kohana/James Shigeta, Jan Kohana/Donna Butterworth, Lani/Marianna Hill, Pua/Irene Tsu, Lehua/Linda Wong, Joanna/Julie Parrish, Betty Kohana/Jan Shepard, Donald Belden/John Doucette, Moki/Philip Ahn, Mr. Cubberson/Grady Sutton, Andy Lowell/Don Collier, Mrs. Barrington/Doris Packer, Mrs. Belden/Mary Treen, Peggy Holden/Gigi Verone. Screenplay, Allan Weiss and Anthony Lawrence. Photography, W. Wallace Kelley. Music, Joseph J. Lilley. Choreography, Jack Regas. Art Direction, Hal Pereira and Walter Tyler. Set Decoration, Sam Comer and Ray Moyer. Special Effects, Romaine Birkmeyer. Costumes, Edith Head. Assistant Director, James Rosenberger. Editor, Warren Low. Songs sung by Elvis: "Paradise Hawaiian Style," "Scratch My Back (Then I'll Scratch Yours)" (duet with Susan Leigh), "Stop Where You Are," "This Is My Heaven," "House of Sand," "Queenie Wahine's Papaya" (sung duet with Donna Butterworth), "Datin'" (in duet with Donna Butterworth), "Drums of the Islands," "A Dog's Life," Donna Butterworth sang "Bill Bailey, Won't You Please Come Home." "Sand Castles" was deleted from the film.

Paradise—Hawaiian Style. Title song of the 1966 movie *Paradise —Hawaiian Style*. The film version has added instrumentation. "Paradise—Hawaiian Style" was used at the beginning of Elvis's Hawaii TV special but it does not appear on the soundtrack album "Elvis: Aloha from Hawaii Via Satellite."

"Paradise—Hawaiian Style" was written by Bill Giant, Bernie Baum, and Florence Kaye and appeared in the Long Playing album "Paradise—Hawaiian Style" (RCA LPM/LSP-3643).

Paradise—Hawaiian Style. RCA LPM/LSP-3643. Released in June 1966 as a 33⅓ rpm Long Playing album. It reached #15 on *Billboard*'s Hot LP chart and achieved sales of over $1 million, qualifying it for a Gold Record. The album featured songs from the 1966 movie *Paradise—Hawaiian Style* plus one bonus song. Songs included—Side 1: "Paradise—Hawaiian Style," "Queenie Wahine's Papaya," "Scratch My Back (Then I'll Scratch Yours)," "Drums of the Islands," "Datin'." Side 2: "A Dog's Life," "A House of Sand," "Stop Where You Are," "This Is My Heaven," "Sand Castles" (bonus).

Paralyzed. Song written by Otis Blackwell and recorded by Elvis in 1956. "Paralyzed"* was released in the United Kingdom as a single, reaching #8 on the charts. It appeared in the Extended Play album "Elvis, Volume 1" (RCA EPA-992) and the following Long Playing albums: "Elvis" (RCA LPM-1382); "Elvis" (RCA LSP-1382 [e]); "Elvis: The Other Sides—Worldwide Gold Award Hits, Volume 2" (RCA LPM-6402).

Paramount Theater. New York City movie theater where, on November 16, 1956, *Love Me Tender* premiered.

The Paramount was the site of Frank Sinatra's Columbus Day appearance in 1944, in which the theater grossed $29,000 —at that time a record.

In 1957 the Paramount grossed $32,000 in one day, when Alan Freed hosted a rock 'n' roll show.

Orville "Happy" Jones, Charlie Fuqua,† and Ivory "Deek" Watson (better known as the Ink Spots) were all once employed by New York City's Paramount Theater.

Across the street from the Paramount Theater on November 16, 1956, was a huge billboard of Phil Silvers as Sgt. Bilko advertising Camel cigarettes.

Parchman Penitentiary. Mississippi state prison where Vernon Presley served nine months (June 1, 1938–February 6, 1939) of a three-year prison term for forgery. Presley was convicted of forging a check of a local farmer, Orville Bean. He sold Bean a calf for $4 and altered the check to read $40. Friends of the Presleys—Forrest L. Bobo and his wife Flora—took Gladys Presley and Elvis to Parchman to visit Vernon on one occasion.

In the late 1920s (1928–29), blues singer Eddie House spent time at Parchman Penitentiary as did blues singer Booker "Bukka" Washington. Mose Allison recorded the song "Parch-

---

*"Paralyzed" inspired Terry Noland and Norman Petty to write "Hypnotised," which the Drifters (with Johnny Moore singing lead) recorded in 1957 (Atlantic 1141).
†Charlie Fuqua is the uncle of Harvey Fuqua, lead singer of Harvey and the Moonglows.

man Farm" (Prestige 130), as did the Kingston Trio as "Parchman Farm Blues" (Decca 31806), in 1965.

Parker, Ed. Elvis's bodyguard and personal karate instructor. Ed Parker specialized in Kenpo karate, which consists of chopping and jabbing blows with the hands. Parker appeared in a bit role in the 1978 Peter Sellers comedy *The Revenge of the Pink Panther*. Parker first began instructing Elvis in karate in Los Angeles in 1972. Hawaiian singer Don Ho is a cousin of Ed Parker. Ed Parker, along with author Edgar Rice Burroughs and future boxer eleven-year-old Carl "Bobo" Olson, witnessed the Japanese bombing of Pearl Harbor on December 7, 1941.

Parker, Little Junior. R & B singer, born Herman Parker, Jr. He was nicknamed "Junior" by blues singer Sonny Boy Williamson. Junior Parker recorded for various small labels such as Duke, Peacock, and Sun. It was on Sun that Little Junior Parker and the Blue Flames* first recorded "Mystery Train" (Sun 192), which Parker cowrote with Sam Phillips. The record's label listed the performers as Little Junior's Blue Flames. Elvis also recorded "Mystery Train" for the Sun label but sang it at a faster pace. Little Junior Parker had several hit records during the 1960s.

Parker, Marie. Wife of Col. Tom Parker, who maintained a quiet image during her husband's busy career as Elvis's manager. Marie Parker lent her name for Lisa Marie Presley.

Parker, Pamela. One of Elvis's secretaries, whose job was answering fan mail. Pamela Parker had previously worked for evangelist Oral Roberts.

Parker, Patricia. Hollywood waitress who, on August 21, 1970, brought a paternity suit against Elvis in Los Angeles, claiming that her child, Jason, born on October 19, 1970, was fathered by Elvis. She requested $1,000 a month child support. After nine months of litigation the suit was dropped.

Parker, Thomas Andrew. Promoter and agent, born June 26, 1909, in West Virginia. He began in carnivals and fairs, pushing anything that he thought he could sell. He founded the Great Parker Pony Circus and later Colonel Tom Parker and His Dancing Turkeys, in which Parker placed live turkeys on a hot plate covered with sawdust, accompanied by a record player as the turkeys "danced." In the 1950s Thomas Parker became a manager of such stars as Gene Austin, Hank Snow, Eddy Arnold, and Tommy Sands. On March 15, 1956, he officially became the manager of Elvis Presley for a twenty-five-percent fee. Parker, an honorary colonel since 1953, was Elvis's manager until Elvis's death, never taking on another client. Col. Parker is a shrewd, hard-working, and demanding individual who worked for the financial betterment of both Elvis and himself.

---

*British rocker Georgie Fame in the 1960s employed a band called the Blue Flames.

For this reason, Col. Parker has become controversial. Everyone, including Presley and Parker, was aware of the fact that Elvis's movies were B grade. A number of times Elvis was offered decent dramatic roles—i.e., *Thunder Road* (1958) and *A Star Is Born* (1976)—only to have Parker ruin the deal by asking for too much money. Many believe that Parker was more interested in quantity (money) than in quality (establishing Elvis as a respectable actor). But few people could argue with Parker's success in guiding Elvis's career. There are very few accounts of Elvis ever disagreeing with Parker's decisions and no account of the two ever having anything but a good working relationship and friendship. Parker has also been criticized for his nonchalant attitude, especially as reflected by his attire at the funerals of both Elvis and Vernon Presley—he wore shorts, a colorful shirt, and a baseball cap.

Party. Song that Elvis sang in the 1957 movie *Loving You*. It was sung several times during the movie and the movie versions different slightly from that on record. A different version (with an added verse) can be found on the bootleg albums "Got a Lot o' Livin' to Do" and "Loving You" (Australian). "Party" was covered by the Collins Kids on August 21, 1957, on Columbia Records (41012). Written by Jessie Mae Robinson, "Party" appeared in the Extended Play album "Loving You, Volume 1" (RCA EPA1-1515) and the Long Playing albums "Loving You" (RCA LPM-1515) and "Loving You" (RCA LSP-1515) [e]).

Passing of a King, The. A 1977 Elvis tribute record by Tony Copeland on the ARCO label (ARCO 104).

Pasternak, Joe. Hungarian-born producer of the Elvis movies *Girl Happy* (1965) and *Spinout* (1968).

Pat Boone Sings ... Guess Who? Pat Boone tribute album to Elvis on Dot Records in the 1960s (Dot DLP 25501).

Patch It Up. RCA 47-9916. Released in October 1970 as a 45 rpm single. It reached #11 on *Billboard*'s Hot 100 chart. "You Don't Have to Say You Love Me" was on the flip side. Some sources credit "Patch It Up" with selling over a million copies. Elvis sang "Patch It Up" in the 1970 documentary *Elvis—That's the Way It Is*. The song was written by Eddie Rabbitt and Rory Bourke and appeared in the Long Playing albums "Elvis—That's the Way It Is" (RCA LSP-445) and "Elvis: The Other Sides—Worldwide Gold Award Hits, Volume 2" (RCA LPM-6402).

Patch It Up. RCA 447-0678. Gold Standard Series re-issue of RCA 47-9916.

Patricia Stevens Finishing and Career School. Memphis school, 111 Monroe Ave., that Priscilla Beaulieu attended in the mid-1960s, studying dancing and modeling.

Patty Alice. Name of a black ragdoll that Elvis bought for Linda Thompson in Las Vegas.

Payne, Leon. Blind-born composer (1917–69) who once played in Bob Wills's band the Texas Playboys. In 1949 Leon Payne composed "I Love You Because," which Elvis recorded in July 1954.

Payne, Silas. Black plantation worker, employed by Sam Phillips's father, who taught young Sam many of the blues songs of the day. Payne is reminiscent of another black singer, Tee-Tot, who taught another young southern boy how to play the guitar and sing the blues. The boy's name was Hank Williams.

(There'll Be) Peace in the Valley (For Me). Gospel standard adapted by the Rev. Thomas A. Dorsey in 1939 from the spiritual "We Shall Walk Through the Valley in Peace." Red Foley had a million-seller with "(There'll Be) Peace in the Valley (For Me)" (Decca 14573) in 1951. It was re-issued in 1957.

Elvis sang "(There'll Be) Peace in the Valley (For Me)"* on his third "Ed Sullivan Show" appearance, on January 6, 1957. It appeared in the Extended Play albums "Peace in the Valley" (RCA EPA-4054), and "Peace in the Valley" (RCA EPA-5121) and the following Long Playing albums: "Elvis' Christmas Album" (RCA LOC-1035); "Elvis' Christmas Album" (RCA LSP-1951 [e]); "You'll Never Walk Alone" (RCA Camden CASX-2472); "You'll Never Walk Alone" (Pickwick CAS-2472).

Peace in the Valley. RCA EPA-4054. This was a 45 rpm Extended Play album released in April 1957. It reached #39 on *Billboard*'s Hot 100 chart and #3 on the Extended Play chart. "Peace in the Valley" was Elvis's first religious release. Songs included—Side 1: "(There'll Be) Peace in the Valley (For Me)," "It Is No Secret (What God Can Do)." Side 2: "I Believe," "Take My Hand, Precious Lord."

Peace in the Valley. RCA EPA-5121. This record was a Gold Standard Series re-issue of RCA EPA-4054 (April 1961).

Peacock Suit. Elvis's favorite concert jumpsuit.

Peanut Butter and Mashed Banana Sandwiches. Reportedly one of Elvis's favorite snacks.

Pearl, Minnie. (Sarah Ophelia Colley Cannon) The Queen of Country Comedy. College-graduated country comedienne ("Howw-dee,") who appeared regularly on the "Grand Ole Opry" and on TV's "Hee Haw" series. She wears a hat with a $1.98 price tag on it. Minnie Pearl performed with Elvis in March 1961 at a benefit concert for the U.S.S. *Arizona* Memorial Fund.

Minnie Pearl and Pee Wee King were the two featured performers at the Mississippi-Alabama Fair and Dairy Show in Tupelo in 1945, when Elvis won the second-place prize in

---

*While watching gospel singer Clara Ward sing "Peace in the Valley," teenager Aretha Franklin decided that she wanted to become a singer.

the talent contest (See: Mississippi-Alabama Fair and Dairy Show)

Peary, Hal. Actor who played a doorman in the 1967 movie *Clambake*. Peary had previously played Throckmorton P. Gildersleeve (*The Great Gildersleeve*) on radio and in movies.

Penniman, Richard Wayne. Macon, Georgia, Little Richard was born on Christmas Day 1935. An R & B singer he is known as Little Richard because of his height. After little success for RCA Victor and Duke Records, he recorded a number of hits for the Los Angeles Specialty label. In 1957 Little Richard quit recording to become a minister, only to return to recording with "Crying in the Chapel." Elvis recorded the following songs previously recorded by Little Richard: "Tutti Frutti" (Specialty 561), 1955; "Long Tall Sally" (Specialty 572), 1956; "Rip It Up" (Specialty 579), 1956; "Ready Teddy" (Specialty 579), 1956; "Crying in the Chapel" (Atlantic 2181); "Shake a Hand" (Specialty 670), 1957. Interestingly, Elvis covered both sides of the 45 "Rip It Up"/"Ready Teddy." (See: Thing, The)

Pepper, Gary. Memphis cerebral palsy victim to whom Vernon Presley had been sending $400 a month until Elvis's death.

As president of the Elvis Presley Tankers Fan Club, Gary Pepper regularly placed flowers on Gladys Presley's grave on the anniversary of her death.

Pepper, Sterling. One of a number of men employed as gate guards at Graceland.

Peppermint Twist. Popular 1961 dance craze hit by Joey Dee and the Starliters (Roulette 4401), the house band at New York's Peppermint Lounge in the Knickerbocker Hotel, heard in the 1979 TV movie *Elvis*. "Peppermint Twist" was the song playing on the car radio as Elvis (Kurt Russell) and Priscilla (Season Hubley) were riding together.

Pepsi-Cola. Elvis's favorite drink. Also that of Hugh Hefner. Elvis's grandfather Jessie Presley had been a night watchman for a Pepsi-Cola plant in 1947.

James Dean and Nick Adams made their screen debut in a Pepsi-Cola commercial in 1951.

Bruce Springsteen also claims to be a lover of Pepsi.

Pepsi-Cola was also inspirational in the composing of the Elvis song "All Shook Up." Al Shalimar, an employee of the music-publishing company Hill and Range, was talking to composer Otis Blackwell one day as he was drinking a bottle of Pepsi. As he shook the bottle he said to Blackwell; "Otis, I've got an idea. Why don't you write a song called 'All Shook Up'?" Otis accepted the challenge and wrote the song.

Perfect American Male, The. Book for which Diane St. Clair (Diane McBain) was researching material in the 1966 movie *Spinout*. Her two previous works were *Ten Ways to Trap a Bachelor* and *The Mating Habits of the Single Male*.

Perfect for Parties. RCA SPA-7-37. This was a 45 rpm Extended

Play album available in late 1956. It was never released to the general public; however, you could get it free if you bought a new Victrola phonograph at the nationally advertised sale price of $28.34. Elvis sang "Love Me" and introduced songs by the other artists. Songs included—Side 1: "Love Me" (Elvis), "Anchors Aweigh" (Tony Scott and His Orchestra), "That's a Puente" (Tito Puento and His Orchestra). Side 2: "Rock Me But Don't Roll Me" (Tony Scott and His Orchestra), "Happy Face Baby" (the Three Suns), "Prom to Prom" (Dave Pell Octet).

Perkins, Carl Lee. Disc jockey (WTJS radio in Jackson, Tennessee) turned recording artist. At age thirteen Carl Perkins won a talent show on WTJS when he sang "Home on the Range," winning twenty-five dollars. Perkins, who was born on April 7, 1932, is two days older than country singer Carl Smith. Carl Perkins first recorded for Flip Records, a non-union subsidiary label of Sun Records. His first release was "Movie Magg" (Flip 501). Carl Perkins first met Elvis in Bethel Springs, Tennessee, in 1954. Perkins had his first hit big when he recorded his composition "Blue Suede Shoes" (Sun 234) on December 19, 1955. On March 27, 1956, Carl Perkins was injured in an automobile accident that took the life of his brother Jay, Carl's manager. Disc jockey David Stewart had fallen asleep at the wheel. At the time of the accident, his version of "Blue Suede Shoes" had reached the #4 slot on the charts. The band was en route to New York to appear on national TV on the Ed Sullivan and Perry Como shows.

Elvis recorded Perkin's "Blue Suede Shoes" in 1956 and the Beatles recorded three of his compositions.

Perkins became a part of Johnny Cash's TV show and concerts. He composed the Cash hit "Daddy Sang Bass."

Perkins and Johnny Cash have been close friends ever since their Sun days. There exist several close similarities in their lives. They were both from poor cotton farms on the sides of the Mississippi River (Cash from Arkansas, Perkins from Tennessee). They both began recording at the same time, for the same label, and had their first hits at about the same time. Both have an "X" scar on the forefingers of their left hands from whittling as kids, and both have scars on their right legs from getting tangled in barb-wire fences. Both got involved with drugs, which nearly destroyed their careers.

Chet Atkins once remarked, when Carl Perkins had the #4 record in the country with "Blue Suede Shoes:" "We thought for a while we bought the wrong Sun artist."

The Beatles recorded the following Carl Perkins compositions: "Honey Don't" (flip side of Perkin's "Blue Suede Shoes"); "Everybody's Trying to Be My Baby"; "Matchbox."

Jackson, Mississippi, celebrated Carl Perkins Day on February 4, 1969.

Perkins, Elvis Brooke. Son of actor Tony Perkins and his wife, Berry Berenson. Born in 1976, Elvis Brooke Perkins was named after Elvis Presley.

Perkins, Luther. Member of Johnny Cash's Tennessee Two and the brother of singer Thomas Wayne. Luther Perkins was born on January 8, 1928, seven years to the day prior to Elvis's birth. Perkins died on August 5, 1968. The Bill Black Combo once recorded a tribute record to Perkins titled "Cashin' In (A Tribute to Luther Perkins)" on HI Records (HI 78508).

Perkins, Millie. Female lead (as Betty Lee) in the 1961 movie *Wild in the Country* along with Hope Lange and Tuesday Weld. Millie Perkins won an Oscar for Best Supporting Actress in her debut movie, *Diary of Anne Frank* (1959). She also appeared in the 1968 movie *Wild in the Streets.*

Peters, (Sir) Gerald. Elvis's chauffeur, who had previously served in the same capacity for British Prime Minister Winston Churchill.

Peterson, James B. Civilian barber from Gans, Oklahoma, who gave Elvis his Army haircut at Fort Chaffee, Arkansas, on March 25, 1958. Elvis paid sixty-five cents for the haircut.

Peterson, Ray. Singer born in Denton, Texas, in 1939. Ray Peterson had hits with "Tell Laura I Love Her" (RCA 7745) in 1960 and "Corinna, Corinna" (Dunes 2002) in 1960 (originally recorded by Joe Turner). His first hit record was on RCA Victor in 1959, "The Wonder of You" (RCA 7513), which Elvis recorded in February 1970. Peterson also recorded "Fever" on RCA in 1957.

Petunia, the Gardener's Daughter. Song that Donna Douglas sang in the 1966 movie *Frankie and Johnnie*. It was written by Sid Tepper and Roy C. Bennett. Elvis did record "Petunia, the Gardener's Daughter" and it appeared in the Long Playing albums "Frankie and Johnny" (RCA LPM/LSP-3553) and "Frankie and Johnny" (Pickwick ACL-7007).

Phillips, Dewey Mills. Memphis disc jockey for WHBQ radio, who, on his program "Red, Hot and Blue," first played an Elvis record on July 7, 1954*. He was so taken by the record that he played "That's All Right (Mama)" fourteen times in a row. Later that night, after receiving fourteen telegrams and forty-seven phone calls, Phillips interviewed Elvis, which became his first media interview.

It was Dewey Phillips who played the first Jerry Lee Lewis record over the air on WHBQ in 1956 when he aired "Crazy Arms."

---

*Dewey Phillips was not only the first DJ to play an Elvis record, he was the first DJ to play a Sun Record, when on March 1, 1952, he aired the first record released commercially by Sun Records. The record was "Blues in My Condition"/"Sellin' My Whiskey" (Sun 174) by Jackie Boy and Little Walker.

Dewey Phillips died on September 28, 1968, at age forty-two, the same age as Elvis at the time of his death.

Phillips, Judd. Brother of producer Sam Phillips. Judd Phillips founded the Phillips International record label in 1957, on which Bill Justis had hits with "Raunchy"* (Phillips 3519) in 1957 and "College Man" (Phillips 3422) in 1958. Charlie Rich and Carl Mann also recorded for the label. One story has it that Judd Phillips was standing in front of the Memphis Recording Service while Elvis was out front pacing in the summer of 1953. Judd supposedly encouraged Elvis to go inside and record his first record, a $4 acetate.

Phillips, Sam Cornelius. Born in Florence, Alabama, in 1935, Sam Phillips began in music as a radio station engineer and later as a disc jockey. He worked for the following radio stations: 1942: WLAY, Muscle Shoals, Alabama. 1943: WHSL, Decatur, Alabama. 1945: WLAC, Nashville, Tennessee. 1946–49: WREC, Memphis, Tennessee.

In 1950 Phillips cut two songs for his newly founded record label, Phillips (The "Hottest Thing in the Country"), but the record ("Gotta Let You Go"/"Boogie in the Park" by Joe Hill Louis) was never released.

Later, in 1950, Sam Phillips founded the Memphis Recording Service while living at 1028 Evers Road. (telephone 62-1889).

Phillips began recording demo records, which he sold to other independent record companies such as Chess and Modern Records. Among the artists he recorded were Jackie Brenston, Rosco Gordon, and Ike Turner.

Phillips's most successful record was Jackie Brenston's "Rocket 88,"† which Chess Records bought (Chess 1458).

In February 1952 Sam Phillips started Sun Records, which was based in the same small building, 706 Union Ave., that housed the Memphis Recording Service. His first Sun release came on March 1, 1952, with "Blues in My Condition"/"Sellin' My Whiskey" by Jackie Boy and Little Walter (Sun 174). Among the Sun artists whom Phillips recorded were Rufus Thomas; the Prisonaires; Junior Parker, Little Milton, Doug Poindexter, and the Johnny Burnette Trio, prior to recording Elvis's first record, "That's All Right Mama" in 1954. After the success of Elvis on Sun, other rock-a-billy and country singers came to Phillips's label. Some of these were: Johnny Cash; Carl Perkins; Charlie Feathers; Warren Smith; Roy Orbison; Billy Riley; Sonny Burgess; Jerry Lee Lewis; Ray Harris; Dickey Lee; Charlie Rich; Harold Dorman; Bill Justis; Carl Mann; David Houston; Thomas Wayne; and there were dozens of lesser-known performers. In 1955 Sam Phillips sold Elvis's

---

*"Raunchy" was originally titled "Backwoods."
†Record debut of Ike Turner, who led the band on the record.

contract to RCA Victor in order to obtain needed capital to help groom an up-and-coming artist named Carl Perkins.

In 1968 Sam Phillips sold Sun records, including all stock, to Shelby Singleton. Among the items that changed hands was a box full of Elvis Sun 45s and the Million Dollar Session tapes. The influence of Sam Phillips's small Sun label was major to the field of rock 'n' roll music of the 1950s. Aside from the artists he recorded, numerous other young singers attempted to record the "Sun sound," such as Ricky Nelson and Buddy Holly.

Sam Phillips can be called nothing less than a genius in that he had the talent to recognize talent.

Phillips International. Subsidiary label of Sun Records (1957–66), founded by Judd Phillips. It was located on Madison Ave. in Memphis. It was on this label that Charlie Rich recorded "Lonely Weekend" (Phillips 3552).

Phil Silvers Show, The. Popular situation-comedy TV series of the late 1950s, focusing on Army life. It starred Phil Silvers as Sgt. Ernie Bilko, head of the motor pool at Fort Baxter in Roseville, Kansas (later Camp Fremont in Grove City, California).

For the first six episodes "The Phil Silvers Show" was known as "You'll Never Get Rich" (September 20–October 25, 1955), but the title was changed to capitalize on the popularity of its star.

"The Phil Silvers Show" did a parody on Elvis in 1958 with a character called Elvin Pelvin. The scheming Sgt. Bilko attempted to manage Elvin Pelvin. The episode was titled "Rock and Roll Rookie" and aired on Friday, March 28, 1958, at 9:00 P.M. (See: Elvin Pelvin; Paramount Theater)

Photoplay Gold Medal Awards. Two awards presented to Elvis by *Photoplay* magazine on June 18, 1977, for Favorite Variety Star and Favorite Rock Music Star. These were the last awards presented to Elvis before his death.

Piano. Second musical instrument played by Elvis. On "Lawdy, Miss Clawdy," "Wear My Ring Around Your Neck," and "One-Sided Love Affair" Elvis played the piano. At his concerts he accompanied himself on piano when he sang "Unchained Melody." On his Long Playing album "How Great Thou Art" Elvis played piano on some of the cuts.

Piccadilly Cafeteria. Memphis restaurant, at 123 Madison Ave., where Priscilla modeled for a brief time in the mid-1960s.

Pickwick. Discount record label on which the Elvis albums were released after RCA Victor's discount label. Camden Records went out of business in December 1975.

Pieces of My Life. RCA PB-10401. Released in October 1975 as a 45 rpm single. It reached #33 on *Billboard*'s Country chart. "Bringing It Back" was on the flip side. "Pieces of My Life" was written by Troy Seals and appeared in the Long Playing album "Today" (RCA APL1-1039).

Pierce, Webb. Singer/composer who has had a number of success-ful country hit records. Webb Pierce composed (with Wayne Walker) "How Do You Think I Feel," which Elvis recorded in September 1956. Faron Young and Floyd Cramer were once members of Webb Pierce's band.

Pink and Black. Elvis's favorite colors in the early 1950s.

Pink Cadillac. Automobile that Elvis bought for his mother, Gladys, on September 3, 1956. Elvis still had the car the day he died.

Pioneer, Go Home. A 1957 novel by Richard Powell on which the 1962 movie *Follow That Dream* is based. *Pioneer, Go Home* appeared in *Reader's Digest* in condensed form.

Pirates Den. Club where Robin Ganter (Stella Stevens) sang in the 1962 movie *Girls! Girls! Girls!*.

Pittman, Barbara. Singer whom Elvis dated. Barbara Pittman, who also recorded for Sun Records, recorded the demo for Elvis's *Playing for Keeps*.

Plaisir d'Amour. Classical piece, composed by Jean Paul Martini (1741–1816), which was adapted in 1961 by George Weiss, Hugo Peretti, and Luigi Creatore as "Can't Help Falling in Love," which Elvis recorded in March 1961.

Plantation Rock. Song that Elvis recorded for the 1962 movie *Girls! Girls! Girls!* but it was cut from the final print. "Planta-tion Rock" is not available on record except on the bootleg al-bum, "Plantation Rock."

Plastic Products. Memphis firm, located at 1746 Chelsea Ave., that pressed the records for Sun Records.

Playboy Magazine Hall of Fame. Annual feature in *Playboy* maga-zine in which various musical artists are honored. Elvis was inducted on Feburary 1, 1978. (When *Playboy* was first pub-lished, in 1954, was to have been known as *Stag Party*.)

Playing for Keeps. RCA 20/47-6800. Released in January 1957 as a 78 rpm single and a 45 rpm single. It reached #34 on *Billboard*'s Hot 100 chart and sold over a million copies. "Too Much" was on the flip side. "Playing for Keeps" was written by Stanley A. Kesler and appeared in the following Long Playing albums: "For LP Fans Only" (RCA LPM-1990); "For LP Fans Only" (RCA LSP-1990 [e]); "Elvis: Worldwide 50 Gold Award Hits, Volume 1" (RCA LPM-6401).

Playing with Fire. Song that Elvis recorded for the 1961 movie *Blue Hawaii*, but it was cut from the final print of the film. "Playing with Fire" has never been released by RCA Victor. Written by Fred Wise and Ben Weisman, the song was recorded in 1964 by Terry Stafford (Crusader 105).

Play Misty for Me. A 1971 movie starring Clint Eastwood (first Eastwood-directed film), in which Roberta Flack sang "The First Time Ever I Saw Your Face," which became a #1 hit for her in 1972. Elvis recorded "The First Time Ever I Saw Your Face" in March 1971.

Please Don't Drag That String Around. RCA 47-8188. Released in July 1963 as a 45 rpm single. "(You're The) Devil in Disguise" was on the flip side. "Please Don't Drag That String Around" was written for Elvis by Otis Blackwell and Winfield Scott and appeared in the Long Playing albums "Elvis' Gold Records, Volume 4" (RCA LPM/LSP-3921) and "Elvis: The Other Sides—Worldwide Gold Award Hits, Volume 2" (RCA LPM-6402).

Please Don't Drag That String Around. RCA 447-0641. Gold Standard Series re-issue of RCA 47-8188.

Please Don't Stop Loving Me. RCA 47-8780. Released in March 1966 as a 45 rpm single. It reached #45 on *Billboard*'s Hot 100 chart. "Frankie and Johnny" was on the flip side. Elvis sang "Please Don't Stop Loving Me" in the 1966 movie *Frankie and Johnny*. It was written by Joy Byers and appeared in the Long Playing albums "Frankie and Johnny" (RCA LPM/LSP-3553) and "Frankie and Johnny" (Pickwick ACL-7007)

Please Don't Stop Loving Me. RCA 447-0656. Gold Standard Series re-issue of RCA 47-8780.

Please Release Me. A 45 rpm bootleg single release. The first Elvis bootleg single. The record was released on the Sun label with credit given to "Aaron P., Scotty & Bill." The songs on the record were "Baby, Let's Play House"/"My Baby Is Gone." "My Baby Is Gone" was a slower, bluesier version of "I'm Left, You're Right, She's Gone."

Please Release Me. A 33⅓ rpm British bootleg LP released on the First label. Songs included—Side One: "Fame and Fortune" ("Frank Sinatra-Timex Special"), "Stuck On You" ("Frank Sinatra-Timex Special"), "Teddy Bear," "Got a Lot o' Livin' to Do," "Jailhouse Rock," "A Cane and a High Starched Collar." Side Two: "The Lady Loves Me," "C'mon, Everybody," "Dominique," "Baby, What You Want Me to Do," "My Baby Is Gone," Interview.

Pledging My Love. RCA PB-10998. Released in June 1977 as a 45 rpm single. It reached #1 on *Billboard*'s Hot Country chart (for one week, August 13–20, 1977). "Way Down" was on the flip side. "Pledging My Love" was written by Ferdinand Washington and Don Robey and originally recorded by Johnny Ace* (Duke 136) in 1955. (See: Ace, Johnny)

Pledging My Love. RCA JB-10998. Rare 45 rpm single, released in stereo. It was released in advance of the regular release (RCA PB-10998).

Pocketful of Rainbows. Song that Elvis sang in the 1960 movie *G.I. Blues*. Juliet Prowse sang a few lines with Elvis in the film. In 1961 Dean Hawley released a version of "Pocketful of Rainbows" on Liberty Records. "Pocketful of Rainbows" was

---

*"Pledging My Love" by Johnny Ace was the first song that Stevie Wonder recalls ever hearing.

written by Fred Wise and Ben Weisman and appeared in the Long Playing album "G.I. Blues" (RCA LPM/LSP-2256).

Poems That Touch the Heart. Book that Elvis read on the troopship *General Randall* during his voyage to Bremerhaven, West Germany (September 22–October 1, 1958).

Pointer Sisters. Popular female vocal group made up of sisters Ruth, Anita, Bonnie, and June, the daughters of preacher parents. In 1979 they recorded their biggest hit, "Fire" (Planet 45901), composed by Bruce Springsteen.

Anita and Bonnie were the composers of "Fairytale," recorded by Elvis in March 1975.

Poison Ivy League. Song that Elvis sang in the 1964 movie *Roustabout.* "Poison Ivy League" was written by Bill Giant, Bernie Baum, and Florence Kaye and appeared in the Long Playing album "Roustabout" (RCA LPM/LSP-2999).

Polk Salad Annie. Song written and originally recorded by Tony Joe White (Monument 1104) in 1969. It reached #8 on *Billboard*'s Hot 100 chart. Elvis sang "Polk Salad Annie"* in the 1972 documentary *Elvis on Tour.* "Polk Salad Annie" appeared in the Long Playing albums "On Stage—February, 1970" (RCA LSP-4362) and "Elvis as Recorded at Madison Square Garden" (RCA LSP-4776).

Polynesian Paradise. Title originally considered for the 1966 movie *Paradise—Hawaiian Style.* Prior to *Polynesian Paradise,* it was to have been called *Polynesian Holiday. Hawaiian Paradise* was yet another title considered.

Poor Boy. Song that Elvis sang in the 1956 movie *Love Me Tender.* The film verison has hands clapping and girls screaming. Though Elvis and Vera Matson are credited with writing "Poor Boy," Ken Darby was actually the composer. (See: Darby, Ken) "Poor Boy" appeared in the Extended Play album "Love Me Tender" (RCA EPA-4006) and the following Long Playing albums: "For LP Fans Only" (RCA LSP-1990); "For LP Fans Only" (RCA LPS-1990 [e]): "Elvis: The Other Sides—Worldwide Gold Award Hits, Volume 2" (RCA LPM-6402).

Poor Man's Gold. Song for which only an instrumental track was recorded, on January 15, 1969, at the American Sound Studios. Elvis did not record a vocal track for "Poor Man's Gold."

Popular Tunes Record Shop. Record store, located at 308 Poplar Avenue, that became a hangout for Elvis when he was in high school. The store was founded by Joe Coughi, who also launched Hi Records.

Porkchops. Elvis's favorite food, served with brown gravy and apple pie.

---

*On Tony Joe White's version, producer Billy Swan's voice can be heard at the beginning, saying: "Four."

Porkupine Flats. Home of the Tatum family near Big Smokey Mountain in North Carolina in the 1964 movie *Kissin' Cousins*.

Portland, Maine. Site of the next scheduled concert that Elvis was to have played, on August 17 and 18, 1977, after his last concert in Indianapolis at the Market Square Arena, June 26, 1977.

Portnow, Lillian. Model who gave Elvis a box of cheesecake and kissed him goodbye as he boarded the U.S.S. *Randall* on September 22, 1953. She was the last girl to kiss Elvis goodbye as he sailed to Europe. He was walking up the gangplank when kissed.

Port of Call. Tentative title of the 1967 movie *Easy Come, Easy Go*.

Posey, Sandy. Singer (real name: Martha Sharp) and secretary* employed at the American Sound Studios in Memphis, who, in July 1966, made the top ten with her song "Born a Woman" (MGM). She later sang background for Tommy Roe, Bobby Bare, Skeeter Davis, Joe Tex, Bobby Goldsboro, and for Elvis at the American Sound Studios. The Elvis session in which Sandy Posey sang as a background singer was held between January 13 and 23 and again between February 17 and 22, 1969.

Pot Luck. Title originally considered for the 1968 MGM movie *Speedway*. Another tentative title was *So I'll Go Quietly*.

Pot Luck. RCA LPM/LSP-2523. A 33⅓ rpm Long Playing album that was released in June 1962. It reached #4 on *Billboard's* Hot LP chart. "Pot Luck" achieved sales of over $1 million, qualifying it for a Gold Record. Songs included—Side 1: "Kiss Me Quick," Just for Old Times Sake," "Gonna Get Back Home Somehow," "(Such An) Easy Question," "Steppin' Out of Line," "I'm Yours." Side 2: "Something Blue," "Suspicion," "I Feel That I've Known You Forever," "Night Rider," "Fountain of Love," "That's Someone You Never Forget."

Potomac. Former presidential yacht (owned by Franklin D. Roosevelt) that Elvis gave to Danny Thomas in care of St. Jude's Children's Hospital in Memphis. Elvis purchased the yacht for $55,000 on January 30, 1964. The March of Dimes and the Coast Guard Auxiliary previously rejected it as unsafe.

Pot Pourri. Song that Elvis recorded for the 1962 movie *Girls! Girls! Girls!* but it was cut from the final print. "Pot Pourri" is not available on record.

Pound Dog. A 1956 Elvis novelty song by Lalo Guerrero on L & M Records (L & M 1000).

Pour Les Fans d' Elvis Seulement (For Elvis Fans Only). Elvis novelty album by Johnny Farago on Nobel Records (Nobel 508). The album included ten Elvis songs.

---

*Martha Reeves was a secretary with Motown Records and Minnie Riperton was once a receptionist at Chess Records.

Power of My Love. Song written by Bill Giant, Bernie Baum, and Florence Kaye and recorded by Elvis on February 18, 1969, at the American Sound Studios in Memphis. "Power of My Love" appeared in the Long Playing album "From Elvis in Memphis" (RCA LSP-4155).

Precious Memories. Gladys Presley's favorite hymn. It was sung at her funeral by the Blackwood Brothers Quartet. "Precious Memories" was composed in 1925 by J. B. F. Wright of Tennessee.

Precision Tool. Memphis company, located at 1132 Kansas (telephone WHitehall 8-1652), with which Elvis had a brief factory job in the summer of 1953. This was prior to working for the Crown Electric Company. A story has it that Elvis was fired because of a fight with the foreman over the length of his hair.

Prell, Milton. Principal owner of the Aladdin Hotel in Las Vegas. It was in his private suite that Elvis and Priscilla were married, on May 1, 1967.

Prescription House, The. Memphis drugstore, located at 1737 Madison Ave., where Elvis's prescriptions were filled.

Preseley, Vernon. Misspelling of Vernon Presley's name in the Memphis telephone directory in the 1950s.

Presley, Davada "Dee." Second wife of Vernon Presley; Elvis's stepmother. (See: Stanley, Davada "Dee")

Presley, Elvis, as Composer. Elvis has been credited as the co-author of the following songs—"Don't Be Cruel," "Heartbreak Hotel," "Love Me Tender," "Paralyzed," "That's Someone You Never Forget," "We're Gonna Move," "You'll Be Gone."

Elvis has been credited as arranging or adapting the following songs: "I'm Gonna Walk Dem Golden Stairs," "In My Father's House," "Milky White Way," "Joshua Fit the Battle," "Swing Down Sweet Chariot," "Aloha-Oe," "By and By," "Farther Along," "I'll Take You Home Again Kathleen," "Run On," "I Was Born About Ten Thousand Years Ago," "O Come All Ye Faithful," "O Little Town of Bethlehem," "San Lucia," "See See Rider," "So High," "The First Noel."

Presley, Gladys Love Smith. (April 25, 1912–August 14, 1958) Mother of Elvis Presley. In 1933, at the age of twenty-one she married seventeen-year-old Vernon Elvis Presley. Elvis, born on January 8, 1935, was the couple's only child, as Elvis's brother, Jesse Garon, died at birth.

Gladys worked as a sewing machine operator in Tupelo and later worked as an aide at St. Joseph's Hospital in Memphis. Mother and son were very close, with Elvis always keeping his mother's needs uppermost in his mind. He bought her automobiles and houses and maintained a close relationship with her until her death.

Gladys Presley died of a heart attack, brought on by acute hepatitis, at the Methodist Hospital in Memphis on August 14,

1958, at 3:00 A.M. She was forty-six years old. Her body was buried at Forest Hill Cemetery until it was placed next to that of Elvis at Graceland. Marlon Brando, Dean Martin, Tennessee Ernie Ford, Rick Nelson, and Sammy Davis, Jr., sent remembrances.

Presley, Jesse Garon. Elvis's twin brother, who was stillborn. Jessie Garon was laid in a tiny cardboard box in the front room of the Presley home that same day (January 8, 1935). The next day Jesse was buried in an unmarked grave next to a tree in the Priceville Cemetery, northeast of East Tupelo. Jesse Garon was named for his paternal grandfather, Jessie McClowell Presley.

Presley, Jessie D. McClowell. Paternal grandfather (1896–1973) of Elvis Presley. He married Elvis's grandmother Minnie Mae Hood, of Fulton, Mississippi, in 1913 and divorced her thirty-four years later. In 1947 Jessie married a schoolteacher named Vera Pruitt.

Presley, John Baron. Name that Elvis and Priscilla would have called Lisa Marie had she been a boy.

Presley, Lisa Marie. Elvis and Priscilla's only child. She was born at 5:01 P.M., February 1, 1968 (nine months to the day after Elvis and Priscilla were married), on the fifth floor of the east wing, 6 hours 19 minutes after Priscilla entered the Baptist Memorial Hospital in Memphis. Lisa Marie weighed 6 lbs. 15 oz. and measured 20 inches. Upon the death of Minnie Mae Presley (Elvis's grandmother), Lisa Marie will receive all assets of the estate when she reaches the age of twenty-five. Her middle name, Marie, was given to her in honor of Col. Tom Parker's wife.

Presley, Minnie Mae Hood. Paternal grandmother of Elvis Presley, born on June 17, 1893. She married Jesse D. McClowell Presley in 1913 and was divorced in 1947, after raising five children, one of whom was Vernon, Elvis's father.

Minnie Mae moved into Graceland in the 1960s and lived there until her death on May 8, 1980.

Presley, Patsy. (See: Gamble, Patsy)

Presley, Priscilla. (See: Beaulieu, Priscilla)

Presley, Vernon Elvis. Father of Elvis Presley. Vernon Presley was born in 1916 in Fulton, Mississippi, and died in Memphis, Tennessee, in 1979. Vernon Presley married twenty-one-year-old Gladys Smith in 1933, when he was but seventeen. He and Gladys worked hard in Tupelo, where they made their home, but money was hard to come by. Vernon Presley worked at various jobs such as farmer, truckdriver, and painter. He also worked for the WPA (Works Progress Administration), a branch of F.D.R.'s New Deal Program. In 1938 and 1939 Vernon Presley spent nine months at the Parchman Penitentiary for forgery. In 1948 Vernon Presley moved his family to Memphis, as he had obtained a job at a paint factory there.

After the death of his wife Gladys in 1958 he devoted himself solely to his successful son's career. On July 3, 1960, Vernon Presley married Davada "Dee" Stanley, only to divorce her in May 1977. He was named executor of Elvis's will on August 23, 1977. Vernon Presley died of heart failure on June 26, 1979. He was sixty-three years old. (See: Presley, Gladys; United Paint Company; Stanley, Davada "Dee"; Parchman Penitentiary). Vernon Presley was portrayed by Bing Russell in the 1979 TV movie *Elvis*.

Presley, Vester. Elvis's uncle who married Cletis Smith, the younger sister of Gladys Smith. Vester authored the twenty-five-dollar book *A Presley Speaks*.

Presley Center Courts, Inc. Corporation formed in 1975 by Dr. George Nichopoulos, Joe Esposito, and Michael McMahon, to build and manage ten racquetball-court facilities costing approximately $700,000 each. This was the first commercial venture in which Elvis authorized the use of his name. Elvis was chairman of the board, but he left the company before the end of the first year (1976). Mike McMahon was general manager of the company, which was formed on April 20, 1976.

Presley, Medley, A. A 1978 Elvis tribute record by Bruce Channel on LeCam Records (LeCam 1117).

Presley on Her Mind. Novelty record that made reference to Elvis in the lyrics. It was released on Reserve Records (Reserve 118) by Don Hart in 1957.

Presley Speaks, A. Book by Vester Presley (Elvis's uncle, Vernon's brother) as told to Deda Bonura (Wimmer Brothers Books, 1978).

Presley, the King Cadillac Man. A 1977 Elvis tribute record by Angelmaye North on High Country Records (High Country 108).

Preston, Sandy. Las Vegas chorus girl whom Elvis dated briefly in 1956.

Pretty Boy 11. Nickname of Tulsa McLean's (Elvis) tank crew in the 1960 movie *G.I. Blues*.

Price, Lloyd. New Orleans R & B artist who composed and originally recorded "Lawdy, Miss Clawdy" (Specialty 428) in 1952, which was recorded by Elvis in 1956. The piano player on Lloyd Price's "Lawdy, Miss Clawdy" was Fats Domino. In the early 1950s Price's valet and chauffeur was a young singer named Larry Williams. The Beatles recorded three of Williams's songs.

Price, Ray. The Cherokee Cowboy (Willie Nelson, Roger Miller, and Johnny Paycheck were all members of his band, the Cherokee Cowboys). Ray Price was once a member of Hank Williams's Drifting Cowboys. Ray Price recorded versions of "For the Good Times" (Columbia 45178) and "Release Me" (Columbia 21214), both of which Elvis recorded.

Priceville Cemetery. Burial spot of Jesse Garon Presley, Elvis's twin brother, who was stillborn on January 8, 1935. He was buried in an unmarked grave the next day. Priceville Cemetery is located three miles northeast of Tupelo on Feemster Lake Road. (See: Presley, Jesse Garon)

Pricilla. A 1977 Elvis tribute record by Wally Fowler on Dove Records. (Note: Priscilla is misspelled.) (See: a New Star in Heaven, A)

Priddy, Al. Disc jockey at KEX in Portland, Oregon, who was fired in December 1957 because he played several cuts from "Elvis' Christmas Album." The station management thought the album was in "extremely bad taste." The cuts thought most objectionable were "O Little Town of Bethlehem," "White Christmas," and "Silent Night."

Priest, Pat. Actress who appeared on the TV series "The Munsters" and played Dina Bishop in the 1967 movie *Easy Come, Easy Go*. Pat Priest is the daughter of Ivy Baker Priest, former Treasurer of the United States.

Prima, Louis and Smith, Keeley. Singers (husband and wife) whom Elvis visited backstage at the Sahara Hotel in Las Vegas. It was Keeley Smith who appeared in the 1958 movie *Thunder Road*—the movie that had been offered to Elvis by Robert Mitchum.

Prince of Wales Hotel. Paris hotel where Elvis and his friend Cliff Greaves spent a two-week furlough in June 1959. (See: Lido, The)

Prisonaires, The. Early 1950s black vocal group who recorded on Sun Records. The Prisonaires were inmates at the Tennessee State Prison. The Sun labels read: "Prisonaires Confined to the Tennessee State Prison, Nashville." The group consisted of Johnny Bragg, John Drue, William Stewart, Marcell Sanders, and Ed Thurman. The Prisonaires' biggest Sun release came in 1953 with "Just Walkin' in the Rain."* Lead singer Johnny Bragg once claimed that Elvis helped him with the lyrics on the song. (This is highly unlikely since the record was released in early 1953 and Elvis was in high school at the time).

Pritchett, Nashval Lorene. Elvis's aunt (Vernon's sister). She was ordained Assembly of God minister and was pastor at the First Assembly of God Church in Walls, Mississippi.

Pritchett, William Earl. Uncle of Elvis who was employed at Graceland as a grounds keeper.

Private First Class. Army rank that Elvis achieved on December 27, 1958.

Proby, P.J. Pseudonym of American-born singer James Marcus

---

*Johnnie Ray had a #2 hit and a million-seller in 1956 with "Just Walkin' in the Rain" (Columbia 40729).

Smith. He was one of several singers used to cut Elvis sound-alike demo records of material that Elvis would select to record.

P.J. Proby, not finding success in the U.S. went to England prior to the Beatles' invasion. There he became a pop artist but also became controversial, especially after his pants ripped at a number of live concerts. Because of this, he was eventually forbidden to do live performances in Britain. He has had a number of hit records on the British charts but could never become the star in America that he was in Europe.

In the 1950s P.J. recorded several records under the pseud-onym of Jet Powers.

P.J. Proby portrayed Elvis in London's West End musical *Elvis*.

Throughout his career Proby always claimed that Elvis was a close friend of his.

Professional Stock Car Drivers. Those mentioned in the opening credits of the 1968 movie *Speedway* were Richard Petty, Buddy Baker, Cale Yarborough, Dick Hutcherson, Tiny Lund, O.C. Spencer, and Roy Mayne.

Promised Land. RCA PB-10074. Released in October 1974 as a 45 rpm single. "Promised Land" reached #14 on *Billboard's* Hot 100 chart and #9 on the Country chart. "It's Midnight" was on the flip side. "Promised Land" was written and original-ly recorded by Chuck Berry (Chess 1916) in 1964. Elvis's version of "Promised Land" appeared in the Long Playing album "Promised Land" (RCA APL-0873)

Promised Land. RCA GB-10488. Gold Standard Series re-issue of RCA PB-10074.

Promised Land. RCA APL1-0873. Released in January 1975 as a 33⅓ rpm Long Playing album. "Promised Land" reached #47 on *Billboard's* Hot LP chart and was also available in quadra-sonic. It achieved sales of more than half a million copies, qualifying it for a Gold Record. Songs included—Side 1: "Promised Land," "There's a Honky Tonk Angel (Who Will Take Me Back In)," "Help Me," "Mr. Songman," "Love Song of the Year." Side 2: "It's Midnight," "Your Love's Been a Long Time Coming," "If You Talk in Your Sleep," "Thinking About You," "You Asked Me To."

Property of Notre Dame. Wording on the sweatshirt worn by Sister Michelle (Mary Tyler Moore) in a touch football game in the 1969 movie *Change of Habit*.

Prophet, The. Religious philosophy book by Kahlil Gibran, which Elvis (Kurt Russell) read to Priscilla in the 1979 TV Movie *Elvis. The Prophet* was one of actress Carole Lombard's favorite books and was the favorite of Joan Crawford.

Proud Mary. Song written by John C. Fogerty and originally recorded by Creedence Clearwater Revival (Fantasy 619) in

1969. "Proud Mary" reached #2 on the charts and sold over a million copies. Sonny Charles and the Checkmates, Ltd., also had a successful version (A & M 1127). Ike and Tina Turner's 1971 version of "Proud Mary" (Liberty) became a million-seller.

Elvis sang "Proud Mary" in the 1972 documentary *Elvis on Tour* and it appeared in the Long Playing albums "On Stage—February, 1970" (RCA LSP-4362) and "Elvis as Recorded at Madison Square Garden" (RCA LSP-4776).

Prowse, Juliet. Female lead (as Lili) in the 1960 movie *G.I. Blues*. She was once the fiancée of Frank Sinatra. Elvis dated Juliet Prowse briefly. Juliet appeared in several Sinatra movies as well.

Puff. Lisa Marie Presley's pet white cat.

Puppet on a String. RCA 447-0650. Released in October 1965 as a 45 rpm Gold Standard Series original. It reached #14 on *Billboard*'s Hot 100 chart. Some sources indicate that "Puppet on a String" sold over a million copies. "Wooden Heart" was on the flip side. Elvis sang "Puppet on a String" in the 1965 movie *Girl Happy*. Written by Sid Tepper and Roy C. Bennett, "Puppet on a String" appeared in the following Long Playing albums: "Girl Happy" (RCA LPM/LSP-3338); "Elvis: The Other Sides—Worldwide Gold Award Hits, Volume 2" (RCA LPM-6402); "Elvis Sings for Children (And Grownups Too)" (RCA CPL1-2901).

Puppet on a String. RCA PB-11320. A 45 rpm limited edition single (on green vinyl) released in July 1978, with "(Let Me Be Your) Teddy Bear" on the flip side.

Pure Gold. Title of first licensed album (Opus 91130625) by Elvis to be released in Eastern-bloc countries beginning in 1979. It is the same album as the RCA "Pure Gold." The second album was titled "Elvis," released by GDR in East Germany on the Amiga Records label (Amiga 855630).

Pure Gold. RCA ANL1-0971. Released in March 1975 as a 33⅓ rpm Long Playing album. The album was released by RCA's budget line, the "Pure Gold" series. "Pure Gold" achieved sales of over half a million copies, qualifying it for a Gold Record. Songs included—Side 1: "Kentucky Rain," "Fever," "It's Impossible," "Jailhouse Rock," "Don't Be Cruel." Side 2: "I Got a Woman," "All Shook Up," "Loving You," "In the Ghetto," "Love Me Tender."

Pursuit of Happiness. A 1934 movie starring Francis Lederer and Joan Bennett, which was playing at the Strand Theatre in Tupelo, Mississippi, the day Elvis was born (January 8, 1935).

Pusser, Buford. Sheriff of McNairy County, Tennessee, who came to national prominence fighting organized crime. The 6' 6", 250-lb. Pusser was the subject of three theatrical movies and one made-for-TV movie.* Elvis anonymously sent him a check for a substantial amount after his house was burned down while fighting organized crime. Elvis greatly admired Pusser. Pusser died in an auto accident in 1974.

Put a Little Lovin' on Me. Song recorded by Bobby Bare on RCA Victor. Elvis's name is mentioned in the lyrics.

Put the Blame on Me. Song that Elvis sang in the 1965 movie *Tickle Me.* "Put the Blame on Me" was written by Kay Twomey, Fred Wise, and Norman Blagman and appeared in the Extended Play album "Tickle Me" (RCA EPA-4383) and the Long Playing album "Something for Everybody" (RCA LPM/LSP-2370).

Put Your Hand in the Hand (Of the Man from Galilee). Song written by Gene McLellan and originally recorded by Beth Moore in 1971 on Capitol Records (Capitol 3013). "Put Your Hand in the Hand (Of the Man from Galilee)" by Ocean (Kama Sutra 519), that same year, reached #2 on the charts and sold over a million copies. Elvis recorded "Put Your Hand in the Hand (Of the Man from Galilee)" in 1971 and it appeared in the Long Playing albums "Elvis—Now" (RCA LSP-4671) and "Elvis—A Canadian Tribute" (RCA KKL1-7065).

Q

Quadradisc. Stereo, four-channel record. Elvis was the first artist in history to receive a Gold Record for a quadradisc. He received the award for the 1973 Long Playing album "Elvis: Aloha from Hawaii Via Satellite," which was RCA's first quadradisc. (See: Elvis: Aloha from Hawaii Via Satellite)

Queenie Wahine's Papaya. Song that Elvis sang in the 1966 movie *Paradise—Hawaiian Style.* In the film, Donna Butterworth sang a duet with Elvis. "Queenie Wahine's Papaya" was written by Bill Giant, Bernie Baum, and Florence Kaye and appeared in the Long Playing album "Paradise—Hawaiian Style" (RCA LPM/LSP-3643).

Quinn, Ray. Program manager at radio station WCBM in Baltimore, who was the first to splice together a taped duet of both Elvis and Linda Ronstadt singing versions of "Love Me Tender."

---

*The movies are: *Walking Tall,* (1974), Joe Don Baker; *Walking Tall Part 2* (1975), Bo Svenson; *Final Chapter—Walking Tall* (1977), Bo Svenson; "*A Real American Hero*" (1978 TV), Brian Dennehy.

R

Rabbit, Eddie. Country singer and composer who cowrote two Elvis hits: "Patch It Up" (with Rory Bourke) and "Kentucky Rain" (with Dick Heard). Eddie Rabbitt (real name: Edward Thomas Rabbit) was born in Brooklyn, New York. In 1979, he had a hit with the title song of the Clint Eastwood movie *Every Which Way But Loose.*

Radford Center. Iowa town that was the setting for the 1969 movie *The Trouble with Girls* (*And How to Get Into It*).

Radio Recorders. Los Angeles recording studio, located at 7000 Santa Monica Blvd., where Elvis made his first Hollywood recording session—September 1–3, 1956. Studio B at Radio Recorders was used. Radio Recorders was owned by Thorne Nogar.

Rag Mop. Song written by Johnnie Lee Wills (brother of Bob Wills) and Deacon Anderson (father of Lynn Anderson) and originally recorded by Johnnie Lee Wills (Bullet 696). In 1950 the Ames Brothers (Joe, Gene, Vic, and Ed*) had a #1 hit and million-seller with "Rag Mop" (Coral 60173). The song was so popular that there were three versions in the top ten of the Rhythm and Blues charts (Lionel Hampton, Doc Sausage, and Joe Liggins) and two in the Pop charts (Ralph Flanagan and the Ames Brothers). Elvis attempted to record "Rag Mop" at Sun Records on July 5, 1954, but the take was unacceptable to Sam Phillips. "Rag Mop" remains unreleased to this day.

Rags to Riches. RCA 47-9980. Released in March 1971 as a 45 rpm single. It reached #33 on *Billboard*'s Hot 100 chart. "Where Did They Go, Lord" was on the flip side. "Rags to Riches" was written by Richard Adler and Jerry Ross and originally recorded by Tony Bennett with the Percy Faith Orchestra in 1953 (Columbia 40048). In 1954 the Dominoes† recorded the song for the King label (King 1280). Elvis's version of "Rags to Riches" did not appear in an album.

Rags to Riches. RCA 447-0680. Gold Standard Series re-issue of RCA 47-9980.

Rainbow Records. Lawndale, California, company that produced a seven-inch cardboard Elvis-interview record titled "The Truth About Me." The record was issued on gold cardboard with a

---

*Ed Ames played the Oxford-educated Cherokee Indian Mingo on the TV series "Daniel Boone."
†Two members of the Dominoes were Billy Ward and Clyde McPhatter (replaced by Jackie Wilson when McPhatter left to form the Drifters).

blue label and came on the front cover of the 1956 magazine *Elvis Answers Back*. It played at 78 rpm and was perforated so that it could be removed from the magazine. The interview record was released "By Special Permission of RCA Victor." An identical version of the record, called "Speaks—In Person!" is quite rare. (See: Lynchburg Audio)

Rainbow Rollerdome. Memphis roller skating rink, located at 2881 Lamar Ave., that Elvis rented for the entertainment of his friends and himself. The manager was Joe Pieraccini. The Rainbow Rollerdome was situated next to the Rainbow Lake Swimming Pool.

Rainey, Ma. Blues singer (1886–1939) who first recorded "See See Rider" (also called "C.C. Rider") on Paramount Records in the 1920s. Ma Rainey (real name: Gertrude Pridgett Rainey)* was called the "Mother of the Blues." Her trademark, until it was stolen, was a necklace of gold coins. It was Ma Rainey who discovered blues singer Bessie Smith. (See: See See Rider)

Rainmaker, The. A 1956 Paramount movie starring Burt Lancaster† and Katharine Hepburn. On April 1, 1956, Elvis did a scene from *The Rainmaker* with Frank Faylen for his screen test. In an interview Elvis erroneously stated that he was going to make his acting debut in *The Rainmaker*.

Raised on Rock. RCA APBO-0088. Released in September 1973 as a 45 rpm single. It reached #41 on *Billboard*'s Hot 100 chart. "For Ol' Times Sake" was on the flip side. Elvis recorded "Raised on Rock" at the Stax Studios in Memphis. "Raised on Rock" was written by Mark James and appeared in the Long Playing album "Raised on Rock/For Ol' Times Sake" (RCA APL1-0388).

Raised on Rock. RCA GB-10157. Gold Standard Series original released in January 1975. Although "Raised on Rock" had been released previously (RCA APBO-0088), this Gold Standard Series issue had a different flip side ("If You Talk in Your Sleep"), making it a different record.

Raised on Rock/For Ol' Times Sake. RCA APL1-0388. A 33⅓ rpm Long Playing album released in October 1973. It reached #50 on *Billboard*'s Hot LP chart. The songs in "Raised on Rock/For Ol' Times Sake" were recorded at Stax Studios in Memphis and at Elvis's Palm Springs, California, home. Songs included—Side 1: "Raised on Rock," "Are You Sincere," "Find Out What's Happening," "I Miss You," "Girl of Mine." Side 2: "For Ol' Times Sake," "If You Don't Come Back," "Just a Little Bit," "Sweet Angeline," "Three Corn Patches."

Ram, Buck. Manager and songwriter for two 1950s rhythm

---

*Another Ma Rainey (real name: Lilian Glover) was popular in Memphis in the 1960s/1970s. Also known as Big Memphis Ma Rainey, she made some recordings for Sun.
†Lancaster's role was actively sought by Bing Crosby.

and blues groups: the Penguins and the Platters. In 1956 Mercury Records wanted to sign the Penguins, but Buck Ram insisted that they sign both groups. Mercury signed the Platters just to get the Penguins. The Penguins never had a hit for Mercury Records, but the Platters had a string of successes. Buck Ram was a cowriter (with Walter Kent and Kim Gannon) of "I'll Be Home for Christmas," which Elvis recorded in September 1957).

Randall, U.S.S. General. Troopship (P115) on which Elvis traveled (with 1,400 other soldiers) to Bremerhaven, West Germany. He left New York City on September 22, 1958, and arrived in Bremerhaven on October 1. Charlie Hodge also sailed on the U.S.S. *General Randall,* sharing the same room with Elvis at Elvis's request.

During World War II, Soupy Sales* served aboard the U.S.S. *General Randall.* The ship appeared in the 1956 movie *Away All Boats.*

Randle, Bill. Cleveland disc jockey (on radio station WERE) who was the first disc jockey outside the south to play Elvis records on a regular basis (1955). Bill Randle had a Saturday-morning show on CBS in New York City and commuted from Cleveland once a week. In the fall of 1955 Bill Randle was approached by Arnold Shaw, general professional manager of the Edward B. Marks Music Corp. Shaw asked Randle to play some Elvis records on his CBS radio program. Randle thought that Elvis was a bit too much for the New York audience, but he did start playing the records on WERE. The audience response was phenomenal. This was one of the major factors in getting national exposure for Elvis.

Bill Randle introduced Elvis on his third appearance on "Stage Show," February 11, 1956.

The Diamonds received a recording contract with Mercury Records through Bill Randle's influence. He convinced Coral Records to sign the Johnny Burnette Trio and told Don George that his adaptation of "The Yellow Rose of Texas" had pop potential. (See: Circle Theater; Day in the Life of a Number One D.J., A)

Randolph, Homer "Boots." Popular saxophone player and Nashville session artist. Boots Randolph played saxophone and vibes in many of Elvis's recordings in the 1960s (beginning on April 3, 1960). In 1963 Randolph had a big hit of his own with "Yakety Sax" (Monument 804).

Boots Randolph is the only musician to have played for both Elvis Presley and Buddy Holly. With Holly he played in the following recordings: "Rock Around with Ollie Vee" (Decca 30434); "Modern Don Juan" (Decca 30166); "You Are My One Desire" (Decca 30543).

---

*Born Milton Hines, Soupy Sales is now his legal name.

Range Round-Up. Comedy sketch featuring Elvis, Steve Allen, Imogene Coca, and Andy Griffith on "The Steve Allen Show" on July 1, 1956.

Ray, Johnnie. A 1950s ballad singer known as the "Prince of Wails" and the "Nabob of Sob" because of his shrieking singing style. (Johnnie Ray learned his singing style from rhythm and blues singer Lavern Baker.) Johnnie Ray's biggest hits were "Cry" (Okeh 6840)* (#1 for eleven weeks) and the flip side, "Little White Cloud That Cried" (#2), and "Just Walkin' in the Rain" (#2)—all were million-sellers.

Elvis met Johnnie Ray backstage at the Desert Inn in Las Vegas in 1956.

RCA. Brand of the two color TVs that Elvis had mounted in the ceiling of his bedroom at Graceland. They were installed by Charles R. Church. (See: Church, Charles R.)

RCA Consolette. Monaural mixing console, type 76-D, that was used by the Memphis Recording Service and Sun Records in producing Elvis's first records ("My Happiness"/"That's When Your Heartaches Begin"; "Casual Love"/"I'll Never Stand in Your Way"; "That's All Right (Mama)"/"Blue Moon of Kentucky"). The console (serial #1011) was previously used in a Florida radio station. Sam Phillips used it for several years at Sun Records.

RCA DJ-56. Special disc jockey Extended Play album featuring "Too Much" and "Playing for Keeps," by Elvis, on one side, and "Chantez Chantez" and "Honky Tonk Heart," by Dinah Shore, on the other side.

RCA DJ-7. Special disc jockey Extended Play album featuring "Love me Tender" and "Any Way You Want Me (That's How I Will Be)," by Elvis, on one side, and "Welcome to the Club" and "I Won't Be Rockin' Tonight," by Jean Chapel, on the other side.

RCA Victor. Highly successful record company founded in 1901. On November 22, 1955, RCA Victor A & R man Steve Sholes purchased Elvis's contract from Sam Phillips for RCA. Sholes offered $25,000 from RCA and $15,000 from Hill and Range to purchase Hi-Lo Music. Several other record labels were also making bids at the time. Columbia dropped out at $15,000 and Atlantic at $25,000. Elvis was given $5,000 against his royalties, which he used to purchase a new Cadillac. The purchase of Elvis's contract was a daring feat by Sholes at the time; in 1955, $40,000 was a large amount of money. Steve Sholes's boldness did pay off, for Elvis went on to become RCA Victor's greatest asset with worldwide record sales in 1978 in excess of 500 million units. The signing of Elvis to the RCA Victor label took place at the Warwick Hotel in New York City. (See: Hi-Lo; X Records; Sholes, Steve)

---

*The Four Lads sang back-up on "Cry" and "Little White Cloud That Cried."

Reach Out to Jesus. Gospel song by Ralph Carmichael, which Elvis recorded in 1971. "Reach Out to Jesus" appeared in the Long Playing album "He Touched Me" (RCA LSP-4690).

Read All About It. Song that Shelley Fabares and Nita Talbot sang in the 1965 movie *Girl Happy*. "Read All About It" has never been released by RCA.

Reader's Digest Presents Elvis Presley. A 33⅓ rpm single, made of plastic, issued by *Reader's Digest* to promote its boxed set. Brian Matthew introduced excerpts of interviews and songs that were typical of Elvis's career.

Ready for Love. Song that Elvis is reported to have recorded, although it has never been released in any form.

Ready Teddy. Song written by Robert (Bumps) Blackwell and John Marascalo and originally recorded by Little Richard in June of 1956 (Specialty 579). "Rip It Up" was on the flip side; so, Elvis had the distinction of covering both sides of a Little Richard single. Elvis recorded "Ready Teddy" at Radio Recorders in Hollywood on September 3, 1956. Before Elvis recorded it, fifty percent of the publishing rights were relinquished by Venice Music, Inc., to Elvis Presley Music, Inc. On September 9, 1956, "Ready Teddy" was sung by Elvis on his first appearance on "The Ed Sullivan Show." "Ready Teddy" appeared in the Extended Play album "Elvis, Volume 2" (RCA EPA-993) and the Long Playing albums, "Elvis" (RCA LPM-1382) and "Elvis" (RCA LSP-1382 [e]).

Ready Teddy. RCA CR-25. Special disc jockey 45 rpm single. The record was one-sided.

Reagan, Maureen. Actress who played Lorraine in the 1964 movie *Kissin' Cousins*. Maureen Reagan is the daughter of former actor and U.S. President Ronald Reagan* and actress Jane Wyman.

Real Elvis, The. RCA EPA-940. This was a 45 rpm Extended Play Album released in September 1956. Songs included—Side 1: "Don't Be Cruel," "I Want You, I Need You, I Love You." Side 2: "Hound Dog," "My Baby Left Me."

Real Elvis, The. RCA EPA-5120. This record was a Gold Standard Series re-issue of RCA EPA-940 (April 1961).

Real History of Rock 'n' Roll, The. A 33⅓ rpm album released by Candlelite Records (Candlelite 1002). It contained a one-hour narration by Wayne Stierle on Elvis's career from 1954 to '69.

Rebel Without a Cause. A 1955 movie starring James Dean, Natalie Wood, Sal Mineo, and Nick Adams. *Rebel Without a Cause* was one of Elvis's favorite movies. He watched it so many times that he could recite James Dean's dialogue from

---

*As a Captain in the Army, Ronald Reagan signed Major Clark Gable's discharge papers on June 12, 1944, in Culver City, California.

memory. In the 1979 TV movie *Elvis,* Kurt Russell (as Elvis) watched *Rebel Without a Cause* at Graceland.

Reconsider Baby. Song written and originally recorded by Lowell Fulson in 1954 (Checker 804). Elvis recorded "Reconsider Baby" in 1960 and it appeared in the Long Playing album "Elvis Is Back" (RCA LPM/LSP-2231).

Redding, Otis. Soul singer from Macon, Georgia. Otis Redding recorded for the Memphis-based Volt Records. (Volt Records, a subsidiary of Stax, was created for Redding's releases.) Originally, Otis Redding was a chauffeur for a Macon, Georgia, group, the Pinetoppers, headed by Johnny Jenkins. He drove Jenkins and the group to Memphis for an audition with Stax Records. The audition resulted in Jim Stewart of Stax signing Redding to a long-term contract. After he was killed in a plane crash on December 19, 1967, near Madison, Wisconsin, Otis Redding's biggest hit was released—"(Sittin' On) The Dock of the Bay."

Otis Redding replaced Elvis as the Top Male Vocalist in Great Britain in 1967.

Red Dots, The. Group that supposedly backed Elvis on the bogus 1954 recording of "Tell Me Pretty Baby." On the label, the song was credited to the Red Dots. (See: Tell Me Pretty Baby)

Red, Hot, and Blue. Radio program on Memphis station WHBQ, hosted by Dewey Phillips. "Red, Hot, and Blue,"* which was on from 9:00 P.M. to midnight in the 1950s, aired mostly rhythm and blues and rock-a-billy music. It was on this program, on July 7, 1954, that an Elvis record was first played. Dewey Phillips helped to introduce many rhythm and blues and rock-a-billy artists. (See: Phillips, Dewey)

Red River Valley. Instrumental song playing on the jukebox during a barroom fight in which Vince Everett (Elvis) accidentally killed a man (1957 movie *Jailhouse Rock*). "Red River Valley," which was originally titled "The Bright Mohawk Valley" was used twice as the theme song of classic movies: *The Grapes of Wrath,* (1940), and *The Ox-Bow Incident,* (1943).

Red Seal. RCA label used only once on an Elvis record, the 1958 album "Elvis' Golden Records" (RCA RB-16069), in England.

Redwing, Rodd. Chickasaw Indian stuntman who played Lige, an Indian brave, in the 1969 movie *Charro!*. Rodd Redwing taught Clayton Moore (who portrayed the Lone Ranger on TV) to handle a gun expertly. He also taught Gail Davis† (TV's Annie Oakley).

Red, Hot, and Blue was also a 1936 movie, in which Bob Hope and Ethel Merman introduced the Cole Porter song, "It's De-Lovely."
†Gail Davis was such a sharpshooter that she would occasionally perform trick shots with Wild West shows.

Reed, Jerry. Atlanta, Georgia-born (March 20, 1937) guitarist, singer, composer, session musician, and actor. He wrote two Elvis hit records, "Guitar Man" (1967) and "U.S. Male" (1968), in which he played lead guitar. Jerry Reed also composed the songs "A Thing Called Love" and "Talk About the Good Times," which Elvis also recorded. In 1967 Jerry Reed recorded "Tupelo Mississippi Flash," an Elvis novelty record. He has appeared in four movies with Burt Reynolds: *W. W. and the Dixie Dance Kings* (1975); *Gator* (1976); *Smokey and the Bandit* (1977); *Smokey and the Bandit II* (1980).

Reed, Jimmy. Blues singer who began recording for Chicago's Vee Jay Records in December 1953. Jimmy Reed's first major hit was "You Don't Have to Go" (Vee Jay 119) in 1955.

Elvis recorded three songs that Jimmy Reed had previously recorded: "Ain't That Loving You, Baby"; "Baby, What You Want Me to Do"; "Big Boss Man."

Reeves, Glen. Singer-disc jockey who in 1956 recorded the demo record of "Heartbreak Hotel" for Elvis.

Reeves, Jim. Country music star of the 1950s and '60s. Jim Reeves and Tex Ritter* both hail from Panola County, Texas. "Gentleman" Jim Reeves played minor-league baseball for the St. Louis Cardinals' farm team in Lynchburg, Virginia, until a leg injury ended his career. (Roy Acuff and Charlie Pride also played minor-league baseball). In the early 1950s he was a staff announcer for radio station KWKH in Shreveport, Louisiana.

Jim Reeves had many top ten hits, ranking #3 behind Eddy Arnold and Webb Pierce for the most top ten records. Even after his death in a plane crash on July 31, 1964, Mary Reeves, Jim's widow, continued to release his recordings.

Jim Reeves was elected to the Country Music Hall of Fame in 1967.

Elvis recorded three Jim Reeves hits: "I Love You Because"; "He'll Have to Go"; "Welcome to My World."

Reflections. An Elvis newsletter that began in April 1979, by Charlie Hodge and Dick Grob.

Regal High School. New Orleans high school that Danny Fisher (Elvis) attended in the 1958 movie *King Creole*.

Regal Pharmacy. Drugstore where Danny Fisher's (Elvis) father obtained employment in the 1958 movie *King Creole*.

Reid, Don S. Member of the famed country singing group the Statler Brothers.† Though primarily a country group, the Statler Brothers reached #4 on the Pop charts in early 1966 with

---

*Tex Ritter is the father of actor John Ritter ("Three's Company" TV series) and is the only person elected to both the Cowboy Hall of Fame and the Country Music Hall of Fame.

†The Statler Brothers were discovered by Johnny Cash. Group members include: Don Reid, Harold Reid (Don's older brother), Lew DeWitt, and Phil Balsley.

"Flowers on the Wall." In 1973 Don Reid composed "Susan When She Tried," which Elvis recorded in 1975.

Relax. Song that Elvis sang in the 1963 movie *It Happened at the World's Fair*. The Jordanaires sang back-up for Elvis. "Relax" was written by Sid Tepper and Roy C. Bennett and appeared in the Long Playing albums "It Happened at the World's Fair" (RCA LPM/LSP-2697) and "Mahalo from Elvis" (Pickwick ACL-7064).

Release Me (And Let Me Love Again). Song written by Eddie Miller and W. S. Stevenson (Dub Williams) and originally recorded by Jimmy Heap in 1954. Little Esther Phillips had a million-seller with "Release Me (And Let Me Love Again)" in 1962 (Lenox 5555), as did Englebert Humperdinck in 1967. "Release Me (And Let Me Love Again)" is the world's most-performed country music song (collective sales by all artists have been over 12 million copies). In 1967 the Music Operators of America called it the most popular song of the year in juke box play.

Elvis recorded "Release Me (And Let Me Love Again)" in 1970 and it appeared in the Long Playing albums "On Stage—February, 1970" (RCA LSP-4362) and "Welcome to My World" (RCA APL1-2274).

Reno Brothers, The. Original title of the 1956 movie *Love Me Tender*. The name was changed to capitalize on Elvis's singing popularity. Ken Darby was asked to compose four songs for the soundtrack—"Love Me Tender" was one of them. *The Reno Brothers* was a novel by Maurice Geraghty.

Report to the Nation, Pt. 1/Pt. 2. An Elvis novelty record by Winkly and Nutly, in which "Fame and Fortune," "(Let's Have A) Party," and "We Want Elvis" are heard. It was released on the MK label (MK 101) in 1960.

Requiem for Elvis. A 1977 Elvis tribute record by Jackie Kahane on Raintree Records (Raintree 2206).

Return of the All American Boy. Novelty Elvis answer record by Billy Adams on Nau-Voo Records (Nau-Voo 45-805).

Return to Sender. RCA 47-8100. Released in October 1962 as a 45 rpm single. It reached #2 on *Billboard*'s Hot 100 chart, #5 on the Rhythm and Blues chart, and #1 in the United Kingdom (for three weeks, December 15, 1962–January 6, 1963). "Return to Sender" sold over a million copies. "Where Do You Come From" was on the flip side. Elvis sang "Return to Sender" in the 1962 movie *Girls! Girls! Girls!;* however, the record was released prior to the film—the opposite of the way it was usually done. "Return to Sender" was written by Otis Blackwell and Winfield Scott and appeared in the following Long Playing albums: "Girls! Girls! Girls!" (RCA LPM/LSP-2621); "Elvis: Worldwide 50 Gold Award Hits, Volume 1" (RCA LPM-6401); "Elvis" (RCA DPL2-0056 [e]).

Return to Sender. RCA 447-0683. Gold Standard Series re-issue of RCA 47-8100.

Reynolds, Burt. Highly paid Hollywood actor who attended Elvis's private funeral. Burt Reynolds's father was once the chief of police in Riviera Beach, Florida. Burt played football at Florida State and was drafted by the Baltimore Colts but turned down the offer. Burt Reynolds was the first man to pose nude for the centerfold of *Cosmopolitan* magazine (April 1972).

Rhee, Kang. Owner of the Kang Rhee Institute of Self Defense, Inc., in Memphis (1911 Poplar Ave.). Kang Rhee was a good friend of Elvis and one of Elvis's martial arts instructors. He specialized in Tae Kwon Do karate, which emphasizes the feet.

Rhoades, Calvin. U. S. Army M/Sgt. who gave Private Elvis his Asiatic Flu shot (March 26, 1958).

Rhythm and Blues Charts. The first white artists to make the top ten of the R & B charts were: January 1952: Johnnie Ray, "Cry." July 1955: Bill Haley and His Comets, "Rock Around the Clock." March 1956: Carl Perkins, "Blue Suede Shoes." April 1956: Elvis Presley, "Heartbreak Hotel." August 1956: Buchanan and Goodman, "Flying Saucer." September 1956; Elvis Presley, "Hound Dog"/"Don't Be Cruel."

R.I.A.A. Recording Industry Association of America. The R.I.A.A. audits record companies and certifies record sales, presenting a Gold Disc award for million-sellers. Perry Como* received the first R.I.A.A. Gold Disc award for "Catch a Falling Star" on March 14, 1958. Elvis's first Gold Disc award was for "Hard Headed Woman" on August 11, 1958.

Rich, Charlie. Country singer, nicknamed the "Silver Fox," who recorded from the mid-1950s until the early '70s before achieving national popularity. While in the U.S. Air Force he formed a group called the Velvetones. Charlie Rich recorded for Sam Phillips's Phillips International Records label. Phillips thought that Charlie Rich came the closer to copying Elvis than any other Sun artist. Rich composed songs for Johnny Cash, Jerry Lee Lewis, and Elvis. It is Charlie Rich's voice heard on the Jerry Lee Lewis "Am I to Be the One" release. Charlie Rich last saw Elvis alive in the elevator of the Liberty Bowl Memorial Stadium prior to a football game in 1976. Charlie Rich composed "I'm Coming Home," which Elvis recorded in 1961.

Rich, John. Director of the 1964 movie *Roustabout* and the 1966 movie *Easy Come, Easy Go*.

Richardson, Jane. Home-service adviser for the Memphis Housing

---

*Perry Como, like Elvis, had a street named after him—Perry Como Avenue (formerly Third Avenue) in his hometown, Cannonsburg, Pennsylvania. Como was the first vocalist to have two releases each reaching 2 million in sales at the same time ("Till the End of Time" and "If I Loved You," both in 1946).

Authority in the 1940s and '50s. Mrs. Richardson visited the Presleys in early 1949 to determine whether they qualified for financial assistance. The Presleys were qualified and, on September 20, moved into an apartment at the Lauderdale Courts, 185 Winchester Street. (See: 185 Winchester Street)

Richmond, Ted. Producer of the 1963 movie *It Happened at the World's Fair*.

Riding the Rainbow. Song that Elvis sang in the 1962 movie *Kid Galahad*. "Riding the Rainbow" was written by Fred Wise and Ben Weisman and appeared in the Extended Play album "Kid Galahad" and the Long Playing albums "I Got Lucky" (RCA Camden CAL-2533) and "I Got Lucky" (Pickwick CAS-2533).

Righteous Brothers, The. Singing duo composed of Bill Medley and Bobby Hatfield. The Righteous Brothers were originally called the Paramours, but Ray Maxwell of Moonglow Records had them change their name because black fans called their music "righteous." Their sound was so black-oriented that rhythm and blues radio stations played their songs. The Righteous Brothers helped to create the sound known as "blue-eyed soul."

In late 1964, the Righteous Brothers' biggest hit, "You've Lost That Lovin' Feelin'," was released. It reached #1 on the charts and easily sold over a million copies. Elvis recorded "You've Lost That Lovin' Feelin' " in 1970 and '72.

Right This Way Folks. Title originally considered for the 1964 movie *Roustabout*.

Rio Seco, Texas. Fictitious U.S.–Mexico border town in which the 1969 movie *Charro!* was set.

Rip It Up. Song written by Robert Blackwell and John Marascalco and originally recorded by Little Richard in 1956 (Specialty 579). Little Richard's version of "Rip It Up" sold over a million copies. Elvis recorded "Rip It Up" on September 3, 1956, and it appeared in the Extended Play album "Elvis, Volume 1" (RCA EPA-992) and the following Long Playing albums: "Elvis" (RCA LPM-1382); "Elvis" (RCA LSP-1382 [e]); "Elvis: The Other Sides—Worldwide Gold Award Hits, Volume 2" (RCA LPM-6402).

Rising Sun. Palomino horse, bought for $3,500, that was one of Elvis's favorites. Rising Sun's stable was called the "House of Rising Sun"—a play on words from the 1964 hit song by the Animals (which was based on a traditional black folk song often sung by Josh White).

Ritchie, Martin. Fourteen-year-old Chicago youth who died of electrocution in an attempt to hang an effigy of Elvis in 1956.

Rittenband, Laurence J. Santa Monica, California, judge who granted Elvis and Priscilla their divorce on October 11, 1973.

Ritter's Park Hotel. Plush hotel in Bad Homburg, West Germany, where Elvis, his father, and his grandmother stayed while looking for a house to rent (October 1958).

Rival, The. Song that Ann-Margret sang in the 1964 movie *Viva Las Vegas.* "The Rival" has never been released on record.

Rivera, Geraldo. Investigative reporter for the ABC-TV series "20/20" hosted by Hugh Downs. On the September 13, 1979, episode, titled "The Elvis Cover-up," Geraldo Rivera revealed a convincing case for a cover-up of Elvis's death. The report revealed Elvis's drug usage before his death and the amount of prescriptions authorized by Dr. George Nichopoulos. On June 9, 1971, Geraldo Rivera MC'd Elvis's press conference at the Las Vegas Hilton Hotel. Geraldo Rivera is the former son-in-law of author Kurt Vonnegut, Jr.

Robards, Jason. Actor and father of Academy Award-winning actor Jason Robards, Jr. In the 1961 movie *Wild in the Country* Jason Robards, Sr., (1893–1963) played Judge Parker —his last movie role. On radio he portrayed the title role on "Chandu the Magician."

Robbins, Marty. Country music singer and songwriter. Marty Robbins made his "Grand Ole Opry" debut on January 7, 1953. He races stock cars as a hobby and raced in the Daytona 500 in 1972.

Marty Robbins toured with Elvis in early 1955. He recorded "That's All Right (Mama)" (Columbia 21351) on December 7, 1954—the first person to "cover" an Elvis recording. Marty Robbins's 1959 hit (#1 and a million-seller), "El Paso," was the first record over four minutes in length to reach #1.

In 1973 Elvis recorded a Marty Robbins composition, "You Gave Me a Mountain," which was a tremendous hit for Frankie Laine in 1969.

Robertson, Dale. Hollywood actor with whom Elvis helped to promote Easter Seals. Dale Robertson was seen as a member of the audience in the 1970 documentary *Elvis—That's the Way It Is.*

Dale Robertson is known primarily for his western movie roles and starred in two TV westerns: "Tales of Wells Fargo" (1957–62) and "The Iron Horse" (1966–68).

Robertson, Don. Singer and musician who was born in Peking, China, in 1922. Don Robertson's father was the head of the Department of Medicine at Peking's Union Medical College.

In 1956 Don Robertson had a #9 hit and million-seller with his own composition, "The Happy Whistler" (Capitol 3391). On that recording, he also did the whistling.* Floyd Cramer's slip-note style of piano playing was learned from Robertson.

Don Robertson is a prolific writer of songs. He composed

---

*Don Robertson also whistled the theme of the TV series "The Andy Griffith Show."

Lorne Greene's 1960 hit "Ringo" (#1 and a million seller). Other songs include: "I Really Don't Want to Know"; "Please Help Me, I'm Falling"; I Love You More and More Everyday." Don Robertson composed twelve songs for Elvis, including: "Anything That's Part of You"; "They Remind Me Too Much of You"; "I'm Yours."

Robey, Don. Founder of Peacock Records of Houston in 1949, and discoverer of Johnny Ace. In July 1952 Peacock obtained the Duke label. Don Robey (with Ferdinand Washington) composed "Pledging My Love," which both Johnny Ace (1954) and Elvis (1976) recorded.

Robinson, Red. Canadian disc jockey who interviewed Elvis in Vancouver, British Columbia, on August 31, 1957, at the Empire Stadium. Red Robinson claims to have been the first Canadian disc jockey to play Elvis records over the air.

Red Robinson is the narrator of the Long Playing album "Elvis—A Canadian Tribute," for which Robinson received a double Platinum Award (over 100,000 units sold in Canada). In 1977 he released the album "The Elvis Tapes." (See: Elvis—A Canadian Tribute; Elvis Tapes, The)

Rock & Role Heaven, Pt. 1/Rock & Roll Heaven, Pt. 2. An Elvis novelty record by the Flares on which Elvis's name and "All Shook Up" are mentioned. It was released by Press Records (Press 2800) in 1962.

Rock & Roll King. A 1977 Elvis tribute recorded by Carl Jones on C.J. Records (CJ 675).

Rockabilly Party. An Elvis novelty record by Hugo and Luigi in which Elvis's name and "All Shook Up" are mentioned in the lyrics: released by Roulette Records (Roulette 4012) in 1957.

Rock-a-Hula Baby. RCA 47-7968. Released in November 1961 as a 45 rpm single. It reached #23 on *Billboard*'s Hot 100 chart and #1 in the United Kingdom (for four weeks, February 24–March 24, 1962). "Rock-a-Hula Baby" sold over a million copies. Elvis sang it in the 1961 movie *Blue Hawaii.* "Rock-a-Hula Baby" was written by Fred Wise, Ben Weisman, and Dolores Fuller and appeared in the following Long Playing albums: "Blue Hawaii" (RCA LPM/LSP-2426); "Elvis: World-wide 50 Gold Award Hits, Volume 1" (RCA LPM-6401); "Elvis in Hollywood" (RCA DLP2-0168).

Rock-a-Hula Baby. RCA 447-0635. Gold Standard Series re-issue of RCA 47-7968.

Rock Around the Clock. A 1955 hit record by Bill Haley and His Comets (Decca 29124). It was the theme of the 1955 movie *The Blackboard Jungle,* starring Glenn Ford (the movie was banned in Great Britain for eleven years). "Rock Around the Clock" is the biggest-selling rock 'n' roll record of all time (over 25 million copies sold) and was the first record to sell a million copies in Great Britain. The song was the original theme of the TV series "Happy Days" and the first song played in the 1973 movie *American Graffiti*. "Rock Around the Clock" was also heard in the 1978 movie *Superman*. Elvis sang part of "Rock Around the Clock" at one of his early concerts in Kingsport, Tennessee (September 22, 1955).

Rockefeller, Winthrop. Former Arkansas governor and brother of Nelson A. Rockefeller, who bought Elvis's prize cattle when Elvis sold the Circle G Ranch in 1969.

Rock Era (A Tribute to the King), Pt. 1, The/The Rock Era (A Tribute to the King), Pt. 2. An Elvis tribute record by the Phantom of Rock, released on Patti Records (Patti 10000) in 1973. The record chronologized Elvis's career.

Rockin' at the Drive-In. A 1958 Elvis novelty record by the Beavers, which made reference to Elvis (Capitol 3956).

Rockin' Little Sally. Song that Elvis is reported to have recorded, although it has never been released in any form.

Rockin' with Elvis New Year's Eve. A 33⅓ rpm bootleg double LP released on the Spirit of America label in 1977. This album (Spirit of America HNY 7677) included Elvis's entire concert appearance in Pittsburgh on New Year's Eve, December 31, 1976. The inside sleeve of the album had advertisements for six other bootleg albums. Songs included—Side 1: "Also Sprach Zarathustra," "See See Rider," "I Got a Woman," "Amen," "Big Boss Man," "Love Me," "Fairytale." Side 2: "You Gave Me a Mountain," "Jailhouse Rock," Presentation of Liberty Bell by Jim Curtin, "It's Now or Never" (with Introduction by Sherril Nielson), "My Way," "Funny How Time Slips Away," "Auld Lang Syne," Introduction of Vernon and Lisa Presley, "Blue Suede Shoes," "Trying to Get to You." Side 3: "Polk Salad Annie," Introductions to Band, "Early Morning Rain," "What'd I Say," "Johnny B. Goode," Ronnie Tutt drum solo, Jerry Scheff solo, Sonny Brown piano solo, "Love Letters," "Hail, Hail, Rock 'n' Roll," "Fever," "Hurt." Side 4: "Hound Dog," "Are You Lonesome Tonight," "Reconsider Baby," "Little Sister," "Unchained Melody," "Rags to Riches," "Can't Help Falling in Love."

Rock My Soul. A 33⅓ rpm bootleg LP released in 1975 on the Teddy Bear label (Teddy Bear Imp 1108). Songs included were from the *Elvis on Tour* soundtrack.

Rock 'n' Roll ABC's. An Elvis novelty record by Freddy Cannon,* in which Elvis's name is mentioned. It was released by MCA Records (MCA 40269).

Rock 'n' Roll Tragedy. An Elvis novelty record by the Chestnuts, in which "All Shook Up" was heard. "Rock 'n' Roll Tragedy"/"I'm So Blue" was released on the Nightrain label (Nightrain 906).

---

*Freddy Cannon (real name: Frederick Anthony Picariello) once met Elvis in 1959, Elvis complementing him on his latest record, "Talahassee Lassie" (Swan 4031), which Elvis had bought.

Rock of Ages. Gospel standard sung at Gladys Presley's funeral, on August 16, 1958, by the Blackwood Brothers. "Precious Memories" was also sung.

Rock On and On and On. A 1977 Elvis tribute record by Doug Koempel on Chart Action Records.

Rodeo. Original title of the 1965 movie *Tickle Me* when it was planned in 1958.

Rodgers, Jimmie. The "Father of Country Music," who died of tuberculosis on May 26, 1933, at the age of thirty-six. Jimmie Rodgers's first recording was "The Soldier's Sweetheart," on August 4, 1927.* Nicknamed the "Singing Brakeman" because he once worked for the Mobile and Ohio Railroad, James Charles Rodgers was the first person to be elected to the Country Music Hall of Fame (November 3, 1961).

On May 26, 1955, Elvis performed in a concert at the Jimmie Rodgers Memorial Day Celebration in Meridian, Mississippi.

Rol-Tan. Brand of blunt-tip cigars smoked by Elvis.

Rolls-Royce. Elvis purchased his first Rolls-Royce on March 18, 1961.

Romanelli, Carl. Sculptor of the 6-foot, 400-pound bronze statue of Elvis placed in the lobby of the Las Vegas Hilton Hotel. The statue was dedicated by Priscilla Presley on September 8, 1978.

Rondstadt, Linda. Female singer of superstar dimensions, Linda Ronstadt began as the lead singer for the Stone Poneys in 1964 (the group's biggest hit, "Different Drummer," was co-composed by Mike Nesmith), quitting to become a solo artist. Originally, several members who later became the Eagles were in her back-up group. In 1978 soulful Ms. Ronstadt cut a version of "Love Me Tender" that began getting a lot of air play and even more when a Baltimore disc jockey spliced her version with that of Elvis (both versions were sung at the same tempo). (See: Love Me Tender)

Rookies, The. ABC television series (1972–76) starring George Stanford Brown,† Sam Melville, Michael Ontkean, Kate Jackson,‡ and Gerald S. O'Laughlin. Linda Thompson made her TV debut on an episode of "The Rookies" titled 'Shadow of a Man." (See: Thompson, Linda)

Rooks, Nancy. Black cook and maid at Graceland for eleven years. Elvis once gave her a 1974 Pontiac Ventura—the first new car she ever owned.

Roosevelt Hotel. New Orleans hotel, one-half block from the French Quarter, where Elvis stayed in 1958 while shooting on

---

*On the same day that Rodgers auditioned for Ralph Peer of Victor Records in Bristol, Virginia, on August 1, 1927, A. P. Carter and Maybelle Carter were also present to audition, an incredible coincidence.
†Son-in-law of TV actor James Daly.
‡Daughter-in-law of actress Stella Stevens.

location for the movie *King Creole*. Elvis reserved the entire tenth floor.

Rooster. Symbol of Sun Records. The rooster appeared on the labels of the 78 rpm records—but not the 45 rpm records. Sun discontinued 78 rpm records in 1958, as did most other companies.

Rose, Fred. Evansville, Indiana, born (1897–1954) pianist who founded the Acuff-Rose Music Publishing Company in 1942. He played piano in Hank Williams's early recordings. In 1961 Rose was elected to the Country Music Hall of Fame. His son Wesley is a music publisher today. Fred Rose composed (with Zeb Turner) "It's a Sin," which Elvis recorded in 1961.

Ross Carpenter. Elvis's role as a nightclub singer in the 1962 movie *Girls! Girls! Girls!*

R.O.T.C. Reserve Officers' Training Corps, formed on October 21, 1916. Elvis belonged to R.O.T.C. while a sophomore at Humes High School. In later years Elvis bought new uniforms for the R.O.T.C. drill team.

ROUSTABOUT. Paramount, 1964. Premiered New York City November 12, 1964 (101 min). Elvis's sixteenth movie. Producer, Hal B. Wallis. Associate Producer, Paul Nathan. Director, John Rich. Cast: Charlie Rogers/Elvis Presley, Maggie Morgan/Barbara Stanwyck, Cathy Lean/Joan Freeman, Joe Lean/Leif Erickson, Mme. Mijanou/Sue Ane Langdon, Harry Carver/Pat Buttram, Marge/Joan Staley, Arthur Nielsen/Dabbs Greer, Fred/Steve Brodie, Sam/Norman Grabowski, Lou/Jack Albertson, Hazel/Jane Dulo, Cody Marsh/Joel Fluellen, Gus/Arthur Levy, Dick/Toby Reed, Ernie/Ray Kellogg, Viola/Marianna Hill, Cora/Beverly Adams, B.J./Lester Miller, Little Egypt/Wilda Taylor, Bill the Midget/Billy Barty, College Student/Raquel Welch, The Jordanaires/The Jordanaires Screenplay, Allan Weiss and Anthony Lawrence. Photography, Lucien Ballard. Music, Joseph J. Lilley. Choreography, Earl Barton. Art Direction, Hal Pereira and Walter Tyler. Set Decoration, Sam Comer and Robert Benton. Special Effects, Paul K. Lerpae. Costumes, Edith Head. Technical Adviser, Col. Tom Parker. Assistant Director, Michael Moore. Editor, Warren Low. Songs sung by Elvis: "Roustabout," "Carney Town," "Poison Ivy League," "One Track Heart," "Wheels on My Heels," "Hard Knocks," "It's a Wonderful World," "Little Egypt," "It's Carnival Time," "Big Love, Big Heartache," "There's a Brand New Day on the Horizon." "Roustabout" was backed by the Mello Men although credited to the Jordanaires. Movie debut of Raquel Welch.

Roustabout. Title song of the 1964 movie *Roustabout*. Even though the Jordanaires are credited with singing back-up, it was actually the Mello Men who did the singing. They gave up their copyright claim and were paid by the hour for their services. The film version of "Roustabout" has additional instrumentation. "Roustabout" was written by Bill Giant, Bernie Baum, and Florence Kaye and appeared in the Long Playing albums "Roustabout" (RCA LPM/LSP-2999) and "Elvis in Hollywood" (RCA DPL2-0168).

Roustabout. RCA SP-45-139. Special 45 rpm promotional release. "One Track Heart" was on the flip side.

Roustabout. RCA LPM/LSP-2999. A 33⅓ rpm Long Playing album released in October 1964. It reached #1 on *Billboard*'s Hot LP chart (for one week, January 2–9, 1965). "Roustabout" received a Gold Record for sales totaling over $1 million. It featured songs from the 1964 movie *Roustabout*. Songs included—Side 1: "Roustabout," "Little Egypt," "Poison Ivy League," "Hard Knocks," "It's a Wonderful World," "Big Love, Big Heartache." Side 2: "One Track Heart," "It's Carnival Time," "Carny Town," "There's a Brand New Day on the Horizon," "Wheels on My Heels."

Rowan, Elwyn "Rip." U.S. Army captain and Memphis recruiter in the late 1950s. Capt. Rowan recruited Elvis in 1958.

Rowland, Dave. A member of the Stamps Quartet in 1973. Dave Rowland left to form the successful country music trio Dave and Sugar.*

Royal Records. Record company that bought the master of Vince Everett's (Elvis) first record from Geneva Records in the 1957 movie *Jailhouse Rock*. (See: Laurel Records)

Rubberneckin'. RCA 47-9768. Released in November 1969 as a 45 rpm single. It reached #6 on *Billboard*'s Hot 100 chart. "Don't Cry, Daddy" was on the flip side. "Don't Cry, Daddy"/ "Rubberneckin' " sold over a million copies and received a Gold Disc award from the R.I.A.A. "Rubberneckin' " was sung in the 1969 movie *Change of Habit*. It was written by Dory Jones and Bunny Warren and appeared in the following Long Playing albums: "Almost in Love" (RCA Camden CAS-2440); "Almost in Love" (Pickwick CAS-2440); "Double Dynamite" (Pickwick DL2-5001).

Rubberneckin'. RCA 447-0674. Gold Standard Series re-issue of RCA 47-9768.

Runaway. A million-seller and #1 record (for four weeks, April 24–May 22, 1961) for Del Shannon (Big Top 3067). "Runaway" was written by Del Shannon (real name: Charles Westover) and Max T. Crook. Elvis recorded "Runaway" in 1969 and it appeared in the Long Playing album "On Stage—February, 1970" (RCA LSP-4362).

Running Scared. Song written by Joe Melson and Roy Orbison back in 1952 and finally recorded by Roy Orbison in 1961, reaching #1 (Monument 438). Elvis recorded this song and

---

*Sugar is made up of Vicki Hackman Baker and Sue Powell. Dave and Sugar's first record, "Queen of the Silver Dollar," became a huge hit. Their second record, "The Door Is Always Open," went to #1.

"Cryin' in December" in 1976. Elvis was dissatisfied with the songs, and they were never released.

Running Wild. A 1956 Hal Wallis film starring Mamie Van Doren, William Campbell, and Keenan Wynn. On "The Ed Sullivan Show" of January 6, 1957, Sullivan incorrectly stated that, on his return to Hollywood, Elvis was going to start filming *Running Wild*. (Actually, the movie Elvis was to begin filming was *Loving You*.)

Run On. Traditional gospel song arranged and recorded by Elvis on May 25, 1966—the first Elvis recording session produced by Felton Jarvis. "Run On" was the first song recorded during the session. "Run On" appeared in the Long Playing album "How Great Thou Art" (RCA LPM/LSP–3758).

Rusk, Johnny. An Elvis impersonator since 1972. Johnny Rusk began in Seattle, Washington, nightclubs.

Russell, Bing. Veteran film actor and father of actor Kurt Russell. Bing Russell had a continuing role as Deputy Clem Poster on the TV western series "Bonanza." He portrayed Vernon Presley in the 1979 TV movie *Elvis*. Since Kurt Russell portrayed Elvis in the movie, father and son portrayed father and son. (See: Russell, Kurt)

Russell, Kurt. Actor who made his film debut in the 1963 movie *It Happened at the World's Fair* (he played a small boy who kicked Elvis in the leg).

Kurt Russell has appeared in three TV series: "The Travels of Jaimie McPheeters" (Charles Bronson, as Linc Murdock, and the four eldest Osmond Brothers, as the Kissel children, also appeared in the series); "The New Land"; "The Quest."

In 1978 Kurt Russell, who had been known previously for his work in Walt Disney films, was chosen from over 700 actors to portray Elvis in the TV movie *Elvis*. On March 17, 1979, Russell married his costar, Season Hubley.

Russell, Leon. Musician who played piano for the soundtrack recordings of many Elvis movies. Leon Russell was previously a member of the rock group the Hawks* (which evolved into the Band). He has backed Jerry Lee Lewis, been a studio musician for Phil Spector, played with the Rolling Stones, and produced recordings for Bob Dylan. Leon Russell played piano for both George Harrison and Bob Dylan at the famed "Concert for Bangladesh," August 1, 1971. David Gates and Russell both attended the same high school in Tulsa, Oklahoma, playing in the school band.

Russell, Nipsey. Comedian who opened Elvis's concerts in Lake Tahoe, Nevada, from July 20 to August 2, 1971. Nipsey Russell is well known for his amusing poems and his many appearances on TV game shows.

---

*The Hawks backed singer Ronnie Hawkins, whose biggest hit record was "Mary Lou" (Roulette 4177) in 1959.

Russwood Park. Memphis park where Elvis performed a benefit concert on July 4, 1956. Elvis and his band were backed by the Bobby Morris Orchestra.

Rusty Wells. Elvis's role as a musician in the 1965 movie *Girl Happy*.

Ryan, Shiela. Twenty-two-year-old *Playboy* playmate whom Elvis dated in 1975. Shiela Ryan married actor James Caan in January 1976. She graced the cover of the October 1973 issue of *Playboy* magazine.*

Ryman Auditorium. Nashville, Tennessee, building from which WSM radio broadcast the "Grand Ole Opry" (1942–74). Ryman Auditorium was named for riverboat captain Thomas Ryman and originally served as a tabernacle. The TV series "The Johnny Cash Show" was broadcast from the auditorium between 1969 and 1971.

Elvis once performed at the Ryman Auditorium. (See: Grand Ole Opry)

S

6. Number of tiers on Elvis and Priscilla's five-foot-high wedding cake.

6 Feet. Elvis's height. In the 1965 movie *Harum Scarum,* Johnny Tyronne's (Elvis) height was given as six-foot-two.

7. Number on Lucky Jackson's (Elvis) racing car in the 1964 movie *Viva Las Vegas.*

16. Number of coaches in Elvis's 1955 song "Mystery Train." Ironically, there were sixteen limousines in Elvis's funeral caravan.

17. Number of portraits of Elvis hanging throughout Graceland at the time of his death.

$63.80. Monthly government disability check received by Toby Kwimper (Elvis Presley) for hurting his back during an Army judo lesson at Fort Dix in the 1962 movie *Follow That Dream.*

66. Number of cards included in the Elvis Presley Bubble Gum Card collection. © Boxcar Enterprises, Inc., 1978. Licensed by Factors Etc., Inc., Bear, Delaware (See: Factors Etc.).

'68 Comeback, The. A 33⅓ bootleg album on the Memphis King label that featured material from Elvis's "comeback" appearance on the 1968 NBC-TV special "Elvis" (December 3). Songs included—Side 1: "Nothingville," "Guitar Man," "Let

---

*Marilyn Monroe graced the cover of the first edition of *Playboy* (December 1953).

317

Yourself Go," "Guitar Man," "Big Boss Man," "If I Can Dream," "Memories," "Let Yourself Go." Side 2: "It Hurts Me," "Trouble," "Guitar Man," "Sometimes I Feel Like a Motherless Child," "Where Could I Go But to the Lord," "Saved," "A Little Less Conversation."

75. Number of G.I.s, including Sgt. Elvis Presley, that were transported home from Frankfurt, West Germany (Rhein Main A.F.B.), to McGuire A.F.B. in New Jersey (March 3, 1960).

$78. Elvis's monthly salary as a private upon first entering the Army in 1958. It was down from $400,000 a month as a civilian.

706 Union Street. Memphis address of Sun Records and the Memphis Recording Service, both of which were owned and operated by Sam Phillips. The telephone number was JAckson 7-7197. Brad Suggs, on Phillips International Records, recorded a song titled "706 Union" (Phillips 3545).

6239. Vince Everett's (Elvis) prisoner number in the 1957 movie *Jailhouse Rock* (later in the movie when he performed the "Jailhouse Rock" sequence, his number was 6240).

Sad Sack. A 1957 movie starring Jerry Lewis, based on the George Baker comic-strip character. The movie was being shown at the Grand Theater in Amarillo, Texas, on the same bill as Tex Warner's Rough Ridin' Ramblers and Deke Rivers (Elvis) in the 1957 movie *Loving You.*

Sagal, Boris. Director of the 1965 movie *Girl Happy.*

Sahara Tahoe. Lake Tahoe hotel in Stateline, Nevada, where Elvis appeared on five occasions: August 2, 1971; May 4–20, 1973; May 16–26, 1974; October 11–14, 1974; April 30–May 9, 1976.

Salem, Marc. Philadelphia man who, on August 12, 1977, predicted Elvis's death. He placed his written prediction inside an aspirin box that was baked into a pretzel. This was done under the guidance of Arlen Spector, former Philadelphia district attorney. He not only predicted Elvis's death but gave the headlines: *Daily News*: "The King Is Dead"; *National Enquirer*: "The King Dies at 42"; *Bulletin*: "Elvis Dies"; All headlines were as he predicted.

Salk Vaccine. Vaccine against polio, developed by Jonas Salk in 1954. In 1968 Elvis posed for photographs as he was being given a Salk Vaccine shot in front of his daughter, Lisa Marie.

Salute. A 1960 Elvis novelty record by Jimmy Tennant on Warwick Records (Warwick 533).

Sand Castles. Song that Elvis recorded for the 1966 movie *Paradise—Hawaiian Style*, but it was cut from the final print of the film. "Sand Castles" was written by Herb Goldberg and David Hess and appeared in the Long Playing album "Paradise —Hawaiian Style" (RCA LPM/LSP-3643).

Sanders, Bud. Elvis impersonator from El Paso, Texas.

318

Sanders, Denis. Director of the 1970 documentary *Elvis: That's the Way It is.*

Sands, Tommy Adrian. Singer, actor, and one-time husband of Nancy Sinatra (1960–65). He was discovered by Col. Tom Parker, who was his manager from when he was twelve until he was sixteen years old. Sands was one of the people who informed the colonel about Elvis, as he had toured with Elvis in Texas and appeared on the bill with him on the "Louisiana Hayride." Paula Prentiss and Tommy Sands were classmates at Lamar High School in Houston, Texas. Sands played an Elvis-like character in the TV play "The Singing Idol" and in the 1958 movie *Sing, Boy, Sing.* (See: Singing Idol, The; Sing, Boy, Sing; Chenault's)

Sands of the Desert. Johnny Tyronne (Elvis) movie that premiered in the Near East country of Babelstan in the 1965 movie *Harum Scarum.*

Santa, Bring My Baby Back (To Me). Christmas song written by Aaron Schroeder and Claude DeMetrius and recorded by Elvis in 1957. "Santa, Bring My Baby Back (To Me)" appeared in the Extended Play album "Elvis Sings Christmas Songs" (RCA EPA-4108) and the following Long Playing albums: "Elvis' Christmas Album" (RCA LOC-1035); (RCA LPM-1951); (RCA LPM-1951 [e]); RCA Camden CAL-2428); (Pickwick CAS-2428).

Santa Claus Is Back in Town. RCA 447-0647. Released in November 1965 as a 45 rpm Gold Standard Series original. "Blue Christmas" was on the flip side. In December 1977 this record was re-issued. Written by Jerry Leiber and Mike Stoller, "Santa Claus Is Back in Town" appeared in the Extended Play album "Elvis Sings Christmas Songs" (RCA EPA-4108) and the following Long Playing albums: "Elvis' Christmas Album" (RCA LOC-1035); (RCA LPM-1951); (RCA LPM-1951 [e]); (RCA Camden CAL-2428); (Pickwick CAS-2428).

Santa Fe Road Race. Sports car race won by Mike McCoy (Elvis) in the 1966 movie *Spinout.*

Santa Lucia. Song that Elvis sang in the 1964 movie *Viva Las Vegas.* In the movie version, Ann-Margret hums along with Elvis at the beginning of "Santa Lucia" and then talks with Cesare Danova during the rest of the song. "Santa Lucia" is an old standard that Elvis rearranged to suit his style. It appeared in the following Long Playing albums: "Elvis for Everyone" (RCA LP/LSP-3450); "Burning Love and Hits from His Movies, Volume 2" (RCA Camden CAS-2595); "Burning Love and Hits from His Movies, Volume 2" (Pickwick CAS-2595).

Saperstein, Hank. Associate of Col. Tom Parker in 1956, who was the merchandising and exploitation manager for Elvis and Col. Parker, establishing Factors Etc., Inc., to merchandise Elvis memorabilia. He previously merchandized Wyatt Earp, Lone Ranger, and Lassie products.

Satellite Supplement, The. A 45 rpm bootleg single on the Shaker label. The record consisted of two songs from the studio session of the "Elvis: Aloha from Hawaii" TV special. The songs were "Blue Hawaii" and "Hawaiian Wedding Song."

Satellite Supplement, The. A 45 rpm bootleg single on the Shaker label. The record consisted of "Ku-u-i-po" (from the "Elvis: Aloha from Hawaii" TV special) and "Nostalgia Party" (a 1950s novelty song with Elvis and other artists).

Satisfied. One-minute-fifteen-second gospel song that Elvis, Scotty Moore, and Bill Black are believed to have taped just prior to the famous incident when Elvis began singing "That's All Right (Mama)" on July 5, 1954. "Satisfied" was composed and performed by gospel singer Martha Lou Carson on the "Grand Old Opry" in 1952. "Satisfied" is yet to be released by RCA Victor.

Saucedo, Rick. Talented Elvis impersonator who refers to himself as the "Prince of Rock and Roll." He played the lead in the Broadway play *The Living Legend*. Saucedo's lipcurl is one of the best among those of the Elvis impersonators.

Saved. Song written by Jerry Leiber and Mike Stoller and originally recorded by LaVern Baker (Atlantic 2099) in 1961. Elvis sang "Saved" in the 1968 NBC-TV special "Elvis" and it appeared in the Long Playing album "Elvis—TV Special" (RCA LPM-4088).

Save the Last Dance for me. Mystery song that suddenly appeared on radio in November 1978. Radio stations began playing the song and asking their audiences to listen to the other voice singing with Jerry Lee Lewis on the record. The voice was supposedly that of Elvis, who had recorded the session with Lewis when they were both recording for Sun Records. Further speculation was that Elvis's name couldn't be mentioned due to a conflict of ownership between Sun and RCA Victor Records. The truth of the matter is that "Save the Last Dance for Me" was actually composed by Doc Pomus and Mort Shuman for the Drifters in 1960, five years after Elvis had left Sun Records. The song was a spliced version of "Save the Last Dance for Me," which Jerry Lee Lewis recorded (in stereo) in 1963 (Sun 367). The voice on the recording was not that of Elvis but of Elvis sound-alike Jimmy Ellis (spliced in 1978). This phony recording is another product of the highly imaginative Shelby Singleton (See: Singleton, Shelby; Sun Records)

Scatter. Elvis's pet chimpanzee. It developed a penchant for straight scotch and bourbon and eventually died of cirrhosis of the liver. He was with Elvis both at Graceland and in Los Angeles.

Scheff, Jerry. Electric bass player who performed in Elvis's band in later years. Scheff was previously a member of the rock group the Doors.

Schilling, Jerry. Elvis's bodyguard and manager of the Sweet

Inspirations and later the Beach Boys. He married Myrna Smith, a member of the Inspirations.

Schroeder, Aaron. One-time manager of singer Gene Pitney, who co-composed a number of Elvis songs, such as—"Good Luck Charm" (with Wally Gold), "I Was the One" (with Claude DeMetrius, Hal Blair, Bill Pepper), "Anyway You Want Me" (with Cliff Owens), "I Got Stung" (with David Hill), "A Big Hunk o' Love" (with Sid Wyche), "Stuck on You" (with J. Leslie McFarland), "It's Now or Never" (with Wally Gold), "Santa Bring My Baby Back (To Me)" (with Claude DeMetrius), "Young and Beautiful" (with Abner Silver), "Shoppin' Around" (with Sid Tepper and Roy C. Bennett).

Schulten, Marjorie. Army Lt. Colonel who served as public information officer at Fort Hood, Texas, when Elvis arrived there in 1958.

Schwalb, Ben. Producer of the 1965 Allied Artists movie *Tickle Me*.

Scotch. Magnetic recording tape used by Sam Phillips to record the Elvis sessions at Sun Records.

Scott, Lizabeth. Female lead (as Glenda Markle) in the 1957 movie *Loving You*. Lizabeth Scott (born Emma Matzo,) was Humphrey Bogart's leading lady in the 1947 movie *Dead Reckoning*. Lizabeth Scott, Barbara Stanwyck, and Joan Blondell hold the distinction of being the only women to play leading roles with both Bogart and Presley.

Scott Heyward. Elvis's role as a millionaire's son who swapped places with a water-ski instructor in the 1967 movie *Clambake*.

Scout Jeep Driver. Duty Elvis held while stationed in Friedberg, West Germany. He had to know everything possible about the condition of the roads. He also chauffeured his platoon sergeant, Master Sergeant Ira Jones.

Scratch My Back (Then I'll Scratch Yours). Song that Elvis sang in the 1966 movie *Paradise—Hawaiian Style*. In the film, Suzanne Leigh did a duet with Elvis. "Scratch My Back (Then I'll Scratch Yours)" was written by Bill Giant, Bernie Baum, and Florence Kaye and appeared in the Long Playing album "Paradise—Hawaiian Style" (RCA LPM/LSP-3643).

Scrivener, Mildred. History teacher at Humes High School and Elvis's homeroom teacher during his senior year. She put Elvis in the annual variety show, which she produced. Elvis received more applause than anyone else and was asked to do an encore.

Sedaka, Neil. Singer who spans the mid-1950s through the '70s. He wrote and recorded numerous hit songs. He and Howard Greenfield scored Connie Francis's debut movie, *Where the Boys Are* (1960). He composed the hit "Oh! Carol" (RCA 7595) in dedication to composer Carole King. Arthur Rubinstein selected Neil Sedaka as the best classical pianist in New York City in 1956. Neil Sedaka composed (with Phil Cody) "Solitaire," which Elvis recorded in 1976.

Seeing Is Believing. Song written by Red West and Glen Spreen and recorded by Elvis in 1971. "Seeing Is Believing" appeared in the Long Playing album "He Touched Me" (RCA LSP-4690).

See See Rider. Traditional folk song written and recorded by Big Bill Broonzy (real name: William Lee Conley Broonzy, 1893–1958) under the title "C.C. Rider,"* on Perfect Records (PE-0313) in the 1920s. Ma Rainey had a version called "See See Rider Blues" in the 1920s and again in 1943 (Paramount 12252). Ray Charles recorded "See See Rider" in 1949 (Swingtime 217). In 1962 LaVern Baker had a hit with a stepped-up version titled "See See Rider" (Atlantic 2167); this is the version that Elvis copied. Under the title "C.C. Rider,"† Chuck Willis (Atlantic 1130) reached #12 on the Pop charts in 1957. "C.C. Rider" by Mitch Ryder and the Detroit Wheels was the theme song of the 1970 movie *C.C. and Company*, starring Ann-Margret and New York Jets quarterback Joe Namath. Elvis sang "See See Rider" in the 1972 documentary *Elvis on Tour,* the 1973 TV special "Elvis: Aloha from Hawaii," and the 1977 CBS-TV special "Elvis in Concert." "See See Rider" was the first song in most of Elvis's later concerts and he was credited on the albums with arranging it. It appeared in the following Long Playing albums: "On Stage—February, 1970" (RCA LSP-4362); "Elvis: Aloha from Hawaii Via Satellite" (RCA VPSX-6089); "Elvis Recorded Live on Stage in Memphis" (RCA CPL1-0606); "Elvis in Concert" (RCA APL2-2587).

See the U.S.A. the Elvis Way. RCA EPAS-4386. This is a 45 rpm Extended Play album. Songs included: "Memphis, Tennessee"; "Blue Moon of Kentucky"; "New Orleans"; "Viva Las Vegas." This album contains the only stereo version of "Viva Las Vegas."

Self-Realization Fellowship. Philosophy, founded by Yogi Paramahansa Yogananda, that Elvis became involved with briefly in the early 1970s.

Sellers, Peter. Elvis's favorite comedy actor. Peter Sellers‡ was born on September 8, 1925, the same day as actor Cliff Robertson. In 1963 John Lennon named his favorite actors as Robert Mitchum and Peter Sellers.

Sentimental Journey. Popular World War II ballad by Les Brown and his orchestra, with Doris Day (Columbia 36769). "Sentimental Journey" was the first million-seller by both Les Brown and Doris Day. It was written by Les Brown, Bud Green, and Ben Homer, and, popularized in 1945, it reached #1 for nine weeks. Les Brown adopted "Sentimental Journey" as his theme

---

*C. C. Rider was a black expression meaning "Country Circuit Preacher."
†Willis's "C.C. Rider" was the first stroll dance record.
‡Sellers, Stephen Stills, and Ringo Starr have all lived in the same house in Surrey, England.

song. On October 3, 1945, Becky Harris won first prize at the Mississippi-Alabama Fair and Dairy Show singing "Sentimental Journey." Ten-year-old Elvis won second place. "Sentimental Journey" was one of several songs played by the Army Band when Elvis boarded the U.S.S. *General Randall* for West Germany. (See: Harris, Becky; Mississippi-Alabama Fair and Dairy Show)

Sentimental Me. Song written by Jimmy Cassin and Jim Morehead and popularized by the Ames Brothers (Coral 60140) in 1950. Elvis recorded "Sentimental Me" in 1961 and it appeared in the following Long Playing albums: "Separate Ways" (RCA Camden CAS-2611); "Separate Ways" (Pickwick CAS-2611); "Double Dynamite" (Pickwick DL2-5001).

Separate Ways. RCA 74-0815. Released in November 1972 as a 45 rpm single. It reached #20 on *Billboard*'s Hot 100 chart and #10 on the Country chart. "Separate Ways" was reputed to have sold over a million copies. "Always on My Mind" was on the flip side. Elvis sang "Separate Ways" in the 1972 documentary *Elvis on Tour*. Written by Red West and Richard Mainegra, "Separate Ways" reflected on Elvis and Priscilla's separation. It appeared in the following Long Playing albums: "Separate Ways" (RCA Camden CAS-2611); "Separate Ways" (Pickwick CAS-2611); "Double Dynamite" (Pickwick DL2-5001).

Separate Ways. RCA GB-10486. Gold Standard Series re-issue of RCA 74-0815.

Separate Ways. RCA Camden CAS-2611. Released in January 1973 as a 33⅓ rpm Long Playing album. "Separate Ways" reached #46 on *Billboard*'s Hot LP chart. Songs included— Side 1: "Separate Ways," "Sentimental Me," "In My Way," "I Met Her Today," "What Now, What Next, Where To." Side 2: "Always on My Mind," "I Slipped, I Stumbled, I Fell," "Is It So Strange," "Forget Me Never," "Old Shep."

Separate Ways. Pickwick CAS-2611. A re-issue of RCA Camden CAS-2611 in December 1975.

Seth, Larry. Elvis impersonator, nicknamed the "Big El." (See: Elvis Lives)

Shafer, Paul. Executive from the Malco Theaters, Inc., who obtained the films for Elvis's private parties.

Shake a Hand. Song written by Joe Morris and originally recorded by Faye Adams (Herald* 416), who had a million-seller with it in 1953. Red Foley also had a hit with "Shake a Hand" (Decca 28839) in 1953. Little Richard recorded a version in 1957 (Specialty 670). Elvis recorded "Shake a Hand" in 1975 and it appeared in the Long Playing album "Today" (RCA APL1-1039).

---

*"Shake a Hand" was the first release for Herald Records, begun by Al Silver in 1953.

Shake, Rattle and Roll. RCA 20/47-6642. Released in September 1956 as a 78 rpm single and a 45 single. "Lawdy, Miss Clawdy" was on the flip side. "Shake, Rattle and Roll" was written by Charles Calhoun (a pseudonym for Jesse Stone) and originally recorded by Joe Turner (Atlantic 1026) in 1954. On April 12, 1954.* Bill Haley and His Comets (Decca 29204) covered Joe Turner's version of "Shake, Rattle and Roll," using less suggestive lyrics. It reached #12 on *Billboard*'s Hot 100 chart and sold over a million copies. On Haley's Decca recording the song is listed as a fox trot. Elvis sang "Shake, Rattle and Roll" in his third "Stage Show" appearance (February 11, 1956). It appeared in the Extended Play album "Elvis Presley" (RCA EPA-830) and the Long Playing albums "For LP Fans Only" (RCA LPM-1990) and "For LP Fans Only" (RCA LSP-1990 [e]).

Shake, Rattle and Roll. RCA 447-0615. Gold Standard Series reissue of RCA 20/47-6642.

Shake That Tambourine. Song that Elvis sang in the 1965 movie *Harum Scarum*. "Shake That Tambourine" was written by Bill Giant, Bernie Baum, and Florence Kaye and appeared in the Long Playing album "Harum Scarum" (RCA LPM/LSP-3468).

Shannon, Del. Del Shannon (real name: Charles Westover) recorded "Runaway" (Big Top 3067) in 1961, which was #1 in both the U. S. and the U. K. Elvis recorded "Runaway" in 1969. Shannon composed Peter and Gordon's 1965 hit "I Go to Pieces." In 1962 he was the first American artist to record a John Lennon-Paul McCartney composition, when he recorded "From Me to You" (Big Top 3112).

Shapiro, Dr. Max. Los Angeles dentist who makes house calls. He supplied Elvis with "medication" while Elvis resided in Southern Califonia.

SHARE. Hollywood women's charity to which Elvis donated his $35,000 1964 Rolls-Royce in 1968. The Rolls-Royce was auctioned off to raise funds for their charities.

Shap, Nancy. Wardrobe assistant whom Elvis dated. He met her in 1961 while filming *Flaming Star*.

Shaver, Sean. Photographer who has taken over 80,000 photos of Elvis. He was Elvis's official photographer.

Shaw, Arnold. Music publisher (vice-president of Hill and Range Music), record producer, and general professional manager for the Edward B. Marks Music Corporation in the 1950s. Arnold Shaw helped to get Elvis Presley signed by RCA.

In the fall of 1955, Elvis was still a regional phenomenon; he hadn't yet broken nationally. With a national base, Colonel Parker could get top dollar for Elvis's Sun contract. Parker asked Arnold Shaw to get Elvis's records played in the North.

---

*Bill Haley and His Comets recorded "Rock Around the Clock" (Decca 29124) on the same day.

Shaw asked disc jockey Bill Randle of WERE in Cleveland to program Elvis. Soon after, Elvis began receiving national notoriety and, on November 22, 1955, RCA purchased Elvis's Sun contract. (See: RCA Victor; Randle, Bill)

She Can't Find Her Keys. A 1962 song by Paul Peterson* on Colpix Records (Colpix 620) that made reference to "Presley Records."

Shelby County Deputy Sheriff. Honorary, nonsalaried law enforcement position to which Elvis was sworn in on September 1, 1970.

Shelby County, Tennessee. Originally the home of Dr. John Carpenter (Elvis) in the 1969 movie *Change of Habit*.

Shepherd, Cybill. Model and actress whom Elvis dated after his separation from Priscilla in 1972.

Sheppard, T.G. Country singer (real name: Bill Browden) through whom Elvis met Linda Thompson after Sheppard had invited Linda to a private movie showing at the Memphian Theatre. Elvis gave Sheppard a customized GMC bus in 1975.

Sherlock. Basset hound on TV's "Steve Allen Show" to whom tuxedo-clad Elvis sang "Hound Dog" on Sunday, July 1, 1956.

Sherry, Dorothy. Thirty-two-year-old housewife who claims to have talked to the dead Elvis in a series of séances. Her story is told in Hans Holzer's book *Elvis Presley Speaks*.

She's a Machine. Song that Elvis recorded for the 1967 movie *Easy Come, Easy Go*, but it was not used. "She's a Machine" was written by Joy Byers and appeared in the following Long Playing albums: "Singer Presents Elvis Singing Flaming Star and Others" (RCA PRS-279); "Elvis Sings Flaming Star" (RCA Camden CAS-2304); "Elvis Sings Flaming Star" (Pickwick CAS-2304).

She's Not You. RCA 47-8041. Released in July 1962 as a 45 rpm single. It reached #5 on *Billboard*'s Hot 100 chart and #13 on the Rhythm and Blues chart. "She's Not You" was #1 in the United Kingdom (for three weeks, September 15–October 6). "She's Not You" sold over a million copies. "Just Tell Her Jim Said Hello" was on the flip side. Written by Jerry Leiber, Mike Stoller, and Doc Pomus, "She's Not You" appeared in the Long Playing albums "Elvis' Golden Records, Volume 3" RCA LPM–LSP-2765) and "Elvis: Worldwide 50 Gold Award Hits, Volume 1" (RCA LPM-6401).

She's Not You. RCA 447-0637. Gold Standard Series re-issue of RCA 47-8041.

She Thinks I Still Care. RCA PB-10857. Released in December 1976 as a 45 rpm single. It reached #31 on *Billboard*'s Hot 100 chart and #1 on the Country chart. "Moody Blue" was on the flip side. Five copies of the record were pressed on translu-

---

*Paul Peterson later became a professional writer, creating the crime-fighter novel series *The Smuggler*.

cent blue plastic (the same as the "Moody Blue" album). "She Thinks I Still Care" was written by Dickie Lee and originally recorded by George Jones (United Artists 424) in 1962. Jones's version reached #1 on the Country charts. Elvis's version of "She Thinks I Still Care" appeared in the Long Playing albums "Moody Blue" (RCA AFL1-2428) and "Our Memories of Elvis" (RCA AQL1-3279).

She Was the Sunshine of Our Home. Phrase on Gladys Presley's grave marker in front of the larger ten-foot monument.

She Wears My Ring. Song written by husband and wife team Boudleaux and Felice Bryant and originally recorded by Ray Orbison on Monument Records and then by Ray Price (Columbia 44628) 1968. Elvis recorded "She Wears My Ring" at the Stax Studios in Memphis in 1973. It appeared in the Long Playing albums "Good Times" (RCA CPL1-0475) and "Our Memories of Elvis, Volume 2" (RCA AQL1-3448).

Shindig. ABC-TV show (September 16, 1964–January 5, 1966,) hosted by Jimmy O'Neill. Reportedly, it was one of Elvis's favorite TV programs. The Blossoms, who later backed Elvis in in 1968 recording session, appeared as regulars on the show. Some of the musicians who appeared in "Shindig" are: Glen Campbell; David Gates; Leon Russell; Billy Preston; Glen Hardin; Delaney Bramlett; James Burton. (See: Blossoms, The; O'Neill, Jimmy)

Sholes, Steve. Graduate of Rutgers University and a member of the Country Music Hall of Fame (1967). Sholes was an RCA Victor executive until his death, in 1968. Sholes moved to Nashville to record a number of artists for the RCA Victor label, such as Hank Snow, Pee Wee King, and Johnny and Jack. It was Steve Sholes who signed Elvis to the RCA Victor label in 1955.

Steve Sholes replaced Joe Carlton as head of RCA's A & R department. Joe Carlton left to join ABC Paramount Records where he met a young singer named Jack Scott. Carlton then established his own Carlton label on which Scott and a runner-up in the 1959 Miss America contest, Anita Bryant, had a number of hits.

Shook, Jerry. Bass player in Elvis's back-up-group. He previously played with the Association.*

Shooting Star. Air Force aerobatic team of which 2d Lt. Josh Morgan (Elvis) was a member in the 1960 movie *Kissin' Cousins*. (In reality no such team exists; the real Air Force team is called the Thunderbirds.)

Shoppin' Around. Song that Elvis sang in the 1960 movie *G.I. Blues*. Horns were added to the film version. "Shoppin 'Around" was written by Sid Tepper, Roy C. Bennett, and Aaron

---

*The Association's biggest hits were "Along Comes Mary" (Valiant 741), and "Cherish" (Valiant 747), both released in 1966.

326

Schroeder and appeared in the Long Playing album "G.I. Blues" (RCA LPM LSP-2256).

Shore, Sammy. Comedian who opened many of Elvis's live concerts in the 1970s. He was replaced by Jackie Kahane.

Shot in the Dark, A. A 1964 Blake Edwards movie starring Peter Sellers and Elke Sommer, the second movie in the *Pink Panther* series. It was one of Elvis's favorite movies, along with *Dr. Strangelove* (1964). (See: *Dr. Strangelove*)

Shout It Out. Song that Elvis sang in the 1966 movie *Frankie and Johnny*. It was written by Bill Giant, Bernie Baum, and Florence Kaye. "Shout It Out" appeared in the Long Playing albums "Frankie and Johnny" (RCA LPM/LSP-3553) and "Frankie and Johnny" (Pickwick ACL-7007).

Sideburns. Part of Elvis's hair style, along with a ducktail cut first worn by him at age sixteen while a student in high school. The style of wearing sideburns was named for General Ambrose Burnsides, who served with the Union Army during the Civil War and became the first president of the National Rifle Association in 1871.

Sidney, George. Director of the 1964 movie *Viva Las Vegas*.

Siebert, Ursula. Girl whom Elvis dated in Germany, where they were both involved in an automobile accident in which neither was injured.

Siegel, Don. Director of the 1960 movie *Flaming Star*. Siegel previously directed *Invasion of the Body Snatchers* (1956), *Coogan's Bluff* (1958), and *Dirty Harry** (1972).

Signs of the Zodiac. Song that Elvis sang in the 1969 movie *The Trouble with Girls* (*And How to Get Into It*); Marlyn Mason sang duet with Elvis. "Signs of the Zodiac" has never been released by RCA, but it does appear on the Dutch bootleg LP "From Hollyood to Vegas."

Silent Night. One of the most popular Christmas carols of all time. Father Joseph Mohr (1792–1848), of the Church of St. Nicholas in Oberndorf, Austria, composed the poem, "Stille Nacht, Heilige Nacht" (the original title was "Song from Heaven"), after visiting the home of a poor woodcutter. He saw similarities between the woodcutter's new baby and the birth of Christ centuries earlier. Mohr had his organist, Franz Gruber (1787–63), write some music for the poem and they sang it at midnight mass with guitar accompaniment (the pipe organ had broken down). In the spring of 1819, Karl Mauracher, organ builder and repairman, came to fix Father Mohr's Grotien pipe organ. Franz Gruber played "Stille Nacht, Heilige Nacht" on the organ, and Mauracher fell in love with the tune. He took a copy of the tune back to his home in Zillertall Valley. In 1831 Karl Mauracher arranged the carol

---

*In "Dirty Harry" Don Siegel made a cameo appearance.

for four children's voices and had Joseph, Caroline, Andreas, and Amalie Strasser sing it. While the children were singing "Still Nacht, Heilige Nacht" at the Leipzig Trade Fair in 1832, they were invited to sing for the King and Queen in the Royal Saxon Court Chapel in Pleissenburg Castle on Christmas Eve, 1832. The carol quickly gained international popularity. "Stille Nacht, Heilige Nacht" was translated into English by the Rev. John Freeman Young (1820–85) in 1863. "Silent Night" was recorded by Bing Crosby on June 8, 1942, in Los Angeles, with the Max Terr Choir and John Scott Trotter's Orchestra. Reportedly, "Silent Night" backed with "Adeste Fideles" (Decca Records) has sold over 30 million copies through the years and has surpassed "White Christmas" as the best-selling record of all time. Elvis recorded "Silent Night" in 1957 and it appeared in the Extended Play album "Christmas with Elvis" (RCA EPA-4340) and the following Long Playing albums: "Elvis' Christmas Album" (RCA LOC-1035); (RCA LPM-1951); (RCA LPM 1951 [e]); (RCA Camden CAS-2428); (Pickwick CAS-2428).

Silverado. Ghost town in the 1965 movie *Tickle Me.*

Silver Bells. Christmas carol written by Jay Livingston and Ray Evans* and introduced by Bob Hope and Marilyn Maxwell† in the 1951 movie *The Lemon Drop Kid.* Bing Crosby and Carol Richard had a tremendously popular hit with "Silver Bells" (Decca Records) in 1951. Elvis recorded "Silver Bells" in 1971 and it appeared in the Long Playing albums "Elvis Sings the Wonderful World of Christmas" (RCA LSP-4579) and "Elvis Sings the Wonderful World of Christmas" (RCA AN11-1936).

Simon, Paul. Highly talented singer/composer who at one time was half of the duo Simon and Garfunkel. He and Carole King once recorded demo records as the Cosines. Melissa Manchester was one of Simon's students when he taught at New York University. Elvis recorded the Paul Simon composition "Bridge Over Troubled Water" in 1970.

Sinatra, Frank. Very successful singer (nicknamed "Ole Blue Eyes) who spanned the 1940s to the present. He began as a member of the Hoboken Four and appeared as a regular on radio's "Your Hit Parade." He won an Oscar for Best Supporting Actor for the 1953 movie *From Here to Eternity.* It was on Sinatra's TV special that Elvis made his first TV appearance after his release from the Army. Sinatra's eldest daughter, Nancy, co-starred with Elvis in the 1968 movie *Spinout.*

Sinatra, Nancy. Daughter of Frank and Nancy Sinatra. Born

---

*Jay Livingston and Ray Evans have written numerous TV themes, including: "Bonanza"; "Mister Ed"; "Mr. Lucky"; "77 Sunset Strip."
†Marilyn Maxwell was born Marvel Maxwell.

Sandra Sinatra on June 8, 1940, Nancy* appeared with her father on "The Frank Sinatra-Timex Special," aired May 12, 1960, in which Elvis was featured. Nancy Sinatra, Jr., costarred (as Susan Jacks) with Elvis in the 1968 movie *Speedway*. She sang "Your Groovy Self" in the movie. On August 30, 1969, Elvis, his wife, Priscilla, and Vernon and Dee Presley all attended Nancy Sinatra's opening at the Las Vegas International Hotel.

Sing, Boy, Sing. A 1958 movie starring Tommy Sands as the Elvis-like character Ewell Walker. This movie was an expanded version of "The Singing Idol," which was presented on TV in 1957. Elvis's good friend Nick Adams had a part in the movie. (See: Sands, Tommy; Singing Idol, The)

Sing, Boy, Sing. Title song of the Twentieth Century-Fox picture *Sing, Boy, Sing,* recorded on Capitol Records (Capitol 3867) by Tommy Sands in 1958. The song was composed by Tommy Sands and Rod McKuen.

Singer. Sewing machine manufacturer,† sponsor of Elvis's NBC-TV special, "Elvis," broadcast Tuesday, December 3, 1968, 9:00 P.M. (EST). The special was shown in Britain on BBC-2 TV on December 31, 1968, without commercials. A special album titled "Singer Presents Elvis Singing Flaming Star and Others" was released in 1968 through Singer stores with Singer's name on the album cover.

Singer Presents Elvis Singing Flaming Star and Others. PRS-279. Released in November 1968 as a 33⅓ rpm Long Playing album. "Singer Presents Elvis Singing Flaming Star and Others" was available only at Singer Sewing Centers in conjunction with the December 3, 1968, NBC-TV special "Elvis." In 1969 the album was re-issued by RCA as "Elvis Sings Flaming Star" (RCA Camden CAS-2304). In December 1975 it was again re-issued, by Pickwick (Pickwick CAS-2304). Songs included—Side 1: "Flaming Star," "Wonderful World," "Night Life," "All I Needed Was the Rain," "Too Much Monkey Business." Side 2: "Yellow Rose of Texas/The Eyes of Texas," "She's a Machine," "Do the Vega," "Tiger Man."

Singing Idol, The. TV play presented on NBC's Kraft Theatre, January 30, 1957, starring Tommy Sands as the Elvis-like

---

*Songwriter Jimmy Van Heusen, a descendant of Stephen Foster, wrote (with comedian Phil Silvers) the song "Nancy with the Laughin' Face" for Nancy when she was five years old. A similar incident occurred when a songwriter named Jack Lawrence composed the song "Linda" in 1946, about his attorney's little girl Linda Eastman. Today, Linda Eastman is Mrs. Paul McCartney.

†The Beatles dedicated their 1965 movie *Help!* to Mr. Elias Howe, who in 1846 invented the sewing machine. When Elvis was a child, his mother, Gladys Presley, worked long and hard hours for several clothing manufacturers in Tupelo. The industrial sewing machines she used were manufactured by Singer, the same company that would one day sponsor a television special starring her son.

character Ewell Walker. Elvis was originally requested to play the lead role in "The Singing Idol" but turned it down. Sands sang "Hep Dee Hootie" and "Teenage Crush." The play was later expanded into the 1958 movie *Sing, Boy, Sing*, which also starred Tommy Sands.

Singing Tree. Song written by Owens and Solberg that Elvis recorded in 1967. "Singing Tree" appeared as a bonus song in the Long Playing album "Clambake" (RCA LPM/LSP-3893).

Singleton, Shelby. Highly successful record producer. Among his many hit records was "Wooden Heart" (Smash 1708) by Joe Dowell, which Singleton produced in 1961. In 1968 he founded Plantation Records, which produced the million-selling single by Jeannie Riley, "Harper Valley P.T.A." (Plantation 3). In 1969 Shelby Singleton bought Sun Records from Sam Phillips. Singleton began releasing many of the Johnny Cash, Roy Orbison, Carl Perkins, and Charlie Rich material on Sun International Records. Always an innovator, Singleton released albums with lifetime guarantees against wearing out (for one dollar Sun International would replace the record). In 1978 Singleton brought out a series of mysterious duet records, featuring Jerry Lee Lewis and someone sounding like Elvis on the "Save the Last Dance for Me" and "Am I To Be the One." These were cuts from an album titled "Duets" but did not reveal who Lewis was singing with. In 1979 Singleton released a mysterious album titled "Orion." (It was the very next album that Sun International released after the "Duets" album (Sun 1011) Shelby Singleton today owns the famed Million Dollar Session tapes, kept safely in a bank vault. He has, as yet unsuccessfully negotiated with RCA Victor a plan to legally release the tapes that would be mutually beneficial to both parties.

Sing, You Children. Song that Elvis sang in the 1967 movie *Easy Come, Easy Go*. The Mello Men sang vocal back-up in this song. "Sing, You Children" was written by Gerald Nelson and Fred Burch and appeared in the Extended Play album "Easy Come, Easy Go" (RCA EPA-4387) and Long Playing albums "You'll Never Walk Alone" (RCA Camden CALX-2472) and "You'll Never Walk Alone" (Pickwick CAS-2472).

Sing You Sinners. Title originally considered for the 1958 movie *King Creole*. In 1938 Bing Crosby appeared in a Paramount movie titled *Sing You Sinners*.

Sir Swivel Hips. One of Elvis's many nicknames.

Sis and Buzzy. Sister and brother of Susie Jessup (Dolores Hart) in the 1957 movie *Loving You*.

Sitton, Ray. Member of the Memphis Mafia off and on through the years.

Sixteen Tons. Recorded by Tennessee Ernie Ford (Capitol 3262). Elvis's "Love Me Tender" sales beat out "Sixteen Tons," which previously held the record for the fastest pace set by a million-seller, reaching a million fourteen days after release. "Love Me

Tender" sold a million copies prior to its release. "Sixteen Tons" was written by Merle Travis in 1947. Merle Travis played a G.I. in the 1953 movie *From Here to Eternity*, singing "Reenlistment Blues." Today one of Elvis's music companies owns the publishing rights to "Sixteen Tons."

Skippy Peanut Butter. Favorite food of Elvis as a young boy in Tupelo. When company appeared he would hide the jar for fear of it being eaten.

Skylar, Alexis. Twenty-four-year-old woman who announced that she was to marry Elvis in 1974. Although some newspapers carried the account, it proved to be a hoax.

Sleepy Eyed John. (See: Lepley, John)

Slemansky, Hank. Elvis's original martial arts instructor; Slemansky was killed in Vietnam in the 1960s.

Slicin' Sand. Song that Elvis sang in the 1961 movie *Blue Hawaii*. "Slicin' Sand" was written by Sid Tepper and Roy C. Bennett and appeared in the Long Playing album "Blue Hawaii" (RCA LPM/LSP-2426).

Slowly But Surely. Song that Elvis sang in the 1965 movie *Tickle Me.* "Slowly But Surely" was written by Sid Wayne and Ben Weisman and appeared in the Extended Play albums "Tickle Me" (RCA EPA-4383) and "Fun in Acapulco" (RCA LPM/LSP-2756).

Small, Edward. Producer of the 1966 movie *Frankie and Johnny.*

Smash Hits, Presley Style. Elvis tribute album by Emi and Hamlyn Group on MFP Records.

Smith, Ann Dewey. Wife of Vernon Presley's attorney, Beecher Smith, III, and one of the three witnesses of Elvis's will.

Smith, Beecher, III. Vernon Presley's attorney. He was one of three persons who witnessed Elvis's will.

Smith, Billy. Member of the Memphis Mafia. Billy, Elvis's maternal cousin, took care of Elvis's wardrobe and served as valet. He once doubled for Annette Day in the 1968 movie *Double Trouble.*

Smith, Bobby. Cousin of Elvis. Bobby Smith died on September 13, 1968, of a heart attack at the age of twenty-six.

Smith, Carrol "Junior." Cousin of Elvis and close friend who accompanied him on trips in the 1950s. Carrol Smith was with Elvis when he went to New York to film "The Steve Allen Show" in 1956. Junior Smith died in 1958.

Smith, Clettes. Elvis's aunt and Gladys Presley's younger sister. Clettes married Vernon Presley's brother, Vestor.

Smith, Gene. Member of the Memphis Mafia. As Elvis's maternal cousin he was employed for ten years in the capacity of chauffeur.

Smith, Gladys Love. Maiden name of Elvis's mother. Gladys Smith was also the real name of actresses Mary Pickford and Alexis Smith. (See: Presley, Gladys)

Smith, John. One of Elvis's uncles, John Smith died on October 6, 1968. He had been employed as a Graceland guard.

Smith, Travis. Gate guard at Graceland and one of Elvis's uncles (Gladys Presley's brother). He also was caretaker of the Circle G Ranch.

Smokey Mountain Boy. Song that Elvis sang in the 1964 movie *Kissin' Cousins.* "Smokey Mountain Boy" was written by Lenore Rosenblatt and Victor Millrose and appeared in the Long Playing album "Kissin' Cousins" (RCA LPM/LSP-2894).

Smorgasbord. Song that Elvis sang in the 1966 movie *Spinout.* In the film, Elvis changed the lyrics. Instead of "I'll take the dish I please, and please the dish I take," Elvis sang: "I'll take the dish I please, and take the please I dish." "Smorgasbord" was written by Sid Tepper and Roy C. Bennett and appeared in the Long Playing album "Spinout" (RCA LPM/LSP-3702).

Snoopy. One of the two Great Danes that Elvis bought for Priscilla (the other was Brutus). Snoopy eventually became Lisa Marie's dog.

Snow, Hank. Clarence Eugene Snow, born in Liverpool, Nova Scotia, in 1914. In 1954 Snow became a client of Col. Tom Parker. On January 7, 1949, Hank Snow debuted on the "Grand Ole Opry," with the same lack of audience enthusiasm as was given Elvis in 1954. Hank Snow originally wrote and recorded "I'm Moving On," which Elvis recorded in January 1967. It was Hank Snow who introduced Elvis in his appearance on the "Grand Ole Opry,"* September 25, 1954.

Snowbird. Song written by Gene MacLellan and originally recorded by Anne Murray in 1970. "Snowbird" reached #8 on *Billboard*'s Hot 100 chart and sold over a million copies. Anne Murray received her Gold Record on November 10, 1970, on the TV series "The Merv Griffin Show." In 1971 Chet Atkins won a Grammy Award for his instrumental version of "Snowbird." Elvis recorded "Snowbird" in 1970 and it appeared in the Long Playing album "Elvis Country" (RCA LSP-4460).

Snowman's League. An Elvis fan club established in the 1950s by Col. Tom Parker.

So Close, Yet So Far (From Paradise). Song that Elvis sang in the 1965 movie *Harum Scarum.* "So Close, Yet So Far (From Paradise)" was written by Joy Byers and appeared in the Long Playing albums "Harum Scarum" (RCA LPM/LSP-3468) and "Mahalo from Elvis" (Pickwick CL-7064).

Softly as I Leave You. RCA PB-11212. Released in March 1978 as a 45 rpm single. "Unchained Melody" was on the flip side. "Softly as I Leave You" was written by G. Calabrese, A. DeVita, and Hal Shaper and originally recorded by Matt Monroe (Liberty 55449) in 1962. Frank Sinatra had a popular version of

---

*The segment in which Snow introduced Elvis was sponsored by Kellogg's Cornflakes.

the song in 1964 (Reprise 0301). "Softly as I Leave You" by Elvis was taken from a live concert. Charlie Hodge sang duet. It was nominated for a Grammy Award in 1978. "Softly as I Leave You" hasn't appeared on an RCA album.

So Glad You're Mine. Song written and originally recorded by Arthur Crudup (RCA 20-1949) in 1946. Elvis recorded "So Glad You're Mine" in 1956 and it appeared in the Extended Play album "Elvis, Volume 2" (RCA EPA-993) and the Long Playing albums "Elvis" (RCA LPM-1382) and "Elvis" (RCA LSP-1382 [e]).

So High. Gospel song arranged and recorded by Elvis in 1966. "So High" appeared in the Long Playing album "How Great Thou Art" (RCA LPM/LSP-3758).

So High. RCA SP-45-162. Special 45 rpm promotional release. "How Great Thou Art" was on the flip side.

So I'll Go Quietly. Title originally considered for the 1968 movie *Speedway.*

Soklow, Herbert F. Producer of the 1970 documentary *Elvis— That's the Way It Is.*

Soldier Boy. Song written in Korea in 1951 by David Jones and Larry Banks (although credited to David Jones and Teddy Williams) and originally recorded by the Four Fellows (Glory 234) in 1955. Elvis recorded "Soldier Boy" in 1960 and it appeared in the Long Playing album "Elvis Is Back" (RCA LPM/LSP 2231).

Sold Out. A 33⅓ rpm bootleg album on the E.P. label. Songs included: Side 1: "Burning Love," "Lawdy, Miss Clawdy," "T-R-O-U-B-L-E," "I'm Leavin'," "When the Snow Is on the Roses," "Need Your Lovin' Every Day," "Little Sister/ Get Back," "Steamroller Blues," "Rock Medley," "Walk the Lonesome Road," "Help Me Make It Through the Night," "Faded Love." Side 2: "Heartbreak Hotel," "One Night," "Reconsider Baby," "Mystery Train," "Tiger Man," "Jailhouse Rock," "Teddy Bear"/"Don't Be Cruel," "I John," "Softly as I Leave You," "It's Now or Never," "My Babe," "Sweet Sweet Spirit," "I'm Leaving It Up To You," "I Got a Woman," "What'd I Say."

Solitaire. RCA PB-11533. Released in April 1979 as a 45 rpm single. "Are You Sincere" was on the flip side. "Solitaire" reached #10 on *Billboard*'s Country chart. Song written by Neil Sedaka and Phil Cody and originally recorded by Sedaka in an album (Kirshner KES 117) in 1971. "Solitaire" was popularized by the Carpenters (A & M 1721) in 1975. Elvis recorded "Solitaire" at Graceland in 1976 and it appeared in the Long Playing albums "From Elvis Presley Boulevard, Memphis, Tennessee" (RCA APL1-1506) and "Our Memories of Elvis" (RCA AQL1-3279).

Somebody Bigger Than You and I. Gospel song written by Lang, Heath, and Burke and recorded by Elvis in 1966. "Somebody

Bigger Than You and I" appeared in the Long Playing albums "How Great Thou Art" (RCA LPM/LSP-3758) and "He Walks Beside Me" (RCA AFL1-2772).

Something. Song written by George Harrison and originally recorded by the Beatles (Apple 2654) in 1969. It sold over a million copies. Elvis sang "Something" in the 1973 TV special "Elvis: Aloha from Hawaii' and it appeared in the Long Playing album "Elvis: Aloha from Hawaii Via Satellite" (RCA VPSX-6089).

Something Blue. Song written by Paul Evans and Al Byron and recorded by Elvis in 1962. "Something Blue" appeared in the Long Playing album "Pot Luck" (RCA LPM/LSP-2523).

Something for Everybody. RCA LPM/LSP-2370. A 33⅓ rpm Long Playing album that was released in June 1961. It reached #1 on *Billboard*'s Hot LP chart. "Something for Everybody" had advertisements for the single "Wild in the Country" and the EP "Elvis by Request" on the covers. Also, on the back cover was a picture from the movie *Wild in the Country*. Songs included—Side 1: "There's Always Me," "Give Me the Right," "It's a Sin," "Sentimental Me," "Starting Today," "Gently." Side 2: "I'm Comin' Home," "In Your Arms," "Put the Blame on Me," "Judy," "I Want You with Me," "I Slipped, I Stumbled, I Fell."

Something for the Girls. Title originally considered for the 1957 movie *Loving You*. Another title considered was *The Lonesome Cowboy*.

Sometimes I Feel Like a Motherless Child. Black spiritual that the Blossoms sang in the 1968 NBC-TV special "Elvis."

Somewhere Elvis Is Smiling. Keith Bradford's 1977 tribute record on Nu-Sound Records (Nu-Sound 77).

Songfellows. Gospel group for which Elvis auditioned in 1954 at the Memphis auditorium when it was believed that one of the members was leaving. The Songfellows was a group of young singers associated with the well-known Blackwood Brothers Quartet. Elvis asked to join because Cecil Blackwood was leaving to join the Blackwood Brothers. Elvis couldn't join because he had just signed with Sun Records (See: Sumner, J.D.; Blackwood Brothers)

Song of the Shrimp. Song that Elvis sang in the 1962 movie *Girls! Girls! Girls!*. Written by Sid Tepper and Roy C. Bennett, "Song of the Shrimp" appeared in the Long Playing album "Girls! Girls! Girls"! (RCA LPM/LSP-2621)

Sonny and Cher. Husband and wife singing duet originally billed as Caesar and Cleo. Born Salvatore Philip Bono and Cherilyn Sakisian La Pierre, the couple was divorced in 1974. Sonny and Cher turned down roles in the 1968 movie *Speedway*. The couple's only movie appearances have been in *Wild on the Beach* (1965), *Good Times* (1967), and *Chastity* (1969).

Sotheby Park-Bernet. New York auction house that inventoried Elvis's possessions after his death.

Sound Advice. Song that Elvis sang in the 1962 movie *Follow That Dream*. The film version of "Sound Advice" had a whistling introduction. It was written by Bill Giant, Bernie Baum, and Florence Kaye and appeared in the Long Playing album "Elvis for Everyone" (RCA LPM/LSP-3450)

Sounding Story, The. First book written about Elvis. It was written in Germany by Peter de Vecchi prior to 1959.

Sound of Your Cry, The. RCA 48-1017. Released in September 1971 as a 45 rpm single—the only Presley single to be issued with a "48" prefix. "It's Only Love" was on the flip side. "The Sound of Your Cry" was written by Bill Giant, Bernie Baum, and Florence Kaye and never appeared in an album.

Sound of Your Cry, The. RCA 447-0684. Gold Standard Series re-issue of RCA 48-1017

Sour Apple Award. Negative award conferred on Elvis by the Hollywood Women's Press Club for Least Cooperative Actor of the Year (1967). At the same presentation Natalie Wood received the Least Cooperative Actress award.

South, Joe. Composer and singer who made the charts with the Capitol Records releases "Games People Play," "Rose Garden," and "Walk a Mile in My Shoes." Elvis recorded South's composition "Walk a Mile in My Shoes" in 1970.

Southern Made Doughnuts. Product for which Elvis did commercials while performing as a regular on the "Louisiana Hayride" in October of 1954. ("You can get 'em piping hot after four P.M., You can get 'em piping hot, Southern made doughnuts hits the spot, You can get 'em piping hot after four P.M.) No known copies of this commercial exist today.

Spangler's Rest. Motel where Glenn Tyler (Elvis) and Betty Lee (Millie Perkins) spend the night, in separate cabins, in the 1961 movie *Wild in the Country*.

Spanish Eyes. Song written originally as an instrumental by Bert Kaempfert called "Moon Over Naples." Charles Singleton and Eddy Snyder wrote lyrics to the song and retitled it "Spanish Eyes." Al Martino's* Capitol recording (Capitol 5542) in 1965 sold over a million copies and reached #15 on *Billboard*'s Hot 100 chart. When Elvis sang "Spanish Eyes" at his live performances, Sherril Nielson sang duet with him. "Spanish Eyes" appeared in the Long Playing albums "Good Times" (RCA LPL1-0475) and "Our Memories of Elvis" (RCA AOL1-3279).

Spearhead. The Second Armored Division to which Elvis was

---

*In the 1950s, Al Martino won first prize on "Arthur Godfrey's Talent Scouts." He was encouraged to become a singer by Mario Lanza. Al Martino made his film debut as singer Johnny Fontaine in the 1972 movie *The Godfather*.

assigned. The division was commanded by General George Smith Patton* during World War II.

Specialist Fourth Class. Army rank that Elvis achieved on June 1, 1959. With the promotion, Elvis began to receive $135.30 a month.

Special Palm Sunday Programming. RCA SP 33-461. Special disc-jockey promotional album. The album included a "Complete half-hour program with spot announcements and selections from the RCA Victor album "How Great Thou Art" (LPM/LSP-3758). Disc jockeys were to play the album on Palm Sunday, March 19, 1967.

Special Projects, Inc. Beverly Hills firm that handled the Elvis products in the 1950s and '60s. It was owned by Hank G. Saperstein and Howard Bell (Saperstein also took over the administration of the Elvis Presley National Fan Club). The company also handled products for the Long Ranger and Ding Dong School.

Spector, Phil. Teenage millionaire who created the "Wall of Sound" on records by the Righteous Brothers, the Crystals, the Ronettes, Darlene Love, etc. He later produced for the Beatles ("Let It Be"). During the 1960s Phil Spector produced some of the demo records of material sent to Elvis. He co-wrote "You've Lost That Lovin' Feeling," which Elvis recorded. He is the only man to produce for both Elvis (indirectly) and the Beatles. (See: Love, Darlene)

SPEEDWAY. MGM, 1968. Premiered Charlotte, North Carolina, June 12, 1968 (94 min). Elvis's twenty-seventh movie. Producer, Douglas Laurence. Director, Norman Taurog. Cast: Steve Grayson/Elvis Presley, Susan Jacks/Nancy Sinatra, Kenny Donford/Bill Bixby, R. W. Hepworth/Gale Gordon, Abel Esterlake/William Schallert, Ellie Esterlake/Victoria Meyerink, Paul Dado/Ross Hagen, Birdie Kebner/Carl Ballentine, Lloyd Meadow/Robert Harris, Debbie Esterlake/Michele Newman, Juan Medala/Poncie Ponce, Carrie Esterlake/Courtney Brown, Billie Esterlake/Dana Brown, Annie Esterlake/Patti Jean Keith, Ted Simmons/Harper Carter, Billie Jo/Christopher West, Mike/Carl Reindel, The Cook/Harry Hickox, Mary Ann/Miss Beverly Hills, Dumb Blonde/Gari Hardy, Lori/Charlotte Considine, Race Announcer/Sandy Reed, The Jordanaires/The Jordanaires. Screenplay, Phillip Shuken. Photography, Joseph Ruttenberg. Music, Jeff Alexander. Art Direction, George W. Davis and Leroy Coleman. Set Decoration, Henry Grace and Don Greenwood, Jr. Special Visual Effects, Carroll L. Shepphird. Assistant Director, Dale Hutchinson. Editor, Richard Farrell. Songs sung by Elvis: "Speedway," "He's Your Uncle, Not Your Dad," "Who Are You (Who Am I)," "Let Yourself

---

*Patton was the first American to enter the Olympic Pentathlon when it was introduced in 1912; he finished fifth.

Go," "Your Time Hasn't Come Yet, Baby," "There Ain't Nothing Like a Song" (duet with Nancy Sinatra). "Your Groovy Self" was sung by Nancy Sinatra.

Speedway. Title song of the 1968 movie *Speedway*. "Speedway" was written by Mel Glazer and Steven Schlaks and appeared in the Long Playing album "Speedway" (RCA LSP-3989).

Speedway. RCA LSP-3989. Released in June 1968 as a 33⅓ rpm Long Playing album. "Speedway" reached #82 on *Billboard*'s Hot LP chart. It contained songs from the 1968 movie *Speedway* plus five bonus songs. Monaural copies (LPM-3989) of "Speedway" are extremely rare. Songs included—Side 1: "Speedway," "There Ain't Nothing Like a Song" (duet with Nancy Sinatra), "Your Time Hasn't Come Yet, Baby," "Who Are You (Who Am I)," "He's Your Uncle, Not Your Dad," "Let Yourself Go." Side 2: "Your Groovy Self" (Nancy Sinatra only), "Five Sleepy Heads" (bonus), "Western Union" (bonus), "Mine" (bonus), "Goin' Home" (bonus), "Suppose" (bonus).

Spelling, Aaron. Producer of the 1958 movie *King Creole*. He was Carolyn Jones's husband at the time.

SPINOUT. MGM, 1966. Premiered Los Angeles November 23, 1966 (93 min). Elvis's twenty-second film. Producer, Joe Pasternak. Associate Producer, Hank Moonjean. Director, Norman Taurog. Cast: Mike McCoy/Elvis Presley, Cynthia Foxhugh/Shelly Fabares, Diana St. Clair/Diane McBain, Les/Deborah Walley, Susan/Dodie Marshall, Curly/Jack Mullaney, Lt. Tracy Richards/Will Hutchins, Philip Short/Warren Berlinger, Larry/Jimmy Hawkins, Howard Foxhugh/Carl Betz, Bernard Ranley/Cecil Kellaway, Violet Ranley/Una Merkel, Blodgett/Frederic Worlock, Harry/Dave Barry, The Jordanaires/The Jordanaires. Screenplay, Theodore J. Flicker and George Kirgo. Photography, Daniel L. Fapp. Music, George Stoll. Choreography, Jack Baker. Art Direction, George W. Davis and Edward Carfagno. Set Direction, Henry Grace and Hugh Hunt. Special Visual Effects, J. McMillan Johnson and Carroll L. Shepphird. Technical Adviser, Col Tom Parker. Assistant Director, Claude Binyon, Jr. Editor, Rita Roland. Songs sung by Elvis: "Adam and Evil," "Stop, Look and Listen," "All That I Am," "Am I Ready," "Smorgasbord," "Never Say Yes," "Beach Shack," "I'll Be Back," "Spinout."

Spinout. RCA 47-8941. Released in October 1966 as a 45 rpm single. It reached #40 on *Billboard*'s Hot 100 chart. "Spinout" reportedly sold over a million copies. "All That I Am" was on the flip side. Written by Sid Wayne, Ben Weisman, and Darrell Fuller, "Spinout" was the title song of the 1966 movie of the same name. It appeared in the Long Playing albums "Spinout" (RCA LPM/LSP-3702) and "Elvis in Hollywood" (RCA DPL2-0168).

Spinout. RCA 447-0658. Gold Standard Series re-issue of RCA 47-8941.

Spinout. RCA LPM/LSP-3702. Released in October 1966 as a 33⅓ rpm Long Playing album. It reached #18 on *Billboard*'s Hot LP chart. "Spinout" contained songs from the 1966 movie *Spinout* plus three bonus songs. Songs included—Side 1: "Stop, Look and Listen," "Adam and Evil," "All That I Am," "Never Say Yes," "Am I Ready," "Beach Shack." Side 2: "Spinout," "Smorgasbord," "I'll Be Back," "Tomorrow Is a Long Time" (bonus), "Down in the Alley" (bonus), "I'll Remember You" (bonus).

Spirit of America Records. Bootleg company that released the double album "Rockin' with Elvis New Year's Eve."

Spreckles, Judy. Heiress to a sugar fortune who was romantically linked to Elvis in 1957–58. She was millionaire Adolph Spreckles's sixth wife. (Another wife of Spreckles was Kay Williams, who in 1955 became Clark Gable's fifth wife).

Spring Fever. Song that Elvis sang in the 1965 movie *Girl Happy*. Written by Bill Giant, Bernie Baum, and Florence Kaye, "Spring Fever" appeared in the Long Playing album "Girl Happy" (RCA LPM/LSP-3338).

Springfield, Dusty. Female British star who was once part of the folk group the Springfields. She recorded "You Don't Have to Say You Love Me" (Philips 40371) in 1966. Elvis later recorded the song in 1970.

Spy Who Loved Me, The. A 1977 James Bond movie starring Roger Moore. It was the last movie that Elvis saw in public, as he had rented the Southbrook Theatre on Tuesday evening, August 9, 1977.

Staff Sergeant. Highest rank achieved by Elvis while in the Army (1958–60).

Stage Show. CBS-TV series, starring Tommy and Jimmy Dorsey and produced by Jackie Gleason, in which Elvis made his national TV debut, on January 28, 1956. "Stage Show" was originally a summer replacement for "The Jackie Gleason Show." It entered the fall 1955 lineup, preceding Gleason's "The Honeymooners." Presley signed for six Saturday-night appearances at $1,250 each. In March 1956 Bobby Darin made his TV debut on "Stage Show." Elvis sang the following songs: January 28, 1956: "Blue Suede Shoes," "Heartbreak Hotel" (with Dorsey Orchestra). February 4, 1956: "Tutti Frutti," "I Was the One." February 11, 1956: "Shake, Rattle and Roll" (with "Flip, Flop and Fly" ending), "I Got a Woman." February 18, 1956: "Baby Let's Play House," "Tutti Frutti." March 17, 1956: "Blue Suede Shoes," "Heartbreak Hotel." March 24, 1956: "Money Honey," "Heartbreak Hotel."

Stamps Quartet. Vocal group lead by J.D. Sumner, that sang back-up for Elvis at his concerts. Members were: Ed Enoch; Ed Hill; Larry Strickland; Buck Buckles.

Stand By Me. Gospel song written by Dr. C.H. Tindley,* founder of the Tindley Methodist Church in Philadelphia (where blues singer Bessie Smith was buried, on October 4, 1937). Elvis was credited with arranging and adapting "Stand By Me" on the only album in which it appeared, "How Great Thou Art" (RCA LPM/LSP-3758).

Standing Room Only. RCA LSP-4762. Projected Long Playing album that was never released. "Standing Room Only" was to have contained songs from Elvis's live performances at the Hilton Hotel in Las Vegas (February 14–17, 1972) and studio tracks from Hollywood (March 17–19, 1972).

Stanley, William "Billy" Job. Elvis's stepbrother, the son of Dee Stanley Presley.

Stanley, Bill. Davada Elliot's first husband (married February 1, 1949). While in the U.S. Army in Europe, he served as General George S. Patton's bodyguard during World War II.

Stanley, Davada "Dee." Vernon Presley's second wife, Elvis's stepmother. Vernon met Davada Stanley in West Germany while Elvis was in the Army. The Huntsville, Alabama, woman at the time was in the process of divorcing her husband, an Army sergeant. Vernon Presley and Davada Stanley were married on July 3, 1960, in a private ceremony at the home of her brother. Elvis did not attend because he was filming *G.I. Blues* (1960). Vernon Presley filed for divorce in May 1977, citing irreconcilable differences. It was reported on November 15, 1977, that Davada Stanley had received a Dominican Republic divorce.

Stanley, David. Stepbrother of Elvis. He was employed as a security man at Graceland at the time of Elvis's death. David Stanley is the son of Dee Stanley Presley.

Stanley, Richard "Rick" Earl. Stepbrother of Elvis, who worked at Graceland the night of Elvis's death. Under orders from Elvis, Ricky delivered to Elvis two packets of pills, which contributed to the death of the musician. Rick Stanley is the son of Dee Stanley Presley.

Stanwyck, Barbara. Great veteran movie actress, born Ruby Stevens. She was nominated four times for Best Actress for an Academy Award. In 1939 she married actor Robert Taylor. Barbara Stanwyck starred in the TV series "The Big Valley." Barbara Stanwyck played the female lead (as Maggie Morgan) in the 1964 movie *Roustabout* (the role was turned down by Mae West). Barbara Stanwyck is a member of the National Cowboy Hall of Fame.

Star Is Born, A. Movie filmed on four occasions over the years:

---

*Songwriter Thomas A. Dorsey was inspired by Dr. Tindley to move from the blues field to the gospel field, where he became one of the greatest writers of gospel songs.

What Price Hollywood (1932)—Constance Bennett and Neil Hamilton; *A Star Is Born* (1937)—Janet Gaynor and Fredric March; *A Star Is Born* (1954)—Judy Garland and James Mason; *A Star Is Born* (1976)—Barbara Streisand and Kris Kristofferson. It was for the last version that Streisand wanted to co-star with Elvis in what would have been his best screen role, but Col. Parker couldn't come to an agreement, as he wanted $1 million rather than to settle for a percentage of the movie's gross. Kenny Loggins also turned down the lead in *A Star Is Born*.

Starkey, Gerald. Police doctor to whom Elvis gave a Lincoln Continental Mark IV on January 14, 1976. (See: Kennedy, Jerry)

Starlight Wrangles. Country band headed by Doug Poindexter, who appeared in the local clubs in Memphis and who cut a few records for the Sun label. Both Bill Black and Scotty Moore were members of the group. It is believed that Elvis once appeared with the band in a club in Memphis in 1954. Sam Phillips originally considered to have the Starlight Wrangles back Elvis, but when two of the band's members, Bill Black and Scotty Moore first began backing Elvis the sound they created filled the bill. An agreement was made between Elvis, Bill Black, and Scotty Moore, that Elvis would receive 50% of their future earnings, with Bill and Scotty each receiving 25%. The members of the Starlight Wranglers were: Scotty Moore (guitar); Bill Black (bass); Millard Yeo (fiddler); Clyde Rush (guitar); Tommy Seals (steel guitar). Doug Poindexter recorded one song for Sun—"Now She Cares No More for Me"/"My Kind of Carrying On" (Sun 202) in 1954.

Starr, Kay. One of Elvis's two favorite female singers (the other being Patti Page) as stated in an interview with Red Robinson in Vancouver, British Columbia, on August 31, 1957.

Starr, Ringo. Ex-member of the most successful musical group of all time, the Beatles, born Richard Starkey. Elvis once gave Ringo Starr a cowboy holster, which Ringo proudly displays today in his Weybridge, Surrey, home (See: Beatles, The)

Starting Today. Song written by Don Robertson for Elvis in 1961. "Starting Today" appeared in the Long Playing album "Something for Everybody" (RCA LPM/LSP-2370).

Startin' Tonight. Song that Elvis sang in the 1965 movie *Girl Happy*. "Startin' Tonight" was written by Lenore Rosenblatt and Victor Millrose and appeared in the Long Playing album "Girl Happy" (RCA LPM/LSP-3338).

Star Wars. A 1977 movie starring Mark Hamill, Harrison Ford, Carrie Fisher, and Alec Guinness. It has become the largest-grossing movie of all time. Elvis tried to obtain a print of *Star Wars* to show Lisa Marie on the night of August 15, 1977, but was unable to be so. He died the next day.

Statue Inscription at the Las Vegas Hilton Hotel.

ELVIS AARON PRESLEY

MEMORIES OF ELVIS WILL ALWAYS BE WITH US. NONE OF US REALLY, TOTALLY, KNOW HOW GREAT A PERFORMER HE WAS. ALL OF US AT THE LAS VEGAS HILTON WERE PROUD TO PRESENT ELVIS IN OUR SHOWROOM. THE DECORATIONS IN THE HOTEL, THE BANNERS, THE STREAMERS, "ELVIS, ELVIS" ALWAYS CREATED GREAT EXCITEMENT WITH HIS LOYAL FANS AND FRIENDS. THE LAS VEGAS HILTON WAS ELVIS' HOME AWAY FROM HOME. HIS ATTENDANCE RECORDS ARE A LEGEND. WE WILL MISS HIM. THANKS, ELVIS, FROM ALL OF US,

BARRON HILTON

Statue of a King. A 1977 Elvis tribute record by Ronnie McDowell on Compass Records (Compass 009).

Stax Recording Studios. Memphis recording studios, on McLemore Ave., founded by Jim Stewart and his sister Estelle Axton in 1960, and utilized by Elvis for part of his Memphis recording sessions. Stax Records was originally named Satellite Records, on which the Markeys recorded their 1961 hit "Last Night" (Satellite 107). The building used was the old Capitol Cinema.

Stay Away. RCA 47-9465. Released in March 1968 as a 45 rpm single. It reached #67 on *Billboard*'s Hot 100 chart. Reportedly "Stay Away" sold a million copies. "U. S. Male" was on the flip side. Written by Sid Tepper and Roy C. Bennett, "Stay Away" used the melody of "Greensleeves." It was sung by Elvis in the 1968 movie *Stay Away, Joe* and appeared in the Long Playing albums "Almost in Love" (RCA CAS-2440) (the second pressing in 1973) and "Almost in Love" (Pickwick CAS-2440).

Stay Away. RCA 447-0664. Gold Standard Series re-issue of RCA 47-9465.

Stay Away. RCA MTR-243. Special 45 rpm Extended Play promotional release. Songs included—Side 1: "Stay Away," "U. S. Male." Side 2: "Guitar Man," "Big Boss Man."

STAY AWAY, JOE. MGM, 1968. Premiered Birmingham, Alabama, March 8, 1968 (101 min). Elvis's twenty-sixth movie. Producer, Douglas Laurence. Director, Peter Tewksbury. Cast: Joe Lightcloud/Elvis Presley, Charlie Lightcloud/Burgess Meredith, Glenda Callahan/Joan Blondell, Annie Lightcloud/Katy Jurado, Grandpa/Thomas Gomez, Hy Slager/Henry Jones, Bronc Hoverty/L.Q. Jones, Mamie Callahan/Quentin Dean, Mrs. Hawkins/Anne Seymour, Lorne Hawkins/Angus Duncan, Congressman Morrissey/Douglas Henderson, Frank Hawk/Michael Lane, Mary Lightcloud/Susan Trustman, Hike Bowers/Warren Vanders, Bull Shortgun/Buck Kartalian, Connie Shortgun/Maurishka, Marlene Standing Rattle/Caitlin Wyles, Billie-Jo Hump/Marya Christen, Jackson He-Crow/Del "Sonny" West, Little Deer/Jennifer Peak, Dep. Sheriff Hank Matson/Bret Parker, Orville Witt/Michael Keller, Salesman/

Dick Wilson, Indian/David Cadiente, Judge Nibley/Harry Harvey, Sr., Workman/Joe Esposito, Announcer/Robert Lieb, The Jordanaires/The Jordanaires. Screenplay, Burt Kennedy and Michael A. Hoey. Photography, Fred Koenekamp. Music, Jack Marshall. Art Direction, George W. Davis and Carl Anderson. Set Decoration, Henry Grace and Don Greenwood, Jr. Assistant Director, Dale Hutchinson. Editor, George W. Brooks. Songs Sung by Elvis: "Stay Away, Joe," "All I Needed Was the Rain," "Dominick," "Lovely Mamie," "Stay Away."

Stay Away, Joe. Song that Elvis sang in the 1968 movie *Stay Away, Joe.* "Stay Away, Joe" was written by Sid Wayne and Ben Weisman. It appeared in the following Long Playing albums: "Let's Be Friends" (RCA Camden CAS-2408); "Let's Be Friends" (Pickwick CAS-2408); "Almost in Love" (RCA Camden CAS-2440) (the 1970 pressing only). In the 1973 pressing of "Almost in Love," "Stay Away, Joe" was removed from the album and "Stay Away" was substituted. The 1975 Pickwick release of "Almost in Love" does not include "Stay Away, Joe."

Steadfast, Loyal, and True. Song that Elvis sang in the 1958 movie *King Creole.* "Steadfast, Loyal, and True" was the school song of Royal High School, the school that Danny Fisher (Elvis) attended. Written by Jerry Leiber and Mike Stoller, "Steadfast, Loyal, and True" is the official theme song of the International Elvis Presley Appreciation Society. It appeared in the Long Playing albums "King Creole" (RCA LPM-1884) and "King Creole" (RCA LSP-1884 [e]).

Steamroller Blues. RCA 74-0910. Released in March 1973 as a 45 rpm single. It reached #17 on *Billboard*'s Hot 100 chart and #31 on the Country chart. "Fool" was on the flip side. "Steamroller Blues" was written by James Taylor and first appeared in his 1970 album "Sweet Baby James" (Warner Bros. 1843). Elvis sang "Steamroller Blues" in the 1973 TV special "Elvis: Aloha from Hawaii" and it appeared in the Long Playing album "Elvis: Aloha from Hawaii via Satellite" (RCA VPSX-6089).

Steamroller Blues. RCA GB-10156. Gold Standard Series re-issue of RCA 74-0910.

Stefaniak, Elisabeth. Adopted daughter of Army Sfc. Raymond L. McCormick, she was Elvis's secretary in Bad Nauheim, Germany.

Steppin' Out of Line. Song that Elvis recorded for the 1961 movie *Blue Hawaii,* but it was cut from the final print of the film. In the movie, Elvis told Jenny Maxwell, "You're steppin' out of line." At that point, the song is cut. "Steppin' Out of Line" was written by Fred Wise, Ben Weisman, and Dolores Fuller and appeared in the Long Playing album "Pot Luck" (RCA LPM/LSP-2523).

Steve Allen Show, The. TV series, hosted by comedian, composer, and musician Steve Allen. It was Steve Allen who composed the lyrics to the Academy Award-winning song "Picnic." Elvis appeared on the "Steve Allen Show" on July 1, 1956. He was instructed to attire himself in evening dress and not to dance while he sang. Elvis did a skit with Allen, Imogene Coca, and Andy Griffith, singing a few lines about Tonto Candy Bars. Among the artists who made their TV debuts on "The Steve Allen Show" are: Johnny Burnette, Jerry Lee Lewis, and Trini Lopez. Elvis sang "I Want You, I Need You, I Love You" and "Hound Dog."

Steve Garvey Junior High School. School in Lindsay, California, named for Los Angeles Dodgers' baseball player Steve Garvey when the principal let the students choose the school's name. (They originally chose Elvis Presley Junior High, but it was vetoed). Steve Garvey Jr. High is only the second school in the world to be named after a baseball player. Walter Johnson High in Bethesda, Maryland, was the first.

Steve Grayson. Elvis's role, as a race car driver in the 1968 movie *Speedway.*

Stevens, Connie. Actress and singer dated by Elvis in 1961. Connie Stevens had previously been married to singer Eddie Fisher. (See: Hawaiian Village Hotel; Barrett, Rona)

Stevens, Stella. Female lead, as Robin Ganter, in the 1962 movie *Girls! Girls! Girls!.* Stella Stevens was *Playboy*'s Playmate of the Month in January 1960. Stella Stevens became the mother-in-law of actress Kate Jackson when Kate married Stella's son, Andrew Stevens, on August 23, 1978.

Stevenson, Venetia. Hollywood actress and daughter of movie star Anna Lee Venetia* and director Robert Stevenson (*Mary Poppins*, 1964) whom Elvis dated in 1958. While Elvis was in the Army, Venetia Stevenson once flew to West Germany to spend some time with him. She later married singer Don Everly.

Stiles, Gloria. Maiden name of Terri Taylor who claims Elvis Presley fathered her child, Candy Jo. (See: Fuller, Candy Jo; Taylor, Terri)

Strand Theatre. Memphis theatre where the world premiere of *Loving You* took place July 9, 1957. The film was shown at 9:15 A.M., 11:05 A.M., 12:55 P.M., 2:45 P.M., 4:35 P.M., 6:25 P.M., 8:15 P.M., 10:05 P.M.

St. Joseph's Hospital. Memphis medical facility, at 264 Jackson Ave., where Gladys Presley worked as a nurse's aide, 1949–50.

Stoll, Fred. Gatekeeper at Graceland for fourteen years.

Stone, Jesse. Composer/musical arranger for Atlantic Records. He arranged and orchestrated Chick Willis's "C.C. Rider," among other releases. Elvis recorded the following Jesse Stone compositions: "Down in the Valley"; "Like a Baby"; "Money

---

*Real name: Joanne Winnifrith.

Honey"; "Shake, Rattle and Roll" (composed under the pseudonym of Charles Calhoun). Had Atlantic Records obtained Elvis from Sun in 1955, chances are Jesse Stone would have become Elvis's producer.

Stone, Mike. Karate expert who, in January 1972, became the bodyguard for record producer Phil Spector. It was in this capacity at the Las Vegas Hilton that Elvis first met Mike, suggesting he become Priscilla's karate instructor. On August 5, 1973, Ed Parker introduced Mike Stone to Priscilla; the two became good friends and eventually lovers.

Stone for Danny Fisher, A. A 1952 novel by Harold Robbins, on which the movie *King Creole* was based. In the book, Danny Fisher was a boxer; in the movie, a singer. In the book, the location was New York City; in the film, New Orleans.

Stop, Look and Listen. Song that Elvis sang in the 1966 movie *Spinout*. "Stop, Look and Listen" was written by Joy Byers and appeared in the Long Playing album "Spinout" (RCA LPM/LSP-3702).

Stop Where You Are. Song that Elvis sang in the 1966 movie *Paradise—Hawaiian Style*. The instrumental breaks are longer in the film version. "Stop Where You Are" was written by Bill Giant, Bernie Baum, and Florence Kaye and appeared in the Long Playing album "Paradise—Hawaiian Style" (RCA LPM/LSP-3643).

Storm, Tempest. Las Vegas stripper, romantically involved with Elvis in 1957.

Story of Elvis Presley, The. Novelty song by Jim Ford on Drumfire Records (Drumfire 2). The song made reference to Elvis and "Heartbreak Hotel."

Strada, Al. Elvis's wardrobe man at Graceland (one of several whom Elvis employed over the years).

Stranger in My Own Home Town. Song written by Percy Mayfield and recorded by Elvis at the American Sound Studios in Memphis on February 17, 1969. "Stranger in My Own Home Town" appeared in the Long Playing albums "From Memphis to Vegas/From Vegas to Memphis" (RCA LSP-6020) and "Elvis—Back in Memphis" (RCA LSP-4429).

Stranger in the Crowd. Song written by Winfield Scott and recorded by Elvis in 1970. Elvis sang "Stranger in the Crowd" in the 1970 documentary *Elvis—That's the Way It Is* and it appeared in the Long Playing album "Elvis—That's the Way It Is" (RCA LSP-4445).

Strauss, Ron. Co-pilot of Elvis's Convair 880 jet; reportedly he earned $39,000 a year.

Streisand, Barbra. First performer to appear at the International Hotel in Las Vegas, opening on July 2, 1969. Elvis was the second performer, opening on July 26, after Streisand's successful appearance. Barbra Streisand would have been Elvis's leading lady had Elvis accepted her offer to star in the movie *A*

Star Is Born. Barbra Streisand and Neil Diamond sang in the same school chorus at New York's Eramus High School. In 1978 Barbra Streisand broke Elvis's record for the highest-paid entertainer in Las Vegas, when she signed for $350,000 a week at the Riviera Hotel.

Strictly Elvis. RCA EPA-994. This was a 45 rpm Extended Play album released in January 1957. Songs included—Side 1: "Long Tall Sally," "First in Line." Side 2: "How Do You Think I Feel," "How's the World Treating You."

Stuck on You. RCA 47-7740. Released in March 1960 as a 45 rpm single. It reached #1 on *Billboard*'s Hot 100 chart (for four weeks, April 25–May 23) and #6 on the Rhythm and Blues chart. "Stuck on You" was Elvis's first release after being discharged from the Army. It sold over 2 million copies (advance orders were 1,275,077 copies). "Fame and Fortune" was on the flip side. Elvis sang "Stuck on You" on "The Frank Sinatra-Timex Special" (May 12, 1960). Written by Aaron Schroeder and J. Leslie McFarland, "Stuck on You" appeared in the following Long Play albums: "Elvis' Golden Records, Volume 3" (RCA LPM/LSP-2765); "Elvis: Worldwide 50 Gold Award Hits, Volume 1" (RCA LPM-6401); "Elvis" (RCA DPL1-0056 [e]).

Stuck on You. RCA 447-0627. Gold Standard Series re-issue of RCA 47-7740.

Stuck on You. RCA 61-7740. A 45 rpm "Living Stereo" release— Elvis's first. "Fame and Fortune" was on the flip side.

Student Prince, The. A 1927 silent movie starring Norma Shearer* and Ramon Novarro. The movie was advertised on a theater marquee on Main Street in Radford Center, Iowa in the 1960 movie *The Trouble with Girls (And How To Get Into It).*

Stuff. Black poodle owned by Elvis's aunt.

Sturgeon, Phillip. Doctor who gave Elvis his blood-group test in 1971 to prove that he was not the father of Jason Parker, as claimed by Jason's mother, Patricia Parker.

Stuttering. Speech defect that occurred when Elvis either talked rapidly or was nervous. In one scene in the 1964 movie *Kissin' Cousins,* Elvis was seen and heard to stutter slightly. Country singer Mel Tillis consistently stutters when he talks, yet when he sings the stuttering disappears.

Stutz Blackhawk Coup. Custom automobile purchased by Elvis on September 10, 1971, from dealer Jules Meyers at a cost of $38,500. Annual production of the car was 100. It was custom handcrafted in Italy from mostly American parts and included a General Motors frame, suspension, and 490 h.p. engine. Elvis purchased the very first Stutz Blackhawk. On the way to a car

---

*Norma Shearer, nicknamed the "First Lady of the Screen," and wife of Irving Thalberg, had previously been a model posing for noted artists James Montgomery Flagg and Charles Dana Gibson.

wash, Elvis's driver totaled the car. Elvis owned three Stutz Bearcats, giving one to Dr. Elias Ghanem.

Such a Night. RCA 47-8400. Released in July 1964 as a 45 rpm single. It reached #16 on *Billboard's* Hot 100 chart. "Never Ending" was on the flip side. "Such a Night" was written by Lincoln Chase* and originally recorded by Clyde McPhatter and the Drifters (Atlantic 1019) in 1954. Johnnie Ray also recorded a version of "Such a Night" (Columbia 40020) in 1954, but it was banned from the air because of its suggestive lyrics. Elvis's version of "Such a Night" appeared in the Long Playing albums "Elvis Is Back" (RCA LPM/LSP-2231) and "Elvis—A Legendary Performer, Volume 2" (RCA CPL1-1349).

Such a Night. RCA 447-0645. Gold Standard Series re-issue of RCA 47-8400.

Such a Night/Such a Night. RCA JB-50170. Special 45 rpm promotional release. One version of "Such a Night" was from the Long Playing album "Elvis Is Back" (RCA LSP-2231), and the other version was from the Long Playing album "Elvis—A Legendary Performer, Volume 2" (RCA CPL1-1349).

Sullivan, Ed. Newspaper columnist and host of TV variety shows "Toast of the Town" and the "Ed Sullivan Show," nicknamed the "Great Stoneface." He was portrayed by comedian Will Jordon on numerous occasions. (See: Jordon, Will) On his September 9, 1956, show, Ed was to have introduced Elvis, but on August 6 he was involved in a head-on automobile accident that put him in the hospital. He missed his next five shows. For the Elvis appearance Charles Laughton was the substitute host.

Summer Kisses, Winter Tears. Song recorded by Elvis for the 1960 movie *Flaming Star,* but it was cut from the final print of the film. "Summer Kisses, Winter Tears" was written by Fred Wise, Ben Weisman, and Jack Lloyd and appeared in the Extended Play album "Elvis By Request" (RCA LPC-128) and the Long Playing album "Elvis for Everyone" (RCA LPM/LSP-3450).

Sumner, Donnie. A member of the Stamps Quartet and a member of Voice, both of which were back-up vocal groups for Elvis.

Sumner, J.D. Bass singer who had been a friend of Elvis since Elvis was fourteen. Sumner has sung with the Blackwood Brothers. His vocal group, the Stamps, backed Elvis in many recording sessions and concerts. The Stamps consist of Donnie Sumner, Bill Baize, Ed Enoch, and Ed Wideman.

Sun Also Rises, The. Novel written by Ernest Hemingway in 1926. It was mentioned in the 1969 movie *The Trouble with Girls (And How To Get Into It).*

Sun International. Company set up by Shelby Singleton to release

---

*Lincoln Chase is the husband of singer Shirley Ellis, for whom he has composed her novelty hit songs *"The Nitty Gritty"* and *"The Name Game."*

those songs he acquired when he bought Sun Records in July 1969. Singleton acquired 4,000 original master recordings. (See: Singleton, Shelby; "Save the Last Dance for Me")

Sun Records. Memphis record label founded by Sam Phillips in 1952. Prior to establishing his own label, Phillips leased his recordings of Howlin' Wolf, B.B. King, Walter Horton, Little Junior Parker, and Bobby Blue Bland to various labels, including Chess Records and RPM Records. The recording studio was located at 706 Union Street, where the Memphis Recording Service was also located. In the late 1950s, Sun Records moved to 639 Madison Ave., the present-day home of Sam Phillips's Recording Service, Inc. Shelby Singleton bought Sun Records in 1963, moving the firm to Nashville. The original Sun building later sold it, housed a plumbing company and then an automobile-parts firm. The building was somewhat restored by Grayline Tours after Elvis's death. "Blue in My Condition"/ "Sellin' My Whiskey" by Jackie Boy and Little Walter (Jack Kelly and Walter Horton) was the first Sun recording (Sun 1974). (See: Phillips, Sam; Singleton, Shelby; Flip Records; Parker, Little Junior)

Sun Records Releases of Elvis. Sun 209: "That's All Right (Mama)"/"Blue Moon of Kentucky" (July 1954). Sun 210: "Good Rockin' Tonight"/"I Don't Care If the Sun Don't Shine" (September 1954). Sun 215: "Milkcow Blues Boogie"/"You're a Heartbreaker" (January 1955). Sun 217: "I'm Left, You're Right, She's Gone"/"Baby Let's Play House" (April 1955). Sun 223: "Mystery Train"/"I Forgot to Remember to Forget" (August 1955).

Other songs Elvis recorded for Sun, but which were later released by RCA Victor, were: "Blue Moon"; "Harbor Lights"; "I'll Never Let You Go (Little Darlin')"; "I Love You Because"; "Just Because"; "Trying to Get to You." RCA Victor has also released some alternate takes of the Sun sessions.

Elvis recorded the following songs for Sun, which were never released: "Always Late (With Your Kisses)"; "Blue Guitar"; "Crying Heart Blues"; "Down the Line"; "Give Me More, More, More"; "Gone"; "Night Train to Memphis"; "Oakie Boogie"; "Satisfied"; "Sunshine"; "Tennessee, Saturday Night"; "That's the Stuff You Gotta Watch"; "Uncle Penn." There are other songs that Elvis recorded for Sun, but their authenticity has yet to be verified.

Sunrise Hospital. Medical facility in Las Vegas where Elvis went on several occasions.

Sunshine. Unreleased Elvis Sun recording of 1955.

Sun Years, The. Sun 1001. A 33⅓ Long Playing album released by Sun International in 1977, shortly after Elvis's death. Written and produced by Shelby Singleton, Jr., "The Sun Years" was an historical documentary of the years 1954 and 1955. Narration on the album was provided by Gilbert Blasingame, Jr.

347

Excerpts of all of Elvis's released Sun recordings were included, as well as some of his unreleased material. Side 1: "The Sun Years" (Contained parts from actual recording sessions with the voice of Sam Phillips, the voice of Elvis Presley, plus excerpts of Elvis Presley's Sun recordings, issued and unissued). Side 2: "Interviews And Music" (Contained interviews by Jay Thompson at Wichita Falls, Texas, Charlie Walker at San Antonio, Texas, plus various other rare Elvis Presley talking intros on stage and television).

Superstar Outtakes. A 33⅓ rpm bootleg album. Songs included— Side 1: "Steve Allen Show" (July 1, 1956): "I Want You, I Need You, I Love You," "Hound Dog," Comedy sketch, 1968 NBC-TV special "Elvis": "Let Yourself Go," "It Hurts Me." Side 2: "Las Vegas" (August 1969): "Yesterday/Hey Jude," Elvis talks; introduction of the band, "Happy Birthday, James Burton," "In the Ghetto," "Suspicious Minds," "What'd I Say," "Can't Help Fallin' in Love," "Bridge Over Troubled Water."

Superstition Inn. Motel where Elvis and his friends stayed while filming location shots at Apache Junction (outside Phoenix, Arizona) for the 1969 movie *Charro!*.

Suppose. Song that Elvis recorded for the 1968 movie *Speedway*, but it was cut from the final print of the film. Rumor has it that "Suppose" is included in the prints in Malaya. "Suppose" was written by Dee and Goehring. It appeared in the Long Playing album "Speedway" (RCA LSP-3989).

Surber, Raymond. Automobile salesman at Schilling Lincoln-Mercury (987 Union Ave.) where, on September 23, 1974, Elvis bought his entire stock of Lincoln Continental Mark IVs. The total sale was over $60,000. Surber's commission was approximately $4,000.

Surrender. RCA 47-7850. Released in February 1961 as a 45 rpm single. It reached #1 on *Billboard*'s Hot 100 chart (for two weeks, March 20–April 3) and also #1 in the United Kingdom (for five weeks, May 14–June 18). "Surrender" sold over 5 million copies. "Lonely Man" was on the flip side. "Surrender" was a comtemporary version of the 1911 Italian ballad "Torna a Sorrento" ("Come back to Sorrento"), which was written by G.D. de Curtis and E. de Curtis. Doc Pomus and Mort Shuman added English words in 1960. "Surrender" appeared in the following Long Playing albums: "Elvis' Golden Records, Volume 3" (RCA LPM/LSP 2765); "Elvis: Worldwide 50 Gold Award Hits, Volume 1" (RCA LPM-6401); "Elvis" (RCA DPL2-0056 [e]); "Elvis—A Legendary Performer, Volume 3" (RCA CPL2-3082).

Surrender. RCA 447-0630. Gold Standard Series re-issue of RCA 47-7850.

Surrender. RCA 37-7850. A 33⅓ rpm single release—the first released by RCA. "Lonely Man" was on the flip side.

Surrender. RCA 61-7850. A 45 rpm "Living Stereo" release. "Lonely Man" was on the flip side.

Surrender. RCA 68-7850. A 33⅓ rpm "Living Stereo" single— the only one by Elvis released by RCA. "Lonely Man" was on the flip side.

Susan When She Tried. Song written by Don S. Reid and originally recorded by the Statler Brothers (Mercury 73625) in 1975. Elvis recorded "Susan When She Tried" in 1975 and it appeared in the Long Playing album "Today" (RCA APL1-1039).

Susie Q. Hit song by Dale Hawkins (Checker 863) in 1957. Lead guitarist on the record was James Burton (who would later play for Elvis). Elvis sang only a line or two of "Susie Q" in one of his 1970s concerts.

Suspicion. RCA 447-0639. Released in April 1964 as a 45 rpm Gold Standard Series original. "Kiss Me Quick" was on the flip side. "Suspicion" was written by Doc Pomus and Mort Shuman and originally recorded by Elvis on March 19, 1962. Elvis's version, however, was not released as a single until two months after Terry Stafford's (Crusader 101) in 1964. Stafford's version of "Suspicion" reached #3 on *Billboard*'s Hot 100 chart and sold over a million copies. "Suspicion," by Elvis, appeared in the Long Playing album "Pot Luck" (RCA LPM/LSP-2523).

Suspicion. Album released in 1964 by Terry Stafford on Crusader Records (Crusader 1001). Four Elvis songs were included in the album.

Suspicious Minds. RCA 47-9764. Released in August 1969 as a 45 rpm single. It reached #1 on *Billboard*'s Hot 100 chart (for one week, November 1–8) and #2 in the United Kingdom. "Suspicious Minds" sold well over a million copies. "You'll Think of Me" was on the flip side. Elvis sang "Suspicious Minds" in the 1970 documentary *Elvis—That's the Way It Is,* in the 1972 documentary *Elvis on Tour,* and the 1973 TV special "Elvis: Aloha from Hawaii." The version that appeared on the single release was the product of splicing three takes, adding horns, and overdubbing Elvis's group. "Suspicious Minds" was written by Mark James and appeared in the following Long Playing albums: "From Memphis to Vegas/ From Vegas to Memphis" (RCA LSP-6020); "Elvis: Worldwide 50 Gold Award Hits, Volume 1" (RCA LPM-6401); "Elvis in Person" (RCA LSP-4428); "Elvis as Recorded at Madison Square Garden" (RCA LSP-4776); "Elvis: Aloha from Hawaii Via Satellite" (RCA VPSX-6089).

Suspicious Minds. RCA 447-0673. Gold Standard Series re-issue of RCA 47-9764.

Suzore No. 2 Theater. Neighborhood theater (279 N. Main) that Elvis frequented during high school. On July 7, 1954 (the night Dewey Phillips first played "That's All Right [Mama]"), Elvis went to the Suzore No. 2 Theater to see a movie because he was too shy to hear his own record. The movie he saw was *The Best Years of Our Lives* (1946). (See: Best Years of Our Lives, The)

Swan, Billy. One-time gate guard at Graceland. Prior to becoming a recording artist and later a producer, he and Kris Kristofferson were employed as janitors at the Columbia Records studio in Nashville. Billy Swan composed and recorded "I Can Help" in 1974, which Elvis recorded in March 1975.

Sweet Angeline. Song written by Arnold, Martin, and Morrow and recorded by Elvis in 1973. The instrumental tracks were recorded at the Stax Studios in Memphis and Elvis's voice track was cut at his home in Palm Springs, California. "Sweet Angeline" appeared in the Long Playing album "Raised on Rock"/"For Ol' Times Sake" (RCA APL1-0388).

Sweet Bird of Youth. A 1962 movie based on the play by Tennessee Williams (Thomas Lanier Williams) for which Elvis was considered for the lead role of Chance Wayne. Because Elvis would have been portrayed as a "bad guy," Col. Parker turned down the offer, allowing Paul Newman to win the part.

Sweet Caroline. Song written and originally recorded by Neil Diamond in 1969. "Sweet Caroline" (UNI 55136) reached #4 on *Billboard*'s Hot 100 chart and sold over a million copies. Elvis recorded "Sweet Caroline" in 1970 and sang it in the 1970 documentary *Elvis—That's the Way It Is*. It appeared in the Long Playing album "On Stage—February, 1970" (RCA LSP-4362).

Sweet Inspirations. Black female vocal group which sang back-up for Elvis in concert dates and some recording sessions for eight years. The trio originally was the back-up vocal group for Aretha Franklin. Members were: Emily "Cissy" Houston; Myrna Smith; Estelle Brown; Sylvia Shenwell. The vocal group recorded a number of songs for Atlantic Records, the most successful being "Sweet Inspiration"* in 1968. Elvis asked to use the group after he had heard them on record. After Elvis's death, the Sweet Inspirations joined Rick Nelson's show and are today a solo act.

Sweetpea. Gladys Presley's pet dog at the time of her death. Sweetpea was named for the adopted son of the cartoon sailor, Popeye.

Swing Down, Sweet Chariot. RCA 447-0652. Released in February 1966 as 45 rpm Gold Standard original. "Milky White Way" was on the flip side. "Swing Down, Sweet Chariot" was based on an old black spriritual known as "Swing Low, Sweet Chari-

---

*The group was not named after the song. The song was written for the group. Two of Aretha Franklin's sisters, Carolyn and Erma, were original members of the group.

ot."* Elvis sang "Swing Down, Sweet Chariot" in the 1968 movie *The Trouble with Girls* (*And How to Get Into It*) and it appeared in the Long Playing albums "His Hand in Mine" (RCA LPM/LSP-2328) and "His Hand in Mine" (RCA ANL1-1319).

Swingers. Las Vegas casino in the 1964 movie *Viva Las Vegas*. Lucky Jackson (Elvis) led a group of rowdy Texans out of the casino, singing "The Yellow Rose of Texas" and "The Eyes of Texas."

Sylvia. Song written by Geoff Stephens and Les Reed and recorded by Elvis in 1970. "Sylvia" appeared in the Long Playing album "Elvis—Now" (RCA LSP-4671).

T

2. Number of the Ferris wheel seat ridden by Elvis and Joan Freeman in the "It's a Wonderful World" sequence of the 1964 movie *Roustabout*.

2-447. Tennessee state license plate number of Elvis's Harley-Davidson motorcycle in 1956.

2D-33501. The 1958 Tennessee license number of the Cadillac that Elvis drove to the Army induction center on Monday, March 24, 1958.

2X-139. The 1962 Tennessee license number of Elvis's Gold Cadillac. (See: Gold Cadillac).

12. Size of Elvis's Army combat boots.

$12.75. Reportedly, the price Vernon Presley paid for Elvis's first guitar† in January 1946. Elvis was taught to play the guitar by his two uncles, Johnny Smith and Vester Presley. (See: Bobo, Forrest L.)

13. Number of songs released on the soundtrack of Elvis's thirteenth movie, *Fun in Acapulco* (1963).

21. Number of recruits Elvis was put in charge of on the bus

---

*Numerous artists have recorded versions of the song, including: Dave Barbour and his wife Peggy Lee (Capitol 375); Benny Goodman (Victor 25492); Paul Robeson (the Rutgers All American End) (Victor 20068); the Ink Spots (Decca 1230); Bing Crosby (Decca 1809); the Sophisticates (Decca 1808). The Champs recorded a rock 'n' roll instrumental version in 1958 titled "Chariot Rock" (Challenge 59018).

†Other first guitars include: Chuck Berry ($4); B.B. King ($8); Lonnie Mack ($10); George Benson ($15); Denny Dia (of Steely Dan) ($5); Pop Staple (of the Staple Singers) ($5). Buddy Holly bought Waylon Jennings his first bass guitar. Steve Miller was given his first guitar and lessons from Les Paul (Steve was five years old). Bill Haley made his first guitar out of cardboard.

ride from the Army induction center in Memphis to Fort Chaffee, Arkansas (March 24, 1958).

.22 Savage. Elvis's favorite pistol.

24. Number of teddy bears that Elvis once claimed he won at a carnival in 1956.

25%. Believed to be Col. Tom Parker's cut of Elvis's income for his managerial/agent services.

29 Royal Street. Home address of Danny Fisher (Elvis) in the 1958 movie *King Creole*.

30 Weeks. Longest time that any Elvis song remained on *Billboard*'s Pop chart. This distinction belongs to "All Shook Up," March–October 1957. "Mystery Train" and "I Forgot to Remember to Forget" stayed on the Country chart for a total of forty weeks (August 1955–January 1956).

33 Movies. Number of movies, including two documentaries, in which Elvis appeared. He turned down several opportunities, among them: the lead in *Thunder Road* (1958); an opportunity to sing two songs in *Bye Bye Birdie* (1963); a starring role in *A Star Is Born* (1976). Elvis's screen test was a scene from *The Rainmaker* (1954).

211 Lookout Mountain. Los Angeles address of Greg Nolan's (Elvis) apartment in the 1968 movie *Live a Little, Love a Little*.

260 Pounds. Extreme weight held by Elvis prior to his death.

282. Number of teddy bears Elvis received for Christmas in 1956. Elvis made the statement on the "Ed Sullivan Show" of January 6, 1957.

311 Surrey Road. Home address, in the St. John's Wood section of London, of Jill Conway (Annette Day) in the 1967 movie *Double Trouble*.

317X. Miracle surface on RCA Victor records, beginning with the Long Playing album "Blue Hawaii."

328. Apartment number of the Presleys in the Lauderdale Courts at 185 Winchester Street.

398 Cypress Street. Address of the small apartment house to which the Presleys moved on January 7, 1953, after being evicted from 185 Winchester Street by the Memphis Housing Authority. The monthly rent there was fifty-two dollars. In April the Presleys moved to 462 Alabama Street.

1350 Leadera Circle. Palm Springs, California, address of an estate leased by Elvis.

2001: A Space Odyssey. A 1968 movie, directed by Stanley Kubrick, that used "Also Sprach Zarathustra," by Richard Strauss, as its theme. (See: Also Sprach Zarathustra)

2001 Enigma. Interesting mathematical computation relating to various dates in Elvis's life, all of which have the sum of 2001.

Month Elvis died ___	8	Day Elvis was born ___	8
Day Elvis died	16	Day Elvis died _____	16
Year Elvis died ____1977		Age Elvis died _____	42
	2001	Year Elvis was born ___1935	
			2001

2414 Lamar Avenue. Memphis address to which the Presleys moved in late 1954. Their telephone number was 37-4185. They remained there until mid-1955, when Elvis bought a home at 1414 Getwell. In 1968, the home on Lamar Ave. was converted to the Tiny Tot Nursery School.

$2,424. Cost of the train trip from Memphis to Hollywood for Elvis and six of his buddies when they rented a private railroad car in 1960. Elvis was scheduled to begin filming *G.I. Blues*.

3,116. Number of floral arrangements delivered to Elvis's mausoleum on August 17–18, 1977.

3764 Elvis Presley Boulevard. Memphis address of Graceland. Elvis Presley Boulevard was formerly Highway 51 South.

$10,000. Amount of money that Laurel Goodwin (Laurel Dodge) paid to purchase the sailing vessel *The West Wind* from Wesley Johnson (Jeremy Slate). The vessel had previously belonged to Ross Carpenter's (Elvis) late father. Laurel bought it to give to Ross.

$10,000. Amount of money that actor Johnny Tyronne (Elvis) agreed to pay Zacha (Jay Novello)—a member in good standing of the Honorable Guild of Marketplace Thieves—if Zacha would take him to safety, in the 1965 movie *Harum Scarum*.

$12,250. Amount of Union payroll taken by the Reno Brothers when they robbed a Union train on April 10, 1865, in the 1956 movie *Love Me Tender*. In actuality, the first train robbery in U. S. history took place on October 6, 1866, when the Ohio and Mississippi Railroad was robbed for $10,000 at Seymour, Indiana. The name of the gang that robbed that train was the Reno Brothers.

204843. California license plate number of Charlie Roger's (Elvis) motorcycle in the 1964 movie *Roustabout*.

$220,000. Amount of jewelry given away by Elvis during a performance in Asheville, North Carolina (July 22–24, 1975).

$250,000. Amount received by Priscilla Presley for the rights to Elvis's private home movies in 1979. They included footage of his wedding and stag parties.

2571459. Elvis's Tennessee driver's license number, issued on September 18, 1975.

332-4748. Elvis's unlisted telephone number at Graceland in the 1970s.

276571A139060. Vehicle identification number of Elvis's 1971 Stutz Blackhawk. (See: Stutz Blackhawk)

Taj. Capitol city of Lunarkand and the location of the royal palace of King Toranshad (Philip Reed) in the 1965 movie *Harum Scarum.*

Take Good Care of Her. RCA APBO-0196. Released in January 1974 as a 45 rpm single. It reached #39 on *Billboard*'s Hot 100 chart and #4 on the Country chart. "I've Got a Thing About You, Baby" was on the flip side. "Take Good Care of Her" was written by Ed Warren and Arthur Kent and originally recorded by Adam Wade (Coed 546) in 1961. Elvis's version of "Take Good Care of Her" appeared in the Long Playing albums "Good Times" (RCA CPL1-0475) and "Our Memories of Elvis" (RCA AQL1-3279).

Take Good Care of Her. RCA GB-10485. Gold Standard Series re-issue of RCA APBO-0196.

Take Me to the Fair. Song that Elvis sang in the 1963 movie *It Happened at the World's Fair.* The Mello Men backed Elvis on this song. In the film, a banjo was the only instrumental backing Elvis had on "Take Me to the Fair." It was written by Sid Tepper and Roy C. Bennett and appeared in the Long Playing album "It Happened at the World's Fair" (RCA LPM/LSP-2697).

Take My Hand, Precious Lord. Gospel song written by Thomas A. Dorsey. Elvis recorded "Take My Hand, Precious Lord" in 1957 and it appeared in the Extended Play albums "Peace in the Valley" (RCA EPA-4054) and "Peace in the Valley" (RCA EPA-5121) and the following Long Playing albums: "Elvis' Christmas Album" (RCA LOC-1035); "Elvis' Christmas Album" (RCA LPM-1951); "Elvis' Christmas Album" (RCA LSP-1951 [e]); "You'll Never Walk Alone" (RCA Camden CALX-2472); "You'll Never Walk Alone" (Pickwick CAS-2472).

Talk About the Good Times. Song written and originally recorded by Jerry Reed (RCA 9804) in 1970. Elvis recorded "Talk About the Good Times" in 1973 and it appeared in the Long Playing album "Good Times" (RCA CPL1-0475).

Tankel, Toll, and Leavitt. Los Angeles law firm that acted on behalf of Priscilla Presley in her divorce proceedings in 1973. They charged that Elvis didn't make a full disclosure of his assets to Priscilla.

Taurog, Norman. Former child actor and director of the popular movies *The Adventures of Tom Sawyer* (1938), *Boy's Town* (1938), and *Young Tom Edison* (1940). He directed the following Elvis movies: *G.I. Blues* (1960), *Blue Hawaii* (1961), *Girls! Girls! Girls!* (1962), *It Happened at the World's Fair* (1963), *Tickle Me* (1964), *Spinout* (1966), *Double Trouble* (1967), *Speedway* (1968), *Live a Little, Love a Little* (1968).

Taylor, James. Singer and composer of numerous hit songs, including: "Fire and Rain"; "You've Got a Friend"; "Carolina in My Mind." Peter Asher (of Peter and Gordon) is James Taylor's manager. James Taylor is married to singer Carly

Simon, daughter of Richard Simon, the co-founder of the publishing firm of Simon and Shuster. Taylor's younger sister, Kate, and brother, Livingston, are also recording artists.

Elvis recorded James Taylor's "Steamroller Blues" in 1973 and '74.

Taylor, Terri. Nebraska woman who, it is claimed, fathered a child by Elvis Presley. According to Terri Taylor, she first met Elvis in 1955 in Bossier City, Louisiana. She was fifteen years old and traveling and performing as a singer. It was while Elvis was performing in Lincoln and Omaha, Nebraska, in February or March of 1957, that Terri Taylor (maiden name: Gloria Stiles) became pregnant with Elvis's child. On December 22, 1956, at St. Elizabeth's Hospital in Lincoln, Nebraska, her child, Candy Jo, was born. Reportedly, Elvis telephoned Terri Taylor and sent her a few checks through the years.

Although several people substantiate Terri Taylor's story, the records indicate that Elvis did not perform in Nebraska in 1957. (See: Fuller, Candy Jo)

Taylor's Restaurant. Restaurant located at 710 Union Ave., next door to Sun Records. The Sun artists, including Elvis, would meet at Taylor's Restaurant (telephone JA6-9509) to eat and talk. Taylor's Restaurant was established in 1949. In the mid-1950s, while recording with Sun Records, Roy Orbison lived in a two-room apartment above the restaurant. Jack Clement once humorously stated that the secret of Sun Records was the popularity of Taylor's Restaurant.

TCB. *T*aking *C*are of *B*usiness.* This was Elvis's business motto and working philosophy. Elvis gave fourteen-carat gold ID bracelets to his male friends with TCB and their nicknames inscribed on them. The letters TCB appeared with lightning bolts through them. The lightning bolt symbolized the West Coast Mafia. Elvis was buried with a diamond ring bearing the initials TCB. (See: TLC)

TCB Band. Name sometimes applied to the band that backed Elvis on tour.

TCB Records. Record label that released the 1977 bootleg album "Cadillac Elvis."

Technical Adviser: Col. Tom Parker. Credit that appeared in some Elvis films.

Teddy Bear. Cute toy bear created in 1902 by Morris Michton, founder of the Ideal Toy Company. Michton named the toy after President Theodore Roosevelt. The original toy bear is on display at the Smithsonian Institute.

---

*"Taking Care of Business" was the title of the NBC-TV special broadcast on December 9, 1968, featuring Diana Ross and the Supremes, and the Temptations. The soundtrack album sold over a million copies. The Supremes and the Temptations first appeared together on "The Ed Sullivan Show." "Takin' Care of Business" was a hit record by Bachman-Turner Overdrive (Mercury 73487) in 1974.

Elvis began collecting teddy bears after a rumor was started that he did collect them. Fans sent him thousands for his nonexistent collection. On December 26, 1957, Elvis donated a truckload of teddy bears to the National Foundation for Infantile Paralysis.

(Let Me Be Your) Teddy Bear. RCA 20/47-7000. Released in June 1957 as a 78 rpm single and a 45 rpm single. It reached #1 on *Billboard*'s Hot 100 chart (for seven weeks, July 15–September 2), #1 on the Country chart, and #1 on the Rhythm and Blues chart—one of four songs to reach #1 on all three *Billboard* charts. (The other three were "Don't Be Cruel," "All Shook Up," and "Jailhouse Rock.") "(Let Me Be Your) Teddy Bear" sold over a million copies. "Loving You" was on the flip side. "(Let Me Be Your) Teddy Bear" was written by Kal Mann and Bernie Lowe for Elvis because of his fondness for teddy bears. It was sung in the 1957 movie *Loving You* and the 1977 CBS-TV special "Elvis in Concert." "(Let Me Be Your) Teddy Bear" appeared in the Extended Play album: "Loving You, Volume 1" (RCA LPM-1515); and the following Long Playing albums: "Loving You" (RCA LSP-1515 [e]); "Elvis' Golden Records" (RCA LPM-1707); "Elvis' Golden Records" (RCA LSP-1707 [e]); "Elvis: Worldwide 50 Gold Award Hits, Volume 1" (RCA LPM-6401); "Elvis as Recorded at Madison Square Garden" (RCA LSP-4776); "Elvis" (RCA DPL2-0056 [e]); "Elvis in Concert" (RCA APL2-2587); "Elvis —A Canadian Tribute" (RCA KKL1-7065); "Elvis Sings for Children (And Grownups Too)" (RCA CPL1-2901).

(Let Me Be Your) Teddy Bear. RCA 447-0620. Gold Standard Series re-issue of RCA 20/47-7000.

(Let Me Be Your) Teddy Bear. RCA PB-11320. A 45 rpm limited edition single (on green vinyl) released in July 1978, with "Puppet on a String" on the flip side.

Teddy Bear of Zizipompom. French poodle that Elvis obtained in October 1960.

Ted Jackson. Role played by Elvis (as a Navy frogman) in the 1967 movie *Easy Come, Easy Go*.

Teen Parade. Magazine that contained the plastic record, "The Truth About Me," in a 1956 issue. (See: Lynchburg Audio)

TELEVISION APPEARANCES OF ELVIS. 1955: "Louisiana Hayride," March 5, 1956: "Stage Show" (CBS), January 28—8:00 P.M. E.S.T., February 4—8:00 P.M. E.S.T., February 11—8:00 P.M. E.S.T., February 18—8:00 P.M. E.S.T., March 17 —8:30 P.M. E.S.T., March 24—8:30 P.M. E.S.T. "The Milton Berle Show" (NBC), April 3—8:00 P.M. E.S.T., June 5—10:00 P.M. E.S.T. "The Steve Allen Show" (NBC), July 1—8:00 P.M. E.S.T. "The Ed Sullivan Show" (CBS), September 9—8:00 P.M. E.S.T., October 28—8:00 P.M. E.S.T. 1957: "The Ed Sullivan Show" (CBS), January 6—8:00 P.M. E.S.T., "Dance Party" (WHBQ, Memphis). 1960: "The Frank Sinatra-Timex Special"

(ABC), May 12—9:30 P.M. E.S.T. 1968: "Elvis" (NBC Singer special), December 3—9:00 P.M. E.S.T. 1973: "Elvis: Aloha from Hawaii" (Worldwide), January 14—12:00 P.M. (Hawaiian time). "Elvis: Aloha from Hawaii" (NBC), April 4—8:30 P.M. E.S.T. 1977: "Elvis in Concert" (CBS) October 3—8:00 P.M. E.S.T.

Tell Me Pretty Baby. Song released as a 45 rpm record in 1978 with allegations that it was Elvis's first recording. Supposedly, it was recorded at Audio Recorders in Phoenix, Arizona, in 1954. "Tell Me Pretty Baby" was composed by Andrew Lee Jackson and in 1978 was "rereleased" on the Elvis Classic label (EC-5478). The song is on both sides of the record and lasts 2 minutes 12 seconds.

The music was published by the Golgotha Publishing Company.

In an affidavit signed by Pete Falco on July 6, 1978, he stated that he paid Elvis $15 to record "Tell Me Pretty Baby" with his group, the Red Dots. Vernon Presley contested the song's authenticity, stating that Elvis was never in Phoenix in 1954 and never recorded for any company prior to Sun Records. Singer Michael Conley later admitted making the fake recording, although his manager, Hal Freeman, stated that Conley lied.

Tell Me Why. RCA 47-8740. Released in January 1966 as a 45 rpm single. It reached #33 on *Billboard*'s Hot 100 chart. "Blue River" was on the flip side. Originally recorded by Marie Knight (Wing 90069) in 1956, "Tell Me Why" was written by Titus Turner and sold over a million copies for Elvis. "Tell Me Why" appeared in the Long Playing album "Elvis: The Other Sides—Worldwide Gold Award Hits, Volume 2" (RCA LPM-6402).

Tell Me Why. RCA 447-0655. Gold Standard Series re-issue of RCA 47-8740.

Tender Feeling. Song that Elvis sang in the 1964 movie *Kissin' Cousins*. "Tender Feeling" was written by Bill Giant, Bernie Baum, and Florence Kaye and appeared in the following Long Playing albums: "Kissin' Cousins" (RCA LPM/LSP-2894); "Burning Love and Hits from His Movies, Volume 2" (RCA Camden CAS-2595); "Burning Love and Hits from His Movies, Volume 2" (Pickwick CAS-2595).

Tender Trap, The. Popular song by Frank Sinatra from the 1955 movie *The Tender Trap*, starring Frank Sinatra and Debbie Reynolds (Carolyn Jones and Lola Albright also appeared).

The theme song, "The Tender Trap," was played during a scene in *Jailhouse Rock* (1957) when Elvis and Jennifer Holden were swimming.

Tennessee Board of Medical Examiners. Medical governing board that, in September 1979, charged Dr. George Nichopoulos with gross negligence in overprescribing of drugs for his patient,

357

Elvis Presley. Dr. Nichopoulos was accused of prescribing 5,684 pills for Elvis in the seven months before his death. Among the pills were Quaaludes, Dexedrine, and Demeral, a narcotic painkiller.

Tennessee Karate Institute. Memphis marital arts studio, located at 1372 Overton Park (above a Rexall drugstore), founded by Red West and Bobby Wren (a first cousin of Elvis). Elvis gave a ninety-minute demonstration and lecture on karate on July 29, 1974.

Tennessee Partner. Song supposedly recorded by Elvis, although no record exists.

Tennessee, Saturday Night. Song, composed by Billy Hughes, recorded by Red Foley (Decca 46292) and Foley's son-in-law, Pat Boone (Dot 15377), in 1954. Elvis sang "Tennessee, Saturday Night" on the "Louisiana Hayride" in 1955. "Tennessee, Saturday Night" was recorded by Elvis but has never been released by Sun Records.*

Ten Outstanding Young Men of America. Award presented to Elvis on January 9, 1971, by the U. S. Jaycees. Others selected were: Ron Ziegler; Jim Goetz; William Bucha; Wendall Cherry; George J. Todaro; Dr. Mario R. Capecchi; Thomas Atkins; Thomas Coll; Walker S. Humann. They received their awards from U. S. Jaycee president, Gordon Thomas.

Tewksbury, Peter. Director of the 1968 movie *Stay Away, Joe* and the 1969 movie *The Trouble with Girls (And How to Get Into It)*. He previously directed the TV series "My Three Sons" and "Father Knows Best."

Texarkana, Texas. Texas-Arkansas border town where, in 1955, Col. Tom Parker first saw Elvis performing. Elvis was singing on stage at a movie theater.

Tex Warner and His Rough Ridin' Ramblers. Band with which Deke Rivers (Elvis) sang in the 1957 movie *Loving You*. Tex's (Wendell Corey) real first name was Walter.

Thank You, Elvis. A 1977 Elvis tribute record by Brendan "Big Eight" Boyer on the Hawk label (Hawk 411).

Thanks to the Rolling Sea. Song that Elvis sang in the 1962 movie *Girls! Girls! Girls!*. "Thanks to the Rolling Sea" was written by Ruth Batchelor and Bob Roberts and appeared in the Long Playing album "Girls! Girls! Girls!" (RCA LPM/LSP-2621).

That Last Encore. A 1977 Elvis tribute record by Jim Fagan on the Webcor label (Webcor 101).

That's All Right (Mama). Sun 209. Released on July 19, 1954, as a 78 rpm single and a 45 rpm single. "Blue Moon Of Kentucky" was on the flip side. Elvis recorded "That's All Right (Mama)" on the evening of July 5, 1954—his first commercial recording session. "That's All Right (Mama)"/"Blue Moon Of

---

*"Tennessee Saturday Night" appeared on a bootleg 45 rpm record credited to Elvis, Scotty, and Bill (Sun 252).

Kentucky" sold less than twenty thousand copies and reached #3 on Memphis's Country charts.

On the evening of July 7, at approximately 9:30, Dewey Phillips, disc jockey on Memphis radio station WHBQ, first aired "That's All Right (Mama)." Later in 1954, Marty Robbins became the first artist to cover an Elvis Presley record when he recorded "That's All Right (Mama)" (Columbia 21351). It outsold Elvis's version.

Arthur "Big Boy" Crudup composed and originally recorded "That's All Right (Mama)" in 1946. Its original title was "I Don't Know It." In 1949 Crudup again recorded the song on RCA Victor backed with "Crudup's After Hours" (RCA Victor 50-0000).*

That's All Right (Mama). Sun 1129. A 45 rpm single originally released without any artist listed on the label. After a lawsuit by RCA, Sun re-issued the record, listing Jimmy Ellis as the artist. Conjecture is that "That's All Right (Mama)" is an outtake from an early Sun session and that it's really Elvis on the record.

That's All Right (Mama). RCA 20/47-6380. A 78 rpm and a 45 rpm re-issue of the Sun original (Sun 209). "That's All Right (Mama)" was sung by Elvis on the 1977 CBS-TV Special, "Elvis In Concert" and in the documentaries *Elvis—That's The Way It Is* (1970) and *Elvis On Tour* (1972). It appeared in the Extended Play album "A Touch of Gold, Volume 2" (RCA EPA-5101) and the following Long Playing albums: "For LP Fans Only" (RCA LPM-1990), "For LP Fans Only" (RCA LSP-1990 [e]), "Elvis As Recorded At Madison Square Garden" (RCA LSP-4776), "Elvis—A Legendary Performer, Volume 1" (RCA CPL1-0341), "The Elvis Presley Sun Collection" (RCA Starcall HY-1001), "Elvis—The Sun Sessions" (RCA APM1-1675), "The Sun Years" (Sun 1001), and "Elvis In Concert" (RCA APL2-2587).

That's All Right (Mama). RCA 447-0601. Gold Standard Series re-issue of RCA 20/47-6380.

That's Amore—That's Love. Song written by Jack Brooks and Harry Warren and introduced by Dean Martin in the 1953 Martin and Lewis comedy *The Caddy* (directed by Norman Taurog). "That's Amore—That's Love" (Capitol 2589) reached #2 on the charts and was Dean Martin's first million-seller.

Some people believe that Elvis sang "That's Amore—That's Love" on stage at the Eagle's Nest in Memphis in October 1953. Introduced by Dewey Phillips, Elvis was backed by the house band—Johnny Long's Orchestra. If this is true, this would have been Elvis's first professional appearance, prior to

---

*The RCA Victor 50-0000 series was for Rhythm and Blues artists beginning in 1949.

recording for Sun Records, and would indicate that Elvis had every intention of becoming a professional singer.

That's How I Will Be. Subtitle of "Any Way You Want Me," recorded by Elvis on July 2, 1956.

That's Someone You Never Forget. RCA 47-9115. Released in May 1967 as a 45 rpm single. It reached #92 on *Billboard*'s Hot 100 chart. "Long Legged Girl (With the Short Dress On)" was on the flip side. "That's Someone You Never Forget" was written by Red West and Elvis and appeared in the Long Playing album "Pot Luck" (RCA LPM/LSP-2523).

That's Someone You Never Forget. RCA 447-0660. Gold Standard Series re-issue of RCA 47-9115.

That's the Stuff You Gotta Watch. Unreleased Elvis Sun recording of 1955.

That's When Your Heartaches Begin. RCA 20/47-6870. Released in March 1957 as a 78 rpm single and a 45 rpm single. It reached #58 on *Billboard*'s Hot 100 chart and sold over a million copies. "All Shook Up" was on the flip side. "That's When Your Heartaches begin" was the second song that Elvis ever recorded ("My Happiness" was the first), in the summer of 1953. (See: Keisker, Marion; Memphis Recording Service) It was written by William J. Raskin,* Billy Hill, and Fred Fisher in 1940. The Inkspots had a popular recording of "That's When Your Heartaches Begin" (Decca 25505) in 1950. Elvis's version of "That's When Your Heartaches Begin" appeared in the following Long Playing albums: "Elvis' Golden Records" (RCA LPM-1707); "Elvis' Golden Records" (RCA LSP-1707 [e]); "Elvis: Worldwide 50 Gold Award Hits, Volume 1" (RCA LPM-6401).

That's When Your Heartaches Begin. RCA 447-0660. Gold Standard Series re-issue of RCA 20/47-6870.

There Ain't Nothing Like a Song. Song that Elvis sang in the 1968 movie *Speedway*. Nancy Sinatra sang a duet with Elvis. "There Ain't Nothing Like a Song" was written by Joy Byers and William Johnston and appeared in the Long Playing album "Speedway" (RCA LSP-3989).

There Goes My Everything. RCA 47-9960. Released in December 1970 as a 45 rpm single. It reached #21 on *Billboard*'s Hot 100 chart and #9 on the Country chart. "I Really Don't Want to Know" was on the flip side. "There Goes My Everything" was written by Dallas Frazier about the broken marriage of two of his friends in 1965. Jack Greene recorded the song in 1966 (Decca 32023) and it became the Country Music Association Song of the Year in 1967. Englebert Humperdinck's version of "There Goes My Everything" (London 59036) in 1967 sold over a million copies and reached #20 on the charts. Elvis's

---

*William J. Raskin also wrote "Wagon Wheels" and "Empty Saddles," among others.

version appeared in the Long Playing albums "Elvis Country" (RCA LSP-4460) and "Elvis: The Other Sides—Worldwide Gold Award Hits, Volume 2" (RCA LPM-6402).

There Goes My Everything. RCA 447-0679. Gold Standard Series re-issue of RCA 47-9960.

There Is No God But God. Religious song written by Bill Kenny (former lead singer of the Ink Spots) and recorded by Elvis in 1971. "There Is No God But God" appeared in the Long Playing album "He Touched Me" (RCA LSP-4690).

There Is So Much World to See. Song that Elvis sang in the 1967 movie *Double Trouble*. "There Is So Much World to See" was written by Sid Tepper and Ben Weisman. It appeared in the Long Playing album "Double Trouble" (RCA LPM/LSP-3787).

There's a Brand New Day on the Horizon. Song that Elvis sang in the 1964 movie *Roustabout*. The film version differs from that on record. "There's a Brand New Day on the Horizon" was written by Joy Byers and appeared in the Long Playing album "Roustabout" (RCA LPM/LSP-2999).

There's a Fire Below. Song written by Jerry Scheff, Elvis's bass player. The instrumental tracks were recorded on the night of October 30–31, 1976. No record exists of Elvis recording "There's a Fire Below"; however, Felton Jarvis has stated that Elvis *did* record a vocal track.

There's a Honky Tonk Angel (Who Will Take Me Back In). RCA PB-11679. Released in August 1979 as a 45 rpm single. It reached #6 on *Billboard*'s Hot Country chart. "I've Got a Feelin' in My Body" was on the flip side. "There's a Honky Tonk Angel (Who Will Take Me Back In)" was written by Troy Seals and Denny Rice and recorded by Conway Twitty (MGM 40173) in 1974. Twitty's version reached #1 on *Billboard*'s Hot Country chart. "There's a Honky Tonk Angel (Who Will Take Me Back In)" appeared in the Long Playing albums "Promised Land" (RCA APL1-0873) and "Our Memories of Elvis, Volume 2" (RCA AQL1-3448).

There's Always Me. RCA 47-9287. Released in August 1967 as a 45 rpm single. It reached #56 on *Billboard*'s Hot 100 chart. "Judy" was on the flip side. "There's Always Me" was written for Elvis by Don Robertson and appeared in the Long Playing album "Something for Everybody" (RCA LPM/LSP-2370).

There's Always Me. RCA 447-0661. Gold Standard Series re-issue of RCA 47-9287.

There's Gold in the Mountains. Song that Elvis sang in the 1964 movie *Kissin' Cousins*. "There's Gold in the Mountains" was written by Bill Giant, Bernie Baum, and Florence Kaye and appeared in the Long Playing album "Kissin' Cousins" (RCA LPM/LSP-2894).

They Remind Me Too Much of You. RCA 47-8134. Released in January 1963 as a 45 rpm single. It reached #53 on *Billboard*'s

Hot 100 chart. "One Broken Heart for Sale" was on the flip side. Elvis sang "They Remind Me Too Much of You" in the 1963 movie *It Happened at the World's Fair*. "They Remind Me Too Much of You" was written by Don Robertson for Elvis and appeared in the following Long Playing albums: "It Happened at the World's Fair" (RCA LPM/LSP-2697); "Elvis: The Other Sides—World Wide Gold Award Hits, Volume 2" (RCA LPM-6402); "Elvis Sings Hits from His Movies, Volume 1" (RCA Camden CAS-2567); "Elvis Sings Hits from His Movies, Volume 1" (Pickwick CAS-2567); "Elvis in Hollywood" (RCA DPL2-0168).

They Remind Me Too Much of You. RCA 447-0640. Gold Standard Series re-issue of RCA 47-8134.

Thing, The. Original title of Little Richard's hit record "Long Tall Sally" (Specialty 572). Both Elvis and the Beatles have recorded "Long Tall Sally." "Long Tall Sally" was the biggest-selling record in Specialty Record's history.

Thing Called Love, A. Song written by Jerry Reed and originally recorded by Jimmy Dean (RCA 9454) in 1968. Johnny Cash also had a popular version of "A Thing Called Love" (Columbia 45534). Elvis recorded the song in 1971 and it appeared in the Long Playing album "He Touched Me" (RCA LSP-4690).

Thinking About You. RCA PB-10191. Released in January 1975 as a 45 rpm single. "My Boy" was on the flip side. "Thinking About You" was written by Tim Baty and appeared in the Long Playing albums "Promised Land" (RCA APL1-0873) and "Our Memories of Elvis, Volume 2" (RCA AQL1-3448).

Thinking About You. RCA GB-10489. Gold Standard Series re-issue of RCA PB-10191.

This Is Living. Song that Elvis sang in the 1962 movie *Kid Galahad*. It was originally titled "Let's Live a Little." "This Is Living" was written by Fred Wise and Ben Weisman and appeared in the Extended Play album "Kid Galahad" (RCA EPA-4371) and the Long Playing albums "C'mon Everybody" (RCA Camden CAL-2518) and "C'mon Everybody" (Pickwick CAS-2518).

This Is My Heaven. Song that Elvis sang in the 1966 movie *Paradise—Hawaiian Style*. The film version has added instrumentation. "This Is My Heaven" was written by Bill Giant, Bernie Baum, and Florence Kaye and appeared in the Long Playing album "Paradise—Hawaiian Style" (RCA LPM/LSP-3643).

This Is Our Dance. Song written by Les Reed and Geoff Stephens and recorded by Elvis in 1970. "This Is Our Dance" appeared in the Long Playing album "Love Letters from Elvis" (RCA LSP-4530).

This Is the Story. Song written by Arnold, Morrow, and Martin and recorded by Elvis at the American Sound Studios in

Memphis on January 13, 1969. "This Is the Story" appeared in the Long Playing albums "From Memphis to Vegas/From Vegas to Memphis" (RCA LSP-6020) and "Elvis—Back In Memphis" (RCA LSP-4429).

Thomas, B.J. Born in Houston, Texas; singer and composer whose full name is Billy Joe Thomas. In 1969 he recorded the theme song of the movie *Butch Cassidy and the Sundance Kid*, a Burt Bacharach—Hal David composition titled "Raindrops Keep Falling on My Head." In August 1970 Elvis recorded B.J. Thomas's 1970 hit "I Just Can't Help Believing." Both B.J. Thomas and Elvis have recorded Hank Williams's "I'm So Lonesome I Could Cry."

Thomas, Gordon. President of the U. S. Jaycees, who gave Elvis an award on January 9, 1971, for being one of the Ten Outstanding Young Men of America.

Thomas, Rufus R & B singer, born on March 26, 1917, in Cayce, Mississippi. Rufus Thomas was a disc jockey on Memphis radio station WDIA in the 1950s. He recorded "Tiger Man (King of the Jungle)" for Sun Records on June 30, 1953 (Sun 188). In 1963 he recorded "Walking the Dog"* for Stax Records. Rufus Thomas is the father of soul singer Carla Thomas, the "Queen of the Memphis Sound," whose biggest hits were "Gee Whiz (Look at His Eyes)"† (Atlantic 2086) in 1961 and "B-A-B-Y" (1966). (Carla has a degree in English literature from Howard University.) Elvis recorded "Tiger Man" in 1968. (See: Hound Dog; Bear Cat)

Thompson, Jay. Disc jockey who interviewed Elvis in Wichita Falls, Texas, in early 1956.

Thompson, Linda Diane. Twenty-three-year-old, 5′ 9″, 36-23-36, 125-pound, former Miss Tennessee (1972), who was romantically involved with Elvis. She was the third runner-up in the Miss U.S.A. Pageant. Miss Thompson lived with Elvis at Graceland from 1972 to '76. She is presently a regular on the TV series "Hee Haw."

Thompson, Sam. Security guard at Graceland and one of Elvis's bodyguards in the 1970s. He is the brother of Linda Thompson.

Thornton, Willie Mae. Blues artist, born October 11, 1926. Willie Mae Thornton is the daughter of a minister. Influenced by Bessie Smith, she in turn influenced Janis Joplin, who recorded her "Ball and Chain." In August 1952, in Los Angeles, Willie Mae Thornton (backed by Johnny Otis on vibes and Peter "Guitar" Lewis on lead guitar) originally recorded "Hound Dog" (Peacock 1612). In the same session she recorded "They Call Me Big Mama," the origin of her nickname, "Big Mama."

---

*Thomas recorded several records based on the dance called "The Dog": "The Dog"; "Walking the Dog"; "Can Your Monkey Do the Dog"; "Somebody Stole My Dog."
†Stax Records' first Gold Record, distributed through Atlantic Records.

She received only $500 for her version of "Hound Dog." Willie Mae Thornton traveled with the Johnny Otis's Rhythm and Blues Caravan in the early 1950s. (See: Otis, Johnny)

Thorpe, Richard. Director of the 1967 movie *Jailhouse Rock* and the 1963 movie *Fun in Acapulco.* Richard Thorpe (real name: Rollo Smolt Thorpe) also directed *Huckleberry Finn** (1939), *The Great Caruso* (1951), and *The Prisoner of Zenda* (1952).

Three Blazes, The. Combo formed by Tulas McLean (Elvis) in the 1960 movie *G.I. Blues.*

Three Corn Patches. Song written by Jerry Leiber and Mike Stoller and originally recorded by T-Bone Walker† (Reprise 2X56483) in 1973. Elvis recorded "Three Corn Patches" at the Stax Studios in Memphis and it appeared in the Long Playing album "Raised on Rock/For Ol' Times Sake" (RCA APL1-0388).

Three Dog Night. Rock group that first recorded the Hoyt Axton composition "Never Been to Spain," in 1971. Elvis recorded the song in 1972. "Three Dog Night" is an Australian Aborigine expression—on extremely cold nights, the Aborigines sleep with three of their dogs.

Thrill of Your Love. Song written by Stan Kesler and recorded by Elvis in 1960. "Thrill of Your Love" appeared in the Long Playing album "Elvis Is Back" (RCA LPM/LSP-2231).

Through My Eyes. Title of the revealing autobiography that Elvis planned to author, prior to his death.

Thunderbird Lounge. Memphis site (750 Adams Ave.) of Elvis's New Year's Eve party on December 31, 1968. The house band was Flash and the Board of Directors and guest musicians included B.J. Thomas, Ronnie Milsap, and Billy Lee Riley.

Thunder Road. A 1958 movie starring Robert Mitchum. The lead role was offered to Elvis but he turned it down.

The movie's theme song, "The Ballad of Thunder Road" (Capitol 3986), which made the *Billboard* charts in 1958, was composed and recorded by Robert Mitchum. Robert Mitchum's son, James, made his movie debut as Robert's brother.

Thursday. Day of the week on which both Elvis and Vernon Presley were buried (Elvis: August 18, 1977; Vernon: June 28, 1979).

TICKLE ME. Allied Artists, 1965. Premiered Atlanta, Georgia, May 28, 1965 (90 Min.) Elvis's eighteenth movie. Producer, Ben Schwalb. Director, Norman Taurog. Cast: Lonnie Beale/Elvis Presley, Pam Merritt/Jocelyn Lane, Vera Radford/Julie Adams, Stanley Potter/Jack Mullaney, Estelle Penfield/Merry Anders, Hilda/Connie Gilchrist, Brad Bentley/Edward Faulk-

---

*Director Norman Taurog, who directed nine Elvis movies, also directed a version of *Huckleberry Finn*, released in 1933.

†T-Bone Walker (real name: Aaron Thibeaux Walker) was part-Cherokee Indian and as a boy served as a guide for blues singer Blind Lemon Jefferson.

ner, Deputy Sturdivant/Bill Williams, Henry the Gardener/ Louis Elias, Adolph the Chef/John Dennis, Janet/Laurie Benton, Clair Kinnamon/Linda Rogers, Sybyl/Ann Morell, Ronnie/Lilyan Chauvin, Evelyn/Jean Ingram, Mildred/Francine York, Pat/Eve Bruce, Gloria/Jackie Russell, Donna/Angela Greene, Dot/Peggy Ward, Polly/Dorian Brown, Ophelia/Inez Pedroza, Mr. Dabney/Grady Sutton, Mrs. Dabney/Dorothy Conrad, Barbara/Barbara Werle, Mabel/Allison Hayes. Screenplay, Elwood Ullman and Edward Bernds. Photography, Loyal Griggs. Music, Walter Scharf. Choreography, David Winters. Art Direction, Arthur Lonergan. Set Decoration, Arthur Krams. Costumes, Leah Rhodes. Assistant Director, Artie Jacobson. Editor, Archie Marshek. Songs sung by Elvis: "(It's A) Long Lonely Highway," "Night Rider," "It Feels So Right," "Dirty, Dirty Feeling (Si Seulement!)" "(Such An) Easy Question," "Put the Blame on Me," "I'm Yours," "I Feel That I've Known You Forever," "Slowly But Surely."

Tickle Me. RCA EPA-4383. This was a 45 rpm Extended Play album released in July 1965. It reached #70 on *Billboard*'s Hot 100 chart. Songs included—Side 1: "I Feel That I've Known You Forever," "Slowly But Surely." Side 2: "Night Riders," "Put the Blame on Me," "Dirty, Dirty Feeling."

Tidwell, John. Superintendent of Tupelo's Parks and Recreation Department. (See: Elvis Presley Park)

Tiger Man. Elvis's karate nickname at Kang Rhee's Karate School.

Tiger Man (King of the Jungle). Song written by J.H. Lewis and S. Burns and originally recorded by Rufus Thomas (Sun 188) in 1953. "Tiger Man (King of the Jungle)" was playing on the Crown Electric pick-up truck driven by Elvis (Kurt Russell) in the 1979 TV movie *Elvis*.

Elvis sang "Tiger Man (King of the Jungle)" in the August 17, 1969, rerun of the NBC-TV special "Elvis." (In the original broadcast of the special, on December 3, 1968, "Blue Christmas" was sung.) "Tiger Man (King of the Jungle)" was also sung in the 1970 documentary *Elvis—That's the Way It Is* and appeared in the following Long Playing albums: "Singer Presents Elvis Singing Flaming Star and Others" (RCA PRS-279); "Elvis Sings Flaming Star" (RCA Camden CAS-2304); "Elvis Sings Flaming Star" (Pickwick CAS-2304); "From Memphis to Vegas/From Vegas to Memphis" (RCA LSP-6020); "Elvis in Person" (RCA LSP-4428).

Tillotson, Johnny. Former country disc jockey (Palatka, Florida, radio station WWPF). He became popular in both the country and the pop field ("Poetry in Motion" [Cadence 1384] went to #2 on the charts). As a singer and composer he wrote the Hank Locklin hit "Send Me the Pillow That You Dream On" (RCA 7127) and sang the theme song of the TV series "Gidget" (starring Sally Field). In 1969 Elvis recorded the

Tillotson composition "It Keeps Right on A-Hurtin'," which Tillotson had recorded in 1962 (Cadence 1418). (See: Jacksonville, Florida)

Tipler, James R. Elvis's employer at Crown Electric Company. (See: Crown Electric Company)

Tipley, Coleman, III. RCA Victor Records executive who signed the contract that sent Elvis from the Sun label to that of RCA Victor on November 22, 1955.

Tip Toe Through the Tulips (With Me). Song written by Al Dubin and Joseph A. Burke in 1929 for the motion-picture musical *Gold Diggers of Broadway*. Tiny Tim (real name: Herbert Khaury) revived "Tip Toe Through the Tulips (With Me)" (Reprise 0679) in 1968. Elvis did a parody of the song during one of the live tapings for the 1968 NBC-TV special "Elvis" (June 27, 1968, Burbank Studios).

Tjader, Cal. Renowned jazz musician who played on the Elvis *"Easy Come, Easy Go"* film soundtrack.

TJ's. Memphis nightclub in which Elvis held a few New Year's Eve parties.

TLC. *T*ender *L*oving *C*are.* Elvis gave gold necklaces to his girlfriends and to the wives and girlfriends of his male friends. The letters TLC, with a lightning bolt through them, appeared on the necklaces. The lightning bolt symbolized the West Coast Mafia.

To a Heart That's True. Subtitle of "Don't Be Cruel." The full, correct title is "Don't Be Cruel" (To a Heart That's True)."

Toast of the Town. Name often mistakenly credited to the Ed Sullivan series on which Elvis first appeared (September 9, 1956). Actually, the series was called "Toast of the Town" from June 20, 1948, until September 18, 1955. When Elvis appeared, the show was then being called "The Ed Sullivan Show." Charles Laughton, Bob Hope, Jackie Gleason, and Martin and Lewis (among others) made their TV debuts on "Toast of the Town." (See: Ed Sullivan Show, The)

Toby Kwimper. Elvis's role in the 1962 movie *Follow That Dream*.

Today. RCA APL1-1039. A 33⅓ rpm Long Playing album released in June 1975. It reached #57 on *Billboard*'s Hot LP chart. "Today" was available in quadrasonic, also. Songs included—Side A: "T-R-O-U-B-L-E," "And I Love You So," "Susan When She Tried," "Woman Without Love," "Shake a Hand." Side B: "Pieces of My Life," "Fairytale," "I Can Help," "Bringin' It Back," "Green, Green Grass of Home."

Today, Tomorrow, and Forever. Song that Elvis sang in the 1964 movie *Viva Las Vegas*. "Today, Tomorrow, and Forever" was written by Bill Giant, Bernie Baum, and Florence Kaye

---

*In 1960 Jimmie Rodgers recorded a song titled "T.L.C. (Tender Love and Care)" (Roulette 4218).

and was based on "Liebestraume," composed by Franz Liszt* in 1850. It appeared in the Extended Play album "Viva Las Vegas" (RCA EPA-4385) and the Long Playing albums "C'mon Everybody" (RCA Camden CAL-2518) and "C'mon Everybody" (Pickwick CAS-2518).

To Elvis in Heaven. A 1977 Elvis tribute record by Vicki Knight on American Sound Records (American Sound 3096).

To Kill a Mocking Bird. A 1962 movie, from the Pulitzer Prize-winning novel by Harper Lee, starring Gregory Peck. Peck (who turned down the lead role in *High Noon*) won an Academy Award for Best Actor, for his portrayal of Atticus Finch. Gregory Peck was the first native Californian to win an Oscar. *To Kill a Mockingbird* was one of Elvis's favorite movies.

To Know Him Is to Love Him. A 33⅓ rpm bootleg LP released by Black Belt Records, which featured songs recorded by Elvis live in Las Vegas and Lake Tahoe. Songs included—Side 1: "Trouble," "Raised on Rock," "Steamroller Blues," "Sweet Inspirations," "Help Me Make It Through the Night," "More"/"Suspicious Minds," "Please Release Me," "I, John." Side 2: "Folsom Prison Blues"/"I Walk the Line," "Until It's Time for You to Go," "Fever," "I'm Leavin'," "Memphis, Tennessee" (Pt. 1 and Pt. 2), Elvis Introduces Bobby Darin, "Can't Help Falling in Love/Closing."

Tomorrow Is a Long Time. One of two songs written by Bob Dylan that Elvis recorded (the other was "Don't Think Twice, It's All Right"). Elvis recorded "Tomorrow Is a Long Time" in 1966 and it appeared in the Long Playing album "Spinout" (RCA LPM/LSP-3702).

Tomorrow Never Comes. Song written by Ernest Tubb and Johnny Bond and recorded by Ernest Tubb (Blue Bird 6106) and by Slim Whitman (Imperial 66441). Elvis recorded "Tomorrow Never Comes" in 1970 and it appeared in the Long Playing album "Elvis Country" (RCA LSP-4460).

Tomorrow Night. Song written by Sam Coslow and Will Grosz in 1939. Lonnie Johnson had a million-seller with "Tomorrow Night" in 1948 on King Records. Elvis recorded "Tomorrow Night" in 1955 while still with Sun Records. On March 18, 1965, a new instrumental track was recorded by RCA. Musicians in that session were: Chet Atkins, guitar; Grady Martin, guitar; Henry Strzelecki, bass; Buddy Harman, drums; Charlie McCoy, harmonica; the Anita Kerr Singers, vocal backing. "Tomorrow Night" appeared in the Long Playing album "Elvis for Everyone" (RCA LPM/LSP-3450).

---

*Hungarian-born pianist and composer Franz Liszt was the father-in-law of composer Richard Wagner. One of Liszt's piano students was Katharine Delaney O'Hara, mother of author John O'Hara.

Tonight Is So Right for Love. Song that Elvis sang in the 1960 movie *G.I. Blues.* "Tonight Is So Right for Love" was based on the classic by Jacques Offenbach (1819–80), "Bacarolle." Because of copyright problems, "Tonight Is So Right for Love" couldn't be released in the non-English-speaking countries of the world. Instead, "Tonight's All Right for Love" (similar lyrics, but based on an entirely different song) was recorded for insertion in the foreign releases of *G.I. Blues.* (See: Tonight's All Right for Love) "Tonight Is So Right for Love" was an adaptation by Joe Lilly, Abner Silver, and Sid Wayne. It appeared in the following Long Playing albums: "G.I. Blues" (RCA LPM/LSP-2256); "Burning Love and Hits from His Movies, Volume 2" (RCA Camden CAS-2495); "Burning Love and Hits from His Movies, Volume 2" (Pickwick (CAS-2595).

Tonight's All Right for Love. Song that Elvis recorded for the non-English-speaking version of the 1960 movie *G.I. Blues.* Because of a copyright problem, "Tonight Is So Right for Love," which appeared in the English version of the film, couldn't be used. "Tonight's All Right for Love" was an adaptation by Abner Silver, Sid Wayne, and Joe Lilly of the Johann Strauss (1825–99) classic, "Tales from Vienna Woods" (1868). It appeared in the Long Playing album "Elvis—A Legendary Performer, Volume 1" (RCA CPL1-0341). The version on the album, however, is an edited version. The complete song was released as a single in Germany.

Tonto Candy Bars. Jingle sung by Elvis in a skit on "The Steve Allen Show" on July 1, 1956. Steve Allen, Andy Griffith, and Imogene Coca were also in the skit. Tumbleweed (Elvis) stated that Tonto Bars were made by the Kemo-Sabe Candy Company of Ptomaine, Texas.

Tony Sheridan and the Elvis Presley Band. Album recorded by Tony Sheridan in 1978. Tony Sheridan was the singer whom the Beatles backed in recordings made in Hamburg, Germany. On the recordings the Beatles were credited as the Beat Brothers.

Too Big For Texas. Original song considered for the 1967 movie *Clambake.*

Toof, Grace. Aunt of Mrs. Ruth Brown Moore, the woman from whom Elvis purchased Graceland in 1957. Graceland was named for Grace Toof. (See: Graceland)

Too Late Blues. A 1961 movie starring Bobby Darin in the role of John Wakefield, which was first offered to Elvis.

Too Much. RCA 20/47-6800. Released in January 1957 as a 78 rpm single and a 45 rpm single. It reached #2 on *Billboard*'s Hot 100 chart, #5 on the Country chart, and #7 on the Rhythm and Blues chart. "Too Much" sold well over a million copies. "Playing for Keeps" was on the flip side. Elvis sang "Too Much" in his third appearance on "The Ed Sullivan Show"—January 6, 1957. "Too Much," first recorded in 1954 by Bernard Hardison (Republic 7111), was written by Lee

Rosenberg and Bernard Weinman. (Rosenberg gave the song to Elvis as the singer was boarding a train for Los Angeles in 1956.) The song appeared in the Extended Play album "A Touch of Gold, Volume 3" (RCA EPA-5141) and the following Long Playing albums: "Elvis' Golden Records" (RCA LPM-1707); "Elvis' Golden Records" (RCA LSP-1707 [e]); "Elvis: Worldwide 50 Gold Award Hits, Volume 1" (RCA LPM-6401).

Too Much. RCA 447-0617. Gold Standard Series re-issue of RCA 20/47-6800.

Too Much Monkey Business. Song written and originally recorded by Chuck Berry (Chess 1635) in 1956. Elvis recorded "Too Much Monkey Business"* in 1968 and it appeared in the following Long Playing albums: "Singer Presents Elvis Singing Flaming Star and Others' (RCA PRS-279); "Elvis Sings Flaming Star" (RCA Camden CAS-2304); "Elvis Sings Flaming Star" (Pickwick Cas-2304).

Toot Toot Tootsie (Goo' Bye). Song written by Gus Kahn, Ernie Erdman, and Dan Russo for the 1922 Broadway musical *Bombo*, starring Al Jolson. "Toot Toot Tootsie (Goo' Bye)" was sung by Jolson in the first talking movie, *The Jazz Singer*† (1927).

In the 1969 movie *The Trouble with Girls (And How to Get Into It)*, the mayor's daughter, Lily-Jeanne (Linda Sue Risk), sang "Toot Toot Tootsie (Goo' Bye)."

Torme, Mel. Popular crooner of the 1940s and '50s, nicknamed the "Velvet Fog." Mel Torme (real name: Melvin Howard Torme) was the voice of Joe Corntassel on the radio series "Little Orphan Annie."

A prolific songwriter, Mel Torme wrote "The Christmas Song," which was a big hit for Nat "King" Cole (Capitol 3561) in 1946. He sang "Blue Moon" in the 1948 movie *Words and Music* and recorded "Comin' Home" (Atlantic 2165) in 1962. "Comin' Home" was used as the theme for introducing the members of Elvis's T.C.B. Band.

Torna a Sorrento. Italian ballad ("Come Back to Sorrento") written in 1911 by G. D. de Curtis (words) and E. de Curtis (music). "Torna a Sorrento" was adapted by Doc Pomus and Mort Shuman in 1960 as "Surrender."

Touch of Gold, A, Volume 1. RCA EPA-5088. This was a 45 rpm Extended Play album originally issued in the Gold Standard Series in April 1959 and re-issued in April 1961. Songs included—Side 1: "Hard Headed Woman," "Good Rockin' Tonight." Side 2: "Don't," "I Beg of You."

Touch of Gold, A, Volume 2. RCA EPA-5101. This was a 45 rpm

---

*Freddy Welles (previous member of Paul Revere and the Raiders) recorded an album in 1973 titled "Too Much Monkey Business."
†The 1928 Warner Bros. movie *Lights of New York* was the first *all-talking* movie, although subtitles were still used throughout the film.

Extended Play album originally issued in the Gold Standard Series in October 1959 and re-issued in April 1961. Songs included—Side 1: "Wear My Ring Around Your Neck," "One Night." Side 2: "Treat Me Nice," "That's All Right (Mama)."

Touch of Gold, A, Volume 3. RCA EPA-5141. This was a 45 rpm Extended Play album originally issued in the Gold Standard Series in February 1960 and re-issued in April 1961. Songs included—Side 1: "All Shook Up," "Don't Ask Me Why." Side 2: "Too Much," "Blue Moon of Kentucky."

Town House. Saloon in the Mexican town of Rio Seco in the 1969 movie *Charrol*.

Treat Me Nice. RCA 20/47-7035. Released in September 1957 as a 78 rpm single and a 45 rpm single. It reached #27 on *Billboard*'s Hot 100 chart and #1 on the Rhythm and Blues chart. "Treat Me Nice" sold over a million copies. "Jailhouse Rock" was on the flip side. Elvis sang "Treat Me Nice" in the 1957 movie *Jailhouse Rock*. Written by Jerry Leiber and Mike Stoller, "Treat Me Nice" appeared in the Extended Play album "A Touch of Gold, Volume 2" (RCA EPA-5101) and the following Long Playing albums: "Elvis' Golden Records" (RCA LPM-1707); "Elvis' Golden Records" (RCA LSP-1707 [e]); "Elvis: Worldwide 50 Gold Award Hits, Volume 1" (RCA LPM-6401).

Treat Me Nice. RCA 447-0619. Gold Standard Series re-issue of RCA 20/47-7035.

Tree Publishing Company. Nashville music-publishing firm (located at 905 16th Street S.) founded in 1956 by Jack Stapp. Tree Publishing Company obtained "Heartbreak Hotel" as one of its first songs.

Tribble, Iladean. Forty-four-year-old widow, with four adult children, who claimed that she and Elvis were to be married at the First Baptist Church in Athens, Alabama, on April 17, 1976. Earlier that month she placed the announcement in the local paper. Five hundred people showed up for the wedding. Her mother, Mrs. Homer McLamore, then finally realized that they had been victims of a hoax.

Tribute to a King. An Elvis novelty song by Bobby Wallace on Okie Records (Okie 5597).

Tribute to Elvis, A. An Elvis tribute album by Golden Ring on Arc Records (Arc 823). The album featured twelve Elvis songs.

Tribute to Elvis, Memories of You, A. A 1977 Elvis tribute song by Connie Lynn on American Sound Records (American Sound 3102).

Tribute to Elvis' Mother. An Elvis tribute song by Red River Dave on Marathon Records.

Tribute to Elvis Presley. An Elvis tribute album by Vince Eager on Avenue Records (Avenue 093). The album featured twelve Elvis songs.

Troubadour from Memphis, The. A 1977 Elvis tribute song by Jean Sampson on Lighthouse Records. (Lighthouse 3000).

Trouble. Song that Elvis sang in the 1958 movie *King Creole*. "Trouble" was written by Jerry Leiber and Mike Stoller and has been recorded in later years by the Osmonds and Suzi Quatro, among others. It appeared in the Extended Play album "King Creole, Volume 2" (RCA EPA-4321) and the following Long Playing albums: "King Creole" (RCA LPM-1884); "King Creole" (RCA LSP-1884 [e]); "Elvis—TV Special (RCA LPM-4088); "Elvis: The Other Sides—Worldwide Gold Award Hits, Volume 2" (RCA LPM-6402).

T-R-O-U-B-L-E. RCA PB-10278. Released in April 1975 as a 45 rpm single. It reached #35 on *Billboard*'s Hot 100 chart and #11 on the Country chart. "Mr. Songman" was on the flip side. "T-R-O-U-B-L-E" was written by Jerry Chesnut and appeared in the Long Playing album "Today" (RCA APL1-1039).

T-R-O-U-B-L-E. RCA GB-10487. Gold Standard Series re-issue of RCA PB-10278.

Trouble in Vegas. A 33⅓ rpm bootleg LP. Songs included— Side 1: "C'mon Everybody, "Dominique," "Memphis, Tennessee" (Las Vegas, 1973), "Hound Dog" (Las Vegas, 1972), "A Big Hunk o' Love" (Las Vegas, 1972), "Got a Lot o' Livin' to Do," "Treat Me Nice," 1956 Interview, "Witchcraft" ("The Frank Sinatra-Timex Special"). "Wild in the Country." Side 2: "An American Trilogy" (Las Vegas, 1972), "My Baby Is Gone," "Baby, What You Want Me to Do" (Las Vegas, 1969), "A Cane and a High Starched Collar," "The Lady Loves Me."

TROUBLE WITH GIRLS, THE. MGM, 1969. Premiered New York City December 10, 1969 (97 min). Elvis's thirtieth movie. Producer, Lester Welch. Associate Producer, Wilson McCarthy. Director, Peter Tewksbury. Cast: Walter Hale/Elvis Presley, Charlene/Marylyn Mason, Betty/Nicole Jaffe, Nita Bix/Sheree North, Johnny/Edward Andrews, Mr. Drewcolt/ John Carradine, Mr. Morality/Vincent Price, Carol/Anissa Jones, Maude/Joyce van Patten, Willy/Pepe Brown, Harrison Wilby/Dabney Coleman, Mayor Gilchrist/Bill Zuckert, Mr. Perper/Pitt Herbert, Clarence/Anthony Teague, Constable/ Med Flory, Smith/Robert Nichols, Olga Prchlik/Helene Winston, Yale/Kevin O'Neal, Rutgers/Frank Welker, Princeton/ John Rubinstein, Amherst/Chuck Briles, Mrs. Gilchrist/Patsy Garrett, Lyly-Jeanne/Linda Sue Risk, Cabbie/Charles P. Thompson, 1st Farmhand/Leonard Rumery, 2d Farmhand/ William M. Paris, 3d Farmhand/Kathleen Rainey, Soda Jerk/ Hal James Pederson, Chowderhead/Mike Wagner, Iceman/Brett Parker, The Cranker/Duke Snider, Choral Society/Pacific Palisades High School Madrigals. Screenplay, Arnold and Lois Peyser. Photography, Jacques Marquette. Music, Billy Strange. Choreography, Jonathan Lucas. Art Direction, George W. Davis and Edward Carfagno. Set Decoration, Henry Grace and

Jack Mills. Costumes, Bill Thomas. Assistant Director, John Clark Bowman. Editor, George W. Brooks. Songs Sung by Elvis: "Clean Up Your Own Backyard," "Almost," "Swing Down, Sweet Chariot," "Violet (Flower of N.Y.U.)" "Signs of the Zodiac" (duet with Marilyn Mason), "Whiffenpoof Song."

True Love. Song composed by Cole Porter and introduced by Bing Crosby and Grace Kelly in the 1956 motion-picture musical *High Society*. The recording of "True Love" (Capitol 3507)* by Crosby and Kelly sold over a million copies. It was Grace Kelly's only recording.

Elvis recorded "True Love" in 1957 and it appeared in the Extended Play album "Loving You, Volume 1" (RCA EPA1-1515) and the Long Playing albums "Loving You" (RCA LPM-1515) and "Loving You" (RCA LSP-1515 [e]).

True Love Travels on a Gravel Road. Song written by Dallas Frazier and Al Owens. It was recorded by Elvis in 1969 at the American Sound Studios in Memphis. "True Love Travels on a Gravel Road" appeared in the Long Playing album "From Elvis in Memphis" (RCA LSP-4155).

Truth About Me, The. A 1956 interview record in which Elvis talked about himself and his career. (See: Lynchburg Audio; Rainbow Records)

Truth About Elvis, The. Book by Jess Stearn with Larry Geller, published in 1980 by Jove Books.

Trying to Get to You. RCA 20/47-6639. Released in September 1956 as a 78 rpm single and a 45 rpm single. "I Love You Because" was on the flip side. "Trying to Get to You" was written by Rose Marie McCoy and Charlie Singleton and originally recorded by Roy Orbison and the Teen Kings (JEWEL 101). Elvis recorded "Trying to Get to You" in 1955 while still with Sun Records. He taped the song for the 1968 NBC-TV special "Elvis," but it was not used. "Trying to Get to You" appeared in the Extended Play albums "Elvis Presley" (RCA SPD-22) and "Elvis Presley" (RCA SPD-23) and the following Long Playing albums: "Elvis Presley" (RCA LPM-1254); "Elvis Presley" (RCA LSP-1254 [e]); "Elvis—A Legendary Performer, Volume 1" (RCA CPL1-0341); "Elvis Recorded Live on Stage in Memphis" (RCA CPL1-0606); "The Elvis Presley Sun Collection" (RCA Starcall Hy-1001); "Elvis—The Sun Sessions" (RCA APM1-1675).

Trying to Get to You. RCA 447-0612. Gold Standard Series reissue of RCA 20/47-6639.

Tschechowa, Vera. Teenage German actress occasionally dated by Elvis while he was stationed in West Germany (1958–60).

Tubb, Ernest. Composer (with Johnny Bond) of "Tomorrow Never Comes," which Elvis recorded in 1970.

---

*The flip side of "True Love" was "Well Did You Evah," a duet by Frank Sinatra and Bing Crosby.

As a young lad, in 1936 Jimmie Rodgers's widow gave Ernest Tubb one of her husband's guitars. In 1940 Tubb began a long association with Decca Records. His record store, the Ernest Tubb Record Shop in Nashville (at 417 Broadway), is world famous. Ernest Tubb wrote and recorded "I'm Walkin' the Floor Over You," which has been recorded by several people including Bing Crosby.

In 1965 Ernest Tubb was elected to the Country Music Hall of Fame.

Tucker, Tommy. Checker Records artist whose biggest hit was his own composition, "Hi-Heel Sneakers" (Checker 1067) in 1964. Elvis recorded "High Heel Sneakers" (note the spelling change) in 1967. Tommy Tucker (real name: Robert Higgenbotham) was a Golden Gloves boxer in the early 1950s.

Tuesday. Day of the week on which both Elvis and Vernon Presley died (Elvis: August 16, 1977; Vernon; June 26, 1979).

Tulsa McLean. Elvis's role (as an Army soldier) in the 1960 movie *G.I. Blues.*

Tumbleweed Presley. Name of the cowboy character that Elvis played on TV in a sketch on "The Steve Allen Show." Steve Allen, Andy Griffith, and Imogene Coca appeared with Elvis in that sketch, which was telecast on July 1, 1956.

Tumbling Tumbleweeds. Song composed in 1934 by Bob Nolan, leader of the Sons of the Pioneers, and recorded by them (Decca 46027). "Tumbling Tumbleweeds" was sung by Bob Nolan in the 1935 Gene Autry film *Tumbling Tumbleweeds.* Elvis sang one line of this song at the Fadel home in Houston, Texas, in 1958.

Tupelo. A 1961 blues song by John Lee Hooker on Vee Jay Records (Vee Jay 366), telling about the great flood of 1936 in Tupelo, Mississippi (through which the Presleys lived).

Tupelo Garment Company. Milltown, Mississippi, firm (on S. Green Street) where Gladys Presley was employed as a sewing machine operator. This was shortly after her marriage to Vernon Presley in 1933.

Tupelo Hardware Company. Main Street store in Tupelo, Mississippi, where, in 1946, Gladys Presley bought Elvis a guitar. Mr. F.L. Bobo, the proprietor, sold Gladys the instrument. (See: Bobo, Forrest L.)

Tupelo, Mississippi. Lee County town credited as the birthplace of Elvis Presley on January 8, 1935, at 12:20 P.M. Actually, Elvis was born in East Tupelo, which wasn't annexed by Tupelo until 1948. The population of Tupelo at the time of Elvis's birth was approximately six thousand. Previously, it was called Gum Pond. Tupelo is Chickasaw for "lodging place." In 1936, Tupelo, Mississippi, was the first town to be provided with electricity by the Tennessee Valley Authority (TVA). Machine Gun Kelley (real name: George Barnes) once robbed a bank in the town.

Several country entertainers hail from Tupelo. Ray Harris, a Sun artist in the 1950s, was from Tupelo, as were the Miller Sisters, Elsie Jo Miller and Mildred Wages. The Miller Sisters recorded a record for Sam Phillips's Flip label in April 1955: "Someday You Will Pay"/"You Didn't Think I Would."

Tupelo Mississippi Flash. A 1967 song recorded by Jerry Reed on RCA Victor Records (RCA 9334) about a mythical Beauregard Rippy from Tupelo, Mississippi. It was a satire on Elvis. A version was also recorded by Tom Jones.

Turn Around, Look at Me. Song written by Jerry Capshart in 1961 and recorded by Glen Campbell (Crest 1087)—his first chart release. In 1968 the Vogues had a #4 hit and million-seller with "Turn Around, Look at Me." Elvis sang only a line or two of the song in one of his concerts in the 1970s.

Turtles, Berries and Gumbo. Song in the 1958 movie *King Creole*. It is sung in the form of an exchange between two black street vendors in the opening sequence of the movie. "Turtles, Berries and Gumbo" was written by Al Wood and Kay Twomey.

Tutt, Ronnie. Drummer for Elvis during his live concerts, who also appeared in a number of recording sessions.

Tutti Frutti. RCA 47-6466. A 45 rpm disc jockey "record preview." "One-sided Love Affair" was on the flip side. On the regular release, RCA 20/47-6636, "Blue Suede Shoes" was on the flip side.

Tutti Frutti. RCA 20/47-6636. Released in September 1956 as a 78 rpm single and 45 rpm single. "Blue Suede Shoes" was on the flip side. Elvis sang "Tutti Frutti" on the Dorsey Brothers' "Stage Show" on February 4 and February 18, 1956.

"Tutti Frutti" was written by Dorothy La Bostrie,* Richard Penniman ("Little Richard"), and Joe Lubin and recorded by Little Richard in 1955 (Specialty 561). Little Richard's version sold over 3 million copies and reached #21 on the charts.

"Tutti Frutti," by Elvis, appeared in the following Extended Play albums: "Elvis Presley" (RCA EPA-747); "Elvis Presley" (RCA EPB-1254); "Elvis Presley" (RCA SPD-22); "Elvis Presley" (RCA SPD-23). "Tutti Frutti" also appeared in the Long Playing albums "Elvis Presley" (RCA LPM-1254) and "Elvis Presley" (RCA LSP-1254 [e]).

Tuttti Frutti. RCA 447-0609. Gold Standard Series re-issue of RCA 20/47-6636.

TV Guide. Television magazine, published by Triangle Publications in Radnor, Pennsylvania, since the April 3–9, 1953, issue. The premiere edition contained a cover photo of Lucille Ball and her three-month-old son, Desiderio Arnaz, IV (Desi Arnaz, Jr.). Its September 8–14, 1956, issue featured Elvis on the cover and an article, "The Plain Truth About Elvis Presley," by Paul Wilder, on the inside. Elvis was featured on the cover of

---

*Dorothy La Bostrie rewrote the original suggestive lyrics of the song.

two editions: September 8–14, 1956, and May 7–13, 1960 (with Frank Sinatra).

TV Guide Presents Elvis Presley. RCA 8705. A 45 rpm record considered by many collectors to be the most valuable record in the world.* The record was made in 1956 and sent to radio and TV stations. It consisted of only one side: band 1—"Pelvis" Nickname (:19); band 2—Adults' Reaction (:34); band 3—First Public Appearance (:54); band 4—How "Rockin' Motion" Started (:44). Two special inserts were sent with the record. One insert suggested questions for the announcer to ask, to match Elvis's responses on the record. The other insert featured a photo of the September 8–14, 1956, issue of *TV Guide*. It related the story of how the interview came to be.

"TV Guide Presents Elvis Presley" was recorded by Paul Wilder, a reporter for *TV Guide,* in Lakeland, Florida.

TV Guide Presents Elvis Presley. A 33⅓ rpm bootleg album released on the Graceland label. It featured: Side 1: Songs from "The Steve Allen Show" (July 1, 1956), "TV Guide Presents Elvis" (1956). Side 2: Hy Gardener Interview (1956), Songs from "The Frank Sinatra-Timex Special" (May 12, 1960).

Tweedle Dee. Hit song for LaVern Baker in 1954 on Atlantic Records (Atlantic 1047) and by "Her Nibs"† Georgia Gibbs (Mercury 70517). Elvis sang "Tweedle Dee" in the "Louisiana Hayride" in 1954. Floyd Cramer played piano while Jimmy Day played steel guitar. The song was composed by Winfield Scott and a recording of the song by Elvis (sung in the "Louisiana Hayride" in December 1954) appears on a number of bootleg records including Sun 526.

Twelfth of Never, The. Song written by Paul Francis Webster and Jerry Livingston in 1956 and originally recorded by Johnny Mathis (Columbia 40993). In 1973 Donny Osmond had a million-seller and #8 hit with "The Twelfth of Never." Elvis sang "The Twelfth of Never" in a few concerts and one of those versions appeared in the bootleg LP "Elvis Special, Volume 2."

Twenty Days and Twenty Nights. Song written by Ben Weisman and Clive Westlake and recorded by Elvis in 1970. "Twenty Days and Twenty Nights" appeared in the Long Playing album "Elvis—That's the Way It Is" (RCA LSP-4445).

Twinkletown Farm. Name of the Circle G Ranch prior to Elvis's purchase of it.

Twist Me Loose. Song that Elvis recorded for the 1962 movie *Girls! Girls! Girls!,* but it was cut from the final print. "Twist

---

*The record considered the second most valuable is "My Bonnie"/"The Saints" by Tony Sheridan and the Beat Brothers (the Beatles) on the German Polydor label (Polydor 24–673A). The most valuable rhythm and blues record to date is the 1952 version of "Stormy Weather" by the Five Sharps (Jubilee 5104). The 78 rpm version will sell for $4000. Some collectors consider this to be *the* most valuable record.

†Georgia Gibbs's nickname of "Her Nibs" was coined by Garry Moore.

Me Loose" is the only "Twist" song Elvis ever recorded. It is not available on record.

Twitty, Conway. Tremendously successful country singer (real name: Harold Lloyd Jenkins) who, early in his career, sounded much like Elvis Presley. Even his speech was similar to Elvis's.

Conway Twitty originally recorded for Sun Records under his real name.* After changing his name (he looked at a map and spotted the two towns of Conway, Arkansas and Twitty, Texas), he composed "It's Only Make Believe" (MGM 12677) in seven minutes during an intermission at the Flamingo Hotel in Las Vegas. Conway Twitty's recording of the song reached #1 on *Billboard*'s Hot 100 chart and sold over a million copies in 1958.

The Elvis-like character in the play and movie, *Bye Bye Birdie*, had a name that satirized Twitty's—Conrad Birdie.

In 1964 Conway Twitty recorded two Elvis songs: "My Baby Left Me"/"Such a Night" (ABC Paramount 10550). From 1967 to 1977, every single release (thirty-five) of Twitty's reached #1 on the Country charts. He has recorded a number of songs with Loretta Lynn. His back-up band was called the Lonely Blue Boys prior to being changed to the Twitty Birds.

Tyler, Judy. Female lead (as Peggy Van Alden) in the 1957 movie *Jailhouse Rock*. She previously played Princess Summerfall Winterspring on the TV series "Howdy Doody Time." *Jailhouse Rock* was her last movie appearance, as she was killed in an automobile accident on July 3, 1957, near Billy the Kid, Wyoming. After Judy Tyler's death, Elvis couldn't stand to watch *Jailhouse Rock*.

U

U.F.O. Unidentified Flying Object. Sightings of a U.F.O. are "close encounters of the first kind." On June 24, 1947, while flying near Mt. Rainier, in Oregon, Kenneth Arnold filed the first official U.F.O. sighting. He had spotted nine U.F.O.s that day.

Elvis once watched a U.F.O. execute erratic maneuvers over Memphis. Since President Jimmy Carter had filed a U.F.O. sighting, Elvis was in good company. Others who have reported U.F.O. sightings include: John Lennon (August 23, 1974, in

---

*He recorded three Sun masters as Harold Jenkins and The Rockhousers in 1956, none of which were ever released: "Born to Sing the Blues," "Crazy Dreams," and "Give Me Some Love."

New York City); Cliff Robertson* (in 1965); Jackie Gleason; Senator Barry Goldwater.

ULL 501. California license plate number of Elvis's Rolls-Royce. Elvis bought the automobile from Coventry Motors in Beverly Hills.

Unchained Melody. RCA PB-11212. Released in March 1978 as a 45 rpm stereo single. "Softly as I Leave You" was on the flip side. "Unchained Melody" was originally the theme (sung by Todd Duncan) of the 1955 movie *Unchained*, starring Elroy "Crazy Legs" Hirsch and Barbara Hale. Al Hibbler's (Decca 29441) 1955 recording of "Unchained Melody" sold over a million copies and reached #5 on the charts. Les Baxter's† Orchestra (Capitol 3055) and Roy Hamilton (Epic 9102) also had successful recordings. Written by Hy Zaret and Alex North, "Unchained Melody" was recorded by Elvis on April 25, 1977, at the Civic Center in Saginaw, Michigan. His only accompaniment was his own piano playing. RCA later added organ, bass, and percussion to the instrumental track. "Unchained Melody" appeared in the Long Playing album "Moody Blue" (RCA AFL1-2428).

Uncle Penn. Unreleased song recorded by Elvis in 1955 while he was still with Sun Records. "Uncle Penn" was written in 1951 by Bill Monroe (recorded on Columbia 46283) about his real-life Uncle Penn (Pendleton Vandiver). It was also recorded by Porter Wagoner (RCA 6494). Elvis sang the song in many concerts in 1955 and '56, including that in Richmond, Virginia, on June 30, 1956. On the "Louisiana Hayride" TV show (March 5, 1955), Elvis sang "Uncle Penn." It appeared on a bootleg single in 1956.

United Paint Company. Memphis firm, located at 446 Concord Ave., for which Vernon Presley worked (1951–55). His income was $2,000 a year.

Unit No. 6. Memphis Fire Department rescue vehicle that arrived at Graceland shortly after 2:30 P.M. on August 16, 1977.

University of Nevada. School at which Rusty Martin (Ann-Margret) was enrolled in the 1964 movie *Viva Las Vegas*.

University of Tennessee—Memphis. Wording on the sweatshirt worn by Dr. John Carpenter (Elvis) in a touch football game in the 1969 movie *Change of Habit*.

University Park Cleaners. Laundry, located at 613 McLean Blvd. in Memphis, owned by Carney Moore in the 1950s. Carney Moore employed his brother Scotty after Scotty's tour in the service. It was while working there that Scotty Moore became a member of the Starlight Wranglers. The mother of singer

---

*Cliff Robertson was born the same day as Peter Sellers—September 8, 1925.

†Les Baxter was once a member of Mel Torme's vocal group, the Meltones.

Tammy Wynette once worked for Carney Moore at University Park Cleaners.

Until It's Time for You to Go. RCA 74-0619. Released in January 1972 as a 45 rpm single. It reached #40 on *Billboard*'s Hot 100 chart and #68 on the Country chart. "We Can Make the Morning" was on the flip side. "Until It's Time for You to Go" was written by Buffy Sainte-Marie* and introduced by her in a 1965 album titled "Many a Mile." She later had a hit single with the song in 1970. Elvis sang "Until It's Time for You to Go" in the 1972 documentary *Elvis on Tour*, and it has appeared in the Long Playing albums "Elvis Now" (RCA LSP-4671) and "Elvis—A Canadian Tribute" (RCA KKL1-7065).

Until It's Time For You To Go. RCA 447-0685. Gold Standard Series original that was released in July 1973. Though "Until It's Time for You to Go" had been released as a single previously (RCA 74-0619), this Gold Standard Series issue had a different flip side ("An American Trilogy"), making it a different record.

Up Above My Head. Song that Elvis sang in the 1968 TV special "Elvis." "Up Above My Head" was written for Elvis by W. Earl Brown. The song appeared in the Long Playing album "Elvis—TV Special" (RCA LPM-4088).

U.S. Male. RCA 47-9465. Released in March 1968 as a 45 rpm single. It reached #28 on *Billboard*'s Hot 100 chart and #55 on the Country chart. "Stay Away" was on the flip side. "U.S. Male" was written by Jerry Reed, who played lead guitar in this recording. "U.S. Male" appeared in the following Long Playing albums: "Almost in Love" (RCA Camden CAS-2440); "Almost in Love" (Pickwick CAS-2440); "Double Dynamite" (Pickwick DL2-5001).

U.S. Male. RCA 447-0664. Gold Standard Series re-issue of RCA 47-9465

V

Vail, Colorado. Ski resort where Elvis vacationed in January 1976. On January 14 he gave away three new Cadillacs and two new Lincoln Continental Mark IVs. Three police department employees, a doctor, and a TV newsman were the lucky recipients. (See: Kumpf Lincoln-Mercury)

---

*Buffy Sainte-Marie was born on a Cree Indian Reservation in Saskatchewan, Canada.

Vallee, Rudy. Singer of the 1920s and '30s who was one of the most popular crooners of the pre-Bing Crosby era. Vallee (real name: Hubert Prior Vallee) used a megaphone when singing, which became his trademark. He sang "Empty Saddles" at the funeral of Tom Mix in October 1940. Rudy Vallee, whose theme song is "My Time Is Your Time,"* appeared in Elvis's 1968 movie *Live a Little, Love a Little,* in the role of Penlow.

Vancouver, British Columbia. Canadian city that was the site of an Elvis concert on August 31, 1957. Prior to performing at the Empire Stadium in Vancouver, Elvis held one of his few press conferences. He performed in Canada only three times. The other two appearances were in Toronto and Ottawa. (See: Elvis Tapes, The; Robinson, Red)

Vanderhoof, Bruce. San Francisco disc jockey at radio station KYA, who, in 1957, played "Love Me Tender" at various speeds fourteen consecutive times to protest his station's policy of banning Elvis songs from the air between 10:00 A.M. and 4:00 P.M. For his actions, Vanderhoof was fired.

Vanilla. Reportedly, Elvis's favorite flavor of ice cream.

Van Kuyk, Andre. Rumored to be the name with which Col. Tom Parker was born. It is said that he was Dutch-born.

Van Man, Inc. Elkhart, Indiana, firm, owned by Luther Roberts, that customized a Dodge van for Elvis. Elvis was prompted to buy a van because he liked Conway Twitty's so much.

Van Natta, Thomas F. Army Major-General who commanded the 3d Armored Division in West Germany at the time that Elvis served there.

Vegas Records. Bootleg label from Canada that released a two-record 45 rpm Extended Play album featuring eight songs from Elvis's 1971 Las Vegas shows. Songs included—Record 1 (Vegas 45001), Side 1: "Never Been to Spain," "Lord, You Gave Me a Mountain." Side 2: "Proud Mary," "Love Me." Record 2 (Vegas 45002), Side 1: "I'm Leavin' It Up to You," "An American Trilogy." Side 2: "Hound Dog," "A Big Hunk o' Love."

Velvet, Jimmy. Recording artist ("It's Almost Tomorrow" [Philips 40314] and "We Belong Together" [Cub 9105]) and good friend of Elvis. Jimmy Velvet toured with Elvis in the mid-1950s. He has stated that he had a premonition of Elvis's death. While attending Paxton High School in Jacksonville, Florida, Velvet's English teacher was Mae Axton. (See: Axton, Mae Boren)

Venus Room. Showroom at the New Frontier Hotel, where Elvis made his Las Vegas debut (April 23–29, 1956). Comedian

---

*Rudy Vallee and His Collegians introduced "My Time Is Your Time" in the U. S. at the Heigh-Ho Club in New York City. He sang the song in the 1957 movie *The Helen Morgan Story.* On July 28, 1933, Rudy Vallee became the very first recipient of a singing telegram, when a delivery boy sang "Happy Birthday" to him.

Shecky Greene and the Freddie Martin Orchestra appeared on the same bill. (See: New Frontier Hotel)

Vesco, Robert L. Fugitive financier who fled the U. S. in 1972 just before being indicted in connection with a Securities and Exchange Commission fraud investigation. In January 1975, Elvis made a $75,000 deposit on Vesco's Boeing 707 jetliner. Total purchase price was to have been $775,000. The plane was included in the bankruptcy sale of one of Vesco's companies. Its renovated interior housed a gymnasium, a sauna, and a discotheque. During the bankruptcy proceedings, the jetliner was parked at Newark International Airport.

Elvis's offer for the Boeing 707 was withdrawn when a telegram was received from agents of Vesco threatening to have the plane seized if it ever landed outside the U. S.

Vicious Circle, The. Original subtitle of Elvis's hit song "In the Ghetto," composed by Mac Davis. RCA asked for and received permission to drop the subtitle. The correct, full title is "In the Ghetto (The Vicious Circle)."

Victory Gun. Napoleonic, twelve-pound cannon covered with bronze, silver, and gold. It was the cannon that fired the last shot against Mexican ruler Ferdinand Maximilian, freeing the country of his rule. The cannon was the subject of the 1969 movie *Charro!*.

Villiger Keil. Elvis's favorite brand of cigars. Villiger Keil is a German brand.

Vince Everett. Elvis's role in the 1957 movie *Jailhouse Rock*. (See: Everett, Vince)

Vincent, Gene. Rock-a-billy singer (real name: Eugene Vincent Craddock) from Norfolk, Virginia, who was born at about the same time as Elvis (February 11, 1935). He was one of the early rock 'n' roll artists, reaching the charts in 1956 with "Be-Bop-a-Lula" (Capitol 3405). Prior to 1956, Vincent had served in Korea with the Navy. After the military, he won an Elvis-impersonation contest and became the first artist to perform in black leather. Capitol signed him to their label in hopes of competing with Elvis. Gene Vincent's backup group was called the Blue Caps. Tommy Facenda, who had the 1960 hit "High School U.S.A.,"* was once a member of the Blue Caps.†

Vino, Dinero y Amor. Song that Elvis sang in the 1963 movie *Fun in Acapulco*. "Vino, Dinero y Amor" was written by Sid

---

*Twenty-eight different regional versions of "High School U.S.A." were recorded on Atlantic Records (Atlantic 2051–2078). Each regional version incorporated the names of well-known high schools in the area in which it was released. The Memphis version, which mentioned Humes High, was Atlantic 2072. The original version of "High School U.S.A." was recorded by Facenda on Legrand Records with Gary "U.S." Bonds as one of the backup vocalists. When Atlantic Records bought the master, they at first considered having Bobby Darin record the song.

†Other members have been: "Galloping" Cliff Gallup; "Wee" Willie Williams; "Be Bop" Harrell; "Jumpin'" Jack Neal (bass).

Tepper and Roy C. Bennett and appeared in the Long Playing album "Fun in Acapulco" (RCA LPM/LSP-2756).

Violet (Flower of N.Y.U.) Song that Elvis sang part of in the 1969 movie *The Trouble with Girls* (*And How to Get Into It*). "Violet (Flower of N.Y.U.)" lasted just fifteen seconds and has never been released by RCA. The song does, however, appear on bootleg albums. "Violet" was sung to the tune of "Aura Lee."

VIVA LAS VEGAS. MGM, 1964. Premiered New York City April 20, 1964 (86 min). Elvis's fifteenth movie. Producers, Jack Cummings and George Sidney. Director, George Sidney. Cast: Lucky Jackson/Elvis Presley, Rusty Martin/Ann-Margret, Count Elmo Mancini/Cesare Danova, Mr. Martin/William Demarest, Shorty Farnsworth/Nicky Blair, Jack Carter/Jack Carter, Swanson/Robert B. Williams, Big Gus Olso/Bob Nash, Baker/Roy Engel, Driver/Ford Dunhill, Mechanic/Barnaby Hale, Head Captain/Ivan Triesault, M.C./Eddie Quillan, Francois/Francis Raval, Delivery Boy/Rick Murray, Race Official/Larry Kent, Starter/Howard Curtis, Race Announcer/Alan Fordney. Screenplay, Sally Benson. Photography, Joseph Biroc. Music, George Stoll. Choreography, David Winters. Art Direction, George W. Davis and Edward Carfagno. Set Decoration, Henry Grace and George R. Nelson. Costumes, Don Feld. Assistant Director, Milton Feldman. Editor, John McSweeney, Jr. Songs sung by Elvis: "Viva Las Vegas," "If You Think I Don't Need You," "I Need Somebody to Lean On," "The Lady Loves Me" (duet with Ann-Margret), "C'mon Everybody," "Tomorrow and Forever," "Santa Lucia," "The Yellow Rose of Texas," "What'd I Say," "The Eyes of Texas." Ann-Margret sang "The Rival" and "Appreciation."

Viva Las Vegas. RCA 47-8360. Released in May 1964 as a 45 rpm single. It reached #29 on *Billboard*'s Hot 100 chart. "Viva Las Vegas" was a million-seller worldwide. "What'd I Say" was on the flip side. Written by Doc Pomus and Mort Shuman, "Viva Las Vegas" was the title song of the 1964 movie of the same name and appeared in the Long Playing albums "Elvis: Worldwide 50 Gold Award Hits, Volume 1" (RCA LPM-6401) and "Elvis in Hollywood" (RCA DPL2-0168).

"Viva Las Vegas" was released in true stereo in New Zealand on an Extended Play album, "See the U.S.A. the Elvis Way" (RCA EPAS-4386)—the only version released in stereo.

Viva Las Vegas. RCA 447-0646. Gold Standard Series re-issue of RCA 47-8360.

Viva Las Vegas. RCA EPA-4382. This was a 45 rpm Extended Play album released in July 1964. It reached #92 on *Billboard*'s Hot 100 chart. Songs included—Side 1: "If You Think I Don't Need You" "I Need Somebody to Lean On." Side 2: "C'mon Everybody," "Today, Tomorrow and Forever."

Vocal Groups. The following vocal groups sang back-up for Elvis in his records and his live performances: Amigos; Anita Kerr Singers; Blossoms; Carol Lombard Trio; Holladays; Hugh Jarrett Singers; Imperials Quartet; J. D. Sumner and the Stamps; Jordanaires; Jubilee Four; Ken Darby Singers; Mello Men; Nashville Edition; Sweet Inspirations; Voice.

Voice. Vocal group that backed Elvis in some recordings and live concerts from 1973 to '75. The members of Voice were Donnie Sumner, Tim Batey, and Sherril Nielson. Donnie Sumner also sang with J. D. Sumner and the Stamps.

W

W2349687. Air Force service number of PFC Midge Riley (Cynthia Pepper) in the 1964 movie *Kissin' Cousins*.

Wade, Elvis (a.k.a. Wade Cummins). Elvis Presley impersonator, beginning in 1968.

Wakely, Jimmy. Popular singer of the 1940s, appearing in movies with Roy Rogers and Gene Autry. Merle Haggard and Spade Cooley have both played in Jimmy Wakely's band. Wakely has recorded duets with Margaret Whiting. Jimmy Wakely is the composer of "I'll Never Let You Go (Little Darlin')," which Elvis recorded in January 1955. Jimmy Wakely was born February 16, 1914, seven days after Ernest Tubb (February 9) and two days before Pee Wee King (February 18). Wakely was once asked about his opinion of Elvis. His reply was: "Man, he's great! Fifteen years ago, I wrote a song called 'I'll Never Let You Go (Little Darlin')' and nothing happened. Presley put it into one of his albums and so far I've gotten $4,300 in royalties."

Wald, Jerry. Producer of the 1961 Twentieth Century-Fox movie *Wild in the Country*.

Walk a Mile in My Shoes. Song written and originally recorded by Joe South (Capitol 2704) in 1969. It reached #12 on *Billboard*'s Hot 100 chart. Elvis recorded "Walk a Mile in My Shoes" in 1970 and it appeared in the Long Playing album "On Stage—February, 1970" (RCA LSP-4362).

Walker, Cindy. Cowriter (with Eddy Arnold) of the song "You Don't Know Me," which Elvis recorded in February 1967. Cindy Walker's grandfather, F.L. Finland, is the composer of the popular hymn "Hold to God's Unchanging Hands."

Walker, Gary. Former member of the Walker Brothers (real name: Gary Leeds) Gary Walker once played drums in Elvis's band when the regular drummer was ill.

Wallace, Bill "Superfoot". Former World Middleweight karate champion who was one of Elvis's martial arts instructors.

Wallace, Don. Tulsa, Oklahoma, disc jockey whose 18,000-signature petition was presented to Elvis on "The Steve Allen Show" on July 1, 1956. The petition was a request to see more of Elvis on television.

Walley, Deborah. Actress whom Elvis dated while the two were making the 1966 movie *Spin Out*.

Wallis, Hal B. Producer of the following Elvis movies: *Loving You* (1957, Paramount), *King Creole* (1958, Paramount), *G.I. Blues* (1960, Paramount), *Blue Hawaii* (1961, Paramount), *Girls! Girls! Girls!* (1962, Paramount), *Fun in Acapulco* (1963, Paramount), *Roustabout* (1964, Paramount), *Paradise—Hawaiian Style* (1965, Paramount), *Easy Come, Easy Go* (1966, Paramount).

Walls Have Ears, The. Song that Elvis sang in the 1962 movie *Girls! Girls! Girls!*. The film version of "The Walls Have Ears" had added sound-effects simulating crashing walls. It was written by Sid Tepper and Roy C. Bennett and appeared in the Long Playing album "Girls! Girls! Girls!". (RCA LPM/LSP-2521).

Walter Gulick. Elvis's role as a boxer in the 1962 movie *Kid Galahad*.

Walter Hale. Elvis's role as a theatrical show manager in the 1969 movie *The Trouble with Girls (And How to Get Into It)*.

Warren, Charles Marquis. Director of the 1969 movie *Charro!*.

Warwick Hotel. New York City hotel, located at 54th Street and Avenue of the Americas, where Col. Tom Parker and RCA executive Steve Sholes signed the contract making Elvis an RCA artist (November 22, 1955). While appearing on the Dorsey Brothers' "Stage Show" (January–March 1956), Elvis, Scotty Moore, and Bill Black stayed at the Warwick Hotel (Elvis in Room 527). They also stayed at the Warwick while making all three appearances on "The Ed Sullivan Show." (See: Shaw, Arnold; RCA Records)

Washington Street. New York City street on which the free clinic run by Dr. John Carpenter was located in the 1969 movie *Change of Habit*.

Waters, Dickie. Instructor who taught Elvis to water ski in 1957.

Waters, Muddy. R & B composer and singer (real name: McKinley Morganfield) of the late 1940's and '50s. Muddy Waters's song "Rollin' Stone" (the title of which influenced the naming of a group and a magazine) was Chess Records' first hit record (Chess 1426), in 1950. In 1957 Waters wrote and recorded "Got My Mojo Working," which was recorded by Elvis in 1970.

Watz Matta You. Sloppily written nickname on the side of 2d Lt. Josh Morgan's (Elvis) F84 Thunderjet in the 1964 movie *Kissin' Cousins*.

Way Down. RCA PB-10998. Released in June 1977 as a 45 rpm single. It reached #18 on *Billboard*'s Hot 100 chart, #1 on the Country chart (for one week, August 13–20), and #14 on the Easy Listening chart. "Way Down" sold over a million copies. "Pledging My Love" was on the flip side. "Way Down" was recorded at Graceland on the night of October 29–30, 1976. It was written by Layng Martine, Jr., and appeared in the Long Playing albums "Moody Blue" (RCA AFL1-2428) and "Our Memories of Elvis, Volume 2" (RCA AQL1-3448).

Way Down. RCA JB-10998. Rare 45 rpm promotional single, released in stereo. It was released in advance of RCA PB-10998.

Wayne, Thomas. Singer who, in 1959, recorded the hit record, "Tragedy"* (Fernwood 109; released in 1961 on Capehart 5009), which became a classic. Thomas Wayne (full name: Thomas Wayne Perkins) was a graduate of Humes High School† in Memphis, as was Elvis. His brother, Luther Perkins, was the lead guitarist for Johnny Cash. Thomas Wayne composed (with Bill Rice) "Girl Next Door Went a'Walking," which Elvis recorded in April 1960. In 1971 Thomas Wayne was killed in a Memphis automobile accident.

WDIA. Black Memphis rhythm and blues radio station at 2074 Union Ave., which Elvis listened to in the early 1950s. It was advertised as "America's Only 50,000 Watt Negro Radio Station" (1070 KC). Rufus Thomas, a disc jockey at WDIA, recorded one of the first releases for the Sun label, with "Bear Cat" (Sun 181) in 1953. Blues singer B. B. King also served as a DJ for WDIA. James Mattis, another disc jockey at WDIA, founded Duke Records of Houston, on which Johnny Ace and Bobby Blue Bland recorded. Duke's sister label, Peacock, released Willie Mae Thornton's version of "Hound Dog." Joe Hill Lewis, another Sun artist, had a show on WDIA.‡

WDIA Goodwill Review. Concert held in Memphis on December 22, 1956. The artists were: Elvis Presley; Little Junior Parker; Earl Malone; B.B. King; Bobby Blue Bland.

Wearin' That Loved On Look. Song written by Dallas Frazier and Al Owens and recorded by Elvis in 1969. "Wearin' That Loved

---

*Scotty Moore produced "Tragedy."
†There exist a number of situations where two future singers attended the same high school at the same time. For example:
David Gates and Leon Russell attended the same Tulsa, Oklahoma, high school, where they played in the same band. David Bowie and Peter Frampton attended the same British school. Bowie's art teacher was Peter Frampton's father. Rod Stewart and Raymond Davies played football for the same school team in England. Tommy Sands and Paula Prentiss were classmates at Lamar High School in Houston, Texas. Kenny Rogers and Mickey Newberry were schoolmates at Jefferson Davis High in Houston, Texas. And, of course, the most famous combination, Barbra Streisand and Neil Diamond attended Eramus Hall High in New York City, singing together in the same school choir.
‡Mike Bloomfield once recorded a song titled "WDIA."

On Look" appeared in the Long Playing album "From Elvis in Memphis" (RCA LSP-4155).

Wear My Ring Around Your Neck. RCA 20/47-7240. Released in April 1958 as a 78 rpm single and a 45 rpm single. It reached #3 on *Billboard*'s Hot 100 chart, #3 on the Country chart, and #7 on the Rhythm and Blues chart. "Wear My Ring Around Your Neck" sold over a million copies (advance orders alone were for over a million). "Doncha' Think It's Time" was on the flip side. "Wear My Ring Around Your Neck" was written by Bert Carroll and Russell Moody and appeared in the Extended Play album "A Touch of Gold, Volume 2" (RCA EPA-5101) and the following Long Playing albums: "50,000,-000 Elvis Fans Can't Be Wrong—Elvis' Gold Records, Volume 2" (RCA LPM-2075); "50,000,000 Elvis Fans Can't Be Wrong—Elvis' Gold Records, Volume 2" (RCA LSP-2075 [e]); "Elvis: Worldwide 50 Gold Award Hits, Volume 1" (RCA LPM-6401).

Wear My Ring Around Your Neck. RCA 447-0622. Gold Standard Series re-issue of RCA 20/47-7240.

Wear My Ring Around Your Neck. RCA SP-45-76. Special 45 rpm promotional release. "Don't" was on the flip side.

Webb, Robert D. Director of the 1956 movie *Love Me Tender*.

Webb, Trent. Driver of the hearse (#25) that took Elvis's body to Forest Hill Cemetery on August 18, 1977.

We Call on Him. RCA 47-9600. Released in April 1967 as a 45 rpm single. "You'll Never Walk Alone" was on the flip side. Although "We Call on Him" never reached the charts, some sources indicate that it sold over a million copies. Written by Fred Karger, Sid Wayne, and Ben Weisman, "We Call on Him" appeared in the Long Playing albums "You'll Never Walk Alone" (RCA Camden CALX-2472) and "You'll Never Walk Alone" (RCA CAS-2472).

We Call on Him. RCA 447-0665. Gold Standard Series re-issue of RCA 47-9600.

We Can Make the Morning. RCA 74-0619. Released in January 1972 as a 45 rpm single. "Until It's Time for You to Go" was on the flip side. "We Can Make the Morning" was written by Jay Ramsey and appeared in the Long Playing album "Elvis—Now" (RCA LSP-4671).

We Didn't Get Enough of You. A 1977 Elvis tribute song by Pickin' Post Records artist Nancy Jewell. (Pickin' Post 8830).

Weisbart, David. Producer of the following Elvis movies: *Love Me Tender* (1956, Twentieth Century-Fox), *Flaming Star* (1960, Twentieth Century-Fox), *Follow That Dream* (1962, United Artists), *Kid Galahad* (1962, United Artists). Weisbart also produced the 1955 James Dean movie, *Rebel Without a Cause*, in which both Natalie Wood and Nick Adams appeared.

Weisman, Ben. Co-composer of fifty-seven songs for Elvis, including "Fame and Fortune," "Rock-a-Hula Baby," and "Follow That Dream." Ben Weisman composed "You Can Do It" for Dobie Gray. The first song Weisman composed for Elvis was "First in Line" and his first movie song was "Got a Lot o' Livin' to Do." Ben Weisman appears frequently on the CBS-TV daytime serial "The Young and the Restless," as a pianist in the Club Allegro.

Weiss, Allan. Author of the screenplays for the following Elvis movies: *Blue Hawaii* (1961). *Fun in Acapulco* (1963), *Roustabout* (1964), *Paradise—Hawaiian Style* (1966), *Girls! Girls! Girls!* (1962), *Easy Come, Easy Go* (1967).

Weiss, Gene. Man who tried to sell Elvis to Columbia Records, but Mitch Miller wasn't interested.

Welch, Lester. Producer of the 1969 movie *The Trouble with Girls (And How to Get Into It)*.

Welch, Raquel. Actress (born Raquel Tejada in Chicago on September 5, 1940) who made her screen debut as a college student in the 1964 movie *Roustabout*.

Welcome Aboard. One of two titles originally considered for the 1962 movie *Girls! Girls! Girls!*. The other title was *A Girl in Every Port*.

Welcome Home Elvis. A 1977 Elvis tribute song by Billy Joe Burnette on Gusto-Starday Records (Gusto-Starday 167).

Welcome Home Elvis. A 1977 Elvis tribute song by Daddy Bob on the Bertram-International label (Bertram-International 1835).

Welcome to My World. Country song written by Ray Winkler and John Hathcock and originally recorded by Jim Reeves (RCA 8289) in 1963. Elvis sang "Welcome to My World" in the 1973 TV special "Elvis: Aloha from Hawaii," and it appeared in the Long Playing albums "Elvis: Aloha from Hawaii Via Satellite" (RCA UPSX-6089) and "Welcome to My World" (RCA APL1-2274).

Welcome to My World. RCA APL1-2274. A 33⅓ rpm Long Playing album released in March 1977. It reached #44 on *Billboard*'s Hot LP chart and #4 on the Hot Country LP chart. "Welcome to My World" sold in excess of 500,000 copies, qualifying it for a Gold Record. It contained the following songs: Side 1: "Welcome to My World," "Help Me Make It Through the Night," "Release Me (And Let Me Love Again)," "I Really Don't Want to Know," "For the Good Times." Side 2: "Make the World Go Away," "Gentle on My Mind," "I'm So Lonesome I Could Cry," "Your Cheatin' Heart," "I Can't Stop Loving You."

Weld, Tuesday. Female lead (as Noreen) in the 1961 movie *Wild in the Country*, along with Hope Lange and Millie Perkins. Tuesday Weld was born Susan Ker Weld on Thursday, August 27, 1943. She made her movie debut in the 1957 movie *Rock, Rock, Rock*, with Connie Francis dubbing her singing voice. Tuesday played Dobie Gillis's first love, Thalia Menniger, in the TV series "The Many Loves of Dobie Gillis"* between 1959 and '60. In 1975 she married Dudley Moore.

Wella Corporation. Hair-care company with which Priscilla Presley signed a three-year contract in 1979. The company had already helped to launch the careers of Farrah Fawcett, Jaclyn Smith, and Cheryl Ladd. Her first TV commercial was shown on all three networks on October 31, 1979.

We'll Be Together. Song that Elvis sang in the 1962 movie *Girls! Girls! Girls!*. The Amigos were background vocalists in "We'll Be Together." It was written by Charles O'Curran and Dudley Brooks and appeared in the following Long Playing albums: "Girls! Girls! Girls!" (RCA LPM/LSP-2621); "Burning Love and Hits from His Movies, Volume 2" (RCA Camden CAS-2595); "Burning Love and Hits from His Movies, Volume 2" (Pickwick CAS-2595).

We'll Have a Blue Christmas, Elvis. A 1977 Elvis tribute song by Jim Matthews† on Music Emporium Records.

WELO. Tupelo, Mississippi, radio station (580 K.C. on the dial), located at 212 S. Spring Street, that first broadcast Elvis. WELO broadcast, live, the annual talent show at the Mississippi-Alabama Fair and Dairy Show on October 3, 1945. Ten-year-old Elvis sang "Old Shep." (See: Harris, Becky; Mississippi-Alabama Fair and Dairy Show)

Wendell. Cat owned by Elvis. Wendell was named for actor Wendell Corey, who appeared with Elvis in the 1957 movie *Loving You.*

We're Coming in Loaded. Song that Elvis sang in the 1962 movie *Girls! Girls! Girls!*. "We're Coming in Loaded" was written by Otis Blackwell and Winfield Scott and appeared in the Long Playing album "Girls! Girls! Girls!". (RCA LPM/LSP-2621).

We're Gonna Live It Up. Song that Elvis is believed to have recorded for the 1957 movie *Loving You.* It was cut from the final print of the film. "We're Gonna Live It Up" is not mentioned in any of the recording sessions notes.

We're Gonna Move. Song that Elvis sang in the 1956 movie *Love Me Tender.* Although Elvis and Vera Matson are credited with writing "We're Gonna Move," Ken Darby was actually the composer. (See: Darby, Ken) "We're Gonna Move" appeared in the Extended Play album "Love Me Tender" (RCA EPA-4006) and the following Long Playing albums: "A Date with Elvis" (RCA LPM-2011) "A Date with Elvis" (RCA LSP-2011 [e]); "Elvis: The Other Sides—Worldwide Gold Award Hits, Volume 2" (RCA LPM-6402).

We Remember Elvis. Book by Wanda June Hill, published by Morgan Press, in Palos Verdes, in 1978. In the book, Ms. Hill

---

*Warren Beatty also appeared in the TV series, playing Milton Armitage, and Ryan O'Neal played bit roles as a high school student.
†On the label, Jim Matthews was credited as "The Singing Surgeon."

has reproduced supposed telephone conversations, poetry, and correspondence of and by Elvis.

We're Sure Gonna Miss You, Old Friend. A 1977 Elvis tribute song by Jack Hickox on Constellation Records.

West, Delbert "Sonny". Six-foot-two-inch-tall cousin of Red West. He first met Elvis at Humes High and later went to work for him, taking care of Elvis's vehicles. Sonny West appeared in the 1968 movie *Stay Away, Joe.*

West, Newton Thomas. Red West's father, who died the same day as Elvis's mother, Gladys Presley—August 14, 1958.

West, Pat Boyd. One of Elvis's personal secretaries, married to Red West since 1961.

West, Robert "Red", Gene. Close friend of Elvis and member of the Memphis Mafia. He is the cousin of Delbert "Sonny" West. West first met Elvis in high school, where he was a year behind Elvis. For years West was employed as Elvis's bodyguard. A man of many talents, Red West became a movie stuntman, appearing in numerous movies including *Spartacus* (1960). He married one of Elvis's secretaries, Pat Boyd. In Memphis, Red West operated the Tennessee Karate Institute. He wrote a number of songs that Pat Boone, Ricky Nelson, and Johnny Rivers put on record. He also wrote "If Every Day Could Be Like Christmas" and "Holly Leaves and Christmas Trees," which Elvis recorded. While attending Jones Junior College, Red West played in the Junior Rose Bowl in Pasadena after his school won the state championship. Red West appeared in the following Elvis movies: *Flaming Star* (1960) as an Indian, *Wild in the Country* (1961) as Hank, *Blue Hawaii* (1961) as a party guest, *Follow That Dream* (1962) as a bank guard, *Girls! Girls! Girls!* (1962) as a sailor who played bongos, *It Happened at the World's Fair* (1963) as Fred, *Roustabouts* (1964) as a carnival worker, *Tickle Me* (1965) in a fight scene, *Harum Scarum* (1965) as an assassin, *Clambake* (1967) as an ice cream vender. He also appeared in three Robert Conrad TV series: "The Wild Wild West"; "Baa Baa Black Sheep" (as Sgt. Andy Micklin, 1977–78); "The Duke." In 1979 he made a Chevy truck TV commercial. In the 1969 TV movie *Elvis,* Red West was portrayed by Robert Gray.

Western Union. Song that Elvis recorded for the 1968 movie *Speedway,* but it was never used. "Western Union" was written by Sid Tepper and Roy C. Bennett and appeared in the Long Playing album "Speedway" (RCA LSP-3989).

Westinghouse Credit Corporation. Memphis lending institution (located at 3003 Airways Blvd.) through which Elvis financed (in the Mobile Home Division)—the many mobile homes he bought for the Memphis Mafia and their wives or girlfriends. The mobile homes were hauled to the Circle G Ranch, where they remained. One of the few times, if not the *only* time, that Elvis bought anything on credit.

Westmoreland, Kathy. Soprano singer who toured with Elvis in his concert appearances and who can be heard in many Elvis recordings between 1970 and '77.

West Side Story. A 1960 movie starring Natalie Wood* and Richard Beyer, which won an Academy Award for Best Picture of the Year, as did the two supporting actors, Rita Moreno and George Chakiris. Elvis was offered the lead role in the movie but turned it down. Elvis seriously dated two of the leading actresses in the movie version—Natalie Wood and Rita Moreno.

Westwind. Sailboat previously owned by Ross Carpenter's (Elvis) late father in the 1962 movie *Girls! Girls! Girls!*. Wesley Johnson (Jeremy Slate) bought it from Mr. Carpenter for $6,000. Ross wanted to buy it from Johnson but couldn't afford it. Laurel Dodge (Laurel Godwin), Ross's wealthy girlfriend, bought it for Ross, but he made her sell it. He decided to build a new boat after marrying Laurel.

What a Wonderful Life. Song that Elvis sang in the 1962 movie *Follow That Dream*. Written by Sid Wayne and Jay Livingstone, "What a Wonderful Life" appeared in the Extended Play album "Follow That Dream" (RCA EPA-4368) and the Long Playing albums "I Got Lucky" (RCA Camden CAL-2533) and "I Got Lucky" (Pickwick CAS-2533)

What Did They Do Before Rock and Roll. A 1962 novelty song by Paul Peterson and Shelley Fabares on Colpix Records (Colpix 631). Elvis was mentioned in the lyrics.

What'd I Say. RCA 47-8360. Released in May 1964 as a 45 rpm single. It reached #21 on *Billboard*'s Hot 100 chart. "Viva Las Vegas" was on the flip side. Elvis sang "What'd I Say" in the 1964 movie *Viva Las Vegas* and the 1970 documentary *Elvis— That's the Way It is*. "What'd I Say" was written and originally recorded by Ray Charles (Atlantic 2031) in 1959 (titled "What'd I Say, Pt. 1"/"What'd I Say, Pt. 2"). It reached #6 on *Billboard*'s Hot 100 chart and was Ray Charles's first million-seller. Other popular versions of "What'd I Say" were by Jerry Lee Lewis and His Pumping Piano (Sun 356) in 1961 and Bobby Darin (Atco 6221) in 1962. Elvis's version of "What'd I Say" appeared in the Long Playing albums "Elvis' Gold Records, Volume 4" (RCA LPM/LSP-3921) and "Elvis in Concert" (RCA APL2-2587).

What'd I Say. RCA 447-0646. Gold Standard Series re-issue of RCA 47-8360.

What Every Woman Lives For. Song that Elvis sang in the 1966 movie *Frankie and Johnny*. "What Every Woman Lives For" was written by Doc Pomus and Mort Shuman and appeared in the Long Playing albums "Frankie and Johnny" (RCA LPM/LSP-3553) and "Frankie and Johnny" (Pickwick ACL-7007).

---

*Marni Nixon, the mother of singer Andrew Gold, sang for Natalie Wood in the film.

What Now My Love. Song written by French composers P. Delanoe and Gilbert Becaud (and originally recorded by Becaud) in 1962 under the title, "Et maintenant." In 1966 (A & M SP 4114) Herb Alpert and the Tijuana Brass had a million-selling album titled "What Now My Love"* containing the popular song of the same name. Elvis sang "What Now My Love" in the 1973 TV special "Elvis: Aloha from Hawaii," and it appeared in the Long Playing album "Elvis: Aloha from Hawaii Via Satellite" (RCA VPSX-6089).

What Now, What Next, Where To. Song written by Don Robertson and Hal Blair and recorded by Elvis in 1963. "What Now, What Next, Where To" appeared in the following Long Playing ablums: "Double Trouble" (RCA LPM/LSP-3787); "Separate Ways" (RCA Camden CAS-2611), and "Separate Ways" (Pickwick CAS-2611).

What's She Really Like. Song that Elvis sang in the 1960 movie *G.I. Blues*. In the film version, Elvis sings "What's She Really Like" while he's in the shower. It lasts only twenty seconds. Written by Sid Wayne and Abner Silver, "What's She Really Like" appeared in the Long Playing album "G.I. Blues" (RCA LPM/LSP 2256).

What Will We Do Without You? A 1978 Elvis tribute song by Bobby Fisher (Mark 004).

WHBQ. Memphis radio station, located in the Chisca Hotel at 272 S. Main, that became the first station to play an Elvis record, on July 7, 1954. (See: Phillips, Dewey; Red, Hot, and Blue)

Wheeler, Kate. Girl dated occasionally by Elvis in 1956.

Wheeler, Treatise, III. Eighteen-year-old Memphis driver who ran into the teenage girls Juanita Joanne Johnson (nineteen) and Alice Marie Hovartar (nineteen) of Monroe, Tennessee, at 4:00 A.M., August 18, 1977. He drove his 1963 Ford Fairlane into a crowd of Elvis mourners and, after hitting the two girls drove off, only to be caught by the Memphis police. A third women was injured, Tammy J. Baiter (seventeen) of St. Clair, Missouri. He was charged with drunk driving, two counts of second-degree murder, leaving the scene of an accident, public drunkenness, and reckless driving.

Wheels on My Heels. Song that Elvis sang in the 1964 movie *Roustabout*. "Wheels on My Heels" was written by Sid Tepper and Roy C. Bennett and appeared in the Long Playing album "Roustabout" (RCA LPM/LSP-2999).

When Elvis Marches Home Again. A 1960 novelty record by the Sophisticates released on ViVa records (ViVa 61).

When I'm Over You. Song written by Shirl Milete and recorded

---

*"What Now My Love" was the first eight-track stereo cartridge to be awarded the Gold Cartridge Award for sales exceeding $1 million.

by Elvis in 1970. "When I'm Over You" appeared in the Long Playing album "Love Letters from Elvis" (RCA LSP-4530).

When It Rains, It Really Pours. Song written and originally recorded by William Robert "Billy the Kid" Emerson* (Sun 214) in 1955. (It was released the same day as Elvis's "Milkcow Blues Boogie"/"You're a Heartbreaker"—January 8, 1955). Elvis recorded "When It Rains, It Really Pours" in 1957 and it appeared in the Long Playing album "Elvis for Everyone" (RCA LPM/LSP-3450).

When My Blue Moon Turns to Gold Again. Country song written by Wiley Walker and Gene Sullivan and originally recorded by Walker on Columbia Records in 1941. Maurice Woodward "Tex" Ritter had a popular version of "When My Blue Moon turns to Gold Again" (Capitol 1977) in 1949. Elvis recorded the song for the 1968 TV special "Elvis," but it was not included in the telecast. "When My Blue Moon Turns to Gold Again" appeared in the Extended Play album "Elvis, Volume 1" (RCA EPA-992) and the following Long Playing albums: "Elvis" (RCA LPM 1382); "Elvis" (RCA LSP-1382 [e]); "Elvis: The Other Sides—Worldwide Gold Award Hits, Volume 2" (RCA LPM-6402).

When You Wore a Tulip and I Wore a Big Red Rose. Popular vaudeville song written by Jock Mahoney and Percy Wenrich in 1914. "When You Wore a Tulip and I Wore a Big Red Rose" was sung in several movies over the years, including *Larceny in Music* (1942), *Hello, Frisco, Hello* (1943), and *Cheaper By the Dozen* (1950). In the 1969 Elvis movie *The Trouble with Girls* (*And How to Get Into It*), a young girl sang the song.

Where Could I Go But to the Lord. Gospel song composed by J. B. Coats that Elvis sang in the 1968 NBC-TV special "Elvis." "Where Could I Go But to the Lord" appeared in the Long Playing albums "How Great Thou Art" (RCA LPM/LSP-3758) and "Elvis—TV Special" (RCA LPM 4088).

Where Did They Go, Lord. RCA 47-9980. Released in March 1971 as a 45 rpm single. It reached #33 on *Billboard*'s Hot 100 chart and #55 on the Country chart. "Rags to Riches" was on the flip side. "Where Did They Go, Lord," according to some sources, sold over a million copies. It was written by Dallas Frazier and Al Owens and appeared in the Long Playing album "He Walks Beside Me" (RCA AFL1-2772).

Where Did They Go, Lord. RCA 447-0680. Gold Standard Series re-issue of RCA 47-9980.

Where Do I Go from Here. Song written by country singer Hank Williams, which Elvis recorded in 1972. "Where Do I Go from Here" appeared in the Long Playing album "Elvis" (RCA APL1-0283).

---

*"Billy the Kid" Emerson was once a member of Ike Turner's Kings of Rhythm band.

Where Do You Come From. RCA 47-8100. Released in October 1962 as a 45 rpm single. It reached #99 on *Billboard*'s Hot 100 chart. Despite its poor chart showing, "Where Do You Come From" was credited with selling over a million copies. "Return to Sender" was on the flip side. "Where Do You Come From" was written by Ruth Batchelor and Bob Roberts and sung by Elvis in the 1962 movie *Girls! Girls! Girls!*. It appeared in the Long Playing albums "Girls! Girls! Girls!" (RCA LPM/LSP-2621) and "Elvis: Worldwide 50 Gold Award Hits, Volume 1" (RCA LPM-6401).

Where Do You Come From. RCA 447-0638. Gold Standard Series re-issue of RCA 47-8100.

Where No One Stands Alone. Gospel song written by Mosie Lister and recorded by Elvis in 1966. "Where No One Stands Alone" appeared in the Long Playing album "How Great Thou Art" (RCA LPM/LSP-3758).

WHHM. Memphis country-music radio station, located on Sterich Blvd., on which disc jockey "Sleepy-Eyed" John Lepley first played "Blue Moon of Kentucky" in July 1954. "Blue Moon of Kentucky" was the country side of Elvis's first record, Sun 209. Dewey Phillips of WHBQ was the first disc jockey to play the rhythm and blues side, "That's All Right (Mama)."* (See: Lepley, John "Sleepy-Eyed"; Phillips, Dewey)

Whiffenpoof Song, The. Theme song of the Yale University singing club, the Whiffenpoofs. The music to "The Whiffenpoof Song" was written by Guy Scull, circa 1894. In 1909 Mead Minnigerode and George S. Pomeroy loosely adapted the words from *Gentlemen Rankers*, a poem by Rudyard Kipling. The song has been recorded by Bing Crosby, Robert Merrill, Rudy Vallee, and the Sons of the Pioneers. "The Whiffenpoof Song" appeared in the 1950 movie *Riding High*. Elvis sang a few lines of the school song in the 1969 movie *The Trouble with Girls (And How to Get Into It.)*

Whipshaw, Miss. Director of the orphanage where Deke Rivers was raised in the 1957 movie *Loving You*.

Whirling Dervish of Sex. Term applied to Elvis in 1956 by the Rev. Charles Howard Graff of St. John's Episcopal Church in Greenwich Village, New York City.

Whistling Blues. Song that Elvis may have recorded for the 1960 movie *G.I. Blues*. "Whistling Blues" did not appear in the film, nor is it available on record.

Whistling Tune, A. Song that Elvis sang in the 1962 movie *Kid Galahad*. The version that appeared in the movie was different from that on records. Written by Sherman Edwards and Hal David, "A Whistling Tune" was originally scheduled to be in

---

*Although Lepley is credited as being the first to play "Blue Moon of Kentucky," it is hard to believe that Dewey Phillips would play the same record over and over, receive numerous phone calls and telegrams, and not once flip the record over to hear what was on the other side.

the 1962 movie *Follow That Dream*, but it was not used. It appeared in the Extended Play album "Kid Galahad" (RCA EPA-4371) and the Long Playing albums "C'mon Everybody" (RCA Camden CAL-2518) and "C'mon Everybody" (Pickwick CAS-2518).

White. Color of the telephone at Elvis's bedside at Graceland.

White, Bergen. Arranger of the strings and horns heard on "Moody Blue" and "She Thinks I Still Care."

White, Carrie. Beverly Hills hair stylist who occasionally cut Elvis's hair (at thirty-five dollars per visit) when he was in Hollywood.

White, Kitty. Female voice heard in the song "Crawfish" in the 1958 movie *King Creole*.

White, Tony Joe. Country artist, singer, and composer who recorded for Monument Records. His compositions recorded by Elvis are: "Polk Salad Annie," "I've Got a Thing About You," "Rainy Night in Georgia" (sung live in the documentary *Elvis On Tour*).

White Christmas. Best-selling song of all time, with over 30 million copies sold. "White Christmas" was written by Irving Berlin in 1942 for the film *Holiday Inn* and recorded by Bing Crosby (Decca 18429A) on May 29 of that year. Crosby* was backed by the John Scott Trotter Orchestra and the Ken Darby Singers. Originally, the opening line of "White Christmas" was "I'm sitting here in Beverly Hills, dreaming of a White Christmas." Due to the insistence of Jack Kapp, Irving Berlin deleted the line from the song. "God Rest Ye Merry Gentlemen" was on the flip side of Bing Crosby's record. Several artists have recorded "White Christmas" through the years, including Freddie Martin and His Orchestra (million-seller in 1942), Frank Sinatra (million-seller in 1944), and the Drifters (1954). Elvis recorded "White Christmas" in 1957 based on the Drifters' arrangement (Atlantic 1048) of 1954. It appeared in the Extended Play album "Christmas with Elvis" (RCA EPA-4340) and the following Long Playing albums: "Elvis' Christmas Album" (RCA LOC-1035); "Elvis' Christmas Album" (RCA LPM-1951); "Elvis' Christmas Album" (RCA LSP-1951 [e]); "Elvis' Christmas Album" (RCA Camden CAL-2428); "Elvis' Christmas Album" (Pickwick CAS-2428).

Whitehaven. Former suburb of Memphis where Graceland is located, at 3764 Elvis Presley Blvd. Annexed by Memphis in 1969, Whitehaven is in South Memphis.

Whitehaven Bowling Lane. Memphis bowling establishment where Elvis occasionally bowled.

Whitehaven High School. School, located at 4851 Elvis Presley

---

*Bing Crosby was the first artist to record for Decca Records (August 8, 1934). Decca was founded by Jack Kapp. Crosby's (and Decca's) first record was "I Love You Truly"/"Just a Wearyin' for You" (Decca DE-100).

Blvd., where Elvis rented the stadium to play football with his friends. Elvis, who played end, would hire an official to call the game.

Whitehaven Music. Music-publishing company of which Elvis owned part interest.

Whitman, Slim. Pseudonym of country singer/yodeler Otis Dewey. Slim Whitman was on the same bill with Elvis in Elvis's first stage appearance, July 30, 1954. They appeared in Memphis to a crowd of 2,000. Whitman was the first country entertainer to perform at the London Palladium. He is a Capricorn, as was Elvis.

Whoa. Elvis's first spoken word in films. He said it to stop his plow horses. His second word was "Brett" and his third was "Vince." "They told us you were dead" was his first full line (1956 movie *Love Me Tender*).

Who Am I. Song by Charles "Rusty" Goodman that Elvis recorded in February 1969 at the American Sound Studios in Memphis. "Who Am I" appeared in the following Long Playing albums: "You'll Never Walk Alone" (RCA Camden CALX-2472); "You'll Never Walk Alone" (Pickwick CAS-2472); "He Walks Beside Me" (RCA AFL1-2772).

Who Are You (Who Am I). Song that Elvis sang in the 1968 movie *Speedway*. "Who Are You (Who Am I)" was written by Sid Wayne and Ben Weisman. It appeared in the Long Playing album "Speedway" (RCA LSP-3989).

Whole Lotta Shakin' Goin' On. Song written by Dave Williams and Sunny David and originally recorded by the Commodores on Dot Records in 1955. Jerry Lee Lewis had a tremendous hit with "Whole Lotta Shakin' Goin' On" (Sun 267) in 1957. It reached #3 on *Billboard*'s Hot 100 chart, #1 on the Country chart, and #1 on the Rhythm and Blues chart. ("Whole Lotta Shakin' Goin' On" was the only song by an artist other than Elvis to become #1 on both the Country and Rhythm and Blues charts.) Through the years, Jerry Lee Lewis's "Whole Lotta Shakin' Goin' On" has sold over 3 million copies.* Elvis sang "Whole Lotta Shakin' Goin' On" in the 1973 TV special "Elvis: Aloha from Hawaii" and it appeared in the following Long Playing albums: "Elvis Country" (RCA LSP-4460); "Elvis: Aloha from Hawaii Via Satellite" (RCA VPSX-6089); "Elvis Recorded Live on Stage in Memphis" (RCA CPL1-0606).

Who Needs Money. Song that Elvis sang in the 1967 movie *Clambake*. Will Hutchins sang a duet with Elvis; however, the voice heard was not really Hutchins's. "Who Needs Money" was written by Randy Starr and appeared in the Long Playing album "Clambake" (RCA LPM/LSP-3893).

---

*The two musicians who backed up Jerry Lee Lewis, Roland James on drums and Jimmy Van Eaton on guitar, were members of Billy Lee Riley's Little Green Men.

Who's Lonesome Tonight, Act III (Pt. 1). Song recorded in 1961 by Redd Dogg on Del-fi Records. It was an answer record to Elvis's "Are You Lonesome Tonight."

Why Me Lord. Song written and originally recorded as "Why Me," by Kris Kristofferson in 1973, achieving sales of over a million copies. Elvis recorded "Why Me Lord" in 1974 and it appeared in the Long Playing album "Elvis Recorded Live on Stage in Memphis" (RCA SPL1-0606).

Wiere Brothers. Comedy team: Harry, Herbert, and Sylvester. They appeared as Belgian detectives in the 1967 movie *Double Trouble*.

Wilbank, June. Girl whom Elvis dated on three occasions in 1958.

WILD IN THE COUNTRY. Twentieth Century-Fox, 1961. Premiered Memphis, Tennessee, June 15, 1961 (114 min). Elvis's seventh movie. Producer, Jerry Wald. Director, Philip Dunne. Cast: Glenn Tyler/Elvis Presley, Irene Sperry/Hope Lange, Noreen/Tuesday Weld, Betty Lee Parsons/Millie Perkins, Davis/Rafer Johnson, Phil Macy/John Ireland, Cliff Macy/Gary Lockwood, Uncle Rolfe/William Mims, Dr. Underwood/Raymond Greenleaf, Monica George/Christina Crawford, Flossie/Robin Raymond, Mrs. Parsons/Doreen Lang, Mr. Parsons/Charles Arnt, Sarah/Ruby Goodwin, Willie Dace/Will Corry, Professor Larson/Alan Napier, Judge Parker/Jason Robards, Sr., Bartender/Harry Carter, Sam Tyler/Harry Sherman, Hank Tyler/Bobby West, State Trooper/Elisha M. Mott, Spangler/Walter Baldwin, Huckster/Mike Lally, Mr. Dace/Joe Butham, Conductor/Hans Moebus, Doctor/Linden Chiles, Jr., Coroner/Jack Orrison. Screenplay, Clifford Odets. Photography, William C. Mellor. Music, Kenyon Hopkins. Art Direction, Jack Martin Smith and Preston Ames. Set Decoration, Walter M. Scott and Stuart A. Reiss. Costumes, Don Feld. Assistant Director, Joseph E. Rickards. Editor, Dorothy Spencer. Songs Sung by Elvis: "In My Way," "I Slipped, I Stumbled, I Fell," "Husky Dusky Day" (with Hope Lange) "Wild in the Country." Sonny West played a bit part in the film. The movie was originally released without Elvis singing. The film did so badly at the box offices that it was recalled soon after release and had songs added to it.

Wild in the Country. RCA 47-7880. Released in May 1967 as a 45 rpm single. It reached #26 on *Billboard*'s Hot 100 chart. "I Feel So Bad" was on the flip side. "Wild in the Country" was written by Hugo Peretti, Luigi Creatore, and George Weiss and sung by Elvis over the credits of the 1961 movie *Wild in the Country.* On the English LP "Elvis for Everyone," maracas were added to the instrumental track. "Wild in the Country" appeared in the Long Playing albums "Elvis: The Other Sides— Worldwide Gold Award Hits, Volume 2" (RCA LPM-6402) and "Elvis in Hollywood" (RCA DPL2-0168).

Wild in the Country. RCA 447-0631. Gold Standard Series re-issue of RCA 47-7880.

Wild in the Country. RCA 37-7880. A 33⅓ rpm single release. "I Feel So Bad" was on the flip side.

Wild in the Country. RCA 61-7880. A 45 rpm "Living Stereo" release. "I Feel So Bad" was on the flip side.

Wiley, Sharon. Girl whom Elvis seriously dated in the 1950s.

Wilkinson, John. Guitarist with the band that backed Elvis at the International Hotel in Las Vegas in 1969.

William Morris Agency. Large talent agency through which Col. Tom Parker used to book Elvis's early concerts. The William Morris Agency received a ten-percent commission. (See: Lastfogel, Abe)

Williams, Andy. Popular ballad singer who was a member of the Williams Brothers as a youth. The group dubbed the back-up singing for Bing Crosby on "Would You Like to Swing on a Star" in the 1944 movie *Going My Way*. As a fourteen-year-old, Andy sang for Lauren Bacall in her movie debut, *To Have and to Have Not* (1945). He recorded two songs that were later recorded by Elvis: "Are You Sincere" and "The Hawaiian Wedding Song."

Williams, Ernestine. Graceland maid for five years.

Williams, Hiram "Hank". Highly popular singer and composer who wrote and sang from the heart. His country band was the Drifting Cowboys. On June 11, 1949, Hank Williams made his debut at the Grand Ole Opry, singing "Lovesick Blues" over and over again at the audience's request. During his short life span (1923–53) Hank Williams wrote a vast list of country songs that are classics today. On January 1, 1953, Williams's chauffeur, Charles Carr, found him dead in the back seat of his Cadillac. Williams's second wife, Billie Jean Jones, was also married to Johnny Horton when Horton died. In 1961 Williams was elected to the Country Music Hall of Fame. Some of Williams's compositions were: "Cold Cold Heart"; "Hey Good Lookin'"; "Half as Much"; "Jambalaya"; "Move It Over"; and "Your Cheatin' Heart" and "I'm So Lonesome I Could Cry," which Elvis recorded in his 1977 album "Welcome to My World." Like Elvis, at the age of twelve Williams entered a talent contest, singing "WPA Blues." He won fifteen dollars.

Williams, Maurice. Lead singer of the Gladiolas and later the Zodiacs. Williams's biggest hit with the Zodiacs was, "Stay" (Herald 552) in 1960. He composed "Little Darlin'," which the Gladiolas recorded in 1957 (Excello 2101). Elvis recorded "Little Darlin' " in 1977.

Williams, Tery and Samuels, Jeff. Two men who attempted to sell illegal copies of a photograph of Elvis in his coffin. They were arrested for theft of the photo, which belonged to the *National Enquirer*. The pair sold a negative for $20,000. (See: Last Photograph)

Willis, Chuck. Late blues singer called the "Sheik of the Blues" and "King of the Stroll" when he introduced "C.C. Rider" (Atlantic 1130) in 1957. Chuck Willis died during an operation on April 10, 1958. His last hit record was, ironically, titled "What Am I Living For" backed with "Hang Up My Rock and Roll Shoes" (Atlantic 1179). Elvis recorded two Chuck Willis hits, "C.C. Rider" and "Feel So Bad."

Willis Brothers. Country-western group (Guy, Skeeter, and Willis) that was once managed by Col. Parker. The group toured for many years with Eddy Arnold.

Willow Weep for Me*. One of the songs that Elvis is believed to have sung at the Lido Night Club in Paris on February 18, 1959, during an impromptu thirty-minute stage show.

Wills, James "Bob". Member of the Country Music Hall of Fame, born on March 6, 1906, in Limestone Co., Texas. Bob Wills's Texas Playboys was the first country band to include drums. Because drums were taboo on the "Grand Ole Opry," the drummer played behind the curtain. Bob Wills, along with his brother John, composed and first recorded "Faded Love." Elvis recorded the song in 1970.

Wills, Johnnie Lee. Country bandleader and composer, brother of Bob Wills. With Deacon Anderson he composed "Rag Mop" in 1950, which Elvis recorded in 1954.

Wilson, Jackie. One of Elvis's favorite black artists. At times Wilson was referred to as the "Black Elvis." Jackie Wilson's first hit song, in 1957, titled "Reet Petite," was co-composed by Berry Gordy, Jr.,† the founder of Motown Records. In the 1950s Wilson was a member of Billy Ward and the Dominoes. He replaced Clyde McPhatter, who had just left the group to join the Drifters. In 1975, when Wilson suffered a disabling stroke while singing "Lonely Teardrops" at the Latin Casino nightclub in Cherry Hill, New Jersey, Elvis offered to help pay the hospital bill. Elvis once said to Jackie, upon meeting him in Las Vegas, "I thought it was about time the white Elvis Presley met the black Elvis Presley."

Wiltshire, Michael. Fourteen-year-old boy from Perth, Australia, who won a trip to America by naming all forty-two Elvis songs played during a contest conducted by a radio station a few days after Elvis's death. Wiltshire also wrote a tribute song, called "Elvis Aaron Presley," which he performed at the Memphis Motel.

Winfield, Nigel. Miami entrepreneur who located for Elvis the Convair 880 jet and two other planes, which he then purchased.

---

*Song composed in 1932 by Ann Ronell.
†Berry Gordy, Jr., a former Golden Gloves boxer, founded Motown in 1959 by first establishing the Tamla label on a borrowed $700. His two sisters, Gwen and Anna (founder of Ana Records, on which Barret Strong recorded "Money" in 1960), are married to singers Harvey Fuqua and Marvin Gaye, respectively. Berry Gordy, Jr., is also the father-in-law of Jermaine Jackson of the Jacksons.

Winnebago. Recreational vehicle that Elvis bought in Los Angeles while filming the 1964 movie *Kissin' Cousins*.

Winters, Roland. Veteran Hollywood actor who played Fred Gates in the 1961 movie *Blue Hawaii*. Roland Winters was one of six non-Chinese actors to play Chinese detective Charlie Chan in the movies.

Winter Wonderland. Christmas song written by Dick Smith and Felix Bernard in 1934. Guy Lombardo and His Royal Canadians, with the Andrew Sisters, had a million-seller with "Winter Wonderland" (Decca 23722) in 1946. Through the years "Winter Wonderland," by various artists, has had collective sales of over 45 million. Elvis recorded "Winter Wonderland" in 1971 and it appeared in the Long Playing albums "Elvis Sings the Wonderful World of Christmas" (RCA LSP-4579) and "Elvis Sings the Wonderful World of Christmas" (RCA AML1-1936).

Wisdom of the Ages. Song recorded by Elvis and originally scheduled to appear in the 1965 movie *Harum Scarum*. It was cut from the final print, although rumor has it that some prints do exist, with "Wisdom of the Ages" included. Written by Bill Giant, Bernie Baum, and Florence Kaye, "Wisdom of the Ages" appeared in the Long Playing album "Harum Scarum" (RCA LPM/LSP 3468).

Wise, Dennis. Elvis impersonator who underwent facial surgery to look more like Elvis. His face was revealed on the TV program "Good Morning America" in 1978.

Witchcraft. RCA 47-8243. Released in October 1963 as a 45 rpm single. It reached #37 on *Billboard*'s Hot 100 chart. "Bossa Nova Baby" was on the flip side. "Witchcraft" was written by Dave Bartholomew and Pearl King and originally recorded by the Spiders (Imperial 5366) in 1955. This is *not* the same song that Frank Sinatra popularized in 1958. However, Elvis *did* sing Sinatra's "Witchcraft" on "The Frank Sinatra-Timex Special" in 1960. Elvis's "Witchcraft" appeared in the Long Playing albums "Elvis' Gold Records, Volume 4" (RCA LMP/LSP-3921) and "Elvis: The Other Sides—Worldwide Gold Award Hits, Volume 2" (RCA LPM-6402).

Witchcraft. RCA 447-0642. Gold Standard Series re-issue of RCA 47-8243.

Witchcraft. Song written by Carolyn Leigh and Cy Coleman in 1957 and introduced by Gerry Matthews in a nightclub show called "Take Five." In 1958 Frank Sinatra had a best-selling record with "Witchcraft" (Capitol 3859). On "The Frank Sinatra-Timex Special" (May 12, 1960) Elvis and Sinatra sang a duet; Elvis sang Sinatra's "Witchcraft" while Sinatra sang "Love Me Tender," both ending with "Love Me Tender."

Without a Song. Song composed in 1929 by Edward Eliscu, William Rose, and Vincent Voumans and recorded by Frank Sinatra (Victor 36396). They were the song lyrics that Elvis read in his speech to the audience when he was presented the

Man of the Year award by the Jaycees: "I learned very early in life that, without a song, the day would never end, without a song, a man ain't got a friend, without a song, the road would never end, without a song, so I'll keep singing the song. Goodnight."

Without Him. Gospel song written by Myron Lefevre and recorded by Elvis in 1966. "Without Him" appeared in the Long Playing album "How Great Thou Art" (RCA LPM/LSP-3758).

Without Love (There Is Nothing). Song written by Danny Small and originally recorded by Clyde McPhatter (Atlantic 1117) in 1957. Tom Jones had a million-seller with "Without Love (There Is Nothing)" (Parrot 40045) in 1970. Elvis recorded "Without Love (There Is Nothing)" at the American Sound Studios in Memphis in January 1969. It appeared in the Long Playing albums "From Memphis to Vegas"/"From Vegas to Memphis" (RCA LSP-6020) and "Elvis—Back in Memphis" (RCA LSP-4429).

Without You. First song Elvis recorded for Sam Phillips, at Phillips's suggestion. Phillips wanted to record the song but couldn't locate the black singer who made the demo. It was Marion Keisker's suggestion to call Elvis, which Phillips did. Elvis came running down to the studio and recorded the song on tape. But, no matter how much he tried, it didn't sound right.*

"Without You" was written by a white inmate at Nashville's Maximum Security Prison. Sam Phillips obtained the song while there recording a session with the group the Prisonaires.

Wolf Call. Song that Elvis sang in the 1965 movie *Girl Happy*. The movie version of "Wolf Call" had whistles and wolf barks. "Wolf Call" was written by Bill Giant, Bernie Baum, and Florence Kaye and appeared in the Long Playing album "Girl Happy" (RCA LPM/LSP-3338).

Wolfman Jack. Popular disc jockey (real name: Robert Westing Smith) who played Elvis records in the early 1950s over radio station XERP in Mexico. He portrayed himself in the 1973 movie *American Graffiti*.† In Las Vegas in 1969 Elvis talked about his youthful memories of listening to Wolfman and then he introduced him from the audience.

Woman Without Love. Song written by Jerry Chesnut and recorded by Elvis in 1975. "Woman Without Love" appeared in the Long Playing album "Today" (RCA APL1-1039)

Wonderful World. Song that Elvis sang in the 1968 movie *Live a Little, Love a Little*. Written by Guy Fletcher and Doug Flett. "Wonderful World" appeared in the following Long Playing albums: "Singer Presents Elvis Singing Flaming Star and Oth-

---

*At Memphis State University on August 16, 1979, Judd Phillips played the Sun recording of Elvis singing "Without You."

†The producer of *American Graffiti* attempted to get permission to play an Elvis song or two in the movie, but the cost was prohibitive.

ers" (RCA PRS-279); "Elvis Sings Flaming Star" (RCA Camden CAS-2304); "Elvis Sings Flaming Star" (Pickwick CAS-2304).

Wonderful World of Christmas, The. Christmas song written by Tobias and Frisch and recorded by Elvis in 1971. "The Wonderful World of Christmas" appeared in the Long Playing albums "The Wonderful World of Christmas" (RCA LSP-4579) and "Elvis Sings the Wonderful World of Christmas" (RCA ANL1-1936).

Wonder of You, The. RCA 47-9835. Released in May 1970 as a 45 rpm single. It reached #9 on *Billboard*'s Hot 100 chart, #37 on the Country chart, and #1 in the United Kingdom for (six weeks, August 1–September 12). "The Wonder of You" sold over 2 million copies and was the first "live" single release by Elvis. "Mama Liked the Roses" was on the flip side. "The Wonder of You" was written by Baker Knight and originally recorded by Ray Peterson (RCA 7513) in 1959. Elvis's version of "The Wonder of You" appeared in the Long Playing albums "On Stage—February, 1970" (RCA LSP-4362) and "Elvis: The Other Sides—Worldwide Gold Award Hits, Volume 2" (RCA LPM-6402).

Wonder of You, The. RCA 447-0676. Gold Standard Series reissue of RCA 47-9835.

Wonders You Perform, The. A 1973 studio recording that has never been released in any form. The instrumental track was recorded on July 25, but Elvis never recorded a vocal track.

Wood, Anita. Local Memphis disc jockey (WHHM radio), television personality, and singer who appeared on the "Top Ten Party." After being introduced to Elvis by Cliff Gleaves, she became romantically involved with him in 1958. A Memphis newspaper stated that Elvis was to marry her on the eve of his departure to Germany. In 1958 Elvis gave her a toy French poodle for Christmas named Little Bit. Anita Wood once won a beauty contest and was given a seven-year contract with Paramount Pictures. In 1964 she recorded "Dream Baby"/"This Happened Before" on Sue Records. (See: "I'll Wait Forever")

Wood, Natalie. Hollywood actress, (born Natasha Gurdin), who was given her screen name of Wood by motion-picture executives William Goetz and Leo Spitz in honor of their late friend director Sam Wood (director of several Marx Brothers movies). Elvis dated Ms. Wood in 1956. Newspaper stories accused them of having a "motorcycle romance." In October 1956 Elvis, Natalie, and his parents spent a week together in Memphis. Natalie Wood* has been married to Robert Wagner twice. Natalie Wood and actress Diana Rigg share the same birthdate

---

*The Natalie Wood Award is the Harvard Lampoon's annual award for the year's worst actress. She was the 1967 recipient of the Sour Apple Award. (See: Sour Apple Award)

—July 20, 1938. In the 1973 TV movie *Elvis*, Natalie Wood was portrayed by Abi Young.

Wood, Randy. Founder of Dot Records in Gallatin, Tennessee, in 1951. In early 1955 Sam Phillips attempted to sell Elvis's contract to Randy Wood for $7,500. Wood declined because he already had an up-and-coming artist—Pat Boone—whom he had just acquired from Republic Records. Randy Wood was also the name of the president of Chicago's Vee Jay Records.

Woodbine Cemetery. Cemetery near Allen City where the real Deke Rivers (1878–1934) was buried. It was from his tombstone that the orphan Jimmy Tompkins (Elvis) adopted the name Deke Rivers in the 1957 movie *Loving You*.

Wooden Heart. RCA 447-0720. Released in November 1964 as a 45 rpm Gold Standard Series original. "Blue Christmas" was on the flip side. "Wooden Heart" was recorded by Elvis on April 28, 1960, for the movie *G.I. Blues*. It was sung partly in German and partly in English. It was released as a single in Europe in 1961 and reached #1 in the United Kingdom (for three weeks, March 12–April 12). Sales in West Germany alone (on the Teldec label) were over a million copies. In 1961 Joe Dowell's version of "Wooden Heart" (Smash 1708) reached #1 on *Billboard*'s Hot 100 chart and sold over a million copies. Elvis's 1964 and '65 releases never made the charts. "Wooden Heart" was written by Ben Weisman, Kay Twomey, and Bert Kaempfert, based on the German folk song "Mus I denn zum Stadtele naus." It appeared in the following Long Playing albums: "G.I. Blues" (RCA LPM/LSP-2256); "Elvis: Worldwide 50 Gold Award Hits, Volume 1" (RCA LPM-6401); "Elvis Sings for Children (And Grownups Too)" (RCA CPL1-2901).

Wooden Heart. RCA 447-0650. Gold Standard Series original released in October 1965. Although "Wooden Heart" had been released previously (RCA 447-0720), this Gold Standard Series issue had a different flip side ("Puppet on a String"), making it a different record.

Words. Song written and originally recorded by the Bee Gees (Barry, Robin, and Maurice Gibb) in 1968. "Words" (Atco 6548) sold over a million copies. Elvis sang "Words" in the 1970 documentary *Elvis—That's the Way It Is*, and it appeared in the Long Playing albums "From Memphis to Vegas/From Vegas to Memphis" (RCA LSP-6020) and "Elvis in Person" (RCA LSP-4428).

Working on the Building. Gospel song written by Hoyle and Bowles and originally recorded by the Blackwood Brothers. Elvis recorded "Working on the Building" in 1960 and it appeared in the Long Playing albums "His Hand in Mine" (RCA LPM/LSP-2328) and "His Hand in Mine" (RCA ANL1-1319).

World Loves You Elvis, The. A 1977 Elvis tribute record by Wesley Gillespie on Rome Records (Rome 1017).

World of Our Own, A. Song that Elvis sang in the 1963 movie *It Happened at the World's Fair*. The Mello Men backed Elvis on this song. "A World of Our Own" was written by Bill Giant, Bernie Baum, and Florence Kaye and appeared in the Long Playing album "It Happened at the World's Fair" (RCA LPM/LSP-2697).

Wright, Lou. Psychic who did readings for Elvis (through Charlie Hodge).

WSM. Nashville radio station that broadcasts the "Grand Ole Opry." The National Life and Accident Insurance Company originally owned the radio station and used the call letters WSM, to stand for "We Shield Millions," an advertisement for their insurance company. WSM-FM was the first licensed FM station in the U. S. (See: Grand Ole Opry)

Wuhoberac, Larry. Piano played in Elvis's band at the International Hotel in Las Vegas in 1969.

X

X Records. Subsidiary label of RCA Victor Records established in 1952, for which Joe Delaney, the label's manager, attempted to get Elvis to record in 1955.

It was for X Records that eleven-year-old Frankie Avalon made his recording debut, as a trumpet player, in 1952. He recorded the instrumental "Trumpet Sorrento" (X 0006).

Ironically, it was on the X label (another company) that the Beach Boys made their first recording, "Surfin'" (X 301) in 1962. ("Surfin'" was later released on the Candix label [Candix 331] in 1962.)

Y

Yancey, Becky. One of the office girls at Graceland. She was in Elvis's employ from March 1962 to July 1975. Her starting salary was sixty-five dollars a week. Becky Yancey coauthored (with Clifford Linedecker) the book *My Life with Elvis*.

Yellow Rose, The. Song that Sweet Susie Jessup (Dolores Hart) sang on stage in the 1957 movie *Loving You*.

Yellow Rose of Texas, The. "The Eyes of Texas." Medley sung by Elvis in the 1964 movie *Viva Las Vegas*.

"The Yellow Rose of Texas"* was a marching song written in 1853 by a composer known only as "J.K." It was originally written for minstrel shows. During the Civil War, "The Yellow Rose of Texas" achieved tremendous popularity under the title "The Gallant Hood of Texas"—named for General John B. Hood of the Confederacy. Gene Autry recorded "The Yellow Rose of Texas" in 1933 (Perfect 12912). In 1955 Mitch Miller had a million-seller—his first—with Don George's adaptation of "The Yellow Rose of Texas" (Columbia 40540). In June 1955 Stan Freberg recorded a parody version (Capitol 3249).

"The Eyes of Texas," written by Sinclair, serves as the school song of the University of Texas Longhorns. It was the last song recorded by Ozzie Nelson (Victor 27426). Every time a home run is hit in the Astrodome, "The Eyes of Texas" is played. "The Eyes of Texas" was also sung in the 1969 movie *The Trouble with Girls (And How To Get Into It)* by a quartet of college boys.

Yes, I'm Lonesome Tonight. Answer record to Elvis's "Are You Lonesome Tonight" in 1960. "Yes, I'm Lonesome Tonight" was recorded by Dodie Stevens† (Dot 16167), Thelma Carpenter (Coral 62241), and Jo Anne Perry (Glad 1006).

Yesterday. Song recorded by the Beatles in 1965 (Capitol 5498) and, reportedly, the most recorded song of all time, with 1,186 versions through 1972. "Yesterday,"‡ composed by Paul McCartney, although credited as a John Lennon-Paul McCartney composition, was recorded by Elvis in 1969 and appeared in the Long Playing album "On Stage—February, 1970" (RCA LSP-4362).

Yoga Is as Yoga Does. Song that Elvis sang in the 1967 movie *Easy Come, Easy Go*. Elsa Lanchester sang a duet with Elvis. Several back-up voices are added to the film version. Written by Gerald Nelson and Fred Burch, "Yoga Is as Yoga Does" appeared in the Extended Play album, "Easy Come, Easy Go" (RCA EPA-4387) and the Long Playing albums "I Got Lucky" (RCA Camden CAL-2355) and "I Got Lucky" (Pickwick CAS-2355).

You Asked Me To. Song written by Waylon Jennings and Billy Joe Shaver in 1973. Elvis recorded "You Asked Me To" at Stax Studios in Memphis in December 1973. It appeared in the Long Playing album "Promised Land" (RCA APL1-0873).

You Better Believe It. Possibly, Elvis's favorite expression, since he said it quite often.

---

*In a roadside café, near the end of the 1956 James Dean movie *Giant*, "The Yellow Rose of Texas" was played on a juke box.
†Real name: Geraldine Ann Pasquale.
‡The song's working title had been "Scrambled Egg."

You Can't Say No in Acapulco. Song that Elvis sang in the 1963 movie *Fun in Acapulco*. "You Can't Say No in Acapulco" was written by Sid Feller, Dee Fuller, and Lee Morris and appeared in the Long Playing album "Fun in Acapulco" (RCA LPM/LSP-2756).

You Don't Have a Wooden Heart. Answer record by Bobbi Martin on Coral Records (Coral 62285).

You Don't Have to Say You Love Me. RCA 47-9916. Released in October 1970 as a 45 rpm single. It reached #11 on *Billboard*'s Hot 100 chart and #56 on the Country chart. "Patch It Up" was on the flip side. "You Don't Have to Say You Love Me" was a million-seller for Elvis. It was written by V. Pallavicini and P. Donaggio under the Italian title "Io che non vivo (senzate)." The song was written for the San Remo (Italy) Song Contest in 1965. English lyrics to "You Don't Have to Say You Love Me" were written by Vicki Wickham and Simon Napier-Bell. In 1966 Dusty Springfield reached #3 and sold over a million copies with her recording of the song (Philips 40371). Elvis sang "You Don't Have to Say You Love Me" in the 1970 documentary *Elvis—That's the Way It Is*. It appeared in the following Long Playing albums: "Elvis—That's the Way It Is" (RCA LSP-4445); "Elvis: The Other Sides—Worldwide Gold Award Hits, Volume 2" (RCA LPM-6402); "Elvis as Recorded at Madison Square Garden" RCA LSP-4776).

You Don't Have to Say You Love Me. RCA 447-0678. Gold Standard Series re-issue of RCA 47-9916.

You Don't Know Me. RCA 47-9341. Released in September 1967 as a 45 rpm single. It reached #44 on *Billboard*'s Hot 100 chart. "Big Boss Man" was on the flip side. Elvis sang "You Don't Know Me" in the 1967 movie *Clambake*. The film version was backed by a string section. "You Don't Know Me" was written by Eddy Arnold and Cindy Walker in 1955 and originally recorded by Jerry Vale (Columbia 40710) in 1956. Eddy Arnold had a chart version of the song at about the same time (RCA 6502). In 1960 Lenny Welch recorded "You Don't Know Me" on Archie Bleyer's Cadence Records label (Cadence 1373). In 1962 Ray Charles had a #2 hit record and million-seller with the song (ABC Paramount 10345). "You Don't Know Me" appeared in the following Long Playing albums; "Clambake" (RCA LPM/LSP-3893); "Elvis Sings Hits from His Movies, Volume 1" (RCA Camden CAS-2567); "Elvis Sings Hits from His movies, Volume 1" (Pickwick CAS-2567).

You Don't Know Me. RCA 447-0662. Gold Standard Series re-issue of RCA 47-9341.

You Gave Me a Mountain. Song written by Marty Robbins and originally recorded by Frankie Laine had a big hit on ABC Paramount Records (ABC 11174). Elvis sang it in the 1973 TV special "Elvis: Aloha from Hawaii' and the 1977 CBS-TV special "Elvis in Concert." "You Gave Me a Mountain" appeared in the Long Playing albums "Elvis: Aloha from Hawaii Via Satellite" (RCA VPSX-6089) and "Elvis in Concert" (RCA APL2-2587).

You Gotta Stop. Song that Elvis sang in the 1967 movie *Easy Come, Easy Go.* "You Gotta Stop" was written by Bill Giant, Bernie Baum, and Florence Kaye and appeared in the Extended Play album "Easy Come, Easy Go" (RCA EPA-4387) and the Long Playing albums "I Got Lucky" (RCA Camden CAL-2355) and "I Got Lucky" (Pickwick CAS-2355).

You'll Be Gone. RCA 47-8500. Released in March 1965 as a 45 rpm single. "Do the Clam" was on the flip side. Elvis, Red West, and Charlie Hodge are credited with writing "You'll Be Gone." It appeared in the Long Playing album "Girl Happy" (RCA LPM/LSP-3338).

You'll Never Walk Alone. RCA 47-9600. Released in April 1968 as a 45 rpm single. It reached #90 on *Billboard's* Hot 100 chart. "We Call on Him" was on the flip side. "You'll Never Walk Alone" was written by Oscar Hammerstein, II, and Richard Rodgers in 1945 and introduced by Christine Johnson in the play *Carousel.* In the 1956 movie adaptation of *Carousel,* Claramae Turner sang it. In 1964 Gerry and the Pacemakers recorded a version for Parlophone Records in London. Elvis's version of "You'll Never Walk Alone" was an exact copy of Roy Hamilton's 1954 recording.* It appeared in the following Long Playing albums; "You'll Never Walk Alone" (RCA Camden CALX-2472); "You'll Never Walk Alone" (Pickwick CAS-2472); "Double Dynamite" (Pickwick DL2-5001).

You'll Never Walk Alone. RCA 447-0665. Gold Standard Series re-issue of RCA 47-9600.

You'll Never Walk Alone. RCA Camden CALX-2472. A 33⅓ rpm Long Playing album that was released in March 1971. It reached #69 on *Billboard's* Hot LP chart. Songs included—Side 1: "You'll Never Walk Alone," "Who Am I," "Let Us Pray," "(There'll Be) Peace in the Valley (For Me), "We Call on Him." Side 2: "I Believe," "It Is No Secret (What God Can Do)," "Sing You Children," "Take My Hand, Precious Lord."

You'll Never Walk Alone. Pickwick CAS-2472. A re-issue of RCA Camden CALX-2472 in December 1975.

You'll Think of Me. RCA 47-9764. Released in August 1969 as a 45 rpm single. "Suspicious Minds" was on the flip side. Written by Mort Shuman, Elvis recorded "You'll Think of Me" at the American Sound Studios in Memphis on January 14, 1969. It appeared in the following Long Playing albums: "From Memphis to Vegas/From Vegas to Memphis" (RCA LSP-6020); "Elvis—Back in Memphis" (RCA LSP-4429); "Elvis: The

---

*The musicians who backed Roy Hamilton were members of Duke Ellington's Band.

Other Sides—Worldwide 50 Gold Award Hits, Volume 2"
(RCA LPM-6402).

You'll Think of Me. RCA 447-0673. Gold Standard Series re-issue
of RCA 47-9764.

Young, Faron. Popular country singer who got his start on the
"Louisiana Hayride" radio program in the late 1940s and early
'50s. Faron Young* was born on February 25, 1932, one day
before the birth of Johnny Cash. In the 1950s he appeared in
the movie *The Young Sheriff*, and since that time he has been
called the "Singing Sheriff."

Faron Young has had two million-selling records ("Hello
Walls" in 1962 and "Four in the Morning" in 1972) and is
currently the president of *Music City News*, a country-music
newspaper based in Nashville. Frieda's cat, in the Charles
Schulz comic strip *Peanuts*, is named Faron after the singer.

Faron Young composed "Is It So Strange," which Elvis
recorded in 1957.

Young, Gig. Academy Award-winning actor who portrayed Willy
Grogan in the 1962 movie *Kid Galahad*. Gig Young (real
name: Byron Ellsworth Barr)† was nominated for Best Supporting Actor three times. For his portrayal of Rocky, the
master of ceremonies of the dance marathon in *They Shoot
Horses, Don't They*, Gig Young won his only Oscar. Between
1964 and '65 he starred in the NBC TV series "The Rogues."
Gig Young committed suicide on October 19, 1978.

Young, Victor. Bandleader and composer. He received an Academy Award, posthumously, for his musical scoring of the 1956
movie *Around the World in 80 Days*. Victor Young once
replaced Jack Benny on radio when Benny was fired (in the
1930s). He died on November 11, 1956.

Young was the composer (music), with Edward Heyman
(lyrics), of "Love Letters," which Elvis recorded in May, 1966.

Young and Beautiful. Song that Elvis sang in the 1957 movie
Jailhouse Rock. It was sung three times in the film. In Europe
"Young and Beautiful" was released as a single, backed with
"Lover Doll." Written by Abner Silver and Aaron Schroeder,
"Young and Beautiful" appeared in the Extended Play album
"Jailhouse Rock" (RCA EPA-4114) and the following Long
Playing albums: "A Date with Elvis" (RCA LPM-2011); "A
Date with Elvis" (RCA LSP-2011 [e]); "Elvis: The Other
Sides—Worldwide Gold Award Hits, Volume 2 (RCA LPM-
6402).

Young Dreams. Song that Elvis sang in the 1958 movie *King
Creole*. Written by Aaron Schroeder and Martin Kalmanoff,

*Singer-composer-musician Roger Miller was once a drummer in Faron
Young's band.
†He took his stage name from a character that he played in the 1945
movie *The Gay Sisters*.

"Young Dreams" appeared in the Extended Play album "King Creole, Volume 2" and the following Long Playing albums: "King Creole" (RCA LPM-1884); "King Creole" (RCA LSP-1884 [e]); "Elvis: The Other Sides—Worldwide Gold Award Hits, Volume 2" (RCA LPM-6402).

Youngman, Henny. Comedian, nicknamed the "King of the One-Liners." He appeared on TV's "Stage Show" on March 17, 1956—the fifth appearance of Elvis on that show.

Your Cheatin' Heart. Song written and recorded by Hank Williams in late 1952. "Your Cheatin' Heart" was issued shortly after Williams's death and became the top country record of 1953 and a million-seller (MGM 11416).* Joni James also recorded the song (MGM 11426) in 1953 and had a million-seller. Elvis recorded "Your Cheatin' Heart" in 1958 and it appeared in the Long Playing albums "Elvis for Everyone" (RCA LPM/LSP-3450) and "Welcome to My World" (RCA APL1-2274). (See: Williams, Hank)

Your Cheatin' Heart. A 1964 biographical movie of Hank Williams. George Hamilton portrayed Williams, while the singer's son, Hank Williams, Jr., recorded the soundtrack.

Elvis was considered for the lead role of Hank Williams.

You're a Heartbreaker. Sun 215. Released on January 8, 1955, as a 78 rpm single and a 45 rpm single. "Milkcow Blues Boogie" was on the flip side. "You're a Heartbreaker" was an old country music standard written by Jack Sallee.

You're a Heartbreaker. RCA 20/47-6382. A 78 rpm and a 45 rpm re-issue of the Sun original (Sun 215). "You're a Heartbreaker" appeared in the following Long Playing albums: "For LP Fans Only" (RCA LPM-1990); "For LP Fans Only" (RCA LSP-1990 [e]); "The Elvis Presley Sun Collection" (RCA Starcall HY-1001); "Elvis—The Sun Sessions" (RCA APM1-1675); "The Sun Years" (Sun 1001).

You're a Heartbreaker. RCA 447-0603. Gold Standard Series re-issue of RCA 20/47-6382.

You're Nothin' But a Raccoon. Satirical version of "Hound Dog" that was a big hit for Elvin Pelvin on an episode of the TV series the "Phil Silvers Show" in the 1950s. (See Elvin Pelvin; Phil Silvers Show, The)

You're the Boss. Song that Elvis reportedly recorded for the 1964 movie *Viva Las Vegas.* "You're the Boss" was cut from the final print of the film and has never been released on record.

You're the Brightest Star. Phrase that appeared on the license-plate holder of Elvis's Stutz Bearcat.

Your Groovy Self. Song that Nancy Sinatra sang in the 1968 movie *Speedway.* It appeared in the Long Playing album "Speedway" (RCA LSP-3989). "Your Groovy Self" was writ-

---

*"Kaw-Liga" was on the flip side.

ten by Lee Hazelwood and is the only song to appear on an Elvis album that Elvis did not sing.

Your Love's Been a Long Time Coming. Song written by Rory Bourke, which Elvis recorded at Stax Studios in Memphis on December 15, 1973. "Your Love's Been a Long Time Coming" appeared in the Long Playing albums "Promised Land" (RCA APL1-0873) and "Our Memories of Elvis" (RCA AQL1-3279).

Your Mama Don't Dance. Song originally composed and recorded by Dave Loggins and Jim Messina in 1972 (Columbia 45719). The song was based on the Rooftop Singers' 1963 hit, "Mama Don't Allow" (Vanguard 35020). Elvis sang fifteen seconds of the song as part of a medley of tunes, consisting of "Long Tall Sally," "Whole Lotta Shakin' Going On," "Flip, Flop, Fly," "Jailhouse Rock," and "Hound Dog," on his album "Elvis Recorded Live on Stage in Memphis."

Your Time Hasn't Come Yet, Baby. RCA 47-9547. Released in May 1968 as a 45 rpm single. It reached #72 on *Billboard*'s Hot 100 chart and #50 on the Country chart. "Let Yourself Go" was on the flip side. "Your Time Hasn't Come Yet, Baby" was written by Hirschorn and Kasha and sung by Elvis in the 1968 movie *Speedway*. It appeared in the Long Playing album "Speedway" (RCA LSP-3989).

Your Time Hasn't Come Yet, Baby. RCA 447-0666. Gold Standard Series re-issue of RCA 47-9547.

You've Lost That Lovin' Feelin'. Song that was written by Phil Spector, Barry Mann, and Cynthia Weill and originally recorded by the Righteous Brothers* (Philles 124) in 1964.† It quickly became a million-seller for them. Elvis sang "You've Lost That Lovin' Feelin'" in the 1970 documentary *Elvis—That's the Way It Is,* and it appeared in the Long Playing albums "Elvis—That's the Way It Is" (RCA LSP-4440) and "Elvis as Recorded at Madison Square Garden" (RCA LSP-4776).

Z

Zager, Lt. Jack. Army lieutenant who administered Elvis's mental examination on the day of his induction into the Army—March 24, 1958.

---

*Cher sang background on the Righteous Brothers version.
†In Britain Cilla Black's version entered the charts first, in January 1965, but shortly afterward the Righteous Brothers' version passed hers up and rested in the top position, with Cilla's version sitting at #2.

Zancan, Sandra. Las Vegas showgirl dated by Elvis in 1972, after he and Priscilla had separated.

Zenoff, Judge David. Justice of the Nevada Supreme Court who performed the wedding ceremony for Elvis Presley and Priscilla Beaulieu on May 1, 1967. (See: Aladdin Hotel)

Ziegler, Ronald L. Press secretary for President Richard M. Nixon. Ziegler was one of the Top Ten Young Men of the Year (1971), as selected by the U. S. Jaycees. Elvis was also one of the Ten. In the 1979 TV mini-series "Blind Ambition," Ziegler was portrayed by James Sloyan.

BIBLIOGRAPHY

Books

Atkins, Chet with Neely, Bill. *Country Gentleman*. New York: Ballantine Books, 1975.

Barry, Ron. *All American Elvis*. New Jersey: Phillipsburg, 1976.

Bowser, James W. *Starring Elvis*. New York: Dell Publishing Co., 1977.

Brooks, Tim and Marsh, Erle. *The Complete Directory of Prime Time Network TV Shows 1946–Present*. New York: Ballantine Books, 1979.

Cash, Johnny. *Man in Black*. New York: Warner Books, 1975.

Chalker, Bryan. *Country Music*. Chartwell Books, Inc.

Chapple, Steve and Garofalo, Reebee. *Rock 'n' Roll Is Here to Pay*. Chicago: Nelson Hall, 1977.

Charles, Ray and Ritz, David. *Brother Ray (Ray Charles' Own Story)*. New York: Dial Press, 1978.

Clark, Dick. *Rock, Roll & Remember*. New York: Popular Library, 1978.

Cohn, Nik. *Rock From the Beginning*. New York: Pocket Books, 1970.

Cortez, Diego. *Private Elvis*. Stuttgart, West Germany: Fey, 1978.

Dellar, Fred and Thompson, Roy. *The Illustrated Encyclopedia of Country Music*. New York: Harmony Books, 1977.

Escott, Colin and Hawkins, Martin. *Catalyst—The Sun Records Story*. London: Aquarius Books, 1975.

Ewen, David. *American Popular Songs*. New York: Random House, 1966.

Farren, Mick and Marchbank, Pearce. *Elvis in His Own Words*. New York: Omnibus Press, 1977.

Friedman, Favius. *Meet Elvis Presley*. New York: Scholastic Books, 1971.

Gillett, Charlie. *The Sound of the City*. New York: Dell Publishing Co., 1972.

——. *Making Tracks*. New York: Sunrise Books, 1973.

Goldrosen, John. *The Buddy Holly Story*. New York: Quick Fox, 1979.

Grissim, John. *Country Music: White Man's Blues*. New York: Paperback Library, 1970.

Grove, Martin. *The King Is Dead, Elvis Presley*. New York: Manor Books, 1977.

——. *Elvis the Legend Lives*. New York: Manor Books, 1978.

Hanna, David. *Elvis: Lonely Star at the Top*. New York: Nordon Publications, 1977.

Harbinson, W. A. *The Illustrated Elvis*. New York: Grosset & Dunlap, 1975.

Harris, Sheldon. *Blues Who's Who*. New Rochelle, New York: Arlington House, 1979.

Heibut, Tony. *The Gospel Sound*. New York: Simon and Schuster, 1976.

Hemphill, Paul. *The Nashville Sound*. New York: Ballantine Books, 1970.

Holzer, Hans. *Elvis Presley Speaks*. New York: Manor Books, 1978.

Hopkins, Jerry. *The Rock Story*. New York: Signet Books, 1970.

——. *Elvis*. New York: Warner Paperback Library, 1972.

Jahn, Mike. *Rock from Elvis Presley to the Rolling Stones*. New York: Quadrangle, 1973.

James, Anthony. *Presley: Entertainer of the Century*. New York: Tower Publications, 1977.

Jenkinson, Philip and Warner, Alan. *Celluloid Rock*. New York: Warner Books, 1974.

Kinkle, Roger D. *The Complete Encyclopedia of Popular Music and Jazz 1900–1950* (4 volumes). New Rochelle, New York: Arlington House, 1974.

Krafsur, Richard, Executive Editor. *The American Film Institute Catalog of Motion Pictures 1961–1970*. New York, 1976.

Kramer, Freda. *The Glen Campbell Story*. New York: Pyramid Books, 1970.

Lacker, Marty, Lacker, Patsy, and Smith, Leslie S. *Elvis: Portrait of a Friend*. Memphis: Wimmer Brothers Books, 1979.

Lahr, John and Palmer, Robert. *Baby, That Was Rock & Roll—The Legendary Leiber & Stoller*. New York: Harcourt Brace Jovanovich, 1978.

Laing, Dave. *Buddy Holly*. New York: Macmillan, 1972.

Lichter, Paul. *The Boy Who Dared to Rock: The Definitive Elvis*. Garden City, New York: Dolphin Books, 1978.

Lichter, Paul. *Elvis in Hollywood*. New York: Fireside Books, 1975.

Linedecker, Cliff. *Country Music Stars and the Supernatural*. New York: Dell Publishing Co., 1979.

Logan, Nick and Woffinder, Bob. *The Illustrated Encyclopedia of Rock*. New York: Harmony Books, 1977.

Malone, Bill C. and McCulloh, Judith. *Stars of Country Music*. Chicago: University of Illinois Press, 1975.

Mann, May. *Elvis and the Colonel.* New York: Pocket Books, 1976.

Mann, Richard. *Elvis.* Van Nuys, California: Bible Voice, Inc., 1977.

Marcus, Greil. *Mystery Train.* New York: E.P. Dutton & Co., 1976.

McWhirter, Norris. *Guinness Book of World Records.* New York: Sterling Publishing Co., 1978.

Murrells, Joseph. *The Book of Golden Discs.* London: Barrie & Jenkins, 1978.

Nash, Bruce M. *The Elvis Presley Quizbook.* New York: Warner Books, 1978.

Nite, Norm N. *Rock On.* New York: Thomas Y. Crowell, 1974.

——. *Rock On, Volume II.* New York: Thomas Y. Crowell, 1978.

Oakley, Giles. *The Devil's Music—A History of the Blues.* New York: Taplinger Publishing Company.

Oliver, Paul. *The Story of the Blues.* London: Design Yearbook Limited, 1969.

Osborne, Jerry. *Popular & Rock Records 1948–1978.* Phoenix Arizona: O'Sullivan Woodside and Co., 1978.

——. *55 Years Of Recorded Country/Western Music.* Phoenix, Arizona: O'Sullivan Woodside and Co., 1976.

——. *Record Albums 1948–1978.* Phoenix, Arizona: O'Sullivan Woodside and Co., 1978.

Parish, James Robert. *The Elvis Presley Scrapbook.* New York: Ballantine Books, 1975, 1977.

Parker, Ed. *Inside Elvis.* Orange, California: Rampart House, Ltd., 1978.

Propes, Steve. *Those Oldies But Goodies.* New York: Collier Books, 1973.

——. *Golden Oldies.* Radnor, Pennsylvania: Chilton Book Co., 1974.

——. *Golden Goodies.* Radnor, Pennsylvania: Chilton Book Co., 1975.

Rosenbaum, Helen. *The Elvis Presley Trivia Quiz Book,* New York: Signet Books, 1978.

Rolling Stone. *The Rolling Stone Illustrated History of Rock & Roll.* New York: Rolling Stone Press, 1976.

Shaver, Sean and Noland, Hal. *The Life of Elvis Presley.* Memphis: Timur Publishing, Inc., 1979.

Shaw, Arnold. *Honkers and Shouters.* New York: Collier Books, 1978.

——. *The Rockin' '50s.* New York: Hawthorne Books, 1974.

——. *The World of Soul.* New York: Paperback Library, 1971.

——. *The Rock Revolution.* New York: Paperback Library, 1971.

Shestack, Melvin. *The Country Music Encyclopedia.* New York: Thomas Y. Crowell, 1974.

Stambler, Irwin. *Encyclopedia of Pop, Rock & Soul.* New York: St. Martin's Press, 1974, 1977.

Stambler, Erwin and Landon, Grelun. *Encyclopedia of Folk, Country, and Western Music.* New York: St. Martin's Press, 1969.

Staten, Vince. *The Real Elvis: Good Old Boy.* Dayton, Ohio: Media Ventures, 1978.

Tosches, Nick. *Country: The Biggest Music in America.* New York: Dell Publishing Co., 1977.

West, Red (Sonny West, Dave Hebler, as told to Steve Dunleavy). *Elvis What Happened?* New York: Ballantine Books, 1977.

Williams, Richard. *Out of His Head.* London: Sphere Books Ltd., 1972.

Williams, Roger M. *Sing a Sad Song: the Life of Hank Williams.* New York: Ballantine Books, 1973.

Worth, Fred L. *The Complete Unabridged Super Trivia Encyclopedia.* New York: Warner Books, 1977.

——. *The Country Western Book.* New York: Sterling Publishing Co., 1977.

——. *Thirty Years of Rock 'n Roll Trivia.* New York: Warner Books, 1980.

Wren, Christopher S. "Winners Got Scars Too (The Life of Johnny Cash)." New York: *Country Music Magazine,* 1974.

Yancey, Becky and Linedecker, Cliff. *My Life with Elvis.* New York: Warner Books, 1978.

Zmijewsky, Steven and Boris. *Elvis: The Films and Career of Elvis Presley.* Secaucus, New Jersey: Citadel Press, 1976.

Periodicals

Elvis the Record, Smith, Lacker, Davis, Inc., P.O. Box 18408, Memphis, TN.

Elvis World, Elvis World Ent., P.O. Box 388, Bound Brook, NJ 08805.

Goldmine, Arena Magazine Co., 23745 Elmira Ave., St. Clair Shores, MI.

Record Digest, Record Digest Corp., 8A Sweet Acres Dr., Prescott, AZ 86301.

Record Exchanger, Vintage Records, 804 Webster, Anaheim, CA.

Time Barrier Express, Time Barrier Ent. Inc., Box 1109, White Plains, NY 10602.

Trivia Unlimited, United States Trivia Ass., Ltd., P.O. Box 5213, Lincoln, NB 68505.

ABOUT THE AUTHORS

FRED L. WORTH needs no introduction to trivia fanatics. His book, *The Complete And Unabridged Super Trivia Encyclopedia*, has been called the most comprehensive trivia reference source ever published and the trivia buffs' Bible. Mr. Worth is a member of the board of directors of the National Trivia Hall of Fame and a founder and feature writer of *Trivia Unlimited* magazine. While in the U.S. Air Force, he served as an air traffic controller at a radio site in England. For the past thirteen years, he has been employed by the Federal Aviation Administration as an air traffic controller. Other books by Fred L. Worth include *Thirty Years of Rock 'N Roll Trivia*, *Hollywood Trivia*, and *World War II Super Facts*.

STEVE D. TAMERIUS is the president of the United States Trivia Association, Ltd., and is the editor and publisher of *Trivia Unlimited* magazine. He serves on the board of directors of the National Trivia Hall of Fame. In 1980, Steve Tamerius appeared on over one-hundred-and-fifty radio and television talk shows promoting trivia. He is employed as a REALTOR® and is presently working on a book about the Beatles.

THE PRIVATE LIVES
BEHIND PUBLIC FACES

These biographies tell the personal stories of these well-known figures recounting the triumphs and tragedies of their public and private lives.

☐	13592	CHANGING Liv Ullmann	$2.75
☐	14858	THE SECRET LIFE OF TYRONE POWER	$2.95
☐	20416	HAYWIRE Brooke Hayward	$3.25
☐	14862	THE TWO LIVES OF ERROL FLYNN Michael Freedland	$2.95
☐	14130	GARY COOPER: INTIMATE BIOGRAPHY Hector Arce	$2.75
☐	13824	ELVIS: PORTRAIT OF A FRIEND Lackers & Smith	$2.95
☐	12942	JOAN CRAWFORD: A Biography Bob Thomas	$2.75
☐	14677	MONTGOMERY CLIFT: A Biography Patricia Bosworth	$3.50
☐	13030	SOPHIA: Living and Loving, Her Own Story A. E. Hotchner	$2.75
☐	20121	STRAWBERRY FIELDS FOREVER! John Lennon Remembered Garbarine & Cullman	$2.95
☐	14038	RAGING BULL LaMotta with Carter	$2.50
☐	14551	AN UNFINISHED WOMAN Lillian Hellman	$2.75

Buy them at your local bookstore or use this handy coupon:

We Deliver!
And So Do These Bestsellers.